Ultimate Guide to
Medical Schools

Ultimate Guide to Medical Schools

Josh Fischman and the Staff of U.S.News & World Report

Foreword by Bernadine Healy, M.D.

Anne McGrath, Editor

Robert Morse, Director of Data Research

Ulrich Boser, Associate Editor

Sara Sklaroff, Series Editor

SOURCEBOOKS, INC.®
NAPERVILLE, ILLINOIS

This publication is designed to provide accurate and authoritative information in regard to the subject matter covered. It is sold with the understanding that the publisher is not engaged in rendering legal, accounting or other professional service. If legal advice or other expert assistance is required, the services of a competent professional person should be sought.
—*From a Declaration of Principles Jointly Adopted by a Committee of the American Bar Association and a Committee of Publishers and Associations*

Trademarks: All brand names and product names used in this book are trademarks, registered trademarks, or trade names of their respective holders. Sourcebooks, Inc. is not associated with any product or vendor in this book.

Published by Sourcebooks, Inc.
P.O. Box 4410
Naperville, Illinois 60567-4410
(630) 961-3900 FAX: (630) 961-2168
www.sourcebooks.com

ISBN 1-4022-0290-3
First Edition
Printed and bound in the United States of America
ED 10 9 8 7 6 5 4 3 2 1

Table of Contents

Foreword

On Being a Doctor

by Bernadine Healy, M.D.

Medicine is a way of life. It is a way of knowing and thinking, of seeing the world, and of feeling about people. No one
is born a doctor, and the long road to becoming one requires
unrelenting study, discipline, and the cultivation of unique
talents and skills. But whatever the domain of medical pursuit and however removed from the bedside one's work may
ultimately be, its ethos and raison d'être stems from that
one enduring relationship: physician and patient.

   In our time, this most personal of human services has
burgeoned into a $1.5 trillion enterprise employing one in
ten Americans. It is a growth propelled by the endless fron-
tier of medical discovery, translating into better ways to care
for people. In that sense, a medical career is the intellectual

journey of a lifetime. In a field where the sands shift so quickly and one technology is swept away by another, medical school is not about teaching you all the facts you'll ever need to know. Rather, it is the place in which students are slowly converted from lay people into doctors.

This conversion takes time, with and beyond the books, journals, and professorial pronouncements. Ultimately, one becomes a doctor from an immersion in the unpredictable, varied, and complex ways in which patients fall ill, and the momentous efforts of people and technology to make them well. It comes from learning the secrets of the body, the passages of life from birth to death, the tortured times and the peaceful times of human souls, and the uplifting (and carefully harnessed) power of the physician to make a difference every step along the way. For the best of students, by the time they walk across the stage and accept their medical diploma, doctorhood has seeped into the marrow of their bones, the depth of their hearts. Whatever their chosen line of work, they will always see the world through the lens of a doctor.

That lens is broad. Medicine embraces a continuum of knowledge and practice from the micro to macro level—from the medical scientist in the laboratory, to the doctor at the bedside, to the public health specialist tracking down the latest epidemic anywhere in the world. And along that broad spectrum, one can carve out a professional life of research, teaching, practice or administration, or some combination of all four. There is a place for generalists and specialists, writers and policy wonks, computer jocks and business gurus—all part of a medical community doing something that is in its ultimate purpose about helping another human being.

That the profession helps human beings in a profound and measurable way is in fact why young people dream of being a doctor, and it is the single most common reason medical school applicants give for pursing a medical career. Indeed, it is that perspective that ultimately overrides some of the negative sides of a career in medicine, which in today's world can discourage even the strongest-hearted premed. For medicine as we know it today brings its own set of hassles: managed care, increasing government regulations, and malpractice premiums (and massive malpractice awards), on top of discouraging medical school debt averaging nearly $100,000 at a time when physician's incomes are relatively stagnant.

Although there are two applicants for every medical school slot, and the quality of prospective students is thought to be as good as ever, there is widespread belief among medical school educators that because of these strains, fewer students are interested in applying to medical school now than a decade ago, a phenomenon masked by the dramatic increase in female applicants. But the reality is that no profession—and nothing worth pursuing in life—is free from its own set of hassles. The reward-to-hassle ratio is what counts. It is something each prospective doctor must sort out for himself or herself.

And the rewards of today's medicine are many. The expanding knowledge base is truly compelling and ever changing to the betterment of patient and doctor. There is virtually no illness we cannot make better, if not cure, and with improved drugs and technology and emerging knowledge of human genomes, we see more tailored treatment of individual patients with better results. As for the doctor's personal life, the hours today are more reasonable and controllable than in the past. The solo doc is becoming a rare breed; large group practices and clinics enable medical practitioners to escape the direct brunt of administrative hassles while at the same time gaining camaraderie and an enriched practice environment. Medicine is a tough and fulfilling career, immutably purpose driven, value laden, intellectually stimulating, and emotionally gratifying. But it is a profession that demands the right stuff of those who serve.

Certain deeply held personal qualities are essential; without them, from my perspective as a former medical school dean, students quite simply need not apply. Think hard about them, for they are the essence of the art and the science of being a doctor.

Compassion and generosity. Kindness goes beyond "bedside manner." It is reflected in generosity of time and self, and sensitivity to the unique circumstance of any given situation. Making an extra stop by the room of a lonely patient; giving a worried family member your home phone number; being calm and measured with an ornery, angry, or noncompliant patient. Sickness can bring out the best in people but also the worst, and a physician can lighten a patient's load by being a source of hope, caring, and cheerleading—along with providing technical expertise.

Hard work and grit. It takes a lot of stamina to be part of a world that is always on call in some fashion. The stress might come from a rather mundane struggle with an insurance company for an extra day in the hospital or a needed MRI, or from perseverance against an engulfing bureaucracy. But stress most especially comes from the challenge of caring for the very sick. This demands the courage to make tough medical decisions, and in the face of risk and uncertainty, to proceed with

a risky operation, or embark on a drastic course of medical therapy. It takes grit to confront one's inevitable failures and learn from them—without becoming timid because of them. In their hearts, doctors must live with the confidence that at the end of the day, they did the best they could, and tirelessly so.

Scholarship and good sense. With medical practice reborn almost every day in new knowledge and emerging technology, new approaches are an essential part of medicine, disseminated in hospital corridors, medical rounds, mortality and morbidity conferences, journal clubs, and national medical gatherings. The wise and learned physicians are those who can sift through the flood of new knowledge and the latest evidence to make it apply to any given patient. That's why we teach medicine at the bedside and through individual case studies of real people. And that's why we respect reasoned judgment that often comes out with different advice. Should that 30-year-old woman with a newly discovered benign heart tumor have prompt heart surgery, as is the practice? Of course—but she is six months pregnant and with surgery, risks losing the baby, so dare we wait? The PSA is intermittently elevated in a 55-year-old man. Do you watch, or biopsy? Yes, a lumpectomy is the conventional wisdom for this precancerous change detected by mammogram, but this patient wants a mastectomy as an alternative because she has a breast cancer gene running through her family. Do we go along? The hyperactive child is driving his family to distraction with behaviors that another family could manage better. Do you medicate?

Medical wisdom is about knowing when conventional practice guidelines apply, particularly in the context of the unlimited variables that confound any given patient's illness or circumstance.

The best decisions come from the marriage of scholarship and good sense.

Integrity and trust. Despite the variability of human illness, one of the great insights of medicine is that with regard to reaction to their disease, all patients are fundamentally the same. Though they may show it differently, they share the same fears and vulnerabilities; and have the same needs for comfort, support, and trust. The physician is the focus of that trust, and that is a heavy responsibility. Never give advice that you yourself would not take—or you would not recommend to a loved one. Imagine you are the patient, particularly when the going gets tough. Matters of privacy, conflicts of interest, participation of patients in research trials—these are all issues of trust. Underpinning this essential quality of being a doctor is a quiet reverence for what it means to be a doctor and what it feels like to care—in the deepest sense—for a patient in your charge. The late Dr. George Crile, Jr., a pioneering Cleveland surgeon and son of one of the founders of the Cleveland Clinic, wrote a short passage in his book on cancer back in 1955 that captures the quiet reverence of a profession that has the ability to restore health or even life, and always to relieve human suffering. His words mean as much now as they did then:

No physician, sleepless and worried about a patient, can return to the hospital in the midnight hours without feeling the importance of his faith. The dim corridor is silent; the doors are closed. At the end of the corridor in the glow of the desk lamp, the nurse watches over those who sleep or lie lonely and wait behind closed doors. No physician entering the hospital in these quiet hours can help feeling that the medical institution of which he is a part is in essence religious, that it is built on trust. No physician can fail to be proud that he is part of his patient's faith.

The student who understands that faith is the one who is ready to embark on life as a doctor.

Dr. Healy graduated from Harvard Medical School and spent much of her career caring for patients and teaching and researching at the Johns Hopkins School of Medicine and the Cleveland Clinic Foundation. She served as the dean of the College of Medicine and Public Health at Ohio State University, president of the American Red Cross, and was the first woman to be the director of the National Institutes of Health. Currently she writes health and medical columns for U.S. News & World Report, where she speaks to some 20 million "patients."

Introduction

There are certainly easier careers than medicine. You'll struggle through difficult science courses, indenture yourself for a *long* decade of school and training, and lose countless hours of sleep. The reward? You may end up owing $100,000, being mired in paperwork that robs you of time for patients (or for a life outside of work), and holding a job that leaves you a ripe target for malpractice lawsuits.

And it spite of it all, medicine could be the best choice you ever make. You could be the person who turns pain and suffering into relief and hope. You might solve the mystery of an illness that has stumped generations of doctors. Your colleagues will be extraordinary people. You will see babies safely born, and you will save people's lives.

"I think I have the best job on Earth," says Ronald Drusin, a doctor and associate dean of education at Columbia University's College of Physicians and Surgeons. "Half of my time, I deal with students and help make sure they get the best education. And half the time I'm in practice as a cardiologist, working at our heart transplant center. So I get to see miracles everyday."

> *"I spend my time seeing my patients as people, not just handing out medications. I get to know them."*

"I can't put into words how wonderful this job is," says Cynthia Romero, a family practice doctor in Virginia Beach, Virginia. "I spend my time seeing my patients as people, not just handing out medications. I get to know them, see them again and again and help them to live a healthy lifestyle. And I can see that it makes a big difference in my community."

It sounds ideal—and idyllic. But before you rush into medical school, stop and think about whether the vision of the profession you carry in your head matches today's reality. Medicine has always demanded a lot of physicians, even in the pre-HMO days of small practices and house calls. For many years, however, it has been changing in ways that doctors simply don't like. Lawrence Klein, an internist who enjoys his private practice in Washington, D.C., feels frustrated that increasing bureaucracy and financial pressures steal time from his patients. After all, seeing patients and giving them good care is what drew him to medicine in the first place. Would he go to medical school today? "Yes, but I'd think about it a bit more."

He'd consider, for example, the skyrocketing malpractice insurance premiums now hitting doctors—price hikes that insurers blame on outrageous jury awards in malpractice cases. "It's a dangerous situation for everyone," says Donald Palmisano, president of the American Medical Association. "The costs are forcing doctors to close practices." Indeed, physicians in Pennsylvania, West Virginia, Connecticut, and many other states have held protest marches recently to plead for relief.

Klein would also factor in the pressure that hospitals, practice groups, and HMOs exert on doctors to bring in more revenue by seeing more patients and seeing them faster. And he would certainly think about one unfortunate consequence of rising health care costs: Employers, looking for the best deals, are switching health plans frequently—every two years, in many cases—and that means that patients have to switch doctors, too. As a result of these switches and the hurried patient visits, many physicians find it impossible to build the long-term relationships they feel are so essential to effective patient care. Indeed, fewer med school graduates are even going into primary care, opting instead for specialties such as radiology where they believe they will be insulated from these forces.

Because of the time, vast sums of money, and effort involved, it's important to take a hard look at yourself—your motives, your goals, your personality—before embarking on this course. One undergrad at the University of Virginia, after slogging through organic chemistry and other premed courses, getting top marks, and prepping for and acing the all-important Medical College

Admissions Test (MCAT), began collecting school applications. Then, she remembers, she was sitting in the school library one night and looking across the table at a bunch of med students hunched over their books. "That's all they ever do: work," she said to her best friend. "That's not a life. It's a huge sacrifice. And I don't think I can do that." She didn't.

At least she realized her mismatch early. "Sometimes we have alums who stop med school after two or three years," says Carol Baffi-Dugan, director of health profession advising at Tufts University. "It's not often, but when it happens, it's the saddest thing. They've got debt coming out of their ears. And they've devoted an incredible amount of time and energy learning skills that are not really transferable."

So how can you give yourself a reality test before medical school tests you? The Association of American Medical Colleges poses several general questions, such as: Do I care deeply about other people, their problems, and their pain? Do I enjoy helping people with my skills and knowledge? Do I enjoy learning and gaining new understanding? Do I often dig deeper into a subject than my teacher requires? Surely, your response in all cases ought to be a well-considered and resounding "yes" if you're about to start writing tuition checks. But a "yes" could just as easily foreshadow a brilliant career in social work.

So as you go about measuring your reservoir of empathy and intellectual drive, check your motives, too. "People want to go into medicine for all sorts of reasons," says Noah Raizman, a student at Columbia's College of Physicians and Surgeons. "Sometimes it's money or prestige. And that's just stupid. Look, you'll always make a comfortable living as a doctor. But there's got to be something

more for you to be happy." Larry Sullivan, the pre-health professions advisor at Avila University in Kansas City, Kansas, often sees students who "have 'inherited' the idea of being a doctor. It comes from pressure from their family, or their peers." This, says Baffi-Dugan, is "one of the biggest pitfalls: the idea that 'it's going to make my parents happy.'" Still others want to practice because they've always watched *ER* and have the notion that medicine is dramatic and exciting. They don't consider how little independence doctors often have in real life and how difficult a workplace the health care system can be.

It's also worth considering how well-endowed you are with some specific strengths that seem to stand out in the profession. Admissions directors and advisors agree that good doctors come in a whole range of personality types. "Is every good doctor an extrovert? No," says Baffi-Dugan. But beyond an honest desire to help sick people, good doctors do share some important characteristics, chief among them self-discipline, an ability to think clearly and make decisions in a crisis, and conscientiousness.

A mix of great attention to detail and a desire to strive for high-quality work proves extremely valuable in medical school, too. In an unpublished study of 610 Belgian medical students over six years of their education, "across the board, conscientiousness predicted the strongest performance in medical school," says psychologist Deniz Ortiz of the University of Minnesota in Minneapolis. This finding mirrors an earlier study of 176 English med students, in which teacher references, student personality statements, and personality scores were all compared to see what factor best predicted med school performance, and the winner was conscientiousness.

Why does care and thoroughness mean so much? "You have to have remarkable perseverance to get through medical school," says psychologist Cheryl Weinstein of Harvard Medical School, who studies learning and learning disabilities. "If you are reasonably intelligent and can learn facts, you can get through the MCAT. If you have high intelligence and love science you are likely to get the

"You have to have remarkable perseverance to get through medical school."

references. But once you have to start spending the long hours, once you have to sustain attention and be able to plan and attend, if you don't have [perseverance], you will be found out." Ask yourself: Are you someone who meticulously proofreads a paper before handing it in, not relying on the caprices of computerized spelling and grammar programs to do your work? Did you work extra hours as a hospital volunteer because there was work that needed to be done? And when former professors or former employers write your recommendations, will they note that assignments and projects were never late?

Perhaps the most practical way to research the depth of your commitment is to actually watch what real doctors do. Marilyn Becker, director of admissions for the University of Minnesota Medical School, says that her picks usually have some serious experience in a medical setting before med school, often in a community clinic, a doctor's office, or a hospital. Applicants are strongly encouraged to get this sort of exposure, perhaps part-time while they're in college or over the summers.

Sullivan says that Avila University makes such work a part of a course called Introduction to Health Care Careers. More typically, students arrange it on their own. In college, Virginia Beach doctor Cynthia Romero set herself up with what she calls "mini rotations" by asking different doctors if she could shadow them for a week or more. (And she did this even though she already had more than a passing familiarity with the profession: Her mother is a physician.)

Romero liked what she saw, but for others, work experience can be a jolting reality check. "People volunteered in hospitals and realized they didn't have the patience to see patients," Romero recalls. "Or they couldn't handle the pressure, or they couldn't stand seeing sick children. Some got really upset at the sight of blood." That's a fairly safe sign that you should bail out.

Those who stay the course but aren't truly enthusiastic are easy to identify when you meet them, says Charles Bardes, admissions director at Weill Medical College at Cornell University. "That's why you can't get into medical school without an interview," he notes. What are the signs of true commitment to an activity mentioned in an application? "Did they do this work in a perfunctory way, say for just one hour per week? Were they involved in the leadership of this activity, or did they just show up?" he says. "We try and get a feel for all this when we interview the students." Nor is Becker impressed by someone who emphasizes his or her family's illustrious medical past—two doctor-uncles, a grandfather on the faculty of a renowned med school—as qualifications, rather than a personal passion for the profession.

Raizman, the medical student, is a fan of taking time off after college to put to rest any doubts about your direction. He worked as a chef for a while, and then as a high school teacher. Not only did he gain confidence in his decision to go to med school, but "now I have some sense of professionalism," he says. "Being a doctor is a position of responsibility. You need a solid sense of yourself. School won't teach you that."

Assuming that all this soul searching reveals you're meant to be in medicine, this book is your step-by-step guide to getting there. The first chapter offers snapshots of what you'll experience as a first-year med student, followed by a discussion in Chapter 2 of how to choose a medical school that meets your particular needs. Chapter 3 profiles the life and academics at five very different types of medical schools. In Chapter 4, you'll learn how to fine-tune your application so that your first-choice school chooses you. Chapter 5 is a primer on that all-important topic: financing your education.

Chapter 6 explores second chances, telling you what to do if you don't get accepted the first time. One possibility is to read Chapter 7 for insight on ten other health professions offering some of the same rewards. Beginning on page 85, you'll find a series of exclusive lists that allow you to compare medical schools on all kinds of key attributes: which are the hardest and easiest to get into, for example, and which ones leave graduates with the most and least debt. Finally, in the directory at the back of the book, you'll find detailed information on the country's medical schools, including schools offering the D.O. degree in osteopathy. This alternative medical degree involves a slightly different course of training, which is described in Chapter 2.

As you go through the extensive—some would say excruciating—application process, bear in mind that the interview, recommendation letters, and work experiences act as a final filter. They separate good students who *like* the idea of being a doctor from those who really would *be* a good doctor. Assuming that you possess all of the right qualifications, your best chance of making it through this sieve is to do what Harvard's Weinstein, and several ancient philosophers, suggest: "Know thyself." Perhaps friends, parents, mentors, school counselors, or trusted doctors will be able to ask you all the right questions to help you make this important decision. Regardless, there is only one person who can give the right answer. You.

Chapter One

A Med Student's First Year

Let's say you make it through your premed coursework, do well on the MCATs, and actually get into medical school. What happens next? Rachel Sobel was a young medical writer when she decided that the world she'd been covering as a journalist was something she wanted to experience firsthand. She'd majored in the history of science at Harvard and finished her premed coursework shortly after college. In 2002 she enrolled at the University of California, San Francisco School of Medicine (UCSF). "The process of becoming a physician is exhilarating," she says. "You will learn more about yourself and the world around you than you ever have." Sobel has been chronicling her experiences as a new med student. Here's her report from the front lines.

Fall, Year One

Meet Mr. Danovic

Sirens were blaring when the paramedics wheeled in John Danovic. The twenty-nine-year-old motorcyclist, who had just been laid off from his trucking job, had been drinking. He got hit by a car and thrown from his bike. Blood oozed from wounds in his scalp and chest, and a broken bone was jutting out of one arm.

The scene could have come straight out of any ER, but the case of John Danovic unfolded before my eyes in a lecture hall, not a hospital. The "blood" was actually a viscous burgundy concoction, and the team of doctors and nurses attending to the actor playing Mr. Danovic were my professors.

Welcome to my first lecture at medical school.

Med school isn't famous for its drama, nor is it known for its openness to change. Yet as the Mr. Danovic lecture reveals, change is afoot. Indeed, there is something of a revolution underway, transforming the first years of medical education. Many schools are dramatically revamping their curricula to prepare future physicians for an increasingly fragmented health care system in which any body of biomedical knowledge is bound to be quickly outdated.

Medical education has been virtually unchanged since the early twentieth century, when educators first standardized training. The "2+2" curriculum devoted the first two years to basic science lectures and the last two years to hospital training. Most med schools still use that general framework, but at UCSF and several other places, the first two years would be unrecognizable to a physician who graduated even five years ago.

Forget lectures from 8 a.m. until 5 p.m. Professors here have trimmed away esoteric hard science, keeping only what's essential to patient care. The reasoning is that you don't have to be a biochemist to be a skillful internist. In place of all that lab time, new disciplines are now considered essential to medical training, such as psychology, ethics, and even anthropology. For example, a patient assaulted by a gang (a real victim, unlike Mr. Danovic) talked to us about the psychological dimensions of healing.

David Irby, vice dean of education at UCSF, told me that the school's overhaul was driven in part by studies saying that newly minted M.D.s were unprepared to navigate today's health care system. There was also a widespread sense that medical school, rather than being an inspiring experience, had become a deadening one. Why did education have to be a boring exercise in memorization?

Mr. Danovic's case teaches that it can be otherwise. From him we learned the proper way to insert a chest tube (over the rib so you don't hit the nerves or vessels) and to recognize the signs of shock. Making the material more clinically relevant is not only more compelling but also more practical: According to Irby, study after study suggests that human memory is better wired for narrative than for rote learning.

Another major change taking place in medical training is an increased emphasis on cooperation, which grew out of the frequent observation that new doctors had great difficulty working in teams. You can imagine twenty- and thirty-somethings scoffing at the nursery school notion of cooperative learning, but in fact it's instilled so subtly that it's the way we're learning to think about how medicine works. Grades are pass/fail, which discourages competition. Half our classes take place in small groups, where the only way to learn is from one another. Picture a class where everyone doffs their shirts (women wear sports bras) and students draw on each other with Mr. Sketch markers to learn the complex intertwining of nerves, arteries, and veins of the arm. Being half-naked with classmates in "surface anatomy" isn't exactly a breeding ground for cutthroat rivalry.

Speaking of anatomy, I know my Uncle Peter will ask me over winter break how it went. Before I left for California, he regaled me with tales from his own medical school days—and reminded me to get there early for anatomy to get the best cadaver. I'm bracing for the next "In my day..." speech. But at UCSF, we learn from already dissected cadavers, and there is no competition to get the best one. Instead of spending hours trying to dig out, say, the renal artery, the idea is to save time and learn first from an intact specimen. To be sure, students still do a lot of memorizing. (For the eight wrist bones, remember: Some Lovers Try Positions That They Can't Handle: scaphoid, lunate, triquetrum, pisiform....You get the idea.) And budding surgeons can take a dissection elective, on, say, the abdomen or the pelvis.

No one knows if this new approach will prove better than the old one. Other schools that have made similar switches admit to growing pains. The ultimate measure is whether this generation of M.D.s will be better doctors in the modern health care system. On that, we'll have to wait to hear from the real Mr. Danovic.

Winter, Year One

The Art of Listening

One of my first epiphanies at med school came not from a gray-haired professor nor from *Gray's Anatomy* but from a fellow classmate. During our orientation in the fall, Jane (not her real name) told our entering class at UCSF about her heart surgery just a few weeks earlier.

Jane was a teenager when she first noticed an odd fluttering sensation inside her chest. The doctor did a quick exam and chalked it up to palpitations from too much caffeine. Later, while in college, Jane was getting ready for bed when her heart began racing and her room suddenly started spinning. Different symptoms, different doctor, but the same cursory approach: In this case, the diagnosis was anxiety.

Not until a recent checkup—six years after her initial complaint—did a keen physician find what was really wrong. He took a meticulous history and then listened to her heart with a stethoscope. Medicine's fancy term for this is auscultation: basically, listening to the body's various sounds. According to Jane, this physician "wasn't just going through the motions." He placed the stethoscope on her chest, closed his eyes, and listened for a long time. It paid off. The doc discovered a dangerous murmur, and further tests showed a two-inch hole in the wall between two chambers of her heart. Left untreated, such a defect could have caused heart and lung failure.

I was reminded of Jane's ordeal when I heard that the U.S. Medical Licensing Examination Committee had approved a new requirement for all medical students: a clinical-skills exam. The new test measures two things: communication skills and the ability to gather information through the physical exam. Students will interview and examine a series of "patients" (all actors) and complete a write-up for each one.

Many students were miffed that we would have to shell out an extra $1,000 or more to get licensed—not pocket change, considering that our average debt will close in on $100,000 by graduation. What's more, most schools already offer their own clinical-skills exams. Still, the new test sets important priorities. After all, isn't this what we came to school for, to learn the art of bedside diagnosis?

Kanu Chatterjee, a UCSF cardiologist who is legendary at performing physical examinations, has seen these vital skills atrophy in the profession over time. The repercussions, he says, include not only missed diagnoses but also the erosion of the patient–doctor relationship. Chatterjee trained in the 1950s when a physician's main diagnostic tool was a stethoscope. Now younger doctors rely more on sophisticated technology. He doesn't blame them; there is limited teaching time and technology is powerful. Still, he says, the physical exam "is the only tool to really get to know your patient."

A physical exam includes everything from inspecting a patient's appearance to palpating the abdomen to finding various pulses. As straightforward as that sounds, it is not easy. Last quarter, one of my professors played a recording of aberrant heart sounds during a lecture. I could not identify most of them. He played them again. Was that the abnormal "gallop"? I desperately clung to some fleeting rumble. Or was I just deluding myself into hearing something—anything?

My classmates and I got into medical school based in large part on our aptitude for science. But the art of physical diagnosis calls upon an entirely new sensibility: a heightened ability to listen, and look, and feel. Textbooks and flashcards can't teach these skills. They require practice, more practice, and an entirely new awareness of our own bodies to nourish the senses we have long neglected at the library.

An equally essential part of the bedside exam, obvious as it may seem, is good communication.

In fact, educators who pushed for the new licensing exam say part of the rationale is to weed out poor communicators and encourage schools to emphasize this competency in training. They cite a growing body of literature suggesting that the rising rate of malpractice complaints is linked to poor interpersonal skills.

This quarter, Jane and I took an in-house clinical-skills test. When our grader, a doctor from a nearby hospital, told a colleague she was going to be an evaluator, the colleague quipped: "They still teach that stuff?" Jane looked at me and said: "I can think of a few reasons why."

Spring, Year One

My future life?

The red-headed lady doesn't want her toddler to know she smokes. The man sitting next to her suffered two heart attacks this year and says it's time to quit. Another man, who has asthma, wants cleaner lungs. And in the corner, a transgendered woman undergoing hormone therapy vows to cut back on her two-pack-a-day habit because the combination puts her at increased risk for blood clots.

The motives for quitting might have been familiar, but clearly this was no ordinary smoking cessation meeting. It took place near the end of my first year as a medical student at a shelter in the squalid Tenderloin district of San Francisco, and its participants were a group of determined homeless people. Yes, they had unfathomable troubles to deal with, such as finding work and somewhere permanent to sleep, but they also had an unbending desire to take care of their own health.

The participants inspired not only each other but also the medical students who led the meetings each week. Medical school coursework is rigorous, yet many of us still squeeze in time to volunteer during the classroom years. At UCSF, for example, students set up pediatric health fairs in underserved areas, teach science to high schoolers, and coordinate bone marrow drives, among other things. It is here that we continue to cultivate what brought many of us into medicine in the first place: a desire to serve others through improving health care.

After the first two medical school years, where classroom learning dominates, in the final two years students are immersed in clinical experience and get to funnel all of their idealism, passion, and brain cells into taking care of patients. Enthusiastic friends who are in those years tell me, "you finally get to do what you came here for." Yet, at the same time, students are charged with figuring out their next step—their choice of specialty—and it is quite a complex decision. A new sense of pragmatism emerges.

During my first year, when I was on the wards for a few days during our winter "clinical interlude," I simply wasn't used to the new rhetoric about career choice. A third-year student told me in casual conversation that he wanted to specialize in radiology because of the "great lifestyle." I was shocked at first because I at least expected him to mention something intrinsically attractive about the field, such as its visual elegance or the satisfaction of nailing down diagnoses through images.

But then I began to hear more about this "ROAD to happiness"—radiology, ophthalmology, anesthesia, dermatology. The hours are good and the pay is at the top of the profession. These specialties are so popular that others are getting short shrift. For example, in 2002, less than half of all family practice residencies were filled by recent U.S. graduates.

Indeed, a recent study reported that lifestyle factors, such as adequate time for hobbies and family and control of weekly work hours, are a major reason for recent shifts in specialty career choices. The proportion of students who ranked anesthesiology as their first career choice, for example, went up more than fivefold in the last six years. At the same time, family practice applications have dropped 40 percent and the popularity of general surgery has also significantly declined.

There are many possible reasons why. One explanation is that more and more women are going into medicine and they are choosing more family-friendly fields. Another is that some students quickly become jaded in the modern medical climate. And who could blame them? Their role models are weary. A fourth-year student at an East Coast medical school told me that the attending physicians on his primary care rotation spent the whole time trying to convince him not to go into their field. The sacrifices such specialties call for, the student said, just aren't as appealing during these days of managed care pressures, high malpractice costs, and lower reimbursement rates.

Medical schools are concerned. Harvard's associate dean for student affairs, Nancy Oriol, believes that much of the growing acclaim of "lifestyle specialties" is simply urban legend passed around by students who haven't actually experienced these careers. She advises her students to pick their specialty based on their gut love of the field and then carve out the lifestyle they want once they begin practicing. "If you start off saying 'what are the lifestyle specialties?' then you may miss the ones you really love," she says. In almost every field, Oriol contends, a doctor can find a position that fits his or her choice of hours. There are surgeons who work part time, she says,

How med school works

Though schools vary widely in the courses they teach, most of this variation is grafted on top of a basic curriculum: two years of medical science followed by two years of clinical practice. This is followed by an apprenticeship period, or residency, that lasts from three to seven years. Here's a general outline:

Years One and Two: Coursework covers these topics: anatomy and embryology, physiology, biochemistry, histology, neuroscience, medical genetics, pharmacology, microbiology, pathology, and immunology. These first two years may also include courses on sexuality, nutrition, health care delivery, ethics, and other subjects.

Years Three and Four: You start clinical rotations in hospitals, usually beginning with surgery, family medicine, pediatrics, neuroscience, and obstetrics and gynecology. As you gain experience in patient care, these are followed by more rotations with advanced responsibility. You can also take elective courses in areas such as end-of-life care, psychiatry, or public and community health. Year four is also when students apply for residencies at various hospitals around the country in particular medical specialties. You graduate at the end of four years, and you can put an M.D. or D.O. after your name.

Year Five Postgraduate: You begin the first year of your residency, sometimes called an internship, taking primary responsibility for patient care while being supervised yourself by experienced doctors. Depending on the program—surgery, for instance, is very time-consuming—residencies can last as long as seven years.

Beyond Year Five: There's a lot of hard work involved in residency programs. After completing them successfully and passing national medical exams and state licensing tests, you are a full-fledged physician.

---

and there are academicians in radiology and dermatology who work all the time.

I recently spoke with a friend who is graduating from the University of Pennsylvania medical school. He is going into pediatrics, as did about one-sixth of the Penn class that graduated a year before him. Pediatrics is, on average, the lowest-paying field. "The majority of people," he observes, "still end up doing what their heart has told them to do from the beginning."

Now that I've finished my first year and have some perspective on it, I count my blessings: how privileged I am to be studying medicine and starting to work in the field. I know that in my training there will be elation and frustration, excitement and exhaustion—as there has been for many of my predecessors. Still, in the whirlwind events of a day during my training, I hope to always find meaning in the simple wonders of medicine—like the wonder I witnessed in the Tenderloin, as that group of homeless people threw away their lighters and cigarettes to begin a tough journey toward healthier living.

Chapter Two

Which Is the Right School for You?

There are essentially two ways to choose a medical school. There's the cynical approach: "You don't really have much choice," says one student. That is, you'll apply to the very few schools that might take you, and, if you're lucky "get into one or maybe two. And there you go." In the view of many medical school admissions officers, all schools offer a similarly fine education, anyway, because of medicine's rigid accreditation requirements. (Although their own schools, of course, are better than most, these officers hasten to add.) So what does it matter where you go, in the end?

Then there's the smarter approach, which won't make getting in any easier but greatly improves your odds of thriving if you make it. "Schools really aren't created equal," says Lucy Wall, assistant dean for admissions at the University of Wisconsin Medical School. "There are differences in teaching methods and curriculum, some schools are more research oriented, public schools can be very different environments than private schools....There are lots of things to consider." A school's location can make a huge difference in the kind of experience you have, both academically and in terms of your quality of life. An institution's reputation—whether it's viewed as a topflight research

---

"Schools really aren't created equal....There are lots of things to consider."

---

school or the place to go to become a primary care physician—can influence your chances of getting the residency slot you want after graduation. And since the learning environment is greatly affected by the other students and the campus culture, the most important consideration may be "that gut feeling you get about a school, how comfortable you feel there," says Lauren Oshman, president of the American Medical Student Association and a recent graduate of Baylor College of Medicine in Houston.

Take Fernanda Musa, a first-year student at Columbia University's College of Physicians and Surgeons in New York City. Musa wanted to attend a big-city institution doing cutting-edge research ("our teachers are some of the top names in their fields") where she would see the greatest variety of patients and conditions. Columbia was the perfect fit, she says. "The school culture is so happy. We're a really close, supportive group. We study together, and we also go out to concerts and bars. Most first-year students live together in Bard Hall, and that's where we get this great sense of community."

Jessica Vorpahl, a student at the University of Wisconsin interested in family practice, feels equally thrilled about her Midwestern, primary-care oriented, smaller-town school: "There's absolutely no better place. I'm totally convinced."

The hard numbers—your overall grade point average, your all-important science GPA, and your score on the Medical College Admissions Test—will narrow the field considerably by telling you which schools are within your reach. (See Chapter 4 for tips on figuring out the extent of your reach, then check out the directory at the back of this book for a sense of the numbers needed for entry at each school.) But your proper place in the field will depend on more, much more, than collections of statistics. Examining how the school teaches students (Does it rely on huge lectures? Will you get clinical experience early on or not until the latter half of your med school career?), what its curricular strengths are, what specialties graduates go on to practice, and how current students feel about the school will give you the best chance of finding, like Vorpahl, "no better place."

Consider the school culture

At the University of Iowa's Carver College of Medicine, students from all four years are grouped into small "learning communities" and interact both in class and out. First-year students relish the contact with upperclassmen, who are founts of invaluable advice about choosing courses and figuring out ways to fit all your hospital rotations into a tight schedule. At more traditionally organized schools, such as the University of Chicago Pritzker

School of Medicine, older students can disappear from sight once they start their clinical rotations. "Insanely competitive" is the phrase one student from the University of Alabama School of Medicine used to describe classmates. While the med school at Johns Hopkins University also has a reputation for intense competition, many students there protest that this is a myth—though they concede that, as a group, they tend to drive themselves hard and aren't exactly famous for kicking back and relaxing. At Yale, on the other hand, a policy of optional exams and no grades (students get evaluations from faculty) seems to create a less-pressured atmosphere, aided by the school schedule, which mandates a few weekday afternoons off.

Clearly, getting a feel for the ambience of a school requires some on-the-ground reporting. When you visit campus for your interview—which every med school requires—you'll be taken on a guided tour set up by the admissions office and designed to impress; figure out how to break away and do some independent poking around. One way to gather information is to visit a school early in the application process—before you're called in. Medical school admission offices aren't set up for drop-in visits the way college admissions offices are, so you may not get a lot of help from them. But you can contact alumni from your college at a particular med school, and they should be able to find you people to talk with and places to stay. Once you're on campus, don't be shy about buttonholing a few students and asking them some pointed questions:

What is student life like outside the classroom? Fernanda Musa at Columbia might tell you about the school's P & S Club, a student-run group central to most medical students' social lives that one day is running a wine tasting and another is producing *West Side Story* with students in the starring roles. Sara Brenner, a student at Iowa, reports that in Iowa City, "the world stops for college athletics. This place is overwhelmed by Hawkeye fever, and it's a lot of fun. Everyone goes to football and basketball games. At hospitals, you even see doctors with Hawkeye lapel pins next to their name badges." Hopkins students, in contrast, say they have to work to find extracurricular activities in Baltimore; the fun is there, but you need to dig for it. At Northwestern University's Feinberg School of Medicine, as at Columbia, a social life is easy to come by. First-year students at Northwestern live together in Lake Shore Center, which leads to impromptu gatherings, study support, and therapeutic venting sessions.

How intense is the competition? Generally speaking, a lot less so than you might think. Sure, there are people at Hopkins who are intensely competitive, says student Aima Ahonkhai, "but it hasn't affected me." Study groups and note-sharing are more the norm. Dan Imler, a student at Case Western Reserve University School of Medicine, says, "I had heard students at Case were kind of snobby and I was concerned that might lead to competition, but that's definitely not the case!" At Alabama, too, the "insanity" is more exception than rule. "The students are very helpful if you ask," says student Damion Heersink. "I think there are really only a few people who don't like to help others, and nobody likes them anyway."

Many new med students may *fear* competition because they remember, all too clearly, how fiercely they fought to get into medical school in the first place. But the reality is that once admitted, students feel a kinship with each other—that they're in this often-grueling, often-exhilarating experience together, says Jack Snarr, associate dean for student programs at Northwestern. They want to do well so as to get into a good residency program, but aren't willing to do it by hurting others. "I know what I want to score on an exam, because I know what I'm capable of. But I don't want to get that score by withholding information from another student," says Carrie Castleforte, a student at Wright State University School of Medicine in Dayton, Ohio.

How accessible are the professors? Try to get input from a number of people because opinions may differ a lot within schools: Students who hang back may find they have very little contact with faculty, while more assertive students have no complaints. A lecture format, which predominates during the first years of school at the University of Chicago, for example, will probably make it more difficult to get to know faculty, especially if the school and the lectures are large. In the faculty-led small discussion and problem-solving groups that pepper the first years at Cornell University's Weill Medical College in New York City, by contrast, even the shyest students are soon known by name. At the University of Minnesota School of Medicine at Duluth, where entering class sizes hover around 50 rather than the more typical 100 to 150, faculty and administration "really feel more like family," says student Krista Johnson. "People have open-door policies, and you can just walk in and discuss something if you have a problem or are confused by something."

Yet even at schools like Chicago, professors have office hours. Find out whether they keep them, and whether those who go up and knock on the door are welcome or treated as nuisances. Keep in mind that even though medical schools list particular faculty members as "course directors" in their catalogs, at some schools you may see that professor only at the first lecture and then spend the rest of the semester dealing with assistants.

How welcoming is the school and the student body to people of different backgrounds? You can often tell a lot by just walking around with your eyes open. How diverse does the population seem to be? How much a part of things are the minority students? "We do OK on women here," says Philip Farrell, dean at Wisconsin, where women make up 56 percent of the 2003 entering class, compared to the national average of just under 50 percent. "But we don't do so well on minorities."

Nor do a good many other medical schools, but finding and encouraging would-be minority doctors is a goal that some are now getting serious about. Wisconsin has initiated "pipeline" programs to try and remedy the shortage, running summer science and math workshops for disadvantaged and minority high school students. Some med schools, such as Columbia and the University of California–San Francisco, have tried to build special support networks for minority students to reduce feelings of isolation and deal with any academic troubles. At UCSF, for example, the Medical Scholars Program was started because some underrepresented minority students found a few of the science courses to be tough going. Students who want help can meet twice a week in small workshops to discuss coursework, problem-solving skills, and better ways of organizing their study time. The workshops also serve as social hubs, where students meet one another and forge friendships.

If you can't manage to get to a school in person, some virtual exploration might be in order. Student perspectives can be found on the website of the Student Doctor Network (www.studentdoctor.net), a volunteer not-for-profit group that collects questionnaires about medical schools from premed students who have visited them. "Really laid back, friendly and enjoyable. Interviews were conversational. I had to explain my nontraditional stuff, which I expected (I'm 25). Really got me excited about the school," wrote one visitor to the University of Michigan–Ann Arbor. Another visitor to the same school, however, had this to say: "I got the real picture from some of the students. They told me most people are sons of doctors, or their parents are wealthy benefactors of the school. Lots of Ivy Leaguers too over there, not much room for people without money."

Obviously, student opinions will be just that, and you're sure to get conflicting information. But complaints can clue you in to areas that bear further investigation. The SDN site also features chat rooms where you can quiz students at schools of interest. You can also trade impressions with premeds and med students at another online community, www.medschoolchat.com.

Weigh the location

Beyond student culture, one of the most important features of a school to consider is its address. Location affects the kinds of patients you'll see, the range of diseases you'll be trained in, and the emphasis the school puts on different medical specialties—not to mention whether or not your significant other will have to give up his or her job and follow you out of state.

"An urban setting exposes you to a wide variety of patients, simply because that's the population. And that's going to make you a more well-rounded clinician." says Charles Bardes, admissions director at Cornell, which sits on the east side of Manhattan. It's important, he says, for applicants comparing schools to get a sense of the patient populations when they're visiting campus. "Walk up and down the hospital halls, and talk to students." If the school has a spectrum of hospitals, he says, there will in all likelihood be a spectrum of patients. A student at Cornell, for instance, might spend time in a hospital where a number of

> *"An urban setting exposes you to a wide variety of patients, simply because that's the population."*

patients are elderly and have brittle bones, then move on to a hospital in a poor neighborhood and see pregnant teenagers and children affected by lead poisoning. And because the school is affiliated with the world-renowned Memorial Sloan-Kettering Cancer Center, the student might well see more rare cancers than the average medical student—and the latest in treatment.

But don't take this to mean that all noncity schools will offer you an all-white or otherwise one-dimensional experience. Even though Wisconsin is located in the small city of Madison, for example, it sends students to training sites across the state. They can spend weeks seeing patients in small towns like Chippewa Falls, where many people have adequate health insurance and are easily available for follow-up care. But they can also go to Milwaukee, which has a large Latino population, and where patient care might involve surmounting language barriers that don't exist in Chippewa Falls. That said, schools like Minnesota–Duluth and Iowa, in rural states, do tend to focus more on family

The "other" medical degree

Connor Shannon is the son of a doctor and he knew, very early, that he wanted to be an M.D., too. So after graduating from the University of Colorado, he trained as an emergency medical technician, spent a couple of years working, and applied to 25 medical schools. Because his science background was relatively weak, which in turn "made me not do so well on the MCATs," he was rejected by 23 schools and waitlisted by the remaining two.

In the months that followed, Shannon got to know several doctors with the "other" medical degree—a doctor of osteopathy or D.O.—and began to suspect he might be chasing the wrong kind of training. "I liked [the D.O.s'] bedside manner better," he says. Shannon now attends—and is loving—the Chicago College of Osteopathic Medicine at Midwestern University.

Many medical school advisors recommend applying to a combination of D.O. and M.D. schools right from the start. "Both produce well-trained doctors," says Carol Baffi-Dugan,

program director for health professions advising at Tufts University. Curricula at both cover the same basic scientific principles of medicine, and osteopaths are licensed in all 50 states in surgery, internal medicine, and every other medical discipline.

Where the two schools of medicine differ is in philosophy. Doctors of osteopathy "treat people, not just symptoms," says Karen Nichols, dean of the Chicago College of Osteopathic Medicine. "The course list looks exactly the same, but the M.D.'s focus is on discreet organs. The osteopathic focus is that all of those pieces are interrelated. You can't affect one with out affecting another." That means more than paying simple lip-service to the idea of the "whole" patient: It means examining his or her environment, family, and general situation in life, too. Michael Kuchera, a D.O., describes the emphasis as being on health rather than disease. Not surprisingly, more than 65 percent of the 52,000 licensed osteopaths in the United States are primary care

physicians—in family practice or pediatrics, for example. The American Association of Colleges of Osteopathic Medicine provides a description of osteopathic training, as well as short profiles of 20 schools, on its website (www.aacom.org). The D.O. programs and their contact information are listed in the Directory section of this book.

Beyond their other medical studies, osteopathic students get 200 hours of training in "osteopathic manipulative medicine," a hands-on technique for diagnosis and healing. Limited motion in the lower ribs, for instance, can cause pain in the stomach that seems a lot like irritable bowel syndrome. Identifying the muscle strain in the ribs through manipulation, and then treating it, can relieve the stomach distress. An osteopath learns to apply specific amounts of pressure on a body part, attempting to relax it or stimulate it. While such an approach might have raised eyebrows in the profession a decade or two ago, these days no one—except perhaps the crustiest old M.D.s—dismisses it as New Age nonsense. Manipulative medicine is based on the not-terribly-heretical idea that structures in the body influence function, and that a problem in the structure of one body part can cause problems in the function of other parts.

Nichols cautions students not to think of applying to D.O. schools as a fallback plan. Some of them accept a greater percentage of applicants than do M.D. schools, but many are just as selective. And all D.O. schools are searching for a particular kind of person. "Students have to understand the osteopathic schools are not looking for people who couldn't get into M.D. schools," says Nichols. "I want them to understand the osteopathic philosophy, to have spent time with a D.O. so they can get a strong letter of recommendation." And as for Connor Shannon, he now believes his rejections were a good thing because they allowed him to land where he was always meant to be.

practice medicine because that specialty is much in demand in these areas.

Indeed, public institutions supported by state money generally emphasize medical training targeted to state and local needs. While it's possible to be trained in ophthalmology or oncology at the University of Washington in Seattle, for example, there's a definite push to turn out primary care docs who will stay in the Northwestern corner of the country and practice; 60 percent of graduates do just that. Wisconsin offers many more opportunities to learn about rural health care than does Columbia. At SUNY Downstate Medical Center College of Medicine in Brooklyn, students get exposure to a high-risk obstetrics program because there are so many high-risk pregnancies in that community.

Another way state schools fulfill state objectives is by educating their own residents, and doing so relatively cheaply. "The first issue I usually ask students to think about when thinking about schools is where they live," says John Friede, the health professions advisor at Villanova University in Philadelphia. "Staying in-state can often mean real savings, and getting out of school with less debt." Pennsylvania residents who choose Pennsylvania State University College of Medicine pay about $24,000 per year in tuition, for instance. The school charges students from out of state an extra $10,000 per year. If Pennsylvania residents go to Duluth to study medicine, they pay $46,000, while the Minnesota locals pay $25,000. Likewise, leaving state for a private institution could mean tuition bills of $30,000–40,000 a year. (See Chapter 5 for other strategies for financing your education.)

You'll probably find that staying close to home gives you a better chance of getting in, too. In 2003, for example, the University of California–San Diego School of Medicine had about 3,000 in-state applicants and admitted 120; of about 1,100 applicants from out-of-state, it took just 2. Wisconsin's med school is committed to taking 80 to 90 percent of its students from the Badger State. Finally, of course, a school's location can mean a great deal for your personal life. One of the reasons Columbia works so well for Musa is that her family members, who live in Brazil, find it easy to fly up and visit her on the East Coast; a California school would mean a longer, more expensive trip.

"Staying in-state can often mean real savings, and getting out of school with less debt."

Put prestige in perspective

You might be tempted to pay any amount of money to get your M.D. from a great medical school—a really, really great school. Someplace you've always heard about, like Harvard, or Stanford, or Cornell, or Johns Hopkins, whose name alone says "first-rate education."

Not so fast, says Bardes. As admissions director at Cornell, he can certainly brag about a top-notch faculty and state-of-the-art facilities. He just can't say that Cornell's strengths add up to a quality of education that's significantly better than most others. "The quality range in medical schools is much narrower than in other types of schools," he says. Andrew Frantz, associate dean of admissions at Columbia, which usually scores near the top in the annual *U.S.News & World Report* ranking of med schools, agrees: "For maybe 90 percent of the schools, the quality seems very tight, and very high." Or as Delores Brown, associate dean for admissions at Northwestern's med school, puts it: "For medical training, there is no bad school."

Why would medicine produce such a tight bunch? There are a few reasons. Bardes points out that because the public has a life-and-death interest in highly skilled physicians, the accreditation process for medical schools is unusually elaborate and demanding. That process, overseen by both the Association of American Medical Colleges and the American Medical Association, examines everything from the technology at student clinical sites to the teaching qualifications of the faculty to the curriculum content, ensuring that it covers not just the scientific basis of medicine but also behavioral and socioeconomic aspects. The resulting accreditation reports for any given school are as bulky as a Los Angeles telephone directory. "They ask a lot of questions and want very specific answers," says Wisconsin's Farrell, hefting his school's report off his desk. "There are about 120 certification standards in here. With us, they liked our faculty development program and our mentoring program for students. But they thought we had too many lectures and not enough self-directed study."

Another equalizer? The national standardized tests students must take during their four years in school. Passing the initial U.S. Medical Licensing Examination, which tests knowledge of basic medical science, is required for promotion from the second to the third year, and students have to pass further stages of the test during their final two years in order to graduate. Obviously, failure doesn't just hurt the student: A pattern of failures reflects badly on the school and may jeopardize its accreditation.

Schools that do enjoy an aura of prestige tend to be the ones with the big research programs, says Thomas Langhorne, the prehealth professions advisor at Binghamton University in New York. "These are schools with lots of Nobel Prize winners, or researchers that make discoveries about diseases, or get big grants, and so they get a lot of press," he says. "You read the names 'Harvard' and 'Stanford' a lot. But these are things that, to me, don't have a lot to do with your training to be a physician."

It's not that a strong and active research program is irrelevant; in fact, the research might well enhance your academic experience. If you find yourself drawn to the study of glaucoma or the genetics of antibiotic resistance, for example, it should be relatively easy at a school pulling in lots of grants in these areas to get funding for a short research project, often working alongside a faculty member. The research may also inform course content—indeed, the experts may be teaching the classes. At a smaller school with less research money—say, a state school focused on primary care—you'll have fewer opportunities to "follow your nose" and go in unexpected directions. And anyone who tells you that having Harvard or Cornell on a résumé won't open a few extra doors simply isn't being honest.

In certain cases, however, a great research reputation might actually be a career handicap, says Phyllis Guze, president of the Association of Program Directors in Internal Medicine—the people who run residency programs and thus hire med school graduates for their first job. "You can come from a school with a stellar academic reputation, and depending on the residency you're applying for, that's not going to help you," she says. If she were looking at applicants for an inner-city hospital residency without a big research component, a Stanford résumé wouldn't be the top one on her pile. "It's a school noted for great scholarship and academic physicians," she says, "so why would the student be interested in this kind of hospital? Program directors really think about things like this."

Rather than focusing on reputation, advisors and med school faculty suggest taking a hard look at the concrete—and the metal and the electronics. Good facilities are a harbinger of a good educational experience. Wisconsin's new health sciences building, for

"The quality range in medical schools is much narrower than in other types of schools."

instance, has Ethernet jacks at every classroom desk, so if a lecturer is using a PowerPoint presentation, students can download it right onto their laptops. The University of Pittsburgh School of Medicine is going totally wireless, so students can do the same thing even when sprawled out in a hallway.

Pittsburgh also has installed high-resolution cameras and monitors that cover every inch of its anatomy lab. Typically, when new students are dissecting a cadaver and people at one table find something interesting, like the heart, "a buzz goes through the room and 150 students line up to look," says John Mahoney, the school's assistant dean for medical education. "That takes forever and number 150 probably can't see anything. But with our cameras, an image immediately shows up over every dissecting table, so all students have to do is look up for a great view." Features like these indicate that the school is investing in education, and not neglecting students to pay hospital debts, say.

One aspect of a school's reputation that should matter to you a lot is how well-regarded it is among residency directors who aim to hire the most skilled doctors they can find. Examining the school's record on residency matches will give you a good idea. In general, academic hospitals—those closely affiliated with a university—tend to be more sought after because they are better teaching environments than stand-alone hospitals. And how many of the students get into their top choices? At most schools, 90 percent of graduates get into their first-, second,- or

> "You read the names 'Harvard' and 'Stanford' a lot. But these are things that, to me, don't have a lot to do with your training to be a physician."

third-choice program. If the school reports a lower number, that should be a warning.

There are other signs of trouble, and they have to do with money. If a school is strapped, count on it: You'll be affected. In the late 1990s, for instance, MCP-Hahnemann University School of Medicine in Philadelphia was in dire straits because its hospitals were hemorrhaging money. Morale among faculty was low and researchers had trouble getting the school to pay their bills on time. Since then, Hahnemann has merged with another Philly school to form the Drexel University College of Medicine. There's new management, new money flowing in, new technology, new ownership arrangements for the hospitals, and much more happiness on campus. So check the local newspapers for stories about financial worries. You might even call a broker. If a school or medical center has floated bond issues, agencies like Moody's rate those bonds based on the financial soundness of the institution issuing them.

What and how you'll learn

A school's curriculum and the style faculty use to teach it are crucial elements of your decision, even though the topics covered during the first and second years are pretty much the same wherever you go. Anatomy and embryology, physiology, biochemistry, histology, neuroscience, genetics, pharmacology, microbiology, pathology, and immunology—all are basic science areas that every budding doctor needs to cover.

What varies is the way in which they are taught; many schools present the facts in tried-and-true large lectures, while others emphasize small-group discussions that center around solving problems. Some schools use a mix of the two styles. At Harvard and Pittsburgh, two institutions that rely heavily on "problem-based learning," or PBL, a group of first-year students studying anatomy or immunology or microbiology will meet for, say, 90 minutes to discuss a hypothetical patient with specific symptoms— Mr. X has come to his family doctor complaining of fever and chills—and brainstorm ways to figure out what's wrong. If the course is microbiology, someone might suggest an infection. Then the question becomes: What kind of infection? Everyone goes off to research possible conditions and appropriate diagnostic tests, and the group meets again and again during the week, eventually arriving at a solution: Mr. X has a staph infection. The idea is that by teaching themselves how to solve problems, students are better equipped for the real world. "When they present to you one specific disease and you talk about it in PBL, it really sticks with you," notes Mike Mclaughlin, a

Pittsburgh student. A microbiology lecture on staph, in contrast, might present a list of germs, symptoms they can cause, and antibiotics that might kill them.

Not everyone is a believer in PBL. Noah Raizman, a Columbia student, thinks that while it gives students the needed information, it can also take a lot of extra time. A former teacher, he's used PBL with his own students. "It's great when everyone in the group comes in with a different knowledge base and can exchange information. But the first year of med school is *not* like that. People actually know very little. So you end up spending an awful lot of time running around to the library, looking up basic things. It's not efficient at all." The Columbia faculty agrees with him for the most part and has emphasized lectures, adopting PBL techniques in just a few courses. Jessica Carney, a University of Chicago med student, also feels she gets more with less fuss out of the science lectures that dominate at her school: "You need to have the basic sciences down first in order to do something good later. It might not seem interesting but we can't help patients without it."

Another variation is the way schools serve up the required topics. For example, many are moving away from courses that cover discrete subjects such as microbiology or pharmacology as overviews of the entire body, moving instead toward interdisciplinary "organ-based" courses that examine all aspects of, say, the kidneys. Students learn about kidney anatomy, microbiology, immunology, and the drugs that affect this organ. Next, they might move on to the heart and circulatory system, then go on to the nervous system, and so on throughout the body. "I think it helps you put things together and see how the body actually works," says Duluth student Krista Johnson. Her school, along with Brown, Yale, the University of Texas Medical Branch at Galveston, and many others, have switched to this way of teaching.

> *"You need to have the basic sciences down first in order to do something good later."*

The amount of time spent helping patients—or at the very least seeing patients—is an increasingly important variable, too. For a large part of the last century, the basic science courses during the first years of med school kept students in large lecture halls or with their noses buried in textbooks. Then, in the third year, they'd enter the hospital for clinical training and encounter their first real patients. Often they were ill-prepared. "Our faculty was getting worried that students weren't making the connections between science and patient care that they could be making," says Donald Innes, associate dean for curriculum at the University of Virginia's medical school. That concern was shared nationwide, says Robert Eaglen of the Liaison Committee on Medical Education, the curriculum guidance arm of the Association of American Medical Colleges. Medical schools across the country began revamping their first-year curriculum so that student–patient encounters would occur early on.

It's a welcome change for many students. "I want the science backed up by experience," says

Drew Kalishman, explaining that the promise of early and plentiful experience with patients drew him to the University of New Mexico. As a supplement to time in class, the school places first-year students in local clinics where they work with supervising physicians in actual practice. "Having a real face behind these medical problems is really helpful," Kalishman says. Moreover, students

---

"Our faculty was getting worried that students weren't making the connections between science and patient care that they could be making."

---

learn early how to interact with patients—a skill you can't get from a textbook, says Scott Obenshain, New Mexico's former associate dean for undergraduate medical education. The contact is helpful to patients, too—which is why New Mexico originally started making it happen. "We're in a rural area and we have a great call for physicians who have general skills, rather than specialists," says Obenshain. Case Western pairs students in their first month of school with expectant mothers at local clinics. The students work as patient advocates until these mothers give birth.

Some schools simulate patient interaction instead. Virginia, for instance, uses "standardized patients" in first-year lecture classes. These are not real patients, but people who have been trained to complain of symptoms that are signs of a particular illness. Students learn to take medical histories from working with them and progress to giving them physical exams.

Most schools also now require that first-year students "shadow" practicing physicians on their rounds, perhaps once a week or once a month. But

beware: Not all shadowing experiences are equally useful. "Applicants really should ask if shadowing is an active or passive experience," says Cornell's Bardes, who believes that just sitting around watching the doctor work doesn't do much good. A more active role, which Cornell asks of its students, is to function as a patient advocate or a kind of social worker in a medical clinic, talking to the patient and making sure any concerns are addressed by the medical team. "Not only does that get the student involved with the patient," Bardes says, "it also involves the student with the doctors and nurses directly, and helps the student understand that care is a team effort."

New topics are also shouldering their way into the mix. At Pritzker in Chicago, first-years take a course called Introduction to Clinical Medicine, which gets away from science and into interpersonal relationships and ethics; at Iowa, this course is called Foundations of Clinical Practice. UCSF offers an introduction to pain treatment. And Emory, in Atlanta, teaches Complementary Medical Practices as an elective, in which students visit acupuncture studios and Chinese herbalists. Other schools have added complementary medicine to the curriculum, too, as doctors begin to realize how many of their patients take herbs and supplements.

Finally, although medical students often joke that "C equals M.D." (meaning that you can count on being a doctor as long as you don't flunk out), it's worth considering the way schools on your list handle grades. The traditional "ABC" system may be the most comfortable one for you if you like getting fairly specific feedback about how firm a grasp you have of the material. Some students at Yale, in fact, say that school's relaxed no-grade approach can cause people to slip far behind unless they are highly motivated and disciplined. On the other hand, many students find that simple pass/fail grades relieve some of the pressure that comes with a letter system. Dan Imler at Case Western, who keeps a record of his medical school experiences online at www.medschooldiary.com, says that grading policies helped him choose between Case in Cleveland and Ohio State in Columbus. Ohio State was a lot cheaper and "in a town that felt more like home." Yet he decided on Case largely because the first two years of the program are graded pass/fail. To Imler, that meant the likelihood that Case "might be more humane than the rest," and that there would be less competition and more cooperation with other students. Indeed, Imler's time in school so far has been filled with fun as well as work, and much of the credit goes to his fellow students, he says. "So I'll take my Case Western degree and smile."

Chapter Three

Inside Five Top Schools

There's more than one way to become a doctor—146 ways, in fact, if you count all of the accredited medical schools in the country. (Turn to the Directory for details.) The five top schools profiled in this chapter each typify a different approach to the teaching of medicine. All place highly in the annual *U.S.News & World Report* rankings. Two are public schools, one in a small Midwestern city (the University of Wisconsin in Madison) and the other in a dense, urban West Coast setting (the University of Washington in Seattle). Both of these schools try to meet local needs by turning out world-class primary care doctors, but they do so in very different ways.

The remaining three are private institutions. Duke University, in the Southeast, has an accelerated program of science courses for first-year students, setting them up to do complex research. At Yale University in the Northeast, students don't take exams unless they want to, yet are required to write a thesis. Then there is Johns Hopkins University in the mid-Atlantic, a research power-house whose students serve urban Baltimore when they are not busy in the school's labs.

Of course, each school boasts features that defy the limits of any stereotype: Washington, for instance, creates family doctors while also pulling in more research money than most other schools in the nation. That's why any school you're interested in merits a closer look. To give you a head start, here are profiles, including student and faculty viewpoints, of each member of this medical Fab Five.

University of Wisconsin Medical School

- Madison, Wisconsin
- Public
- Enrollment 2003–2004 academic year: 598
- Overall rank in the 2005 *U.S. News* medical school rankings (research): 25
- Overall rank in the 2005 *U.S. News* medical school rankings (primary care): 3
- Average MCAT score: 10.4
- Average undergraduate GPA: 3.74

Stroll over to Wisconsin's anatomy department and you'll be able to talk to—or take a class from—James Thomson, the scientist who first isolated human stem cells from an embryo, a giant break-through that has raised hopes for dramatic new medical therapies and embroiled the country in an ethical debate over use of these cells. Nearly 600 of Wisconsin's other 1,100 faculty members are involved in leading medical science programs in aging, neuroscience, cancer, and other key areas. The university as a whole pulled in $600 million in research money in 2003, making it one of the top public schools doing this kind of work. So what draws most students to Madison? Surprisingly, *not* the lure of the lab. "I came because we train some of the best primary care physicians around," says student Jennifer Erickson. It's a sentiment her fellow students echo again and again.

Philip Farrell, dean of the medical school, says there's no contradiction here, given Wisconsin's status as both a fine academic institution and a state university. "We have a superb clinical care program; that's absolutely true. It's a core part of our mission. Yet we're also part of this enormous research university." The med school has almost as many Ph.D. students as it does M.D. students; joint M.D./Ph.D. degrees in the Medical Scientist Training Program are also popular. Pioneering research programs on the connection between cancer and nutrition, and on cardiac electrophysi-ology, have spawned courses for medical students. "But yeah," Farrell acknowledges, "we produce fine, caring doctors."

This, then, is the "Wisconsin idea": While the university is tucked away on a narrow isthmus of land, almost cut off by two surrounding beautiful lakes, Mendota and Monona, the medical school itself is a statewide institution. Students do research in Madison at the highly regarded cancer center, for example, but also go to Milwaukee and work with the urban poor, or head out to small towns like Eagle River or Ashland, where they learn about rural health care issues and everyone around knows their names. Feeling a strong responsibility to make sure Wisconsin has the necessary supply of doctors, the university's Board of Regents presses Farrell to reserve 80 to 90 percent of the spots in each entering class for in-state students, many of whom will stay in the area once they get their M.D.

To fan interest in treating patients, the school pairs first- and second-year students with family practice doctors, internists, or pediatricians for a half-day each month. Students themselves run a program called MEDIC (Medical Information Center), which puts them to work advising patients at clinics in the Madison area. For at least six weeks during the third year, the school boots everyone out for rotations in small-town clinics and hospitals throughout the state. "It's not that they absolutely want to push us in that direction, but they definitely want to expose us to that," says student Jessica Vorpahl, who says she feels pulled toward family practice. (The school does look beyond the Dairy State borders: It runs a summer medical clinic in Ecuador, for example.) And the exposure definitely gets results: Since 1999, about 20 percent of each graduating class has gone into family medicine residencies. Internal medicine has drawn an additional 12 to 20 percent, and the third most popular specialty has been pediatrics. In contrast, about five or six percent choose surgery, and a fraction of a percent go into neurology.

Whatever specialty students explore, they do it in close contact with their professors. Particularly at the small-town sites, there's often just one student rotating through at a time, which translates into a lot of attention from teacher-physicians. That's true on campus, too. Faculty members have a reputation for being very approachable and often come in during the evenings to tutor students. "There's a lot of interaction with professors," says Erickson. "When I went to get recommendations for residency programs, there was no shortage of people I could talk to. I was on a first-name basis with a lot of them." Indeed, teaching skill, not just the number of publications or amount of grant

"When I went to get recommendations for residency programs, there was no shortage of people I could talk to."

funding brought in, is weighed more heavily in promotion decisions than at most schools, and junior faculty are assigned a senior faculty mentor to help them along.

The warm, intimate feeling extends to fellow students. "I got into here, and Dartmouth, and Yale," says one third-year student. "This place seemed different. People at Madison take time out of their schedules to stop and discuss the school with you, in the classrooms and in the hallways, because they like it so much. I remember I visited one other school where I didn't see a student all day, and I know they weren't all on vacation." Students call the culture supportive, not competitive; there are even side bets in each class on how many members will end up marrying one another. And while everyone studies hard, people here "also know how to have a good time," says another student. Erickson likes the fact that much of her class is older and brings mature, diverse perspectives to discussions about subjects such as medical ethics.

Not everything about the school gets rave reviews. There are too many basic science lectures, according to some students and faculty. Unlike schools that try to pepper the first year with small-group learning experiences, Wisconsin has retained the large-lecture format. "I'd say that small-group learning is our biggest weakness right now," says Susan Skochelak, the senior associate dean for academic affairs. Adds Vorpahl: "There were six or seven hours of lectures per day during the first year. They don't take attendance, so you don't have to be there. But I felt that much structured time was excessive, at least for me." There are also complaints that the school buildings are old and overcrowded and that there's no student parking.

Class sizes and facilities should be drastically improved in the fall of 2004, when the school's $55 million Health Sciences Learning Center is set to open, giving Wisconsin the most modern medical school building in the country. Numerous classrooms and labs will allow for smaller course sections and discussion groups. The school's separate libraries will be consolidated here and equipped with more computer terminals as well as wireless access. The entire building, in fact, will be wireless heaven, with numerous "hot spots" where students can download course materials and medical data out of the ether. The building will also house Wisconsin's nursing and physician assistant programs, allowing for a lot of cross-pollination of ideas and staff.

Parking spaces are still going to be a problem, however. If that's a big issue for you, Madison is not going to make you happy. But everything else—the patient contact, the access to leading research if you want it, the new building, the famously rich university-made ice cream sold at the student center—makes for some of the best-trained (and happiest) future doctors around.

Duke University School of Medicine

- ■ **Durham, North Carolina**
- ■ **Private**
- ■ **Enrollment 2003–2004 academic year: 470**
- ■ **Overall rank in the 2005 *U.S. News* medical school rankings (research): 4**
- ■ **Overall rank in the 2005 *U.S. News* medical school rankings (primary care): 39**
- ■ **Average MCAT score: 11.9**
- ■ **Average undergraduate GPA: 3.80**

Most medical students spend their third year of school racing around hospitals, going from cardiology units to pediatric wards to try out various clinical specialties. But by Brian Griffith's third year at Duke, he had already been there and done that. Instead, Griffith was holed up in his own little corner of a bustling microbiology lab, surrounded by rows and rows of petri dishes filled with a fungus that can cause meningitis in people with weak immune systems. Griffith, 24, was designing tests to identify genes that help the fungus become virulent. With the support of his mentor and lab chief, geneticist Joseph Heitman, he plans to publish the results of several experiments.

Meanwhile, across town at a Duke clinic, Griffith's classmate Jennifer Kim was interviewing and examining a 100 patients enrolled in a new study on the reliability of various blood pressure monitors. "Blood pressure is used so often for diagnosis and patient status info," says Kim, who hopes to bring better, more reliable devices into hospitals and clinics. "I think this sort of research is key to the practice of medicine."

This notion—that research is the cornerstone of health care—dominates the Duke experience.

To this end, the school packs all basic science classes into the first 11 months, running August through July, instead of spreading them across the first two years as most schools do. The science acceleration gets students into the hospital sooner—during year two instead of year three, so their third year is devoted full-time to research.

Clearly, Duke is not aiming to swell the ranks of family practice docs. Instead, the program is geared toward producing physician-scientists who can easily move between the lab bench and the bedside. "Our current body of knowledge will have nothing to do with the practice of medicine in ten years," says R. Sanders Williams, dean of the school. "We aim to provide graduates with both the tools and the ethos of lifetime scholarship." He notes that a full 40 percent of students go on to pursue dual degrees such as an M.D./Ph.D. or an M.D. combined with a new master's degree in translational medicine, which focuses on turning basic research into clinically useful models.

The pressure can be great here, especially early on, so Duke students must hit the ground running. That early push to cover everything from physiology and neurobiology to pathology in the first year means spending all day, every day in a lecture hall and then a lab. It's difficult, say students, but doable. "We're learning the essentials, not a lot of fluff, because you don't need it," says second-year student Erica Taylor, adding that she felt extremely well-prepared for her clinical rotations. In fact, most students are eager to hit the wards. "I came to med school to practice medicine, to put a white coat on and get out into the hospital—not to sit in a classroom for two years," explains Julius Wilder, now in the fourth year of a combined M.D./Ph.D. program in medical sociology and health policy.

Then it's on to the third year for research. The school pushes this hard, says Edward Halperin, vice dean of the med school, in part because of a belief that would-be doctors need to be able to interpret constantly advancing research. "Just because a study is in the *Journal of*

"We aim to provide graduates with both the tools and the ethos of lifetime scholarship."

---

the American Medical Association doesn't mean it's true," he says. "You have to learn how to critically read scientific literature—*how* do you read what's published and decide when things change research to therapy? And there's no better way to assess the value of research than to do it yourself." The individualized research process requires a lot of initiative and self-motivation—much like the rest of the Duke experience—but gives students exceptional benefits. It provides an opportunity to work closely with a faculty mentor, for one thing, perhaps one of the big names you see on the covers of your textbooks. It can also be an important résumé boost when you start shopping for a residency, particularly if you've published a scientific paper or two, as both Griffith and Kim plan to do.

There are a few complaints about the pace. Some students say that the chock-full first year ignores important areas such as embryology; others say that it's particularly difficult to cover gross anatomy—and dissect a human body—in only nine weeks. (Other schools spend twice as much time teaching these skills.) Currently, Duke is in the midst of revamping its curriculum to better address changes in the field. The traditional first-year lecture courses will be regrouped into three blocks—Molecules and Cells, Normal Body, and Body and Disease—with a focus on individual organ systems rather than broad topics, and more emphasis on interaction and case-based

"There's no better way to assess the value of research than to do it yourself."

learning. In the second year, there will be five weeklong "mini courses" that cover diagnostic exercises and exposure to areas of health care like physical rehabilitation and social work. In addition, the research year will expand from eight to ten months and require a written thesis.

Already, though, both research and clinical opportunities abound throughout the relatively young and rich Duke University Medical Center, a $1.3 billion system closely affiliated with the medical school, encompassing myriad health care providers from the Duke Hospital and Clinics to the Duke Community Hospice. That range provides chances for students to gain exposure to many different areas of medicine. This is perhaps another reason why the vast majority of students here end up focusing on competitive specialties and subspecialties like dermatology, pediatrics, plastic surgery, orthopedics, and radiology, as opposed to primary care or family medicine. A good number go on to obtain coveted residencies in these areas at top institutions, including nearly a quarter at Duke itself. After

they graduate, some 20 percent of Duke students go on to hold academic positions; the remaining 80 percent pursue a wide variety of career paths, from running biotech companies to working in government health organizations. And, yes, a few do serve as physicians in small towns.

Although Duke is filled with one hyperqualified overachiever after another, students say the culture here is overwhelmingly collegial. Many tell tales of sharing notes and study charts with their whole class during the first year, perhaps because students aren't grubbing for A's. The grading system here is pass, fail, and honors; some complain that the latter designation can be arbitrary, but most say they're happy with the results. It helps that faculty are said to be very accessible. In the first year, students are assigned to an advisory dean and meet with that person and a handful of peers for lunch once a week; these gatherings let students discuss current events and schoolwide issues, or simply blow off steam. In the second year, larger groups of 25 congregate to talk about being in the hospital and share important milestones, like delivering a baby for the first time.

This collegiality was crucial, students say, when the unthinkable happened a few years back. In a case that made major headlines, a Duke surgeon infamously botched an organ transplant on a young illegal immigrant named Jesica Santillan, who eventually died. "I think we were all shocked, to say the least," says one third-year student. "But we talked about it a lot [in advising groups and classes] and I think we learned from it. It made me more aware of how vigilant you have to be at all times, even with the most routine things."

In the aftermath, some students say they feel more empowered to speak up to physicians if they notice a mistake or an inconsistency.

In addition to its many academic advantages, Duke, surprisingly, can also provide a relatively inexpensive medical education. The low cost of living in Durham, combined with a famously generous financial aid office, results in a much lower average debt burden: the mean for Duke grads is $77,324, compared to the national average of slightly more than $100,000. That, say students, relieves a lot of anxiety about the future. The med school offers 11 full-tuition scholarships per class; and last year, 65 out of 100 third-year students received research scholarships from sources such as Hughes Medical Institute. And despite the hard work, fourth-year student Jesse Nussbaum says there's plenty of time to hang out with friends and enjoy Durham Bulls minor league baseball and the university's nationally ranked basketball teams. (The comprehensive, student-produced *Duke Med School Made Ridiculously Simple* is a favorite resource for information about how you'll spend your free time, in addition to academics.)

Duke is, in short, a school of tremendous challenges but also tremendous opportunities. Says the school's dean: "Being here is about dreaming big, following your dream, and not being afraid." The fearless thrive and go on to push back the current boundaries of medicine.

Yale University School of Medicine

- **New Haven, Connecticut**
- **Private**
- **Enrollment 2003–2004 academic year: 689**
- **Overall rank in the 2005 *U.S. News* medical school rankings (research): 10**
- **Overall rank in the 2005 *U.S. News* medical school rankings (primary care): 65**
- **Average MCAT score: 11.4**
- **Average undergraduate GPA: 3.71**

When Yale students invite friends from other med schools for some weekend fun, such as skiing or a trip to the ballpark, the response is usually something along the lines of "Are you kidding?" That's because most med students spend their weekends cramming for exams. But not at Yale. Most exams here are optional, anonymous, online self-evaluations. What's more, students get two free afternoons each week. So perhaps it's not surprising that they jokingly refer to laid-back Yale as the "Utopia School of Medicine."

Officially, though, the school's approach is called "The Yale System." It aims to give med students wide latitude in constructing their own educational experiences, akin to Ph.D. programs in, say, genetics or history. And if this is utopia, it requires plenty of self-discipline. "Students must assume more than usual responsibility for their education," reads the school's literature. "Memorization of facts should be far less important than a well-rounded education in fundamental principles, training in methods of investigation, and the acquisition of the scientific habit of mind."

For the academic overachievers who populate Yale's ranks, The System can take some getting used to. It tries to transform students who have previously succeeded by being extremely competitive into team players. "Yale is full of people who are Type A personalities but are trying to be Type B," says second-year student Priya Shete. The reason? Success in modern medicine depends more than ever before on collaboration. There's so much knowledge to absorb and then put into practice that doctors and researchers have to team

---

"Yale is full of people who are Type A personalities but are trying to be Type B."

---

up. "At Yale, it's all about getting through this stuff together," says Shete. "It's not like, 'I won't give you the answer because you'll get a better orthopedics residency.'" Says second-year student Nana Akua Asafu-Agyei: "Students here study for the right reasons. You take self-evaluations to see if you understand the material, not to see who got a 94 percent and who got a 97 percent." The school's size—each class is roughly 100 students—also breeds an intimate, cooperative atmosphere. For second-year students who cycle through a long series of total-immersion modules—a few weeks on the cardiovascular system followed by a few weeks of psychiatry, and so on—classes outside the lectures are invariably tiny. In labs and workshops, class size stays below 20.

But the system has its pitfalls, students say. Basic science lectures for first and second years are often poorly attended, probably due in part to lecturers not taking attendance. And because self-evaluations are optional, some students never get around to taking them, which could mean playing catch-up before taking national licensing exams.

"If one is too liberal in slacking," says first-year student Alex Diaz de Villalvilla, "the system will give you enough rope to hang yourself." Still, most students learn to keep up with the curriculum; Yale's pass rate on the national exams is similar to other top-ranked med schools.

What Yale does require is a thesis, an unusual demand among medical schools. This project, usually begun during the first or second year and completed during the fourth and final year of school, may be lab research or an investigation of clinical, epidemiological, or sociological subjects. Recent papers have examined the stigma attached to AIDS in Africa and the causes of type II diabetes in lab mice. Students doing this work can tap into Yale's resources as a leading research institution (it received $267.1 million in National Institutes of Health grants in 2003), funding thesis-related research through grants and getting access to top faculty for thesis advisors. Meeting with his advisor for the first time, third-year student Ameya Kulkarni remembers "we had a fifteen-minute appointment, and [the advisor] stayed for two hours. His eyes shone as he talked—I didn't think you could get that excited about basic science." Most students secure research funding for the summer between their first and second year, often for overseas projects and thesis-related work. Roughly half of each class takes an extra year to graduate, often to devote a full year to the thesis; in these cases, Yale waives fifth-year tuition.

Because of this program, Yale is known for breeding academic physicians. Even students who aren't drawn to Yale for the thesis often wind up getting hooked on research. Many publish their papers in medical journals. "Our purpose here is to turn out individuals who are going to be the leading physician-scientists in the country," says acting dean Dennis Spencer. "We don't turn out many people who are going to do primary care." Indeed, Yale New Haven Hospital, the school's main teaching hospital, doesn't count family medicine among the residencies it offers, though a large number of Yale students do take residencies in pediatrics.

Despite the heady academic atmosphere, students are not locked in an ivory research tower. The M.D. program puts students in touch with patients early on. From the first year, all students meet weekly to practice taking medical histories from fellow students, then from actual patients—sometimes within the first few weeks of med school. This is a big help when students hit the hospital wards full-time in their third year. One third-year student says he didn't appreciate the weekly meetings until he had to tell a former drug user that he'd need regular kidney dialysis for the rest of his life—a test of interpersonal, rather than medical, skills. "By the time third-year rolls around," he says, "you spend time caring for the patient instead of figuring out how to gather information from them." Even during their time in the hospitals, students are encouraged to take control of their learning. "The structure on the wards is flat as opposed to hierarchical," says Kulkarni. "There's no objection to saying, 'I don't think that's right' to an attending [physician]. Just because they've had all this training doesn't mean they can't be challenged."

During that third year, which can be quite intense, Yale still prides itself on maintaining free afternoons. Most students don't use these to sleep in or goof off, however. Many spend the time doing volunteer work, like educating local school children on AIDS/HIV prevention or creating basic medical records for New Haven's homeless population. An annual auction, organized by students, raises tens of thousands of dollars for the homeless. With plenty of low-income residents, New Haven is flush with volunteer opportunities.

"We don't turn out many people who are going to do primary care."

"You can't be isolated here," says Spencer. "You have to engage in the community." The medical school is also a short walk from Yale's main campus, which allows students to interact with other university departments.

Most of their engagement, however, is at the med school itself, where the administration seems unusually responsive to student input. When a pair of students recently developed a formula that allowed third-year students to schedule their clinical clerkships more easily, administrators agreed to adopt it. And when international students lobbied to extend financial aid to foreign students last year, the school obliged. After all, if a school urges students to take their education into their own hands, it has to face the consequences.

Johns Hopkins University School of Medicine

- Baltimore, Maryland
- Private
- Enrollment 2003–2004 academic year: 476
- Overall rank in the 2005 *U.S. News* medical school rankings (research): 3
- Overall rank in the 2005 *U.S. News* medical school rankings (primary care): 46
- Average MCAT score: 11.0
- Average undergraduate GPA: 3.80

Johns Hopkins researchers invented the implantable pacemaker, discovered restriction enzymes that let geneticists manipulate DNA, and developed CPR. The medical school received $412 million in National Institutes of Health funding in 2003. Hopkins surgeons routinely make newspaper headlines by, say, separating conjoined twins in intricate operations. So what is it like at the bottom of the Hopkins pecking order, as a lowly medical student? Like being taught by the best in the world, says fourth-year student Andy Muck. "Even the greatest researchers there completely feel that part of their job is to train students."

And they should feel teaching is important—modern medical education was born at Hopkins. When the school opened in 1893, most medical institutions offered only lectures—future doctors never laid eyes on a live patient. But Quaker merchant Johns Hopkins stipulated that the medical school carrying his name had to be connected to a hospital with the size and means to train medical students. As a result, Hopkins students learned through hands-on experience. Eventually, this model spread throughout American medical education. Since its founding, the school has been home to over a century of influential medical educators, such as William Osler and William Halsted, inventors of the modern medical residency.

"I think that the tradition here is important," says Frank Herlong, associate dean of student affairs. "And I think we have to be careful that it doesn't become oppressive." He gives the example of the resident who, several years ago, announced that she just wanted to be a regular old doctor, not an academic. A faculty member called her into his office to ask "Where have we failed?" Today, however, Herlong likes to say that Hopkins students are "pluripotent"—like the human embryo's primordial stem cells, they could develop into anything, not just academic physicians. "The person who has been a leader in some small community by influencing the health care for the underserved, that person may not be famous or in the newspaper, but I hope that we would continue to embrace that," he says. Still, more than half of Hopkins graduates spend some part of their career in academic medicine, whether as full professors or as part-timers at local medical schools. Only about 10 percent of graduates focus exclusively on primary care.

Medical education at Hopkins, overall, follows the traditional pattern: science lectures until April of the second year, then just over two years of learning by watching and doing in the hospital. But several years ago, the school reassessed first-year courses, which leapt from biochemistry to genetics to immunology with no attempt to explore the relationships between these topics. Now the curriculum starts with the molecule, builds up to cells, then to organs, and finishes with organ functions in a healthy person. Although lectures dominate in the beginning, most of the teaching in later years happens one-on-one, with a research mentor or on the wards, says pediatrician David Nichols, vice dean for education. "Teaching how to develop a bedside manner—that's really a one-on-one kind of experience," he says. "You can't teach it in a lecture and you can't read about it in a book."

Even before bedside manners are taught, however, Hopkins students begin feeling the research tug: More than 80 percent do some kind of research as an elective, most often in the summer after their first year. When she began school, fourth-year student Aima Ahonkhai was interested in international health. She'd been an anthropology major in college, and often said there was no way anyone was getting her to sit at a lab bench for months at a stretch. "Then all of a sudden here I was working in a lab and, you know, I took a year off to do it." Her research, on how HIV lives in the body even during antiviral treatment, taught her how the lab relates to patient care—in her case, to the international HIV prevention work that she eventually wants to do.

Besides its name for fostering cutting-edge research, Hopkins also has a reputation for generating cutthroat competition. Hopkins takes only 120 of its 6,000 or so applicants every year, so its students are among the best in the country academically. But reputation isn't necessarily reality, Ahonkhai says. "My experience has been that there are always a handful of people who are very, very intensely competitive and that's kind of their thing." She and other students say that most study in groups, helping each other get through the difficult science courses. And during those first few years of school, students spend a great deal of time together, in and out of class.

Professors seem to be supportive as well. After the first exam of her first year, Ahonkhai recalls getting "the worst grade I've ever seen in my life." She went to see the professor and "just started bawling like an idiot." But her prof calmed her down, reassuring her that everyone goes through tough times in medical school, and she wasn't destined to fail. After talking about the situation, Ahonkhai realized she had to overhaul her study habits to focus on learning, not grades. When she had to explain the

"Even the greatest researchers there completely feel that part of their job is to train students."

material to other students in study groups, she finally knew that she had it down pat.

Hopkins' urban home, Baltimore, may be known as "Charm City," but those charms are usually not immediately evident to med students. "Baltimore is a great place once you get to know it, but at first it seems maybe not the most friendly place that I've ever been," says Muck. The hospital and school are wedged into a dense urban campus in rough East Baltimore, although the neighborhood has been improving in recent years. Security officers check IDs by every entrance, and the students consider the hospital campus to be safe. Eventually, they learn to navigate Baltimore's many neighborhoods, such as nightclub-packed Fell's Point and tree-lined, pet-friendly Butchers Hill, and many fall in love with the city. Washington, D.C., is less than an hour away, and students can get to New York City in a few hours. Muck says he spent his spare time exploring Maryland's state parks—in addition to the horse racing scene, which includes the Preakness, Baltimore's leg of the Triple Crown.

The city plays a role in students' education, too. Part of the hospital's mission is to take care of the poor. While students see many unusual cases referred from other hospitals (because Hopkins has so many top specialists), they also tackle the day-to-day health problems of their closest neighbors. Many students work on community health projects: Some teach sex education workshops in Baltimore middle schools, work on a program to introduce local high school kids to health careers, or mentor pregnant teenagers.

While students are working to change the area around the school, the school is working hard to change itself. Committees of faculty and students are discussing an overhaul of the curriculum to take effect in 2006 or 2007. As more and more conditions are treated without a hospital stay, medical students rarely see a patient with pneumonia. Doctors are spending less time with patients, which means new doctors have less time to learn clinical skills, such as listening to the way lung and heart sounds change as people get better or worse. In the next few years, the school will start using more high-tech simulations to train students, such as special mannequins that can be programmed to make different heart sounds and mimic these changes. Another major debate about the curriculum is how new research on genetics will change medical practice—for example, whether doctors should drop the old idea of a sick body as a machine that needs fixing and focus instead on each patient's genes, environment, and personal history.

In the meantime, the school is still turning out new doctors with an impressive entry on their résumés. "To be honest, the name helps a lot," Muck says, but adds that it's more than just a name to him; it's a superior education. "They set me up to do whatever I wanted to do after medical school."

University of Washington School of Medicine

- Seattle, Washington
- Public
- Enrollment 2003–2004 academic year: 790
- Overall rank in the 2005 *U.S. News* medical school rankings (research): 10
- Overall rank in the 2005 *U.S. News* medical school rankings (primary care): 1
- Average MCAT score: 10.4
- Average undergraduate GPA: 3.69

It's puzzling: Why would more than half the graduates of a huge school with an expansive academic research program like the University of Washington School of Medicine go into primary care? And why would so many graduates leave this urban Seattle campus to practice medicine in rural areas, many outside the state?

The answer, it seems, is WWAMI. That's the acronym for five Northwestern states—Washington, Wyoming, Alaska, Montana, and Idaho—that together make up more than a quarter of the land mass in the United States, yet have only one medical school among them. People in these states need good primary care in fields such as family medicine and pediatrics. So for thirty years, all five states have united behind that one school, UW, pooling far-flung resources, doctors, and science faculty at local colleges to bring WWAMI residents to Seattle—and get them back to WWAMI states once they've graduated.

The route many of them take is, for med students, a little unusual. Courtney Paterson, a second-year med student, grew up in Bozeman, Montana, where she also went to college. After getting into UW's medical program, Paterson spent her first year not in Seattle, but at Montana State University, where there is no med school. There she took the basic medical science courses—physiology, microbiology, and so on—with visiting faculty and the school's own science staff. Paterson then went to work for a summer at a clinic in tiny Ronan, Montana (population 1,800) which had six primary care docs and not much else. She followed the doctors around, watching how they did their work, and also did research on local rates of sexually transmitted diseases. She finally set foot on UW's campus at the beginning of her second year—the first time she'd been there since her admissions interview. "It was a little weird to have to mix with all these people who've already been here for a year when I didn't even know where the main office was yet," she says, "But I knew I wasn't alone."

Far from it. Nearly half of the 178 students in Paterson's med school class spent their first year like her, doing basic science at one of four Northwestern schools outside Seattle. More than a hundred UW students spend their first-year summers working side-by-side with local docs in underserved, rural areas. And ultimately more than 50 percent of UW graduates end up practicing medicine in a WWAMI state.

This commitment to rural primary care came about, says Paul Ramsey, the school's dean, because 37 percent of the population in the region lives in rural areas. "Over two billion people in the world have no access to a physician," he says. "Does the world really need more big city specialists?" Not from UW, which has sent graduates everywhere from Kodiak Island, Alaska, to Thermopolis, Wyoming.

Primary care "is just part of the culture" that suffuses UW and its affiliated hospitals, says Kristi Nix. A pediatrics resident at a UW children's hospital in Seattle, Nix works with both students and faculty from the med school. She says that you get a feel, watching the professors, for what it is to be a "good doctor." Nix didn't go to UW for medical school herself, and at other schools, she says, the

"I was in a clinic taking a personal history the first week of my first year."

good doctors all "have labs and see patients half-time and do research eighty hours a week. Out here, most of the docs are living lives as physicians, they're actually taking care of people—and they don't have that aggressive, 'you've got to publish' type of feeling."

Instead, faculty push clinical skills on their students early and often. In both first and second years, students take the required course Introduction to Clinical Medicine, where they are tutored in interviewing skills, usually in small groups of six or seven. "I was in a clinic taking a personal history the first week of my first year," says second-year student Chris Giedt.

In their third and fourth years, when a lot of other med students are touring specialty areas in big teaching hospitals, UW students are encouraged to do their rotations outside Seattle, in more than one hundred WWAMI towns from Pocatello to Coeur d'Alene to Mountain Home. "It's just an unbeatable experience out there," says Joe Woodward, a student who did his family medicine rotation in a five-doctor clinic in eastern

Washington. The doctors there had known their patients for years. In some cases, they were delivering the babies of people they'd delivered. "I saw things I'd never see in an urban hospital with a hundred interns running around," he says.

When students do rotations as far away as Alaska, the isolation puts a premium on developing diverse medical skills. "Out there you have no

---

"Sometimes specialists just take care of a problem, you know? In primary care, your job really is to take care of people."

---

idea what could walk in the door at any moment," says Woodward. "If you can't handle it, the patient gets choppered a hundred miles to someone who can," and the helicopter ride can, for critically injured patients, take too long.

This emphasis on primary care does have its downside. It "can be a good thing as an introduction to medicine, but it's a double-edged sword," says Charlotte Yeomans, a fourth-year student who is torn between hospital-based primary care and infectious diseases. She worries that UW students who don't know what they want to specialize in can easily fall into something like family medicine for lack of extensive exposure to anything else. "It's entirely possible to find yourself at the end of your third year, and you haven't rotated in any other fields." Other students say UW does offer plenty of options outside primary care for those who truly want them. "If you're proactive, it's easy to find [an

advisor] in something else," says Leah Smith, a fourth-year student specializing in internal medicine who made space in her schedule for classes in anesthesiology.

Many of those options come from UW's enormous research presence. Last year, the school scored just over $488 million in grants from the National Institutes of Health, one of the highest totals in the nation. Over 1,600 full-time faculty wend their ways through the fir trees on the shores of Lake Washington each day to the school's Pentagon-sized labyrinth of laboratories. Calling Washington home are 25 members of the Institute of Medicine, and students can also work with dozens of award-winning cancer vaccine researchers at the Fred Hutchinson Cancer Research Center a few miles from campus. Scott Sears, a recent grad on his way to a job as a general internist in Billings, Montana, earned three separate grants at UW to work with the school's collection of human and primate eyeballs, one of the largest in the country, studying ophthalmology and developmental proteins in retinas.

Still, for Paterson and so many of her classmates, the UW road will lead to WWAMI's primary needs. "When I was 16, I wanted to be a brain surgeon," she says. "When I was 18, it was obstetrics/gynecology. I was never interested in family practice until that summer" in Ronan. And after graduation, Paterson plans on heading back to Montana. "Sometimes specialists just take care of a problem, you know? In primary care, your job really is to take care of people."

Chapter Four

Getting In

There are lots of good reasons for wanting to be a doctor. Maybe you think you have a healing touch, or you want to serve the community, or there's something about solving the puzzle of an illness that satisfies your mind and your soul. And there are probably some bad reasons, like doing it for the money, or because your family will be disappointed if you don't make medicine a career. But no matter what the motives, everyone has to jump over the same hurdle: medical school admissions.

It's not an easy leap. More than 34,000 people try to get in every year, yet just 16,000 succeed. And that's only the overall picture. Individual schools can be much more picky. The University of Chicago Pritzker School of Medicine recently received over 5,700 applications for its incoming class of about 100 students. Georgetown University School of Medicine had over 7,000 applicants for about 170 spaces. You do the math.

If you want in, you'd better be *able* to do the math. This is a brainy crowd. Admissions committees are swamped with applications from students whose undergraduate grade point averages hover at 3.4 and who average a score of 27 out of 45 on the Medical College Admission Test (MCAT). Those who attend the most competitive schools consistently score well over 30. "The competition is very intense," says

---

"The competition is very intense. There are a whole bunch of applicants who, in terms of numbers, are all equally qualified."

Greg Goldmakher, a medical school advisor with AdmissionsConsultants, Inc. in Vienna, Virginia. "There are a whole bunch of applicants who, in terms of numbers, are all equally qualified."

To stand out—and get in—applicants must find ways to distinguish themselves from the rest of the premed pack. In this chapter, you'll learn how. *U.S. News* asked admissions directors at the nation's top medical schools to describe what they look for in candidates who get the green light. All of them said good grades and MCATs are a great start. But science smarts are not enough. Admissions committees are looking for unique, highly motivated people who excel in and out of the classroom. "It's a very special segment of the human race," says Andrew Frantz, associate dean of admissions at Columbia University's College of Physicians and Surgeons in New York. "They have to be intelligent, sensitive to others, compassionate, committed to finding joy in their work and they should want to be of service to others." Here are tips to best let you show those traits, along with ways to get the best test scores and grades that you can.

Making the grades

It all starts in the classroom. Science is the backbone of medicine, and no matter how caring or compassionate you may be, medical schools want to know that you can handle the academic material. You will need to complete certain science courses before you can apply to medical school and you should start taking them freshman year, if possible. By the time you apply to medical school, you should have completed one year each (including labs) of chemistry, biology, physics, and organic chemistry. In addition, medical schools often want to see a year of English and a year of math, including a semester of calculus. The American Medical Student Association (AMSA) tells premeds to head for their school's preprofessional health advisor, usually found in the career counseling office, and together plot a course for completing all of the classes.

Tip: Pace yourself. A heavy load of rigorous courses can drag down your performance in each class, so don't take more than two prerequisites a semester.

If you decide to jump on the premed track a bit later—say, well into your sophomore year—you may need to take summer classes to make up for lost time. Find a summer school that is comparable to the one you attend during the school year; admissions committees do take note of the difference. "We are troubled by someone taking one or two semesters of something like organic chemistry at a community college over the summer," says Robert Witzburg, associate dean of admissions at Boston University School of Medicine. But if the course is taken at a school like the one you're already

The "nontraditional" student

There was a time when almost every applicant to medical school came directly from college. No longer. An ever-increasing number are taking time after they graduate to pursue other interests or get some work experience. Called "nontraditional applicants," even though their path is becoming a tradition in itself, these people are often viewed favorably, even prized, by admissions committees. Boston University's medical school admissions office says the school's nontraditional students, many of whom have put off their physician training to work in jobs serving communities without many resources, demonstrate "flexible intelligence" and an ability to interact well with patients. Henry Ralston, associate dean of admissions at the University of California–San Francisco agrees—that's why he encourages premeds to take a year off and get some experience outside of the school setting. "I prefer older students," he says.

But not all schools feel this way, cautions Trina Denton, a nontraditional applicant who served as director of premedical affairs at AMSA, the medical student advocacy group. Some medical schools may worry that applicants who have taken time away from studying will find it hard to get back into the habit. Applicants can ask the schools they are interested in if taking time off could harm their chances of getting in—or better yet, ask for the numbers of nontraditional students in the entering class.

Some nontraditional applicants decide after finishing college that they want to apply to medical school, but have not taken the prerequisite science courses. Such applicants should consider a premed, postbaccalaureate program. You get the basic courses plus the chance to take some advanced electives. At Georgetown University, the postbaccalaureate program "gives students the courses they need so they will qualify as premed despite the fact that they may have majored in poetry," says Douglas Eagles, a former program director. Programs take one to two years and offer students some valuable structure and help when they get ready to take the MCAT and prepare their school applications. Some people find this much easier than going it all alone. And because postbaccalaureate programs can include some of the same courses a first-year med student would take, they let the admissions office see that you can really do the work—because you have.

The Association of American Medical Colleges offers a searchable database to find these programs nationwide. Go to www.aamc.org and search "postbaccalaureate programs." (For a list of several well-regarded programs, see 352.) An alternative is to take the classes on a full- or part-time basis at a local university under a nondegree-seeking status, and med schools will usually accept them. Some are more restrictive, however, so check with the schools before signing up.

studying at, he says, "no one here is going to be bothered by that."

If you plan on using Advanced Placement courses taken during high school to fulfill these requirements, be wary. Many med schools won't accept them, and whether they do or not can depend on your other science courses. Remember, schools want to see that you can handle the mate-

---

> *"The ideal candidate has strong performance in science, but also has taken humanities."*

---

rial. So college students who major in science and also received AP credit can demonstrate they know the basics by performing well in their upper-level science courses. Med schools are more likely to let their AP work count for a college course. But those who do not take more advanced college science classes may not be able to use their AP scores. If you already have an idea about the med schools you want to apply to, check with those admissions offices about their AP credit policies.

This focus on science doesn't mean you have to major in biology or physics. In fact, admissions committees look for students who have challenged themselves academically and taken a broad range of classes throughout their undergraduate years. "The ideal candidate has strong performance in science, but also has taken humanities," says Albert Kirby, dean for admissions at Case Western Reserve University School of Medicine in Cleveland, Ohio. "We love students who are nonscience majors," says William Eley, director of admissions at Emory University School of Medicine in Atlanta, Georgia. "We are

looking for that breadth because it indicates involvement in the human side of medicine."

Indeed, majoring in something nonscientific might actually help you. In a crowd of biology and physics students, that history degree stands out. According to the Association of American Medical Colleges (AAMC), 52 percent of humanities and social science majors who applied were accepted to medical school in 2001. That's actually a little better than the 48 percent of successful applicants who majored in biology.

Tip: Take some humanities courses. Applicants who focus solely on science can be viewed as weaker candidates than those who have performed well across many fields.

Testing, testing

In addition to science classes, undergraduates must take the MCAT, an eight-hour standardized test given by the AAMC. Typically, applicants take the test in April of their junior year, although the MCAT is also given in August. You must preregister at www.aamc.org/mcat. Registration usually begins on February 1 for the April test and on June 1 for the August test. Aim for the April date because then you have August as a fallback if your scores aren't as high as you want. Try to register early because space can be limited at certain testing sites and slots are filled in the order in which they are received. The fee can be paid by credit card or by an electronic money transfer.

Unlike other standardized tests that attempt to predict a student's ability (such as the SAT), the MCAT is content-driven, testing your mastery of the basic science material covered in premed courses.

The test consists of four sections: physical sciences, which includes physics and chemistry; biological sciences, which includes biology and organic chemistry; verbal reasoning; and the writing sample. You can score up to 15 points in each of the two science sections and in verbal reasoning, for a possible total score of 45. (Most med school applicants, successful and unsuccessful, score in the high 20s and low 30s.) The writing sample is graded according to an eleven-letter system that goes alphabetically from "J" (lowest) to "T" (highest).

Obviously, it's best to have completed all of the science prerequisites before you take the test. Even so, to adequately prepare, you should plan to devote between 200 and 300 hours to studying. Many applicants, perhaps as many as three-quarters, choose to take a preparatory class to help them structure their studying and to ensure that they cover all of the material. Princeton Review and Kaplan, Inc., offer widely available courses. You get multiple classroom sessions, prep materials, and practice tests. The courses are expensive, running well over $1,000, but if you are not satisfied with your score, the companies will refund your fee or let you take the course again. (That's not going to help you, however, if you're not satisfied with your score and not satisfied with the course itself.) There are many local prep companies, too. But prep courses certainly aren't a must; if you feel you can be both disciplined and organized in your studying, you can purchase practice tests from the AAMC and a study guide from a bookstore, and prepare on your own.

Tip: Consider prepping. Prep classes can particularly help because they provide proctored practice tests to get you used to the grueling task of sitting and answering questions for eight hours straight.

Taken together, your GPA and MCAT score form the basis of the initial cut medical schools make in their applicant pool. Why? Studies have shown that performance on the MCAT and in undergraduate courses is a reliable predictor of how well an applicant will do during the first two years of medical school.

It takes about two months to get your scores back. If your April MCAT score falls well below what you expected, consider taking the test again in August. Medical schools vary on whether they will use your highest or your most recent score, with some averaging the two. Call admissions offices to find out how they handle the second set. But be warned: Waiting for the August score to come in could slow down the admission committee's review of your application, and when schools offer admissions on a rolling basis, that may reduce your chances of getting a spot.

Apply yourself

Once you have completed the MCAT in April, it is time to start thinking about assembling your application. This is one-stop shopping: Most medical schools use the American Medical College Application Service (AMCAS), a division of the AAMC, to process all the paperwork. You submit one completed application online, and that includes an application form, a personal statement, transcripts from all the undergraduate schools you have attended, and other paperwork, as well as a list of schools you want to apply to. For a fee, AMCAS assembles your application file, verifies it, and forwards it to the schools you have designated. The service also sends along your MCAT scores if you tell them to do so. (If you plan on retaking the test, you have the option to withhold your scores.)

What schools want...and what they don't

Some of our most difficult applicants are the majors from technical schools who took AP English in high school and never took another humanities course. They generally don't do well in the application process.
—Robert Witzburg, associate dean of admissions, Boston University School of Medicine

Don't ask *me* why you should pick our school. It's a turn-off.
—Andrew Frantz, associate dean of admissions, Columbia University College of Physicians and Surgeons in New York

We value individuals who will bring different strengths to the class. If everyone in the class had the same background, it would be dull.
—Albert Kirby, associate dean for admissions, Case Western Reserve University School of Medicine in Cleveland

Write about something you really experienced, not a two-week trip to a developing country where you saw poverty and were moved by it.
—Henry Ralston, associate dean of admissions, UCSF School of Medicine in San Francisco

We are looking for people who can do lots of things well. I like to see someone who is engaged in events and issues, someone who is not just interested in medicine.
—Gaye Sheffler, director of admissions, University of Pennsylvania School of Medicine in Philadelphia

I do not view the goal of the essays as either to entertain me, persuade me that the applicant would be 'fun to teach,' or regale me with stories of wondrous achievements and world travel. I expect applicants to take the writing of the essays seriously.
—Edward Halperin, vice dean, Duke University School of Medicine in Durham, North Carolina

---

The application, along with timelines, resources, and worksheets, is available at www.aamc.org/amcas. You should be able to get the application about mid-March, and the service begins accepting completed applications on June 1. It stops accepting applications two weeks before whatever deadline is set by the medical schools you are applying to, and that's generally from October to mid-December. It is your responsibility to meet these deadlines.

Tip: Double check. Some schools do not use the AMCAS application and rely on some other form instead. Contact the schools you are interested in to see if you need other application materials.

After AMCAS, there's still more application paperwork to deal with. Once the service has sent a copy of your application to each of your chosen medical schools, the schools themselves may send you a "secondary application." Some schools send secondary applications to all applicants, others send them only to those who make the initial cut after a review of GPAs and MCATs. The secondary application usually asks for additional personal essays, letters of recommendation, and an application fee. AMSA recommends that applicants fill out and return secondary applications no later than two weeks after they are received to avoid paperwork pileup.

Because the competition is so steep, plan to send out about 10 to 15 applications, maximizing your chances of success. Include three or four "reach" schools—where you just might have good enough credentials to get in—two back-up schools, and five to ten schools that you have a reasonable chance of getting into. What's a reach and what's a backup? Look at the mean GPA and MCAT scores for the incoming class of each medical school, which you can find in the directory section of this book. If your numbers are higher, you can think of the school as a backup. If they are lower, consider the school a reach—and the greater the gap, the longer the reach. Close matches are just that: By the numbers, you're a good fit. (See Chapter 2 for details about other important factors—things to consider before you worry about your chances for successful admission—in choosing schools.) Of course, the rest of your application has to be strong: Good numbers are ultimately no substitute for a poor essay or lackluster recommendations.

Getting personal

The next phase of application review, if you have the grades and MCAT scores to make it past a school's cut-off points, is when the school tries to get to know you as more than a set of numbers. Admissions committees are keenly interested in learning who you are, based on what you have done and how you express yourself. Here is where your written statements, recommendation letters, and interview come into play.

Keep in mind that medical schools receive thousands of applications from people who appear to be pretty much the same as one another. They have good grades, good MCATs, experience working in a research lab for a summer or two, have worked in a hospital shadowing a physician, and have volunteered with a community organization delivering food to homeless people. These are strong candidates, says Goldmakher—but they are not distinctive. If you want to get into an ultra-competitive school, you will need to be all this and more. That could mean demonstrating a longer commitment to one of these extracurricular activities or to the pursuit of something that is entirely unrelated to medicine, but is challenging nonetheless. The depth of your involvement in a project will indicate to medical schools how important that activity was to you.

Schools really are not looking for any one type of person or set of experiences. They want individuals with traits such as leadership, compassion, commitment, enthusiasm, and competence. For example, athletics can be an excellent way to show that you can work with a team—an important trait in many fields of medicine—as well as demonstrate that you have leadership skills and the ability to make quick decisions. Athletics also demonstrates physical stamina,

"It is very important in medicine to be able to extend yourself emotionally."

which can be important in certain fields, such as surgery. Admissions committees will consider all of these traits, so include hobbies and talents that you are passionate about in your application even if you think they are not relevant to your interest in becoming a doctor. These outside interests reveal a lot to admissions committees about who you are and what you are capable of. Andrew Frantz from Columbia University says he is drawn to applicants with an interest in theater because acting "forces you to put yourself in another person's shoes," he says. "It is very important in medicine to be able to extend yourself emotionally."

Of course, actors and lacrosse goalies still must know something about taking care of people, in sickness and in health. "Applicants need to show that they can deal with illness," says Henry Ralston, associate dean of admissions at the University of California–San Francisco School of Medicine. Volunteering at a hospital or nursing home, shadowing a physician, or even having personal exposure to serious illness, such as a terminally ill family member, are all avenues to gain such experience.

But even here you can find ways to set yourself apart from the typical medical school applicant and further bolster your application. Gaye Sheffler, director of admissions at the University of Pennsylvania School of Medicine, recalls one student who, along with his wife, developed a program for Hispanic residents in his community who were having difficulty accessing health care. That showed inner strength, she says, and an ability to take a project to its end, in addition to hands-on experience in the medical field.

Recommendation letter 101

Letters of recommendation should speak to these experiences or personality traits, and they should be written by people who know you well. It is better to have a letter from someone who can provide details about how you work and what kind of a person you are than one from some well-known professor who only taught you in a 250-student lecture and cannot say very much about you as an individual. If you have been engaged in a variety of activities outside of the classroom, it should not be hard to find people who can write about you in detail. Athletic coaches, employers, and volunteer work supervisors are all good sources of letters.

Tip: Choose wisely. Avoid asking for letters from people like your minister or congressman unless they can speak directly to your ability to lead, teach others, put forth the extra effort, or learn new skills.

Medical schools will want to see letters of recommendation from your college professors. Students who attend large universities may have a harder time establishing a close relationship with their teachers, especially in basic science classes with 100 or more students. The folks at AMSA suggest a way around this problem: Approach professors of larger classes near the beginning of the term to let them know that you will be applying to medical school and may ask them for a letter of recommendation at the end of the semester. Throughout the semester, attend the professor's office hours to ask questions about the material. After the class has ended and your grade has been determined, then make the request for the letter. Bring a copy of your résumé and perhaps your personal statement and be ready to sit down to discuss your interests and desire to become a

Countdown to med school

WHEN	WHAT YOU SHOULD DO
College freshman year and sophomore year	Get some medical experience
	Contact your premed advisor about planning coursework
	Do some community work
	Check out the nonmedical world—don't be one-dimensional
Junior year	
Sept. through Dec.	Take an MCAT prep course if you can afford it
Jan./Feb.	Register for the April MCAT
	Take a prep course if you still need it
March	Last chance to register for April MCAT
April	MCAT test date
May	Start writing your personal statement
June	Turn in AMCAS application; register for August MCAT if you're taking the test again
August	MCAT test date
Senior year	
Sept./Oct./Nov.	Fill out secondary applications and send them in
	Go on interviews
Oct.	Early decision applicants receive admission letters
Jan.	Another chance to register for an MCAT, if you plan to start med school more than a year from now
April	MCAT test date
	Regular admission applicants receive admission letters
May/June	Graduate and start packing for med school

doctor. Make sure you ask the professor if she or he can write a *strong* letter of recommendation on your behalf. If the answer is no, look elsewhere. If it is yes, send a thank-you note two weeks after you ask for the letter, both to be polite and as a gentle reminder to finish the letter in time to meet your application deadlines. (And don't forget to send along a stamped, addressed envelope.)

Your undergraduate school may have a pre-professional committee, generally made up of faculty members from different academic departments and a preprofessional advisor. They will ask you for your academic record, personal statement, letters of recommendation, employment and volunteer experience, and extracurricular activities. You may be called in for an interview as well. Using this information, the committee will write a single letter of recommendation, which you then send to all of the medical schools you are applying to.

Making a statement

The personal statement is your chance to show that you can express a point of view clearly while also explaining a little bit about yourself. It's also probably the hardest part of the application process, prompting a lot of staring at a blank computer screen, multiple drafts, and much anxiety. Here are strategies to make things easier.

Pick a topic that reveals something about you that committee members would not otherwise have known. It should come from your life experiences, such as an event or person that has made a deep impression on you. And it should reflect you and your life in an honest, thoughtful way. "Tell me something I don't know, not just 'I love science and I want to help people,'" says Emory's Eley. "There are moments in life that teach. Tell us about them. It could be about being sick, or a special grandparent, or climbing a mountain."

Structure the personal statement either around a theme or as a chronology, advises Goldmakher. A thematic essay about being sick, for example, might focus on shepherding a friend or family member through illness. Admissions committees want to see that you can write and express yourself well, but they also want to get to know something about your insights and attributes. A chronological essay might focus more on

a series of events or activities and how you grew or changed as a result. One example might be an essay about a year spent abroad.

Tip: Gimmicks are not impressive. Although you want your essay to stand out, avoid tricks that fall flat, such as poems, plays, or mock press releases.

Face to faces

If your written application sparks enough interest, the admissions committee will invite you to visit the school for an interview. At some schools, this will be a one-on-one with a faculty member, but at others you may sit down with a group of senior medical students and professors. Whatever the configuration, interviews have some things in common. Someone is probably going to ask you to elaborate on some experience you wrote about, or will ask you to talk about your interests in medicine or your background. Some typical questions: Why do you want to be a doctor? What makes you think you'll make a good one? What experiences in your life led to this decision? What weaknesses do you struggle against in yourself? The committee is looking for signs that you are mature, confident without being arrogant, and able to communicate well.

You can write passionately about many things in your application, but in an interview, applicants often reveal how truly meaningful an experience was. "If they are doing all of these things because they think it's what they are supposed to do, it will be a boring interview," says Eley. "If they have followed their heart, their eyes will light up, and that's what we look for."

To prepare for the interview, brush up on current events, especially those related to medicine as well as some issues like medical ethics. Goldmakher says that admissions committees generally aren't looking for one particular answer when they ask you these less personal kinds of questions. They are interested in how you think and whether you can see different points of view. He advises his clients to take a deep breath, come up with a few points they want to make, and try to express them clearly. Don't rehearse your answers too much: Admissions directors say canned answers are a good way for an applicant to get, well, canned.

Be sure to know something about the school before you arrive for the interview. It is a big turn-off to admissions committees if they ask you why you are interested in their program and it becomes clear you don't know very much about the school. Take advantage of the chance to ask about something specific to the school—and not something easily answered in the brochure. It shows you have genuine interest. After the interview, remember to send a thank-you note to the people who interviewed you as well as anyone else who helped you throughout the interview day. This is a good way to get them to remember you.

"If they have followed their heart, their eyes will light up, and that's what we look for."

After all this, what's left? You get to sit back and wait for your acceptance letters.

Chapter Five

Finding the Money

Make no mistake: It costs an arm and a leg to become a doctor. The tab at private medical schools—for tuition, living expenses, and books—easily tops $200,000 over four years. At the George Washington University School of Medicine, for instance, the four-year budget is more than $232,000—and that's before allowing for the inevitable tuition increases. Costs are equally high for out-of-state students at public institutions. A nonresident at the University of North Carolina–Chapel Hill School of Medicine will pay more than $225,000. Even in-state students at public medical schools can expect to spend $150,000 or more to earn an M.D. degree.

Most medical students borrow heavily to cover the bills. Total debts in excess of $100,000 are typical for new doctors, and that's not counting whatever they may have borrowed as an undergraduate. Not surprisingly, many young docs continue to feel strapped for cash even after their incomes begin to soar.

How can you limit the damage? While financial aid in the form of grants and scholarships is not as plentiful as it is for undergraduates, most schools do make modest need-based or merit-based awards to some medical students. A handful of outside scholarships are available, too—especially for members of minority groups. Uncle Sam's largesse, in the form of tax credits for the cost of higher education, can also free up some extra cash. And students who are willing to serve in the military or commit to practicing medicine in underserved communities can go to medical school practically for free—or at least have a portion of their debts forgiven.

Even if you do have to borrow a bundle, you can take some comfort in the fact that, with interest rates at historic lows, education debt is as cheap as it ever has been. And through your tax deductions, the federal government will chip in on the interest you do pay. Here's what you need to know to pay for your degree.

Need-based grants might help a little—very little

As you'll probably remember from your undergraduate days, anyone applying for financial aid funds handed out by the federal government has to fill out the Free Application for Federal Student Aid, also known as the FAFSA. That's where you'll start, but the truth is that most medical schools have only a modest amount of money available for need-based grants. They assume that most students will borrow to finance their degrees and will easily be able to repay their debts once they are doctors. At the University of Missouri School of Medicine, for example, only about 43 percent of students receive need-based awards—and they average a measly $2,400 yearly, a drop in the bucket compared to tuition.

Even schools with more money available generally won't meet your full need with grants: There simply aren't enough funds available at the graduate level to fulfill the requirements of students no longer dependent on their parents. At Johns Hopkins University School of Medicine in Baltimore, for instance, the average need-based grant is $16,000; tuition runs about $32,000 for first-year students, who need an estimated $50,900 to cover everything. (The school offers over 300 endowed scholarships to help meet students' financial need.)

You may find that your eligibility for need-based aid varies dramatically from school to school. That's because medical schools, like undergraduate colleges and universities, use different formulas to calculate how big a discrepancy there is between what med school will cost and what your income and assets are. Under the formula used to hand out federal aid, for example, all graduate students are considered *independent*: supporting themselves, regardless of their age or whether they have financial help from their parents. Bottom line: Full-time students at schools using the federal formula will have significant need.

But most medical schools use their own institutional formulas, which classify many students as *dependent*. You'll provide schools with information about your parents' income and assets on additional needs-analysis forms (GAPS–FAS, CSS, and Need Access are the common ones), and the financial aid office will consider those resources to be available to pay the bills—how available varies by school. At the University of Vermont College of Medicine, any student whose family is expected to contribute $10,000 or less to medical school expenses, counting the parents' resources, receives the same amount from the school in a need-based grant: $11,000. At Johns Hopkins, parent resources are weighed on a case-by-case basis. "If someone is the son or daughter of elderly parents, we won't expect much," says Paul T. White, assistant dean for admissions and financial aid. "But there are also children well over 30 whose parents are still supporting them. We consider that," White says.

Parents' income and assets also are used in determining who is eligible for federal Scholarships for Disadvantaged Students. These are need-based awards, specifically for medical students who come from disadvantaged backgrounds, based on family income or ethnicity. The size of the award varies from school to school.

Regardless of which forms are required, be sure to get them in as soon as possible after January. Some aid is awarded on a first-come, first-served basis.

Apply with an eye on the merit money

The medical schools at Johns Hopkins and Harvard do not award any merit scholarships. At the University of Michigan Medical School, by contrast, about one-third of each entering class receives a renewable scholarship ranging from $1,000 to $30,000 a year. At Vanderbilt School of Medicine in Tennessee, about 16 percent of students receive full-tuition scholarships, some based solely on academic merit and extracurricular record (such as the Canby-Robinson Scholarship),

others based on a combination of merit and need. The school also awards money to applicants who will diversify the student body; recipients have included not only students of color, but also students of Jewish background (not so common in the Southeast), students from Appalachian Tennessee, and one recipient who grew up in Montana and was a cowboy, according to J. Harold Helderman, assistant dean for admissions.

Schools that do have merit money to dole out usually base their awards on the admission application. High MCAT scores and undergraduate grades are a big factor, but, like Vanderbilt, many schools are also looking to attract people with varied strengths and backgrounds. Many of the awards are endowed scholarships handed out based on the donor's wishes. One award might be reserved for residents of a certain state or county, for example, another for students studying cardiology or pediatrics.

Search for outside scholarships

Scholarships from foundations, associations, and civic organizations are not as plentiful in medicine as they are for other graduate students, and many are reserved for minority students, residents of specific states or counties, or students concentrating in specific areas of medicine. Regardless, it's well worth checking an online search engine for possibilities. (Good search engines include www.fastweb.com and www.collegenet.com. Also try the excellent listing of grants on Michigan State University's website at www.lib.msu.edu/harris23/grants/3gradinf.htm.) Check with any civic, religious, or community groups you or your family members belong to, as well. And be sure to ask your med school's financial aid officer for other leads.

Shelley Corrigan at the University of Vermont College of Medicine has been able to lead students to a variety of special scholarships—including ones for people with epilepsy and diabetes.

How varied are the opportunities? Here's a sampling of scholarships:

• The Jack Kent Cooke Foundation Graduate Scholarship program (www.jackkentcooke foundation.org) makes approximately 35 awards a year to college seniors or recent grads who are pursuing graduate study. The scholarship pays for full tuition, fees, room, board, and books (up to $50,000 a year) for up to six years of graduate study. Candidates must be nominated by their undergraduate institution.

• The Medical Scientist Training Program (www.nigms.nih.gov/funding/mstp.html) is for students pursuing a combined M.D./Ph.D. degree at one of 41 participating medical schools, including Harvard, Stanford, Tufts, and the University of Michigan. Students accepted into the program, which is funded by the National Institutes of Health, earn full tuition plus a stipend; $20,000 to $25,000 per year is typical.

• The Nicholas Pisacano Family Practice Scholarship is awarded by the American Board of Family Practice (www.fpleaders.org/leaderfrm. html). Five awards of $7,000 per year are made to third-year med school students planning to specialize in family medicine.

• National Medical Fellowships (www.nmf-online.org) are awards of up to $10,000 for med students who have financial need and who are African American, mainland Puerto Rican, Mexican American, American Indian, or native Alaskan or Hawaiian. The group also offers numerous other merit-based fellowships and scholarships for minorities.

Get set to borrow

The average medical student borrows more than $109,000; a quarter borrow more than $150,000, and 7.5 percent borrow more than $200,000, according to the Association of American Medical Colleges. Ultralow interest rates will help ease the sting. And if you shop around for a lender, you may save a bit more in upfront fees.

Federal loans. Government-guaranteed Stafford loans are a staple for most medical students; a typical full-time student borrows the annual maximum of $8,500 in a "subsidized" Stafford loan plus at least a portion of the additional $30,000 allowed each year in "unsubsidized" loans, for a total of up to $38,500 per year. The federal government pays the interest on a subsidized loan while you're in school and for six months after you graduate or drop below half-time status. Interest accrues on the unsubsidized loan while you're a student, so the grand total mounts, but with both types of loan you can delay making payments until after graduation—or even until after your residency. In total, you can borrow up to $189,125 in Stafford loans to finance your education, including whatever you've already taken on as an undergraduate.

To qualify for a subsidized loan, you have to show on your FAFSA form that you have "need" (a gap between what you've got and the cost of school), which is fairly easy to do with medical school costs being so high. If your school participates in the Federal Direct Student Loan Program, you'll borrow directly from the federal government. Otherwise you can choose your own funding source using a list of preferred lenders provided by your school. While all lenders offer the same interest rate on Stafford loans, some waive the up-front origination and guarantee fees (which can run up to 4 percent of the loan amount), some reduce the interest rate in repayment if you sign up for automatic payments or make a certain number of payments on time, and some do both. Rates on these variable-rate loans change every summer, but will not exceed a cap of 8.25 percent. Lately, they've been around 3.4 percent.

Students with high financial need—the FAFSA shows that they're expected to contribute very little or nothing to their medical school education—will also qualify for a Perkins loan of up to $6,000 per year. The interest rate is a fixed 5 percent. While that's a bit higher than the 2004 rate on Stafford loans, it won't rise in future years. In addition, there are no up-front origination fees. The Perkins is a subsidized loan, so no interest accrues until nine months after you graduate or drop below half-time status—or until after your residency if you qualify for a deferment (page 52).

The federal government also makes certain loans available specifically to medical students. Federal Loans for Disadvantaged Students are available to needy students from disadvantaged backgrounds, based on family income or ethnicity. The interest rate is a fixed 5 percent, with no loan fees, and interest is subsidized. Primary Care Loans, which have the same rate and no fees, go to students who agree to enter family medicine, internal medicine, pediatrics, or preventive medicine—and to practice primary care until the loan is fully repaid. There's a big catch, though: The interest rate jumps to 18 percent if you change your mind and practice in another specialty.

Private loans. If the federal loan limits leave you short, private lenders stand ready to lend you up to the full cost of your education, less any financial aid. (Some medical schools also have their own loan programs.) Interest rates tend to be only slightly higher than the rates on Stafford loans, but origination fees can be significantly higher—up to 6 percent of the loan amount—and interest begins accruing right away. Some lenders who market specifically to medical students will even lend you up to $13,000 to cover the costs of traveling to your residency interviews.

Some popular programs include MEDLOANS Alternative Loan Program, from Sallie Mae and the Association of American Medical Colleges (www.aamc.org/students/medloans), Medical Access Loan, from Access Group, Inc. (www.accessgroup.org), CitiAssist Health Profession Loans, from Citibank (www.studentloan.com), and MedAchiever, from KeyBank (www.keybank.com/educate).

To qualify for a private loan, you need a clean credit history—or a cosigner. It's a good idea to check your credit reports for errors before you apply.

Home-equity loans. For students who own a home, a home-equity line of credit is another attractive choice. Rates are low, fees are minimal, and the interest on up to $100,000 in debt is tax deductible if you itemize. If you expect to graduate into a high-paying job, home-equity debt may be a better choice than other debt because you won't qualify to deduct the interest on government or private student loans. Interest on student loans will be fully tax deductible only if your income falls below $50,000 if you're a single taxpayer and below $100,000 if you file jointly. Remember, though, that a home-equity line of credit is secured by your home. Will you be able to make the payments when you're a struggling resident?

Find help paying the money back

At 2004 rates, the payment on $100,000 in Stafford loan debt is nearly $1,000 a month over the standard ten-year repayment term. Those payments usually aren't manageable on a typical resident's pay of $40,000 or so a year. But there are ways to ease the burden.

Deferment and forbearance. Most medical residents with high levels of debt will qualify for an economic hardship deferment on their Stafford loans, which allows them to push off making payments for up to three years. Interest continues to accrue on unsubsidized loans (at the "in-school" rate, which is somewhat lower than the "repayment" rate that kicks in when payments are due) but does not accrue on subsidized loans. After three years, residents can continue to have their payments suspended for the remainder of their residency by requesting "forbearance," during which interest accrues on all loans at the repayment rate. You file an application for deferment or forbearance with your lender.

Flexible repayment options. The standard 10-year repayment term for Stafford loans—which for most new doctors begins after residency ends—can be stretched in various ways to reduce your monthly payments. With an extended repayment plan, for instance, you can lengthen the loan term to up to 30 years. Another option, a graduated repayment schedule that extends over 12 to 30 years, starts you off with lower payments than the standard plan would call for and then ratchets them up annually as your paycheck presumably grows. Income-contingent or income-sensitive repayment plans adjust your payment each year based on your income. In the end, you'll pay more interest over the longer payback periods, but you can always boost your payments as your income rises to pay down the loan more quickly than you're asked to.

Loan consolidation. You may also be able to reduce the interest you pay on Stafford loans by consolidating them when interest rates are low. That locks in current interest rates instead of allowing them to fluctuate annually. You may even be able to consolidate your undergraduate and early medical school loans to take advantage of low rates while you're still in school. For more details on student loan consolidation, see loanconsolidation.ed.gov at the Department of Education's web site, or www.federalconsolidation.org, a website sponsored by Access Group, Inc., a private nonprofit lender.

Student loan interest deduction. You can deduct up to $2,500 a year in student loan interest if you earn less than $50,000 as a single taxpayer or less than $100,000 if you are married and filing jointly. (You can deduct a lesser amount with income up to $65,000 filing singly or $130,000 filing jointly.)

Note to parents: You get to take this deduction on your own return if you're legally obligated to pay back the debt and you claim the student as a dependent on your tax return.

Loan repayment programs. Doctors who agree to practice certain kinds of medicine where there are shortages or who work in underserved areas of the country can qualify to have significant portions of their debt forgiven. Through the National Health Service Corps, for instance, doctors practicing primary care medicine in underserved areas can have up to $50,000 of their debt repaid by the federal government during a two-year minimum service commitment. An additional $35,000 a year in debt repayment is available to doctors who sign up for a third or fourth year of service.

Many states have similar debt repayment programs for doctors who live or are licensed in the state and who practice primary care medicine in-state. Doctors in Massachusetts, for instance, can earn $20,000 a year in debt payments if they work a minimum of two years in a Massachusetts community health center. A listing of state programs is available at the website of the Association of American Medical Colleges, at www.aamc.org/students/financing/repayment.

The National Institutes of Health offers a debt repayment program for employees engaged in various kinds of research, including AIDS research, pediatric research, and clinical research, whose debt load is at least 20 percent of their annual salary. M.D. researchers can have up to $35,000 per year of debt repaid during a two-year service period.

Get a job

One reason M.D. students tally up so much debt is that most cannot work part-time while earning their degree, even during summers. "There is no time to work," says Conway Jones, coordinator of financial aid at the University of Missouri–Columbia School of Medicine. For that reason, most financial aid officers do not include a federal work-study job in financial aid packages for med students. But for students who feel they can handle it, work-study is available and can reduce the need to borrow. An award of $1,500 to $2,000 might typically cover 10 to 15 hours of work a week in the university hospital or in a lab.

In most programs, there is a summer break between the first and second years of med school, after which the academic year runs 11 or 12 months. During the first-year summer break, some students earn extra money assisting faculty

with a research project or participating in a summer preceptorship in which they shadow a doctor in exchange for a stipend. At the University of California–San Francisco, for instance, students can earn $1,000 to $3,200 for a four- to six-week full-time summer preceptorship.

Take advantage of Uncle Sam

If your household income is modest, the federal government offers help in the form of a tax credit or tax deduction for educational expenses. Medical students who qualify will want to take advantage of the Lifetime Learning tax credit, worth $2,000 a year (20 percent of the first $10,000 you spend in tuition and fees each year). You qualify for the full credit if you file a single tax return and your income is $42,000 or less, and for a partial credit if you make up to $52,000. If you're married and filing jointly, the full credit is available when income is less than $85,000, and a partial credit is available up to $105,000. (A tax credit reduces your tax bill dollar for dollar.)

Most full-time medical students won't exceed those thresholds. (In fact, those with little or no income won't benefit at all from the credits because they won't owe any taxes to begin with.) But if you do cross the line—perhaps because you are married and your spouse earns a good income—you may still qualify for a tax deduction for your educational expenses. In 2004 and 2005, students can take a deduction for up to $4,000 in tuition and fees if their incomes don't exceed $65,000 filing singly or $130,000 filing jointly. That's worth up to $1,000 to a taxpayer in the 25 percent tax bracket. Note: You can't take both the credit and the deduction.

If there's time, plan ahead

If you're looking ahead to medical school in the next couple of years and can set aside some savings, take advantage of the tax benefits of a state-sponsored 529 plan. While most investors use these plans to save for a child's undergraduate expenses, the plans generally allow you to open an account and name yourself as the beneficiary. The primary benefit is that the earnings on your savings will be tax-free, and your state may throw in a deduction for your contributions. All 529 plans include investments that are appropriate for adults who will need to tap the money soon, such as bonds and money-market accounts.

While many of the broker-sold 529s impose up-front sales fees that would minimize or offset any tax benefits over just a year or two, many of the direct-sold plans, such as those offered by TIAA-CREF and Vanguard, do not. Several are paying a guaranteed 3 percent or so right now. Not a bad parking place for a couple of years, especially when Uncle Sam isn't claiming any of the gains.

Medical students who are willing to pay for their education with a service commitment to the military or to the National Health Service Corps can start their medical careers with little or no debt. An Armed Forces Health Professions Scholarship, for instance, pays for tuition, fees, books, and supplies, plus a living-expense stipend of about $1,100 a month. After your residency, you repay the armed forces with a year of service for each year of support you received. You can get in touch with an Army, Army Reserve, Navy, or Air Force recruiter for more information. (Anyone who is gay or lesbian will want to keep in mind the military's policy on homosexuality; one website that provides an overview is gaylife.about.com/cs/politicsactivism.)

Students on a National Health Service Corps scholarship also get a free ride that covers tuition, fees, books, and supplies, plus a stipend. The tradeoff: These students agree that, for each year of support, they'll practice a year of primary care medicine in an underserved area, which may be a rural community or even a prison. What if you renege? You'll owe the government three times the amount of your scholarship, plus interest. This is not a commitment to make lightly.

Chapter Six

What If You Don't Get In?

Dreams have a predictable way of taking unpredictable turns. For many, the dream of med school started in childhood with a mini doctor's bag molded in black plastic, and continued through grueling college organic chemistry classes and cram sessions for the MCAT. But for all too many, what comes next is a mailbox full of rejection letters—and an uncertain future. These rude awakenings are unavoidable: Many medical schools accept fewer than 1 in 10 or 15 of those who apply.

So what happens next?

Your first priority should be to put things in perspective. "A lot of high quality kids can't make the cut," says William Harvey, who recently retired after spending years advising aspiring medical students at Earlham College in

Richmond, Indiana. While this sometimes can be the result of unrealistic aspirations, he notes, it may be for reasons as impersonal as that you hail from the same state as a huge number of other applicants that year.

And take heart: You do have options. You can rethink your goals altogether. You can retake your MCATs and get more science courses—perhaps a master's degree—and reapply. Or you can do what thousands of successful doctors have done: study abroad.

Trying again

You might as well start by reassessing your goals. Are you so sure that you belong in medicine that you're really prepared to go through all this again? "The hardest thing about medical school is not getting in, it's getting through," warns Karen Nichols, dean of Midwestern University Chicago College of Osteopathic Medicine. If an honest second look tells you that "you aren't motivated by all the right reasons, you must not come." Adds Nancy Nielsen, senior associate dean at the University at Buffalo School of Medicine and Biomedical Sciences: "Ask [yourself] how badly you want to be a doctor, and if the answer is 'more than anything,' consider reapplying."

That's assuming you've got the grades, of course. You may have spent your last four summers working at an inner-city clinic and every scrap of free time reading journal articles about cancer research, but if your college grades are mediocre, "you can apply till the cows come home, but you're not going to get in" to a U.S. school, says Nielsen. Even if you do have a respectable grade point average, statistics from the Association of American Medical Colleges show that repeat

applicants are less likely than first-timers to be accepted, so you may have to target less-competitive schools this go around.

In any case, ask admissions officers at the schools that sent rejection letters to explain your shortcomings. Often, they're happy to offer insights. The University of Minnesota Medical School–Twin Cities, in fact, sends out rejections with an explicit offer: "I am very willing to speak with applicants by phone or in a personal interview and give them very, very specific information about what they can do to improve their applications," says the director of admissions, Marilyn Becker. Good scores may have been overshadowed by weak essays, flat letters of recommendation, or an unimpressive science background. The tell-all postrejection interview "takes the mystery out of it and gives concrete ideas" about what to do next, Becker says.

If the admissions staff isn't helpful—and even if they are—pose the same question to your undergraduate advisor, says Nichols. "Ask them to be ruthless—and have thick skin." Then apply their answers to the next application. While you're tapping undergrad resources, you might also ask someone in your college admissions office to give you a mock interview. The right answer, expressed in the wrong way, can tank an acceptance. Nichols once had an applicant say, "'I would really like to go to your school because I really don't want to work that hard,'" she says. "What he meant was, 'Your school really understands the importance of a balanced approach.'" The end result: He didn't get in.

It's probably a given that you'll revisit your MCAT scores; taking the test again and raising your numbers will certainly be a big help. So find a study group. Take a prep class. Hire a tutor. And take as many practice tests as you can. Admissions deans further recommend looking critically at your science background and doing whatever you need to do to bolster it. Indeed, one of the best ways to upgrade your application is to get a master's degree in one of the sciences.

It pays to get work or service experience, too; exposure to the health care field will enhance an application, admissions deans say. If grades and MCAT scores are equal, "the person who has a history of volunteering has an edge," Nielsen says. Volunteering for a medical facility that interests you, such as a clinic, a pediatric cancer ward, or a nursing home, underscores your commitment to medicine and desire to learn and can also offer evidence that you've got other valued attributes. Leadership, for example, "is one quality that is highly weighted," says Gregory Vercellotti, senior associate dean for education at the University of Minnesota. So are level-headedness and heart. The admissions committee is on the lookout for "students who have a sense of well-being and balance and can demonstrate compassion," he says.

When your new, improved application is ready to go, don't worry too much that your rejection will taint it. "Given the number of applications and number of students who have to try more than once, there's nothing really adverse about a second application," says Vercellotti. Indeed, it's worth remembering that some people are accepted on the third or occasionally the fourth try.

Looking abroad

During Peter Burke's first two years of college, he was "a student athlete, with more emphasis on 'athlete,'" he says. Though he "got serious" by junior year and worked for a few years as a lab technician after graduation, his early history hurt him when he decided on medical school. "I was always having to explain my first two years in college," he says—and American medical schools were not forgiving. So he joined more than 8,000 Americans currently taking an alternate "offshore" route and went to The American University of the Caribbean School of Medicine, located in St. Maarten.

Many aspiring doctors look at the offshore schools as a poor substitute for U.S. institutions, but the reality is that more than 25 percent of doctors practicing in the United States today got their education outside of the country, according to the American Association of International Medical Graduates. Some 43,000, or 6 percent, of these doctors are United States citizens. "There are a number of international schools that are worth looking at," says former Earlham advisor Harvey. (For a list of foreign schools that educate significant numbers of American students, see page 356.)

Look carefully, though, because the quality of overseas programs varies enormously. Some of the most highly regarded schools in Europe are just as selective as U.S. medical schools and are not known for training Americans who failed to make the cut stateside. Besides AUC, foreign schools that do take large numbers of U.S. citizens—and that have track records for turning out solid doctors—include St. George's University School of Medicine in Grenada, Tel Aviv University Sackler School of Medicine in Israel, and Ross University School of Medicine in Dominica (which is now owned by DeVry University).

How do you determine which schools are worth your time and money? Separating the winners from the losers is a chore made both easier and harder by the Internet, which will probably be your first route to campus. Building an impressive website is much easier than building a high-quality faculty or campus; on the other hand, the Web can be a source of expert advice and an insider's point of view. The American Association of International Medical Graduates (www.aaimg.com) issues reports on schools in different areas of the world, providing pros and cons along with "words of wisdom." The organization evaluates schools using such criteria as

---

"There are a number of international schools that are worth looking at."

---

recruiting practices; basic science curriculum; student concerns like affordable housing and health care; clinical training programs; faculty qualifications; and history of problems with regulatory agencies, licensing boards, student loans, and student records. AAIMG notes whether each school is deficient or meets or exceeds the AAIMG standards. You'll also find a list of schools that don't meet the group's standards.

Approach your search with a similarly critical eye, advises Harvey. The overseas medical schools that cater to Americans follow a curriculum essentially the same as that of U.S. schools—two years of basic sciences followed by two years of clinical rotations in hospitals—in preparation for the same set of licensing exams all U.S. doctors-to-be must pass. But you may find considerable variation in the quality of the faculty (Where did they train? What kind of research are they engaged in? Will you be taught by full-time professors or part-time local practitioners?) and how accessible they are. While a dedicated, permanent staff is ideal, some students note that they have

had excellent courses taught by gifted U.S. professors enjoying the adventure of a year in an exotic locale.

The faculty/student ratio will provide a clue as to how likely you are to get professors' attention; in the U.S., ratios range from 11.9 faculty members per student at Mayo Medical School to 1 professor for every 29 students at the New York College of Osteopathic Medicine. Anyone considering a European or other medical school that doesn't teach in English will want to find out whether there's an English-language program and if foreign students have the same access to faculty as native students do.

To assess how well schools prep students for the U.S. Medical Licensing Examination (USMLE), compare their students' pass rates on "Step 1," the portion of the exam taken after second year, and "Step 2," generally taken during the last clinical year of medical school or around graduation. Pass rates vary. For example, Tel Aviv's Sackler School's most recent pass rate for Step 1 is 98 percent; St. George's in Grenada has a 90 percent pass rate. Lesser schools have lower rates—sometimes much lower. As is true for American medical schools, too, you'll want to find out what type of clinical experience you can expect, and how early. Ask what kind of support services students have available: stress management? counseling? help with study skills?

A number of offshore schools have come and gone in the last several years, particularly in Mexico, Central America, and the Caribbean. So focus from the start on schools with a history. Indeed, before you invest in a place, make sure the place has invested in itself. Be wary of a school operating in rented space—some marginal schools have been known to hold classes in hotels or even private homes—because, as the AAIMG website cautions, "the school that rents a few classrooms has little incentive to remain open during hard times."

Make a visit before you commit so you can gauge quality and viability by sitting in on classes, quizzing students, and checking out the library and labs. While a listing in the "World Directory of Medical Schools," published by the World Health Organization, doesn't guarantee that a school is worthy, being included is considered a good sign. Another tip: The U.S. Department of Education Federal School Code Search (www.fafsa.ed.gov/fotwo405/fslookup.htm) lets you plug in a foreign institution's code number and find out if it can receive and distribute American financial aid.

Find out, too, who the school considers a worthy candidate. At Ross University School of Medicine in Dominica, the class admitted in January 2004 had an average undergraduate GPA of 3.18. And whereas "most U.S. schools are looking at [MCAT scores of] 27 and above, our average was 21," says Andrew Serenyi, director of marketing for the school. At American University of the Caribbean, the incoming classes often include "people who are nurses, paramedics and EMTs; career transfers; people who are young, didn't study well in college and didn't get the grades that they needed; and people who are waitlisted," says Susan Atchley, professor of immunology and director of community services. "They judge you based on what you are doing now instead of on what you did as an 18-year-old," says Burke, who was 28 when he arrived at AUC in September 2000. "But then you have to prove yourself. My class started with 180 [students] and is now about 90. If you're not meeting the criteria you'll get weeded out of the system."

Many students attending offshore schools return to the United States after the second year to do their clinical rotations in U.S. hospitals; before applying to any overseas school, ask if the school is affiliated with clinical sites in the United States. Students often find residencies in the States, too, through the same match system as do their stateside peers (students pick schools and schools pick students and the computer matches them up). The website of the Educational Commission for Foreign Medical Graduates (www.ecfmg.org) walks students through the required steps to a U.S. residency.

The chances of making a match are good for students from reputable international programs who have strong USMLE scores. While some 15,000 students graduate from U.S. medical schools each year, there are about 21,500 postgraduate residency positions available. Among the eligible U.S. citizens attending St. George's University Medical School who applied last year, 99 percent landed U.S. residency positions. Students from Ross University School of Medicine have been offered residencies at such noted hospitals as Yale–New Haven Hospital, Loma Linda University Medical Center in California, Georgetown University Medical Center, and UCLA Medical Center. As you shop for a school, ask those that interest you to provide a contact list of graduates who are now practicing in the U.S., as well as a history of residency placements.

"The great equalizer is standardized tests," says Burke, who says he scored in the 95th percentile on Step 1 and in the 99th on Step 2. Before he finished his fourth year in a cardiology rotation at Providence Hospital in Southfield, Michigan, he was prematched to a residency in internal medicine with the hospital. "From there I hope to get into a fellowship in cardiology," he says.

Finding your Plan B

What do you do if, in the end, your dream is dashed? "You need to think about Plan B: a different career choice," says Harvey.

But Plan B may well be a modification of Plan A: a career in public health or another health-related field, or the pursuit of a Ph.D. in the biological sciences, for example. Carol Baffi-Dugan, who advises undergrads going into health professions at Tufts University in Massachusetts, says the first thing she asks students who have been rejected by a medical school is why they were attracted to medicine in the first place. "Sometimes a student is motivated by an incredible love of science. It may be that that student would be intellectually stimulated and more successful doing a Ph.D.," she says. "But if they say the classic, 'I want to help people and use science,'

then I start to talk about the clinical health professions and the area of public health. Other health professions are playing an increasingly important role in health care delivery." She mentions physician assistants, who can specialize in cardiology or surgery, or nurse practitioners, who can specialize in pediatrics. (For an introduction to a number of health care options, see Chapter 7.)

Baffi-Dugan hopes that the students she advises have at least been thinking about other possibilities all along. At freshman orientation she tells the incoming class, "Look at all areas [in medicine], even if you do decide that a M.D. degree is what you want. You will understand that medical care is a team effort [and] you'll be better prepared." You will also be more likely to make a thoughtful and heartfelt choice. No one wants "the dentist who wanted to be a doctor," says Baffi-Dugan.

Chapter Seven

Other Choices, Other Paths

So you like medicine and you like making people feel better, yet you don't want to be a doctor? Good. Though it may surprise many physicians, there are plenty of good health careers that *don't* take you through medical school. Physical therapy, physician assistant, and nursing are among some of the booming fields in the allied health professions. People working in them say the intellectual challenges, emotional rewards, and relationships with patients are often more satisfying than in the doctor's world. "I can see a patient for ten consecutive weeks, make corrections in their treatment, and see steady progress," says one physical therapist. "How many doctors can do that?"

Here we profile ten such professions, highlighting the pluses and minuses of each, the training needed, tips on how to get into a program or school, and the career and salary outlook. We also list the top three schools in each field (or more in the case of a third-place tie) according to the latest *U.S News & World Report* rankings, which are based on opinion surveys of faculty and administrators at accredited schools. (Note: There are no rankings for EMT and dentistry programs.)

Physician Assistant

Health care has changed enormously over the last 20 years, and as a result, the role physician assistants play in medicine has been transformed. Treating acute illnesses is now less important than preventing them. Widespread use of routine screening and an arsenal of new drugs has made managing chronic illness a top priority. Today, there is a premium on controlling costs, and four of five Americans are enrolled in managed care plans. Health care is delivered not only by physicians but by a team of medical providers, and physician assistants have become some of the team's most sought-after players.

Physician assistants (PAs) are licensed to practice medicine under the supervision of physicians. They are nationally certified after graduating from an accredited program, usually about two years in length, and passing a certifying exam. More than half of the nation's 50,000 PAs specialize in primary care—family medicine, internal medicine, pediatrics, or obstetrics and gynecology. Over a third specialize either in surgery or emergency medicine. They see patients, take histories, evaluate tests, make diagnoses, prescribe drugs, give advice, suture cuts, perform simple surgeries such as biopsies, and more.

"I love the potpourri of family practice," says Julie Theriault, a physician assistant at the Sutter Medical Group in Elk Grove, California, and president-elect of American Academy of Physician Assistants. "I do see some complicated things, and one of the key factors in the job of a PA is knowing when to get the doctor involved. I just had a diabetic patient who was on three medications and yet her blood sugar level was still out of whack. So I called the doctor." Theriault was able to describe the patient's test results and other factors, allowing the physician to make a diagnosis and advise treatment—even though he was located in another office miles away. The ability of one highly paid doctor to supervise a number of PAs who can manage patient care on-site not only cuts costs, it also allows rural and medically vulnerable communities access to care when they may have had none before. A study of primary care providers in two Western states showed that more physician assistants were practicing in rural areas than any other type of provider, and in vulnerable minority and poor communities, physician assistants, along with family physicians and internists, provide the majority of medical services available.

Pluses. PAs end up in much the same place as primary care physicians but spend about half the time in school and probably one-fifth of the money to get there. Salaries are high, and many practices and hospitals work out flexible schedules to allow PAs to have lives outside of work. Women find the PA career—with its high skill levels, good salaries, and flexible hours—particularly rewarding: They make up nearly 60 percent of the profession.

Minuses. Some doctors worry that the huge growth in nonphysician clinicians may lead to competition—rather than cooperation—between doctors and PAs. Physician assistants estimate that they can treat 50 to 75 percent of the complaints that send patients to doctors. The ability of physician assistants to treat so many conditions, coupled with a two- to four-fold increase in the number of PAs and other nonphysician clinicians, has left doctors wondering if there may be less need for M.D.s in the future. Still, Joseph Kaplowe, physician assistant coordinator at New Britain Hospital in New Britain, Connecticut, thinks that's unlikely. "With so many people in the population getting into their 50s and 60s, and that being the age at which people need more health and hospital care, there will be a need for more docs *and* more PAs."

Training. Many of the first PAs were Navy medical corpsmen who had received training and experience in Vietnam, but returned home to find there were no similar positions in the civilian health care system. At the same time, the nation faced a shortage of primary care physicians, particularly in rural and inner-city communities, so PA positions were created for these veterans.

Today most PAs are trained not on the battlefield but in programs that offer a master's degree. The coursework is divided into two parts spread over two years. The preclinical curriculum during the first year includes medical science courses—topics such as pharmacology, signs and symptoms of diseases, and primary care aspects of every medical specialty. The second year con-

sists of clinical clerkships where PA students work with physicians treating patients and managing their cases. Many programs now require a thesis or "capstone" project on a medical topic of interest such as obesity or childhood depression. "PA programs are also beefing up population health—epidemiology, biostatistics, preventative medicine—because these are huge areas of

> *"With so many people in the population getting into their 50s and 60s...there will be a need for more docs and PAs."*

public health now," adds Paul Lombardo, president of the Association of Physician Assistant Programs (www.apap.org). Newly minted PAs must pass a national certification exam, and then must acquire 100 hours of continuing medical education every two years and be recertified every six years.

Tips on getting started. Nationally, there are about two applicants for every opening in PA programs, and at some schools the competition is stiffer. Applicants to PA programs must complete at least two years of college-level courses in basic and behavioral sciences as prerequisites. There are 133 PA programs at various schools across the country, and for about 80 of them applications can be submitted online through a central system, at www.caspaonline.org. At this site, you can click on the schools, look at what their programs offer, and get details on requirements, prerequisites, and more. You can apply to more than one program and add to your list if your application is turned down at your first few choices.

Most PA students already hold undergraduate degrees in a wide variety of fields and have worked in health care for four years before beginning training. At Stony Brook University in New York, where Lombardo is chair of the PA program, the average student is 25. "But the range runs between 19 and 55," he says, and many schools are looking for older applicants.

"The person who has a strong work ethic, who understands they will be part of a team, will be a successful PA applicant."

Kaplowe agrees, and says he believes "the most competitive applicant for PA school is 28 or older and this is a second career for them. They have a liberal arts degree and they understand the way the world works. They'll be able to communicate better to patients, staffs, and to write clearly. The person who has a strong work ethic, who understands they will be part of a team, who understands the boundaries that they work in—he or she will be a successful PA applicant."

Top schools. master's programs, ranked in 2003: 1) Duke University, North Carolina, 2) University of Iowa, 3) (tie) Emory University, Georgia; George Washington University, Washington, D.C.

Outlook. Demand for PAs skyrocketed in 2003 when new limits on the hours that medical residents can work in hospitals took effect. The total number of medical residents in many specialties, such as surgery, is also declining. At New Britain hospital, for example, there were 20 surgical residents in 1986, five in 1990, and this year there are two. PAs have filled the slots to continue the same level of service to patients. The U.S. Department of

Labor estimates that jobs for PAs will increase about 53 percent by 2010, and it is among the fastest growing occupations in the nation. Most PAs have jobs waiting for them when they finish school and pass their certification exam. The average salary for an experienced PA working 32 hours a week is a little over $76,000, the AAPA reports; for PAs practicing less than a year, the salary is about $64,500.

To find out more. The American Academy of Physician Assistants (703-836-2272; www. aapa.org) has extensive resources about schools, training, and careers on its site.

Public Health

Someone with a master's of public health is, traditionally, an M.D. looking to add another credential to the collection. Don't tell that to Cybele Bjorklund. She has a master's in health science from one of the top schools in the country, Johns Hopkins Bloomberg School of Public Health. And Bjorklund never went to med school; rather, she became interested in health policy after working at a television station in her native Indiana. "I decided I'd rather make national policy than cover it," she says. The M.P.H., she decided, would give her the best tools for the job. She's now a senior staff member on Capitol Hill (the Democratic staff director for the health subcommittee of the House of Representatives' powerful Ways and Means Committee), and she's working to overhaul Medicare before it goes bankrupt. "I think it's an incredibly flexible degree," Bjorklund says of the M.P.H. "It gives you a lot of opportunities, without having to get an M.D."

Bjorklund's "unusual" career path is really not

all that odd. The public health field is extraordinarily broad: It embraces epidemiologists, the disease detectives who race to figure out how SARS, West Nile virus, and other new ailments spread; administrators for health plans and hospitals; biostatisticians who crunch numbers for medical research; environmental health experts who deal with toxic waste sites or help reduce workers' exposure to toxic chemicals; and educators who figure out how to teach people to exercise, quit smoking, or get adequate prenatal care. Even something as seemingly non-medical as explaining the level of risk posed by bioterrorism is actually a public health responsibility, says Jennifer Leaning, a professor of international health at Harvard's School of Public Health. "How do you tell politicians or the public about the risk, and how do you train people's attitudes so they pay attention, but not get them so afraid that they tune it out?" she asks. What unites these disparate specialties is that they aim to improve the health of whole groups of people, not just one individual sitting on a doctor's examining table.

Although people are dazzled by medical feats such as open-heart surgery, the tremendous improvements in health and lifespan in the United States over the past century have been due largely to public health campaigns. These efforts have provided safer drinking water, vaccinated children, reduced deaths in childbirth, promoted the use of automobile seatbelts, and pointed out the hazards of smoking to millions and millions of people. Deborah Prothrow-Stith, a professor at Harvard's School of Public Health, sees that people already in health care, as well as those considering the field, are increasingly drawn to public health for exactly

that reason. "Our medical problems are more and more social, cultural, and political. There's a desire to do something that has a larger impact than the one-on-one impact you have as a clinician."

Interest in public health rose after the 2001 anthrax attacks, when contaminated letters were mailed to Florida, New York, and Washington, D.C. "Many people saw public health for the first

"The public health workforce is an eclectic collection of various disciplines."

time on the national news," says Prothrow-Stith. Since then, global outbreaks of infectious diseases such as SARS have kept public health professionals front and center. All of these incidents made it painfully clear that the nation's public health infrastructure, which has been cash-starved for decades, needs considerable improvement to handle such emerging threats. So the federal government has boosted funding for training public health workers and first responders, although professionals say more needs to be done.

Pluses. Public health degrees offer extraordinary flexibility in career choices, from traditional public health tasks such as managing a county health department or working overseas on a vaccination program, to health care management, state and federal government slots, consulting, and research. And schooling for an M.P.H. takes only two years out of your life.

Minuses. Salaries for new M.P.H.s can be well below those of new M.D.s.

Training. It's quite possible to work in public health with just an undergraduate degree. But the field is increasingly looking for credentials. "The public health workforce is an eclectic collection of various disciplines," says Georges Benjamin, executive director of the American Public Health Association, who previously worked as health commissioner for Washington, D.C., and secretary of health for the State of Maryland. "There is a strong movement to develop some kind of common understanding and training for public health workers. We're looking at a certification exam for a minimum level of expertise." Benjamin notes that he doesn't have an M.P.H. although he's been working in public health administration for most of his professional career.

The M.P.H., which usually takes two years, is the most popular degree. Other options include the master of health administration (M.H.A.), the master of science (M.S.), which many schools gear toward new grads with little experience in health, and doctoral degrees that usually take several more years to complete: the doctorate of public health (Dr.PH) and a research-oriented Ph.D. are two examples. Add in the many joint degree programs at universities around the country, such as M.D./M.P.H., J.D./M.P.H., and M.S.W./M.P.H., and there's no lack of choices. Even within the M.P.H., there are five core disciplines to choose among: biostatistics, environmental health, epidemiology, health education/behavioral science, and health services administration. Many schools also offer concentrations in international health, maternal and child health, nutrition, public health practice and program management, and biomedical laboratory science.

Tips on getting started. It helps to have a good grasp of math and science before applying; math-heavy courses such as statistics are tough even for science undergrads. According to the Association of Schools of Public Health, an undergraduate degree in math or biology is good preparation for a concentration in epidemiology or biostatistics; education, psychology, anthropology, or communications are typical majors for people who go on to specialize in health education. By contrast, a degree in biology, chemistry, engineering, agriculture, or earth sciences is considered good preparation for a concentration in environmental health. Because the field, and the graduate programs, are so varied, it's a good idea to have a sense of what subspecialty you're interested in before applying to schools. Haven't a clue? Internships can be invaluable in sorting out whether you'd be happier holed up in a laboratory sequencing the DNA of an emerging virus or teaching parenting skills to a group of teenage, inner-city moms.

Top schools. master's and doctorate programs, ranked in 2003: 1) Johns Hopkins University, Maryland; 2) (tie) Harvard University, Massachusetts; University of North Carolina–Chapel Hill.

Outlook. "There is a real shortage of trained public health personnel," says Tommy Thompson, Secretary of the U.S. Department of Health and Human Services. HHS researchers say more people are needed in epidemiology, biostatistics, environmental and occupational health, nutrition, public health nursing, and preventive medicine. The demand is expected to increase as the American population ages. Salaries for M.P.H. graduates within one year of graduation range from $31,500 to $161,400, according to the Association of Schools of Public Health. The huge variation reflects the fact that for many students, the M.P.H. is a midcareer degree, which they pursue after years of experience in medicine, nursing, or health administration.

To find out more. The American Public Health Association (202-777-2742; www.apha.org) has extensive information on what's new in public health. The Association of Schools of Public Health (202-296-1099; www.asph.org) has specific information about graduate programs.

Nursing

In Victorian England, nursing was routinely considered "menial employment needing neither study nor intelligence." But then came Florence Nightingale, whose lifesaving work during the Crimean War in the mid-1800s transformed the practice into a respected and highly skilled profession. Today, nurses are witnessing an explosion in demand for their services, from geriatric care in nursing homes to cutting-edge work in high-tech medical facilities. There is now a veritable "candy store" of opportunities in the field, says Patricia Rowell, senior policy fellow at the American Nurses Association. Adds Ruth Corcoran, CEO of the National League for Nursing, "The job security is amazing, the salaries are very fair, and it's an opportunity to make a difference every day in work that is appreciated and needed."

This is still an intimate career, requiring empathy and close relationships with patients who may be sick or dying. In general, nurses collect and analyze data on patients' physical and psychological situations, help diagnose ailments, provide continuous care and monitoring, and offer critical support to physicians. But there's more than one kind of nurse, and they are classified by their skill levels.

First come licensed vocational or practical nurses. There are about 404,000 LPNs in the United States and they're typically high school graduates with a year of nursing training from a voca-

tional school or junior college. They work under the direction of higher-level nurses and focus on the physical care of the patient, such as monitoring vital signs, making beds, and caring for some wounds.

Above LPNs are registered nurses. There are 2.2 million RNs in the United States and they make up the majority of the field. They are state-licensed and have earned either an associate degree in nursing from a community college or a bachelor's of science in nursing from a four-year school. Unlike LPNs, they handle medications, complex treatments, patient assessments, and plans for care. RNs can remain generalist nurses and serve in operating rooms, pediatric and maternity wards, rehabilitation centers, or psychiatric units, to name just a few places.

There are more options for students who earn postgraduate degrees, such as a master's in nursing. These are gateways to a variety of specialized paths. Nurse practitioners, for instance, see patients in primary care settings and help set up treatment plans. Clinical nursing specialists provide expert care in fields like oncology. Nurse anesthetists take care of a patient's anesthesia needs during surgery or childbirth. There's also academia: Some highly motivated baccalaureate students go directly into Ph.D. programs that prepare them for teaching and research positions.

Pluses. Many hospitals allow nurses to negotiate their work schedules, which is a boon for working parents. "If you have a child who is in school all day, you may want to work days so you can be home at night," Rowell says. If you want regular hours, you can find them in public health clinics or doctors' offices. Nursing is also a highly mobile profession, with opportunities growing overseas as well. The current nursing shortage means plenty of jobs, and salaries that keep going up. "I tell students that they will be able to plan a career that isn't bounded by anything," says Kathleen Ann Long, president of the American Association of Colleges of Nursing and dean of the University of Florida School of Nursing.

Minuses. Nurses in some hospitals are asked to work different hours every week, or even every day. As an acute care nurse, Rowell worked three separate shifts: Days were 7 a.m. to 3:30 p.m., for five or ten days straight, followed by a couple of days off, and then a stretch of night and evening shifts. "You can't really plan anything more than a month ahead of time," she says.

Training. LPNs start with that one-year vocational training program. The first step in the RN path is usually the associate or bachelor's degree. There are 569 such bachelor's degree programs in the United States, which take four years to complete, and 885 associate degree programs, which take from two to three years. Most bachelor's degree programs require students to first apply for general undergrad admissions. After completing the school's required courses, students may then apply to the nursing program. The University of Washington's school of nursing in Seattle is a good example. It requires students to take ninety credits—usually during freshman and sophomore year—in English composition, problem-solving, statistics, art, sociology, and the sciences before they can begin the nursing program. Applicants also must maintain at least a 2.0 GPA and provide a résumé outlining health care experience (volunteer and paid), a recommendation from a health care provider, and various essays. Once admitted, nursing students take various courses ranging from anatomy to pharmacotherapeutics to ethics. There also are several required clinical practicums. Clinical nurse specialists and other advanced nursing degree candidates take more advanced courses and must do a thesis or research project.

Once students have completed their undergraduate program, there's yet another hurdle: a state license. That means passing a nationally standardized test from the National Council Licensure Examination (NCLEX). Depending on your state nursing board, additional certification may be required for clinical nurse specialists and nurse anesthetists. You can find links to those boards through the National Council of State Boards of Nursing site at www.ncsbn.org.

The cost of a nursing degree varies enormously depending on the program and the school. Community colleges are the least expensive, costing $3,000 to $5,000 per year. At the other end of the spectrum, a private, four-year college can cost more than $20,000 per year.

Tips on getting started. Preparing for a nursing program is no cakewalk. High school students should take the most rigorous college prep courses, especially in biology, chemistry, and math. They must also show excellent writing skills because documentation is a big part of nursing. Clear communication is essential because nurses assess patients and relay information to other health care providers. Each undergraduate nursing program has its own set of admission prerequisites, but there are some basic requirements: the SAT or ACT exam and high school courses in math, biology, chemistry, English, and a foreign language. The American Nurses Association also recommends courses in computer science and the behavioral and social sciences. Rowell says volunteer work in a nursing setting is key for students "to see if it's what they really want to do. We see students drop out because they had an idealized notion of what a nurse was. Try it out a bit."

Top schools. Master's, ranked in 2003: 1) University of Washington; 2) University of California–San Francisco; 3) (tie) University of Michigan–Ann Arbor; University of Pennsylvania.

Outlook: Nursing is one of the nation's top ten occupations in terms of growth: about 1 million new nurses will be needed by 2010 to fill new jobs and replace people retiring from existing ones, according to the Bureau of Labor Statistics. Most of the growth will be in home health care, nursing homes, and the increasing number of clinics, offices, and medical centers that now offer advanced procedures once limited to hospitals. Public health promotion and disease prevention are also big takers. And there are still more opportunities in teaching. The National League for Nursing's Corcoran says that as many as half of the current nursing faculty will retire within the next five to ten years.

Because of these looming gaps, many employers are doing whatever they can to attract and retain qualified nurses. The average annual income for hourly hospital-based RNs is now about $47,000, a 10 percent hike since 2001, according to *RN Magazine*'s 2003 salary survey. Salaried nurses, who typically work in management and administration, now average about $65,000, another 10 percent gain. Nearly one-third of nurses now earn $60,000 or more, while only 18 percent earned that much two years ago, and a mere 11 percent did so in 1999. Generally speaking, nurses in densely populated cities, such as New York and San Francisco, earn more than RNs in less urban areas. Worried about school debt? Nearly seven out of ten full-time RNs are offered tuition reimbursement, and 54 percent can get continuing education reimbursement.

To find out more. The National Student Nurses Association (718-210-0705; www.nsna.org/career) has information about the variety of nursing careers. So does the American Nurses Association (800-274-4ANA; www.ana.org). The American Association of Colleges of Nursing (202-463-6930; www.aacn.nche.edu) has details on schools and programs.

Dentistry

Dentists roll up their sleeves, put on their surgical gloves, and get down to work in patients' mouths. They pull out painful wisdom teeth, fill cavities, and fit prosthetics where teeth used to be; some operate on cleft palates or even do cosmetic surgery. Research has linked oral health to general health, so dentists see their work as helping to keep their patients hale and hearty overall. Dentists work with their hands more than most physicians do, says Laura Neumann, associate executive director for education for the American Dental Association, and that's a stimulating part of the job. "They work in a small space. It requires very fine motor skills," she says. Those skills are applied not only to the mouth's function, but also to its appearance. "We like to say it's an art and a science," says Neumann. "The art that goes into restoring or improving aesthetics can be both challenging and fun, and people always feel good when you've done something like that for them." Over 80 percent of dentists are general practitioners, and most are in private practice. The rest specialize: Orthodontists correct poorly aligned teeth, for instance, while oral surgeons operate in and around the mouth. Other specialties include prosthodontics (restoring or replacing teeth) and periodontics (treating diseases of gums and other structures around the teeth).

Pluses. Dentistry can drastically improve a patient's life without placing the life-and-death stress of medicine on its practitioners. "Sometimes medical problems can be a little bit depressing," says Neumann. But in dentistry, "you tend to deal with less life-threatening situations." Plus dentists get to treat diseases directly, not just by writing prescriptions, and there's a great deal of satisfac-

---

"Sometimes medical problems can be a little bit depressing," but in dentistry, "you tend to deal with less life-threatening situations."

---

tion in that approach. Dentists earn a healthy income, and demands from work don't take over their lives. "Especially if you have your own practice or you're an associate, you can control your hours," Neumann says. That makes it an attractive career for women, she notes. She had three children—one before dental school, one during, and one just after. "I started practicing right away. I'm not going to say it was a piece of cake, but it was doable."

Minuses. In addition to learning how to pull teeth, anyone interested in private practice should be willing to learn how to manage a payroll and a small business. There's also the inescapable fact that people don't like coming to see you. "There's no question that there's a traditional fear or aversion to going to a dentist," says New York City dentist Leslie Seldin, who has a private practice. But with improving technology, he adds, things have gotten much more pleasant for the patient—although they never seem to get used to the sound of the drill.

Training. Dental schools offer a D.D.S (doctor of dental surgery) or the equivalent D.M.D. (doctor of dental medicine); both degrees are universally accepted. Like medical school, dental school lasts four years. In the first two years, students take classes in basic sciences—such as anatomy, microbiology, and physiology—concentrated on the head and neck. They try out techniques on synthetic models or extracted teeth. Since most dentists end up in private practice, courses on management are also part of the dental training. Students learn how to lead a dental team—which usually includes a hygienist and a dental assistant—and follow employment and tax laws.

Students may begin to see real, live patients in their second year, or sooner in some cases. That clinical experience accelerates in the third and fourth years, when they treat patients under the supervision of faculty dentists. A few schools have students rotate through community-based clinics or hospitals, but the majority of clinical work is in dental schools' own clinics.

Before they can practice, dentists have to pass a national written exam and a clinical licensing exam that may vary from state to state. In every state but Delaware, you can start practicing as soon as you get your degree, but about 40 percent of graduates go on to a residency for further training. Some residencies are in dental schools, others in hospitals. The length of residency depends on the specialty. Most general practice residencies are one year, while orthodontics and periodontics take three years and oral surgery takes four years. Some oral surgeons get an M.D. as part of their residency, which takes an additional two years. Having an M.D. can make it easier to get hospital privileges. There are a variety of other programs, such as one- to two-year residencies in public health.

A public health dentist might work for a city, running dental education and screening programs.

Dental school is about as expensive as medical school, and the vast majority of students have to take out loans. In 2003, graduating dentists averaged just over $100,000 in debt. That can make starting a new business risky, so many recent grads join existing practices as associates. The dentist who owns the practice pays them and teaches them how to run a business.

Tips on getting started. Dentistry isn't a fallback for students who don't have high enough numbers to get into medical school. The entering classes of Harvard's medical and dental schools in 2003 had the same average GPA: 3.8. In addition to great grades, schools also usually require students to have had courses in English, biology, chemistry, and physics—these are part of an established predental curriculum, and your school's health advisor can fill you in on other details. Remember, too, that aligning teeth and making sure they look good is also an art—admissions offices take that seriously. Students should consider taking studio art classes to help with their spatial skills, says Marilyn Hoffman, the predental advisor at the University of Utah in Salt Lake City. And get some experience. Hoffman says the schools want applicants to prove they care about dentistry, and part of that proof is spending time with professionals, doing "chairside observation," and shadowing dentists.

Applicants should also decide whether they are most interested in a practice or in doing research: Some dental schools focus on clinical skills, others on scientific research. Schools do try to simplify the application process by using a central service: AADSAS, the Associated American Dental Schools Application Service (www.adea.org), will send your application to all the schools you select.

As part of your application, you have to take the computerized DAT, or Dental Admissions Test. The test covers biology and chemistry, perceptual ability (matching shapes and judging distances), reading comprehension, and math. Registration is online at the American Dental Association's website (www.ada.org; look for their Education and Testing section), and you can schedule the test for almost any time at one of a few hundred testing centers across the country. You can spend $1,000 on a DAT prep class, but Hoffman says it's not necessary if you buy practice tests and study on your own. Some schools also require a manual dexterity test, like carving a piece of chalk or soap to specifications.

Outlook. The U.S. population is growing faster than schools are producing new dentists, and an older generation of dentists is starting to retire. That means more demand. The average income for all dentists in 2000 was $183,000; in a 2002 survey, recent graduates were making an average of $142,000 if they owned their practice or $93,000 if they were nonowners, such as associates in someone else's practice. As with many health professionals, dentists tend to be concentrated in urban centers where there are more patients and it's easier to pay off debt. The federal government and some states will take over loan payments for graduates willing to practice in underserved and rural areas.

To find out more. The American Dental Association has information on careers in dentistry and on the DAT test (312-440-2500; www.ada.org). The American Dental Education Association (1-800-353-2237; www.adea.org) publishes the *Official Guide to Dental Schools* ($35), which describes the programs at U.S. and Canadian schools and explains the application process.

Psychology

Psychologists have moved far beyond the "talking cure" during the century since Sigmund Freud set up his couch in Vienna. Therapists still talk, of course, and still try to cure. But the field has broadened significantly. Through a wide variety of psychotherapies—some short-term, some long, some directed at modifying behavior, some focused on the thinking behind that behavior— psychologists may work with clients to identify and change unhealthy or irrational attitudes that make people dissatisfied with their lives and, in some cases, utterly miserable. They may also test applicants' fitness for jobs using paper-and-pencil questionnaires, perform IQ tests, and do other kinds of assessments. Some teach and do academic research in different topics, such as a culture's effect on the way people feel. School psychologists work with students' behavior problems and may help teachers learn to manage classrooms. Psychologists may also bring their understanding of the mind to bear on physical illnesses, cooperating with physicians to help patients with stress-related ulcers or others who don't stick with their medications.

One thing all psychologists have in common is that they view distress as a complex problem, not one simply rooted in body chemistry or solved solely by antidepressants. "If you see the solutions to mental illness lying in biology, then I'd probably go to medical school," says George Stricker, a clinical psychologist at Adelphi University in Garden City, New York. (Unlike psychiatrists, psychologists can't prescribe drugs—except in New Mexico, where they recently won that right.)

Pluses. When clinical psychologist Tom Olkowski worked in a suburban Colorado school system, he evaluated children and helped them, their families, and teachers understand how the kids could learn better. "When you see a kid who's been struggling doing better in school, that's something tangible," he says. Variety is another advantage: Olkowski's psychology Ph.D. gave him the background in research and theory to work in many fields. In his 30-year career, he has worked not only in schools, but also in a mental health center; written a book on the stress of moving with children; and made two videos for a real estate company on the same topic. Now he practices privately in Denver.

Minuses. Psychology can be stressful, especially when you deal with clients who may turn suicidal or violent. Olkowski adds that doctoral training doesn't prepare you for running a private practice, when you have to know about things like marketing and cash flow. Insurance restrictions on the number of therapy sessions with a client can add to the hassle factor. And training is expensive: Clinical psychologists often emerge from school $30,000 to $60,000 in debt.

Training. In most states, you need a doctorate in order to practice independently, without a doctorate-level psychologist supervising you. To get that doctorate, Ph.D.s used to be the only option for psychologists. But today, the Psy.D. (doctor of psychology) degree has become popular (although there are still more Ph.D. programs than Psy.D. programs). A Ph.D. has more emphasis on original research and requires an extensive dissertation. Students usually spend five years taking classes, doing research, and learning clinical skills, plus at least another year completing the dissertation. Psy.D. programs concentrate more on clinical practice and therapeutic methods. Students still learn how to do research and how to use the findings, but have to write a shorter paper to graduate. The clinical emphasis makes the Psy.D. attractive, but the Ph.D. makes it easier to get an academic job.

All doctoral students also learn the foundations of the discipline, including skills such as assessing patients using a variety of tests and how to practice ethically. Many students study statistics and research design. They also learn the cognitive, social, and biological bases of behavior, which may include classes in neurological and physiological psychology. Many states only license psychologists with doctorates from programs accredited by the American Psychological Association (most programs are APA-accredited). Graduates who want to be licensed as psychologists also have to take a national written exam and, in some states, a separate test that may cover the state's ethical codes and mental health laws. Many states also require that psychologists practice under supervision for a while before they can get an independent license.

Are you doctorate-phobic? Consider a master's in psychology. Master's programs are short—two or three years—and thus relatively cheap. The degree allows you to do marriage and family counseling, mental health counseling, and social work. "If you want to be a practitioner, if you want to work in the field, a master's is a wonderfully sufficient degree," says Margaret Joyal, past president of the Northamerican Association of Masters in Psychology. Master's programs are accredited by the Masters in Psychology Accreditation Council.

Tips on getting started. You don't have to be a psych major in college to get into graduate school, although it may be tougher to work the classes you'll need into your art history major. Most programs require undergrad courses in statistics and experimental psychology. Stricker also recom-

mends getting some experience with emotionally troubled people to be sure you want to work with them professionally. He suggests volunteering with a peer counseling service, for example. If you plan on going to a Ph.D. program, research experience can be very helpful; try finding a professor who will let you volunteer in his or her lab. About half of the U.S. doctoral programs in psychology require applicants to take the Graduate Record Examinations. Some programs also require the psychology subject GRE, which has multiple-choice questions about experimental and natural sciences, social sciences, and general psychology, including the history of the discipline and research design. Scores on these tests are important, but schools place even more emphasis on the applicant's statement of goals, recommendations from professors, and research experience.

Doctoral students who responded to a 1999 survey funded by the Pew Charitable Trusts said one extremely important factor in picking a school was choosing an advisor you can work with. A Ph.D. student and her advisor may work together closely or meet a few times a year, depending on the school and the person, so it's important to choose someone whose style fits your own. It's also a good idea to ask about funding when you're looking at schools to find out how students there are financially supported. Ph.D. students can be carried on an advisor's research grant. But because Psy.D.s are usually offered by smaller schools that don't have a lot of research money, most Psy.D. students have to come up with loans, which means more postgrad debt.

Top schools. Doctorate programs in clinical psychology, ranked in 2004: 1) University of California–Los Angeles; 2) (tie) University of California–Berkeley; University of Wisconsin–Madison.

Outlook. In the most recent survey by the American Psychological Association, in 2001, clinical psychologists in their first few years after graduate school made an average of about $55,000. Average income climbs with experience: Clinical psychologists who had been working for more than thirty years averaged $90,000, and a full 25 percent of these veterans made over $120,000 a year. The academic job market is not good. Many students enter graduate school thinking they're going to be professors, but only a few make it. Although many professors are nearing retirement age now, "I don't think there's ever going to be as many jobs as people," Stricker says. Most psychologists are not academics; they may be in private practice, work in schools or at private testing companies, or practice and do research in any number of settings. Graduates of master's degree programs have little trouble finding work in the public sector—for example, community health centers, child welfare agencies, and prisons. There's lots of work, Joyal says, but it doesn't pay very well. Starting salaries for psychologists with master's degrees tend to be between $30,000 and $40,000.

To find out more. The American Psychological Association (800-374-2721; www.apa.org) has information on psychology careers and education. The APAs *Graduate Study in Psychology* (www.apa.org/books; $24.95 in print, $19.95 for three months' access to the online version) lists psychology programs in the United States and Canada, and is updated yearly. The Pew-funded survey on Ph.D. student experiences (www.phd-survey.org) has a valuable section devoted to psychology.

Physical Therapy

The human body is pretty good at self-repair, knitting torn muscles and fractured bones together after an injury. But sometimes it can't handle the workload alone. Physical therapists help the healing process by flexing stiffened muscles, stretching limbs, and teaching balance to people who have been off their feet for a while. "It's the study of movement and its application, but it's more than that," says Sue Schafer, associate dean of the School of Physical Therapy at Texas Women's University in Dallas, Texas. It's understanding individual needs, she says, and matching them to individual capabilities. When assessing a patient—from a hulking football player to a stroke survivor to a tiny infant—the therapist determines what structures are damaged, and what a patient needs to do to recover—given his or her particular physical limits—and then oversees the appropriate rehabilitation therapy. Techniques include exercise, massage, ultrasound, and heat therapy.

Sports medicine is one of the better known PT subfields, but therapists don't just rehab athletes. Today, for example, they are often called on to work with breast cancer patients, advising them on how to remain active while undergoing chemotherapy and radiation treatments, and also working to reduce postsurgery side effects such as painful swelling of the arms. Although they often work in tandem with occupational therapists, physical therapists focus on increasing mobility and strength and decreasing pain, while occupational therapists tackle the ability to perform specific tasks.

Pluses. Hanging out with professional sports teams and mixing with world-famous ballerinas isn't too shabby, but in reality, very few physical therapists have celeb-studded jobs. The rest relish the opportunity to work extensively one-on-one with patients and see the fruits of their labor in every step that patients make. PTs also have the flexibility to work in either a hospital or private practice, and the range of patients—from kids with cerebral palsy to senior citizens recovering from hip replacement surgery—keeps them on their toes.

Minuses. The work takes a toll on therapists' own bodies. The job can require heavy lifting—moving around large patients or large equipment—and standing or crouching for long periods of time. "It's a physical profession and eventually we have personal limitations," Schafer says. "I don't do well getting on the ground any more and that's what you have to do when you work with children." Other therapists say that the greatest frustration is patients who are not willing to do the work needed for recovery. Physical therapy often demands that patients be not only cooperative, but determined.

Training. Either a master's or doctorate is required to practice. (The Commission on Accreditation in Physical Therapy stopped recognizing baccalaureate professional degrees a few years ago, and by 2020, the American Physical Therapy Association hopes to make the profession an all-doctorate field.) Master's programs usually take two years and teach students basic sciences such as chemistry and biology as well as the psychosocial aspects of disease, intervention and treatment options, and current PT research directions. In addition to classroom work, students receive an average of fifteen weeks of field training at hospitals, rehab centers, schools, or outpatient clinics.

Doctorates, which take about three years, supplement this training with expanded work in areas like pharmacology, radiology, health care management, and pathology. They also insist on more field training—as long as a year. Graduates must pass a national exam as well as fulfill any individual state requirements, which may include additional training to maintain licensure. Tuition rates vary widely by school. The University of South Alabama, a public institution, estimates that state residents will pay about $17,000 over three years, while out-of-state students pay about $35,000. At a private school like New York's Columbia University, tuition over three years can reach about $75,000.

Tips for getting started. To get into a PT program, applicants need some prerequisite undergrad courses, which include psychology, biology, physics, chemistry, statistics, and the humanities. A high GPA in these courses is important, as is performance on the GRE. But program directors warn that numbers alone won't get you in. Applicants need to show a knack for working with people. "You want to be able to talk with your patients and make them feel at ease," says Meredith Harris, chair of physical therapy at Northeastern University. Making that interpersonal connection can be crucial to encouraging a patient to accept therapy, she says. "A lot of people want to be taken care of. We have to convince them to help themselves." Work as a physical therapy assistant (an accredited aide who has completed a two-year program) or volunteer experience at a nursing home or hospital can also make an application shine.

Top schools. Master's and doctorate programs, ranked in 2004: 1) University of Southern California; 2) Washington University in St. Louis; 3) University of Pittsburgh.

Outlook. A graying society is good news for the physical therapy community. As older people lose mobility and strength through disease and accidents, there will be an increased need for PT services.

And as corporations struggle to keep insurance costs down, many are hiring PTs to improve employee health. PTs are even finding work in veterinarians' offices, where they can rehabilitate injured pets. Salaries averaged about $57,000 in 2002, and therapists who work in home health care services can expect more money than hospital employees.

To find out more. The American Physical Therapy Association (703-684-2782; www.apta. org) lists accredited programs and residency and fellowship information and offers financial aid advice.

Occupational Therapy

Most people view occupations as that thing they do from 9 to 5. Occupational therapists don't. While OTs most often help patients with temporary or permanent disabilities function smoothly in the workplace, they handle every aspect of the business of life, from inventing ways for handicapped parents to make lunches for their kids to teaching premature babies the proper movements for nursing. Retired folks don't stare into computer monitors or punch time cards every day, but they can call on occupational therapists to help them relearn how to dress and bathe themselves after a hip replacement or stroke.

As in physical therapy, the long-term goal of occupational therapy is to increase independence. But while physical therapists focus on overall strength and movement, OTs tackle obstacles to particular activities. When consulting with a patient, a therapist must break down an activity into each of its components, whether they are physical, environmental, mental, or behavioral. "Bowling isn't just picking up a ball and rolling it,"

explains Janet Falk-Kessler, director of Columbia University's occupational therapy programs. "It involves everything from posture, bilateral motor coordination, aspects of vision, sound, and strength. It also has social components, like how one behaves in a bowling alley."

It's a field that requires a lot of creative problem-solving. When some of Falk-Kessler's students were working with the homebound elderly, they discovered that the Meals on Wheels packaging was too difficult to open. So the therapists created a tool specifically designed to cut the boxes. For a patient with a brain tumor in the care of St. Louis–based occupational therapist Vicki Kaskutas, the goal was to help him return to his job as an administrator for a large national firm. She prescribed mock meetings and presentations to help the man readjust to the necessary interpersonal situations.

Pluses. Not bound to hospitals, occupational therapists can ply their trade in a range of industries. Some work with architects—helping design accessible homes and buildings—while others, who are interested in mental health, can work with children and teenagers who have anxiety disorders or substance abuse problems, improving their ability to stay on task and interact better with peers and adults.

Minuses. Sometimes patients have difficulty understanding the purpose of therapy. "We're not here to take away the pain. You have to feed your dog and we have to figure out how to do that," explains Kaskutas. Dealing with insurance companies can also be frustrating. "Patients get what their policy covers, not necessarily what they need," says Rebecca Reder, clinical director of the occupational therapy/physical therapy department at Cincinnati Children's Hospital Medical Center.

Training. Undergraduate degrees for OT are

on their way out: As of January 2007, the Accreditation Council for Occupational Therapy Education will only recognize those programs that confer a master's or doctorate. Anyone now enrolling in an undergrad program is going to need summer coursework to finish by the deadline. The new emphasis is on the master's degree, which requires two years of classroom study, including courses in anatomy, sociology, psychology, and biology. This is followed by six to nine months of fieldwork under the guidance of a licensed therapist. Some combined baccalaureate/master's programs can shorten the amount of schooling by a year. A national certification exam is required to practice. Training isn't cheap, with some private schools charging upwards of $30,000 a year, but public schools can offer lower tuition to in-state residents.

Tips for getting started. Proof of a commitment to community service looks stellar on any kind of application, but for almost all occupational therapy programs, it is required. To impress admissions officers, work beyond the minimum number of hours and try to volunteer in hospitals that will allow you to shadow members of the occupational therapy unit. Experience in varied settings, like homeless shelters or schools, helps demonstrate your dedication as well. There are some required undergrad courses, including biology, physiology, and psychology. Programs also examine GPAs and scores on the Graduate Record Exam.

Top schools. Master's and doctorate programs, ranked in 2004: 1) University of Southern California; 2) Boston University, Sargent College of Health & Rehabilitation Sciences; 3) Washington University in St. Louis.

Outlook. The new educational requirements will narrow the pool of people entering the field at the same time as an aging population begins to rely more heavily on occupational therapy services. Thus, the laws of supply and demand predict a rosy employment future. The U.S. Department of Labor notes that limits on health insurance for therapy will stunt growth in the short term, but

> *"Patients get what their policy covers, not necessarily what they need."*

employment rates will exceed the average for all occupations through 2012. The average annual salary for an OT is about $47,000, according to the most recent surveys by the American Occupational Therapy Association, and this is likely to go up after the education requirements crimp the supply. New grads aren't doing too badly today: Their starting salaries hover around the $40,000 mark.

To find out more. The American Occupational Therapy Association (301-652-2682; www. aota.org) has resources on education and snagging a job in the field. The American Occupational Therapy Foundation (301-652-6611, ext. 2250; www.aotf.org) has information on financial aid.

Social Work

When life gets tough, social workers get moving. "Social workers make real life work better," says Gary Bailey, president of the National Association of Social Workers. People at high risk for AIDS, or low-income parents who are caught between the demands of work and the need to find decent child care, have traditionally been able to get counseling and practical help from social workers employed by public welfare agencies and hospitals. Today private companies, including HMOs and for-profit health service organizations, have added social workers to their payroll to advise patients and their families. While specialties aren't strictly defined in the field, most social workers build an area of expertise or gain certification in the areas of family care, public health, or mental health.

Pluses. No surprises here—the positive impact you have is a big reason for doing this job. "I know it sounds hokey. But when you work with people who are sharing their most emotional pains with you and you see them move forward, it means so much," says Suzanne Towns, former director of the Forensic Healthcare Program at the New York City Alliance Against Sexual Assault. Towns, who once worked for the Union Bank of Switzerland, adds that "I wasn't really feeling that when I was working in finance." Many social workers also praise the diversity of the work, which can range from grief counseling to supervising a homeless outreach program. Some social work positions also allow for flexible working hours; private firms, in particular, often hire counselors on a part-time basis.

Minuses. The emotional rewards typically are higher than the monetary ones, and the long, intense hours often lead to burnout. "Social workers work with some of the most seriously troubled individuals in American culture. It takes its toll when that's your job, day in and day out," says Bruce Thyer, dean of the School of Social Work at Florida State University.

Training. Education requirements for social workers vary in each state; the Association of Social Work Boards lists all of them. A master's degree as well as a passing score on a licensing exam are needed for most positions, especially clinical or management ones. However, some entry-level positions, such as child welfare case workers or counseling jobs in the private sector, only call for an undergraduate degree in social work. That degree, offered at many universities, involves the study of social welfare policies and methods. As part of the major, most schools require seminars on dealing with individuals and families, and an internship where students are placed in a public or private social service organization to get hands-on experience dealing with patients.

The master's degree is similar but more intense. In over 150 programs accredited by the Council on Social Work Education, students take two years of classes in social welfare policy and practice, human behavior, and research methods. Other courses may include applied psychology, sociology, and ethics. Budding social workers also need to take a nine-hundred-hour practicum. At the University of Illinois–Urbana-Champaign, for instance, graduate students work Monday through Thursday at anywhere from a school to a nursing home depending on their area of interest; the work typically includes client interviews and case evaluations. On Fridays, students attend a seminar at the school to discuss and learn from their experiences.

An increasing number of graduate schools are offering minors and dual-degree programs for students who want to demonstrate an expertise in a certain area—and get a step ahead in the job market. Columbia University is starting a dual-degree program in social work and international affairs that will help graduates land positions with international organizations like the United Nations. "We know that there isn't a single social problem that requires one profession to intervene," says Jeanette Takamura, dean of the university's School of Social Work. "So why should we offer one single degree?" The program at Columbia takes three years to finish, and students graduate with two master's degrees. The school also offers dual social work degrees in other areas such as urban planning and Jewish studies.

If you want to become a clinical social worker who provides mental health therapy, you need to receive still more training. Clinical social workers who work as psychotherapists, doing in-depth counseling, can receive reimbursement for their services from HMOs. Besides a master's degree, psychotherapists need two years of supervised work experience and a passing score on a clinical licensing test.

While the social work curriculum is often similar at different schools, costs are not. At some private schools such as the University of Southern California, tuition for full-time grad students is close to $30,000 a year—and most students are on financial aid. Public university in-state tuition tends to be about half that.

Tips on getting started. "Social workers are born, not made," says Bailey, who is an assistant professor of social work at Simmons College in Boston. "You need to have passion if you to want to be a social worker. And that passion can't be taught." The best way to demonstrate this kind of dedication is to show it on your résumé, says Shanti Khinduka, dean of the George Warren Brown School of Social Work at Washington University in St. Louis. If you haven't been working in a related field such as teaching or nursing, volunteer experience is very important for an applicant—even as little as spending one evening each week playing cards at a nearby nursing home or one Saturday a month helping mentally-ill children. While universities do not require an undergraduate degree in social work, most schools do give preference to students who have performed well in social sciences courses like psychology and sociology. Many graduate schools of social work do not require applicants to take the Graduate Record Exam but they do want to see a high undergraduate GPA.

"Social workers work with some of the most seriously troubled individuals in American culture."

Top schools. Master's programs, ranked in 2004: 1) University of Michigan–Ann Arbor; 2) Washington University in St. Louis; 3) (tie) Columbia University, New York; University of California–Berkeley; University of Chicago; University of Washington.

Outlook. Although budget cuts have caused recent layoffs in some states such as Ohio and California, the demand for social workers is expected to rise over the next decade. The National Association of Social Workers (NASW) estimates the field to grow by 30 percent by 2010. Most recent graduates have had an easy time finding a job; for example, over 90 percent of the graduates from the University of Minnesota–Twin Cities last year landed a position within three months. Among the fastest growing subspecialties is elder care, says Jean Quam, director of the university's school of social work. "If you look at the demographic changes in the country, the number of older adults is exploding," she says. Newly minted master's graduates typically earn over $30,000. Those with only an undergraduate degree in social work should expect starting salaries of around $25,000. Compensation varies by region, with urban areas offering more money. Suzanne Towns, who graduated from the social work program at Columbia University in 2001, earned over $45,000 in her New York job, while a recent master's program graduate in New Mexico might make as little as $30,000.

> "You need to have passion if you to want to be a social worker. And that passion can't be taught."

To find out more. The National Association of Social Workers (202-408-8600; www.social workers.org) has general information and career advice The Council on Social Work Education (703-683-8080; www.cswe.org) has complete listings of accredited school programs. The Association of Social Work Boards (800-225-6880; www. aswb.org) administers the licensing exams and maintains information on each state's test and license requirements.

Speech-Language Pathology

Humans need to communicate. It's an essential characteristic of the species. But sometimes it doesn't come easy. That's where speech-language pathologists (SLP) come in. They work in hospitals, clinics, schools, corporate offices, or private practice, diagnosing speaking and communication problems and developing treatment plans. For example, children who have trouble articulating certain words and sounds can learn to talk fluently with proper training. For stroke victims who suffer

aphasia—trouble speaking, comprehending, or writing language—early treatment by an SLP can help preserve and improve language skills by using verbal or visual drills and conversational role-playing.

Pluses. Good salaries and opportunities to work in a variety of settings with all kinds of patients keep SLPs happy. Those that tire of working in a hospital, for instance, can easily find another job in a school helping students with speech problems. New SLPs say they are amazed and gratified when they see a struggling student finally turn a corner. "I've seen a child truly develop his phonology skills, apply them to decoding words, and start reading [for the first time] at nine years," says Jodie Barr-Katzen, who works at Baltimore Lab, a division of The Lab School of Washington, a private school for children with learning disabilities. "When he's really sounding out words, it's awesome."

Minuses. "It's not like giving somebody a pill," says Diane Paul-Brown of the American Speech-Language-Hearing Association. Some patients with severe disabilities may never reach normal levels, and their progress can be slow and frustrating. There are also hassles in getting compensation from schools and insurers. (Some pathologists say, however, that even dealing with bureaucracy can be rewarding. "I feel like I'm advocating for a child; there's a lot at stake," says Barr.)

Training. In almost every state, practicing speech-language pathologists must have a master's degree in the field, pass a national licensing exam, and complete a nine-month supervised fellowship. Programs are accredited by a council of the American Speech-Language-Hearing

Association, and a typical master's curriculum involves four semesters and a summer of full-time study. Classes focus on specific disorders. For example, at the University of Maryland–College Park, besides a diagnostic methods course and an audiology course, all students must study aphasia, voice disorders, stuttering, child language disorders, and phonological disorders. They can also take electives such as augmentative communications (using technology to enhance innate ability). Once graduate students have a grasp of their field and its tools, they begin clinical rotations where they learn how to evaluate and diagnose actual patients and design customized courses of treatment. Some programs also require a thesis.

Not surprisingly, in-state tuition at a public school is far less expensive than out of state or private school tuition. New York University, which is private, charges about $3,000 for just one course. But at the University of Iowa in Iowa City, state residents can take three or four courses for less than that sum.

Tips on getting started. Aspiring undergrads can major in speech pathology or communication sciences and disorders, which gives them many of the prerequisite courses for grad school. (Some grad programs only accept applicants with these majors.) The prerequisites include anatomy and physiology of speech, anatomy and physiology of hearing, speech science, hearing science, speech and language development, phonetics, psychology of language, and acoustics.

You're not barred from becoming an SLP if you didn't major in it, however. Some students without this background do postbaccalaureate work before applying to grad programs, while others apply anyway, and are accepted with the provision that they first take a year of make-up classes. Froma Roth, director of graduate studies in Speech-Language

Pathology at the University of Maryland, says that she looks for students with diverse academic backgrounds because the field is very interdisciplinary. Richard Hurtig, chair of the University of Iowa department of speech pathology and audiology, agrees. In the past, his school has accepted music and singing majors with no science background. (They did have to make up a great deal of coursework, however.) In general, schools are looking for high GPAs and GRE scores. Students with better chances of admission usually have volunteered or worked in nursing homes and preschools.

Top schools. Master's programs, ranked in 2004: 1) (tie) University of Iowa; University of Wisconsin–Madison; 3) (tie) Northwestern University, Illinois; Purdue University–West Lafayette, Indiana; University of Washington.

Outlook. Speech-language pathologists are highly sought after in the private sector, school systems, and academia, and demand seems to be growing. According to the U.S. Bureau of Labor Statistics, speech-language pathology is among the top 30 fastest-growing professions. Most of the growth is in clinical positions rather than academia, but many speech-language professors are set to retire in the next five to ten years, and schools are already looking for candidates for tenure-track research and teaching positions. In 2002 the average salary for a speech-language pathologist was about $51,500. In general, SLPs in hospitals and clinics earn more than those in schools.

To find out more. The American Speech-Language-Hearing Association (800-498-2071; www.asha.org) has extensive student materials with a guide to accredited programs by state.

Emergency Medical Technician

On television, EMTs are in the thick of the action, racing around in ambulances, pulling victims from car wrecks, and administering life-saving CPR. Veteran paramedic Connie Meyer of Greeley, Kansas, says some of this is reality TV: The race to save lives can be a major adrenaline rush. But for her there are other rewards. "Only about five percent of calls are really critical," says Meyer. "Sometimes patients call because they're lonely and they don't know what to do." For her the key is providing whatever aid is needed, even if it's just a sympathetic ear. Whether dealing with multiple injuries at a five-alarm fire or tending to an indigent patient who needs a ride to his doctor's office, the job of an EMT is to get to vulnerable people before any other medical help. Those EMTs with the most advanced level of training are called paramedics. With paramedic certification, EMTs can give oral and intravenous drugs, intubate patients so they can breathe, interpret electrocardiograms, and use defibrillators to shock a stopped heart back to life.

Pluses. "The best part of the job is you're helping people when they're at the absolutely worst point in their lives," says Bob Loftus, a member of the Board of Directors of the National Association of EMTs. The work can also be fast-paced and exciting and offer constant variety. People like it so much that most EMTs work as volunteers.

Minuses. The high rate of volunteerism occurs also because it's hard to find a paying job, or at least a paying job you'd want to keep. Many EMTs leave within the first five years because of high stress, on-the-job accidents, irregular hours, long on-call shifts, and very low compensation. Part of the stress is the regular exposure to dis-

eases and risk of physical injuries. But the worst part, says Loftus, "is the patients you don't save."

Training. Requirements vary across states. Students must complete anywhere from one semester to two years of classroom and clinical training and then pass a state test or, in some cases, a national certification exam. (See below for a way to check state Emergency Medical Services websites for information on your state's requirements.) In the past, many hospitals and emergency services ran independent apprenticeships, but these courses have become rare. Today more EMTs do classroom work in community colleges, technical schools, and universities.

There's also a move toward greater standardization of EMT education because the U.S. Department of Transportation has developed criteria for three levels of training. EMT-Basic, sometimes called EMT-1, requires about 110 hours (about one semester) of classwork and field training. Traditionally, after earning an EMT-Basic, many EMTs worked for several years to gain field experience before pursuing the more advanced coursework that ends in an EMT-Intermediate (EMT-2, EMT-3) or the higher EMT-Paramedic certification. However, because EMTs at the intermediate or paramedic level often have an easier time getting jobs and also earn more, some students are forgoing years of work experience and going straight to paramedic courses. Many community colleges now offer two-year paramedic programs where students graduate with an associate's degree.

Tips on getting started. Those who think they can stomach emergency medical work and who are curious about becoming an EMT can get a taste by volunteering to work for a local ambulance service; the company will often train you as a first responder with basic first aid skills. First responders only need about 40 hours of training. If you do well and decide to pursue EMT training, your volunteer organization may help with tuition and costs. Getting into school usually isn't an issue: Most EMT training programs are open enrollment and some don't even require a high school diploma. The tough part is making it through the training.

Outlook. Turnover from EMT burnout will assure new openings, and the U.S. Department of Labor says more of these positions are switching from volunteer to paid. Salaries and benefits are generally better for EMTs working for local governments as part of fire or police departments or emergency services. After seventeen years and several promotions within the Johnson County Med-Act emergency service, Connie Meyer earns $60,000 and is eligible for retirement in seven years. Starting salary in her department is $34,000. Nationally, most EMTs make significantly less than Meyer does, especially if they work for hospitals and private ambulance services. In 2002, the average annual income was about $26,500.

Of course, compensation varies by certification level. According to a 2001 study by the National Registry of Emergency Medical Technicians, the average EMT-Basic earned about $18,000. The average paramedic did quite a bit better, earning more than $34,000. Supervisory positions earn even more. And as health care continues to change, there are signs that paramedics may have

"The best part of the job is you're helping people when they're at the absolutely worst point in their lives."

more options. Though still controversial, some hospitals have begun hiring paramedics as part of the emergency room medical team, where they work alongside doctors and nurses.

To find out more. The National Registry of Emergency Medical Technicians (614-888-4484; www.nremt.org) offers general information about the field as well as links to every state EMS office. EMSmagazine.com also has a good state-by-state survey of EMT training requirements.

How Do the Schools Stack Up?

Which are the hardest and easiest medical schools to get into?

While the number of applications to medical schools has dropped in recent years, it is still extremely hard to get in. Many of the most competitive only accept 1 in 20 of those who apply—or even fewer. Schools are ranked here from most to least selective based on a formula that combines average MCAT scores and undergraduate GPA for the Fall 2003 entering class as well as the school's acceptance rates. Average GPAs and MCATs will give you a sense of the competition.

Most to least selective

	Overall acceptance rate	Acceptance rate (men)	Acceptance rate (women)	Acceptance rate (minorities)	Average undergraduate GPA	Average composite MCAT score (scale: 1-15)	Average MCAT score, verbal reasoning (scale: 1-15)	Average MCAT score, physical sciences (scale: 1-15)	Average MCAT score, biological sciences (scale: 1-15)	Average MCAT score, writing (scale: J-T)
Washington University in St. Louis	11.2%	9.4%	13.5%	12.4%	3.82	12.2	11.3	12.6	12.5	Q
Duke University (NC)	3.7%	3.6%	3.9%	N/A	3.80	11.9	11.2	12.3	12.4	Q
Columbia Univ. Col. of Physicians and Surgeons (NY)	11.0%	11.7%	10.4%	7.3%	3.79	11.7	11.1	12.1	12.0	Q
Harvard University (MA)	4.7%	4.0%	5.4%	4.8%	3.80	11.3	10.6	11.8	11.6	Q
University of Pennsylvania	5.5%	5.1%	6.0%	5.0%	3.78	11.4	10.8	11.7	11.7	Q
University of Michigan–Ann Arbor	8.5%	7.9%	9.1%	9.1%	3.75	11.5	10.7	12.0	11.9	R
Baylor College of Medicine (TX)	7.0%	6.7%	7.4%	8.1%	3.77	11.2	10.6	11.6	11.4	P
Cornell University (Weill) (NY)	4.2%	3.3%	5.1%	5.4%	3.73	11.3	10.6	11.7	11.7	Q
Stanford University (CA)	3.4%	3.0%	3.9%	4.3%	3.75	11.2	10.2	11.6	11.8	Q
University of California–San Francisco	5.6%	5.7%	5.5%	N/A	3.76	11.2	10.4	11.4	11.7	Q
Yale University (CT)	5.7%	4.9%	6.5%	5.8%	3.71	11.4	10.8	11.8	11.7	R
Johns Hopkins University (MD)	5.6%	5.1%	6.0%	3.7%	3.80	11.0	11.0	12.0	11.0	Q
Emory University (GA)	9.8%	9.9%	9.7%	8.4%	3.75	10.9	10.6	11.0	11.1	P
University of California–San Diego	6.4%	6.1%	6.7%	7.3%	3.73	11.0	9.9	11.4	11.6	Q
Vanderbilt University (TN)	7.7%	6.3%	9.4%	9.7%	3.77	10.8	10.2	11.0	11.1	Q
Mayo Medical School (MN)	2.7%	2.6%	2.8%	3.4%	3.78	10.5	9.9	10.4	11.1	Q
University of Pittsburgh	9.9%	9.4%	10.4%	9.3%	3.70	10.9	10.4	11.0	11.2	P
University of California–Los Angeles (Geffen)	4.6%	4.5%	4.8%	5.1%	3.67	10.9	9.9	11.3	11.5	Q
Mount Sinai School of Medicine (NY)	7.9%	7.0%	8.6%	6.7%	3.66	10.9	10.5	11.0	11.2	Q
New York University	29.7%	48.9%	13.3%	19.1%	3.70	11.0	10.3	11.0	11.0	Q
Northwestern University (Feinberg) (IL)	5.4%	6.1%	4.8%	N/A	3.68	10.8	10.4	10.9	11.0	Q
Univ. of Texas Southwestern Medical Center–Dallas	14.9%	15.2%	14.6%	15.0%	3.75	10.6	10.1	10.8	11.0	P
University of Virginia	9.0%	8.8%	9.2%	8.4%	3.70	10.7	10.3	10.9	10.8	P
University of Southern California	7.9%	7.6%	8.3%	6.9%	3.62	10.8	10.1	11.0	11.3	P
University of Wisconsin–Madison	12.1%	10.3%	13.9%	10.1%	3.74	10.4	10.0	9.8	10.3	P
University of California–Irvine	7.6%	7.2%	8.0%	4.6%	3.67	10.5	9.9	10.9	10.7	Q
Case Western Reserve University (OH)	8.3%	8.4%	8.3%	8.2%	3.64	10.6	10.2	10.8	10.9	P
Dartmouth Medical School (NH)	5.2%	4.6%	5.8%	N/A	3.70	10.3	9.8	10.6	10.6	N/A
University of Florida	8.9%	8.6%	9.3%	22.2%	3.72	10.3	9.7	10.7	10.5	O
University of Washington	8.1%	8.8%	7.3%	3.5%	3.69	10.4	10.0	10.3	10.8	P
Georgetown University (DC)	5.5%	4.6%	6.3%	N/A	3.66	10.4	10.1	10.4	10.8	N/A
University of California–Davis	5.3%	5.3%	5.4%	5.7%	3.62	10.6	9.9	10.9	11.0	P
University of Rochester (NY)	7.3%	6.9%	7.6%	8.0%	3.67	10.4	10.1	10.5	10.6	Q
Ohio State University	11.3%	12.3%	10.1%	10.3%	3.63	10.5	9.9	10.6	10.8	P
University of Minnesota–Twin Cities	15.0%	13.1%	17.2%	17.9%	3.67	10.4	10.0	10.3	10.8	P
University of North Carolina–Chapel Hill	7.5%	7.4%	7.7%	7.2%	3.65	10.4	10.2	10.5	10.6	O
University of Colorado Health Sciences Center	10.2%	10.2%	10.2%	5.9%	3.71	10.1	10.1	10.1	10.1	Q
University of Iowa (Roy J. and Lucille A. Carver)	11.9%	10.3%	13.8%	N/A	3.72	10.1	9.9	10.0	10.3	P

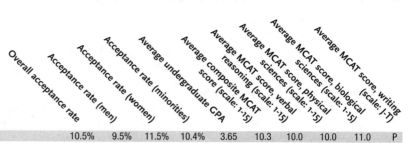

School	Overall acceptance rate	Acceptance rate (men)	Acceptance rate (women)	Acceptance rate (minorities)	Average undergraduate GPA	Average composite MCAT score (scale: 1-15)	Average MCAT score, verbal reasoning (scale: 1-15)	Average MCAT score, physical sciences (scale: 1-15)	Average MCAT score, biological sciences (scale: 1-15)	Average MCAT score, writing (scale: J-T)
Stony Brook University (NY)	10.5%	9.5%	11.5%	10.4%	3.65	10.3	10.0	10.0	11.0	P
Yeshiva University (Albert Einstein) (NY)	10.0%	8.3%	11.7%	N/A	3.64	10.3	9.6	10.5	10.7	Q
Oregon Health & Science University	7.0%	5.5%	8.6%	5.8%	3.65	10.2	9.9	10.2	10.6	P
University of Chicago	9.2%	6.8%	11.5%	8.2%	3.63	10.3	9.8	10.4	10.6	Q
University of Connecticut	8.9%	9.3%	8.5%		3.66	10.2	9.7	10.2	10.6	Q
Jefferson Medical College (PA)	6.1%	4.8%	8.2%	16.5%	3.51	10.7	10.6	10.6	10.9	Q
Medical College of Wisconsin	11.4%	11.3%	11.5%	N/A	3.70	9.9	9.6	10.0	10.0	P
Creighton University (NE)	8.0%	7.4%	8.7%	5.6%	3.70	9.8	9.5	9.9	10.0	P
Tulane University (LA)	5.5%	5.2%	5.8%	3.1%	3.51	10.5	10.2	10.4	10.6	P
University of Alabama–Birmingham	16.7%	17.9%	15.4%	13.7%	3.70	9.8	9.8	9.7	9.9	N/A
University of Massachusetts–Worcester	24.8%	25.2%	24.5%	N/A	3.60	10.3	10.4	10.0	10.5	Q
Indiana University–Indianapolis	18.6%	18.0%	19.4%	N/A	3.69	9.8	9.6	9.9	10.0	P
University of Miami (FL)	10.3%	10.6%	10.0%	7.4%	3.70	9.7	9.5	9.3	10.3	P
University of South Florida	7.3%	7.6%	6.9%	7.6%	3.66	9.8	9.6	9.9	10.1	N/A
Wake Forest University (NC)	5.8%	7.2%	4.2%	N/A	3.60	10.0	10.0	10.0	10.0	P
Brown University (RI)	7.8%	6.9%	8.5%	6.4%	3.60	10.0	9.9	10.0	10.2	Q
St. Louis University	15.5%	15.2%	15.8%	12.0%	3.61	10.0	9.8	9.9	10.3	P
University of Maryland	9.2%	8.1%	10.2%	8.5%	3.63	9.9	9.7	9.8	10.2	P
University of Missouri–Columbia	16.7%	16.1%	17.4%	10.3%	3.72	9.6	9.4	9.4	9.9	O
SUNY–Syracuse	15.0%	14.2%	15.7%	N/A	3.64	9.8	9.4	9.9	10.0	P
Tufts University (MA)	7.5%	7.3%	7.7%	8.0%	3.52	10.2	9.9	10.3	10.5	Q
Loyola University Chicago (Stritch)	9.7%	9.5%	9.8%	5.9%	3.62	9.8	9.6	9.7	10.0	P
UMDNJ-Robert Wood Johnson Medical School	13.4%	12.9%	13.8%	14.0%	3.63	9.8	9.0	10.0	10.2	P
University of Cincinnati	17.4%	18.5%	16.3%	14.2%	3.59	9.9	9.4	10.0	10.3	O
University of Texas Health Science Center–Houston	9.4%	9.9%	9.0%	6.1%	3.64	9.6	9.5	9.5	9.7	P
University of Utah	12.1%	10.9%	14.5%	10.6%	3.63	9.6	9.4	9.4	9.9	O
Medical College of Georgia	17.5%	20.1%	15.0%	6.8%	3.64	9.6	9.5	9.4	10.0	N/A
Texas Tech University Health Sciences Center	7.8%	8.8%	6.9%	6.2%	3.63	9.5	8.9	9.6	9.9	N/A
Medical College of Ohio	13.0%	15.4%	10.5%	N/A	3.61	9.5	9.0	9.6	9.8	N/A
University of Minnesota–Duluth	17.0%	19.6%	14.5%	10.5%	3.67	9.3	8.9	9.4	9.6	Q
University of Nebraska College of Medicine	17.2%	16.8%	17.8%	7.6%	3.65	9.4	9.1	9.3	9.7	N/A
University of Oklahoma	22.2%	24.6%	19.3%	14.9%	3.68	9.3	9.2	9.1	9.6	O
New York Medical College	12.1%	11.7%	12.5%	10.4%	3.50	9.9	9.2	10.3	10.4	Q
University of Kentucky	18.0%	19.2%	16.6%	N/A	3.65	9.3	9.3	9.1	9.6	O
George Washington University (DC)	5.4%	4.4%	6.3%	N/A	3.55	9.5	9.3	9.3	9.8	P
Temple University (PA)	6.8%	7.1%	6.5%	6.0%	3.52	9.7	9.0	10.0	10.0	O
University of Texas Medical Branch–Galveston	8.5%	7.9%	9.1%	8.2%	3.67	9.1	8.7	9.1	9.5	N/A
Eastern Virginia Medical School	13.1%	12.4%	13.7%	N/A	3.48	9.8	9.5	9.8	10.0	N/A
University at Buffalo–SUNY	17.6%	15.4%	19.9%	6.9%	3.57	9.5	9.2	9.6	9.8	P
University of Kansas Medical Center	18.7%	18.7%	18.8%	17.6%	3.63	9.3	9.2	9.1	9.5	N/A
University of Mississippi	50.2%	53.1%	46.8%	38.0%	3.71	9.3	9.6	8.9	9.5	N/A
University of Illinois–Chicago	13.4%	12.7%	14.1%	14.3%	3.51	9.6	N/A	N/A	N/A	N/A
Michigan State University	6.1%	5.2%	7.0%	7.2%	3.50	9.5	9.4	9.2	10.0	P
University of Louisville (KY)	19.2%	19.2%	19.3%	11.9%	3.59	9.3	9.3	9.2	9.5	O
Wayne State University (MI)	18.5%	17.6%	19.5%	14.8%	3.56	9.4	8.8	9.5	9.8	O
Boston University	4.2%	3.8%	4.6%	9.0%	3.49	9.5	9.0	10.0	10.0	Q
Texas A&M University System Health Science Center	10.9%	6.4%	15.0%	15.4%	3.65	8.9	8.3	9.0	9.4	Q
UMDNJ–New Jersey Medical School	15.0%	15.3%	14.7%	N/A	3.47	9.7	9.3	9.7	10.1	O
University of Arkansas for Medical Sciences	22.8%	24.8%	20.7%	22.7%	3.66	9.0	9.0	9.0	9.0	O
West Virginia University	19.5%	18.7%	20.5%	N/A	3.65	9.0	9.1	8.7	9.4	O
Medical University of South Carolina	24.4%	44.2%	5.7%	23.1%	3.57	9.3	9.2	9.1	9.6	N/A

Which are the hardest and easiest medical schools to get into?

	Overall acceptance rate	Acceptance rate (men)	Acceptance rate (women)	Acceptance rate (minorities)	Average undergraduate GPA	Average composite MCAT score (scale: 1-15)	Average MCAT score, verbal reasoning (scale: 1-15)	Average MCAT score, physical sciences (scale: 1-15)	Average MCAT score, biological sciences (scale: 1-15)	Average MCAT score, writing (scale: J-T)
Uniformed Services Univ. of the Health Sciences (MD)	15.5%	15.9%	14.9%	13.7%	3.53	9.4	9.2	9.3	9.7	O
University of New Mexico	17.1%	N/A	N/A	N/A	3.53	9.4	9.5	9.0	9.7	P
Drexel University (PA)	16.0%	13.4%	19.1%	15.6%	3.44	9.7	9.1	9.5	9.7	P
Northeastern Ohio Universities College of Medicine	18.1%	17.3%	18.8%	14.8%	3.61	9.0	9.0	8.9	9.2	P
Southern Illinois University–Springfield	13.0%	11.1%	15.0%	N/A	3.56	9.1	9.1	8.8	9.3	O
University of South Carolina	12.7%	12.1%	13.3%	7.8%	3.56	9.1	9.0	9.0	9.0	O
University of South Dakota	16.9%	14.7%	19.7%	6.2%	3.62	8.9	9.2	8.6	8.8	O
East Tennessee State University (J.H. Quillen)	11.1%	11.2%	11.0%	7.5%	3.51	9.2	9.5	8.9	9.2	O
University of North Dakota	41.0%	37.0%	45.6%	63.6%	3.71	8.7	8.6	8.4	9.0	N/A
Virginia Commonwealth Univ.–Medical College of VA	10.6%	10.4%	10.8%	9.5%	3.46	9.4	9.1	9.4	9.8	N
U. of N. TX Health Sci. Center (TX Col. of Osteopathic Med.)	11.5%	10.3%	12.7%	9.3%	3.59	8.8	8.5	8.7	9.2	N/A
East Carolina University (Brody) (NC)	13.2%	N/A	N/A	N/A	3.60	8.7	8.7	8.5	8.9	O
Oklahoma State Univ. College of Osteopathic Medicine	36.8%	36.3%	37.5%	25.0%	3.62	8.7	9.0	8.0	9.0	O
University of Vermont	6.1%	5.2%	7.1%	3.1%	3.40	9.2	9.2	9.0	9.5	Q
Touro University College of Osteopathic Medicine (CA)	15.9%	17.3%	14.4%	9.9%	3.50	8.7	8.4	8.6	9.0	O
UMDNJ–School of Osteopathic Medicine	11.2%	10.2%	12.1%	12.1%	3.50	8.7	8.0	9.0	9.0	Q
Wright State University (OH)	14.7%	N/A	N/A	N/A	3.49	8.7	8.6	8.5	9.0	O
Kirksville College of Osteopathic Medicine (MO)	17.9%	17.5%	18.4%	17.0%	3.53	8.5	8.5	8.2	8.8	O
Michigan State Univ. College of Osteopathic Medicine	13.1%	11.7%	14.4%	8.0%	3.55	8.2	8.0	7.9	8.7	O
Des Moines University Osteopathic Medical Center (IA)	25.0%	23.0%	27.6%	9.7%	3.50	8.4	8.2	8.2	8.7	O
College of Osteopathic Medicine of the Pacific (CA)	18.7%	16.8%	20.7%	18.9%	3.38	8.6	7.4	8.3	9.0	P
New York College of Osteopathic Medicine	18.0%	16.7%	19.3%	27.7%	3.42	8.0	7.4	8.4	8.4	N
Nova Southeastern Univ. Col. of Osteopathic Med. (FL)	15.7%	15.0%	16.5%	14.4%	3.42	8.0	7.9	7.8	8.3	Q
Philadelphia College of Osteopathic Medicine	12.0%	9.0%	15.0%	6.8%	3.39	8.0	8.0	8.0	8.5	O
Univ. of New England Col. of Osteopathic Medicine (ME)	12.4%	11.4%	13.5%	2.7%	3.31	8.1	8.1	7.6	8.3	Q
West Virginia School of Osteopathic Medicine	18.6%	18.5%	18.8%	10.8%	3.37	7.4	7.8	7.0	7.5	N
Pikeville College School of Osteopathic Medicine (KY)	15.9%	15.8%	16.0%	12.7%	3.31	7.5	7.8	7.0	7.6	N/A

The total cost of an M.D. degree can easily top $200,000 at the most expensive private schools once you factor in living expenses. Private medical schools are ranked here by tuition and fees for the 2003–2004 academic year, with the most expensive at the top. Public institutions follow, sorted by in-state tuition so you can easily see what you might save by sticking close to home.

Private Schools

	Tuition and fees	Room and board
Tufts University (MA)	$40,134	N/A
George Washington University (DC)	$39,285	$17,355
Albany Medical College (NY)	$38,860	N/A
Case Western Reserve University (OH)	$37,904	$15,000
Columbia University College of Physicians and Surgeons (NY)	$37,864	$14,291
St. Louis University	$37,850	$14,411
Northwestern University (Feinberg) (IL)	$37,175	$11,862
Tulane University (LA)	$37,086	$8,826
University of Southern California	$37,076	$9,802
Washington University in St. Louis	$37,032	$8,256
Boston University	$36,980	$10,887
New York Medical College	$36,790	$16,160
University of Pennsylvania	$36,514	$15,005
Yeshiva University (Albert Einstein) (NY)	$36,425	$13,100
Creighton University (NE)	$36,084	$12,500
Stanford University (CA)	$35,682	$17,467
Duke University (NC)	$35,001	$9,306
Harvard University (MA)	$34,776	$15,374
Jefferson Medical College (PA)	$34,565	$12,520
University of Rochester (NY)	$34,317	$14,500
Yale University (CT)	$34,175	$9,650
Drexel University (PA)	$34,100	$10,230
Brown University (RI)	$34,010	$13,482
Georgetown University (DC)	$33,723	$13,085
Dartmouth Medical School (NH)	$33,550	$8,500
Loyola University Chicago (Stritch)	$33,500	$17,250
Johns Hopkins University (MD)	$33,465	$8,386
Emory University (GA)	$33,068	$15,600
Arizona College of Osteopathic Medicine	$32,451	$7,740
Rush University (IL)	$32,268	$8,300
University of Health Sciences College of Osteopathic Medicine (MO)	$32,265	N/A
Vanderbilt University (TN)	$32,157	$8,280
University of Chicago	$32,151	$9,524
Wake Forest University (NC)	$32,056	$13,046
Meharry Medical College (TN)	$31,612	N/A
Touro University College of Osteopathic Medicine (CA)	$31,500	$12,750
University of New England College of Osteopathic Medicine (ME)	$31,355	$10,700
College of Osteopathic Medicine of the Pacific (CA)	$31,155	$10,220
Philadelphia College of Osteopathic Medicine	$31,101	$13,190

Who's the priciest? Who's the cheapest?

Private Schools, cont'd.

	Tuition and fees	Room and board
Cornell University (Weill) (NY)	$31,080	$9,224
New York College of Osteopathic Medicine	$30,678	N/A
Kirksville College of Osteopathic Medicine (MO)	$30,395	$11,398
New York University	$29,750	$9,900
University of Miami (FL)	$28,190	$21,690
Chicago College of Osteopathic Medicine	$28,142	N/A
Des Moines University Osteopathic Medical Center (IA)	$27,400	$12,454
Mercer University (GA)	$26,372	N/A
Medical College of Wisconsin	$26,149	$7,500
Pikeville College School of Osteopathic Medicine (KY)	$26,000	N/A
Morehouse School of Medicine (GA)	$25,376	$10,760
Lake Erie College of Osteopathic Medicine (PA)	$25,195	$10,050
Nova Southeastern University College of Osteopathic Medicine (FL)	$22,490	$11,590
Eastern Virginia Medical School	$21,941	N/A
Rosalind Franklin University of Medicine and Science (IL)	$11,891	N/A
Mayo Medical School (MN)	$11,250	$11,264
Baylor College of Medicine (TX)	$8,688	$17,600

Public Schools

	In-state tuition and fees	Out-of-state tuition and fees	Room and board
East Carolina University (Brody) (NC)	$5,028	$30,144	$17,500
University of Mississippi	$6,715	$12,830	$8,755
Texas A&M University System Health Science Center	$7,770	$20,870	$10,500
University of Texas Medical Branch–Galveston	$8,076	$21,176	N/A
University of North Carolina–Chapel Hill	$8,495	$34,111	$24,666
Texas Tech University Health Sciences Center	$8,683	$21,783	$9,778
University of Texas Southwestern Medical Center–Dallas	$8,932	$22,032	$17,770
U. of North Texas Health Sci. Center (Texas Col. of Osteopathic Medicine)	$9,030	$22,130	$10,098
University of Texas Health Science Center–Houston	$9,480	$22,580	$12,410
Medical College of Georgia	$10,358	$30,562	$13,725
LSU School of Medicine–New Orleans	$10,703	$24,851	$14,499
University of Arizona	$11,578	$20,348	$8,880
University of Nevada–Reno	$11,607	$29,185	N/A
University of New Mexico	$12,122	$31,558	$7,905
University of Arkansas for Medical Sciences	$12,165	$23,807	N/A
Marshall University (WV)	$12,704	$32,534	N/A
University of Washington	$12,848	$29,788	$11,862
University of Alabama–Birmingham	$13,055	$30,827	$10,340
University of Massachusetts–Worcester	$13,102	N/A	$11,350
West Virginia University	$13,440	$31,180	$10,005
University of Utah	$13,886	$25,762	$8,352
University of Kentucky	$14,270	$32,662	$666
Oklahoma State University College of Osteopathic Medicine	$14,550	$30,920	$6,459
University of Kansas Medical Center	$14,961	$29,492	$20,076
University of Oklahoma	$15,136	$35,513	N/A
University of California–Los Angeles (Geffen)	$15,173	$27,418	$14,000
University of Louisville (KY)	$15,204	$36,922	$6,672

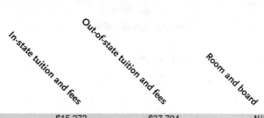

	In-state tuition and fees	Out-of-state tuition and fees	Room and board
West Virginia School of Osteopathic Medicine	$15,272	$37,794	N/A
University of California–San Diego	$15,570	$27,815	$11,134
University of Hawaii–Manoa (Burns)	$15,574	$29,278	N/A
University of South Florida	$15,705	$44,955	$8,690
University of Florida	$15,741	$41,897	$7,816
University of Colorado Health Sciences Center	$15,748	$67,415	$11,160
East Tennessee State University (J.H. Quillen)	$15,855	$31,545	$7,400
University of California–Davis	$15,882	$28,127	$10,803
University of California–San Francisco	$15,977	$28,222	$14,877
University of California–Irvine	$16,202	$28,447	$9,560
University of Tennessee–Memphis	$16,271	$32,185	$13,959
University of North Dakota	$16,383	$42,003	$8,704
University of South Carolina	$16,950	$48,920	$10,050
University of Connecticut	$17,040	$32,340	N/A
SUNY–Brooklyn	$17,145	$30,245	$12,520
Medical University of South Carolina	$17,435	$47,533	$9,830
Stony Brook University (NY)	$17,470	$30,470	$19,350
Wright State University (OH)	$17,532	$24,426	$10,560
University of South Dakota	$17,697	$35,136	$16,480
Wayne State University (MI)	$17,728	$35,969	$18,413
SUNY–Syracuse	$17,900	$30,000	N/A
University at Buffalo–SUNY	$18,000	$31,100	$8,000
Ohio University College of Osteopathic Medicine	$18,015	$26,253	N/A
Southern Illinois University–Springfield	$18,156	$50,452	$8,975
University of Maryland	$18,258	$33,323	$15,450
University of Nebraska College of Medicine	$18,450	$40,829	$13,500
Indiana University–Indianapolis	$18,698	$37,533	$13,405
University of Iowa (Roy J. and Lucille A. Carver)	$19,310	$37,778	$5,940
Northeastern Ohio Universities College of Medicine	$19,371	$37,626	$9,167
University of Missouri–Columbia	$19,572	$38,198	$8,027
University of Cincinnati	$19,662	$34,191	$14,081
Ohio State University	$19,714	$25,853	$6,850
University of Missouri–Kansas City	$19,905	$38,938	$6,659
Virginia Commonwealth University-Medical College of Virginia	$20,023	$35,851	$8,680
University of Michigan–Ann Arbor	$20,525	$31,525	$20,322
Michigan State University	$20,951	$44,751	$11,184
Michigan State University College of Osteopathic Medicine	$20,951	$44,751	$11,184
Medical College of Ohio	$21,089	$40,789	N/A
University of Wisconsin–Madison	$21,728	$32,852	$12,705
UMDNJ–School of Osteopathic Medicine	$21,962	$33,133	$10,000
UMDNJ-Robert Wood Johnson Medical School	$22,167	$33,338	$10,026
University of Virginia	$22,486	$34,486	$13,812
UMDNJ-New Jersey Medical School	$22,491	$33,662	$11,140
University of Illinois–Chicago	$22,780	$50,216	$10,850
University of Vermont	$23,281	$40,001	$10,280
Oregon Health & Science University	$24,462	$34,962	$13,000
University of Minnesota–Twin Cities	$25,266	$33,647	$11,090
Penn State University College of Medicine	$26,422	$36,592	$11,670
University of Minnesota–Duluth	$27,096	$48,604	$12,603
Edward Via Virginia College of Osteopathic Medicine	$29,500	$29,500	$20,000
University of Pittsburgh	$30,644	$36,436	$14,560
Temple University (PA)	$30,665	$37,411	N/A
Mount Sinai School of Medicine (NY)	$33,320	$33,320	$12,300

Which schools award the most and the least financial aid?

Compared to what you're going to need, you may be surprised at how little you get: Medical schools assume that their students will borrow to pay the bills because they'll make enough after graduation to manage the loan payments. However, a lucky few with top scores and undergraduate grades may find a merit award on the table. Schools are ranked here by percentage of students receiving aid.

Private Schools

	% receiving aid of any kind	% receiving loans	% receiving grants/ scholarships	% receiving work-study benefits
Mayo Medical School (MN)	100%	74%	100%	N/A
Medical College of Wisconsin	98%	91%	25%	0%
Des Moines University Osteopathic Medical Center (IA)	96%	90%	21%	N/A
University of Rochester (NY)	95%	89%	45%	20%
Arizona College of Osteopathic Medicine	94%	89%	17%	27%
Creighton University (NE)	94%	82%	19%	0%
Kirksville College of Osteopathic Medicine (MO)	94%	94%	19%	18%
Touro University College of Osteopathic Medicine (CA)	94%	93%	11%	10%
Loyola University Chicago (Stritch)	92%	86%	53%	0%
Philadelphia College of Osteopathic Medicine	92%	91%	51%	16%
College of Osteopathic Medicine of the Pacific (CA)	91%	90%	14%	0%
Duke University (NC)	91%	63%	67%	0%
New York College of Osteopathic Medicine	91%	91%	5%	0%
New York Medical College	91%	91%	14%	3%
Eastern Virginia Medical School	90%	82%	73%	0%
University of New England College of Osteopathic Medicine (ME)	90%	89%	35%	0%
Tulane University (LA)	90%	85%	53%	0%
New York University	88%	88%	58%	14%
University of Southern California	88%	87%	37%	0%
Pikeville College School of Osteopathic Medicine (KY)	87%	96%	67%	N/A
Wake Forest University (NC)	87%	82%	69%	0%
Dartmouth Medical School (NH)	86%	79%	48%	N/A
Drexel University (PA)	86%	76%	8%	2%
Emory University (GA)	86%	76%	57%	0%
Morehouse School of Medicine (GA)	86%	92%	75%	4%
Rush University (IL)	86%	85%	56%	4%
Vanderbilt University (TN)	86%	73%	54%	N/A
Albany Medical College (NY)	85%	84%	37%	15%
University of Pennsylvania	85%	65%	66%	3%
Georgetown University (DC)	84%	93%	42%	1%
Jefferson Medical College (PA)	84%	79%	46%	7%
Nova Southeastern University College of Osteopathic Medicine (FL)	84%	89%	14%	3%
University of Chicago	83%	81%	72%	0%
Cornell University (Weill) (NY)	83%	69%	59%	15%
Columbia University College of Physicians and Surgeons (NY)	82%	72%	55%	9%
Baylor College of Medicine (TX)	81%	70%	55%	14%
Case Western Reserve University (OH)	80%	80%	70%	0%
George Washington University (DC)	80%	80%	24%	0%
University of Miami (FL)	80%	76%	20%	0%

	% receiving aid of any kind	% receiving loans	% receiving grants/ scholarships	% receiving work-study benefits
Washington University in St. Louis	80%	57%	63%	0%
Yale University (CT)	80%	64%	53%	0%
Yeshiva University (Albert Einstein) (NY)	80%	80%	45%	0%
Boston University	79%	76%	34%	0%
Harvard University (MA)	79%	65%	56%	5%
Tufts University (MA)	79%	74%	20%	1%
Johns Hopkins University (MD)	74%	85%	75%	24%
Stanford University (CA)	73%	60%	61%	5%
Northwestern University (Feinberg) (IL)	72%	68%	51%	0%
Brown University (RI)	67%	63%	40%	0%

Public Schools

	% receiving aid of any kind	% receiving loans	% receiving grants/ scholarships	% receiving work-study benefits
University of North Dakota	99%	98%	57%	0%
University of Minnesota–Duluth	98%	97%	55%	0%
University of Nebraska College of Medicine	98%	90%	62%	0%
Ohio State University	98%	88%	51%	0%
University of South Dakota	98%	91%	67%	0%
University of Massachusetts–Worcester	97%	95%	36%	0%
Oklahoma State University College of Osteopathic Medicine	97%	94%	69%	25%
West Virginia School of Osteopathic Medicine	97%	92%	10%	16%
University of California–Irvine	96%	85%	83%	0%
University of Iowa (Roy J. and Lucille A. Carver)	96%	90%	60%	1%
University of Kentucky	96%	83%	62%	7%
Michigan State University College of Osteopathic Medicine	96%	95%	89%	0%
University of Connecticut	95%	90%	45%	0%
University of Kansas Medical Center	95%	88%	84%	0%
University of Missouri–Columbia	95%	95%	43%	0%
Oregon Health & Science University	95%	90%	80%	2%
Michigan State University	94%	91%	83%	0%
University of Colorado Health Sciences Center	93%	87%	69%	4%
University of South Carolina	93%	90%	55%	0%
University of Minnesota–Twin Cities	92%	90%	86%	1%
University of Oklahoma	92%	90%	51%	0%
University of Texas Health Science Center–Houston	92%	92%	40%	0%
University of California–Davis	91%	87%	90%	0%
U. of North Texas Health Sci. Center (Texas Col. of Osteopathic Medicine)	91%	91%	46%	0%
Texas Tech University Health Sciences Center	91%	88%	63%	0%
University of Vermont	91%	84%	62%	0%
University of Washington	91%	85%	60%	0%
East Tennessee State University (J.H. Quillen)	90%	86%	32%	0%

Which schools award the most and the least financial aid?

Public Schools, cont'd.

	% receiving aid of any kind	% receiving loans	% receiving grants/scholarships	% receiving work-study benefits
University of Arkansas for Medical Sciences	90%	88%	44%	1%
University of California–Los Angeles (Geffen)	90%	90%	80%	0%
Southern Illinois University–Springfield	90%	88%	38%	0%
SUNY–Syracuse	90%	90%	N/A	N/A
Indiana University–Indianapolis	89%	87%	33%	0%
University of Mississippi	89%	89%	61%	0%
UMDNJ–School of Osteopathic Medicine	89%	83%	61%	4%
Temple University (PA)	89%	66%	41%	4%
University of Virginia	89%	80%	68%	0%
University of Florida	88%	82%	87%	0%
University of Louisville (KY)	88%	80%	39%	0%
University of Maryland	88%	86%	77%	1%
UMDNJ–New Jersey Medical School	88%	83%	72%	1%
University of Texas Southwestern Medical Center–Dallas	88%	80%	67%	6%
University of California–San Francisco	87%	79%	85%	2%
University of Cincinnati	87%	83%	39%	3%
Medical College of Georgia	87%	78%	38%	11%
Virginia Commonwealth University–Medical College of Virginia	87%	84%	46%	0%
Wayne State University (MI)	87%	86%	36%	2%
University of California–San Diego	86%	82%	70%	2%
University of Michigan–Ann Arbor	86%	74%	56%	0%
Mount Sinai School of Medicine (NY)	86%	75%	48%	12%
East Carolina University (Brody) (NC)	85%	80%	72%	0%
University of New Mexico	85%	84%	83%	0%
University of Pittsburgh	85%	81%	48%	0%
University of South Florida	85%	80%	40%	0%
Stony Brook University (NY)	85%	83%	41%	10%
University of Utah	86%	86%	32%	0%
University of Wisconsin–Madison	85%	85%	25%	0%
West Virginia University	85%	78%	37%	0%
University of North Carolina–Chapel Hill	83%	76%	72%	0%
University of Texas Medical Branch–Galveston	83%	81%	34%	5%
Texas A&M University System Health Science Center	83%	83%	20%	0%
University of Alabama–Birmingham	82%	79%	16%	0%
Medical University of South Carolina	82%	79%	22%	3%
University at Buffalo–SUNY	81%	84%	78%	2%
UMDNJ–Robert Wood Johnson Medical School	80%	80%	30%	10%
Medical College of Ohio	78%	67%	29%	10%
Northeastern Ohio Universities College of Medicine	77%	73%	36%	0%

Which are the largest and smallest medical schools?

As you compare schools, you'll want to pay attention to the total enrollment, the size of the first-year class, and the faculty-to-student ratio. All will have an impact on the schools' personalities, the availability of professors outside of class, and the extent to which you engage with your classmates.

	Total enrollment	% in-state enrollment	Size of first-year class	Faculty-to-student ratio
University of Illinois–Chicago	1,375	83%	313	0.6
New York College of Osteopathic Medicine	1,161	67%	296	N/A
Indiana University–Indianapolis	1,128	94%	280	1.1
Wayne State University (MI)	1,049	93%	257	0.9
Drexel University (PA)	1,019	34%	250	0.4
Philadelphia College of Osteopathic Medicine	1,008	59%	263	0.1
Jefferson Medical College (PA)	933	47%	229	2.3
University of Texas Southwestern Medical Center–Dallas	869	88%	218	1.5
Ohio State University	839	63%	210	1.7
University of Texas Health Science Center–Houston	837	96%	202	1.0
University of Minnesota–Twin Cities	820	77%	165	1.5
University of Texas Medical Branch–Galveston	820	95%	205	1.1
Des Moines University Osteopathic Medical Center (IA)	795	25%	201	N/A
Medical College of Wisconsin	795	51%	205	1.3
University of Washington	790	89%	178	2.4
Temple University (PA)	786	69%	177	0.5
New York Medical College	767	36%	189	1.6
Nova Southeastern University College of Osteopathic Medicine (FL)	760	74%	202	0.1
Yeshiva University (Albert Einstein) (NY)	730	48%	180	3.4
Harvard University (MA)	726	N/A	165	8.8
Medical College of Georgia	717	99%	180	0.7
Virginia Commonwealth University-Medical College of Virginia	716	64%	184	1.0
New York University	712	49%	160	2.4
University of California–Los Angeles (Geffen)	710	96%	121	3.0
University of Kansas Medical Center	707	90%	175	0.7
College of Osteopathic Medicine of the Pacific (CA)	700	75%	174	N/A
Tufts University (MA)	698	33%	170	1.8
Northwestern University (Feinberg) (IL)	695	31%	170	2.3
UMDNJ-New Jersey Medical School	693	99%	170	1.0
University of Alabama–Birmingham	692	86%	160	1.6
Georgetown University (DC)	689	2%	170	1.6
Baylor College of Medicine (TX)	682	85%	168	2.8
Uniformed Services University of the Health Sciences (MD)	681	7%	167	0.4
George Washington University (DC)	675	2%	167	0.9
University of Michigan–Ann Arbor	670	50%	170	2.5
University of Southern California	660	85%	160	1.8
University of North Carolina–Chapel Hill	653	94%	160	1.8
UMDNJ–Robert Wood Johnson Medical School	638	99%	156	1.1
SUNY–Syracuse	631	94%	152	N/A

Which are the largest and smallest medical schools?

	Total enrollment	% in-state enrollment	Size of first-year class	Faculty-to-student ratio
University of California–San Francisco	629	95%	141	2.4
Kirksville College of Osteopathic Medicine (MO)	626	15%	168	0.1
Columbia University College of Physicians and Surgeons (NY)	621	24%	150	3.7
St. Louis University	621	41%	158	0.9
Tulane University (LA)	621	46%	155	0.8
University of Cincinnati	620	82%	161	1.9
Boston University	612	16%	155	1.8
University of Miami (FL)	605	81%	141	1.9
Medical University of South Carolina	604	93%	137	1.4
University of Pennsylvania	603	28%	147	3.3
University of Wisconsin–Madison	598	88%	150	2.0
Medical College of Ohio	593	93%	156	0.5
University of Louisville (KY)	588	87%	149	1.0
University of Pittsburgh	586	41%	145	3.0
University of Maryland	585	85%	150	1.7
University of Oklahoma	585	96%	142	1.1
University of Iowa (Roy J. and Lucille A. Carver)	583	72%	142	1.4
Case Western Reserve University (OH)	581	67%	146	2.9
Washington University in St. Louis	579	8%	122	2.4
University at Buffalo–SUNY	568	100%	135	0.9
University of Arkansas for Medical Sciences	557	99%	147	1.5
University of Virginia	552	68%	140	1.5
Loyola University Chicago (Stritch)	539	49%	140	1.2
Michigan State University College of Osteopathic Medicine	533	93%	143	0.3
University of Colorado Health Sciences Center	526	94%	132	2.5
Texas Tech University Health Sciences Center	515	95%	130	0.8
Albany Medical College (NY)	514	46%	N/A	N/A
Yale University (CT)	507	12%	100	2.9
Touro University College of Osteopathic Medicine (CA)	500	46%	131	0.1
U. of North Texas Health Sci. Center (Texas Col. of Osteopathic Medicine)	492	94%	127	0.4
University of California–San Diego	491	98%	121	1.6
University of New England College of Osteopathic Medicine (ME)	488	25%	121	0.2
Rush University (IL)	487	80%	N/A	N/A
Johns Hopkins University (MD)	476	24%	119	4.3
University of Nebraska College of Medicine	472	89%	118	1.1
Duke University (NC)	470	11%	100	3.3
Stanford University (CA)	463	46%	87	1.8
Mount Sinai School of Medicine (NY)	462	38%	120	4.2
Creighton University (NE)	460	14%	120	0.6
University of Florida	459	96%	116	2.3
Emory University (GA)	454	37%	113	3.5
Michigan State University	438	80%	106	0.7
Wake Forest University (NC)	438	41%	108	1.9
University of Rochester (NY)	433	48%	100	2.8
Eastern Virginia Medical School	432	70%	110	0.7
Northeastern Ohio Universities College of Medicine	430	97%	102	0.6
Stony Brook University (NY)	428	100%	101	1.1
University of Massachusetts–Worcester	425	100%	100	2.0
Oregon Health & Science University	422	64%	107	2.5
University of Chicago	421	38%	104	1.8
University of South Florida	416	100%	115	1.2

	Total enrollment	% in-state enrollment	Size of first-year class	Faculty-to-student ratio
Vanderbilt University (TN)	416	14%	104	3.3
Cornell University (Weill) (NY)	412	52%	101	4.4
University of Utah	410	77%	102	2.2
University of California–Davis	404	100%	96	1.4
University of Vermont	400	29%	100	1.0
University of Mississippi	394	100%	100	1.3
University of California–Irvine	390	99%	92	1.6
University of Kentucky	382	95%	95	1.6
West Virginia University	382	87%	111	1.3
University of Missouri–Columbia	371	98%	96	0.9
Wright State University (OH)	364	97%	91	0.9
UMDNJ–School of Osteopathic Medicine	352	98%	96	0.5
Oklahoma State University College of Osteopathic Medicine	350	89%	88	0.2
West Virginia School of Osteopathic Medicine	336	63%	102	0.1
Brown University (RI)	330	15%	69	1.9
University of Connecticut	309	92%	74	1.3
East Carolina University (Brody) (NC)	304	100%	72	1.2
University of New Mexico	304	98%	75	2.1
University of South Carolina	297	95%	80	0.7
Dartmouth Medical School (NH)	294	10%	78	3.4
Southern Illinois University–Springfield	292	100%	72	1.0
Texas A&M University System Health Science Center	276	94%	70	2.7
Pikeville College School of Osteopathic Medicine (KY)	253	63%	75	0.1
East Tennessee State University (J.H. Quillen)	236	97%	60	1.0
University of North Dakota	226	81%	61	0.6
University of South Dakota	206	98%	50	1.0
Morehouse School of Medicine (GA)	182	59%	52	1.2
Mayo Medical School (MN)	170	27%	44	11.9
Edward Via Virginia College of Osteopathic Medicine	154	29%	154	N/A
University of Minnesota–Duluth	112	91%	53	0.4

How much research does the school support? One prime indicator is the amount of grant money the medical school and its affiliated hospitals are awarded by the National Institutes of Health, the federal research department devoted to medicine. Institutions with an asterisk have received grants to the medical school only.

	Amount of NIH grants in 2003, in millions	Number of NIH grants in 2003	Number of principal investigators associated with NIH-funded grants	Number of full-time faculty associated with NIH research grants
Harvard University (MA)	$977.3	2,299	1,736	3,385
University of Washington	$488.5	1,049	670	1,031
University of Pennsylvania	$462.5	1,273	712	1,048
Johns Hopkins University (MD)	$411.7	943	609	1,351
University of California–Los Angeles (Geffen)	$383.8	1,063	661	1,970
University of California–San Francisco	$383.6	860	583	N/A
Washington University in St. Louis	$373.1	739	456	789
Baylor College of Medicine (TX)	$369.3	959	660	1,280
University of Pittsburgh	$293.7	766	469	528
University of Michigan–Ann Arbor	$287.1	702	483	1,445
Columbia University College of Physicians and Surgeons (NY)	$279.7	676	483	827
Yale University (CT)	$267.1	769	522	898
Duke University*	$259.9	N/A	N/A	N/A
Case Western Reserve University (OH)	$246.7	665	489	1,050
Cornell University (Weill) (NY)	$245.1	807	468	1,019
University of California–San Diego	$241.9	522	287	456
Stanford University*	$222.2	189	177	382
Vanderbilt University (TN)	$220.6	599	301	604
University of Alabama–Birmingham	$210.9	N/A	N/A	N/A
University of North Carolina–Chapel Hill	$209.9	549	297	418
Yeshiva University (Albert Einstein) (NY)	$184.1	438	271	431
University of Texas Southwestern Medical Center–Dallas*	$179.9	456	312	835
Boston University	$173.6	567	345	667
University of Cincinnati	$173.3	571	347	N/A
Northwestern University (Feinberg) (IL)	$171.3	680	316	430
University of Southern California	$166.4	533	269	N/A
Emory University (GA)	$166.0	548	367	763
University of Wisconsin–Madison	$166.0	393	228	362
Oregon Health & Science University	$163.9	504	342	718
Mount Sinai School of Medicine (NY)	$158.4	495	273	601
Ohio State University	$148.3	519	295	509
University of Colorado Health Sciences Center*	$148.1	522	303	275
University of Chicago	$142.9	440	261	359
University of Minnesota–Twin Cities	$140.1	453	265	265
University of Iowa (Roy J. and Lucille A. Carver)	$136.1	370	235	N/A
New York University	$134.2	340	232	763
University of Rochester (NY)	$130.9	382	258	275
Mayo Medical School (MN)	$129.5	337	237	575
University of Virginia*	$123.9	411	258	491
University of Maryland*	$115.3	329	225	499
Wake Forest University*	$105.4	248	158	200
University of Massachusetts–Worcester*	$100.0	360	228	225
Brown University (RI)	$97.2	286	189	229
Indiana University–Indianapolis*	$96.2	290	197	325
Georgetown University (DC)	$91.8	298	183	348
Dartmouth Medical School (NH)	$83.8	310	161	176
Tufts University (MA)	$81.8	257	167	207
Jefferson Medical College (PA)	$81.4	260	143	203
Medical University of South Carolina	$78.5	258	194	328

	Amount of NIH grants in 2003, in millions	Number of NIH grants in 2003	Number of principal investigators associated with NIH-funded grants	Number of full-time faculty associated with NIH research grants
University of Miami (FL)	$75.9	284	167	489
University of Utah	$74.2	182	130	N/A
Medical College of Wisconsin	$73.5	288	181	N/A
University of Florida*	$70.4	330	196	215
University of California–Irvine	$63.6	206	129	343
University of Vermont*	$63.1	148	98	198
Stony Brook University (NY)	$62.5	263	173	207
University of California–Davis	$62.2	226	133	221
University of Texas Health Science Center–Houston	$60.5	193	109	N/A
Virginia Commonwealth University-Medical College of Virginia*	$60.3	230	124	284
UMDNJ-New Jersey Medical School	$60.4	118	92	N/A
Wayne State University*	$58.0	194	145	240
University at Buffalo–SUNY	$57.6	213	157	187
University of Connecticut*	$55.5	188	132	N/A
UMDNJ–Robert Wood Johnson Medical School	$54.2	255	140	276
Tulane University (LA)	$51.9	141	92	134
University of Kentucky*	$51.2	185	120	N/A
University of New Mexico	$49.6	122	77	134
St. Louis University*	$47.3	140	95	157
University of Arkansas for Medical Sciences	$44.8	121	92	57
George Washington University (DC)	$38.6	162	98	240
Medical College of Georgia	$36.9	143	88	N/A
University of Kansas Medical Center	$36.4	108	70	N/A
University of South Florida	$30.9	86	63	N/A
University of Oklahoma*	$30.2	94	62	62
University of Louisville (KY)	$29.2	111	88	135
Temple University (PA)	$28.4	96	56	80
Loyola University Chicago (Stritch)*	$28.1	123	66	106
University of Nebraska College of Medicine	$27.3	82	66	117
New York Medical College	$20.5	57	39	N/A
Uniformed Services University of the Health Sciences*	$18.4	80	59	59
Drexel University*	$18.3	63	61	72
University of Mississippi	$13.5	49	33	60
Medical College of Ohio	$13.4	58	37	71
Texas A&M University System Health Science Center	$13.3	58	58	36
West Virginia University	$12.1	45	35	62
Michigan State University*	$9.9	45	34	N/A
Wright State University*	$9.3	25	18	28
University of South Dakota	$8.5	12	10	26
Creighton University (NE)	$8.2	54	30	43
University of North Dakota*	$8.0	22	16	16
U. of North Texas Health Sci. Center (Texas Col. of Osteopathic Medicine)	$7.9	43	43	78
University of Missouri–Columbia	$7.6	39	30	56
Michigan State University College of Osteopathic Medicine	$7.2	34	25	32
Eastern Virginia Medical School	$5.9	28	19	31
Texas Tech University Health Sciences Center	$4.7	23	16	22
University of South Carolina	$4.6	55	34	59
Southern Illinois University–Springfield*	$4.1	23	17	17
UMDNJ–School of Osteopathic Medicine	$3.7	19	13	22
East Tennessee State University (J.H. Quillen)*	$3.4	23	21	42
East Carolina University (Brody) (NC)	$3.5	16	12	46
Northeastern Ohio Universities College of Medicine	$2.2	16	11	16
University of Minnesota–Duluth*	$1.1	12	8	11
University of New England College of Osteopathic Medicine*	$.7	2	2	3
Oklahoma State University College of Osteopathic Medicine	$.5	4	4	4
Philadelphia College of Osteopathic Medicine	$.5	4	3	5
Kirksville College of Osteopathic Medicine (MO)	$.4	2	2	3
College of Osteopathic Medicine of the Pacific (CA)	$.3	2	3	2

Whose graduates have the most debt? The least?

How much should you expect to borrow? On average, medical school grads who need to take out loans start their residencies with debt of $100,000—and that's not counting any college loans. This table shows the average amount of debt incurred by borrowers in the Class of 2003, from highest to lowest.

	Average medical school debt
Tufts University (MA)	$158,599
Nova Southeastern Univ. Col. of Osteopathic Medicine (FL)	$154,498
New York College of Osteopathic Medicine	$154,000
Philadelphia College of Osteopathic Medicine	$149,813
Touro University College of Osteopathic Medicine (CA)	$149,500
West Virginia School of Osteopathic Medicine	$146,813
Kirksville College of Osteopathic Medicine (MO)	$146,350
College of Osteopathic Medicine of the Pacific (CA)	$145,608
University of Miami (FL)	$144,000
Univ. of New England Col. of Osteopathic Medicine (ME)	$143,000
Creighton University (NE)	$142,236
New York Medical College	$142,000
University of Vermont	$142,000
Des Moines University Osteopathic Medical Center (IA)	$141,114
Albany Medical College (NY)	$140,760
Boston University	$137,983
Georgetown University (DC)	$134,481
Rush University (IL)	$131,900
Arizona College of Osteopathic Medicine	$131,000
Loyola University Chicago (Stritch)	$129,840
Temple University (PA)	$129,120
George Washington University (DC)	$127,202
Wake Forest University (NC)	$126,061
St. Louis University	$125,434
Drexel University (PA)	$124,777
Michigan State University	$122,983
Tulane University (LA)	$122,959
Oregon Health & Science University	$122,524
Pikeville College School of Osteopathic Medicine (KY)	$121,000
Oklahoma State University College of Osteopathic Medicine	$120,000
Medical College of Wisconsin	$118,332
University of Pittsburgh	$117,704
Northwestern University (Feinberg) (IL)	$117,448
Michigan State University College of Osteopathic Medicine	$117,221
Medical College of Ohio	$115,413
Jefferson Medical College (PA)	$113,812
University of Chicago	$112,170
University of Wisconsin–Madison	$110,000
University of Southern California	$109,300
Case Western Reserve University (OH)	$109,200
Texas Tech University Health Sciences Center	$108,149
Stony Brook University (NY)	$107,000
University of Oklahoma	$105,315
Wayne State University (MI)	$104,637

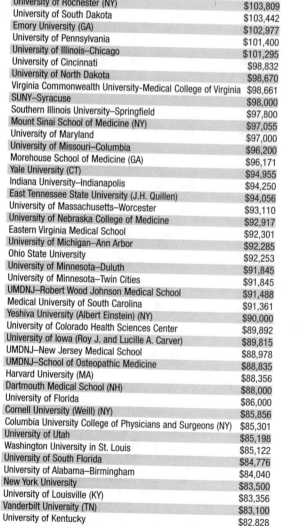

	Average medical school debt
University of Rochester (NY)	$103,809
University of South Dakota	$103,442
Emory University (GA)	$102,977
University of Pennsylvania	$101,400
University of Illinois–Chicago	$101,295
University of Cincinnati	$98,832
University of North Dakota	$98,670
Virginia Commonwealth University-Medical College of Virginia	$98,661
SUNY–Syracuse	$98,000
Southern Illinois University–Springfield	$97,800
Mount Sinai School of Medicine (NY)	$97,055
University of Maryland	$97,000
University of Missouri–Columbia	$96,200
Morehouse School of Medicine (GA)	$96,171
Yale University (CT)	$94,955
Indiana University–Indianapolis	$94,250
East Tennessee State University (J.H. Quillen)	$94,056
University of Massachusetts–Worcester	$93,110
University of Nebraska College of Medicine	$92,917
Eastern Virginia Medical School	$92,301
University of Michigan–Ann Arbor	$92,285
Ohio State University	$92,253
University of Minnesota–Duluth	$91,845
University of Minnesota–Twin Cities	$91,845
UMDNJ–Robert Wood Johnson Medical School	$91,488
Medical University of South Carolina	$91,361
Yeshiva University (Albert Einstein) (NY)	$90,000
University of Colorado Health Sciences Center	$89,892
University of Iowa (Roy J. and Lucille A. Carver)	$89,815
UMDNJ–New Jersey Medical School	$88,978
UMDNJ–School of Osteopathic Medicine	$88,835
Harvard University (MA)	$88,356
Dartmouth Medical School (NH)	$88,000
University of Florida	$86,000
Cornell University (Weill) (NY)	$85,856
Columbia University College of Physicians and Surgeons (NY)	$85,301
University of Utah	$85,198
Washington University in St. Louis	$85,122
University of South Florida	$84,776
University of Alabama–Birmingham	$84,040
New York University	$83,500
University of Louisville (KY)	$83,356
Vanderbilt University (TN)	$83,100
University of Kentucky	$82,828

School	Average medical school debt
Northeastern Ohio Universities College of Medicine	$80,916
U. of N. Texas Health Sci. Center (TX Col. of Osteopathic Med)	$80,172
Johns Hopkins University (MD)	$80,136
University of California–Irvine	$79,767
Brown University (RI)	$79,523
University of Washington	$79,005
University of Kansas Medical Center	$78,915
West Virginia University	$77,747
University of Texas Medical Branch–Galveston	$77,525
Duke University (NC)	$77,324
University of Mississippi	$76,145
University of California–Los Angeles (Geffen)	$75,725
University of Texas Health Science Center–Houston	$73,975
University of South Carolina	$72,728
University of Arkansas for Medical Sciences	$71,537
University of New Mexico	$70,780
University of Virginia	$70,367
University of Texas Southwestern Medical Center–Dallas	$69,600
Mayo Medical School (MN)	$69,184
University of North Carolina–Chapel Hill	$66,386
Texas A&M University System Health Science Center	$66,275
Stanford University (CA)	$64,877
University of Connecticut	$64,000
Medical College of Georgia	$63,017
Baylor College of Medicine (TX)	$61,921
University of California–Davis	$61,833
East Carolina University (Brody) (NC)	$58,114
University of California–San Diego	$56,094
University of California–San Francisco	$55,144
University at Buffalo–SUNY	$54,368
Uniformed Services University of the Health Sciences (MD)	$0

Which schools have the most minority students? The fewest?

If you're looking for a medical school culture that is welcoming to students from a wealth of backgrounds, one way to judge is by the percentage of minority students already there.

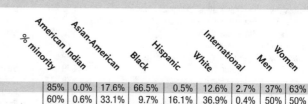

	% minority	American Indian	Asian-American	Black	Hispanic	White	International	Men	Women
Morehouse School of Medicine (GA)	85%	0.0%	17.6%	66.5%	0.5%	12.6%	2.7%	37%	63%
University of California–Los Angeles (Geffen)	60%	0.6%	33.1%	9.7%	16.1%	36.9%	0.4%	50%	50%
Stanford University (CA)	59%	1.7%	35.6%	5.2%	14.7%	39.5%	3.0%	49%	51%
Brown University (RI)	55%	0.0%	29.1%	11.5%	10.0%	43.3%	6.1%	42%	58%
Duke University (NC)	54%	0.4%	17.7%	15.7%	1.9%	47.4%	1.1%	53%	47%
Baylor College of Medicine (TX)	53%	0.7%	33.6%	7.8%	10.6%	46.6%	0.7%	49%	51%
UMDNJ–Robert Wood Johnson Medical School	53%	0.2%	33.2%	14.1%	5.3%	46.2%	0.0%	51%	49%
UMDNJ–New Jersey Medical School	52%	0.1%	29.4%	10.7%	11.7%	47.0%	0.0%	54%	46%
Northwestern University (Feinberg) (IL)	52%	0.6%	41.3%	3.9%	5.8%	42.9%	4.3%	53%	47%
University of Illinois–Chicago	51%	0.5%	33.5%	8.2%	9.5%	46.0%	0.0%	56%	44%
Harvard University (MA)	49%	1.9%	24.8%	13.4%	8.7%	45.0%	4.0%	49%	51%
UMDNJ–School of Osteopathic Medicine	49%	0.3%	23.9%	18.2%	6.8%	50.9%	0.0%	46%	54%
University of Southern California	48%	0.8%	33.2%	4.8%	9.2%	46.5%	2.0%	54%	46%
Cornell University (Weill) (NY)	47%	0.7%	25.5%	14.3%	6.3%	51.5%	0.7%	50%	50%
College of Osteopathic Medicine of the Pacific (CA)	47%	0.3%	38.6%	2.1%	5.1%	44.4%	1.1%	55%	45%
Boston University	45%	0.5%	30.1%	8.7%	6.2%	50.3%	3.1%	54%	46%
University of California–Davis	45%	N/A	N/A	N/A	N/A	N/A	N/A	48%	52%
University of California–San Diego	45%	0.0%	35.2%	2.0%	7.3%	51.3%	0.0%	51%	49%
Tufts University (MA)	45%	0.4%	34.5%	5.6%	4.4%	50.6%	0.7%	52%	48%
Northeastern Ohio Universities College of Medicine	44%	0.7%	37.9%	3.7%	1.6%	56.0%	0.0%	48%	52%
Rush University (IL)	44%	0.8%	34.9%	4.1%	2.5%	56.5%	0.0%	47%	53%
University of Texas Southwestern Medical Center–Dallas	44%	0.2%	26.5%	6.2%	11.0%	52.6%	0.5%	56%	44%
University of California–San Francisco	43%	1.1%	28.8%	5.1%	7.3%	55.8%	0.0%	44%	56%
New York Medical College	43%	0.1%	36.0%	4.0%	3.0%	55.5%	0.1%	49%	51%
University of Michigan–Ann Arbor	43%	0.6%	27.3%	9.9%	5.1%	54.5%	0.0%	56%	44%
New York College of Osteopathic Medicine	43%	0.1%	28.1%	8.9%	5.8%	56.2%	0.3%	46%	54%
University of Texas Medical Branch–Galveston	42%	0.4%	17.3%	7.6%	16.8%	53.7%	0.6%	52%	48%
University of Miami (FL)	41%	0.2%	17.0%	5.6%	18.3%	58.3%	0.0%	49%	51%
Mount Sinai School of Medicine (NY)	41%	1.1%	20.8%	7.6%	11.5%	55.6%	1.3%	45%	55%
New York University	41%	0.0%	31.3%	6.2%	3.8%	50.6%	1.4%	51%	49%
Stony Brook University (NY)	41%	0.2%	27.3%	9.8%	4.0%	58.6%	0.0%	47%	53%
Yale University (CT)	41%	0.6%	23.3%	10.3%	6.5%	49.1%	6.1%	49%	51%
Drexel University (PA)	40%	0.5%	32.6%	5.8%	3.7%	52.3%	0.4%	51%	49%
Johns Hopkins University (MD)	39%	0.4%	25.0%	10.9%	2.7%	58.8%	2.1%	51%	49%
University of California–Irvine	38%	0.0%	30.3%	2.1%	6.2%	61.5%	0.0%	55%	45%
University of Chicago	38%	0.2%	24.5%	11.4%	2.1%	59.1%	2.4%	49%	51%
University of New Mexico	38%	4.3%	6.9%	1.0%	26.3%	60.9%	0.0%	42%	58%
University of Pennsylvania	38%	0.3%	20.9%	8.5%	8.5%	60.5%	1.0%	52%	48%
Temple University (PA)	38%	0.3%	20.5%	11.8%	5.1%	62.3%	0.0%	54%	46%
University of Florida	37%	1.1%	19.4%	7.8%	8.7%	61.2%	0.0%	50%	50%
George Washington University (DC)	36%	0.9%	25.8%	9.2%	2.4%	52.6%	0.9%	45%	55%
University of Maryland	36%	0.0%	22.9%	11.6%	1.0%	60.3%	0.0%	43%	57%
Michigan State University	36%	0.9%	14.6%	11.4%	8.2%	63.7%	1.1%	42%	58%
Albany Medical College (NY)	35%	N/A	N/A	N/A	N/A	N/A	N/A	49%	51%
Case Western Reserve University (OH)	34%	0.0%	18.9%	12.4%	1.4%	63.5%	0.9%	56%	44%
Columbia University College of Physicians and Surgeons (NY)	34%	0.6%	21.1%	7.6%	4.5%	58.6%	4.7%	53%	47%
U. of North Texas Health Sci. Center (Texas Col. of Osteopathic Medicine)	34%	0.6%	25.6%	1.6%	6.5%	65.7%	0.0%	48%	52%

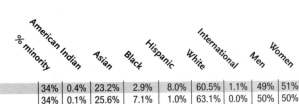

	% minority	American Indian	Asian	Black	Hispanic	White	International	Men	Women
Texas A&M University System Health Science Center	34%	0.4%	23.2%	2.9%	8.0%	60.5%	1.1%	49%	51%
Virginia Commonwealth University–Medical College of Virginia	34%	0.1%	25.6%	7.1%	1.0%	63.1%	0.0%	50%	50%
Washington University in St. Louis	34%	0.5%	24.0%	4.0%	2.2%	57.3%	4.5%	55%	45%
Wayne State University (MI)	34%	0.2%	19.3%	13.0%	1.2%	66.3%	0.0%	53%	47%
Creighton University (NE)	33%	2.0%	24.3%	4.6%	1.7%	65.7%	1.5%	53%	47%
East Carolina University (Brody) (NC)	33%	3.3%	7.6%	19.7%	2.6%	66.8%	0.0%	51%	49%
University of Rochester (NY)	33%	0.2%	19.4%	9.5%	4.4%	64.9%	0.0%	46%	54%
St. Louis University	33%	0.3%	21.7%	8.1%	2.4%	63.3%	0.3%	54%	46%
Nova Southeastern University College of Osteopathic Medicine (FL)	32%	0.8%	16.4%	3.8%	11.2%	62.1%	0.9%	55%	45%
University of Pittsburgh	32%	0.0%	21.8%	8.5%	2.0%	67.6%	0.0%	52%	48%
University of South Florida	32%	2.2%	15.5%	6.0%	8.5%	67.9%	N/A	53%	47%
Wake Forest University (NC)	32%	0.2%	17.1%	10.7%	3.9%	65.1%	3.0%	60%	40%
SUNY–Syracuse	31%	0.3%	23.5%	4.9%	2.7%	67.7%	1.0%	55%	45%
Texas Tech University Health Sciences Center	31%	0.2%	20.4%	1.6%	8.5%	66.2%	0.4%	60%	40%
Yeshiva University (Albert Einstein) (NY)	31%	0.1%	25.3%	5.5%	5.6%	58.5%	2.3%	50%	50%
Georgetown University (DC)	29%	0.1%	16.4%	5.5%	1.5%	69.2%	5.5%	50%	50%
Touro University College of Osteopathic Medicine (CA)	29%	0.0%	26.0%	0.8%	2.6%	55.8%	0.0%	52%	48%
University at Buffalo–SUNY	28%	0.7%	18.1%	6.5%	2.8%	70.6%	0.0%	47%	53%
Eastern Virginia Medical School	28%	0.2%	17.6%	8.6%	1.4%	71.5%	0.0%	47%	53%
University of Texas Health Science Center–Houston	28%	0.4%	11.9%	3.0%	13.0%	69.7%	0.4%	52%	48%
Vanderbilt University (TN)	28%	1.4%	21.4%	3.4%	1.7%	66.3%	4.1%	53%	47%
University of Connecticut	27%	0.3%	12.9%	11.0%	2.9%	69.3%	1.3%	42%	58%
University of North Carolina–Chapel Hill	27%	1.7%	12.4%	11.8%	1.1%	72.7%	0.0%	48%	52%
Tulane University (LA)	27%	0.6%	15.6%	7.4%	3.1%	69.4%	1.6%	56%	44%
University of Virginia	27%	0.0%	19.7%	6.0%	0.9%	71.7%	0.0%	52%	48%
Emory University (GA)	26%	1.1%	14.3%	8.8%	1.3%	69.4%	1.8%	50%	50%
Medical College of Georgia	26%	0.4%	14.1%	8.6%	1.3%	73.9%	0.0%	59%	41%
Ohio State University	26%	0.5%	17.0%	6.7%	2.0%	70.4%	1.1%	57%	43%
Jefferson Medical College (PA)	24%	0.8%	19.9%	1.9%	1.8%	72.5%	2.1%	53%	47%
University of Alabama–Birmingham	23%	1.4%	14.5%	6.4%	0.6%	76.4%	0.4%	59%	41%
University of Cincinnati	23%	0.3%	15.8%	6.6%	0.3%	76.1%	0.0%	60%	40%
Mayo Medical School (MN)	23%	N/A	N/A	N/A	N/A	N/A	N/A	50%	50%
University of Oklahoma	23%	6.8%	14.4%	0.9%	2.4%	57.6%	0.0%	58%	42%
Dartmouth Medical School (NH)	22%	1.4%	13.3%	4.1%	3.4%	71.4%	4.4%	52%	48%
Medical College of Wisconsin	22%	0.8%	15.6%	2.3%	3.5%	75.7%	0.6%	58%	42%
Uniformed Services University of the Health Sciences (MD)	22%	0.7%	14.7%	2.8%	4.1%	76.4%	0.0%	70%	30%
University of Washington	22%	1.4%	14.4%	2.0%	3.9%	75.8%	0.0%	48%	52%
University of Wisconsin–Madison	22%	N/A	N/A	N/A	N/A	N/A	N/A	45%	55%
Edward Via Virginia College of Osteopathic Medicine	21%	0.0%	11.0%	7.1%	3.2%	74.0%	0.6%	52%	48%
University of Kansas Medical Center	21%	1.1%	10.5%	5.9%	3.5%	75.7%	0.0%	55%	45%
Wright State University (OH)	21%	N/A	N/A	N/A	N/A	N/A	N/A	45%	55%
University of Colorado Health Sciences Center	20%	0.6%	8.0%	4.2%	6.8%	80.2%	0.2%	53%	47%
East Tennessee State University (J.H. Quillen)	20%	2.1%	6.8%	9.7%	1.7%	79.7%	0.0%	50%	50%
University of Iowa (Roy J. and Lucille A. Carver)	20%	0.7%	6.5%	3.9%	5.7%	80.4%	0.0%	54%	46%
University of Massachusetts–Worcester	20%	0.7%	14.4%	2.6%	1.9%	79.8%	0.0%	48%	52%
Medical College of Ohio	20%	0.5%	16.7%	1.5%	1.3%	76.6%	2.0%	61%	39%
Medical University of South Carolina	20%	0.5%	7.8%	10.1%	1.5%	78.3%	0.3%	54%	46%
Oklahoma State University College of Osteopathic Medicine	20%	11.1%	4.9%	2.6%	1.4%	78.0%	0.0%	57%	43%
Oregon Health & Science University	20%	8.1%	69.8%	10.5%	7.0%	4.7%	0.0%	45%	55%
Philadelphia College of Osteopathic Medicine	20%	0.2%	10.2%	5.5%	2.9%	79.6%	0.7%	51%	49%
University of South Carolina	20%	0.0%	11.4%	8.1%	0.0%	80.5%	0.0%	53%	47%

Which schools have the most minority students? The fewest?

	% minority	American Indian	Asian	Black	Hispanic	White	International	Men	Women
Southern Illinois University–Springfield	20%	0.3%	11.0%	6.5%	2.1%	80.1%	0.0%	48%	52%
University of Vermont	19%	0.3%	16.8%	0.5%	0.3%	78.5%	1.0%	40%	60%
Indiana University–Indianapolis	18%	0.4%	9.9%	4.8%	2.1%	82.1%	0.7%	55%	45%
University of Minnesota–Twin Cities	18%	2.2%	11.6%	1.6%	2.6%	80.6%	1.5%	52%	48%
University of Louisville (KY)	17%	0.0%	8.2%	7.8%	0.9%	83.2%	0.0%	50%	50%
Loyola University Chicago (Stritch)	17%	0.2%	12.2%	2.2%	1.9%	82.9%	0.0%	52%	48%
Michigan State University College of Osteopathic Medicine	17%	0.2%	12.0%	1.7%	3.4%	82.7%	0.0%	52%	48%
University of Missouri–Columbia	17%	N/A	N/A	N/A	N/A	N/A	N/A	53%	47%
University of Minnesota–Duluth	16%	8.0%	6.3%	0.9%	0.9%	83.9%	0.0%	53%	47%
University of Utah	16%	N/A	N/A	N/A	N/A	N/A	N/A	60%	40%
West Virginia University	15%	0.8%	13.1%	0.5%	1.0%	84.0%	0.3%	58%	42%
Kirksville College of Osteopathic Medicine (MO)	13%	0.8%	11.2%	0.0%	1.1%	81.5%	1.3%	64%	36%
University of Kentucky	12%	0.0%	6.3%	4.5%	0.3%	87.7%	1.3%	56%	44%
University of Mississippi	11%	0.3%	4.3%	6.3%	0.3%	88.8%	0.0%	61%	39%
University of North Dakota	11%	9.7%	0.9%	0.0%	0.4%	88.9%	0.0%	49%	51%
University of Nebraska College of Medicine	10%	0.2%	6.1%	2.8%	1.1%	89.4%	0.0%	62%	38%
University of Arkansas for Medical Sciences	9%	1.2%	1.4%	6.2%	0.6%	90.7%	0.0%	60%	40%
Des Moines University Osteopathic Medical Center (IA)	9%	0.4%	4.4%	1.6%	2.8%	87.9%	0.5%	56%	44%
University of New England College of Osteopathic Medicine (ME)	9%	0.0%	7.6%	0.6%	0.6%	89.8%	1.4%	48%	52%
Pikeville College School of Osteopathic Medicine (KY)	8%	0.4%	4.0%	1.2%	2.4%	91.7%	0.0%	59%	41%
West Virginia School of Osteopathic Medicine	8%	0.3%	6.8%	0.0%	0.9%	92.0%	0.0%	51%	49%
University of South Dakota	4%	2.4%	1.5%	0.0%	0.0%	94.7%	0.0%	57%	43%

If you are interested in family practice, general pediatrics, or general internal medicine, you probably want to consider schools that send most of their graduates on to primary care residency programs.

School	Average % 2001-2003 graduates entering primary care residencies
West Virginia School of Osteopathic Medicine	84.4%
Nova Southeastern Univ. College of Osteopathic Medicine (FL)	83.9%
Pikeville College School of Osteopathic Medicine (KY)	82.0%
U. of N. Texas Health Sci. Center (TX Col. of Osteopathic Med.)	79.8%
Michigan State University College of Osteopathic Medicine	79.0%
Univ. of New England College of Osteopathic Medicine (ME)	74.6%
College of Osteopathic Medicine of the Pacific (CA)	72.0%
University of Minnesota–Duluth	66.9%
University of Massachusetts–Worcester	64.0%
Medical University of South Carolina	63.0%
New York College of Osteopathic Medicine	63.0%
Oklahoma State University College of Osteopathic Medicine	63.0%
University of California–San Diego	63.0%
Touro University College of Osteopathic Medicine (CA)	62.0%
East Tennessee State University (J.H. Quillen)	61.8%
University of Mississippi	61.0%
University of Nebraska College of Medicine	60.0%
University of Vermont	57.2%
Medical College of Georgia	57.0%
University of New Mexico	56.4%
University of Missouri–Columbia	56.1%
University of Arkansas for Medical Sciences	56.0%
SUNY–Syracuse	56.0%
Wright State University (OH)	56.0%
East Carolina University (Brody) (NC)	55.7%
University of Wisconsin–Madison	55.0%
University of Maryland	55.0%
Yeshiva University (Albert Einstein) (NY)	55.0%
Stony Brook University (NY)	53.8%
Brown University (RI)	52.9%
University of Minnesota–Twin Cities	52.9%
New York Medical College	52.5%
University of Connecticut	52.0%
Loyola University Chicago (Stritch)	52.0%
St. Louis University	52.0%
Eastern Virginia Medical School	51.0%
University of South Carolina	51.0%
University of Chicago	50.7%
University of California–Davis	50.0%
Wake Forest University (NC)	50.0%
University of Washington	50.0%
Des Moines University Osteopathic Medical Center (IA)	49.8%
Mount Sinai School of Medicine (NY)	49.0%
University of Southern California	49.0%

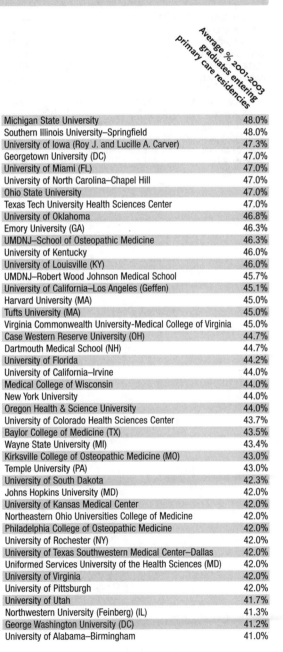

School	Average % 2001-2003 graduates entering primary care residencies
Michigan State University	48.0%
Southern Illinois University–Springfield	48.0%
University of Iowa (Roy J. and Lucille A. Carver)	47.3%
Georgetown University (DC)	47.0%
University of Miami (FL)	47.0%
University of North Carolina–Chapel Hill	47.0%
Ohio State University	47.0%
Texas Tech University Health Sciences Center	47.0%
University of Oklahoma	46.8%
Emory University (GA)	46.3%
UMDNJ–School of Osteopathic Medicine	46.3%
University of Kentucky	46.0%
University of Louisville (KY)	46.0%
UMDNJ–Robert Wood Johnson Medical School	45.7%
University of California–Los Angeles (Geffen)	45.1%
Harvard University (MA)	45.0%
Tufts University (MA)	45.0%
Virginia Commonwealth University-Medical College of Virginia	45.0%
Case Western Reserve University (OH)	44.7%
Dartmouth Medical School (NH)	44.7%
University of Florida	44.2%
University of California–Irvine	44.0%
Medical College of Wisconsin	44.0%
New York University	44.0%
Oregon Health & Science University	44.0%
University of Colorado Health Sciences Center	43.7%
Baylor College of Medicine (TX)	43.5%
Wayne State University (MI)	43.4%
Kirksville College of Osteopathic Medicine (MO)	43.0%
Temple University (PA)	43.0%
University of South Dakota	42.3%
Johns Hopkins University (MD)	42.0%
University of Kansas Medical Center	42.0%
Northeastern Ohio Universities College of Medicine	42.0%
Philadelphia College of Osteopathic Medicine	42.0%
University of Rochester (NY)	42.0%
University of Texas Southwestern Medical Center–Dallas	42.0%
Uniformed Services University of the Health Sciences (MD)	42.0%
University of Virginia	42.0%
University of Pittsburgh	42.0%
University of Utah	41.7%
Northwestern University (Feinberg) (IL)	41.3%
George Washington University (DC)	41.2%
University of Alabama–Birmingham	41.0%

Which schools turn out the most primary care residents? The fewest?

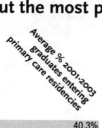

	Average % 2001-2003 graduates entering primary care residencies
Jefferson Medical College (PA)	40.3%
University of Cincinnati	40.0%
Medical College of Ohio	40.0%
Tulane University (LA)	40.0%
Yale University (CT)	40.0%
Stanford University (CA)	39.5%
University of California–San Francisco	39.4%
Texas A&M University System Health Science Center	39.4%
Cornell University (Weill) (NY)	39.0%
Indiana University–Indianapolis	39.0%
UMDNJ-New Jersey Medical School	39.0%
University of Texas Health Science Center–Houston	37.8%
University of Pennsylvania	37.0%

	Average % 2001-2003 graduates entering primary care residencies
Creighton University (NE)	36.7%
University of South Florida	36.4%
University of North Dakota	36.1%
University at Buffalo–SUNY	36.0%
Duke University (NC)	36.0%
Columbia University College of Physicians and Surgeons (NY)	35.8%
Washington University in St. Louis	35.8%
West Virginia University	35.3%
University of Michigan–Ann Arbor	34.6%
Mayo Medical School (MN)	34.0%
Vanderbilt University (TN)	26.0%
Morehouse School of Medicine (GA)	23.0%

Which schools' grads are most likely to stay in state? The least likely?

If you want to stay close to where you study after you graduate, you may want to consider schools whose new doctors choose residencies in-state. Some states also offer incentives to graduates who stay and practice in underserved areas. Doctors in Massachusetts, for instance, can receive as much as $20,000 a year in debt payments if they work at least two years in a Massachusetts community health center.

	Average % 2002-2003 graduates accepting in-state residencies
Michigan State University College of Osteopathic Medicine	87%
University of Southern California	87%
SUNY–Syracuse	86%
University of California–Davis	77%
New York College of Osteopathic Medicine	75%
University of California–Irvine	75%
University of California–Los Angeles (Geffen)	71%
University of California–San Diego	71%
Stony Brook University (NY)	67%
University of California–San Francisco	63%
Wayne State University (MI)	61%
University of Minnesota–Duluth	60%
University of Minnesota–Twin Cities	60%
Oklahoma State University College of Osteopathic Medicine	60%
Yeshiva University (Albert Einstein) (NY)	60%
U. of N. Texas Health Sci. Center (TX Col. of Osteopathic Med.)	59%
Mount Sinai School of Medicine (NY)	58%
Stanford University (CA)	58%
Texas Tech University Health Sciences Center	58%
University of Maryland	57%
New York University	57%
Northeastern Ohio Universities College of Medicine	56%
University of Texas Southwestern Medical Center–Dallas	56%
University of Massachusetts–Worcester	55%
College of Osteopathic Medicine of the Pacific (CA)	55%
Baylor College of Medicine (TX)	54%
UMDNJ–School of Osteopathic Medicine	54%
Wright State University (OH)	54%
University of Arkansas for Medical Sciences	53%
University at Buffalo–SUNY	53%
University of Florida	53%
Harvard University (MA)	53%
University of Texas Health Science Center–Houston	53%
East Carolina University (Brody) (NC)	52%
Rush University (IL)	51%
Philadelphia College of Osteopathic Medicine	50%
Cornell University (Weill) (NY)	49%
Columbia University College of Physicians and Surgeons (NY)	48%
New York Medical College	48%
Nova Southeastern University Col. of Osteopathic Medicine (FL)	48%
Ohio State University	47%

	Average % 2002-2003 graduates accepting in-state residencies
University of Alabama–Birmingham	46%
University of Cincinnati	46%
University of Colorado Health Sciences Center	46%
Michigan State University	46%
University of Mississippi	46%
University of South Florida	46%
Indiana University–Indianapolis	45%
University of Louisville (KY)	45%
Temple University (PA)	45%
University of Washington	45%
Loyola University Chicago (Stritch)	44%
University of Miami (FL)	44%
University of Michigan–Ann Arbor	44%
East Tennessee State University (J.H. Quillen)	43%
University of Pittsburgh	43%
Texas A&M University System Health Science Center	42%
University of South Carolina	41%
Southern Illinois University–Springfield	41%
West Virginia School of Osteopathic Medicine	41%
University of Oklahoma	40%
University of Rochester (NY)	40%
Touro University College of Osteopathic Medicine (CA)	40%
University of Pennsylvania	39%
Eastern Virginia Medical School	38%
Jefferson Medical College (PA)	38%
West Virginia University	38%
Medical College of Ohio	37%
University of Kansas Medical Center	36%
University of Missouri–Columbia	36%
University of Nebraska College of Medicine	36%
Emory University (GA)	35%
University of Iowa (Roy J. and Lucille A. Carver)	34%
University of Wisconsin–Madison	34%
Mayo Medical School (MN)	34%
Medical College of Wisconsin	34%
Vanderbilt University (TN)	34%
Virginia Commonwealth University–Medical College of Virginia	34%
Case Western Reserve University (OH)	33%
University of Kentucky	33%
Northwestern University (Feinberg) (IL)	33%
University of North Carolina–Chapel Hill	32%

Which schools' grads are most likely to stay in state? The least likely?

 Average % 2002-2003 graduates accepting in-state residencies

 Average % 2002-2003 graduates accepting in-state residencies

Tufts University (MA)	32%
Washington University in St. Louis	32%
University of Connecticut	31%
University of South Dakota	31%
Oregon Health & Science University	30%
University of New Mexico	29%
UMDNJ–New Jersey Medical School	29%
Duke University (NC)	28%
University of Utah	28%
Wake Forest University (NC)	28%
Johns Hopkins University (MD)	27%
Medical College of Georgia	27%
UMDNJ–Robert Wood Johnson Medical School	27%
Pikeville College School of Osteopathic Medicine (KY)	27%
St. Louis University	27%

University of Chicago	24%
University of North Dakota	24%
University of Virginia	23%
Tulane University (LA)	22%
Medical University of South Carolina	19%
Yale University (CT)	19%
University of Vermont	18%
Brown University (RI)	14%
University of New England College of Osteopathic Medicine (ME)	14%
Des Moines University Osteopathic Medical Center (IA)	11%
Creighton University (NE)	10%
Dartmouth Medical School (NH)	10%
Morehouse School of Medicine (GA)	9%
Kirksville College of Osteopathic Medicine (MO)	8%

The U.S.News & World Report

Ultimate Medical School Directory

How to use the directory

In the following pages, you'll find in-depth profiles of medical schools fully accredited by the Liaison Committee on Medical Education, plus schools that offer the Doctor of Osteopathy degree accredited by the American Osteopathic Association. The schools are listed alphabetically in two sections: those conferring the M.D. degree, followed by schools of osteopathy.

The data were collected by *U.S. News* from the schools during late 2003 and early 2004. If a medical school did not supply the data requested, or if the data point does not apply to the school, you'll see an N/A, for "not available." Schools that did not return the *U.S. News* questionnaire are listed at the end of the directory.

You may also want to consult the online version of the directory at www.usnews.com, which allows you to do a customized search of our database.

Essential Stats

In addition to the medical school's address and the year the school was founded, you'll find the following key facts and figures here:

Tuition: for the 2003-2004 academic year.

Enrollment: full-time students during the 2003-2004 academic year.

Specialty ranking: the school's 2005 *U.S. News* ranking in various specialty areas, where applicable (the possible areas are women's health, geriatrics, internal medicine, AIDS, drug/alcohol abuse, rural medicine, pediatrics, and family medicine).

GPA and MCAT: The undergraduate grade point averages and Medical College Admission

Test (MCAT) scores shown are for the fall 2003 entering class. The MCAT score is the average of the scores on the verbal, physical sciences, and biological sciences portions of the test.

Acceptance rate: percentage of applicants accepted for the fall 2003 entering class.

U.S. News ranking: A school's overall rank indicates where it sits among its peers in the 2005 ranking of medical schools published by *U.S. News* (at www.usnews.com) and in its annual guide *America's Best Graduate Schools.* Schools are ranked separately in research and primary care, and the schools in the top 60 are ranked numerically. Schools below the top 60 are listed as "unranked."

Admissions

Application website: Many medical schools allow you to complete and submit an application online.

Applicants and acceptees: The acceptance rates for the fall 2003 entering class are broken down by in-state, out-of-state, minority, and international students. The admissions statistics—numbers of applicants and of people interviewed and accepted—are also for the fall 2003 entering class.

Profile of admitted students: Besides the GPA and MCAT scores of fall 2003 entrants, we list the proportion majoring in biological sciences, physical sciences, non-sciences, other health professions, and other disciplines. The percentage who took time off between college and medical school is also shown.

Admission dates and details: We note whether the university uses the American Medical College Application Service (AMCAS), and whether it asks for a second, school-specific application form. Besides key deadlines for applicants to the 2005-2006 first-year class, you'll find information on whether the school has an Early Decision Plan (EDP), whether a personal interview is required for admission, whether admission can be deferred, and what undergraduate coursework is required.

Admissions policy: The text describing admissions policies was written by the schools. *U.S. News* edited the information for style but did not verify it.

Financial Aid

Tuition and other expenses: for the 2003-2004 academic year. For public schools, we list both in-state and out-of-state tuition.

Financial aid profile: The data on financial aid awards and the percentage of students receiving grants, loans, and scholarships are for the 2003-2004 academic year. The average debt burden of borrowers who graduated in 2002 does not include their undergraduate debt.

Student Body Stats

What will your classmates be like? This section supplies the breakdown of male and female students, the in-state enrollments, and the ethnic makeup of the student body during the 2003-2004 academic year (which may not add up to 100 percent due to rounding).

Academic Programs

Besides information on areas of specialization, you can look here for a sense of how early in your training you'll have contact with patients.

Joint degrees awarded: Some medical students pursue a second degree in another university department to marry their interests or gain an edge in the job market. One common joint degree, the M.D./M.B.A., combines medicine and business. Another, for those interested in research, is the M.D./Ph.D. degree. Other degree combos include the M.D. /J.D. (law) and the M.D./M.P.H. (public health).

Research profile: An indicator of how big a role research plays at the medical school is the amount of grant money the faculty brings in. We list the total amount of National Institutes of Health (NIH) grants awarded to the medical school and affiliated hospitals in fiscal 2003.

Curriculum

The text describing the curriculum was provided by the schools. *U.S. News* edited the text for style but did not verify the information.

Faculty Profile

Here, you'll find the number of full-time and part-time teaching faculty during fall 2003, as well as information on whether they teach in the basic sciences or in clinical programs. The full-time faculty/student ratio gives some indication of how accessible your professors are likely to be.

Support Services

How does the school help students deal with the pressure of medical school?

Residency Profile

This section provides data on the residency placements of graduates—the most popular residency and specialty programs chosen by the 2002 and 2003 graduates, plus the proportion of graduates who enter into primary care specialties (family practice, general pediatrics, or general internal medicine). The latter figures are three-year average percentages from 2001-2003 and the proportion of 2002-2003 graduates who accepted in-state residencies.

Albany Medical College

- 47 New Scotland Avenue, Albany, NY 12208
- Private
- Year Founded: N/A
- Tuition, 2003-2004: $38,860
- Enrollment, 2003-2004: 514
- Website: http://www.amc.edu
- Specialty ranking: N/A

3.50 AVERAGE GPA, ENTERING CLASS FALL 2003

9.5 AVERAGE MCAT, ENTERING CLASS FALL 2003

N/A ACCEPTANCE RATE, ENTERING CLASS FALL 2003

Unranked 2005 U.S.NEWS MEDICAL SCHOOL RANKING (RESEARCH)

Unranked 2005 U.S.NEWS MEDICAL SCHOOL RANKING (PRIMARY CARE)

ADMISSIONS
Admissions phone number: (518) 262-5521
Admissions email address: **admissions@mail.amc.edu**

Profile of admitted students
Average undergraduate grade point average: 3.50
MCAT averages (scale: 1-15; writing test: J-T):
  Composite score: 9.5
  Verbal reasoning score: 9.3, Physical sciences score: 9.3,
  Biological sciences score: 9.8, Writing score: P

Dates and details
The American Medical College Application Service
  (AMCAS) application is accepted.
School asks for a school-specific application as part of the
  admissions process.
Oldest MCAT considered for Fall 2005 entry: 2000

Earliest application date for the 2005-2006 first-year class:
  June 1, 2004
Latest application date: November 15, 2004

COSTS AND FINANCIAL AID
Financial aid phone number: (518) 262-5435
Tuition, 2003-2004 academic year: $38,860
Room and board: N/A
Percentage of students receiving financial aid in 2003-04:
  85%
Percentage of students receiving: Loans: 84%,
  Grants/scholarships: 37%, Work-study aid: 15%
Average medical school debt for the Class of 2002:
  $140,760

STUDENT BODY
Fall 2003 full-time enrollment: 514
Men: 49%, Women: 51%, In-state: 46%, Minorities: 35%

Baylor College of Medicine

■ 1 Baylor Plaza, Houston, TX 77030
■ Private
■ Year Founded: 1900
■ Tuition, 2003-2004: $8,688
■ Enrollment, 2003-2004: 682
■ Website: http://public.bcm.tmc.edu
■ Specialty ranking: family medicine: 19, geriatrics: 19, internal medicine: 24, pediatrics: 6, women's health: 19

3.77 AVERAGE GPA, ENTERING CLASS FALL 2003

11.2 AVERAGE MCAT, ENTERING CLASS FALL 2003

7.0% ACCEPTANCE RATE, ENTERING CLASS FALL 2003

13 2005 U.S.NEWS MEDICAL SCHOOL RANKING (RESEARCH)

20 2005 U.S.NEWS MEDICAL SCHOOL RANKING (PRIMARY CARE)

ADMISSIONS

Admissions phone number: **(713) 798-4842**
Admissions email address: **melodym@bcm.tmc.edu**
Application website:
  http://public.bcm.tmc.edu/admissions/suppapp.htm
Acceptance rate: **7.0%**
In-state acceptance rate: **15.5%**
Out-of-state acceptance rate: **3.7%**
Minority acceptance rate: **8.1%**
International acceptance rate: **3.0%**

Fall 2003 applications and acceptees

	Applied	Interviewed	Accepted	Enrolled
Total:	4,097	641	288	168
In-state:	1,160	394	180	131
Out-of-state:	2,937	247	108	37

Profile of admitted students

Average undergraduate grade point average: **3.77**
MCAT averages (scale: 1-15; writing test: J-T):
  Composite score: **11.2**
  Verbal reasoning score: **10.6**, Physical sciences score: **11.6**, Biological sciences score: **11.4**, Writing score: **P**
Proportion with undergraduate majors in: Biological sciences: **50%**, Physical sciences: **21%**, Non-sciences: **14%**, Other health professions: **1%**, Mixed disciplines and other: **14%**
Percentage of students not coming directly from college after graduation: **10%**

Dates and details

The American Medical College Application Service (AMCAS) application is accepted.
School asks for a school-specific application as part of the admissions process.
Oldest MCAT considered for Fall 2005 entry: **2000**
Earliest application date for the 2005-2006 first-year class: **June 1, 2004**
Latest application date: **November 1, 2004**
Acceptance dates for regular application for the class entering in fall 2005:

Earliest: **October 15, 2004**
Latest: **July 26, 2005**
The school considers requests for deferred entrance.
Starting month for the class entering in 2005-2006: **July**
The school has an Early Decision Plan (EDP).
A personal interview is required for admission.

Undergraduate coursework required

Medical school requires undergraduate work in these subjects: biology, English, organic chemistry, inorganic (general) chemistry.

ADMISSIONS POLICY
(TEXT PROVIDED BY SCHOOL):

Baylor College of Medicine participates in the American Medical College Application Service. An application is available at the AMCAS Web site starting in May. Baylor also has a supplemental application.

Among the students enrolled in the class of 2002, 70 percent were Texas residents and 52 percent were women. All entering students had completed work for the baccalaureate degree, and 6 percent had obtained graduate degrees.

The student's record in premedical work offers the Admissions Committee a reasonable basis on which to estimate potential success with the medical school curriculum. The majority of applicants accepted have overall grade-point averages of 3.5 or higher (where 4.0 = A). An overall college GPA of less than B indicates a student might not be able to handle the work of medical school. In evaluating the academic records of applicants, attention is paid to: course selection; academic challenge imposed by the student's curriculum; and the extent to which extracurricular activities and employment might have limited the student's opportunity for high academic achievement. Baylor does not require applicants to major in a scientific field.

All applicants offered places in the first-year class are interviewed personally at Baylor. The Admissions Committee invites for interviews those applicants it perceives to be competitive for admission.

Although high intellectual ability and a record of academic achievement are essential for success in the study of medicine, the Admissions Committee also looks for strong motivation for a career in medicine, human compassion, an abiding interest in the problems of people, leadership skills, the ability to communicate ideas effectively, and a high level of personal integrity. Additional criteria include socioeconomic background, being the first person in the immediate family to graduate from college, multilingual proficiency, responsibilities while attending secondary and/or undergraduate schools, community involvement, and geographic diversity.

COSTS AND FINANCIAL AID

Financial aid phone number: **(713) 798-4603**
Tuition, 2003-2004 academic year: **$8,688**
Room and board: **$17,600**
Percentage of students receiving financial aid in 2003-04: **81%**
Percentage of students receiving: Loans: **70%**, Grants/scholarships: **55%**, Work-study aid: **14%**
Average medical school debt for the Class of 2002: **$61,921**

STUDENT BODY

Fall 2003 full-time enrollment: **682**
Men: **49%**, Women: **51%**, In-state: **85%**, Minorities: **53%**, American Indian: **0.7%**, Asian-American: **33.6%**, African-American: **7.8%**, Hispanic-American: **10.6%**, White: **46.6%**, International: **0.7%**, Unknown: **0.0%**

ACADEMIC PROGRAMS

The school's curriculum gives first-year students substantial contact with patients.
There are opportunities for first- or second-year students to work in community health clinics.
Program offerings: AIDS, drug/alcohol abuse, family medicine, geriatrics, internal medicine, pediatrics, rural medicine, women's health
Joint degrees awarded: M.D./Ph.D., M.D./M.B.A., M.D./M.P.H., M.D./J.D.
Total National Institutes of Health (NIH) grants awarded to the medical school and affiliated hospitals: **$369.3 million**

CURRICULUM
(TEXT PROVIDED BY SCHOOL):

Baylor College of Medicine's curriculum is designed so that students acquire a solid foundation in the scientific concepts underlying medicine, a working knowledge of the core clinical sciences for resident training in any medical specialty, and the skills and attitudes required to be a competent and compassionate physician and lifelong learner. There is a high degree of coordination and integration between the basic and clinical sciences across a curriculum uniquely divided into 1.5 years of preclinical coursework and 2.5 years of highly individualized clinical experiences.

The preclinical curriculum consists of organ-systems-based modules. Baylor's unique approach sequences these modules so that students progressively cycle through the organ systems twice, with normal being emphasized in the first cycle and abnormal in the second. All didactic coursework occurs in the morning, protecting the afternoon for organized, small-group problem solving, skills practice and clinical applications, and independent study. Students benefit from early clinical training exposure, which includes biweekly afternoon preceptors in the offices of nearby community physicians.

The clinical curriculum consists of individually tailored sequences of core clerkships (medicine, pediatrics, obstetrics/gynecology, surgery, psychiatry, family and community medicine, and neurology), selectives (selection of required rotations primarily in the surgical subspecialties), and electives (from over 200 offerings). During the clinical curriculum, Baylor students work with residents, faculty, and community physicians in seven affiliated teaching hospitals and outpatient or ambulatory clinics.

Throughout the entire clinical curriculum, students are freed from rotation duties for one half day per week to participate in other required activities, including the Clinical Application of Biomedical Science course in the second year, the Longitudinal Ambulatory Care Experience course in the third year, and Mechanisms and Management of Disease in the fourth year.

Current and planned dual-degree programs are offered in collaboration with Rice University, the University of Houston, and the University of Texas at Houston.

FACULTY PROFILE (FALL 2003)

Total teaching faculty: **1,891 (full-time)**, **335 (part-time)**
Of full-time faculty, those teaching in basic sciences: **21%**; in clinical programs: **79%**
Of part-time faculty, those teaching in basic sciences: **8%**; in clinical programs: **92%**
Full-time faculty/student ratio: **2.8**

SUPPORT SERVICES

The school offers students these services for dealing with stress: expanded-hour gym access, peer counseling, professional counseling, support groups.

RESIDENCY CHOICES

Most popular residency and specialty programs chosen by the 2002 and 2003 M.D. graduating classes: anesthesiology, dermatology, family practice, internal medicine, internal medicine–pediatrics, neurology, obstetrics and gynecology, ophthalmology, pediatrics, radiology–diagnostic.

WHERE GRADS GO

43.5%
Proportion of 2001-2003 graduates who entered primary care specialties

53.5%
Proportion of 2002-2003 graduates who accepted in-state residencies

ston University

- 715 Albany Street, L-103, Boston, MA 02118
- Private
- **Year Founded:** 1848
- **Tuition, 2003-2004:** $36,980
- **Enrollment, 2003-2004:** 612
- **Website:** http://www.bumc.bu.edu
- **Specialty ranking:** drug/alcohol abuse: 16, pediatrics: 20

3.49	AVERAGE GPA, ENTERING CLASS FALL 2003
9.5	AVERAGE MCAT, ENTERING CLASS FALL 2003
4.2%	ACCEPTANCE RATE, ENTERING CLASS FALL 2003
43	2005 U.S.NEWS MEDICAL SCHOOL RANKING (RESEARCH)
Unranked	2005 U.S.NEWS MEDICAL SCHOOL RANKING (PRIMARY CARE)

ADMISSIONS
Admissions phone number: **(617) 638-4630**
Admissions email address: **medadms@bu.edu**
Application website: **N/A**
Acceptance rate: **4.2%**
In-state acceptance rate: **10.6%**
Out-of-state acceptance rate: **3.8%**
Minority acceptance rate: **9.0%**
International acceptance rate: **2.5%**

Fall 2003 applications and acceptees
	Applied	Interviewed	Accepted	Enrolled
Total:	8,698	945	367	155
In-state:	556	135	59	23
Out-of-state:	8,142	810	308	132

Profile of admitted students
Average undergraduate grade point average: **3.49**
MCAT averages (scale: 1-15; writing test: J-T):
  Composite score: **9.5**
  Verbal reasoning score: **9.0**, Physical sciences score: **10.0**, Biological sciences score: **10.0**, Writing score: **Q**
Proportion with undergraduate majors in: Biological sciences: **73%**, Physical sciences: **6%**, Non-sciences: **10%**, Other health professions: **10%**, Mixed disciplines and other: **1%**
Percentage of students not coming directly from college after graduation: **N/A**

Dates and details
The American Medical College Application Service (AMCAS) application is accepted.
School does not ask for a school-specific application as part of the admissions process.
Oldest MCAT considered for Fall 2005 entry: **2002**
Earliest application date for the 2005-2006 first-year class: **June 1, 2004**
Latest application date: **November 1, 2004**
Acceptance dates for regular application for the class entering in fall 2005:
  Earliest: **December 1, 2004**

Latest: **N/A**
The school doesn't consider requests for deferred entrance.
Starting month for the class entering in 2005-2006:
  August
The school has an Early Decision Plan (EDP).
A personal interview is required for admission.

Undergraduate coursework required
Medical school requires undergraduate work in these subjects: biology, English, organic chemistry, inorganic (general) chemistry, physics, humanities.

ADMISSIONS POLICY
(TEXT PROVIDED BY SCHOOL):
We draw upon a large and highly qualified applicant pool, with more than 80 applicants for every seat in the entering class. Our students represent the full range of geographic, cultural, ethnic, and educational diversity of our pluralistic society, and we believe that this diversity contributes to the strength of the experience for all of us.

COSTS AND FINANCIAL AID
Financial aid phone number: **(617) 638-5130**
Tuition, 2003-2004 academic year: **$36,980**
Room and board: **$10,887**
Percentage of students receiving financial aid in 2003-04: **79%**
Percentage of students receiving: Loans: **76%**, Grants/scholarships: **34%**, Work-study aid: **0%**
Average medical school debt for the Class of 2002: **$137,983**

STUDENT BODY
Fall 2003 full-time enrollment: **612**
Men: **54%**, Women: **46%**, In-state: **16%**, Minorities: **45%**, American Indian: **0.5%**, Asian-American: **30.1%**, African-American: **8.7%**, Hispanic-American: **6.2%**, White: **50.3%**, International: **3.1%**, Unknown: **1.1%**

ACADEMIC PROGRAMS

The school's curriculum gives first-year students substantial contact with patients.

There are opportunities for first- or second-year students to work in community health clinics.

Program offerings: AIDS, drug/alcohol abuse, family medicine, geriatrics, internal medicine, pediatrics, rural medicine, women's health

Joint degrees awarded: M.D./Ph.D., M.D./M.B.A., M.D./M.P.H.

Total National Institutes of Health (NIH) grants awarded to the medical school and affiliated hospitals: **$173.6 million**

CURRICULUM

(TEXT PROVIDED BY SCHOOL):

The basic science curriculum is taught in an innovative format, integrating traditional lecture-style classes with small-group problem seminars and laboratory exercises. There is an emphasis on self-directed learning and teamwork. Patient contact is introduced in the first week of the first-year curriculum, and the formal clinical training in the third and fourth years offers broad-based preparation for postgraduate training in the full range of disciplines that make up modern medicine.

FACULTY PROFILE (FALL 2003)

Total teaching faculty: **1,120 (full-time)**, **1,339 (part-time)**
Of full-time faculty, those teaching in basic sciences: **14%**; in clinical programs: **86%**
Of part-time faculty, those teaching in basic sciences: **N/A**; in clinical programs: **N/A**
Full-time faculty/student ratio: **1.8**

SUPPORT SERVICES

The school offers students these services for dealing with stress: expanded-hour gym access, professional counseling.

Brown University

■ 97 Waterman Street, Box G-A212, Providence, RI 02912-9706
■ Private
■ Year Founded: 1764
■ Tuition, 2003-2004: $34,010
■ Enrollment, 2003-2004: 330
■ Website: http://bms.brown.edu
■ Specialty ranking: drug/alcohol abuse: 13, women's health: 18

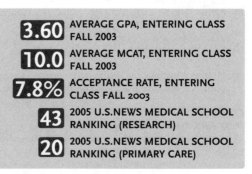

3.60 AVERAGE GPA, ENTERING CLASS FALL 2003

10.0 AVERAGE MCAT, ENTERING CLASS FALL 2003

7.8% ACCEPTANCE RATE, ENTERING CLASS FALL 2003

43 2005 U.S.NEWS MEDICAL SCHOOL RANKING (RESEARCH)

20 2005 U.S.NEWS MEDICAL SCHOOL RANKING (PRIMARY CARE)

ADMISSIONS

Admissions phone number: **(401) 863-2149**
Admissions email address:
medschool_admissions@brown.edu
Application website:
http://bms.brown.edu/admissions/applications
Acceptance rate: **7.8%**
In-state acceptance rate: **26.8%**
Out-of-state acceptance rate: **7.1%**
Minority acceptance rate: **6.4%**
International acceptance rate: **2.5%**

Fall 2003 applications and acceptees
(Acceptees include those in Brown's bachelor's/M.D. program)

	Applied	Interviewed	Accepted	Enrolled
Total:	1,711	46	133	69
In-state:	56	7	15	12
Out-of-state:	1,655	39	118	57

Profile of admitted students
Average undergraduate grade point average: **3.60**
MCAT averages (scale: 1-15; writing test: J-T):
    Composite score: **10.0**
    Verbal reasoning score: **9.9**, Physical sciences score: **10.0**, Biological sciences score: **10.2**, Writing score: **Q**
Proportion with undergraduate majors in: Biological sciences: **41%**, Physical sciences: **7%**, Non-sciences: **41%**, Other health professions: **4%**, Mixed disciplines and other: **7%**
Percentage of students not coming directly from college after graduation: **41%**

Dates and details
The American Medical College Application Service (AMCAS) application is accepted.
School asks for a school-specific application as part of the admissions process.
Oldest MCAT considered for Fall 2005 entry: **1999**
Earliest application date for the 2005-2006 first-year class: **June 1, 2004**
Latest application date: **December 15, 2004**

Acceptance dates for regular application for the class entering in fall 2005:
    Earliest: **January 15, 2005**
    Latest: **September 1, 2005**
The school considers requests for deferred entrance.
Starting month for the class entering in 2005-2006:
    September
The school doesn't have an Early Decision Plan (EDP).
A personal interview is required for admission.

Undergraduate coursework required
Medical school requires undergraduate work in these subjects: biology, organic chemistry, inorganic (general) chemistry, physics, biochemistry, behavioral science, calculus, social sciences.

ADMISSIONS POLICY
(TEXT PROVIDED BY SCHOOL):
All applicants are selected on the basis of academic achievement, faculty evaluations, evidence of maturity, motivation, leadership, integrity, and compassion. Applicants to the M.D./Ph.D. program also are evaluated on the basis of their research accomplishments and potential.

To be eligible for consideration, candidates generally must present a minimum cumulative grade-point average of 3.0 (on a 4.0 scale) in courses taken as a matriculated student at an undergraduate college or graduate school. In addition, applicants must have completed the requirements for a baccalaureate degree prior to matriculation into the medical school. The mean undergraduate GPA for Brown Medical School students is approximately 3.60.

COSTS AND FINANCIAL AID
Financial aid phone number: **(401) 863-1142**
Tuition, 2003-2004 academic year: **$34,010**
Room and board: **$13,482**
Percentage of students receiving financial aid in 2003-04: **67%**
Percentage of students receiving: Loans: **63%**, Grants/scholarships: **40%**, Work-study aid: **0%**
Average medical school debt for the Class of 2002: **$79,523**

STUDENT BODY

Fall 2003 full-time enrollment: 330

Men: 42%, Women: 58%, In-state: 15%, Minorities: 55%,
American Indian: 0.0%, Asian-American: 29.1%,
African-American: 11.5%, Hispanic-American: 10.0%,
White: 43.3%, International: 6.1%, Unknown: 0.0%

ACADEMIC PROGRAMS

The school's curriculum gives first-year students
substantial contact with patients.

There are opportunities for first- or second-year students to
work in community health clinics.

Program offerings: AIDS, drug/alcohol abuse, family
medicine, geriatrics, internal medicine, pediatrics, rural
medicine, women's health

Joint degrees awarded: M.D./Ph.D., M.D./M.P.H.,
M.D./M.S.

Total National Institutes of Health (NIH) grants awarded to
the medical school and affiliated hospitals: **$97.2 million**

CURRICULUM

(TEXT PROVIDED BY SCHOOL):

"The medical program at Brown University has two major
goals for its graduates: that they be broadly and liberally
educated men and women, and that they view medicine as
a socially responsible human service profession.

"We seek students who regard medicine as a noble profession rather than a trade to be learned, as a humanitarian
pursuit as well as a scholarly discipline, and as a unique
lifetime experience. Our graduates must be scientifically
well educated but also capable of approaching problems
from a variety of perspectives, drawing upon the methods of
analysis of the humanist, the social scientist, and the behavioral scientist. We intend that our students follow in the
altruistic tradition of medicine, placing the welfare of their
patients and society above self-interest. We teach our students to view the boundaries of medicine to be wide,
encompassing all of the factors that lead to human disease,
including those of a social, cultural, and economic nature.
We exhort our students to act upon these values by engag-
ing themselves actively in the community, exerting leadership by responding to the needs of those they serve."

These words from the mission statement for the Brown
Medical School proclaim our aspirations for our graduates
and define the nature of the curriculum. Brown Medical
School was the first in the nation to implement a competency-based curriculum. Students must demonstrate competence in nine abilities and a knowledge base. Student
achievement is measured using performance-based methods of assessment.

Brown is the only medical school in the state of Rhode
Island, thus enabling a vast array of resources to be made
available to its students. More than half of the hospital beds
in the state are part of Brown Medical School and its seven
affiliated hospitals, and nearly half of the state's physicians
are on the Brown faculty. Opportunities for clinical research
experience abound.

The curriculum in the first two years of medical school is
a hybrid of traditional discipline-specific, lecture-based
courses in the first year and an organ-system, problem-
based learning approach in the second year. The third and
fourth years consist of 50 weeks of core clerkships and 30
weeks of electives. This highly flexible schedule allows students to individually arrange their course of study. Three
quarters of Brown students take one or more independent
studies—a rate twice as high as the national average.

The flexibility also permits students to undertake a master of public health degree in their fourth year of medical
school. The eighth-semester program encourages students
to take a mini-sabbatical during their last semester of medical school, taking advantage of any of the 2,400 courses
offered at Brown University or those of the Rhode Island
School of Design.

Students are also encouraged to study abroad during
their clinical years. Foreign-studies fellowships are available
on a competitive basis through the International Health
Institute.

Brown prides itself on a curriculum that emphasizes
innovation, creativity, respect for student autonomy, flexibility, social responsibility, and leadership development.

FACULTY PROFILE (FALL 2003)

Total teaching faculty: **631 (full-time)**, **0 (part-time)**

Of full-time faculty, those teaching in basic sciences: **31%**;
in clinical programs: **69%**

Of part-time faculty, those teaching in basic sciences: **N/A**;
in clinical programs: **N/A**

Full-time faculty/student ratio: **1.9**

SUPPORT SERVICES

The school offers students these services for dealing with
stress: expanded-hour gym access, peer counseling, professional counseling, religious support, support groups.

RESIDENCY CHOICES

Most popular residency and specialty programs chosen by
the 2002 and 2003 M.D. graduating classes: emergency
medicine, family practice, internal medicine, obstetrics and
gynecology, orthopedic surgery, pediatrics, psychiatry, radiology–diagnostic, surgery–general.

WHERE GRADS GO

52.9%
*Proportion of 2001-2003 graduates who entered primary
care specialties*

13.5%
*Proportion of 2002-2003 graduates who accepted in-state
residencies*

Case Western Reserve University

- 10900 Euclid Avenue, Cleveland, OH 44106
- Private
- Year Founded: 1843
- Tuition, 2003-2004: $37,904
- Enrollment, 2003-2004: 581
- Website: http://mediswww.cwru.edu
- Specialty ranking: family medicine: 8, internal medicine: 28, pediatrics: 17

3.64 AVERAGE GPA, ENTERING CLASS FALL 2003

10.6 AVERAGE MCAT, ENTERING CLASS FALL 2003

8.3% ACCEPTANCE RATE, ENTERING CLASS FALL 2003

24 2005 U.S.NEWS MEDICAL SCHOOL RANKING (RESEARCH)

31 2005 U.S.NEWS MEDICAL SCHOOL RANKING (PRIMARY CARE)

ADMISSIONS
Admissions phone number: (216) 368-3450
Admissions email address: ack@po.cwru.edu
Application website: N/A
Acceptance rate: 8.3%
In-state acceptance rate: 18.8%
Out-of-state acceptance rate: 6.2%
Minority acceptance rate: 8.2%
International acceptance rate: 0.3%

Fall 2003 applications and acceptees

	Applied	Interviewed	Accepted	Enrolled
Total:	4,504	781	376	146
In-state:	771	317	145	74
Out-of-state:	3,733	464	231	72

Profile of admitted students
Average undergraduate grade point average: 3.64
MCAT averages (scale: 1-15; writing test: J-T):
  Composite score: 10.6
  Verbal reasoning score: 10.2, Physical sciences score: 10.8, Biological sciences score: 10.9, Writing score: P
Proportion with undergraduate majors in: Biological sciences: 66%, Physical sciences: 12%, Non-sciences: 10%, Other health professions: N/A, Mixed disciplines and other: 12%
Percentage of students not coming directly from college after graduation: 33%

Dates and details
The American Medical College Application Service (AMCAS) application is accepted.
School asks for a school-specific application as part of the admissions process.
Oldest MCAT considered for Fall 2005 entry: 2001
Earliest application date for the 2005-2006 first-year class: June 15, 2004
Latest application date: November 1, 2004
Acceptance dates for regular application for the class entering in fall 2005:
  Earliest: October 15, 2004

Latest: N/A
The school considers requests for deferred entrance.
Starting month for the class entering in 2005-2006: July
The school doesn't have an Early Decision Plan (EDP).
A personal interview is required for admission.

Undergraduate coursework required
Medical school requires undergraduate work in these subjects: biology/zoology, English, organic chemistry, inorganic (general) chemistry, physics.

ADMISSIONS POLICY
(TEXT PROVIDED BY SCHOOL):
The Admissions Committee selects students without regard to age, national origin, race, religion, sex, or sexual orientation. With respect to disability, technical standards for admissions are available upon request. The School of Medicine deliberately seeks a diverse student body. Over 20 states of residence and 70 to 80 undergraduate colleges are represented in a typical entering class.

While the committee does not rely on grades and Medical College Admission Test scores alone in the selection process, all students have demonstrated exceptional academic strength. Completed secondary applications are reviewed with great attention given to the candidate's written statements and letters of recommendation in the decision to invite an applicant for an interview.

The school rarely accepts transfer students and then only from Liaison Committee on Medical Education-accredited schools and when the transfer will alleviate an extreme hardship situation.

COSTS AND FINANCIAL AID
Financial aid phone number: (216) 368-3666
Tuition, 2003-2004 academic year: $37,904
Room and board: $15,000
Percentage of students receiving financial aid in 2003-04: 80%
Percentage of students receiving: Loans: 80%, Grants/scholarships: 70%, Work-study aid: 0%

Average medical school debt for the Class of 2002:
$109,200

STUDENT BODY
Fall 2003 full-time enrollment: 581
Men: 56%, Women: 44%, In-state: 67%, Minorities: 34%,
American Indian: 0.0%, Asian-American: 18.9%,
African-American: 12.4%, Hispanic-American: 1.4%,
White: 63.5%, International: 0.9%, Unknown: 2.9%

ACADEMIC PROGRAMS
The school's curriculum gives first-year students
substantial contact with patients.
There are opportunities for first- or second-year students to
work in community health clinics.
Program offerings: AIDS, drug/alcohol abuse, family
medicine, geriatrics, internal medicine, pediatrics, rural
medicine, women's health
Joint degrees awarded: M.D./Ph.D., M.D./M.B.A.,
M.D./M.P.H., M.D./J.D., M.D./M.S., M.D./M.A.
Total National Institutes of Health (NIH) grants awarded to
the medical school and affiliated hospitals: $246.7 million

CURRICULUM
(TEXT PROVIDED BY SCHOOL):
Case School of Medicine offers three paths to the M.D.
degree—the four-year University Program (offered prima-
rily on the university campus, about 130 students per year),
the new five-year Cleveland Clinic Lerner College of
Medicine program (the College Program, offered primarily
at the Cleveland Clinic, 32 students per year), and the
National Institutes of Health-funded Medical Scientist
Training Program (MSTP), in which about 12 students per
year simultaneously pursue an M.D. through the University
Program and a Ph.D. in a basic science field.

The M.D. curriculum for all students includes patient
care experiences and clinical skills education starting at the
beginning of Year 1, an organ-system-based approach to
learning the basic sciences in the first two years, and extensive use of electronic curricular materials.

In the University Program, organ systems courses are
lecture based supplemented by case-based, small-group discussions and problem sets. Patient care in the first two
years involves developing a close relationship with an
obstetrical or geriatric patient. Students also complete a
required number of electives across the four years and can
choose to focus on an area of concentration or select from a
broad range of clinical and nonclinical electives. The
University Program also offers a number of combined-
degree options. Students in the MSTP complete the first
two years of the University Program along with most of
their Ph.D. coursework, then spend three to four years conducting research and preparing a thesis to satisfy Ph.D.
requirements, before returning to the M.D. curriculum.

In the College Program, organ systems courses center on
weekly problem-based learning cases, supplemented by
interactive seminars and labs. Students care for a panel of
patients in the office of a primary care preceptor one half
day per week during the first two years. The College
Program is the only M.D. curriculum in the country
designed to prepare the graduate to become a physician-
investigator by combining an extensive integrated curriculum in basic and clinical research skills with a required
research thesis.

Required clinical clerkships are offered at all major affiliated hospitals in Cleveland and are taken in years 3 to 4 in
the University Program, during the clinical/research thesis
continuum in years 3 to 5 in the College Program, or in the
final two years of the MSTP. Required clerkships include
family medicine, medicine, neurosciences, obstetrics/gyne-
cology, pediatrics, psychiatry, and surgery.

Student advising plays a key role in ensuring success in
each program. Entering students in the University Program
are assigned to an advising dean in one of four societies
and remain members of that society throughout their time
in the program. Students in the MSTP are assigned to one
of the four societies, in addition to choosing a mentor for
their Ph.D. research. Each student in the College Program
has a physician adviser and a research adviser.

FACULTY PROFILE (FALL 2003)
Total teaching faculty: 1,663 (full-time), 2,103 (part-time)
Of full-time faculty, those teaching in basic sciences: 19%;
in clinical programs: 81%
Of part-time faculty, those teaching in basic sciences: 8%;
in clinical programs: 92%
Full-time faculty/student ratio: 2.9

SUPPORT SERVICES
The school offers students these services for dealing with
stress: expanded-hour gym access, peer counseling, professional counseling, religious support, support groups.

RESIDENCY CHOICES
Most popular residency and specialty programs chosen by
the 2002 and 2003 M.D. graduating classes: anesthesiology,
emergency medicine, family practice, internal medicine,
obstetrics and gynecology, orthopedic surgery, pediatrics,
psychiatry, radiology–diagnostic, surgery–general.

WHERE GRADS GO

44.7%

Proportion of 2001-2003 graduates who entered primary care specialties

33.3%

Proportion of 2002-2003 graduates who accepted in-state residencies

Columbia University

COLLEGE OF PHYSICIANS AND SURGEONS

- 630 W. 168th Street, New York, NY 10032
- Private
- Year Founded: 1767
- Tuition, 2003-2004: $37,864
- Enrollment, 2003-2004: 621
- Website: http://cpmcnet.columbia.edu/dept/ps
- Specialty ranking: AIDS: 6, drug/alcohol abuse: 4, internal medicine: 12, pediatrics: 13, women's health: 12

3.79	AVERAGE GPA, ENTERING CLASS FALL 2003
11.7	AVERAGE MCAT, ENTERING CLASS FALL 2003
11.0%	ACCEPTANCE RATE, ENTERING CLASS FALL 2003
8	2005 U.S.NEWS MEDICAL SCHOOL RANKING (RESEARCH)
Unranked	2005 U.S.NEWS MEDICAL SCHOOL RANKING (PRIMARY CARE)

ADMISSIONS

Admissions phone number: **(212) 305-3595**
Admissions email address: **psadmissions@columbia.edu**
Application website: **http://psadmissions.hs.columbia.edu**
Acceptance rate: **11.0%**
In-state acceptance rate: **14.3%**
Out-of-state acceptance rate: **10.2%**
Minority acceptance rate: **7.3%**
International acceptance rate: **19.5%**

Fall 2003 applications and acceptees

	Applied	Interviewed	Accepted	Enrolled
Total:	2,544	1,245	280	150
In-state:	475	269	68	49
Out-of-state:	2,069	976	212	101

Profile of admitted students

Average undergraduate grade point average: **3.79**
MCAT averages (scale: 1-15; writing test: J-T):
   Composite score: **11.7**
   Verbal reasoning score: **11.1**, Physical sciences score: **12.1**, Biological sciences score: **12.0**, Writing score: **Q**
Proportion with undergraduate majors in: Biological sciences: **32%**, Physical sciences: **29%**, Non-sciences: **31%**, Other health professions: **0%**, Mixed disciplines and other: **8%**
Percentage of students not coming directly from college after graduation: **56%**

Dates and details

The American Medical College Application Service (AMCAS) application is accepted.
School asks for a school-specific application as part of the admissions process.
Oldest MCAT considered for Fall 2005 entry: **2000**
Earliest application date for the 2005-2006 first-year class: **June 15, 2004**
Latest application date: **October 15, 2004**
Acceptance dates for regular application for the class entering in fall 2005:
   Earliest: **February 21, 2005**

Latest: **August 20, 2005**
The school considers requests for deferred entrance.
Starting month for the class entering in 2005-2006:
   August
The school doesn't have an Early Decision Plan (EDP).
A personal interview is required for admission.

Undergraduate coursework required

Medical school requires undergraduate work in these subjects: biology, English, organic chemistry, physics, general chemistry.

ADMISSIONS POLICY

(TEXT PROVIDED BY SCHOOL):

Admission is offered to those applicants who have shown the greatest evidence of excellence and leadership potential in both the science and the art of medicine. For classes entering in the past few years, the mean grade-point average has been 3.79 and the mean total Medical College Admission Test score between 35 and 36.

Beyond academic ability, the art of medicine also demands personal qualities of integrity, the ability to relate easily to other people, and concern for their welfare. These qualities are evaluated by several means: the tenor of letters of recommendation, the extent of the applicant's participation in extracurricular and summer activities, the breadth of his or her interests and undergraduate education (the choice of field of concentration is not an important consideration), and the personal interview.

Each year, some applicants are accepted who display extraordinary promise with regard to either the science or the art of medicine, even though they do not meet, in optimal measure, all of the criteria described above.

The Admissions Committee seeks diversity of background, geographical and otherwise, among its applicants; no preference is given to state of residence. Members of underrepresented minority groups are encouraged to apply. Admission is possible for all qualified applicants regardless of sex, race, age, religion, sexual orientation, national origin, or handicap.

COSTS AND FINANCIAL AID

Financial aid phone number: (212) 305-4100
Tuition, 2003-2004 academic year: $37,864
Room and board: $14,291
Percentage of students receiving financial aid in 2003-04:
  82%
Percentage of students receiving: Loans: 72%,
  Grants/scholarships: 55%, Work-study aid: 9%
Average medical school debt for the Class of 2002: $85,301

STUDENT BODY

Fall 2003 full-time enrollment: 621
Men: 53%, Women: 47%, In-state: 24%, Minorities: 34%,
  American Indian: 0.6%, Asian-American: 21.1%,
  African-American: 7.6%, Hispanic-American: 4.5%,
  White: 58.6%, International: 4.7%, Unknown: 2.9%

ACADEMIC PROGRAMS

The school's curriculum gives first-year students
  substantial contact with patients.
There are opportunities for first- or second-year students to
  work in community health clinics.
Program offerings: AIDS, drug/alcohol abuse, family
  medicine, geriatrics, internal medicine, pediatrics, rural
  medicine, women's health
Joint degrees awarded: M.D./Ph.D., M.D./M.B.A.,
  M.D./M.P.H., M.D./J.D.
Total National Institutes of Health (NIH) grants awarded to
  the medical school and affiliated hospitals: $279.7 million

CURRICULUM

(TEXT PROVIDED BY SCHOOL):
Columbia University College of Physicians & Surgeons
(P&S) provides the fundamental scientific basis for the
study of medicine while at the same time coordinating basic
science and clinical subjects throughout four years to make
these connections clear from the start of medical school.

P&S students begin clinical work early in the first year to
acquire the skills and attitudes they will need to see patients
both as individuals and as members of families and communities, and to see themselves as members of a healthcare
team. The cornerstone of the first-year curriculum is a
course called Science Basic to the Practice of Medicine.
Using an interdisciplinary approach, the course weaves
together biochemistry, cell biology, and physiology to
explain how the body works.

The second year is a transitional one, synthesizing the
science of pathophysiology and pharmacology with history
taking and physical diagnosis. Second-year students learn to
take a comprehensive medical history and to conduct a thorough physical examination under faculty supervision at
affiliated hospitals.

The strength and depth of the P&S curriculum is most
evident in the third year, in which the students complete
clerkships in a wide range of clinical disciplines. Clerkship

sites include inner-city, suburban, Indian Health Service,
and rural settings.

In the fourth year, in addition to seven months of electives, students take one of three "back to the classroom"
courses to re-emphasize the foundation of medical knowledge and critical data appraisal in day-to-day patient care
management.

Small-group teaching in the basic sciences is a hallmark
of the curriculum. To become a successful physician, a
medical student must develop the skills and orientation to
pursue lifelong learning. P&S has therefore reduced the
number of required lectures and increased the time students spend working in small groups on case-based, problem-oriented projects. P&S also prepares its graduates to
understand what lies behind the ongoing organizational
changes in American healthcare and how to participate in
these changes.

P&S encourages a greater emphasis on humanism in the
practice of medicine. To affirm their commitment to the
highest ethical principles of the practice of medicine, students entering P&S don a white coat and take the
Hippocratic oath. This ceremony, which was launched at
P&S in 1993, has since been adopted by medical schools
across the nation.

FACULTY PROFILE (FALL 2003)

Total teaching faculty: 2,286 (full-time), 2,811 (part-time)
Of full-time faculty, those teaching in basic sciences: 18%;
  in clinical programs: 82%
Of part-time faculty, those teaching in basic sciences: 6%;
  in clinical programs: 94%
Full-time faculty/student ratio: 3.7

SUPPORT SERVICES

The school offers students these services for dealing with
stress: expanded-hour gym access, peer counseling, professional counseling, religious support.

RESIDENCY CHOICES

Most popular residency and specialty programs chosen by
the 2002 and 2003 M.D. graduating classes: anesthesiology,
emergency medicine, internal medicine, neurological surgery, neurology, orthopedic surgery, pediatrics, psychiatry,
radiology–diagnostic, surgery–general.

WHERE GRADS GO

35.8%
*Proportion of 2001-2003 graduates who entered primary
care specialties*

48.2%
*Proportion of 2002-2003 graduates who accepted in-state
residencies*

Cornell University

WEILL

- 1300 York Avenue at 69th Street, New York, NY 10021
- Private
- Year Founded: 1898
- Tuition, 2003-2004: $31,080
- Enrollment, 2003-2004: 412
- Website: http://www.med.cornell.edu
- Specialty ranking: AIDS: 14, internal medicine: 18

3.73	AVERAGE GPA, ENTERING CLASS FALL 2003
11.3	AVERAGE MCAT, ENTERING CLASS FALL 2003
4.2%	ACCEPTANCE RATE, ENTERING CLASS FALL 2003
12	2005 U.S.NEWS MEDICAL SCHOOL RANKING (RESEARCH)
Unranked	2005 U.S.NEWS MEDICAL SCHOOL RANKING (PRIMARY CARE)

ADMISSIONS

Admissions phone number: **(212) 746-1067**
Admissions email address: **cumc-admissions
@med.cornell.edu**
Application website:
http://www.med.cornell.edu/education/admissions
Acceptance rate: **4.2%**
In-state acceptance rate: **5.2%**
Out-of-state acceptance rate: **3.9%**
Minority acceptance rate: **5.4%**
International acceptance rate: **1.5%**

Fall 2003 applications and acceptees

	Applied	Interviewed	Accepted	Enrolled
Total:	5,307	777	223	101
In-state:	1,200	204	62	39
Out-of-state:	4,107	573	161	62

Profile of admitted students

Average undergraduate grade point average: **3.73**
MCAT averages (scale: 1-15; writing test: J-T):
   Composite score: **11.3**
   Verbal reasoning score: **10.6**, Physical sciences score:
   11.7, Biological sciences score: **11.7**, Writing score: **Q**
Proportion with undergraduate majors in: Biological sciences:
   35%, Physical sciences: **19%**, Non-sciences: **28%**, Other
   health professions: **0%**, Mixed disciplines and other: **19%**
Percentage of students not coming directly from college
   after graduation: **52%**

Dates and details

The American Medical College Application Service
   (AMCAS) application is accepted.
School asks for a school-specific application as part of the
   admissions process.
Oldest MCAT considered for Fall 2005 entry: **2003**
Earliest application date for the 2005-2006 first-year class:
   June 1, 2004
Latest application date: **October 15, 2004**
Acceptance dates for regular application for the class
   entering in fall 2005:

Earliest: **March 1, 2005**
Latest: **August 1, 2005**
The school considers requests for deferred entrance.
Starting month for the class entering in 2005-2006:
   August
The school has an Early Decision Plan (EDP).
A personal interview is required for admission.

Undergraduate coursework required

Medical school requires undergraduate work in these subjects: biology/zoology, English, organic chemistry, inorganic
(general) chemistry, physics.

ADMISSIONS POLICY

(TEXT PROVIDED BY SCHOOL):
Weill-Cornell seeks applicants who uphold the highest academic and personal standards. WMC is among the most
selective medical schools in the nation. Each year the
Committee on Admissions selects 101 students from
among more than 5,000 applicants. The committee seeks
students who are best prepared for future leadership roles
in medicine. In addition to thorough preparation in the
basic sciences, applicants should have a broad liberal arts
education with demonstrated accomplishment in the
humanities and social sciences.

   The committee considers equally students with backgrounds in the basic sciences, social sciences, and liberal
arts. We encourage applicants to pursue premedical curricula that allow them to sample a broad range of academic
disciplines and explore one or more areas in depth.

   Letters of recommendation play an important role in the
committee's assessment of an application. We prefer letters
from persons who know the applicant well to letters from
persons who may be well known but do not know the applicant well personally.

   The committee regards the Medical College Admission
Test as a standardized tool that allows for one form of com-
parison among applicants. There are no cutoffs for MCAT
scores. However, the average total score for the 2003 entering class was 34.

Meaningful participation in extracurricular activities is of extreme interest. Such participation should demonstrate commitment and involvement.

Applicants should explore medicine in some form before entering medical school. The committee also values applicants' research experiences.

The practice of medicine requires the highest level of personal integrity. The committee seeks applicants who show emotional maturity, personal depth, commitment to others' well-being, and ethical and moral integrity.

About 700 applicants are selected for interview. The committee makes acceptance decisions by consensus. While a small number of students are accepted in December, most are accepted in early March.

COSTS AND FINANCIAL AID

Financial aid phone number: **(212) 746-1066**
Tuition, 2003-2004 academic year: **$31,080**
Room and board: **$9,224**
Percentage of students receiving financial aid in 2003-04: **83%**
Percentage of students receiving: Loans: **69%**, Grants/scholarships: **59%**, Work-study aid: **15%**
Average medical school debt for the Class of 2002: **$85,856**

STUDENT BODY

Fall 2003 full-time enrollment: **412**
Men: **50%**, Women: **50%**, In-state: **52%**, Minorities: **47%**, American Indian: **0.7%**, Asian-American: **25.5%**, African-American: **14.3%**, Hispanic-American: **6.3%**, White: **51.5%**, International: **0.7%**, Unknown: **1.0%**

ACADEMIC PROGRAMS

The school's curriculum gives first-year students substantial contact with patients.
There are opportunities for first- or second-year students to work in community health clinics.
Program offerings: AIDS, drug/alcohol abuse, family medicine, geriatrics, internal medicine, pediatrics, women's health
Joint degrees awarded: M.D./Ph.D.
Total National Institutes of Health (NIH) grants awarded to the medical school and affiliated hospitals: **$245.1 million**

CURRICULUM
(TEXT PROVIDED BY SCHOOL):

Key features of the curriculum include: integration of the teaching of the basic and clinical sciences; problem-based learning in the basic sciences; reorganization of the core basic science curriculum into highly integrated block courses; teaching the basic and clinical sciences across the four years of medical school; gradual acquisition of clinical skills in the first two years; a three-year, integrated sequence in public health, behavioral sciences, psychosocial medicine, ethics, and clinical skills; a new primary-care clerkship; and increased flexibility in the scheduling of clerkships and clinical electives.

The first-year curriculum includes:

Molecules to Cells: an integration of biochemistry, cell biology, molecular biology, cellular physiology and biophysics, and the fundamentals of pharmacology.

Fundamentals of Genetic Medicine: the genetic basis of diseases. The course is devoted to all aspects of human genetics, with special emphasis on the molecular basis of genetic disorders.

Human Structure and Function: dedicated to the study of gross anatomy, histology, embryology, physiology of organ systems, and clinical imaging of the normal human body.

Host Defenses: introduces the student to the basic concepts of abnormal human biology and is devoted to the study of general pathology, immunology, and the principles of microbiology and pharmacology.

Medicine, Patients, and Society I: approaches the patient-physician relationship from conceptual and practical perspectives.

The second-year curriculum includes:

Brain and Mind: an integrated course with content ranging from basic neuroscience and gross anatomy of the head and neck to neurological diagnosis and psychopathology.

Basis of Disease: a course organized into nine modules covering the major organ systems.

Medicine, Patients, and Society II: builds upon the principles introduced in Medicine, Patients, and Society I, including an introduction to physical examination.

Introductory Clerkship: a 3-week course designed to provide an orientation to experiences common to all clerkships.

Anesthesia, Ventilation, and Circulation: a one-week introduction to the fundamental principles of anesthesiology.

FACULTY PROFILE (FALL 2003)

Total teaching faculty: **1,811 (full-time)**, **1,828 (part-time)**
Of full-time faculty, those teaching in basic sciences: **10%**; in clinical programs: **90%**
Of part-time faculty, those teaching in basic sciences: **2%**; in clinical programs: **98%**
Full-time faculty/student ratio: **4.4**

SUPPORT SERVICES

The school offers students these services for dealing with stress: professional counseling, religious support, support groups.

RESIDENCY CHOICES

Most popular residency and specialty programs chosen by the 2002 and 2003 M.D. graduating classes: dermatology, emergency medicine, internal medicine, ophthalmology, orthopedic surgery, otolaryngology, pediatrics, psychiatry, radiology–diagnostic, surgery–general.

WHERE GRADS GO

39.0%
Proportion of 2001-2003 graduates who entered primary care specialties

49.2%
Proportion of 2002-2003 graduates who accepted in-state residencies

Creighton University

- 2500 California Plaza, Omaha, NE 68178
- Private
- Year Founded: 1878
- Tuition, 2003-2004: $36,084
- Enrollment, 2003-2004: 460
- Website: http://medicine.creighton.edu
- Specialty ranking: N/A

3.70	AVERAGE GPA, ENTERING CLASS FALL 2003
9.8	AVERAGE MCAT, ENTERING CLASS FALL 2003
8.0%	ACCEPTANCE RATE, ENTERING CLASS FALL 2003
Unranked	2005 U.S.NEWS MEDICAL SCHOOL RANKING (RESEARCH)
Unranked	2005 U.S.NEWS MEDICAL SCHOOL RANKING (PRIMARY CARE)

ADMISSIONS

Admissions phone number: **(402) 280-2799**
Admissions email address: **medschadm@creighton.edu**
Application website: **http://medicine.creighton.edu**
Acceptance rate: **8.0%**
In-state acceptance rate: **15.9%**
Out-of-state acceptance rate: **7.6%**
Minority acceptance rate: **5.6%**
International acceptance rate: **8.7%**

Fall 2003 applications and acceptees

	Applied	Interviewed	Accepted	Enrolled
Total:	3,948	588	315	120
In-state:	189	46	30	14
Out-of-state:	3,759	542	285	106

Profile of admitted students

Average undergraduate grade point average: **3.70**
MCAT averages (scale: 1-15; writing test: J-T):
  Composite score: **9.8**
  Verbal reasoning score: **9.5**, Physical sciences score: **9.9**,
  Biological sciences score: **10.0**, Writing score: **P**
Proportion with undergraduate majors in: Biological
  sciences: **55%**, Physical sciences: **19%**, Non-sciences:
  17%, Other health professions: **9%**, Mixed disciplines
  and other: **0%**
Percentage of students not coming directly from college
  after graduation: **4%**

Dates and details

The American Medical College Application Service
  (AMCAS) application is accepted.
School asks for a school-specific application as part of the
  admissions process.
Oldest MCAT considered for Fall 2005 entry: **2002**
Earliest application date for the 2005-2006 first-year class:
  June 1, 2004
Latest application date: **December 1, 2004**
Acceptance dates for regular application for the class
  entering in fall 2005:
  Earliest: **October 15, 2004**

Latest: **N/A**
The school considers requests for deferred entrance.
Starting month for the class entering in 2005-2006:
  August
The school has an Early Decision Plan (EDP).
A personal interview is required for admission.

Undergraduate coursework required

Medical school requires undergraduate work in these subjects: biology, English, organic chemistry, inorganic (general) chemistry, physics.

ADMISSIONS POLICY
(TEXT PROVIDED BY SCHOOL):

The Medical College Admission Test and three years of
accredited college work are mandatory. Preference is given,
however, to holders of the baccalaureate degree. Applicants
may take the MCAT in the fall of the year preceding their
entry into medical school. All requirements must be completed by June prior to entry. Coursework must include
eight hours of general biology with lab; eight hours of inorganic or general chemistry with lab; eight to 10 hours of
organic chemistry with lab; eight hours of general physics
with lab; and six hours of English. Advanced study in
human biology, especially biochemistry and/or genetics, is
strongly encouraged. Applicants may pursue a baccalaureate
degree with any major in science or liberal arts (except military science). Nonscience majors should elect to take
advanced science study to the extent possible.

Consideration will be given to all of the qualities considered necessary in a physician. Intellectual ability and curiosity, emotional maturity, honesty, and proper motivation, in
addition to proven scholastic ability, are of the utmost
importance. A record that includes significant service to
humanity and medical experience is deemed important.

The school reserves the right to require a formal, on-
campus interview of every applicant selected. There are no
restrictions placed on applicants because of race, religion,
sex, national or ethnic origin, age, disability, or status as a
disabled veteran or veteran of the Vietnam era. Candidates
are not restricted by state of residence.

Creighton University values diversity in its medical classes. Creighton considers the nontraditional applicant to be a positive influence. Advantage is given to applicants who have undertaken their preprofessional education at Creighton University. It is suggested that no candidate apply whose cumulative or science grade-point average is below 3.2.

The American Medical College Application Service application is the principal source of information on the candidates.

COSTS AND FINANCIAL AID
Financial aid phone number: **(402) 280-2666**
Tuition, 2003-2004 academic year: **$36,084**
Room and board: **$12,500**
Percentage of students receiving financial aid in 2003-04: **94%**
Percentage of students receiving: Loans: **82%**, Grants/scholarships: **19%**, Work-study aid: **0%**
Average medical school debt for the Class of 2002: **$142,236**

STUDENT BODY
Fall 2003 full-time enrollment: **460**
Men: **53%**, Women: **47%**, In-state: **14%**, Minorities: **33%**, American Indian: **2.0%**, Asian-American: **24.3%**, African-American: **4.6%**, Hispanic-American: **1.7%**, White: **65.7%**, International: **1.5%**, Unknown: **0.2%**

ACADEMIC PROGRAMS
The school's curriculum gives first-year students substantial contact with patients.
There are opportunities for first- or second-year students to work in community health clinics.
Program offerings: drug/alcohol abuse, family medicine, internal medicine, pediatrics, rural medicine, women's health
Joint degrees awarded: M.D./Ph.D.
Total National Institutes of Health (NIH) grants awarded to the medical school and affiliated hospitals: **$8.2 million**

CURRICULUM
(TEXT PROVIDED BY SCHOOL):
Students participate in an integrated curriculum that incorporates basic and clinical science in all four years.

The educational program has been divided into four components. Component 1, Biomedical Fundamentals, serves as the foundation of the educational program, followed by more complex basic science information presented in a clinically relevant context in Component 2. This component consists of a series of organ-based and disease-based courses. Component 3 consists of required core clerkships emphasizing basic medical principles and acquisition of core clinical skills in a variety of inpatient and ambulatory settings.

Component 4 provides additional responsibilities for patient care, including an eight-week block of critical care medicine, a four-week surgery elective, a four-week primary care subinternship, and 24 weeks of elective study.

Clinical experience is a prominent part of the curriculum in all components, beginning with the physical-diagnosis instruction in the first year. Students interact with standardized patients in the first year and are assigned to longitudinal clinics during the second year. The curriculum also integrates ethical and societal issues into all four components. Instructional methodology utilizes case-based, small-group sessions and computer-assisted instruction in all components. A close faculty-student relationship provides for mentoring and advising of students in choosing courses that will broaden their backgrounds for careers in medicine, as well as satisfying their special interests.

Competency-based evaluation is used in all components, and the students are graded on a pass/fail/honors system. Students compete against standards and not against one another.

FACULTY PROFILE (FALL 2003)
Total teaching faculty: **267 (full-time)**, **24 (part-time)**
Of full-time faculty, those teaching in basic sciences: **20%**; in clinical programs: **80%**
Of part-time faculty, those teaching in basic sciences: **13%**; in clinical programs: **88%**
Full-time faculty/student ratio: **0.6**

SUPPORT SERVICES
The school offers students these services for dealing with stress: expanded-hour gym access, peer counseling, professional counseling, religious support, support groups.

RESIDENCY CHOICES
Most popular residency and specialty programs chosen by the 2002 and 2003 M.D. graduating classes: anesthesiology, emergency medicine, family practice, internal medicine, obstetrics and gynecology, orthopedic surgery, pediatrics, psychiatry, radiology–diagnostic, surgery–general.

WHERE GRADS GO
36.7%
Proportion of 2001-2003 graduates who entered primary care specialties

9.5%
Proportion of 2002-2003 graduates who accepted in-state residencies

Dartmouth Medical School

- 3 Rope Ferry Road, Hanover, NH 03755-1404
- Private
- Year Founded: 1797
- Tuition, 2003-2004: $33,550
- Enrollment, 2003-2004: 294
- Website: http://www.dartmouth.edu/dms
- Specialty ranking: family medicine: 22, rural medicine: 17

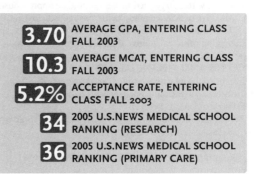

3.70 AVERAGE GPA, ENTERING CLASS FALL 2003

10.3 AVERAGE MCAT, ENTERING CLASS FALL 2003

5.2% ACCEPTANCE RATE, ENTERING CLASS FALL 2003

34 2005 U.S.NEWS MEDICAL SCHOOL RANKING (RESEARCH)

36 2005 U.S.NEWS MEDICAL SCHOOL RANKING (PRIMARY CARE)

ADMISSIONS

Admissions phone number: **(603) 650-1505**
Admissions email address:
DMS.admissions@dartmouth.edu
Application website:
**http://www.dartmouth.edu/dms/admissions/
instrs_to_applicants.shtml**
Acceptance rate: **5.2%**
In-state acceptance rate: **25.0%**
Out-of-state acceptance rate: **4.9%**
Minority acceptance rate: **N/A**
International acceptance rate: **N/A**

Fall 2003 applications and acceptees

	Applied	Interviewed	Accepted	Enrolled
Total:	5,010	588	260	78
In-state:	68	33	17	12
Out-of-state:	4,942	555	243	66

Profile of admitted students

Average undergraduate grade point average: **3.70**
MCAT averages (scale: 1-15; writing test: J-T):
Composite score: **10.3**
Verbal reasoning score: **9.8**, Physical sciences score: **10.6**, Biological sciences score: **10.6**, Writing score: **N/A**
Proportion with undergraduate majors in: Biological sciences: **47%**, Physical sciences: **28%**, Non-sciences: **17%**, Other health professions: **0%**, Mixed disciplines and other: **8%**
Percentage of students not coming directly from college after graduation: **63%**

Dates and details

The American Medical College Application Service (AMCAS) application is accepted.
School asks for a school-specific application as part of the admissions process.
Oldest MCAT considered for Fall 2005 entry: **2002**
Earliest application date for the 2005-2006 first-year class:
June 1, 2004
Latest application date: **November 1, 2004**

Acceptance dates for regular application for the class entering in fall 2005:
Earliest: **December 15, 2004**
Latest: **N/A**
The school considers requests for deferred entrance.
Starting month for the class entering in 2005-2006:
August
The school doesn't have an Early Decision Plan (EDP).
A personal interview is required for admission.

Undergraduate coursework required

Medical school requires undergraduate work in these subjects: biology, organic chemistry, inorganic (general) chemistry, physics, calculus, general chemistry.

ADMISSIONS POLICY
(TEXT PROVIDED BY SCHOOL):

Dartmouth Medical School is committed to medical education based solidly in biomedical science and clinical practice, which will support each student's eventual choice of career in clinical practice, education, and/or research. In each entering class, the school seeks a student body with academic excellence and social diversity. Although the vast majority of DMS students (94 percent in recent years) come from out of state, Dartmouth also has a commitment to provide residents of New Hampshire with the opportunity to study medicine. A similar commitment applies to Maine residents.

Specific requirements for admission include one year (eight semester hours) each of general chemistry, organic chemistry, biology, and physics. A half year of calculus is required, a full year recommended. A semester of biochemistry is encouraged but not required. Successful applicants should have facility in written and spoken English.

All candidates are expected to present scores from the Medical College Admission Test. Also required is the equivalent of at least three years' college work at an American or Canadian college or university.

DMS looks for students who will do well academically, communicate well with patients and colleagues, respect and uphold the role of the physician, keep a commitment to lifelong learning, and handle well the problem-solving and decision-making challenges that a physician faces.

Dartmouth receives about 5,000 applications for roughly 80 places in the entering class. Approximately 10 percent of applicants are interviewed in Hanover.

Most incoming students have presented MCAT scores above 10 and a grade-point average above 3.6. However, the committee extends serious consideration to all candidates who present special qualities or characteristics, even if their credentials fall below these levels. It is the long-standing policy of Dartmouth Medical School to support equality of opportunity for all persons, regardless of race or ethnic background.

COSTS AND FINANCIAL AID

Financial aid phone number: **(603) 650-1919**
Tuition, 2003-2004 academic year: **$33,550**
Room and board: **$8,500**
Percentage of students receiving financial aid in 2003-04: **86%**
Percentage of students receiving: Loans: **79%**, Grants/scholarships: **48%**, Work-study aid: **N/A**
Average medical school debt for the Class of 2002: **$88,000**

STUDENT BODY

Fall 2003 full-time enrollment: **294**
Men: **52%**, Women: **48%**, In-state: **10%**, Minorities: **22%**, American Indian: **1.4%**, Asian-American: **13.3%**, African-American: **4.1%**, Hispanic-American: **3.4%**, White: **71.4%**, International: **4.4%**, Unknown: **2.0%**

ACADEMIC PROGRAMS

The school's curriculum gives first-year students substantial contact with patients.
There are opportunities for first- or second-year students to work in community health clinics.
Program offerings: AIDS, drug/alcohol abuse, family medicine, geriatrics, internal medicine, pediatrics, rural medicine, women's health
Joint degrees awarded: M.D./Ph.D., M.D./M.B.A., M.D./M.P.H.
Total National Institutes of Health (NIH) grants awarded to the medical school and affiliated hospitals: **$83.8 million**

CURRICULUM
(TEXT PROVIDED BY SCHOOL):
One hundred years ago, medical school was a four-year program. Today, medical school still takes four years, yet there is exponentially more to learn—and advances in medical science, medical skills, and medical technology proliferate each year.

The response of Dartmouth Medical School is to develop dynamic learners: physicians who have the tools, the skills, the confidence, and the motivation to keep questioning, discovering, and building their knowledge throughout their professional lives. Our New Directions curriculum mixes lectures, small-group sessions, problem-based learning, computer-assisted instruction, preceptorships, interdisciplinary

coursework, and independent study. The medical education programs at Dartmouth include: the four-year M.D. program, which enrolls about 65 new students each year; the Brown-Dartmouth program, in which approximately 15 students spend two years at Dartmouth and then two years at the Brown Medical School, receiving their M.D. degree from Brown; joint M.D./M.B.A. and M.D./Ph.D. programs; and other master's and doctoral programs.

Year 1 of the M.D. curriculum introduces students to the basic and fundamental biomedical sciences and to the normal structure and function of the human organism. Working with community physicians, students begin to develop clinical skills.

Year 2 exposes students to an integrated, organ-system-based, multidisciplinary examination of pathophysiology, pharmacology, genetics, pathology, and medicine. Students continue to study with their community preceptors.

In Year 3, students strengthen and apply clinical skills in the principal branches and disciplines of medicine, working in both hospital and ambulatory settings. The clerkships cover all of medicine's major specialties and primary-care fields; all clinical instructors are DMS faculty. Students' diverse clerkship experiences provide them with a solid basis for making career choices.

The fourth year is largely made up of electives and some required rotations, joined in the spring by a series of back to the campus "courses designed to prepare the student for a lifetime of continued learning as a physician."

FACULTY PROFILE (FALL 2003)

Total teaching faculty: **1,014 (full-time)**, **719 (part-time)**
Of full-time faculty, those teaching in basic sciences: **8%**; in clinical programs: **92%**
Of part-time faculty, those teaching in basic sciences: **3%**; in clinical programs: **97%**
Full-time faculty/student ratio: **3.4**

SUPPORT SERVICES

The school offers students these services for dealing with stress: expanded-hour gym access, peer counseling, professional counseling, religious support, support groups.

RESIDENCY CHOICES

Most popular residency and specialty programs chosen by the 2002 and 2003 M.D. graduating classes: anesthesiology, emergency medicine, family practice, internal medicine, obstetrics and gynecology, orthopedic surgery, pediatrics, psychiatry, radiology–diagnostic, surgery–general.

WHERE GRADS GO

44.7%
Proportion of 2001-2003 graduates who entered primary care specialties

10.2%
Proportion of 2002-2003 graduates who accepted in-state residencies

xel University

- 2900 Quenn Lane, Philadelphia, PA 19129
- Private
- Year Founded: 1848
- Tuition, 2003-2004: $34,100
- Enrollment, 2003-2004: 1,019
- Website: http://www.drexel.edu/med
- Specialty ranking: women's health: 21

3.44 AVERAGE GPA, ENTERING CLASS FALL 2003

9.7 AVERAGE MCAT, ENTERING CLASS FALL 2003

16.0% ACCEPTANCE RATE, ENTERING CLASS FALL 2003

Unranked 2005 U.S.NEWS MEDICAL SCHOOL RANKING (RESEARCH)

Unranked 2005 U.S.NEWS MEDICAL SCHOOL RANKING (PRIMARY CARE)

ADMISSIONS

Admissions phone number: **(215) 991-8202**
Admissions email address: **Medadmis@drexel.edu**
Application website: **http://www.aamc.org**
Acceptance rate: **16.0%**
In-state acceptance rate: **29.2%**
Out-of-state acceptance rate: **14.4%**
Minority acceptance rate: **15.6%**
International acceptance rate: **N/A**

Fall 2003 applications and acceptees

	Applied	Interviewed	Accepted	Enrolled
Total:	5,613	1,638	899	250
In-state:	623	284	182	71
Out-of-state:	4,990	1,354	717	179

Profile of admitted students

Average undergraduate grade point average: **3.44**
MCAT averages (scale: 1-15; writing test: J-T):
  Composite score: **9.7**
  Verbal reasoning score: **9.1**, Physical sciences score: **9.5**,
  Biological sciences score: **9.7**, Writing score: **P**
Proportion with undergraduate majors in: Biological
  sciences: **N/A**, Physical sciences: **N/A**, Non-sciences:
  N/A, Other health professions: **N/A**, Mixed disciplines
  and other: **N/A**
Percentage of students not coming directly from college
  after graduation: **32%**

Dates and details

The American Medical College Application Service
  (AMCAS) application is accepted.
School asks for a school-specific application as part of the
  admissions process.
Oldest MCAT considered for Fall 2005 entry: **2002**
Earliest application date for the 2005-2006 first-year class:
  June 1, 2004
Latest application date: **December 1, 2004**
Acceptance dates for regular application for the class
  entering in fall 2005:
  Earliest: **October 15, 2004**

Latest: **N/A**
The school considers requests for deferred entrance.
Starting month for the class entering in 2005-2006:
  August
The school has an Early Decision Plan (EDP).
A personal interview is required for admission.

Undergraduate coursework required

Medical school requires undergraduate work in these subjects: biology, English, organic chemistry, inorganic (general) chemistry, physics, general chemistry.

ADMISSIONS POLICY
(TEXT PROVIDED BY SCHOOL):

The College of Medicine seeks highly qualified and motivated students who demonstrate the desire, intelligence,
integrity, and emotional maturity to become excellent physicians. Because of the college's unique background, we
encourage nontraditional applicants and are committed to a
diverse student body.

Our Admissions Committee has a positive attitude
toward students who are interested in medicine as a second
career. We see students who have a firm grasp of the biological and physical sciences as well as broad educational experiences in other areas, regardless of the field of study.
Students who have demonstrated a commitment to the
service of others are given strong consideration.

In accordance with this institution's historic commitment, women, students interested in careers as generalist
physicians, those who come from Pennsylvania, and those
who come from populations that are underrepresented in
medicine are particularly encouraged to apply. Applicants
must be U.S. citizens or permanent residents.

Applications are complete when the medical school
receives a verified American Medical College Application
Service application, a secondary application with the $75
fee, and premedical letters of recommendation. An
Admissions Committee member will then review the application in its entirety. Grade-point average, Medical College
Admission Test scores, adviser recommendations, the essay,

extracurricular activities, and so on are all taken into consideration when choosing whom to interview.

Typically, about 10 percent of applicants are invited for interviews, which are conducted by both an experienced faculty member and a current medical student.

Applicants may be accepted, put on a wait list, or rejected. The process takes about six weeks from interview to receipt of a decision letter.

COSTS AND FINANCIAL AID

Financial aid phone number: **(215) 991-8210**
Tuition, 2003-2004 academic year: **$34,100**
Room and board: **$10,230**
Percentage of students receiving financial aid in 2003-04: 86%
Percentage of students receiving: Loans: **76%**, Grants/scholarships: **8%**, Work-study aid: **2%**
Average medical school debt for the Class of 2002: **$124,777**

STUDENT BODY

Fall 2003 full-time enrollment: **1,019**
Men: **51%**, Women: **49%**, In-state: **34%**, Minorities: **40%**, American Indian: **0.5%**, Asian-American: **32.6%**, African-American: **5.8%**, Hispanic-American: **3.7%**, White: **52.3%**, International: **0.4%**, Unknown: **4.7%**

ACADEMIC PROGRAMS

The school's curriculum gives first-year students substantial contact with patients.
There are opportunities for first- or second-year students to work in community health clinics.
Program offerings: AIDS, drug/alcohol abuse, family medicine, geriatrics, internal medicine, pediatrics, women's health
Joint degrees awarded: M.D./Ph.D., M.D./M.B.A., M.D./M.P.H.
Total National Institutes of Health (NIH) grants awarded to the medical school and affiliated hospitals: **N/A**

CURRICULUM

(TEXT PROVIDED BY SCHOOL):
With its dedication to academic and clinical excellence, Drexel University College of Medicine has earned national recognition as an institution that provides innovation in medical education. Medical students are trained to consider each patient's case and needs in a comprehensive integrated manner. The medical college is dedicated to preparing "physician healers"—doctors who practice the art, science, and skill of medicine.

Students choose between two innovative academic curricula for their first two years of study. Both options prepare students to pursue a career as either a generalist or specialist. Both stress problem solving, lifelong learning skills, and the coordinated teaching of basic science with clinical medicine. Both tracks give early exposure to clinical skills training by using standardized patients.

The Interdisciplinary Foundations of Medicine curriculum integrates basic science courses and presents them through clinical symptom-based modules. Each first-year module features relevant material from the perspective of several basic and behavioral science disciplines. By the end of the first year, the basic and behavioral science courses have presented their entire core content. In the second year, students study basic and clinical sciences using an organ-system approach.

Students who choose the Program for Integrated Learning, a problem-based curriculum, learn primarily in small groups. There are seven 10-week blocks over the first two years. Each block contains 10 case studies, detailing real patient issues. The cases serve as the stimulus and context for students to search out the information they need to understand, diagnose, and treat clinical problems. Laboratories and lectures complement the case studies.

The third year is devoted to required clinical clerkship rotations in medicine, family medicine, obstetrics and gynecology, pediatrics, psychiatry, and surgery. Students spend 30 percent of their clinical time in expanded ambulatory care experiences.

The fourth-year curriculum is structured in the form of "pathways," courses that give students a well-rounded educational experience with some focus on potential careers. The pathway system is structured so that students take both required courses and electives.

FACULTY PROFILE (FALL 2003)

Total teaching faculty: **406 (full-time)**, **80 (part-time)**
Of full-time faculty, those teaching in basic sciences: **19%**; in clinical programs: **81%**
Of part-time faculty, those teaching in basic sciences: **6%**; in clinical programs: **94%**
Full-time faculty/student ratio: **0.4**

RESIDENCY CHOICES

Most popular residency and specialty programs chosen by the 2002 and 2003 M.D. graduating classes: anesthesiology, emergency medicine, family practice, internal medicine, obstetrics and gynecology, ophthalmology, pediatrics, psychiatry, radiology–diagnostic, surgery–general.

Duke University

- **DUMC, Durham, NC 27710**
- **Private**
- **Year Founded:** 1930
- **Tuition, 2003-2004:** $35,001
- **Enrollment, 2003-2004:** 470
- **Website:** http://dukemed.duke.edu
- **Specialty ranking:** AIDS: 9, drug/alcohol abuse: 13, family medicine: 10, geriatrics: 4, internal medicine: 4, pediatrics: 10, women's health: 10

3.80 AVERAGE GPA, ENTERING CLASS FALL 2003

11.9 AVERAGE MCAT, ENTERING CLASS FALL 2003

3.7% ACCEPTANCE RATE, ENTERING CLASS FALL 2003

4 2005 U.S.NEWS MEDICAL SCHOOL RANKING (RESEARCH)

39 2005 U.S.NEWS MEDICAL SCHOOL RANKING (PRIMARY CARE)

ADMISSIONS

Admissions phone number: **(919) 877-2985**
Admissions email address: **armst002@mc.duke.edu**
Application website: **http://dukemed.duke.edu**
Acceptance rate: **3.7%**
In-state acceptance rate: **N/A**
Out-of-state acceptance rate: **N/A**
Minority acceptance rate: **N/A**
International acceptance rate: **N/A**

Fall 2003 applications and acceptees

	Applied	Interviewed	Accepted	Enrolled
Total:	5,205	807	193	100
In-state:	N/A	N/A	N/A	9
Out-of-state:	N/A	N/A	N/A	91

Profile of admitted students

Average undergraduate grade point average: **3.80**
MCAT averages (scale: 1-15; writing test: J-T):
    Composite score: **11.9**
    Verbal reasoning score: **11.2**, Physical sciences score: **12.3**, Biological sciences score: **12.4**, Writing score: **Q**
Proportion with undergraduate majors in: Biological sciences: **47%**, Physical sciences: **25%**, Non-sciences: **18%**, Other health professions: **0%**, Mixed disciplines and other: **10%**
Percentage of students not coming directly from college after graduation: **10%**

Dates and details

The American Medical College Application Service (AMCAS) application is accepted.
School asks for a school-specific application as part of the admissions process.
Oldest MCAT considered for Fall 2005 entry: **2001**
Earliest application date for the 2005-2006 first-year class: **June 1, 2004**
Latest application date: **November 15, 2004**
Acceptance dates for regular application for the class entering in fall 2005:
    Earliest: **March 1, 2005**

Latest: **August 1, 2005**
The school considers requests for deferred entrance.
Starting month for the class entering in 2005-2006:
    August
The school doesn't have an Early Decision Plan (EDP).
A personal interview is required for admission.

Undergraduate coursework required

Medical school requires undergraduate work in these subjects: biology, English, organic chemistry, inorganic (general) chemistry, physics, calculus.

ADMISSIONS POLICY
(TEXT PROVIDED BY SCHOOL):

Duke University School of Medicine's approach to the identification, recruitment, and matriculation of students for the study of medicine is guided by our desire to select those candidates who will benefit maximally from the educational and experiential resources and unique curricula at Duke Med.

The missions of the school, to train scholars and leaders for medicine across a broad spectrum of career opportunities, are embodied in specific parameters that describe those qualities necessary for the study of medicine in the new millennium. This means that in addition to prediction of academic success using bottom-line grade-point average, Medical College Admission Test scores, academic honors, and detailed review of the breadth, depth, and level of academic rigor in undergraduate and graduate transcripts, the Admissions Committee evaluates the impact that the following factors have contributed toward the kind of humanism necessary for the needs of our increasingly diverse society:

1) Sustained participation in and leadership of campus and community service activities.

2) The need to work to support a student's education.

3) Where applicable, the demands imposed by varsity athletics.

4) Family educational achievement, resources, and socioeconomic background and the obstacles that these may

introduce to accelerate or impede the achievement of an applicant's educational goals.

5) Significant exposure to medicine through volunteer experiences in clinical settings.

6) Exposure to research through experiences in research laboratories.

Through the American Medical College Application Service and Duke supplemental application and required interview process, we are able to gain insight into the impact that students' academic and experiential activities have had on the development of compassion, altruism, leadership, professionalism, oral/written communication skills, humanism, intellectual curiosity, critical thinking, and problem-solving skills, all of which are compelling attributes for those to whom the healthcare of the country will be entrusted. Duke University School of Medicine seeks applicants from diverse communities, including but not limited to geographically, culturally, socially, economically, intellectually, and racially diverse populations.

COSTS AND FINANCIAL AID

Financial aid phone number: **(919) 684-6649**
Tuition, 2003-2004 academic year: **$35,001**
Room and board: **$9,306**
Percentage of students receiving financial aid in 2003-04: **91%**
Percentage of students receiving: Loans: **63%**, Grants/scholarships: **67%**, Work-study aid: **0%**
Average medical school debt for the Class of 2002: **$77,324**

STUDENT BODY

Fall 2003 full-time enrollment: **470**
Men: **53%**, Women: **47%**, In-state: **11%**, Minorities: **54%**, American Indian: **0.4%**, Asian-American: **17.7%**, African-American: **15.7%**, Hispanic-American: **1.9%**, White: **47.4%**, International: **1.1%**, Unknown: **15.7%**

ACADEMIC PROGRAMS

The school's curriculum gives first-year students substantial contact with patients.
There are opportunities for first- or second-year students to work in community health clinics.
Program offerings: drug/alcohol abuse, family medicine, geriatrics, internal medicine, pediatrics, rural medicine
Joint degrees awarded: M.D./Ph.D., M.D./M.B.A., M.D./M.P.H., M.D./J.D., M.D./M.S.
Total National Institutes of Health (NIH) grants awarded to the medical school and affiliated hospitals: **N/A**

CURRICULUM
(TEXT PROVIDED BY SCHOOL):
The Duke medical school curriculum emphasizes the development of independent thinkers committed to the generation, conservation, and dissemination of knowledge regarding the causes, prevention, and treatment of human disease.

The Duke curriculum is unique in that all required basic science coursework is taken in the first year. In the second year, students do the core required clinical rotations. The third year is a year of scholarship in which about two thirds of the class pursue laboratory or clinical research. Approximately one third of the students pursue combined degree programs (M.D./Ph.D., M.D./M.P.H., M.D./M.S. in clinical research, M.D./J.D., M.D./M.B.A.). During the fourth year, students return to clinical rotations or clinical electives.

FACULTY PROFILE (FALL 2003)
Total teaching faculty: **1,534 (full-time)**, **17 (part-time)**
Of full-time faculty, those teaching in basic sciences: **9%**; in clinical programs: **91%**
Of part-time faculty, those teaching in basic sciences: **0%**; in clinical programs: **100%**
Full-time faculty/student ratio: **3.3**

SUPPORT SERVICES
The school offers students these services for dealing with stress: expanded-hour gym access, peer counseling, professional counseling, religious support, support groups.

RESIDENCY CHOICES
Most popular residency and specialty programs chosen by the 2002 and 2003 M.D. graduating classes: dermatology, internal medicine, obstetrics and gynecology, ophthalmology, orthopedic surgery, otolaryngology, pediatrics, radiology–diagnostic, surgery–general, internal medicine/pediatrics.

WHERE GRADS GO

36.0%
Proportion of 2001-2003 graduates who entered primary care specialties

27.6%
Proportion of 2002-2003 graduates who accepted in-state residencies

East Carolina University

BRODY

- 600 Moye Boulevard, Greenville, NC 27858-4354
- Public
- Year Founded: 1975
- Tuition, 2003-2004: In-state: $5,028; Out-of-state: $30,144
- Enrollment, 2003-2004: 304
- Website: http://www.ecu.edu/bsomadmissions
- Specialty ranking: family medicine: 15, rural medicine: 4

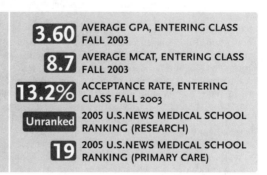

3.60	AVERAGE GPA, ENTERING CLASS FALL 2003
8.7	AVERAGE MCAT, ENTERING CLASS FALL 2003
13.2%	ACCEPTANCE RATE, ENTERING CLASS FALL 2003
Unranked	2005 U.S.NEWS MEDICAL SCHOOL RANKING (RESEARCH)
19	2005 U.S.NEWS MEDICAL SCHOOL RANKING (PRIMARY CARE)

ADMISSIONS

Admissions phone number: **(252) 744-2202**
Admissions email address: **somadmissions@mail.ecu.edu**
Application website: **N/A**
Acceptance rate: **13.2%**
In-state acceptance rate: **17.7%**
Out-of-state acceptance rate: **0.0%**
Minority acceptance rate: **N/A**
International acceptance rate: **N/A**

Fall 2003 applications and acceptees

	Applied	Interviewed	Accepted	Enrolled
Total:	899	453	119	72
In-state:	671	453	119	72
Out-of-state:	228	0	0	0

Profile of admitted students

Average undergraduate grade point average: **3.60**
MCAT averages (scale: 1-15; writing test: J-T):
   Composite score: **8.7**
   Verbal reasoning score: **8.7**, Physical sciences score: **8.5**,
   Biological sciences score: **8.9**, Writing score: **O**
Proportion with undergraduate majors in: Biological
   sciences: **49%**, Physical sciences: **22%**, Non-sciences:
   24%, Other health professions: **4%**, Mixed disciplines
   and other: **1%**
Percentage of students not coming directly from college
   after graduation: **65%**

Dates and details

The American Medical College Application Service
   (AMCAS) application is accepted.
School asks for a school-specific application as part of the
   admissions process.
Oldest MCAT considered for Fall 2005 entry: **2002**
Earliest application date for the 2005-2006 first-year class:
   June 1, 2004
Latest application date: **November 15, 2004**
Acceptance dates for regular application for the class
   entering in fall 2005:
   Earliest: **October 15, 2004**

Latest: **August 15, 2005**
The school doesn't consider requests for deferred entrance.
Starting month for the class entering in 2005-2006:
   August
The school has an Early Decision Plan (EDP).
A personal interview is required for admission.

Undergraduate coursework required

Medical school requires undergraduate work in these subjects: biology/zoology, English, organic chemistry, inorganic (general) chemistry, physics.

ADMISSIONS POLICY
(TEXT PROVIDED BY SCHOOL):

Factors considered by Admissions Committee members as they review applicants to the Brody School of Medicine encompass the intellectual, personal, and social development of each individual. In order to assess these areas, the committee uses a variety of data, including grades and other indicators of academic achievement; performance on the Medical College Admission Test and any other available standardized tests; the personal, professional, and employment experiences of the applicant; evaluations from faculty members who have taught the applicant; letters of reference from employers, acquaintances, and other individuals; interviews conducted by members of the Admissions Committee; and any other pertinent information.

Since there are no rigid cutoffs or formulas used in the selection of medical students, each applicant is viewed as an individual. All available information is considered in order to best determine that applicant's character and qualifications for the study of medicine.

The Brody School of Medicine acknowledges its responsibility as a state-supported school to select students and train physicians who will meet the needs of all residents of North Carolina. In meeting this responsibility, the Brody School of Medicine seeks competent students of diverse personalities and backgrounds. In particular, special effort is made to include in each entering class students from a variety of geographical, economic, and ethnic groups. It follows that all applicants are evaluated by the Admissions Committee without regard to race, religion, sex, color, national origin, age, or disability.

Since the Brody School of Medicine is a state-supported medical school, very strong preference is given to qualified residents of North Carolina who apply for admission. No out-of-state students have been admitted in nearly 20 years.

COSTS AND FINANCIAL AID

Financial aid phone number: **(252) 744-2278**

Tuition, 2003-2004 academic year: **In-state: $5,028; Out-of-state: $30,144**

Room and board: **$17,500**

Percentage of students receiving financial aid in 2003-04: **85%**

Percentage of students receiving: Loans: **80%**, Grants/scholarships: **72%**, Work-study aid: **0%**

Average medical school debt for the Class of 2002: **$58,114**

STUDENT BODY

Fall 2003 full-time enrollment: **304**

Men: **51%**, Women: **49%**, In-state: **100%**, Minorities: **33%**, American Indian: **3.3%**, Asian-American: **7.6%**, African-American: **19.7%**, Hispanic-American: **2.6%**, White: **66.8%**, International: **0.0%**, Unknown: **0.0%**

ACADEMIC PROGRAMS

The school's curriculum gives first-year students substantial contact with patients.

There are opportunities for first- or second-year students to work in community health clinics.

Program offerings: drug/alcohol abuse, family medicine, internal medicine, pediatrics, rural medicine

Joint degrees awarded: M.D./Ph.D., M.D./M.B.A., M.D./M.P.H.

Total National Institutes of Health (NIH) grants awarded to the medical school and affiliated hospitals: **$3.5 million**

CURRICULUM

(TEXT PROVIDED BY SCHOOL):

The medical school curriculum has been carefully developed and is regularly monitored and adjusted to reflect the changes occurring in contemporary medical education and practice. The curriculum provides a logical integration of basic science and clinical science knowledge over the four-year span.

Early experience in the patient care setting is achieved through individual preceptorships at physician offices throughout the state and through contact with both standardized and clinic patients in the Doctoring and Clinical Skills course in the first two years. Innovative teaching methods such as small-group discussions, computer-assisted instruction, and use of standardized patients are employed wherever appropriate during the entire four years, as a complement to the traditional venues of the lecture hall and the laboratory.

The third- and fourth-year clinical experiences are gained at a major regional teaching hospital center, outpatient clinics, and physician office settings as students progress through the six major clinical areas. The fourth year includes opportunities to explore medical topics, specialties, and individually designed selectives. Research projects are encouraged and supported through the medical student research program in the first and second years.

FACULTY PROFILE (FALL 2003)

Total teaching faculty: **352 (full-time), 36 (part-time)**

Of full-time faculty, those teaching in basic sciences: **19%**; in clinical programs: **81%**

Of part-time faculty, those teaching in basic sciences: **19%**; in clinical programs: **81%**

Full-time faculty/student ratio: **1.2**

SUPPORT SERVICES

The school offers students these services for dealing with stress: peer counseling, professional counseling, religious support, support groups.

RESIDENCY CHOICES

Most popular residency and specialty programs chosen by the 2002 and 2003 M.D. graduating classes: anesthesiology, emergency medicine, family practice, internal medicine, internal medicine–pediatrics, obstetrics and gynecology, orthopedic surgery, pediatrics, psychiatry, surgery–general.

WHERE GRADS GO

55.7%

Proportion of 2001-2003 graduates who entered primary care specialties

51.5%

Proportion of 2002-2003 graduates who accepted in-state residencies

stern Virginia Medical School

- 721 Fairfax Avenue, PO Box 1980, Norfolk, VA 23501-1980
- Private
- Year Founded: 1973
- Tuition, 2003-2004: $21,941
- Enrollment, 2003-2004: 432
- Website: http://www.evms.edu
- Specialty ranking: N/A

3.48 AVERAGE GPA, ENTERING CLASS FALL 2003

9.8 AVERAGE MCAT, ENTERING CLASS FALL 2003

13.1% ACCEPTANCE RATE, ENTERING CLASS FALL 2003

Unranked 2005 U.S.NEWS MEDICAL SCHOOL RANKING (RESEARCH)

57 2005 U.S.NEWS MEDICAL SCHOOL RANKING (PRIMARY CARE)

ADMISSIONS

Admissions phone number: **(757) 446-5812**
Admissions email address: **nanezkf@evms.edu**
Application website: **http://www.evms.edu/admissions**
Acceptance rate: **13.1%**
In-state acceptance rate: **19.2%**
Out-of-state acceptance rate: **10.7%**
Minority acceptance rate: **N/A**
International acceptance rate: **N/A**

Fall 2003 applications and acceptees

	Applied	Interviewed	Accepted	Enrolled
Total:	2,565	633	335	110
In-state:	719	303	138	60
Out-of-state:	1,846	330	197	50

Profile of admitted students

Average undergraduate grade point average: **3.48**
MCAT averages (scale: 1-15; writing test: J-T):
 Composite score: **9.8**
 Verbal reasoning score: **9.5**, Physical sciences score: **9.8**,
 Biological sciences score: **10.0**, Writing score: **N/A**
Proportion with undergraduate majors in: Biological
 sciences: **51%**, Physical sciences: **34%**, Non-sciences: **4%**,
 Other health professions: **0%**, Mixed disciplines and
 other: **12%**
Percentage of students not coming directly from college
 after graduation: **25%**

Dates and details

The American Medical College Application Service
 (AMCAS) application is accepted.
School asks for a school-specific application as part of the
 admissions process.
Oldest MCAT considered for Fall 2005 entry: **2002**
Earliest application date for the 2005-2006 first-year class:
 June 1, 2004
Latest application date: **November 15, 2004**
Acceptance dates for regular application for the class
 entering in fall 2005:
 Earliest: **October 15, 2004**

Latest: **N/A**
The school considers requests for deferred entrance.
Starting month for the class entering in 2005-2006:
 August
The school has an Early Decision Plan (EDP).
A personal interview is required for admission.

Undergraduate coursework required

Medical school requires undergraduate work in these subjects: biology, organic chemistry, inorganic (general) chemistry, physics.

ADMISSIONS POLICY
(TEXT PROVIDED BY SCHOOL):

As a medical school dedicated since its inception to the
healthcare needs of eastern Virginia, EVMS shows preference to applicants from the Commonwealth of Virginia,
especially legal residents of Hampton Roads. For an applicant to be considered as an in-state Virginia resident, he or
she must have been legally domiciled in the
Commonwealth of Virginia for at least one year prior to
matriculation.

Out-of-state students who have strong academic credentials and the personal traits valued by EVMS are also
encouraged to apply. Applicants from rural or other underserved regions and those who have been disadvantaged or
underrepresented for economic, racial, or social reasons,
and who possess the motivation and aptitude required for
the study of medicine, are also strongly encouraged to
apply.

The body of knowledge a physician must assimilate is
vast and complex. For this reason, EVMS requires academic
excellence of those students admitted to the medical school.
The Committee on Admissions gauges an applicant's academic ability by his or her performance in undergraduate
courses and scores on the Medical College Admission Test.
The MCAT and a minimum of 100 semester hours at an
accredited American or Canadian university are required.

Coursework must include one year each of biology, general chemistry, organic chemistry, and physics, all with lab
work. Applicants are expected to have grades of C or better

in all required courses. Credits earned through Advanced Placement programs or the College Level Examination Program are acceptable. Applicants may enhance their chances of acceptance by taking graduate coursework in natural science.

COSTS AND FINANCIAL AID
Financial aid phone number: **(757) 446-5813**
Tuition, 2003-2004 academic year: **$21,941**
Room and board: **N/A**
Percentage of students receiving financial aid in 2003-04: **90%**
Percentage of students receiving: Loans: **82%**, Grants/scholarships: **73%**, Work-study aid: **0%**
Average medical school debt for the Class of 2002: **$92,301**

STUDENT BODY
Fall 2003 full-time enrollment: **432**
Men: **47%**, Women: **53%**, In-state: **70%**, Minorities: **28%**, American Indian: **0.2%**, Asian-American: **17.6%**, African-American: **8.6%**, Hispanic-American: **1.4%**, White: **71.5%**, International: **0.0%**, Unknown: **0.7%**

ACADEMIC PROGRAMS
The school's curriculum gives first-year students substantial contact with patients.
There are opportunities for first- or second-year students to work in community health clinics.
Program offerings: AIDS, drug/alcohol abuse, family medicine, geriatrics, internal medicine, pediatrics, rural medicine
Joint degrees awarded: M.D./M.P.H.
Total National Institutes of Health (NIH) grants awarded to the medical school and affiliated hospitals: **$5.9 million**

CURRICULUM
(TEXT PROVIDED BY SCHOOL):
The mission of the M.D. program is to educate medical students who will be noted for their excellence in practice, human values, collegiality, and scientific curiosity and rigor.

The curriculum is designed to educate compassionate, skillful physician-scientists, with an emphasis on preparation of physicians for residency training in the primary care disciplines. Excellence in patient care requires a firm foundation in the medical sciences and clinical skills, combined with an empathetic attitude and the ability to apply the scientific method to the solution of medical problems.

To meet the challenges created by the rapid development of new technologies and new understanding in medical science, the physician of the future will need not only accurate current information but also the ability to obtain, evaluate, and assimilate information about the rapid advances in medicine. Essential to this ability is a habit of critical scientific inquiry. With the increasing complexity of medicine,

deductive reasoning and problem solving become increasingly important.

With these concepts in mind, the EVMS curriculum is designed to: provide a firm foundation in medical sciences and clinical skills; address medical problems using the best available medical evidence; cultivate habits of independent learning and scholarship; help students recognize the broad social and economic responsibilities of members of the medical profession; encourage the development of self-awareness and communication skills; and emphasize human values in the practice of medicine.

The instructional approach at EVMS emphasizes an integrated program of basic and clinical sciences from the first week of medical school throughout all four years of study. Students participate as active learners in a carefully sequenced program designed to achieve competency in all areas required for the general professional education of the physician. Small study groups help students develop their interpersonal skills, professional attitudes, and problem-solving abilities. The four-year curriculum includes both interdisciplinary and discipline-based instruction. Progress toward achieving the expected professional competence is assessed periodically through the Professional Skills Center in all four years and through standardized testing.

FACULTY PROFILE (FALL 2003)
Total teaching faculty: **317 (full-time)**, **63 (part-time)**
Of full-time faculty, those teaching in basic sciences: **14%**; in clinical programs: **86%**
Of part-time faculty, those teaching in basic sciences: **2%**; in clinical programs: **98%**
Full-time faculty/student ratio: **0.7**

SUPPORT SERVICES
The school offers students these services for dealing with stress: peer counseling, professional counseling, religious support.

RESIDENCY CHOICES
Most popular residency and specialty programs chosen by the 2002 and 2003 M.D. graduating classes: anesthesiology, emergency medicine, family practice, internal medicine, obstetrics and gynecology, orthopedic surgery, otolaryngology, pediatrics, radiology–diagnostic, surgery–general.

WHERE GRADS GO
51.0%
Proportion of 2001-2003 graduates who entered primary care specialties

37.6%
Proportion of 2002-2003 graduates who accepted in-state residencies

ast Tennessee State University

J.H. QUILLEN

- PO Box 70694, Johnson City, TN 37614
- Public
- Year Founded: 1974
- Tuition, 2003-2004: In-state: $15,855; Out-of-state: $31,545
- Enrollment, 2003-2004: 236
- Website: http://qcom.etsu.edu
- Specialty ranking: family medicine: 26, rural medicine: 3

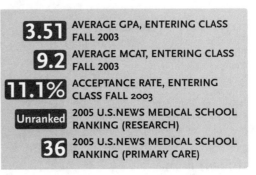

3.51 AVERAGE GPA, ENTERING CLASS FALL 2003

9.2 AVERAGE MCAT, ENTERING CLASS FALL 2003

11.1% ACCEPTANCE RATE, ENTERING CLASS FALL 2003

Unranked 2005 U.S.NEWS MEDICAL SCHOOL RANKING (RESEARCH)

36 2005 U.S.NEWS MEDICAL SCHOOL RANKING (PRIMARY CARE)

ADMISSIONS

Admissions phone number: (423) 439-2033
Admissions email address: sacom@mail.etsu.edu
Application website: http://www.aamc.org
Acceptance rate: 11.1%
In-state acceptance rate: 22.5%
Out-of-state acceptance rate: 3.3%
Minority acceptance rate: 7.5%
International acceptance rate: N/A

Fall 2003 applications and acceptees

	Applied	Interviewed	Accepted	Enrolled
Total:	1,035	186	115	60
In-state:	423	148	95	57
Out-of-state:	612	38	20	3

Profile of admitted students

Average undergraduate grade point average: 3.51
MCAT averages (scale: 1-15; writing test: J-T):
   Composite score: 9.2
   Verbal reasoning score: 95, Physical sciences score: 8.9,
   Biological sciences score: 9.2, Writing score: O
Proportion with undergraduate majors in: Biological
   sciences: 45%, Physical sciences: 22%, Non-sciences:
   10%, Other health professions: 7%, Mixed disciplines
   and other: 16%
Percentage of students not coming directly from college
   after graduation: 33%

Dates and details

The American Medical College Application Service
   (AMCAS) application is accepted.
School asks for a school-specific application as part of the
   admissions process.
Oldest MCAT considered for Fall 2005 entry: 2002
Earliest application date for the 2005-2006 first-year class:
   June 1, 2004
Latest application date: December 1, 2004
Acceptance dates for regular application for the class
   entering in fall 2005:
   Earliest: October 15, 2004

Latest: N/A
The school considers requests for deferred entrance.
Starting month for the class entering in 2005-2006:
   August
The school has an Early Decision Plan (EDP).
A personal interview is required for admission.

Undergraduate coursework required

Medical school requires undergraduate work in these subjects: biology/zoology, English, organic chemistry, physics,
general chemistry.

ADMISSIONS POLICY
(TEXT PROVIDED BY SCHOOL):

Quillen's multilevel review process employs consideration
of the qualities important in making a successful physician
and meeting the stated goals and values of both Quillen and
ETSU. This whole-person concept evaluates applicants on
the basis of objective and subjective criteria: demonstrated
academic achievement, Medical College Admission Test
scores, letters of recommendation, pertinent extracurricular
work and research experience, evidence of nonscholastic
accomplishment, motivation for the study and practice of
medicine, and interest in a primary-care practice in a rural
or underserved area.

Because Quillen College of Medicine is a state-supported
institution, preference for admission is given to Tennessee
residents. Out-of-state applicants from the contiguous
Appalachian region interested in primary-care medicine
may receive a higher admissions priority than other nonresident applicants. There are no quotas or set-asides; all applicants are considered in the same competitive pool using the
same policies, procedures, and Admissions Committee
members.

Through its 25-year history, Quillen's admissions process
has proved to consistently produce a diverse student body
with high graduation rates, with more than half of the graduates entering a field of primary care, often in underserved
rural regions.

COSTS AND FINANCIAL AID

Financial aid phone number: **(423) 439-2035**
Tuition, 2003-2004 academic year: **In-state: $15,855;** Out-of-state: **$31,545**
Room and board: **$7,400**
Percentage of students receiving financial aid in 2003-04: **90%**
Percentage of students receiving: Loans: **86%,** Grants/scholarships: **32%,** Work-study aid: **0%**
Average medical school debt for the Class of 2002: **$94,056**

STUDENT BODY

Fall 2003 full-time enrollment: **236**
Men: **50%,** Women: **50%,** In-state: **97%,** Minorities: **20%,** American Indian: **2.1%,** Asian-American: **6.8%,** African-American: **9.7%,** Hispanic-American: **17%,** White: **79.7%,** International: **0.0%,** Unknown: **0.0%**

ACADEMIC PROGRAMS

The school's curriculum gives first-year students substantial contact with patients.
There are opportunities for first- or second-year students to work in community health clinics.
Program offerings: AIDS, drug/alcohol abuse, family medicine, geriatrics, internal medicine, pediatrics, rural medicine
Joint degrees awarded: **N/A**
Total National Institutes of Health (NIH) grants awarded to the medical school and affiliated hospitals: **N/A**

CURRICULUM

(TEXT PROVIDED BY SCHOOL):
The James H. Quillen College of Medicine has a modification of the traditional two-plus-two medical school curriculum. The first year provides the biomedical science basis for understanding normal human anatomy and function while the second year builds on this base with an introduction to the altered anatomic and physiologic states produced by microorganisms and disease. Biomedical statistics, anatomy, physiology, biochemistry, and cell and tissue biology are taught in the first year; immunology, neuroscience, microbiology, pathology, and pharmacology in the second. Psychological development, psychosocial issues, and the behavioral basis for psychiatric disease are introduced in the first year and continue through the second year.

The first-year Communication Skills and Clinical Skills courses complement each other and use standardized patients to teach and evaluate students in an introduction to the skills that form the basis for the practice of medicine. The students spend an afternoon each week seeing patients with a physician. During the first-year spring break, students have an additional weeklong preceptorship in a physician's office. Clinical Skills continues in the second year and is closely linked with the Practicing Medicine course. These combined courses provide an introduction to clinical thinking and problem solving.

The third year consists of six eight-week clerkships: family medicine, internal medicine, pediatrics, obstetrics and gynecology, psychiatry, and surgery. Students are given supervised responsibility for patient care and required to become a part of the clinical care team.

The fourth year consists of four months of required "selective" experiences, four months of electives, and a one-month "keystone course." Each student selects a one-month experience from each of the following categories: ambulatory, inpatient, intensive care, and subspecialty. Electives allow students to address individual learning needs. The keystone month brings the entire class back together the month before graduation and combines a guest lecture series with practical workshops and advanced cardiac life support training, designed to prepare the graduate for starting internship. U.S. Medical Licensing Examination steps 1 and 2 are required for graduation.

Quillen has a generalist track and a rural primary care track (RPCT). Up to 25 percent of an entering class may apply for admission to RPCT. In addition to the core curriculum, RPCT students participate in an interdisciplinary rural primary-care curriculum. RPCT students spend 20 percent of their time in this curriculum during the first two years and one third of their junior-year clerkship experiences in a rural primary care setting. RPCT students are in an experiential learning environment in an interdisciplinary clinical setting from the first month in medical school.

FACULTY PROFILE (FALL 2003)

Total teaching faculty: **236 (full-time), 51 (part-time)**
Of full-time faculty, those teaching in basic sciences: **26%;** in clinical programs: **74%**
Of part-time faculty, those teaching in basic sciences: **2%;** in clinical programs: **98%**
Full-time faculty/student ratio: **1.0**

SUPPORT SERVICES

The school offers students these services for dealing with stress: expanded-hour gym access, peer counseling, professional counseling, religious support.

RESIDENCY CHOICES

Most popular residency and specialty programs chosen by the 2002 and 2003 M.D. graduating classes: emergency medicine, family practice, internal medicine, obstetrics and gynecology, orthopedic surgery, pediatrics, psychiatry, surgery–general.

WHERE GRADS GO

61.8%
Proportion of 2001-2003 graduates who entered primary care specialties

42.9%
Proportion of 2002-2003 graduates who accepted in-state residencies

Emory University

- 1440 Clifton Road NE, Atlanta, GA 30322-4510
- Private
- Year Founded: 1854
- Tuition, 2003-2004: $33,068
- Enrollment, 2003-2004: 454
- Website: http://www.med.emory.edu
- Specialty ranking: AIDS: 15, internal medicine: 21

3.75 AVERAGE GPA, ENTERING CLASS FALL 2003

10.9 AVERAGE MCAT, ENTERING CLASS FALL 2003

9.8% ACCEPTANCE RATE, ENTERING CLASS FALL 2003

19 2005 U.S.NEWS MEDICAL SCHOOL RANKING (RESEARCH)

42 2005 U.S.NEWS MEDICAL SCHOOL RANKING (PRIMARY CARE)

ADMISSIONS

Admissions phone number: **(404) 727-5660**
Admissions email address: **medadmiss@emory.edu**
Application website: **N/A**
Acceptance rate: **9.8%**
In-state acceptance rate: **19.7%**
Out-of-state acceptance rate: **8.6%**
Minority acceptance rate: **8.4%**
International acceptance rate: **18.4%**

Fall 2003 applications and acceptees

	Applied	Interviewed	Accepted	Enrolled
Total:	3,391	734	332	113
In-state:	350	125	69	36
Out-of-state:	3,041	607	263	77

Profile of admitted students

Average undergraduate grade point average: **3.75**
MCAT averages (scale: 1-15; writing test: J-T):
Composite score: **10.9**
Verbal reasoning score: **10.6**, Physical sciences score: **110**, Biological sciences score: **11.1**, Writing score: **P**
Proportion with undergraduate majors in: Biological sciences: **40%**, Physical sciences: **25%**, Non-sciences: **19%**, Other health professions: **0%**, Mixed disciplines and other: **16%**
Percentage of students not coming directly from college after graduation: **38%**

Dates and details

The American Medical College Application Service (AMCAS) application is accepted.
School asks for a school-specific application as part of the admissions process.
Oldest MCAT considered for Fall 2005 entry: **2001**
Earliest application date for the 2005-2006 first-year class: **June 1, 2004**
Latest application date: **October 15, 2004**
Acceptance dates for regular application for the class entering in fall 2005:
Earliest: **October 7, 2004**

Latest: **July 15, 2004**
The school considers requests for deferred entrance.
Starting month for the class entering in 2005-2006: **July**
The school doesn't have an Early Decision Plan (EDP).
A personal interview is required for admission.

Undergraduate coursework required

Medical school requires undergraduate work in these subjects: biology, English, organic chemistry, inorganic (general) chemistry, physics, humanities, behavioral science, social sciences, general chemistry.

ADMISSIONS POLICY
(TEXT PROVIDED BY SCHOOL):

When you apply to Emory, we will look at you as an individual. To be a competitive applicant, we recommend that you present a file that features a strong academic record; recommendations from those who can attest to both your work in the classroom as well as your personal character, compassion, integrity, and motivation for a career in medicine; exposure to patients in a clinical setting; and evidence of your interests in areas outside of medicine.

There are eight recommended steps that need to be completed in the application process and that can be easily downloaded at the Emory Web site. It is to your advantage to apply though the American Medical College Application Service and complete your application as early as possible, as Emory receives thousands of applications for our entering class of 112 students. Your file will not be screened for an interview until the Office of Medical Education and Student Affairs receives your AMCAS application, Medical College Admission Test scores, recommendations, and supplemental application with fee payment. If you have specific questions about how to improve your application, please contact your premed adviser or visit our Web site.

COSTS AND FINANCIAL AID

Financial aid phone number: **(800) 727-6039**
Tuition, 2003-2004 academic year: **$33,068**
Room and board: **$15,600**

Percentage of students receiving financial aid in 2003-04:
86%
Percentage of students receiving: Loans: 76%,
Grants/scholarships: 57%, Work-study aid: 0%
Average medical school debt for the Class of 2002:
$102,977

STUDENT BODY
Fall 2003 full-time enrollment: 454
Men: 50%, Women: 50%, In-state: 37%, Minorities: 26%,
American Indian: 1.1%, Asian-American: 14.3%, African-
American: 8.8%, Hispanic-American: 1.3%, White:
69.4%, International: 1.8%, Unknown: 3.3%

ACADEMIC PROGRAMS
The school's curriculum gives first-year students
substantial contact with patients.
There are opportunities for first- or second-year students to
work in community health clinics.
Program offerings: AIDS, drug/alcohol abuse, family
medicine, geriatrics, internal medicine, pediatrics, rural
medicine, women's health
Joint degrees awarded: M.D./Ph.D., M.D./M.P.H.
Total National Institutes of Health (NIH) grants awarded to
the medical school and affiliated hospitals: $166.0 million

CURRICULUM
(TEXT PROVIDED BY SCHOOL):
Come to Emory, and you'll partake in a medical curriculum
that is continually extending its program into areas beyond
the bounds of traditional medical education for the benefit
of the student and society. It is a combination of lectures,
laboratory work, research opportunities, conferences,
demonstrations, examinations, clinical instruction, and
small- group discussions, including problem-based learning
and interaction with patient actors in a clinical skills/stan-
dardized patient program.
    The first two years of basic science coursework are con-
ducted on the Emory campus with enhanced patient contact
and experience that includes problem-based learning and
clinical instruction. Emory students are well prepared to

begin caring for patients when they transition into the more
clinical two years of the program. Dual-degree programs
offer in-depth opportunities to pursue research and public-
health projects.
    The vast number of outpatient and inpatient visits within
the Emory Healthcare environment and throughout the
state of Georgia offers students a rewarding experience
within a broad range of facilities. Couple this with more
than 1,400 dedicated faculty, and the medical curriculum
makes Emory a rich environment for learning clinical medicine and providing important research opportunities.

FACULTY PROFILE (FALL 2003)
Total teaching faculty: 1,583 (full-time), 133 (part-time)
Of full-time faculty, those teaching in basic sciences: 10%;
in clinical programs: 90%
Of part-time faculty, those teaching in basic sciences: 2%;
in clinical programs: 98%
Full-time faculty/student ratio: 3.5

SUPPORT SERVICES
The school offers students these services for dealing with
stress: expanded-hour gym access, peer counseling, professional counseling, religious support, support groups.

RESIDENCY CHOICES
Most popular residency and specialty programs chosen by
the 2002 and 2003 M.D. graduating classes: anesthesiology,
dermatology, emergency medicine, family practice, internal
medicine, neurology, obstetrics and gynecology, ophthalmology, orthopedic surgery, pediatrics, surgery–general.

WHERE GRADS GO

46.3%
*Proportion of 2001-2003 graduates who entered primary
care specialties*

34.5%
*Proportion of 2002-2003 graduates who accepted in-state
residencies*

Georgetown University

- 3900 Reservoir Road NW, Med-Dent Building, Washington, DC 20057
- Private
- **Year Founded:** 1851
- **Tuition, 2003-2004:** $33,723
- **Enrollment, 2003-2004:** 689
- **Website:** http://www.gumc.georgetown.edu
- **Specialty ranking:** N/A

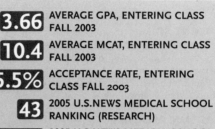

3.66 AVERAGE GPA, ENTERING CLASS FALL 2003

10.4 AVERAGE MCAT, ENTERING CLASS FALL 2003

5.5% ACCEPTANCE RATE, ENTERING CLASS FALL 2003

43 2005 U.S.NEWS MEDICAL SCHOOL RANKING (RESEARCH)

Unranked 2005 U.S.NEWS MEDICAL SCHOOL RANKING (PRIMARY CARE)

ADMISSIONS
Admissions phone number: **(202) 687-1154**
Admissions email address:
  medicaladmissions@georgetown.edu
Application website: **N/A**
Acceptance rate: **5.5%**
In-state acceptance rate: **12.2%**
Out-of-state acceptance rate: **5.4%**
Minority acceptance rate: **N/A**
International acceptance rate: **N/A**

Fall 2003 applications and acceptees

	Applied	Interviewed	Accepted	Enrolled
Total:	7,547	1,136	413	170
In-state:	41	9	5	0
Out-of-state:	7,506	1,127	408	170

Profile of admitted students
Average undergraduate grade point average: **3.66**
MCAT averages (scale: 1-15; writing test: J-T):
  Composite score: **10.4**
  Verbal reasoning score: **10.1**, Physical sciences score: **10.4**, Biological sciences score: **10.8**, Writing score: **N/A**
Proportion with undergraduate majors in: Biological sciences: **55%**, Physical sciences: **10%**, Non-sciences: **18%**, Other health professions: **8%**, Mixed disciplines and other: **9%**
Percentage of students not coming directly from college after graduation: **57%**

Dates and details
The American Medical College Application Service (AMCAS) application is accepted.
School asks for a school-specific application as part of the admissions process.
Oldest MCAT considered for Fall 2005 entry: **2002**
Earliest application date for the 2005-2006 first-year class:
  June 1, 2004
Latest application date: **November 1, 2004**
Acceptance dates for regular application for the class entering in fall 2005:

Earliest: **October 1, 2004**
Latest: **August 17, 2005**
The school considers requests for deferred entrance.
Starting month for the class entering in 2005-2006:
  August
The school doesn't have an Early Decision Plan (EDP).
A personal interview is required for admission.

Undergraduate coursework required
Medical school requires undergraduate work in these subjects: biology, English, organic chemistry, inorganic (general) chemistry, physics, mathematics.

ADMISSIONS POLICY
(TEXT PROVIDED BY SCHOOL):
A secondary application packet is mailed to each applicant who applies to the School of Medicine through the American Medical College Application Service. The packet provides applicants with information on the application requirements, process and procedures, and selection factors of the Committee on Admissions.

Georgetown University School of Medicine requires the Medical College Admission Test and a minimum of three years of college (90 semester hours, including the standard basic science core courses) and a personal essay unique to Georgetown University School of Medicine for consideration of admission. Upon completion of the secondary application process, the applicant's file is personally read during an administrative review. While a solid preparation in the sciences is essential, a broad background in the humanities and computer science is also important. An applicant must not only present a strong academic profile but also demonstrate well-developed noncognitive qualities. The Committee on Admissions selects students on the basis of academic achievement, character, maturity, and motivation. In rendering its decisions, the committee evaluates the applicant's entire academic record, performance on the MCAT, college premedical advisory committee evaluations, letters of recommendation, essays, healthcare-related experiences, and personal interview. The interview evaluates the applicant's motivation, maturity, compassion, commitment to serving others, problem-solving abilities, sense of humor, and reasons for and interest in applying to Georgetown.

The Committee on Admissions meets biweekly to make final decisions on interviewed applicants. Members base their votes on all aspects of the application without a weight or score being assigned to any individual aspect. The School of Medicine does not discriminate on the basis of race, sex, creed, sexual orientation, age, handicap, or national or ethnic origin. Neither citizenry nor residency plays any role in the selection process.

COSTS AND FINANCIAL AID
Financial aid phone number: **(202) 687-1693**
Tuition, 2003-2004 academic year: **$33,723**
Room and board: **$13,085**
Percentage of students receiving financial aid in 2003-04: **84%**
Percentage of students receiving: Loans: **93%**, Grants/scholarships: **42%**, Work-study aid: **1%**
Average medical school debt for the Class of 2002: **$134,481**

STUDENT BODY
Fall 2003 full-time enrollment: **689**
Men: **50%**, Women: **50%**, In-state: **2%**, Minorities: **29%**, American Indian: **0.1%**, Asian-American: **16.4%**, African-American: **5.5%**, Hispanic-American: **1.5%**, White: **69.2%**, International: **5.5%**, Unknown: **1.7%**

ACADEMIC PROGRAMS
The school's curriculum gives first-year students substantial contact with patients.
There are opportunities for first- or second-year students to work in community health clinics.
Program offerings: AIDS, drug/alcohol abuse, family medicine, geriatrics, internal medicine, pediatrics, rural medicine, women's health
Joint degrees awarded: M.D./Ph.D., M.D./M.B.A., M.D./M.S.
Total National Institutes of Health (NIH) grants awarded to the medical school and affiliated hospitals: **$91.8 million**

CURRICULUM
(TEXT PROVIDED BY SCHOOL):
The first two years at Georgetown provide students with an early introduction to the patient, as well as to the spiritual and ethical dimensions of medicine. In the first and second years, departmental courses provide the student with the scientific knowledge basic to the practice of medicine, including the anatomic and chemical characteristics of the normal body and the changes that are produced by diseases, drugs, and other agents. First-year courses are particularly concerned with how bodily organs interact. Finally, students are introduced to the care of patients; the fundamental principles and theories of clinical ethics; the broader demographic and policy dimensions of the American healthcare system; and the role of spirituality in the experience of

health and illness as well as in the physician-patient relationship.

A focus of the second year is the study of disease processes, especially those caused by microbes; the body's own immunological defenses against microbes, as well as other pathological agents; and the principles governing the action of pharmacological agents, their major uses, and their consequences. In addition, students continue their introduction to clinical practice through ambulatory care experiences and through a course in physical diagnosis. They also continue their study of clinical ethics. Finally, students take an interdepartmental course called Clinical Problem Solving, which provides a bridge to the clinical emphasis of the third and fourth years.

The third year contains 48 weeks divided into four 12-week blocks. The student serves clinical clerkships in medicine, surgery, pediatrics, obstetrics/gynecology, neurology, psychiatry, and family medicine.

The fourth year contains 44 weeks of instructional time and provides the student with substantial but supervised responsibility in the clinical management of patients. Patient experience is gained during six weeks on the medical and surgical services as an acting intern, 12 weeks on a primary/ambulatory rotation that includes emergency medicine, and a selection of two other four-week rotations.

FACULTY PROFILE (FALL 2003)
Total teaching faculty: **1,095 (full-time)**, **1,795 (part-time)**
Of full-time faculty, those teaching in basic sciences: **20%**; in clinical programs: **80%**
Of part-time faculty, those teaching in basic sciences: **5%**; in clinical programs: **95%**
Full-time faculty/student ratio: **1.6**

SUPPORT SERVICES
The school offers students these services for dealing with stress: expanded-hour gym access, professional counseling, religious support, support groups.

RESIDENCY CHOICES
Most popular residency and specialty programs chosen by the 2002 and 2003 M.D. graduating classes: emergency medicine, family practice, internal medicine, obstetrics and gynecology, orthopedic surgery, pediatrics, radiology–diagnostic, surgery–general, transitional year.

WHERE GRADS GO

	47.0%		

Proportion of 2001-2003 graduates who entered primary care specialties

N/A			

Proportion of 2002-2003 graduates who accepted in-state residencies

George Washington University

■ 2300 Eye Street NW, Room 713W, Washington, DC 20037
■ Private
■ **Year Founded:** 1821
■ **Tuition, 2003-2004:** $39,285
■ **Enrollment, 2003-2004:** 675
■ **Website:** http://www.gwumc.edu
■ **Specialty ranking:** N/A

3.55 AVERAGE GPA, ENTERING CLASS FALL 2003

9.5 AVERAGE MCAT, ENTERING CLASS FALL 2003

5.4% ACCEPTANCE RATE, ENTERING CLASS FALL 2003

Unranked 2005 U.S.NEWS MEDICAL SCHOOL RANKING (RESEARCH)

Unranked 2005 U.S.NEWS MEDICAL SCHOOL RANKING (PRIMARY CARE)

ADMISSIONS

Admissions phone number: **(202) 994-3506**
Admissions email address: **medadmit@gwu.edu**
Application website: **http://www.gwumc.edu/edu/admis**
Acceptance rate: **5.4%**
In-state acceptance rate: **12.5%**
Out-of-state acceptance rate: **5.4%**
Minority acceptance rate: **N/A**
International acceptance rate: **36.4%**

Fall 2003 applications and acceptees

	Applied	Interviewed	Accepted	Enrolled
Total:	7,412	1,128	402	167
In-state:	40	10	5	1
Out-of-state:	7,372	1,118	397	166

Profile of admitted students

Average undergraduate grade point average: **3.55**
MCAT averages (scale: 1-15; writing test: J-T):
   Composite score: **9.5**
   Verbal reasoning score: **9.3**, Physical sciences score: **9.3**,
   Biological sciences score: **9.8**, Writing score: **P**
Proportion with undergraduate majors in: Biological sciences: **37%**, Physical sciences: **4%**, Non-sciences: **28%**, Other health professions: **3%**, Mixed disciplines and other: **26%**
Percentage of students not coming directly from college after graduation: **N/A**

Dates and details

The American Medical College Application Service (AMCAS) application is accepted.
School asks for a school-specific application as part of the admissions process.
Oldest MCAT considered for Fall 2005 entry: **2002**
Earliest application date for the 2005-2006 first-year class: **June 1, 2004**
Latest application date: **December 1, 2004**
Acceptance dates for regular application for the class entering in fall 2005:
   Earliest: **October 15, 2004**

Latest: **N/A**
The school considers requests for deferred entrance.
Starting month for the class entering in 2005-2006: **August**
The school has an Early Decision Plan (EDP).
A personal interview is required for admission.

Undergraduate coursework required

Medical school requires undergraduate work in these subjects: biology, biology/zoology, English, organic chemistry, inorganic (general) chemistry, physics.

ADMISSIONS POLICY

(TEXT PROVIDED BY SCHOOL):
As the 11th-oldest medical school in the country, the George Washington University has a rich history of being at the forefront of medical technology. The School of Medicine and Health Sciences is enriched by the diversity of its more than 600 medical students. Four of every 10 students hold undergraduate degrees in the liberal arts. In the fall 2003 entering class, 36 states were represented plus the District of Columbia, with the top five states being California, Maryland, New York, Virginia, and Pennsylvania. The entering class ranged in age from 20 to 43 years old, with an average age of 24. Females made up 56 percent of the entering class.

The initial overall evaluation is based on data contained in the American Medical College Application Service and supplemental applications. This evaluation screens applicants on the basis of academic performance; Medical College Admission Test scores; extracurricular, health-related, research, and work experiences; and evidence of nonscholastic accomplishments. Evidence of strong performance in recent, relevant coursework is to an applicant's advantage. Some additional consideration is given to applicants from the District of Columbia and its metropolitan area as well as to applicants from GWU's undergraduate schools.

The next phase of the selection procedure depends on careful examination of personal comments and letters of recommendation. The most promising applicants are then invited for a personal interview either at the school or with a regional interviewer. The last phase includes the review by the Committee on Admissions of the entire dossier. This phase is designed to select academically prepared students with motivation and personal characteristics the committee considers important in future physicians. There is no discrimination in the selection process because of race, gender, religion, age, marital status, sexual orientation, disability, or national or regional origin.

COSTS AND FINANCIAL AID

Financial aid phone number: **(202) 994-2960**
Tuition, 2003-2004 academic year: **$39,285**
Room and board: **$17,355**
Percentage of students receiving financial aid in 2003-04: **80%**
Percentage of students receiving: Loans: **80%**, Grants/scholarships: **24%**, Work-study aid: **0%**
Average medical school debt for the Class of 2002: **$127,202**

STUDENT BODY

Fall 2003 full-time enrollment: **675**
Men: **45%**, Women: **55%**, In-state: **2%**, Minorities: **36%**, American Indian: **0.9%**, Asian-American: **25.8%**, African-American: **9.2%**, Hispanic-American: **2.4%**, White: **52.6%**, International: **0.9%**, Unknown: **8.3%**

ACADEMIC PROGRAMS

The school's curriculum gives first-year students substantial contact with patients.
There are opportunities for first- or second-year students to work in community health clinics.
Program offerings: AIDS, drug/alcohol abuse, family medicine, geriatrics, internal medicine, pediatrics, women's health
Joint degrees awarded: M.D./Ph.D., M.D./M.P.H.
Total National Institutes of Health (NIH) grants awarded to the medical school and affiliated hospitals: **$38.6 million**

CURRICULUM

(TEXT PROVIDED BY SCHOOL):

The George Washington University School of Medicine and Health Sciences provides a diverse spectrum of learning opportunities. These include lectures, laboratories, small groups, problem-based-learning tutorials, and traditional clinical clerkships and electives. Most courses utilize computer-assisted instructional materials and are delivered with Web-based course management software tools. Assessment techniques include National Board of Medical Examiners subject examinations, multiple choice and essay examinations, practical examinations, and structured faculty observations. We incorporate extensive assessment of clinical skills utilizing standardized patients. Training in and evaluation of interviewing skills, technical skills, communication skills, physical diagnosis skills, and clinical decision making are completed in our state-of-the-art Clinical

Learning/Simulation Center throughout the four-year curriculum. Students must pass steps 1 and 2 of the U.S. Medical Licensing Examination in order to graduate.

The first two years include traditional disciplinary courses in the basic and clinical sciences. Year 1 is divided on a "structure-function" continuum; the second year is structured on an organ-based interdisciplinary model. A comprehensive note service is provided. This includes lecture transcripts, audiotapes, and digital streaming audio.

The Practice of Medicine (POM) course runs throughout the four years. During the first two years, it includes small-group instruction in the doctor-patient relationship (interviewing, physical diagnosis), the Clinical Apprenticeship Program (office-based practice experience one half day every other week), and problem-based-learning tutorials. In years 3 and 4, POM incorporates ongoing instruction in the doctor-patient relationship with issues in professionalism, ethics, epidemiology/medical decision making, and cultural competency. There is a required research project that spans the two years.

The third year includes six core clinical clerkships in surgery, internal medicine, primary care, psychiatry, obstetrics and gynecology, and pediatrics. Several short elective opportunities are offered.

Year 4 includes required neuroscience, emergency medicine, anesthesiology, and acting internship (medicine or pediatrics) clerkships with up to six months of elective time.

FACULTY PROFILE (FALL 2003)

Total teaching faculty: **638 (full-time)**, **1,760 (part-time)**
Of full-time faculty, those teaching in basic sciences: **15%**; in clinical programs: **85%**
Of part-time faculty, those teaching in basic sciences: **4%**; in clinical programs: **96%**
Full-time faculty/student ratio: **0.9**

SUPPORT SERVICES

The school offers students these services for dealing with stress: professional counseling.

RESIDENCY CHOICES

Most popular residency and specialty programs chosen by the 2002 and 2003 M.D. graduating classes: anesthesiology, emergency medicine, family practice, internal medicine, obstetrics and gynecology, ophthalmology, orthopedic surgery, pediatrics, radiology–diagnostic, surgery–general.

WHERE GRADS GO

41.2%			

Proportion of 2001-2003 graduates who entered primary care specialties

N/A			

Proportion of 2002-2003 graduates who accepted in-state residencies

Harvard University

- 25 Shattuck Street, Boston, MA 02115-6092
- Private
- Year Founded: 1782
- Tuition, 2003-2004: $34,776
- Enrollment, 2003-2004: 726
- Website: http://www.hms.harvard.edu
- Specialty ranking: AIDS: 3, drug/alcohol abuse: 2, geriatrics: 6, internal medicine: 2, pediatrics: 1, women's health: 1

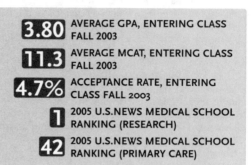

3.80 AVERAGE GPA, ENTERING CLASS FALL 2003

11.3 AVERAGE MCAT, ENTERING CLASS FALL 2003

4.7% ACCEPTANCE RATE, ENTERING CLASS FALL 2003

1 2005 U.S.NEWS MEDICAL SCHOOL RANKING (RESEARCH)

42 2005 U.S.NEWS MEDICAL SCHOOL RANKING (PRIMARY CARE)

ADMISSIONS
Admissions phone number: **(617) 432-1550**
Admissions email address:
   admissions_office@hms.harvard.edu
Application website: **N/A**
Acceptance rate: **4.7%**
In-state acceptance rate: **8.5%**
Out-of-state acceptance rate: **4.4%**
Minority acceptance rate: **4.8%**
International acceptance rate: **52%**

Fall 2003 applications and acceptees

	Applied	Interviewed	Accepted	Enrolled
Total:	5,367	722	250	165
In-state:	354	54	30	21
Out-of-state:	5,013	668	220	144

Profile of admitted students
Average undergraduate grade point average: **3.80**
MCAT averages (scale: 1-15; writing test: J-T):
   Composite score: **11.3**
   Verbal reasoning score: **10.6**, Physical sciences score: **11.8**, Biological sciences score: **11.6**, Writing score: **Q**
Percentage of students not coming directly from college after graduation: **48%**

Dates and details
The American Medical College Application Service (AMCAS) application is accepted.
School asks for a school-specific application as part of the admissions process.
Oldest MCAT considered for Fall 2005 entry: **2001**
Earliest application date for the 2005-2006 first-year class: **June 1, 2004**
Latest application date: **October 15, 2004**
Acceptance dates for regular application for the class entering in fall 2005:
   Earliest: **March 4, 2005**
   Latest: **March 4, 2005**
The school considers requests for deferred entrance.

Starting month for the class entering in 2005-2006:
   September
The school doesn't have an Early Decision Plan (EDP).
A personal interview is required for admission.

Undergraduate coursework required
Medical school requires undergraduate work in these subjects: biology, organic chemistry, inorganic (general) chemistry, physics, humanities, demonstration of writing skills, calculus.

ADMISSIONS POLICY
(TEXT PROVIDED BY SCHOOL):
The Faculty of Medicine accepts applications from current students in good standing and graduates of accredited colleges. Applicants must present evidence that their intellectual and personal credentials are of such quality as to predict success in the study and practice of medicine. Academic excellence is expected. Students are encouraged to take advanced courses, if qualified, since the Committee on Admissions takes the level of courses into account when considering academic performance.

Selection is based on a total and comparative appraisal of the candidates' suitability for medicine. Although applicants are expected to have demonstrated aptitude in the biological and physical sciences during their undergraduate years, narrow specialization in science to the exclusion of the humanities and social sciences is undesirable. A study at the Harvard Medical School has shown that students are successful in their medical studies regardless of undergraduate concentration, providing that they have had adequate science preparation. Students are urged to strive not for specialized training but for a balanced and liberal education. No preference is given to applicants who have majored in science over those who have majored in humanities.

In addition to academic records, the information considered by the Committee on Admissions includes the essay written by the student, Medical College Admission Test scores, extracurricular activities, summer occupations, and life experiences. Any experience in the health field, including research or community work, is also noted as well as the comments contained in letters of evaluation. We look for evidence of integrity, maturity, concern for others, leadership potential, and an aptitude for working with people.

Interviews are scheduled selectively, and all invitations for interview are issued by early January. The Committee on Admissions welcomes applications from qualified students representing groups that historically have had few members in the field of medicine.

COSTS AND FINANCIAL AID
Financial aid phone number: **(617) 432-1575**
Tuition, 2003-2004 academic year: **$34,776**
Room and board: **$15,374**
Percentage of students receiving financial aid in 2003-04: **79%**
Percentage of students receiving: Loans: **65%**, Grants/scholarships: **56%**, Work-study aid: **5%**
Average medical school debt for the Class of 2002: **$88,356**

STUDENT BODY
Fall 2003 full-time enrollment: **726**
Men: **49%**, Women: **51%**, In-state: **N/A**, Minorities: **49%**, American Indian: **1.9%**, Asian-American: **24.8%**, African-American: **13.4%**, Hispanic-American: **8.7%**, White: **45.0%**, International: **4.0%**, Unknown: **2.2%**

ACADEMIC PROGRAMS
The school's curriculum doesn't give first-year students substantial contact with patients.
There are opportunities for first- or second-year students to work in community health clinics.
Program offerings: AIDS, drug/alcohol abuse, family medicine, geriatrics, internal medicine, pediatrics, rural medicine, women's health
Joint degrees awarded: M.D./Ph.D., M.D./M.P.H.
Total National Institutes of Health (NIH) grants awarded to the medical school and affiliated hospitals: **$977.3 million**

CURRICULUM
(TEXT PROVIDED BY SCHOOL):
The Harvard Medical School offers two distinct curricula that are designed to accommodate the extraordinary variety of interests, educational backgrounds, and career goals that characterize the student body; to provide a general medical education for all kinds of physicians; and to serve as the foundation for later career specialization.

The New Pathway is a radical restructuring of the traditional medical school curriculum that gives students not only a core of biomedical and clinical knowledge but also provides the skills, tools, and attitudes that will enable them to become lifelong learners, to use new information, and—most important—to provide better patient care. Basic science and clinical content are interwoven throughout the four years. In the first- and second-year interdisciplinary

block courses, a problem-based approach emphasizing small-group tutorials and self-directed learning is complemented by laboratories, conferences, and lectures. Clinical skills and the patient-doctor relationship are addressed in a three-year longitudinal sequence; instruction in taking patient histories begins in the first weeks of school. The third and fourth years emphasize experiences in direct patient care through clinical clerkships conducted in hospitals and institutions.

The Health Sciences and Technology (HST) curriculum is oriented toward students with a declared interest in a biomedical research career or a strong interest and background in quantitative or molecular science. It is particularly appropriate for students who are planning interdisciplinary research careers in academic medicine. The approach is quantitative and rigorous and emphasizes modern biology, biotechnology, engineering, and physical sciences. Courses in the first two years are taught at HMS and MIT. The curriculum affords students the opportunity to take advantage of elective courses offered at Harvard's Graduate School of Arts and Sciences and MIT's Graduate School of Science and Engineering. HST students join students of New Pathway for clinical clerkships in the third and fourth years. An M.D. thesis is required for graduation.

FACULTY PROFILE (FALL 2003)
Total teaching faculty: **6,357 (full-time)**, **2,616 (part-time)**
Of full-time faculty, those teaching in basic sciences: **3%**; in clinical programs: **97%**
Of part-time faculty, those teaching in basic sciences: **2%**; in clinical programs: **98%**
Full-time faculty/student ratio: **8.8**

SUPPORT SERVICES
The school offers students these services for dealing with stress: professional counseling, religious support, support groups.

RESIDENCY CHOICES
Most popular residency and specialty programs chosen by the 2002 and 2003 M.D. graduating classes: dermatology, emergency medicine, internal medicine, obstetrics and gynecology, ophthalmology, orthopedic surgery, pediatrics, psychiatry, radiology–diagnostic, surgery–general.

WHERE GRADS GO
45.0%
Proportion of 2001-2003 graduates who entered primary care specialties

53.0%
Proportion of 2002-2003 graduates who accepted in-state residencies

ndiana University–Indianapolis

- 1120 South Drive, Indianapolis, IN 46202
- Public
- Year Founded: 1903
- Tuition, 2003-2004: In-state: $18,698; Out-of-state: $37,533
- Enrollment, 2003-2004: 1,128
- Website: http://www.medicine.iu.edu
- Specialty ranking: internal medicine: 28

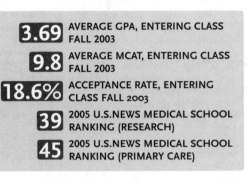

3.69 AVERAGE GPA, ENTERING CLASS FALL 2003

9.8 AVERAGE MCAT, ENTERING CLASS FALL 2003

18.6% ACCEPTANCE RATE, ENTERING CLASS FALL 2003

39 2005 U.S.NEWS MEDICAL SCHOOL RANKING (RESEARCH)

45 2005 U.S.NEWS MEDICAL SCHOOL RANKING (PRIMARY CARE)

ADMISSIONS
Admissions phone number: **(317) 274-3772**
Admissions email address: **inmedadm@iupui.edu**
Application website: **http://www.aamc.org**
Acceptance rate: **18.6%**
In-state acceptance rate: **50.9%**
Out-of-state acceptance rate: **4.9%**
Minority acceptance rate: **N/A**
International acceptance rate: **18.2%**

Fall 2003 applications and acceptees
	Applied	Interviewed	Accepted	Enrolled
Total:	2,029	873	378	280
In-state:	605	535	308	267
Out-of-state:	1,424	338	70	13

Profile of admitted students
Average undergraduate grade point average: **3.69**
MCAT averages (scale: 1-15; writing test: J-T):
  Composite score: **9.8**
  Verbal reasoning score: **9.6**, Physical sciences score: **9.9**,
  Biological sciences score: **10.0**, Writing score: **P**
Proportion with undergraduate majors in: Biological
  sciences: **49%**, Physical sciences: **23%**, Non-sciences:
  17%, Other health professions: **2%**, Mixed disciplines
  and other: **9%**
Percentage of students not coming directly from college
  after graduation: **N/A**

Dates and details
The American Medical College Application Service
  (AMCAS) application is accepted.
School does not ask for a school-specific application as part
  of the admissions process.
Oldest MCAT considered for Fall 2005 entry: **2001**
Earliest application date for the 2005-2006 first-year class:
  June 15, 2004
Latest application date: **December 15, 2004**
Acceptance dates for regular application for the class
  entering in fall 2005:
  Earliest: **October 15, 2004**

Latest: **August 20, 2005**
The school considers requests for deferred entrance.
Starting month for the class entering in 2005-2006:
  August
The school has an Early Decision Plan (EDP).
A personal interview is required for admission.

Undergraduate coursework required
Medical school requires undergraduate work in these subjects: biology, organic chemistry, inorganic (general) chemistry, physics.

ADMISSIONS POLICY
(TEXT PROVIDED BY SCHOOL):
Indiana University School of Medicine requires the following elements in undergraduate study: a minimal number of
required science courses; a significant number of courses in
the humanities and social and behavioral sciences; and
competency in written and spoken English.

It is strongly recommended that the applicant complete a
B.A. or B.S. degree in an accredited U.S. or Canadian
school. The minimum amount of college coursework
required is three academic years. The following science
coursework is required for admission: one year each of general chemistry, organic chemistry, physics, and biological
sciences. Each course must have a laboratory component.

Every grade becomes a part of the academic record and is
calculated in the cumulative grade-point average. Greater
weight is given to the quality of work than to the number of
hours completed.

Preference will be given to applicants who are Indiana
residents. Some nonresidents are accepted each year.
Nonresidents with significant ties to the state of Indiana
may be given greater consideration.

The School of Medicine participates in the American
Medical College Application Service. Applicants must
complete the Web-based application on the AMCAS site
and direct the service to forward the application to
Indiana University. IUSM participates in the early admission program.

Indiana residents with a GPA of 3.2 on a 4.0 scale and a Medical College Admission Test score of at least 22 are eligible for an interview. In general, nonresident applicants must have a GPA of at least 3.8 and superior MCAT scores. The MCAT is required of all applicants.

Students are offered places in the class on the basis of scholarship, character, personality, references, MCAT performance, and a personal interview. Indiana University School of Medicine does not discriminate on the basis of age, color, disability, ethnicity, gender, marital status, national origin, race, religion, sexual orientation, or veteran status.

COSTS AND FINANCIAL AID

Financial aid phone number: **(317) 274-1967**
Tuition, 2003-2004 academic year: **In-state: $18,698; Out-of-state: $37,533**
Room and board: **$13,405**
Percentage of students receiving financial aid in 2003-04: **89%**
Percentage of students receiving: Loans: **87%**, Grants/scholarships: **33%**, Work-study aid: **0%**
Average medical school debt for the Class of 2002: **$94,250**

STUDENT BODY

Fall 2003 full-time enrollment: **1,128**
Men: **55%**, Women: **45%**, In-state: **94%**, Minorities: **18%**, American Indian: **0.4%**, Asian-American: **9.9%**, African-American: **4.8%**, Hispanic-American: **21%**, White: **82.1%**, International: **0.7%**, Unknown: **N/A**

ACADEMIC PROGRAMS

The school's curriculum gives first-year students substantial contact with patients.
There are opportunities for first- or second-year students to work in community health clinics.
Program offerings: AIDS, drug/alcohol abuse, family medicine, geriatrics, internal medicine, pediatrics, rural medicine, women's health
Joint degrees awarded: M.D./Ph.D., M.D./M.B.A., M.D./M.P.H., M.D./M.S., M.D./M.A.
Total National Institutes of Health (NIH) grants awarded to the medical school and affiliated hospitals: **N/A**

CURRICULUM

(TEXT PROVIDED BY SCHOOL):
The IU School of Medicine was among the first schools to adopt a competency-based curriculum to help students grow to become better physicians. The curriculum provides students with excellent clinical training balanced by the development of strong interpersonal and professional skills.

Introduction to Clinical Medicine, a two-year science course, bridges the basic sciences to clinical medicine. Year 1 focuses on the doctor-patient relationship. Learning occurs in groups of eight students and two preceptors. Each group meets throughout the year, and students conduct several patient interviews. By the end of the second year, stu-

dents perform, record, and present a full patient history and physical findings, an assessment, and basic treatment plan. The internal medicine preceptor program in the second year is rated the highest preceptor experience by students, according to a 2001 poll.

In years 3 and 4, IUSM students have access to a variety of clinical settings in Indianapolis and around the state as they rotate through their electives. Fourth-year students have the unique opportunity to pursue electives for six months, a large amount of time when compared with other U.S. medical schools.

In 1999-2000, the school initiated a curriculum consisting of nine competencies: effective communications; basic clinical skills; using science to guide diagnosis, management, therapeutics, and prevention; lifelong learning; self-awareness, self-care, and personal growth; social and community contexts of healthcare; moral reasoning and ethical judgment; problem solving; and professionalism and role recognition.

The school's evaluation system includes grades of honors, high pass, pass, and fail. Students also are evaluated in the nine competency areas. Two transcripts are awarded to students upon graduation: One details grades while the other details students' progress through the competencies. To graduate, students must pass all course requirements, competency requirements, and steps 1 and 2 of the U.S. Medical Licensing Examination.

FACULTY PROFILE (FALL 2003)

Total teaching faculty: **1,229 (full-time)**, **73 (part-time)**
Of full-time faculty, those teaching in basic sciences: **22%**; in clinical programs: **78%**
Of part-time faculty, those teaching in basic sciences: **10%**; in clinical programs: **90%**
Full-time faculty/student ratio: **1.1**

SUPPORT SERVICES

The school offers students these services for dealing with stress: expanded-hour gym access, peer counseling, professional counseling, religious support, support groups.

RESIDENCY CHOICES

Most popular residency and specialty programs chosen by the 2002 and 2003 M.D. graduating classes: anesthesiology, emergency medicine, family practice, internal medicine, obstetrics and gynecology, orthopedic surgery, pediatrics, psychiatry, radiology–diagnostic, surgery–general.

WHERE GRADS GO

39.0%
Proportion of 2001-2003 graduates who entered primary care specialties

45.3%
Proportion of 2002-2003 graduates who accepted in-state residencies

Jefferson Medical College

- 1025 Walnut Street, Room 100, Philadelphia, PA 19107-5083
- Private
- Year Founded: 1824
- Tuition, 2003-2004: $34,565
- Enrollment, 2003-2004: 933
- Website: http://www.tju.edu
- Specialty ranking: N/A

3.51 AVERAGE GPA, ENTERING CLASS FALL 2003

10.7 AVERAGE MCAT, ENTERING CLASS FALL 2003

6.1% ACCEPTANCE RATE, ENTERING CLASS FALL 2003

50 2005 U.S.NEWS MEDICAL SCHOOL RANKING (RESEARCH)

57 2005 U.S.NEWS MEDICAL SCHOOL RANKING (PRIMARY CARE)

ADMISSIONS

Admissions phone number: **(215) 955-6983**
Admissions email address:
   JMC.admissions@jefferson.edu
Application website: **http://www.jefferson.edu**
Acceptance rate: **6.1%**
In-state acceptance rate: **17.9%**
Out-of-state acceptance rate: **4.4%**
Minority acceptance rate: **16.5%**
International acceptance rate: **12.8%**

Fall 2003 applications and acceptees

	Applied	Interviewed	Accepted	Enrolled
Total:	7,499	744	461	229
In-state:	960	204	172	102
Out-of-state:	6,539	540	289	127

Profile of admitted students

Average undergraduate grade point average: **3.51**
MCAT averages (scale: 1-15; writing test: J-T):
   Composite score: **10.7**
   Verbal reasoning score: **10.6**, Physical sciences score: **10.6**, Biological sciences score: **10.9**, Writing score: **Q**
Proportion with undergraduate majors in: Biological sciences: **44%**, Physical sciences: **22%**, Non-sciences: **11%**, Other health professions: **6%**, Mixed disciplines and other: **10%**
Percentage of students not coming directly from college after graduation: **40%**

Dates and details

The American Medical College Application Service (AMCAS) application is accepted.
School asks for a school-specific application as part of the admissions process.
Oldest MCAT considered for Fall 2005 entry: **2001**
Earliest application date for the 2005-2006 first-year class:
   June 1, 2004
Latest application date: **November 15, 2004**
Acceptance dates for regular application for the class entering in fall 2005:

Earliest: **October 15, 2004**
   Latest: **August 2, 2005**
The school considers requests for deferred entrance.
Starting month for the class entering in 2005-2006:
   August
The school has an Early Decision Plan (EDP).
A personal interview is required for admission.

Undergraduate coursework required

Medical school requires undergraduate work in these subjects: biology, organic chemistry, inorganic (general) chemistry, physics.

ADMISSIONS POLICY

(TEXT PROVIDED BY SCHOOL):
The medical profession is a career for those prepared for a lifetime of service to the ill regardless of diagnosis. It has as its objective the development of professional men and women prepared to adhere to the highest standards of conduct and behavior asked of few others in our society.

A strong preparation in the sciences basic to medical school studies is advised. Courses taken should be supplemented by laboratory experiences. Studies in the humanities and the social and behavioral sciences and the development of effective writing skills are strongly suggested.

The Medical College Admission Test and a baccalaureate degree from an accredited college or university in the United States or Canada are required.

The selection of students is made after careful consideration of many factors: college attended, academic record, letters of recommendation, MCAT scores, performance in nonacademic areas, and assessment by the Committee on Admissions, following a personal interview, of motivation, maturity, compassion, dedication, integrity, and commitment. Almost every applicant selected for interview has demonstrated a commitment to community service through volunteer work.

Jefferson Medical College is committed to providing equal opportunities without regard to race, color, national and ethnic origin, religion, sex, age, disability, sexual orientation, or veteran status. Preference is given to Pennsylvania residents. Special consideration may also be given to offspring of faculty and alumni, to applicants whose background is underrepresented in medicine, and to applicants in JMC's cooperative programs with a number of colleges and universities in Pennsylvania. Each year, as the official medical school of Delaware, JMC provides for up to 20 places for Delaware residents in Jefferson's first-year class. The Physician Shortage Area Program admits students from rural areas and small towns who are committed to practicing family medicine in these areas.

COSTS AND FINANCIAL AID
Financial aid phone number: (215) 955-2867
Tuition, 2003-2004 academic year: $34,565
Room and board: $12,520
Percentage of students receiving financial aid in 2003-04: 84%
Percentage of students receiving: Loans: 79%, Grants/scholarships: 46%, Work-study aid: 7%
Average medical school debt for the Class of 2002: $113,812

STUDENT BODY
Fall 2003 full-time enrollment: 933
Men: 53%, Women: 47%, In-state: 47%, Minorities: 24%, American Indian: 0.8%, Asian-American: 19.9%, African-American: 1.9%, Hispanic-American: 1.8%, White: 72.5%, International: 2.1%, Unknown: 1.0%

ACADEMIC PROGRAMS
The school's curriculum gives first-year students substantial contact with patients.
There are opportunities for first- or second-year students to work in community health clinics.
Program offerings: AIDS, drug/alcohol abuse, family medicine, geriatrics, internal medicine, pediatrics, rural medicine, women's health
Joint degrees awarded: M.D./Ph.D., M.D./M.B.A., M.D./M.P.H., M.D./M.H.A.
Total National Institutes of Health (NIH) grants awarded to the medical school and affiliated hospitals: $81.4 million

CURRICULUM
(TEXT PROVIDED BY SCHOOL):
Jefferson Medical College seeks to provide its students with learning opportunities that will enable them to acquire fundamental knowledge and skills in the basic and clinical sciences as well as develop professional behaviors.

JMC is committed to helping its students understand the tentative nature of scientific conclusions and to encouraging students to assume responsibility for their own education. Recognizing that our students have multiple backgrounds and goals, and will pursue varied careers, educational opportunities at Jefferson incorporate sufficient flexibility to address this diversity.

Two years of preclinical instruction are provided in areas of basic science followed by two years of clinical instruction. However, there is considerable integration across the four years. For example, the preclinical curriculum includes

patient contact in the first year, and the clinical curriculum includes basic science reinforcement in the last year.

During the first year, Jefferson students focus on the function of the human organism in its physical and psychosocial context. Coursework provides first-year students with a strong basic science grounding. Clinical coursework focuses on the doctor-patient relationship, medical interviewing and history taking, the human developmental trajectory, behavioral science principles, and core clinical skills and reasoning.

In addition to increasing emphasis on clinical skills, the curriculum shifts in the second year to the study of pathophysiology and disease. After an introductory block of general pathology and general pharmacology, the subjects of immunology, microbiology, and systems-based pharmacology, pathology, and clinical medicine are presented as an interdisciplinary curriculum. The curriculum includes small-group sessions.

The clinical curriculum consists of 84 weeks, including six-week core rotations in family practice, obstetrics and gynecology, pediatrics, psychiatry, and general surgery, as well as 12 weeks of internal medicine in the third year. The fourth year includes 16 weeks of elective time and required rotations in the surgical subspecialties, neurology/rehabilitation medicine, outpatient and inpatient subinternships, and courses in advanced basic science and emergency medicine/advanced clinical skills.

FACULTY PROFILE (FALL 2003)
Total teaching faculty: 2,192 (full-time), 958 (part-time)
Of full-time faculty, those teaching in basic sciences: 10%; in clinical programs: 90%
Of part-time faculty, those teaching in basic sciences: 8%; in clinical programs: 92%
Full-time faculty/student ratio: 2.3

SUPPORT SERVICES
The school offers students these services for dealing with stress: expanded-hour gym access, peer counseling, professional counseling, religious support, support groups.

RESIDENCY CHOICES
Most popular residency and specialty programs chosen by the 2002 and 2003 M.D. graduating classes: anesthesiology, dermatology, emergency medicine, family practice, internal medicine, orthopedic surgery, pediatrics, radiology–diagnostic, surgery–general.

WHERE GRADS GO
| 40.3% |
Proportion of 2001-2003 graduates who entered primary care specialties

| 37.5% |
Proportion of 2002-2003 graduates who accepted in-state residencies

Johns Hopkins University

- 733 N Broadway, Baltimore, MD 21205
- Private
- Year Founded: 1893
- Tuition, 2003-2004: $33,465
- Enrollment, 2003-2004: 476
- Website: http://www.hopkinsmedicine.org
- Specialty ranking: AIDS: 2, drug/alcohol abuse: 1, geriatrics: 1, internal medicine: 1, pediatrics: 2, women's health: 4

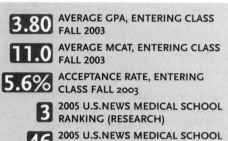

3.80 AVERAGE GPA, ENTERING CLASS FALL 2003

11.0 AVERAGE MCAT, ENTERING CLASS FALL 2003

5.6% ACCEPTANCE RATE, ENTERING CLASS FALL 2003

3 2005 U.S.NEWS MEDICAL SCHOOL RANKING (RESEARCH)

46 2005 U.S.NEWS MEDICAL SCHOOL RANKING (PRIMARY CARE)

ADMISSIONS

Admissions phone number: **(410) 955-3182**
Admissions email address: **somadmiss@jhmi.edu**
Application website:
   http://www.hopkinsmedicine.org/admissions
Acceptance rate: **5.6%**
In-state acceptance rate: **7.7%**
Out-of-state acceptance rate: **5.4%**
Minority acceptance rate: **3.7%**
International acceptance rate: **5.4%**

Fall 2003 applications and acceptees

	Applied	Interviewed	Accepted	Enrolled
Total:	4,265	658	237	119
In-state:	313	63	24	18
Out-of-state:	3,952	595	213	101

Profile of admitted students

Average undergraduate grade point average: **3.80**
MCAT averages (scale: 1-15; writing test: J-T):
   Composite score: **11.0**
   Verbal reasoning score: **11.0**, Physical sciences score:
   12.0, Biological sciences score: **11.0**, Writing score: **Q**
Proportion with undergraduate majors in: Biological
   sciences: **52%**, Physical sciences: **21%**, Non-sciences:
   19%, Other health professions: **2%**, Mixed disciplines
   and other: **6%**
Percentage of students not coming directly from college
   after graduation: **45%**

Dates and details

The American Medical College Application Service
   (AMCAS) application is accepted.
School asks for a school-specific application as part of the
   admissions process.
Oldest MCAT considered for Fall 2005 entry: **2000**
Earliest application date for the 2005-2006 first-year class:
   June 1, 2004
Latest application date: **October 15, 2004**
Acceptance dates for regular application for the class
   entering in fall 2005:

Earliest: **October 15, 2004**
Latest: **April 30, 2005**
The school considers requests for deferred entrance.
Starting month for the class entering in 2005-2006:
   September
The school has an Early Decision Plan (EDP).
A personal interview is required for admission.

Undergraduate coursework required

Medical school requires undergraduate work in these subjects: biology, organic chemistry, inorganic (general) chemistry, physics, humanities, behavioral science, calculus.

ADMISSIONS POLICY

(TEXT PROVIDED BY SCHOOL):

All applicants must be or have previously been in attendance at a fully accredited institution in the country where
the academic work was completed. Prospective applicants
who have exclusively studied outside the United States, in
most cases, must have their academic coursework supplemented by a year or more of coursework in an accredited
U.S. university.

The applicant must arrange for an official transcript to be
sent to Johns Hopkins from each college or university
attended outside the United States. The committee requires
that all of the coursework submitted in fulfillment of admission requirements must be evaluated on the basis of a traditional grading system. Grades of Pass or Credit will be
considered acceptable for only a limited number of courses.

Applicants for admission must fulfill the following seven
prerequisites:

Mathematics: one year of calculus or statistics. Advanced
Placement credit for calculus, acceptable to the student's
undergraduate college, may be used in fulfillment of the
Hopkins math requirement.

General chemistry: one year with lab. Applicants with
acceptable Advanced Placement credit for general chemistry
must take one additional semester of advanced college
chemistry with lab.

Organic chemistry: one year with lab. A semester of bio-chemistry with lab may be substituted for the second semester of organic chemistry.

Biology: one year with lab. Advanced Placement credit may not be used to satisfy the biology requirement.

Physics: one year of general physics with lab. Advanced Placement credit for physics, acceptable to the student's undergraduate college, may be used in fulfillment of the Hopkins physics requirement.

Humanities, social, and behavioral sciences: Applicants are required to complete at least 24 semester hours in these disciplines. The TOEFL exam for foreign applicants is not needed to apply to the School of Medicine. However, the applicant must be proficient in spoken and written English.

Each applicant must have received the bachelor's (B.A. or B.S.) degree prior to matriculation.

COSTS AND FINANCIAL AID

Financial aid phone number: (410) 955-1324
Tuition, 2003-2004 academic year: $33,465
Room and board: $8,386
Percentage of students receiving financial aid in 2003-04: 74%
Percentage of students receiving: Loans: 85%,
  Grants/scholarships: 75%, Work-study aid: 24%
Average medical school debt for the Class of 2002:
  $80,136

STUDENT BODY

Fall 2003 full-time enrollment: 476
Men: 51%, Women: 49%, In-state: 24%, Minorities: 39%,
  American Indian: 0.4%, Asian-American: 25.0%,
  African-American: 10.9%, Hispanic-American: 2.7%,
  White: 58.8%, International: 2.1%, Unknown: 0.0%

ACADEMIC PROGRAMS

The school's curriculum gives first-year students
  substantial contact with patients.
There are opportunities for first- or second-year students to
  work in community health clinics.
Program offerings: AIDS, drug/alcohol abuse, family
  medicine, geriatrics, internal medicine, pediatrics
Joint degrees awarded: M.D./Ph.D.
Total National Institutes of Health (NIH) grants awarded to
  the medical school and affiliated hospitals: $411.7 million

CURRICULUM

(TEXT PROVIDED BY SCHOOL):
The regular M.D. curriculum comprises four academic years. The academic requirements of this program can be combined with graduate study leading to a master's or Ph.D. degree. The course of instruction is based on a core of required basic sciences and clinical courses, supplemented with ample elective time for special advanced study.

The first year primarily centers on normal human structure and function. Required courses include Molecules and Cells, Anatomy (including developmental biology), Neuroscience and Introduction to Behavioral Science, and

Clinical Epidemiology and Organ Systems. The year also begins a four-year course, The Physician and Society, involving ethics, history of medicine, cultural arts, the physician-patient relationship, and the role of physicians in prevention and research. In the Introduction to Medicine course, students spend time working with a community-based, private-practice physician.

Second-year students study the causes and effects of diseases in Pathology and Human Pathophysiology. They also learn about the action of drugs in Pharmacology. Students are introduced to the elements of history taking, physical examination, and clinical medicine.

Beginning in the final quarter of the second year, each student follows an educational program adapted to his or her particular interests and needs. Clinical clerkships are devoted to the study of health and disease. The student is introduced to practical clinical problems through instruction conducted largely in small groups; correlative study involving two or more clinical fields is common. Elective courses available in every department range from direct participation in current biomedical research to advanced clinical work. Students may elect, within certain limits, the order in which they pursue the required instruction.

The total number of students in each class of the regular four-year program is limited to 120. Admissions with advanced standings to the second or third years are restricted.

FACULTY PROFILE (FALL 2003)

Total teaching faculty: 2,057 (full-time), 1,173 (part-time)
Of full-time faculty, those teaching in basic sciences: 10%;
  in clinical programs: 90%
Of part-time faculty, those teaching in basic sciences: 3%;
  in clinical programs: 97%
Full-time faculty/student ratio: 4.3

SUPPORT SERVICES

The school offers students these services for dealing with stress: expanded-hour gym access, peer counseling, professional counseling, support groups.

RESIDENCY CHOICES

Most popular residency and specialty programs chosen by the 2002 and 2003 M.D. graduating classes: anesthesiology, emergency medicine, internal medicine, ophthalmology, orthopedic surgery, otolaryngology, pediatrics, psychiatry, radiology–diagnostic, surgery–general.

WHERE GRADS GO

42.0%			

Proportion of 2001-2003 graduates who entered primary care specialties

26.5%			

Proportion of 2002-2003 graduates who accepted in-state residencies

ola University Chicago

STRITCH

- 2160 S. First Avenue, Building 120, Maywood, IL 60153
- Private
- Year Founded: 1915
- Tuition, 2003-2004: $33,500
- Enrollment, 2003-2004: 539
- Website: http://www.meddean.lumc.edu
- Specialty ranking: N/A

3.62 AVERAGE GPA, ENTERING CLASS FALL 2003

9.8 AVERAGE MCAT, ENTERING CLASS FALL 2003

9.7% ACCEPTANCE RATE, ENTERING CLASS FALL 2003

Unranked 2005 U.S.NEWS MEDICAL SCHOOL RANKING (RESEARCH)

Unranked 2005 U.S.NEWS MEDICAL SCHOOL RANKING (PRIMARY CARE)

ADMISSIONS

Admissions phone number: (708) 216-3229
Admissions email address: N/A
Application website: N/A
Acceptance rate: 9.7%
In-state acceptance rate: 16.7%
Out-of-state acceptance rate: 7.9%
Minority acceptance rate: 5.9%
International acceptance rate: N/A

Fall 2003 applications and acceptees

	Applied	Interviewed	Accepted	Enrolled
Total:	3,547	619	343	140
In-state:	705	204	118	59
Out-of-state:	2,842	415	225	81

Profile of admitted students

Average undergraduate grade point average: 3.62
MCAT averages (scale: 1-15; writing test: J-T):
  Composite score: 9.8
  Verbal reasoning score: 9.6, Physical sciences score: 9.7,
  Biological sciences score: 10.0, Writing score: P
Proportion with undergraduate majors in: Biological
  sciences: 46%, Physical sciences: 13%, Non-sciences:
  14%, Other health professions: 1%, Mixed disciplines
  and other: 26%
Percentage of students not coming directly from college
  after graduation: 38%

Dates and details

The American Medical College Application Service
  (AMCAS) application is accepted.
School asks for a school-specific application as part of the
  admissions process.
Oldest MCAT considered for Fall 2005 entry: 2001
Earliest application date for the 2005-2006 first-year class:
  June 1, 2004
Latest application date: November 15, 2004
Acceptance dates for regular application for the class
  entering in fall 2005:
  Earliest: October 15, 2004

Latest: N/A
The school considers requests for deferred entrance.
Starting month for the class entering in 2005-2006: July
The school doesn't have an Early Decision Plan (EDP).
A personal interview is required for admission.

Undergraduate coursework required

Medical school requires undergraduate work in these subjects: biology/zoology, organic chemistry, inorganic (general) chemistry, physics.

ADMISSIONS POLICY
(TEXT PROVIDED BY SCHOOL):

Premedical students interested in applying for admission to
Loyola's Stritch School of Medicine must apply through the
American Medical College Application Service no later than
November 15 of the year preceding desired entrance into
medical school. After screening, some applicants are invited
to complete a Stritch supplemental application, which
includes short-answer and essay questions that allow students to comment on their personal experiences and
insights. Completed applicant files also include letters of
recommendation and a $60 application fee, unless it is
waived.

  Applicants who present academic credentials that indicate they are capable of succeeding in the rigors of a medical education will be evaluated for evidence of the personal
qualifications they can bring to the medical profession.
Essential characteristics include an interest in lifelong learning, integrity, compassion, and the ability to assume responsibility. Of particular concern will be an applicant's
exploration of the field of medicine, the nature of the motivation to enter this career, and the degree of involvement in
extracurricular activities.

  Each year approximately 600 applicants are invited to
interview with members of the Committee on Admissions
at Loyola's medical center campus. Generally, applicants are
notified of their status within one month of the interview
date. Once the class has been filled, most interviewed candidates are placed on an alternate list and considered for
acceptance as positions in the class become available.

Applicants must earn a bachelor's degree prior to matriculation into the medical school. Any course of study is acceptable. Coursework in molecular biology and genetics is strongly recommended, and an introduction to statistics is helpful.

Applicants must submit scores from the Medical College Admission Test. The MCAT should be taken in the spring of the year in which application is made to Loyola and should be repeated if one's scores are not near the national averages.

COSTS AND FINANCIAL AID
Financial aid phone number: **(708) 216-3227**
Tuition, 2003-2004 academic year: **$33,500**
Room and board: **$17,250**
Percentage of students receiving financial aid in 2003-04: **92%**
Percentage of students receiving: Loans: **86%**, Grants/scholarships: **53%**, Work-study aid: **0%**
Average medical school debt for the Class of 2002: **$129,840**

STUDENT BODY
Fall 2003 full-time enrollment: **539**
Men: **52%**, Women: **48%**, In-state: **49%**, Minorities: **17%**, American Indian: **0.2%**, Asian-American: **12.2%**, African-American: **2.2%**, Hispanic-American: **1.9%**, White: **82.9%**, International: **0.0%**, Unknown: **0.6%**

ACADEMIC PROGRAMS
The school's curriculum gives first-year students substantial contact with patients.
There are opportunities for first- or second-year students to work in community health clinics.
Program offerings: AIDS, drug/alcohol abuse, family medicine, geriatrics, internal medicine, pediatrics, women's health
Joint degrees awarded: **N/A**
Total National Institutes of Health (NIH) grants awarded to the medical school and affiliated hospitals: **N/A**

CURRICULUM
(TEXT PROVIDED BY SCHOOL):
Stritch School of Medicine is a Catholic and Jesuit institution where individuals from a variety of backgrounds and traditions come together and learn the demanding art and science of medicine. Stritch emphasizes personal growth, excellence in academics and character, strong personal work ethic, openness to the spiritual dimensions of life, and a clear intent of developing women and men who will serve others. We encourage individual achievement and have high standards to bring out the best in all our students, but we also prize teamwork, good communication, and development of an atmosphere where students are good friends, help one another, and work cooperatively. We foster a strong

ethical framework that emphasizes respect for human life and dignity and considers medicine a profession dedicated to the service of others. We welcome students with strong backgrounds in academics, service work, and a variety of life experiences who are open to personal reflection, willing to learn about dimensions of caring that go beyond the physical, and show respect for those of differing cultures, backgrounds, faiths, and experiences.

Years 1 and 2 provide a combination of instruction in the basic sciences and in developing skills in communicating with patients, taking a history, and performing a physical examination. All courses feature a combination of lecture and small-group experiences. Some have required laboratory sessions. Practical experience is provided by the Introduction to the Practice of Medicine course.

During the third and fourth years, students participate in required and elective clerkships. Third-year required clerkships include internal medicine, surgery, family medicine, obstetrics/gynecology, pediatrics, and psychiatry. Clerkships combine inpatient experience with extensive time in the ambulatory setting, using one of the private office settings available to students and taking advantage of the Loyola University Hospital, the adjoining Hines Veterans Affairs Hospital, and community hospitals.

FACULTY PROFILE (FALL 2003)
Total teaching faculty: **638 (full-time), 699 (part-time)**
Of full-time faculty, those teaching in basic sciences: **10%**; in clinical programs: **90%**
Of part-time faculty, those teaching in basic sciences: **2%**; in clinical programs: **98%**
Full-time faculty/student ratio: **1.2**

SUPPORT SERVICES
The school offers students these services for dealing with stress: peer counseling, professional counseling, religious support, support groups.

RESIDENCY CHOICES
Most popular residency and specialty programs chosen by the 2002 and 2003 M.D. graduating classes: anesthesiology, emergency medicine, family practice, internal medicine, obstetrics and gynecology, pediatrics, internal medicine/pediatrics.

WHERE GRADS GO
52.0%
Proportion of 2001-2003 graduates who entered primary care specialties

43.5%
Proportion of 2002-2003 graduates who accepted in-state residencies

Mayo Medical School

- 200 First Street SW, Rochester, MN 55905
- Private
- Year Founded: 1972
- Tuition, 2003-2004: $11,250
- Enrollment, 2003-2004: 170
- Website: http://www.mayo.edu/mms
- Specialty ranking: internal medicine: 14

3.78 AVERAGE GPA, ENTERING CLASS FALL 2003

10.5 AVERAGE MCAT, ENTERING CLASS FALL 2003

2.7% ACCEPTANCE RATE, ENTERING CLASS FALL 2003

22 2005 U.S.NEWS MEDICAL SCHOOL RANKING (RESEARCH)

52 2005 U.S.NEWS MEDICAL SCHOOL RANKING (PRIMARY CARE)

ADMISSIONS

Admissions phone number: (507) 284-3671
Admissions email address:
medschooladmissions@mayo.edu
Application website: **http://www.aamc.org**
Acceptance rate: 2.7%
In-state acceptance rate: 4.9%
Out-of-state acceptance rate: 2.4%
Minority acceptance rate: 3.4%
International acceptance rate: N/A

Fall 2003 applications and acceptees

	Applied	Interviewed	Accepted	Enrolled
Total:	2,417	314	65	44
In-state:	283	44	14	11
Out-of-state:	2,134	270	51	33

Profile of admitted students

Average undergraduate grade point average: 3.78
MCAT averages (scale: 1-15; writing test: J-T):
 Composite score: 10.5
 Verbal reasoning score: 9.9, Physical sciences score:
 10.4, Biological sciences score: 11.1, Writing score: Q
Proportion with undergraduate majors in: Biological
 sciences: 18%, Physical sciences: 7%, Non-sciences: 7%,
 Other health professions: 5%, Mixed disciplines and
 other: 63%
Percentage of students not coming directly from college
 after graduation: N/A

Dates and details

The American Medical College Application Service
 (AMCAS) application is accepted.
School does not ask for a school-specific application as part
 of the admissions process.
Oldest MCAT considered for Fall 2005 entry: 2002
Earliest application date for the 2005-2006 first-year class:
 July 1, 2004
Latest application date: November 1, 2004
Acceptance dates for regular application for the class
 entering in fall 2005:

 Earliest: October 15, 2005
 Latest: May 15, 2005
The school considers requests for deferred entrance.
Starting month for the class entering in 2005-2006: July
The school has an Early Decision Plan (EDP).
A personal interview is required for admission.

Undergraduate coursework required

Medical school requires undergraduate work in these subjects: biology, organic chemistry, inorganic (general) chemistry, physics, biochemistry.

ADMISSIONS POLICY
(TEXT PROVIDED BY SCHOOL):

Mayo Medical School enrolls students with superior academic credentials, leadership characteristics, and a sincere
desire to commit their lives to service. Recognizing the
strength of diversity, we encourage individuals with diverse
backgrounds to apply. Equal opportunity and access are
embraced throughout the admissions process.

Once an applicant has completed the standardized telephone and on-campus interviews, his or her application is
presented to the Admissions Committee for discussion and
deliberation. The Admissions Committee meets weekly
from October through March. A periodic review of all
ranked candidates will occur every four to six weeks, at
which time several appointment offers are made.

Those applicants not receiving appointments during this
review will receive notification of their "hold status." During
each subsequent periodic review, however, all previously
reviewed applicants remain eligible to receive appointment
offers. This periodic and rolling admissions process allows
for all applicants to remain active for admissions consideration, irrespective of their interview dates.

U.S. citizenship or permanent resident status is required
for admission. All M.D. program applicants must obtain a
baccalaureate degree from an accredited institution of
higher education in the United States or Canada prior to
matriculation. No major field is preferred. Mayo Medical
School does not routinely accept transfer students.

The following courses are required: one year of biology and/or zoology; one year of inorganic chemistry (with lab); one year of organic chemistry (with lab); one year of physics (with lab); and one course in biochemistry.

Applicants must complete the Medical College Admission Test. Only MCAT scores reported within three years of the application year are considered in admission decisions.

COSTS AND FINANCIAL AID

Financial aid phone number: **(507) 284-4839**
Tuition, 2003-2004 academic year: **$11,250**
Room and board: **$11,264**
Percentage of students receiving financial aid in 2003-04: **100%**
Percentage of students receiving: Loans: **74%**, Grants/scholarships: **100%**, Work-study aid: **N/A**
Average medical school debt for the Class of 2002: **$69,184**

STUDENT BODY

Fall 2003 full-time enrollment: **170**
Men: **50%**, Women: **50%**, In-state: **27%**, Minorities: **23%**

ACADEMIC PROGRAMS

The school's curriculum gives first-year students substantial contact with patients.
There are opportunities for first- or second-year students to work in community health clinics.
Program offerings: AIDS, drug/alcohol abuse, family medicine, geriatrics, internal medicine, pediatrics, rural medicine, women's health
Joint degrees awarded: M.D./Ph.D., M.D./M.P.H., M.D./M.S.
Total National Institutes of Health (NIH) grants awarded to the medical school and affiliated hospitals: **$129.5 million**

CURRICULUM

(TEXT PROVIDED BY SCHOOL):
Mayo's innovative, patient-based curriculum is characterized by two prominent features: extensive patient interaction starting in the first year and integration of the basic sciences into all segments of the curriculum.

Mayo Medical School annually enrolls 42 students in three related medical degree programs: M.D. program, enrolling 34 students per year; M.D./Ph.D. program, enrolling six students per year; and M.D./O.M.S. program, enrolling two students per year.

Patient contact begins early in the first year and increases commensurate with student progress. The integration of basic and clinical sciences occurs in a manner that strengthens basic science concepts; stresses the patient orientation appropriate for an undergraduate medical school; and uses a variety of active, problem-oriented, faculty-guided, and self-learning techniques to aid student comprehension.

Curriculum integration is promoted by the organization of course material into broad functional units that span several curricular years. The curricular units are: The Organ; The Patient, Physician, and Society; The Scientific Foundations of Medical Practice; Clinical Experiences; and The Research Semester.

This curricular organization promotes content integration of the basic and clinical sciences and between basic and clinical science.

FACULTY PROFILE (FALL 2003)

Total teaching faculty: **2,027 (full-time)**, **N/A (part-time)**
Of full-time faculty, those teaching in basic sciences: **9%**; in clinical programs: **91%**
Of part-time faculty, those teaching in basic sciences: **N/A**; in clinical programs: **N/A**
Full-time faculty/student ratio: **11.9**

SUPPORT SERVICES

The school offers students these services for dealing with stress: peer counseling, professional counseling, religious support, support groups.

RESIDENCY CHOICES

Most popular residency and specialty programs chosen by the 2002 and 2003 M.D. graduating classes: anesthesiology, dermatology, emergency medicine, family practice, internal medicine, obstetrics and gynecology, pediatrics, radiology–diagnostic, surgery–general.

WHERE GRADS GO

34.0%
Proportion of 2001-2003 graduates who entered primary care specialties

34.0%
Proportion of 2002-2003 graduates who accepted in-state residencies

Medical College of Georgia

- 1120 15th Street, Augusta, GA 30912
- Public
- Year Founded: 1828
- Tuition, 2003-2004: In-state: $10,358; Out-of-state: $30,562
- Enrollment, 2003-2004: 717
- Website: http://www.mcg.edu/som/index.html
- Specialty ranking: N/A

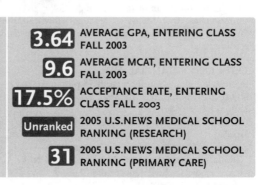

3.64 AVERAGE GPA, ENTERING CLASS FALL 2003

9.6 AVERAGE MCAT, ENTERING CLASS FALL 2003

17.5% ACCEPTANCE RATE, ENTERING CLASS FALL 2003

Unranked 2005 U.S.NEWS MEDICAL SCHOOL RANKING (RESEARCH)

31 2005 U.S.NEWS MEDICAL SCHOOL RANKING (PRIMARY CARE)

ADMISSIONS

Admissions phone number: **(706) 721-3186**
Admissions email address: **stdadmin@mail.mcg.edu**
Application website: **N/A**
Acceptance rate: **17.5%**
In-state acceptance rate: **30.1%**
Out-of-state acceptance rate: **0.8%**
Minority acceptance rate: **6.8%**
International acceptance rate: **N/A**

Fall 2003 applications and acceptees

	Applied	Interviewed	Accepted	Enrolled
Total:	1,448	473	253	180
In-state:	825	453	248	177
Out-of-state:	623	20	5	3

Profile of admitted students

Average undergraduate grade point average: **3.64**
MCAT averages (scale: 1-15; writing test: J-T):
　Composite score: **9.6**
　Verbal reasoning score: **9.5**, Physical sciences score: **9.4**,
　Biological sciences score: **10.0**, Writing score: **N/A**
Proportion with undergraduate majors in: Biological
　sciences: **57%**, Physical sciences: **18%**, Non-sciences:
　9%, Other health professions: **5%**, Mixed disciplines and
　other: **11%**
Percentage of students not coming directly from college
　after graduation: **N/A**

Dates and details

The American Medical College Application Service
　(AMCAS) application is accepted.
School asks for a school-specific application as part of the
　admissions process.
Oldest MCAT considered for Fall 2005 entry: **2002**
Earliest application date for the 2005-2006 first-year class:
　June 1, 2004
Latest application date: **November 1, 2004**
Acceptance dates for regular application for the class
　entering in fall 2005:
　Earliest: **October 15, 2004**

Latest: **N/A**
The school considers requests for deferred entrance.
Starting month for the class entering in 2005-2006:
　August
The school has an Early Decision Plan (EDP).
A personal interview is required for admission.

Undergraduate coursework required

Medical school requires undergraduate work in these subjects: biology/zoology, English, organic chemistry, inorganic
(general) chemistry, physics, molecular and cell biology.

ADMISSIONS POLICY
(TEXT PROVIDED BY SCHOOL):

The Admissions Committee strives to identify and accept
applicants who will help meet the healthcare needs of a
widely dispersed and highly diverse population in Georgia.
We seek applicants with academic ability, personal attributes, and interests that are consistent with our institution's
mission and that produce quality physicians. The
Admissions Committee expects applicants to have experience shadowing physicians and volunteering in a clinical
setting.

Information used for assessing an individual's academic
accomplishments, personal attributes, and interests
includes but is not limited to the applicant's: responsibilities prior to application to medical school; involvement in
extracurricular and community activities; ethnic, socioeconomic, and cultural background; region of residence with
respect to its health professional needs; commitment to
practice in underserved areas of Georgia; letters of recommendation by the premedical adviser and two personal references; motivation and potential for serving as a physician;
personal interviews; performance on the Medical College
Admission Test; and college grades, including undergraduate, graduate, and postbaccalaureate. Preference is given to
residents of Georgia. No more than 5 percent of the entering class each year can be nonresidents of the state of
Georgia.

COSTS AND FINANCIAL AID

Financial aid phone number: **(706) 721-4901**

Tuition, 2003-2004 academic year: **In-state: $10,358; Out-of-state: $30,562**

Room and board: **$13,725**

Percentage of students receiving financial aid in 2003-04: **87%**

Percentage of students receiving: Loans: **78%**, Grants/scholarships: **38%**, Work-study aid: **11%**

Average medical school debt for the Class of 2002: **$63,017**

STUDENT BODY

Fall 2003 full-time enrollment: **717**

Men: **59%**, Women: **41%**, In-state: **99%**, Minorities: **26%**, American Indian: **0.4%**, Asian-American: **14.1%**, African-American: **8.6%**, Hispanic-American: **1.3%**, White: **73.9%**, International: **0.0%**, Unknown: **1.7%**

ACADEMIC PROGRAMS

The school's curriculum gives first-year students substantial contact with patients.

There are opportunities for first- or second-year students to work in community health clinics.

Program offerings: AIDS, drug/alcohol abuse, family medicine, geriatrics, internal medicine, pediatrics, rural medicine, women's health

Joint degrees awarded: M.D./Ph.D.

Total National Institutes of Health (NIH) grants awarded to the medical school and affiliated hospitals: **$36.9 million**

CURRICULUM

(TEXT PROVIDED BY SCHOOL):

During the two preclinical years, students acquire the building blocks of basic science that underlie medical practice and the skills required for clinical decision making and patient interaction. The modular content of the curriculum is taught in lectures, labs with integrated clinical conferences, and small-group activities.

In the first semester of Year 1, the introductory Molecular Cell Biology module provides a foundation for the basic sciences. It is followed by the Cellular and Systems Structures module, which introduces students to gross anatomy, histology, and development. In the second semester, biochemistry and physiology are taught in the Cellular and Systems Processes module while the Brain and Behavior module gives students an understanding of the interplay between psychiatry and neuroscience. The yearlong Essentials of Clinical Medicine emphasizes family, cultural, and population aspects of healthcare; communication skills and information retrieval and analysis; health promotion/disease prevention; ethics; history taking with children and adults; and a community project. The ECM is a two-year sequence that emphasizes skills needed for success in the third year. In Year 2, ECM addresses interviewing and physical exam, common medical problems, and interdisciplinary topics such as ethics, nutrition, and the impact of behavior on

health while highlighting principles of patient care for each stage of life. Cellular and Systems Disease States is a yearlong module running in parallel that exposes students to medical microbiology, pathology, and pharmacology. Grading is A through F, with a C constituting a passing grade. Passing the U.S. Medical Licensing Examination Step 1 is a requirement for promotion to Year 3.

Year 3 consists of required core clerkships in internal medicine (12 weeks), pediatrics (six weeks), family medicine (six weeks), obstetrics/gynecology (six weeks), surgery (eight weeks), psychiatry (six weeks), and neurology (four weeks). Core clerkships take place at the Medical College of Georgia Hospitals and Clinics, the Children's Medical Center, and other sites throughout Georgia. Students may rotate to affiliated community hospitals for part of the core curriculum.

During Year 4, students must complete four-week rotations in emergency medicine and critical care, and an acting internship in medicine, family medicine, pediatrics, surgery, and obstetrics/gynecology. The remainder of Year 4 is for elective study, which can include both clinical and research courses. Evaluation during the clinical years is based on assessment of knowledge, clinical skills, and professional behavior, using an A-to-F scale. Passing the USMLE Step 2 is a requirement for graduation.

FACULTY PROFILE (FALL 2003)

Total teaching faculty: **502 (full-time), 64 (part-time)**

Of full-time faculty, those teaching in basic sciences: **14%**; in clinical programs: **86%**

Of part-time faculty, those teaching in basic sciences: **6%**; in clinical programs: **94%**

Full-time faculty/student ratio: **0.7**

SUPPORT SERVICES

The school offers students these services for dealing with stress: peer counseling, professional counseling, religious support, support groups.

RESIDENCY CHOICES

Most popular residency and specialty programs chosen by the 2002 and 2003 M.D. graduating classes: anesthesiology, emergency medicine, family practice, internal medicine, obstetrics and gynecology, orthopedic surgery, otolaryngology, pediatrics, psychiatry, surgery–general.

WHERE GRADS GO

57.0%

Proportion of 2001-2003 graduates who entered primary care specialties

27.0%

Proportion of 2002-2003 graduates who accepted in-state residencies

edical College of Ohio

- 3000 Arlington Avenue, Toledo, OH 43614
- Public
- Year Founded: 1969
- Tuition, 2003-2004: In-state: $21,089; Out-of-state: $40,789
- Enrollment, 2003-2004: 593
- Website: http://www.mco.edu
- Specialty ranking: N/A

3.61 AVERAGE GPA, ENTERING CLASS FALL 2003

9.5 AVERAGE MCAT, ENTERING CLASS FALL 2003

13.0% ACCEPTANCE RATE, ENTERING CLASS FALL 2003

Unranked 2005 U.S.NEWS MEDICAL SCHOOL RANKING (RESEARCH)

Unranked 2005 U.S.NEWS MEDICAL SCHOOL RANKING (PRIMARY CARE)

ADMISSIONS

Admissions phone number: **(419) 383-4229**
Admissions email address: **admissions@mco.edu**
Application website: **N/A**
Acceptance rate: **13.0%**
In-state acceptance rate: **26.7%**
Out-of-state acceptance rate: **5.4%**
Minority acceptance rate: **N/A**
International acceptance rate: **13.9%**

Fall 2003 applications and acceptees

	Applied	Interviewed	Accepted	Enrolled
Total:	2,441	437	318	156
In-state:	873	273	233	117
Out-of-state:	1,568	164	85	39

Profile of admitted students

Average undergraduate grade point average: **3.61**
MCAT averages (scale: 1-15; writing test: J-T):
   Composite score: **9.5**
   Verbal reasoning score: **9.0**, Physical sciences score: **9.6**,
   Biological sciences score: **9.8**, Writing score: **N/A**
Proportion with undergraduate majors in: Biological
   sciences: **49%**, Physical sciences: **21%**, Non-sciences:
   21%, Other health professions: **8%**, Mixed disciplines
   and other: **1%**
Percentage of students not coming directly from college
   after graduation: **N/A**

Dates and details

The American Medical College Application Service
   (AMCAS) application is accepted.
School asks for a school-specific application as part of the
   admissions process.
Oldest MCAT considered for Fall 2005 entry: **2002**
Earliest application date for the 2005-2006 first-year class:
   June 1, 2004
Latest application date: **December 15, 2004**
Acceptance dates for regular application for the class
   entering in fall 2005:
   Earliest: **October 15, 2004**

Latest: **August 1, 2005**
The school considers requests for deferred entrance.
Starting month for the class entering in 2005-2006:
   August
The school has an Early Decision Plan (EDP).
A personal interview is required for admission.

Undergraduate coursework required

Medical school requires undergraduate work in these subjects: biology, English, organic chemistry, inorganic (general) chemistry, physics, mathematics.

ADMISSIONS POLICY
(TEXT PROVIDED BY SCHOOL):

The Medical College Admission Test is required unless the student is accepted through the MEDStart program. A baccalaureate degree is required. A comprehensive command and understanding of the English language are essential.

Beyond these requirements, concentration in humanities, sciences, or other areas is viewed with equal favor. Close attention will be paid to the general scope of the applicant's academic background and to whether or not there is an adequate understanding of the physical, biological, chemical, and social sciences and some reasonable sensitivity to the humanities. In selecting applicants, the Medical College of Ohio looks more for evidence of general competence and capability than for specific areas of study.

Students are admitted on the basis of individual qualifications, regardless of sex, religion, race, age, or disability.

COSTS AND FINANCIAL AID

Financial aid phone number: **(419) 383-3631**
Tuition, 2003-2004 academic year: **In-state: $21,089; Out-of-state: $40,789**
Room and board: N/A
Percentage of students receiving financial aid in 2003-04: **78%**
Percentage of students receiving: Loans: **67%**,
   Grants/scholarships: **29%**, Work-study aid: **10%**
Average medical school debt for the Class of 2002:
   $115,413

STUDENT BODY

Fall 2003 full-time enrollment: 593
Men: 61%, Women: 39%, In-state: 93%, Minorities: 20%,
  American Indian: 0.5%, Asian-American: 16.7%,
  African-American: 1.5%, Hispanic-American: 1.3%,
  White: 76.6%, International: 2.0%, Unknown: 1.3%

ACADEMIC PROGRAMS

The school's curriculum doesn't give first-year students
  substantial contact with patients.
There are opportunities for first- or second-year students to
  work in community health clinics.
Program offerings: family medicine, geriatrics, internal
  medicine, pediatrics, rural medicine
Joint degrees awarded: M.D./Ph.D., M.D./M.P.H.
Total National Institutes of Health (NIH) grants awarded to
  the medical school and affiliated hospitals: **$13.4 million**

CURRICULUM

(TEXT PROVIDED BY SCHOOL):

The curriculum of the Medical College of Ohio is composed
of an integrated basic science/clinical science four-year
approach to medical education, with emphasis on clinically
oriented objectives and problem-based learning.

The first year is devoted to integrated blocks of cellular
and molecular biology, growth and development, human
structure and neuroscience, and behavioral science. Each of
these sections will have a corresponding integrated clinical,
applied component. Also included will be Introduction to
Primary Care, which runs concurrently throughout the first
two years.

The second year is composed of Immunity and Infection,
an integrated systems course involving pathology, pharmacology, and physiology. During the first two years, approximately 45 percent of the student's time will be spent in a
nonlecture format, with emphasis placed on small-group
interaction. Students are required to pass Step 1 of the U.S.
Medical Licensing Examination before beginning their third
year and Step 2 prior to graduation.

The last two years of the curriculum are devoted to
mandatory clerkships in internal medicine, surgery, pediatrics, obstetrics and gynecology, neurology, psychiatry, family practice, and electives. All students are required to rotate
through a clinical Area Health Education Center, accounting for 10 percent of their total clerkship time.

FACULTY PROFILE (FALL 2003)

Total teaching faculty: **285 (full-time), 35 (part-time)**
Of full-time faculty, those teaching in basic sciences: 26%;
  in clinical programs: **74%**
Of part-time faculty, those teaching in basic sciences: 20%;
  in clinical programs: **80%**
Full-time faculty/student ratio: 0.5

SUPPORT SERVICES

The school offers students these services for dealing with
stress: expanded-hour gym access, peer counseling, professional counseling, support groups.

RESIDENCY CHOICES

Most popular residency and specialty programs chosen by
the 2002 and 2003 M.D. graduating classes: anesthesiology,
emergency medicine, family practice, internal medicine,
obstetrics and gynecology, orthopedic surgery, pediatrics,
radiology–diagnostic.

WHERE GRADS GO

40.0%
*Proportion of 2001-2003 graduates who entered primary
care specialties*

36.5%
*Proportion of 2002-2003 graduates who accepted in-state
residencies*

Medical College of Wisconsin

- 8701 Watertown Plank Road, Milwaukee, WI 53226
- Private
- Year Founded: N/A
- Tuition, 2003-2004: $26,149
- Enrollment, 2003-2004: 795
- Website: http://www.mcw.edu/acad/admission
- Specialty ranking: N/A

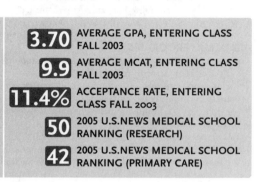

3.70 AVERAGE GPA, ENTERING CLASS FALL 2003

9.9 AVERAGE MCAT, ENTERING CLASS FALL 2003

11.4% ACCEPTANCE RATE, ENTERING CLASS FALL 2003

50 2005 U.S.NEWS MEDICAL SCHOOL RANKING (RESEARCH)

42 2005 U.S.NEWS MEDICAL SCHOOL RANKING (PRIMARY CARE)

ADMISSIONS

Admissions phone number: **(414) 456-8246**
Admissions email address: **medschool@mcw.edu**
Application website: **N/A**
Acceptance rate: **11.4%**
In-state acceptance rate: **32.3%**
Out-of-state acceptance rate: **8.2%**
Minority acceptance rate: **N/A**
International acceptance rate: **2.9%**

Fall 2003 applications and acceptees

	Applied	Interviewed	Accepted	Enrolled
Total:	3,694	579	422	205
In-state:	493	206	159	99
Out-of-state:	3,201	373	263	106

Profile of admitted students

Average undergraduate grade point average: **3.70**
MCAT averages (scale: 1-15; writing test: J-T):
   Composite score: **9.9**
   Verbal reasoning score: **9.6**, Physical sciences score:
   10.0, Biological sciences score: **10.0**, Writing score: **P**
Proportion with undergraduate majors in: Biological
   sciences: **45%**, Physical sciences: **39%**, Non-sciences:
   16%, Other health professions: **N/A**, Mixed disciplines
   and other: **N/A**
Percentage of students not coming directly from college
   after graduation: **N/A**

Dates and details

The American Medical College Application Service
   (AMCAS) application is accepted.
School asks for a school-specific application as part of the
   admissions process.
Oldest MCAT considered for Fall 2005 entry: **2002**
Earliest application date for the 2005-2006 first-year class:
   June 1, 2004
Latest application date: **November 1, 2004**
Acceptance dates for regular application for the class
   entering in fall 2005:
   Earliest: **October 15, 2004**

Latest: **N/A**
The school considers requests for deferred entrance.
Starting month for the class entering in 2005-2006:
   August
The school has an Early Decision Plan (EDP).
A personal interview is required for admission.

Undergraduate coursework required

Medical school requires undergraduate work in these subjects: biology, English, organic chemistry, inorganic (general) chemistry, physics, mathematics.

ADMISSIONS POLICY

(TEXT PROVIDED BY SCHOOL):
The Admissions Committee bases its decisions on a
thoughtful appraisal of each candidate's suitability for the
profession of medicine. Decisions are based upon scholastic
record, Medical College Admission Test scores, recommendations, involvement in college and community activities,
the personal interview, and also by the less tangible qualities
of personality, character, and maturity.

COSTS AND FINANCIAL AID

Financial aid phone number: **(414) 456-8208**
Tuition, 2003-2004 academic year: **$26,149**
Room and board: **$7,500**
Percentage of students receiving financial aid in 2003-04:
   98%
Percentage of students receiving: Loans: **91%**,
   Grants/scholarships: **25%**, Work-study aid: **0%**
Average medical school debt for the Class of 2002:
   $118,332

STUDENT BODY

Fall 2003 full-time enrollment: **795**
Men: **58%**, Women: **42%**, In-state: **51%**, Minorities: **22%**,
   American Indian: **0.8%**, Asian-American: **15.6%**,
   African-American: **2.3%**, Hispanic-American: **3.5%**,
   White: **75.7%**, International: **0.6%**, Unknown: **1.5%**

ACADEMIC PROGRAMS

There are opportunities for first- or second-year students to work in community health clinics.

Program offerings: family medicine, geriatrics, internal medicine, pediatrics, rural medicine, women's health

Joint degrees awarded: M.D./Ph.D.

Total National Institutes of Health (NIH) grants awarded to the medical school and affiliated hospitals: **$73.5 million**

CURRICULUM

(TEXT PROVIDED BY SCHOOL):

The M.D. curriculum at the Medical College of Wisconsin consists of carefully sequenced learning experiences that enable students to acquire the knowledge and skills that are necessary for the effective practice of medicine.

The learning activities of the first two years are a mix of traditional curriculum formats (lectures, labs, dissection, and discussion groups) and newer educational methods—computer-aided instruction, problem-based learning, and independent study options. There are mentor experiences and a medical interviewing course utilizing standardized patients.

During the third and fourth years of study, education shifts from the lecture hall and laboratory to the bedside. Required clerkships in a variety of patient care settings enable third-year students to draw from their working knowledge of the basic medical sciences as they begin to participate in the care of patients. They develop the skills necessary to diagnose and treat those patients.

Fourth-year students continue their training in required and elective experiences. By choosing electives that meet their individual educational needs, students gain experiences that enhance their autonomy and prepare them to enter the specialty of their choice.

FACULTY PROFILE (FALL 2003)

Total teaching faculty: **1,039 (full-time)**, 77 **(part-time)**

Of full-time faculty, those teaching in basic sciences: **11%**; in clinical programs: **89%**

Of part-time faculty, those teaching in basic sciences: **29%**; in clinical programs: **71%**

Full-time faculty/student ratio: **1.3**

SUPPORT SERVICES

The school offers students these services for dealing with stress: expanded-hour gym access, peer counseling, professional counseling.

RESIDENCY CHOICES

Most popular residency and specialty programs chosen by the 2002 and 2003 M.D. graduating classes: anesthesiology, emergency medicine, family practice, internal medicine, orthopedic surgery, pathology–anatomic and clinical, pediatrics, surgery–general, transitional year.

WHERE GRADS GO

44.0%

Proportion of 2001-2003 graduates who entered primary care specialties

34.0%

Proportion of 2002-2003 graduates who accepted in-state residencies

dical University of South Carolina

- 171 Ashley Avenue, Charleston, SC 29425
- Public
- Year Founded: 1824
- Tuition, 2003-2004: In-state: $17,435; Out-of-state: $47,533
- Enrollment, 2003-2004: 604
- Website: http://www.musc.edu
- Specialty ranking: drug/alcohol abuse: 12

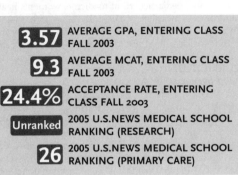

3.57 AVERAGE GPA, ENTERING CLASS FALL 2003

9.3 AVERAGE MCAT, ENTERING CLASS FALL 2003

24.4% ACCEPTANCE RATE, ENTERING CLASS FALL 2003

Unranked 2005 U.S.NEWS MEDICAL SCHOOL RANKING (RESEARCH)

26 2005 U.S.NEWS MEDICAL SCHOOL RANKING (PRIMARY CARE)

ADMISSIONS

Admissions phone number: **(843) 792-3813**
Admissions email address: **ohlandtg@musc.edu**
Application website: **http://www.musc.edu/es/apply**
Acceptance rate: **24.4%**
In-state acceptance rate: **47.9%**
Out-of-state acceptance rate: **4.0%**
Minority acceptance rate: **23.1%**
International acceptance rate: **N/A**

Fall 2003 applications and acceptees

	Applied	Interviewed	Accepted	Enrolled
Total:	784	328	191	137
In-state:	363	295	174	132
Out-of-state:	421	33	17	5

Profile of admitted students

Average undergraduate grade point average: **3.57**
MCAT averages (scale: 1-15; writing test: J-T):
  Composite score: **9.3**
  Verbal reasoning score: **9.2**, Physical sciences score: **9.1**,
  Biological sciences score: **9.6**, Writing score: **N/A**
Proportion with undergraduate majors in: Biological
  sciences: **50%**, Physical sciences: **20%**, Non-sciences:
  29%, Other health professions: **0%**, Mixed disciplines
  and other: **1%**
Percentage of students not coming directly from college
  after graduation: **49%**

Dates and details

The American Medical College Application Service
  (AMCAS) application is accepted.
School asks for a school-specific application as part of the
  admissions process.
Oldest MCAT considered for Fall 2005 entry: **2000**
Earliest application date for the 2005-2006 first-year class:
  June 1, 2004
Latest application date: **December 1, 2004**
Acceptance dates for regular application for the class
  entering in fall 2005:
  Earliest: **October 15, 2004**

Latest: **March 15, 2005**
The school considers requests for deferred entrance.
Starting month for the class entering in 2005-2006:
  August
The school has an Early Decision Plan (EDP).
A personal interview is required for admission.

ADMISSIONS POLICY

(TEXT PROVIDED BY SCHOOL):

The College of Medicine is a participant in the American
Medical College Application Service (AMCAS). The applica-
tion-filing period is from April 1 to December 1 prior to the
year in which the applicant wishes to enter. AMCAS will
forward the applications to the medical school after June 1
for preliminary screening by the Admissions Committee.
All applicants who apply through AMCAS are requested to
complete a supplemental application for MUSC. Before a
final admission decision is made, three personal interviews—with an Admissions Committee member, a MUSC
faculty member, and a South Carolina private physician—
are required. Offers of acceptance are made on a rolling
basis; final decisions on all applications are made by mid-
March.

Medical College Admission Test (MCAT) scores and a
minimum of three years of college work (90 semester
hours) are required for admission. Preference is given to
applicants who have earned a baccalaureate degree.
Students who choose to major in a science should select a
broad range of studies outside the sciences as well. Because
the MCAT requires knowledge of the natural sciences, students should consider studying college courses in introductory biology, introductory physics, general chemistry, and
organic chemistry.

South Carolina residency is a primary admission consideration. Selection is based on a total evaluation of the applicant. Intellectual capability for successful performance in
medical school is evaluated by reviewing an applicant's
cumulative undergraduate grade-point average and MCAT
scores. Those passing the academic cutoff are invited for
interviews. Noncognitive skills desirable in future physicians are evaluated during the interviews. These traits

include emotional stability, integrity, reasoning skills, enthusiasm, brightness, and genuine concern for others. Applicants who demonstrate a strong humanitarian commitment, those who have participated in community services, and those who have tested their desire for medicine by working in a healthcare setting are highly valued.

COSTS AND FINANCIAL AID
Financial aid phone number: **(843) 792-2536**
Tuition, 2003-2004 academic year: **In-state: $17,435; Out-of-state: $47,533**
Room and board: **$9,830**
Percentage of students receiving financial aid in 2003-04: **82%**
Percentage of students receiving: Loans: **79%**, Grants/scholarships: **22%**, Work-study aid: **3%**
Average medical school debt for the Class of 2002: **$91,361**

STUDENT BODY
Fall 2003 full-time enrollment: **604**
Men: **54%**, Women: **46%**, In-state: **93%**, Minorities: **20%**, American Indian: **0.5%**, Asian-American: **7.8%**, African-American: **10.1%**, Hispanic-American: **1.5%**, White: **78.3%**, International: **0.3%**, Unknown: **1.5%**

ACADEMIC PROGRAMS
The school's curriculum doesn't give first-year students substantial contact with patients.
There are opportunities for first- or second-year students to work in community health clinics.
Program offerings: drug/alcohol abuse, family medicine, geriatrics, internal medicine, pediatrics, rural medicine
Joint degrees awarded: M.D./Ph.D.
Total National Institutes of Health (NIH) grants awarded to the medical school and affiliated hospitals: **$78.5 million**

CURRICULUM
(TEXT PROVIDED BY SCHOOL):
The goal of the College of Medicine is to produce caring and competent physicians who are capable of succeeding in their postgraduate career. The four-year program, which leads to an M.D. degree, is divided into two years of preclinical instruction, which consists of education in the basic sciences and an introduction into clinical medicine, followed by two years of clinical science education.

During the first two years, the curriculum addresses four major objectives: provision of basic science concepts; acquisition of problem-solving strategies; development of skills that permit the performance of an adequate history and physical examination; and an introduction to the role of the physician in society. Throughout, emphasis is placed on small-group instruction. The curriculum provides opportu-

nities for independent, self-directed learning. As a result, students are being exposed earlier to certain clinical skills.

The junior year consists of eight clinical core clerkships: eight weeks each of family medicine/rural medicine, internal medicine, obstetrics/gynecology, pediatrics, and surgery, as well as four weeks each of family medicine, psychiatry, Dean's Rural Primary Care, and neurology. During the clerkships, emphasis is placed on the development of clinical, interpersonal, and professional competence. In addition, students participate in the Foundations in Clinical Medicine. This course is designed to integrate basic and clinical sciences utilizing small-group discussions and patient-case scenarios.

During the senior year, students take a minimum of eight four-week rotations. The student is required to take a clinical externship and one month each of surgery, psychiatry, and internal medicine. The remaining four blocks are elective and can be taken at approved sites throughout the state or country. In addition, students are required to complete and satisfactorily pass the Clinical Practice Exam. The clinical offerings of the Area Health Education Centers throughout the state play an integral part in the college's clinical curriculum.

FACULTY PROFILE (FALL 2003)
Total teaching faculty: **828 (full-time), 98 (part-time)**
Of full-time faculty, those teaching in basic sciences: **24%**; in clinical programs: **76%**
Of part-time faculty, those teaching in basic sciences: **11%**; in clinical programs: **89%**
Full-time faculty/student ratio: **1.4**

SUPPORT SERVICES
The school offers students these services for dealing with stress: expanded-hour gym access, professional counseling.

RESIDENCY CHOICES
Most popular residency and specialty programs chosen by the 2002 and 2003 M.D. graduating classes: anesthesiology, emergency medicine, family practice, internal medicine, obstetrics and gynecology, pediatrics, psychiatry, radiology–diagnostic, surgery–general, internal medicine/pediatrics.

WHERE GRADS GO

63.0%
Proportion of 2001-2003 graduates who entered primary care specialties

19.0%
Proportion of 2002-2003 graduates who accepted in-state residencies

Michigan State University

■ A110 E. Fee Hall, East Lansing, MI 48824
■ Public
■ **Year Founded:** 1964
■ **Tuition, 2003-2004:** In-state: $20,951; Out-of-state: $44,751
■ **Enrollment, 2003-2004:** 438
■ **Website:** http://www.chm.msu.edu
■ **Specialty ranking:** family medicine: 12, rural medicine: 9

3.50 AVERAGE GPA, ENTERING CLASS FALL 2003

9.5 AVERAGE MCAT, ENTERING CLASS FALL 2003

6.1% ACCEPTANCE RATE, ENTERING CLASS FALL 2003

Unranked 2005 U.S.NEWS MEDICAL SCHOOL RANKING (RESEARCH)

18 2005 U.S.NEWS MEDICAL SCHOOL RANKING (PRIMARY CARE)

ADMISSIONS

Admissions phone number: **(517) 353-9620**
Admissions email address: **MDadmissions@msu.edu**
Application website: **N/A**
Acceptance rate: **6.1%**
In-state acceptance rate: **11.8%**
Out-of-state acceptance rate: **2.8%**
Minority acceptance rate: **7.2%**
International acceptance rate: **2.5%**

Fall 2003 applications and acceptees

	Applied	Interviewed	Accepted	Enrolled
Total:	2,850	362	173	106
In-state:	1,025	251	121	85
Out-of-state:	1,825	111	52	21

Profile of admitted students

Average undergraduate grade point average: **3.50**
MCAT averages (scale: 1-15; writing test: J-T):
  Composite score: **9.5**
  Verbal reasoning score: **9.4**, Physical sciences score: **9.2**, Biological sciences score: **10.0**, Writing score: **P**
Proportion with undergraduate majors in: Biological sciences: **54%**, Physical sciences: **14%**, Non-sciences: **22%**, Other health professions: **2%**, Mixed disciplines and other: **8%**
Percentage of students not coming directly from college after graduation: **22%**

Dates and details

The American Medical College Application Service (AMCAS) application is accepted.
School asks for a school-specific application as part of the admissions process.
Oldest MCAT considered for Fall 2005 entry: **2002**
Earliest application date for the 2005-2006 first-year class: **June 1, 2004**
Latest application date: **November 15, 2004**
Acceptance dates for regular application for the class entering in fall 2005:
  Earliest: **October 15, 2004**
  Latest: **April 15, 2005**
The school considers requests for deferred entrance.
Starting month for the class entering in 2005-2006: **August**
The school has an Early Decision Plan (EDP).
A personal interview is required for admission.

Undergraduate coursework required

Medical school requires undergraduate work in these subjects: biology, English, organic chemistry, inorganic (general) chemistry, physics, humanities, mathematics, social sciences.

ADMISSIONS POLICY

(TEXT PROVIDED BY SCHOOL):

All application materials are reviewed prior to an initial decision. Approximately 800 applicants will be invited to complete the secondary application. Because MSU/CHM is a state school, approximately 80 percent of the entering class will be Michigan residents.

The college seeks to admit a class that is academically competent, reflective of both the rural and urban character of Michigan, and representative of a wide spectrum of personalities, backgrounds, and talents. Students who have the desire and aptitude to become physicians but who may be disadvantaged because of economic, cultural, or educational background or family circumstances are encouraged to apply.

From approximately 3,000 applicants reviewed by the Committee on Admissions, approximately 400 applicants will be invited to Interview Day at the East Lansing campus for interviews with faculty and medical students. Selection is based on many factors, including grade-point average, both year to year and cumulative; Medical College Admission Test scores; fit with the school's mission; relevant community service experience; clinical experience; interviewers' assessments of motivation, ability to communicate, problem-solving ability, maturity, and suitability for the MSU program; state of residence; and potential to contribute to the overall quality of the entering class.

COSTS AND FINANCIAL AID

Financial aid phone number: **(517) 353-5188**

Tuition, 2003-2004 academic year: **In-state: $20,951; Out-of-state: $44,751**

Room and board: **$11,184**

Percentage of students receiving financial aid in 2003-04: **94%**

Percentage of students receiving: Loans: **91%**, Grants/scholarships: **83%**, Work-study aid: **0%**

Average medical school debt for the Class of 2002: **$122,983**

STUDENT BODY

Fall 2003 full-time enrollment: **438**

Men: **42%**, Women: **58%**, In-state: **80%**, Minorities: **36%**, American Indian: **0.9%**, Asian-American: **14.6%**, African-American: **11.4%**, Hispanic-American: **8.2%**, White: **63.7%**, International: **1.1%**, Unknown: **0.0%**

ACADEMIC PROGRAMS

The school's curriculum gives first-year students substantial contact with patients.

There are opportunities for first- or second-year students to work in community health clinics.

Program offerings: AIDS, drug/alcohol abuse, family medicine, geriatrics, internal medicine, pediatrics, rural medicine, women's health

Joint degrees awarded: M.D./M.S., M.D./M.H.A.

Total National Institutes of Health (NIH) grants awarded to the medical school and affiliated hospitals: **N/A**

CURRICULUM

(TEXT PROVIDED BY SCHOOL):

The curriculum is divided into three blocks that integrate basic biological, behavioral, and social sciences using a developmental approach to learning; early teaching of clinical skills; attention to professional development; and clinical training utilizing a community-integrated approach.

Block 1 is a three-semester experience in which fundamental basic science concepts and principles are presented in a structured, discipline-based format. A mentor group, a longitudinal patient care experience, and both independent and supplementary learning experiences complemented by a clinical correlations course integrate basic science information.

Block 2 is a two-semester experience in which advanced basic science concepts are organized in an integrated, problem-based format. Emphasis is on small-group instruction and problem solving. A clinical context for learning basic science concepts is also provided. Clinical-skills training continues along with special topics seminars, which deal with contemporary issues in society and medicine.

Block 3 includes 56 weeks of required and 20 weeks of elective clerkships. Students experience a variety of hospital and ambulatory care environments in one of the six community campus settings. The required clerkships include one in family practice/primary care.

FACULTY PROFILE (FALL 2003)

Total teaching faculty: **326 (full-time), 28 (part-time)**

Of full-time faculty, those teaching in basic sciences: **49%**; in clinical programs: **51%**

Of part-time faculty, those teaching in basic sciences: **32%**; in clinical programs: **68%**

Full-time faculty/student ratio: **0.7**

SUPPORT SERVICES

The school offers students these services for dealing with stress: professional counseling, support groups.

RESIDENCY CHOICES

Most popular residency and specialty programs chosen by the 2002 and 2003 M.D. graduating classes: anesthesiology, emergency medicine, family practice, internal medicine, obstetrics and gynecology, pediatrics, psychiatry, radiology–diagnostic, surgery–general, internal medicine/pediatrics.

WHERE GRADS GO

48.0%
Proportion of 2001-2003 graduates who entered primary care specialties

46.0%
Proportion of 2002-2003 graduates who accepted in-state residencies

Morehouse School of Medicine

- 720 Westview Drive SW, Atlanta, GA 30310
- Private
- Year Founded: 1975
- Tuition, 2003-2004: $25,376
- Enrollment, 2003-2004: 182
- Website: http://www.msm.edu
- Specialty ranking: N/A

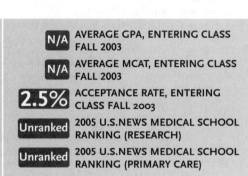

N/A	AVERAGE GPA, ENTERING CLASS FALL 2003
N/A	AVERAGE MCAT, ENTERING CLASS FALL 2003
2.5%	ACCEPTANCE RATE, ENTERING CLASS FALL 2003
Unranked	2005 U.S.NEWS MEDICAL SCHOOL RANKING (RESEARCH)
Unranked	2005 U.S.NEWS MEDICAL SCHOOL RANKING (PRIMARY CARE)

ADMISSIONS

Admissions phone number: **(404) 752-1650**
Admissions email address: **mdadmissions@msm.edu**
Application website: **N/A**
Acceptance rate: **2.5%**
In-state acceptance rate: **N/A**
Out-of-state acceptance rate: **N/A**
Minority acceptance rate: **N/A**
International acceptance rate: **N/A**

Fall 2003 applications and acceptees

	Applied	Interviewed	Accepted	Enrolled
Total:	2,047	244	52	52
In-state:	N/A	N/A	N/A	N/A
Out-of-state:	N/A	N/A	N/A	N/A

Profile of admitted students

Percentage of students not coming directly from college after graduation: **12%**

Dates and details

The American Medical College Application Service (AMCAS) application is accepted.
School asks for a school-specific application as part of the admissions process.
Oldest MCAT considered for Fall 2005 entry: **2002**
Earliest application date for the 2005-2006 first-year class: **June 1, 2004**
Latest application date: **December 1, 2004**
Acceptance dates for regular application for the class entering in fall 2005:
  Earliest: **December 5, 2004**
  Latest: **June 20, 2005**
The school considers requests for deferred entrance.
Starting month for the class entering in 2005-2006: **July**
The school has an Early Decision Plan (EDP).
A personal interview is required for admission.

Undergraduate coursework required

Medical school requires undergraduate work in these subjects: biology, English, organic chemistry, physics, mathematics, general chemistry.

COSTS AND FINANCIAL AID

Financial aid phone number: **(404) 752-1655**
Tuition, 2003-2004 academic year: **$25,376**
Room and board: **$10,760**
Percentage of students receiving financial aid in 2003-04: **86%**
Percentage of students receiving: Loans: **92%**, Grants/scholarships: **75%**, Work-study aid: **4%**
Average medical school debt for the Class of 2002: **$96,171**

STUDENT BODY

Fall 2003 full-time enrollment: **182**
Men: **37%**, Women: **63%**, In-state: **59%**, Minorities: **85%**, American Indian: **0.0%**, Asian-American: **17.6%**, African-American: **66.5%**, Hispanic-American: **0.5%**, White: **12.6%**, International: **2.7%**, Unknown: **0.0%**

ACADEMIC PROGRAMS

The school's curriculum gives first-year students substantial contact with patients.
There are opportunities for first- or second-year students to work in community health clinics.
Program offerings: AIDS, drug/alcohol abuse, family medicine, internal medicine, pediatrics, rural medicine, women's health
Joint degrees awarded: M.D./M.P.H.
Total National Institutes of Health (NIH) grants awarded to the medical school and affiliated hospitals: **N/A**

FACULTY PROFILE (FALL 2003)

Total teaching faculty: **225 (full-time), 34 (part-time)**
Of full-time faculty, those teaching in basic sciences: **26%**; in clinical programs: **74%**
Of part-time faculty, those teaching in basic sciences: **6%**; in clinical programs: **94%**
Full-time faculty/student ratio: **1.2**

SUPPORT SERVICES

The school offers students these services for dealing with stress: expanded-hour gym access, peer counseling, professional counseling, religious support, support groups.

RESIDENCY CHOICES

Most popular residency and specialty programs chosen by the 2002 and 2003 M.D. graduating classes: family practice, internal medicine, obstetrics and gynecology, ophthalmology, pediatrics, psychiatry, surgery–general, internal medicine/pediatrics.

WHERE GRADS GO

23.0%

Proportion of 2001-2003 graduates who entered primary care specialties

9.0%

Proportion of 2002-2003 graduates who accepted in-state residencies

Mount Sinai School of Medicine

- 1 Gustave L. Levy Place, Box 1475, New York, NY 10029
- Public
- Year Founded: 1963
- Tuition, 2003-2004: In-state: $33,320; Out-of-state: $33,320
- Enrollment, 2003-2004: 462
- Website: http://www.mssm.edu
- Specialty ranking: AIDS: 19, geriatrics: 3, internal medicine: 28

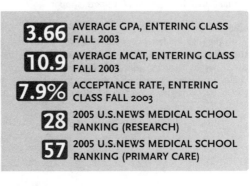

3.66 AVERAGE GPA, ENTERING CLASS FALL 2003

10.9 AVERAGE MCAT, ENTERING CLASS FALL 2003

7.9% ACCEPTANCE RATE, ENTERING CLASS FALL 2003

28 2005 U.S.NEWS MEDICAL SCHOOL RANKING (RESEARCH)

57 2005 U.S.NEWS MEDICAL SCHOOL RANKING (PRIMARY CARE)

ADMISSIONS

Admissions phone number: **(212) 241-6696**
Admissions email address: **admissions@mssm.edu**
Application website: **N/A**
Acceptance rate: **7.9%**
In-state acceptance rate: **11.0%**
Out-of-state acceptance rate: **6.8%**
Minority acceptance rate: **6.7%**
International acceptance rate: **3.8%**

Fall 2003 applications and acceptees

	Applied	Interviewed	Accepted	Enrolled
Total:	4,202	726	331	120
In-state:	1,103	248	121	46
Out-of-state:	3,099	478	210	74

Profile of admitted students

Average undergraduate grade point average: **3.66**
MCAT averages (scale: 1-15; writing test: J-T):
  Composite score: **10.9**
  Verbal reasoning score: **10.5**, Physical sciences score: **11.0**, Biological sciences score: **11.2**, Writing score: **Q**
Proportion with undergraduate majors in: Biological sciences: **41%**, Physical sciences: **14%**, Non-sciences: **36%**, Other health professions: **0%**, Mixed disciplines and other: **9%**
Percentage of students not coming directly from college after graduation: **60%**

Dates and details

The American Medical College Application Service (AMCAS) application is accepted.
School asks for a school-specific application as part of the admissions process.
Oldest MCAT considered for Fall 2005 entry: **2002**
Earliest application date for the 2005-2006 first-year class: **June 1, 2004**
Latest application date: **November 1, 2004**
Acceptance dates for regular application for the class entering in fall 2005:
  Earliest: **November 1, 2004**

Latest: **August 15, 2005**
The school considers requests for deferred entrance.
Starting month for the class entering in 2005-2006:
  August
The school has an Early Decision Plan (EDP).
A personal interview is required for admission.

Undergraduate coursework required

Medical school requires undergraduate work in these subjects: biology, English, organic chemistry, inorganic (general) chemistry, physics, mathematics.

ADMISSIONS POLICY
(TEXT PROVIDED BY SCHOOL):

Mount Sinai seeks to attract individuals of diverse backgrounds who have the ability and potential to become physician-scholars dedicated to excellence in their chosen career paths. Applicants for admission are considered based on their total qualifications. We assess intellectual capability, academic achievement, motivation for a career in medicine, community service, leadership abilities, enthusiasm for shaping one's own learning experience, and personal maturity. We give no preference to in-state applicants. We are seeking students who are dedicated to becoming the next generation of leaders in a constantly changing profession. We pride ourselves in a class that has broad representation of geography, undergraduate colleges, fields of study, race, gender, and previous accomplishments.

COSTS AND FINANCIAL AID

Financial aid phone number: **(212) 241-5245**
Tuition, 2003-2004 academic year: **In-state: $33,320; Out-of-state: $33,320**
Room and board: **$12,300**
Percentage of students receiving financial aid in 2003-04: **86%**
Percentage of students receiving: Loans: **75%**, Grants/scholarships: **48%**, Work-study aid: **12%**
Average medical school debt for the Class of 2002: **$97,055**

STUDENT BODY

Fall 2003 full-time enrollment: 462
Men: 45%, Women: 55%, In-state: 38%, Minorities: 41%,
American Indian: 1.1%, Asian-American: 20.8%,
African-American: 7.6%, Hispanic-American: 11.5%,
White: 55.6%, International: 1.3%, Unknown: 2.2%

ACADEMIC PROGRAMS

The school's curriculum gives first-year students
substantial contact with patients.
There are opportunities for first- or second-year students to
work in community health clinics.
Program offerings: AIDS, drug/alcohol abuse, family
medicine, geriatrics, internal medicine, pediatrics,
women's health
Joint degrees awarded: M.D./Ph.D., M.D./M.B.A.,
M.D./M.P.H.
Total National Institutes of Health (NIH) grants awarded to
the medical school and affiliated hospitals: **$158.4 million**

CURRICULUM

(TEXT PROVIDED BY SCHOOL):

Mount Sinai School of Medicine offers an innovative, newly
revised four-year curriculum that promotes early patient
exposure and interaction during the first two years and integration of clinical medicine with the basic sciences throughout all four years. Interdisciplinary courses and clerkships
are a highlight of the curriculum. Vertical integration of
new disciplines and continuous themes (ethics, evidence-
based medicine, and communication skills, etc.) are organized in a matrix throughout the curriculum, we call them
Courses Without Walls. The Art and Science of Medicine, a
two-year course, integrates many of the non-basic science
aspects of doctoring: communication, history and physical
exam, law, and societal issues. Although lectures have been
retained in the first two years, the school has replaced large-
group formats with interactive, small groups and laboratory
experiences.

Clinical content permeates the Year 1 and 2 courses, with
clinical preceptors in many of the case-based sessions.
There is an emphasis on self-directed and active learning
with assessment of skills and competency. MSSM encourages research and scholarly pursuits. There is an elective
component of the curriculum in years 1 and 2 and students
are encouraged to participate in community-based voluntary
experiences.

In years 3 and 4, the clerkships are organized into modular sequences with greater flexibility for students. Mount
Sinai services a diverse community of patients with a rich
complex network of affiliates that participate in our educational environment. Students experience an introduction to
clinical skills during the week before the modules begin and
an intersession was implemented during the spring of the
third year. Students participate in an integrated problem-

based learning exercise and have an opportunity to integrate
knowledge, skills, and attitudes of clinical practice through
various didactic and small group experiences. Students have
ample elective time in the third and fourth years to develop a
niche or sample various clinical disciplines, participate in
research, or complete other advanced degrees.

Two new courses have been implemented, Critical Care
and Anatomic Radiology, in the fourth year with an
advanced clinically focused experience with an integration
of physiology and anatomy. Many innovative resources are
available to students and faculty including a Web-based curriculum for all courses and clerkships, a Web-based assessment tool for all educational offerings, access to the human
simulator, and access to the standardized patient center.
Our faculty resources are abundant for individualized educational experiences, research exposure, and career counseling. Our students are assessed in many ways but a unique
feature is our comprehensive skills assessments which take
place at the end of year 2 and again at the end of year 3. The
clinical curriculum at MSSM is designed to promote self-
directed learning, enhanced information retrieval skills,
clinical problem solving and reasoning, and scientific
inquiry through diverse, innovative, and integrated educational offerings.

FACULTY PROFILE (FALL 2003)

Total teaching faculty: **1,924 (full-time), 256 (part-time)**
Of full-time faculty, those teaching in basic sciences: **17%**;
in clinical programs: **83%**
Of part-time faculty, those teaching in basic sciences: **4%**;
in clinical programs: **96%**
Full-time faculty/student ratio: **4.2**

SUPPORT SERVICES

The school offers students these services for dealing with
stress: professional counseling, support groups.

RESIDENCY CHOICES

Most popular residency and specialty programs chosen by
the 2002 and 2003 M.D. graduating classes: anesthesiology,
emergency medicine, internal medicine, neurology, obstetrics and gynecology, otolaryngology, pediatrics, psychiatry,
radiology–diagnostic, surgery–general.

WHERE GRADS GO

49.0%
*Proportion of 2001-2003 graduates who entered primary
care specialties*

58.0%
*Proportion of 2002-2003 graduates who accepted in-state
residencies*

w York Medical College

- **Admin. Building, Office of Admissions, Valhalla, NY 10595**
- **Private**
- **Year Founded:** 1860
- **Tuition, 2003-2004:** $36,790
- **Enrollment, 2003-2004:** 767
- **Website:** http://www.nymc.edu
- **Specialty ranking:** N/A

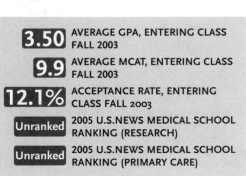

3.50 AVERAGE GPA, ENTERING CLASS FALL 2003

9.9 AVERAGE MCAT, ENTERING CLASS FALL 2003

12.1% ACCEPTANCE RATE, ENTERING CLASS FALL 2003

Unranked 2005 U.S.NEWS MEDICAL SCHOOL RANKING (RESEARCH)

Unranked 2005 U.S.NEWS MEDICAL SCHOOL RANKING (PRIMARY CARE)

ADMISSIONS

Admissions phone number: **(914) 594-4507**
Admissions email address: **mdadmit@nymc.edu**
Application website:
http://www.nymc.edu/admit/medical/info/proced.htm
Acceptance rate: **12.1%**
In-state acceptance rate: **17.3%**
Out-of-state acceptance rate: **10.7%**
Minority acceptance rate: **10.4%**
International acceptance rate: **N/A**

Fall 2003 applications and acceptees

	Applied	Interviewed	Accepted	Enrolled
Total:	**6,495**	**1,332**	**785**	**189**
In-state:	**1,361**	**359**	**235**	**65**
Out-of-state:	**5,134**	**973**	**550**	**124**

Profile of admitted students

Average undergraduate grade point average: **3.50**
MCAT averages (scale: 1-15; writing test: J-T):
  Composite score: **9.9**
  Verbal reasoning score: **9.2**, Physical sciences score:
  10.3, Biological sciences score: **10.4**, Writing score: **Q**
Proportion with undergraduate majors in: Biological
  sciences: **40%**, Physical sciences: **15%**, Non-sciences:
  20%, Other health professions: **3%**, Mixed disciplines
  and other: **22%**
Percentage of students not coming directly from college
  after graduation: **66%**

Dates and details

The American Medical College Application Service
  (AMCAS) application is accepted.
School asks for a school-specific application as part of the
  admissions process.
Oldest MCAT considered for Fall 2005 entry: **2001**
Earliest application date for the 2005-2006 first-year class:
  June 1, 2004
Latest application date: **December 15, 2004**
Acceptance dates for regular application for the class
  entering in fall 2005:

Earliest: **December 6, 2004**
Latest: **July 31, 2005**
The school considers requests for deferred entrance.
Starting month for the class entering in 2005-2006:
  August
The school has an Early Decision Plan (EDP).
A personal interview is required for admission.

Undergraduate coursework required

Medical school requires undergraduate work in these subjects: biology, English, organic chemistry, inorganic (general) chemistry, physics.

ADMISSIONS POLICY
(TEXT PROVIDED BY SCHOOL):

The Committee on Admissions selects students after carefully considering all those factors of intellect, character, and
personality that point toward their ability to become
informed and caring physicians. This basic platform must
include a history of academic excellence. Although the
majority of students have had undergraduate majors in the
sciences, it is not at all a requirement or a factor in selection. We welcome applicants with a broad education in the
humanities who have completed their premed requirements in a postbaccalaureate program.

In addition to purely academic factors, we look for students who show clear evidence through their activities of
strong motivation toward medicine and a sense of dedication to the service of others. Personal qualities of character
and personality are evaluated from letters of recommendation, the personal statement, and the interview. New York
Medical College does not deny admission to any applicant
on the basis of race, gender, religion, national origin, age, or
handicap.

COSTS AND FINANCIAL AID

Financial aid phone number: **(914) 594-4491**
Tuition, 2003-2004 academic year: **$36,790**
Room and board: **$16,160**
Percentage of students receiving financial aid in 2003-04:
  91%

Percentage of students receiving: Loans: **91%**,
   Grants/scholarships: **14%**, Work-study aid: **3%**
Average medical school debt for the Class of 2002:
   $142,000

STUDENT BODY

Fall 2003 full-time enrollment: **767**
Men: **49%**, Women: **51%**, In-state: **36%**, Minorities: **43%**,
   American Indian: **0.1%**, Asian-American: **36.0%**,
   African-American: **4.0%**, Hispanic-American: **3.0%**,
   White: **55.5%**, International: **0.1%**, Unknown: **1.2%**

ACADEMIC PROGRAMS

The school's curriculum gives first-year students
   substantial contact with patients.
There are opportunities for first- or second-year students to
   work in community health clinics.
Program offerings: AIDS, drug/alcohol abuse, family
   medicine, geriatrics, internal medicine, pediatrics, rural
   medicine, women's health
Joint degrees awarded: M.D./Ph.D., M.D./M.P.H.
Total National Institutes of Health (NIH) grants awarded to
   the medical school and affiliated hospitals: **$20.5 million**

CURRICULUM

(TEXT PROVIDED BY SCHOOL):
New York Medical College's goal is to provide a general professional education that prepares students for all career
options in medicine. There is emphasis on critical thinking,
evidence-based decision mathroughout the entire curriculum. Particular strengths include an integrated four-year
curriculum in biomedical ethics; a rigorous subinternship
in medicine or pediatrics; and a required fourth-year rotation in geriatric medicine or chronic care pediatrics.
Noncredit electives in medical Spanish and medical humanities are offered during the preclinical years. International
medical electives are available during the fourth year. An
optional Summer Research Fellowship Program is offered
between the first and second years. The college sponsors a
wide array of community-oriented service programs.

   In addition to traditional lectures and laboratory exercises, the basic science courses utilize small-group learning,
clinical correlation sessions, case-based discussions, problem-based learning, and computer-assisted instruction.
Particular emphasis in the second year is placed on self-
directed learning. Throughout the first and second years, all
students have a longitudinal clinical experience through
assignment to physician preceptors. The third-year clerkships include substantial ambulatory and emergency
department experience. The family medicine clerkship is
entirely community-based. There is a palliative-care compo-

nent of the medicine clerkship. All students gain experience
in medical informatics and in the application of personal
digital assistants (PDAs) to the clinical setting. In the
fourth-year subinternship, students are expected to function
at the level of a beginning resident.

   New York Medical College utilizes an array of evaluation
tools to assess student performance. These include in-house
written exams; laboratory practical exams, including
autopsy; participation in interactive small-group tutorials
and problem-solving exercises; case presentations, discussions, and write-ups; Harvey cardiology simulator sessions;
observed clinical interviews and physical examinations; formal observed supervised clinical evaluations; evidence-
based medicine projects; and standardized checklist rating
forms with narrative comments for clinical clerkships. Most
basic science courses and all third-year clerkships require a
passing score on the relevant National Board of Medical
Examiners subject examination (shelf exam). U.S. Medical
Licensing Examination Step 1 is required for promotion
into fourth year. USMLE Step 2 is required for graduation.

FACULTY PROFILE (FALL 2003)

Total teaching faculty: **1,261 (full-time)**, **129 (part-time)**
Of full-time faculty, those teaching in basic sciences: **10%**;
   in clinical programs: **90%**
Of part-time faculty, those teaching in basic sciences: **4%**;
   in clinical programs: **96%**
Full-time faculty/student ratio: **1.6**

SUPPORT SERVICES

The school offers students these services for dealing with
stress: expanded-hour gym access, peer counseling, professional counseling, religious support, support groups.

RESIDENCY CHOICES

Most popular residency and specialty programs chosen by
the 2002 and 2003 M.D. graduating classes: anesthesiology, emergency medicine, family practice, internal medicine, obstetrics and gynecology, pediatrics, physical
medicine and rehabilitation, psychiatry, radiology–diagnostic, surgery–general.

WHERE GRADS GO

52.5%
*Proportion of 2001-2003 graduates who entered primary
care specialties*

47.5%
*Proportion of 2002-2003 graduates who accepted in-state
residencies*

New York University

- 550 First Avenue, New York, NY 10016
- Private
- Year Founded: 1841
- Tuition, 2003-2004: $29,750
- Enrollment, 2003-2004: 712
- Website: http://www.med.nyu.edu/som/medsch/index.html
- Specialty ranking: AIDS: 8, drug/alcohol abuse: 10, internal medicine: 24

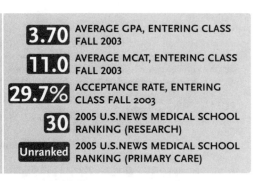

3.70 AVERAGE GPA, ENTERING CLASS FALL 2003

11.0 AVERAGE MCAT, ENTERING CLASS FALL 2003

29.7% ACCEPTANCE RATE, ENTERING CLASS FALL 2003

30 2005 U.S.NEWS MEDICAL SCHOOL RANKING (RESEARCH)

Unranked 2005 U.S.NEWS MEDICAL SCHOOL RANKING (PRIMARY CARE)

ADMISSIONS

Admissions phone number: **(212) 263-5290**
Admissions email address: **admissions@med.nyu.edu**
Application website:
   http://www.med.nyu.edu/som/medsch/download.html
Acceptance rate: **29.7%**
In-state acceptance rate: **N/A**
Out-of-state acceptance rate: **N/A**
Minority acceptance rate: **19.1%**
International acceptance rate: **N/A**

Fall 2003 applications and acceptees

	Applied	Interviewed	Accepted	Enrolled
Total:	3,178	846	943	160
In-state:	N/A	N/A	N/A	N/A
Out-of-state:	N/A	N/A	N/A	N/A

Profile of admitted students

Average undergraduate grade point average: **3.70**
MCAT averages (scale: 1-15; writing test: J-T):
   Composite score: **11.0**
   Verbal reasoning score: **10.3**, Physical sciences score:
   11.0, Biological sciences score: **11.0**, Writing score: **Q**
Proportion with undergraduate majors in: Biological
   sciences: **45%**, Physical sciences: **35%**, Non-sciences:
   20%, Other health professions: **0%**, Mixed disciplines
   and other: **N/A**
Percentage of students not coming directly from college
   after graduation: **10%**

Dates and details

The American Medical College Application Service
   (AMCAS) application is accepted.
School asks for a school-specific application as part of the
   admissions process.
Oldest MCAT considered for Fall 2005 entry: **2001**
Earliest application date for the 2005-2006 first-year class:
   June 1, 2004
Latest application date: **November 1, 2004**
Acceptance dates for regular application for the class
   entering in fall 2005:

Earliest: **December 15, 2004**
Latest: **N/A**
The school considers requests for deferred entrance.
Starting month for the class entering in 2005-2006:
   August
The school doesn't have an Early Decision Plan (EDP).
A personal interview is required for admission.

Undergraduate coursework required

Medical school requires undergraduate work in these subjects: biology, English, organic chemistry, inorganic (general) chemistry, physics.

ADMISSIONS POLICY
(TEXT PROVIDED BY SCHOOL):

The selection process involves judging the applicant on the
basis of several criteria, among them intelligence, preparedness, motivation, and aptitude. In the evaluation, account is
taken of the candidate's excellence in coursework at the college level; of his or her capacities as judged by college
instructors, premedical committees, and other similar
mechanisms provided by the colleges; of the results of a
personal interview at the New York University School of
Medicine; and of the results of the Medical College
Admission Test. Although most entering first-year students
range in age between 21 and 24, there is no upper age limit.
Indeed, older candidates of exceptional merit are given serious consideration for admission. Applications from women
have always been welcomed. In recent years, women have
constituted 50 percent or more of the entering class.

   It is not possible to interview all applicants. Only those
students who, on the basis of application data, appear to
merit serious consideration for admission are selected for
interview. The strength of the applicant pool is such that in
recent years interviews have been granted to only 25 percent
of the candidates who apply. The Committee on Admissions
notifies all those candidates whom it wishes to interview.

   If accepted, the student is given a two-week interval
before a response is required. Matriculation is accomplished by sending a letter of acceptance and a deposit of
$100 to the Committee on Admissions. The deposit is

applied to the first-year tuition and is refundable until May 1. Final registration becomes official only after the student has completed satisfactorily all admission requirements and has passed a physical examination given by the Student Health Service.

Students who have failed in another medical school are not eligible to apply for admission to the New York University School of Medicine.

COSTS AND FINANCIAL AID
Financial aid phone number: **(212) 263-5286**
Tuition, 2003-2004 academic year: **$29,750**
Room and board: **$9,900**
Percentage of students receiving financial aid in 2003-04: **88%**
Percentage of students receiving: Loans: **88%**, Grants/scholarships: **58%**, Work-study aid: **14%**
Average medical school debt for the Class of 2002: **$83,500**

STUDENT BODY
Fall 2003 full-time enrollment: **712**
Men: **51%**, Women: **49%**, In-state: **49%**, Minorities: **41%**, American Indian: **0.0%**, Asian-American: **31.3%**, African-American: **6.2%**, Hispanic-American: **3.8%**, White: **50.6%**, International: **1.4%**, Unknown: **6.7%**

ACADEMIC PROGRAMS
The school's curriculum gives first-year students substantial contact with patients.
There are opportunities for first- or second-year students to work in community health clinics.
Program offerings: AIDS, drug/alcohol abuse, family medicine, geriatrics, internal medicine, pediatrics, rural medicine, women's health
Joint degrees awarded: M.D./Ph.D.
Total National Institutes of Health (NIH) grants awarded to the medical school and affiliated hospitals: **$134.2 million**

CURRICULUM
(TEXT PROVIDED BY SCHOOL):
The central goal of the curriculum is to create leaders in every field of medical endeavor, to create physician-scholars who approach the practice of medicine with intellectual discipline, compassion, and professionalism. Throughout their careers, such individuals will apply the scientific method and critical thinking to advance both patient care and medical knowledge.

Curriculum reform is constant. Continuing efforts are made to identify the factors that will better enable students to use the scientific principles of medicine in the evaluation and treatment of the sick. In this process, students work closely with the faculty to contribute to the improvement of the educational program.

In the fall of 2001, the School of Medicine implemented a new curriculum. Under this unique and innovative program, the basic science courses were reorganized into thematic modules composed of interrelated units such as Macroscopic Structure and Development of the Human Body, Cell Structure and Function, Tissues and Organs, Host Defense, Mechanisms of Disease, and the Skills and Science of Doctoring. Traditional lecture hours were reduced, and the educational program now employs teaching methodologies that are specifically designed to nurture an increasingly independent and self-reliant student.

The clinical sciences core curriculum consists of nine core clerkships in medicine, surgery, pediatrics, psychiatry, obstetrics and gynecology, neurology, ambulatory care, critical care, and an acting internship in advanced medicine. Although the basic element of teaching in the clinical clerkship is bedside instruction, skills are developed through multiple media that reinforce interactive, interdisciplinary learning. Topics introduced in the preclinical years are revisited in renewed depth through case-based exercises. The transition to clinical sciences is facilitated by a two-week, interdepartmental clerkship orientation. Entry into the final year of medical school begins with a thematic selective in advanced science. Students select from a palette of topics drawn from the frontiers of translational medicine and biomedical technology.

FACULTY PROFILE (FALL 2003)
Total teaching faculty: **1,699 (full-time)**, **3,476 (part-time)**
Of full-time faculty, those teaching in basic sciences: **24%**; in clinical programs: **72%**
Of part-time faculty, those teaching in basic sciences: **5%**; in clinical programs: **95%**
Full-time faculty/student ratio: **2.4**

SUPPORT SERVICES
The school offers students these services for dealing with stress: expanded-hour gym access, peer counseling, professional counseling, religious support, support groups.

RESIDENCY CHOICES
Most popular residency and specialty programs chosen by the 2002 and 2003 M.D. graduating classes: emergency medicine, internal medicine, neurology, obstetrics and gynecology, ophthalmology, orthopedic surgery, pediatrics, psychiatry, radiology–diagnostic, surgery–general.

WHERE GRADS GO
44.0%
Proportion of 2001-2003 graduates who entered primary care specialties

57.0%
Proportion of 2002-2003 graduates who accepted in-state residencies

ortheastern Ohio Universities

COLLEGE OF MEDICINE

- 4209 State Route 44, PO Box 95, Rootstown, OH 44272-0095
- Public
- Year Founded: 1973
- Tuition, 2003-2004: In-state: $19,371; Out-of-state: $37,626
- Enrollment, 2003-2004: 430
- Website: http://www.neoucom.edu
- Specialty ranking: N/A

3.61	AVERAGE GPA, ENTERING CLASS FALL 2003
9.0	AVERAGE MCAT, ENTERING CLASS FALL 2003
18.1%	ACCEPTANCE RATE, ENTERING CLASS FALL 2003
Unranked	2005 U.S.NEWS MEDICAL SCHOOL RANKING (RESEARCH)
Unranked	2005 U.S.NEWS MEDICAL SCHOOL RANKING (PRIMARY CARE)

ADMISSIONS
Admissions phone number: **(330) 325-6270**
Admissions email address: **admission@neoucom.edu**
Application website:
   http://www.neoucom.edu/students/ADMI
Acceptance rate: **18.1%**
In-state acceptance rate: **N/A**
Out-of-state acceptance rate: **N/A**
Minority acceptance rate: **14.8%**
International acceptance rate: **N/A**

Fall 2003 applications and acceptees
	Applied	Interviewed	Accepted	Enrolled
Total:	1,402	337	254	102
In-state:	878	309	N/A	95
Out-of-state:	524	28	N/A	7

Profile of admitted students
Average undergraduate grade point average: **3.61**
MCAT averages (scale: 1-15; writing test: J-T):
   Composite score: **9.0**
   Verbal reasoning score: **9.0**, Physical sciences score: **8.9**, Biological sciences score: **9.2**, Writing score: **P**
Proportion with undergraduate majors in: Biological sciences: **77%**, Physical sciences: **7%**, Non-sciences: **8%**, Other health professions: **3%**, Mixed disciplines and other: **5%**
Percentage of students not coming directly from college after graduation: **19%**

Dates and details
The American Medical College Application Service (AMCAS) application is accepted.
School asks for a school-specific application as part of the admissions process.
Oldest MCAT considered for Fall 2005 entry: **2003**
Earliest application date for the 2005-2006 first-year class: **June 3, 2004**
Latest application date: **November 3, 2004**
Acceptance dates for regular application for the class entering in fall 2005:

Earliest: **November 20, 2004**
Latest: **August 27, 2005**
The school doesn't consider requests for deferred entrance.
Starting month for the class entering in 2005-2006: **August**
The school has an Early Decision Plan (EDP).
A personal interview is required for admission.

Undergraduate coursework required
Medical school requires undergraduate work in these subjects: organic chemistry, physics.

ADMISSIONS POLICY
(TEXT PROVIDED BY SCHOOL):
A candidate for the M.D. degree must be able to demonstrate intellectual-conceptual, integrative, and quantitative abilities; skills in observation, communication, and motor functions; and mature behavioral and social attributes. For a more detailed explanation of the above, please contact the Office of Admissions at (800) 686-2511.

NEOUCOM is a publicly chartered and funded institution in the state of Ohio. Therefore, as a result of this public support, its charter mandates giving admission preference to residents of the state of Ohio, as defined by the Board of Regents.
• Only U.S. citizens and permanent residents may be considered for admission to NEOUCOM; candidates must have such status upon application.

COSTS AND FINANCIAL AID
Financial aid phone number: **(330) 325-6479**
Tuition, 2003-2004 academic year: **In-state: $19,371; Out-of-state: $37,626**
Room and board: **$9,167**
Percentage of students receiving financial aid in 2003-04: **77%**
Percentage of students receiving: Loans: **73%**, Grants/scholarships: **36%**, Work-study aid: **0%**
Average medical school debt for the Class of 2002: **$80,916**

STUDENT BODY

Fall 2003 full-time enrollment: 430

Men: 48%, Women: 52%, In-state: 97%, Minorities: 44%,
American Indian: 0.7%, Asian-American: 37.9%,
African-American: 3.7%, Hispanic-American: 1.6%,
White: 56.0%, International: 0.0%, Unknown: 0.0%

ACADEMIC PROGRAMS

The school's curriculum doesn't give first-year students
substantial contact with patients.

There are opportunities for first- or second-year students to
work in community health clinics.

Program offerings: AIDS, drug/alcohol abuse, family
medicine, geriatrics, internal medicine, pediatrics, rural
medicine

Joint degrees awarded: N/A

Total National Institutes of Health (NIH) grants awarded to
the medical school and affiliated hospitals: $2.2 million

CURRICULUM
(TEXT PROVIDED BY SCHOOL):

Students of the Northeastern Ohio Universities College of
Medicine (NEOUCOM) receive quality medical education
that not only emphasizes the science of medicine but also
the art of healing.

One important component of the NEOUCOM educational experience is the Center for Studies of Clinical
Performance. The CSCP consists of 16 state-of-the-art exam
rooms where students from the first through the fourth
year of medical school enhance their clinical and communication skills by examining standardized patients, who are
people from the community trained to portray patients with
illness. The student-patient interactions are recorded, and
members of the clinical faculty rate the students according
to multiple criteria. This nationally recognized program
helps students to grow into highly skilled, compassionate
physicians.

The first-year student receives instruction in basic medical science courses that emphasize the normal structure
and function of the human body, the mechanisms by which
these are maintained, and the factors leading to injury and
disease. The behavioral sciences program teaches the normal development of an individual's mental, personal, and
social capabilities, as well as principles for application in
clinical problem solving and in the medical interview.
Interdisciplinary instruction also is given in geriatrics, community health, and human sexuality. First-year students
experience healthcare in a variety of settings (both in and
outside of the hospital setting) through the ambulatory care
experience program.

The sophomore medical year serves as the bridge from
classroom and laboratory basic science work to clinical

applications in hospitals and ambulatory settings. Students
are on the Rootstown campus two days per week and are
learning in small groups in NEOUCOM's affiliated hospitals three days per week.

The junior medical year provides theoretical and practical
foundations in the clinical disciplines. Working with clinical
faculty and residents in our eight major teaching hospitals,
NEOUCOM students learn diagnostic and therapeutic
skills, gain experience in patient management, and examine
the ethical dilemmas of contemporary medicine.

Guided by advisers and working within a set of requirements, seniors design their own curricula based on their
educational and career priorities. Throughout the year, students take at least five clinical electives, balanced across four
major categories. Three required courses must also be
taken, including the primary-care preceptorship, community medicine, and human values in medicine (HVM).
HVM courses help students gain awareness of their own
and others' value systems and their role in the physician-
patient relationship. At least 30 HVM credits must be
earned throughout the four years of medical school.

FACULTY PROFILE (FALL 2003)

Total teaching faculty: 255 (full-time), 1,690 (part-time)

Of full-time faculty, those teaching in basic sciences: 18%;
in clinical programs: 82%

Of part-time faculty, those teaching in basic sciences: 7%;
in clinical programs: 93%

Full-time faculty/student ratio: 0.6

SUPPORT SERVICES

The school offers students these services for dealing with
stress: expanded-hour gym access, peer counseling, professional counseling.

RESIDENCY CHOICES

Most popular residency and specialty programs chosen by
the 2002 and 2003 M.D. graduating classes: anesthesiology,
emergency medicine, family practice, internal medicine,
obstetrics and gynecology, orthopedic surgery, pediatrics,
physical medicine and rehabilitation, psychiatry,
surgery–general.

WHERE GRADS GO

42.0%

Proportion of 2001-2003 graduates who entered primary
care specialties

56.0%

Proportion of 2002-2003 graduates who accepted in-state
residencies

Northwestern University

FEINBERG

- 303 E. Chicago Avenue, Morton Building 1-606, Chicago, IL 60611
- Private
- Year Founded: 1859
- Tuition, 2003-2004: $37,175
- Enrollment, 2003-2004: 695
- Website: http://www.nums.nwu.edu
- Specialty ranking: AIDS: 17, internal medicine: 23, pediatrics: 16, women's health: 17

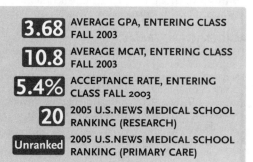

3.68	AVERAGE GPA, ENTERING CLASS FALL 2003
10.8	AVERAGE MCAT, ENTERING CLASS FALL 2003
5.4%	ACCEPTANCE RATE, ENTERING CLASS FALL 2003
20	2005 U.S.NEWS MEDICAL SCHOOL RANKING (RESEARCH)
Unranked	2005 U.S.NEWS MEDICAL SCHOOL RANKING (PRIMARY CARE)

ADMISSIONS

Admissions phone number: **(312) 503-8206**
Admissions email address: **med-admissions@ northwestern.edu**
Application website: **http://www.med-admissions. northwestern.edu**
Acceptance rate: **5.4%**
In-state acceptance rate: **N/A**
Out-of-state acceptance rate: **N/A**
Minority acceptance rate: **N/A**
International acceptance rate: **N/A**

Fall 2003 applications and acceptees

	Applied	Interviewed	Accepted	Enrolled
Total:	5,957	631	323	170
In-state:	860	117	N/A	46
Out-of-state:	5,097	514	N/A	124

Profile of admitted students

Average undergraduate grade point average: **3.68**
MCAT averages (scale: 1-15; writing test: J-T):
  Composite score: **10.8**
  Verbal reasoning score: **10.4**, Physical sciences score: **10.9**, Biological sciences score: **11.0**, Writing score: **Q**
Proportion with undergraduate majors in: Biological sciences: **52%**, Physical sciences: **22%**, Non-sciences: **24%**, Other health professions: **0%**, Mixed disciplines and other: **2%**
Percentage of students not coming directly from college after graduation: **33%**

Dates and details

The American Medical College Application Service (AMCAS) application is accepted.
School asks for a school-specific application as part of the admissions process.
Oldest MCAT considered for Fall 2005 entry: **2002**
Earliest application date for the 2005-2006 first-year class: **June 1, 2004**
Latest application date: **November 1, 2004**

Acceptance dates for regular application for the class entering in fall 2005:
  Earliest: **November 19, 2004**
  Latest: **February 25, 2005**
The school considers requests for deferred entrance. Starting month for the class entering in 2005-2006: **August**
The school doesn't have an Early Decision Plan (EDP).
A personal interview is required for admission.

Undergraduate coursework required

Medical school requires undergraduate work in these subjects: biology, English, organic chemistry, inorganic (general) chemistry, physics.

ADMISSIONS POLICY
(TEXT PROVIDED BY SCHOOL):

The Committee on Admissions seeks applicants who have demonstrated academic excellence, leadership qualities, intellectual curiosity, and personal maturity. Applicants should be liberally educated men and women who have studied in some depth subjects beyond the conventional required premedical courses. The Medical School has a particular interest in students with promise as physician-scholars. Experience in research and evidence of a commitment to medicine as a service profession are also positive factors for selection.

The Medical School maintains the richest possible educational environment through the enrollment of a diverse student body, one that represents applicants from underrepresented populations, those having prior work experience, and students from all areas of the United States and from around the world. No preference is given to Illinois residents.

The equivalent of three years of college is the minimum required for entrance. While a bachelor's degree is not required, it is preferred. The following coursework is recommended: modern biology (one year), general physics (one year), inorganic chemistry (one year), organic chemistry (one year), and English (one year). The Medical College Admission Test is required of all applicants.

Applications from international students are welcome, provided that at least three years of coursework have been completed at an accredited U.S. or Canadian college or university. This policy applies to all applicants, regardless of their citizenship status.

An American Medical College Application Service application, submitted electronically, is required. Selected applicants will be asked to submit a supplemental application, processing fee, and letters of recommendation.

Interviews are held from September through mid-February at the school, on the Chicago campus of Northwestern University. All decisions are mailed to applicants by the end of February of the matriculation year.

COSTS AND FINANCIAL AID
Financial aid phone number: (312) 503-8722
Tuition, 2003-2004 academic year: $37,175
Room and board: $11,862
Percentage of students receiving financial aid in 2003-04: 72%
Percentage of students receiving: Loans: 68%, Grants/scholarships: 51%, Work-study aid: 0%
Average medical school debt for the Class of 2002: $117,448

STUDENT BODY
Fall 2003 full-time enrollment: 695
Men: 53%, Women: 47%, In-state: 31%, Minorities: 52%, American Indian: 0.6%, Asian-American: 41.3%, African-American: 3.9%, Hispanic-American: 5.8%, White: 42.9%, International: 4.3%, Unknown: 1.3%

ACADEMIC PROGRAMS
The school's curriculum gives first-year students substantial contact with patients.
There are opportunities for first- or second-year students to work in community health clinics.
Program offerings: AIDS, drug/alcohol abuse, family medicine, geriatrics, internal medicine, pediatrics, rural medicine, women's health
Joint degrees awarded: M.D./Ph.D., M.D./M.B.A., M.D./M.P.H.
Total National Institutes of Health (NIH) grants awarded to the medical school and affiliated hospitals: $171.3 million

CURRICULUM
(TEXT PROVIDED BY SCHOOL):
The first- and second-year curriculum is composed of three courses. Each course is interdisciplinary and draws faculty from a number of departments. There are two courses in the basic medical sciences. Each involves approximately 10 hours of lecture per week for the entire academic year, complemented by problem-based-learning sessions, laboratories, and small-group discussions and tutorials. Structure-Function, the first-year course, begins with a review of cell and molecular biology, genetics, and signal transduction, then addresses gross and microscopic anatomy, biochemistry, and physiology. In the second year,

The Scientific Basis of Medicine begins with an overview of immunology, microbiology, and infectious diseases and then details the pathology, pathophysiology, and pharmacology specific to each organ system.

The Medical Decision Making course occupies three short blocks of time in the first and second years. This course allows students to develop knowledge and skills in information management, epidemiology, biostatistics, and clinical problem solving.

The course Patient, Physician & Society is devoted to the development of clinical skills and professional perspectives, and provides each student opportunity to develop mentoring relationships with faculty preceptors. The class is divided into four "colleges," each led by an experienced clinician. Colleges meet two afternoons per week throughout the first two years. One afternoon offers learning experiences centered around clinical skills development and the provision of an integrated biopsychosocial perspective on illness and patient care. The other afternoon's course sequence addresses medical ethics and humanities, public health, and health policy.

The third year requires 48 weeks of rotation through clerkships in the major clinical disciplines. In the fourth year, three specific clinical experiences are required: a six-week acting internship in either internal medicine or pediatrics, a four-week clerkship in emergency medicine, and a two-week clerkship in physical medicine and rehabilitation. The remainder of the fourth year consists of elective clerkships and research experiences.

FACULTY PROFILE (FALL 2003)
Total teaching faculty: 1,607 (full-time), 176 (part-time)
Of full-time faculty, those teaching in basic sciences: 12%; in clinical programs: 88%
Of part-time faculty, those teaching in basic sciences: 0%; in clinical programs: 100%
Full-time faculty/student ratio: 2.3

SUPPORT SERVICES
The school offers students these services for dealing with stress: professional counseling, support groups.

RESIDENCY CHOICES
Most popular residency and specialty programs chosen by the 2002 and 2003 M.D. graduating classes: anesthesiology, emergency medicine, family practice, internal medicine, obstetrics and gynecology, ophthalmology, orthopedic surgery, pediatrics, radiology–diagnostic, surgery–general.

WHERE GRADS GO

41.3%
Proportion of 2001-2003 graduates who entered primary care specialties

32.5%
Proportion of 2002-2003 graduates who accepted in-state residencies

Ohio State University

- 200 Meiling Hall, 370 W. Ninth Avenue, Columbus, OH 43210-1238
- Public
- Year Founded: 1834
- Tuition, 2003-2004: In-state: $19,714; Out-of-state: $25,853
- Enrollment, 2003-2004: 839
- Website: http://medicine.osu.edu
- Specialty ranking: N/A

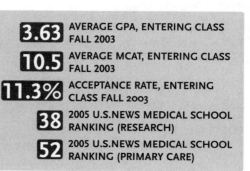

3.63 AVERAGE GPA, ENTERING CLASS FALL 2003

10.5 AVERAGE MCAT, ENTERING CLASS FALL 2003

11.3% ACCEPTANCE RATE, ENTERING CLASS FALL 2003

38 2005 U.S.NEWS MEDICAL SCHOOL RANKING (RESEARCH)

52 2005 U.S.NEWS MEDICAL SCHOOL RANKING (PRIMARY CARE)

ADMISSIONS

Admissions phone number: **(614) 292-7137**
Admissions email address: **medicine@osu.edu**
Application website: **http://www.aamc.org**
Acceptance rate: 11.3%
In-state acceptance rate: 20.2%
Out-of-state acceptance rate: 7.3%
Minority acceptance rate: 10.3%
International acceptance rate: 9.1%

Fall 2003 applications and acceptees

	Applied	Interviewed	Accepted	Enrolled
Total:	3,276	683	369	210
In-state:	1,001	368	202	130
Out-of-state:	2,275	315	167	80

Profile of admitted students

Average undergraduate grade point average: 3.63
MCAT averages (scale: 1-15; writing test: J-T):
 Composite score: 10.5
 Verbal reasoning score: 9.9, Physical sciences score: 10.6, Biological sciences score: 10.8, Writing score: P
Proportion with undergraduate majors in: Biological sciences: 59%, Physical sciences: 21%, Non-sciences: 11%, Other health professions: 4%, Mixed disciplines and other: 5%
Percentage of students not coming directly from college after graduation: 3%

Dates and details

The American Medical College Application Service (AMCAS) application is accepted.
School asks for a school-specific application as part of the admissions process.
Oldest MCAT considered for Fall 2005 entry: **2002**
Earliest application date for the 2005-2006 first-year class: **June 1, 2004**
Latest application date: **November 1, 2004**
Acceptance dates for regular application for the class entering in fall 2005:
 Earliest: **October 15, 2004**

Latest: **August 15, 2005**
The school considers requests for deferred entrance.
Starting month for the class entering in 2005-2006:
 August
The school has an Early Decision Plan (EDP).
A personal interview is required for admission.

Undergraduate coursework required

Medical school requires undergraduate work in these subjects: biology, biology/zoology, organic chemistry, inorganic (general) chemistry, physics, general chemistry.

ADMISSIONS POLICY
(TEXT PROVIDED BY SCHOOL):

Application for admission is initiated through the American Medical College Application Service (AMCAS). Applicants designating Ohio State University on the AMCAS application will receive an email from the College of Medicine directing them to the Web-based secondary application. Applications are reviewed upon receipt of the AMCAS application, the secondary application, and Medical College Admission Test scores. Applicants have access to the status of their application in real time, including: receipt of AMCAS application; receipt of secondary application; interview invitation, with capability to confirm or reschedule via the Web; and admissions decision, with a multimedia message for accepted students.

On-site interviews are conducted from mid-September through March. Admission decisions are made on a rolling monthly basis. Applicants interviewing in September are notified of their admission decision on October 15. Applicants interviewing in October though March are notified on the first business day of the month following their interview.

The College of Medicine and Public Health Admissions Committee will evaluate applicants by competitive admission standards. Along with strong academic performance, we look for self-motivated, compassionate applicants with strong integrity and interpersonal skills to match the intellectual, physical, and emotional capacities needed to master the medical curriculum. Diverse interests and backgrounds are helpful in establishing a balanced view of society necessary for success in medical practice. We encourage applicants to include subjects such as philosophy, literature, writing, history, arts, and languages in the traditional undergraduate premedical curriculum.

Applicants must embody high ethical standards, especially honesty and concern for others, and must be free of substance abuse, addictions, and violent behaviors. They must also possess the skills required to practice direct patient care. No specific undergraduate curriculum or college major is required. However, the prerequisite requirements must be met prior to matriculation. In addition, coursework in biochemistry or cellular and molecular biology is strongly recommended.

COSTS AND FINANCIAL AID

Financial aid phone number: **(614) 292-8771**
Tuition, 2003-2004 academic year: **In-state: $19,714; Out-of-state: $25,853**
Room and board: **$6,850**
Percentage of students receiving financial aid in 2003-04: **98%**
Percentage of students receiving: Loans: **88%**, Grants/scholarships: **51%**, Work-study aid: **0%**
Average medical school debt for the Class of 2002: **$92,253**

STUDENT BODY

Fall 2003 full-time enrollment: **839**
Men: **57%**, Women: **43%**, In-state: **63%**, Minorities: **26%**, American Indian: **0.5%**, Asian-American: **17.0%**, African-American: **6.7%**, Hispanic-American: **2.0%**, White: **70.4%**, International: **1.1%**, Unknown: **2.3%**

ACADEMIC PROGRAMS

The school's curriculum gives first-year students substantial contact with patients.
There are opportunities for first- or second-year students to work in community health clinics.
Program offerings: AIDS, drug/alcohol abuse, family medicine, geriatrics, internal medicine, pediatrics, rural medicine, women's health
Joint degrees awarded: M.D./Ph.D., M.D./M.B.A., M.D./M.P.H., M.D./J.D., M.D./M.H.A.
Total National Institutes of Health (NIH) grants awarded to the medical school and affiliated hospitals: **$148.3 million**

CURRICULUM

(TEXT PROVIDED BY SCHOOL):

All preclinical students are enrolled in two courses throughout both preclinical years—Patient-Centered Medicine (PCM) and Physician Development (PD). PCM is taught in a small-group, case-based format and deals with topics including ethics, professionalism, self-care, diversity, and substance abuse, as well as a community project. PD includes the doctor-patient relationship, clinical interviewing, and physical examination, and a geriatric longitudinal care experience. A newly constructed clinical skills laboratory is available to assist instruction through the use of standardized patients and simulations.

The preclinical curriculum also allows students to choose between two curricular pathways for the core scientific content—Integrated (IP) and Independent Study (ISP). IP is a two-year curriculum that integrates basic and clinical sciences in organ-specific modules. It was implemented in 2002. ISP presents the curriculum in an independent study format guided by written learning objectives related to readings. ISP has a 30-year history of success. Ohio State requires successful completion of U.S. Medical Licensing Examination Step 1 to continue into the clinical portion of the curriculum.

The third year consists of six- to 12-week blocks of the core clinical clerkships: internal medicine (eight weeks), pediatrics (eight weeks), psychiatry/neurology (eight weeks), surgery (six weeks), obstetrics/gynecology (six weeks), and ambulatory (12 weeks). All core clerkships must be taken at one of the affiliated teaching hospitals.

The fourth year consists of four-week blocks, of which four blocks must be selected from the Differentiation of Care (DOC) selectives and four are elective choices. Three blocks are available for preparation for USMLE Step 2, residency interviews, or vacation. All DOC selectives must be taken at an affiliated institution. Electives may be taken at any location, including a variety of international health experiences. Successful completion of USMLE Step 2 is required prior to graduation.

FACULTY PROFILE (FALL 2003)

Total teaching faculty: **1,450 (full-time), 1,061 (part-time)**
Of full-time faculty, those teaching in basic sciences: **21%**; in clinical programs: **79%**
Of part-time faculty, those teaching in basic sciences: **8%**; in clinical programs: **92%**
Full-time faculty/student ratio: **1.7**

SUPPORT SERVICES

The school offers students these services for dealing with stress: expanded-hour gym access, professional counseling, support groups.

RESIDENCY CHOICES

Most popular residency and specialty programs chosen by the 2002 and 2003 M.D. graduating classes: anesthesiology, emergency medicine, family practice, internal medicine, internal medicine–pediatrics, ophthalmology, orthopedic surgery, pediatrics, psychiatry, surgery–general.

WHERE GRADS GO

47.0%
Proportion of 2001-2003 graduates who entered primary care specialties

47.0%
Proportion of 2002-2003 graduates who accepted in-state residencies

Oregon Health & Science University

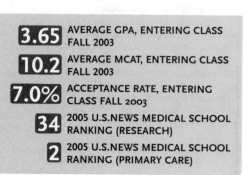

- 3181 S.W. Sam Jackson Park Road, L102, Portland, OR 97239-3098
- Public
- Year Founded: 1887
- Tuition, 2003-2004: In-state: $24,462; Out-of-state: $34,962
- Enrollment, 2003-2004: 422
- Website: http://www.ohsu.edu
- Specialty ranking: family medicine: 3, rural medicine: 20

3.65	AVERAGE GPA, ENTERING CLASS FALL 2003
10.2	AVERAGE MCAT, ENTERING CLASS FALL 2003
7.0%	ACCEPTANCE RATE, ENTERING CLASS FALL 2003
34	2005 U.S.NEWS MEDICAL SCHOOL RANKING (RESEARCH)
2	2005 U.S.NEWS MEDICAL SCHOOL RANKING (PRIMARY CARE)

ADMISSIONS

Admissions phone number: (503) 494-2998
Admissions email address: N/A
Application website:
  http://www.ohsu.edu/som/dean/md/admissions
Acceptance rate: 7.0%
In-state acceptance rate: 21.2%
Out-of-state acceptance rate: 5.2%
Minority acceptance rate: 5.8%
International acceptance rate: N/A

Fall 2003 applications and acceptees

	Applied	Interviewed	Accepted	Enrolled
Total:	2,740	468	192	107
In-state:	316	178	67	55
Out-of-state:	2,424	290	125	52

Profile of admitted students

Average undergraduate grade point average: 3.65
MCAT averages (scale: 1-15; writing test: J-T):
  Composite score: 10.2
  Verbal reasoning score: 9.9, Physical sciences score:
  10.2, Biological sciences score: 10.6, Writing score: P
Proportion with undergraduate majors in: Biological
sciences: 40%, Physical sciences: 15%, Non-sciences:
22%, Other health professions: 0%, Mixed disciplines
and other: 23%
Percentage of students not coming directly from college
after graduation: 72%

Dates and details

The American Medical College Application Service
  (AMCAS) application is accepted.
School asks for a school-specific application as part of the
  admissions process.
Oldest MCAT considered for Fall 2005 entry: 2001
Earliest application date for the 2005-2006 first-year class:
  June 15, 2004
Latest application date: October 15, 2004
Acceptance dates for regular application for the class
  entering in fall 2005:

Earliest: **November 15, 2000**
  Latest: **August 15, 2000**
The school doesn't consider requests for deferred entrance.
Starting month for the class entering in 2005-2006:
  August
The school doesn't have an Early Decision Plan (EDP).
A personal interview is required for admission.

Undergraduate coursework required

Medical school requires undergraduate work in these subjects: biology, English, organic chemistry, inorganic (general) chemistry, physics, biochemistry, humanities,
mathematics, demonstration of writing skills, social sciences, general chemistry.

ADMISSIONS POLICY

(TEXT PROVIDED BY SCHOOL):
Candidates for admission are considered comparatively on
the basis of: assessment of motivation, ability to communicate, problem-solving ability, and maturity; review of overall
scholastic record; review of Medical College Admission Test
scores; review of letters of recommendation; understanding
and appreciation of healthcare issues and/or biomedical
research; and interest in rural health, underserved areas,
and primary care.

With respect to the M.D./Ph.D. combined degree program, candidates are also assessed on their commitment to
and potential for biomedical research.

Applicants are selected for admission regardless of race,
gender, age, religion, national origin, color, marital status,
or disabilities.

The School of Medicine gives preference to residents of
Oregon. Preference is also given to nonresidents of Oregon
who fit into one or more of the following categories: applicants from Montana and Wyoming certified under the
Western Interstate Commission on Higher Education program; members of underrepresented ethnic/racial groups;
applicants to the M.D./Ph.D. and M.D./M.P.H. combined
degree programs; and applicants with superior achievements, such as academics, related experiences, and so on.

All applicants must have U.S. citizenship or resident alien status with a green card indicating permanent residency in the United States.

COSTS AND FINANCIAL AID

Financial aid phone number: **(503) 494-7800**
Tuition, 2003-2004 academic year: **In-state: $24,462; Out-of-state: $34,962**
Room and board: **$13,000**
Percentage of students receiving financial aid in 2003-04: **95%**
Percentage of students receiving: Loans: **90%**, Grants/scholarships: **80%**, Work-study aid: **2%**
Average medical school debt for the Class of 2002: **$122,524**

STUDENT BODY

Fall 2003 full-time enrollment: **422**
Men: **45%**, Women: **55%**, In-state: **64%**, Minorities: **20%**, American Indian: **8.1%**, Asian-American: **69.8%**, African-American: **10.5%**, Hispanic-American: **7.0%**, White: **4.7%**, International: **0.0%**, Unknown: **0.0%**

ACADEMIC PROGRAMS

The school's curriculum gives first-year students substantial contact with patients.
There are opportunities for first- or second-year students to work in community health clinics.
Program offerings: AIDS, drug/alcohol abuse, family medicine, geriatrics, internal medicine, pediatrics, rural medicine, women's health
Joint degrees awarded: M.D./Ph.D., M.D./M.P.H.
Total National Institutes of Health (NIH) grants awarded to the medical school and affiliated hospitals: **$163.9 million**

CURRICULUM

(TEXT PROVIDED BY SCHOOL):
The goal of the School of Medicine curriculum is to present a four-year continuum that balances emphasis on the scientific basis of medicine with early clinical experience; offers progressive patient-care responsibilities for students; and permits students to individualize their educational programs as well as enhance their independent-learning and problem-solving skills. The sciences basic to medicine are presented in an interdisciplinary format, focusing initially on the scientific principles of medicine and ultimately progressing to disease process.

Highlights include: centralized responsibility; integrated and multidisciplinary basic science courses with enhanced clinical relevance and logical sequencing; lecture and non-lecture learning balanced in half-day sessions; courses given in a series to avoid competing with other courses; instructional objective-based education; early and longitudinal clinical preceptorship; required clinical experience in a rural and/or underserved area; strong emphasis on ambulatory and primary care; and performance-based assessment of students utilizing standardized patients.

FACULTY PROFILE (FALL 2003)

Total teaching faculty: **1,038 (full-time)**, **278 (part-time)**
Of full-time faculty, those teaching in basic sciences: **11%**; in clinical programs: **89%**
Of part-time faculty, those teaching in basic sciences: **13%**; in clinical programs: **87%**
Full-time faculty/student ratio: **2.5**

SUPPORT SERVICES

The school offers students these services for dealing with stress: expanded-hour gym access, peer counseling, professional counseling, religious support, support groups.

RESIDENCY CHOICES

Most popular residency and specialty programs chosen by the 2002 and 2003 M.D. graduating classes: anesthesiology, emergency medicine, family practice, internal medicine, obstetrics and gynecology, pediatrics, psychiatry, radiology–diagnostic, surgery–general, urology.

WHERE GRADS GO

44.0%
Proportion of 2001-2003 graduates who entered primary care specialties

30.0%
Proportion of 2002-2003 graduates who accepted in-state residencies

Southern Illinois University–Springfield

- 801 N. Rutledge, PO Box 19620, Springfield, IL 62794-9620
- Public
- Year Founded: 1970
- Tuition, 2003-2004: In-state: $18,156; Out-of-state: $50,452
- Enrollment, 2003-2004: 292
- Website: http://www.siumed.edu
- Specialty ranking: family medicine: 14, rural medicine: 17

3.56 AVERAGE GPA, ENTERING CLASS FALL 2003

9.1 AVERAGE MCAT, ENTERING CLASS FALL 2003

13.0% ACCEPTANCE RATE, ENTERING CLASS FALL 2003

Unranked 2005 U.S.NEWS MEDICAL SCHOOL RANKING (RESEARCH)

39 2005 U.S.NEWS MEDICAL SCHOOL RANKING (PRIMARY CARE)

ADMISSIONS

Admissions phone number: **(217) 545-6013**
Admissions email address: **admissions@siumed.edu**
Application website: **N/A**
Acceptance rate: **13.0%**
In-state acceptance rate: **17.7%**
Out-of-state acceptance rate: **0.6%**
Minority acceptance rate: **N/A**
International acceptance rate: **N/A**

Fall 2003 applications and acceptees

	Applied	Interviewed	Accepted	Enrolled
Total:	1,139	282	148	72
In-state:	827	277	146	72
Out-of-state:	312	5	2	0

Profile of admitted students

Average undergraduate grade point average: **3.56**
MCAT averages (scale: 1-15; writing test: J-T):
  Composite score: **9.1**
  Verbal reasoning score: **9.1**, Physical sciences score: **8.8**,
  Biological sciences score: **9.3**, Writing score: **O**
Proportion with undergraduate majors in: Biological sciences: **53%**, Physical sciences: **17%**, Non-sciences: **18%**, Other health professions: **2%**, Mixed disciplines and other: **10%**
Percentage of students not coming directly from college after graduation: **40%**

Dates and details

The American Medical College Application Service (AMCAS) application is accepted.
School asks for a school-specific application as part of the admissions process.
Oldest MCAT considered for Fall 2005 entry: **2002**
Earliest application date for the 2005-2006 first-year class: **June 1, 2004**
Latest application date: **November 15, 2004**
Acceptance dates for regular application for the class entering in fall 2005:
  Earliest: **October 15, 2004**

Latest: **August 15, 2005**
The school considers requests for deferred entrance.
Starting month for the class entering in 2005-2006:
  August
The school doesn't have an Early Decision Plan (EDP).
A personal interview is required for admission.

ADMISSIONS POLICY
(TEXT PROVIDED BY SCHOOL):

SIU School of Medicine begins by looking for applications with competitive grade-point averages and Medical College Admission Test scores. Applicants are expected to have a good foundation in the natural sciences, social sciences, and humanities and facility in writing and speaking the English language. The Admissions Committee also looks for evidence of responsibility, maturity, integrity, social awareness, compassion, service orientation, proper motivation, exploration of medicine as a career, and good interpersonal skills. We also look for identification with the goals and nature of the school, since our mission is to help the people of central and southern Illinois in meeting their present and future healthcare needs through education, clinical service, and research. SIU also stresses primary care, and a majority of our graduates have always entered primary-care specialties.

Applications are accepted from Illinois residents who are U.S. citizens or foreign citizens with a permanent resident visa. Preference is given to established residents of downstate Illinois and other underserved locations in the state of Illinois (including rural and inner-city areas). A limited number of out-of-state residents are considered for the M.D./J.D. program only. Applicants should display evidence of participation in extracurricular and volunteer activities and employed positions.

COSTS AND FINANCIAL AID

Financial aid phone number: **(217) 545-2224**
Tuition, 2003-2004 academic year: **In-state: $18,156; Out-of-state: $50,452**
Room and board: **$8,975**
Percentage of students receiving financial aid in 2003-04: **90%**

Percentage of students receiving: Loans: **88%**,
Grants/scholarships: **38%**, Work-study aid: **0%**
Average medical school debt for the Class of 2002:
$97,800

STUDENT BODY

Fall 2003 full-time enrollment: **292**
Men: **48%**, Women: **52%**, In-state: **100%**, Minorities: **20%**,
American Indian: **0.3%**, Asian-American: **11.0%**,
African-American: **6.5%**, Hispanic-American: **2.1%**,
White: **80.1%**, International: **0.0%**, Unknown: **0.0%**

ACADEMIC PROGRAMS

The school's curriculum gives first-year students
substantial contact with patients.
There are opportunities for first- or second-year students to
work in community health clinics.
Program offerings: AIDS, drug/alcohol abuse, family
medicine, geriatrics, internal medicine, pediatrics, rural
medicine, women's health
Joint degrees awarded: M.D./J.D.
Total National Institutes of Health (NIH) grants awarded to
the medical school and affiliated hospitals: **N/A**

CURRICULUM

(TEXT PROVIDED BY SCHOOL):
SIU School of Medicine is a public medical school established in 1970 and focused on the healthcare needs of
downstate Illinois. We have always been a leader in medical
education and recognized for innovative teaching and testing techniques, including a competency-base curriculum,
the use of simulated patients, and courses in medical
humanities. (Most U.S. medical schools studied our curriculum before updating theirs in the 1980s.)

The overall focus of our curriculum is on clinical case-
based, self-directed learning in a small-group setting. Our
goal is to foster the integration of basic and clinical science
knowledge as students solve patient problems. Students
work toward competency, focusing on what they should
learn rather than on what teachers want to teach. Our community-based structure places students in physicians' offices
and local hospitals so they are educated as adult learners in
the real world of medicine. Clinical experiences also include
continuity clinic assignments and a doctoring curriculum.
These extensive clinical activities in all four years help students become caring and competent physicians.

We continue SIU's emphasis on treating patients as people rather than solely as medical conditions in various ways,
including emphasizing community healthcare and the psychosocial issues of medicine. Development of lifelong learning skills also is important in our program.

FACULTY PROFILE (FALL 2003)

Total teaching faculty: **306 (full-time)**, **907 (part-time)**
Of full-time faculty, those teaching in basic sciences: **46%**;
in clinical programs: **54%**
Of part-time faculty, those teaching in basic sciences: **20%**;
in clinical programs: **80%**
Full-time faculty/student ratio: **1.0**

SUPPORT SERVICES

The school offers students these services for dealing with
stress: peer counseling, professional counseling, support
groups.

RESIDENCY CHOICES

Most popular residency and specialty programs chosen by the
2002 and 2003 M.D. graduating classes: anesthesiology,
emergency medicine, family practice, internal medicine,
obstetrics and gynecology, pediatrics, psychiatry,
radiology–diagnostic, surgery–general, internal
medicine/pediatrics.

WHERE GRADS GO

48.0%
*Proportion of 2001-2003 graduates who entered primary
care specialties*

41.0%
*Proportion of 2002-2003 graduates who accepted in-state
residencies*

Stanford University

- 300 Pasteur Drive, Suite M121, Stanford, CA 94305
- Private
- **Year Founded:** 1858
- **Tuition, 2003-2004:** $35,682
- **Enrollment, 2003-2004:** 463
- **Website:** http://www.med.stanford.edu
- **Specialty ranking:** AIDS: 15, geriatrics: 15, internal medicine: 9, pediatrics: 8, women's health: 12

3.75	AVERAGE GPA, ENTERING CLASS FALL 2003
11.2	AVERAGE MCAT, ENTERING CLASS FALL 2003
3.4%	ACCEPTANCE RATE, ENTERING CLASS FALL 2003
8	2005 U.S.NEWS MEDICAL SCHOOL RANKING (RESEARCH)
Unranked	2005 U.S.NEWS MEDICAL SCHOOL RANKING (PRIMARY CARE)

ADMISSIONS

Admissions phone number: **(650) 723-6861**
Admissions email address: **admissions@med.stanford.edu**
Application website: **http://www.aamc.org**
Acceptance rate: **3.4%**
In-state acceptance rate: **3.5%**
Out-of-state acceptance rate: **3.4%**
Minority acceptance rate: **4.3%**
International acceptance rate: **5.0%**

Fall 2003 applications and acceptees

	Applied	Interviewed	Accepted	Enrolled
Total:	5,445	556	186	87
In-state:	2,024	216	71	34
Out-of-state:	3,421	340	115	53

Profile of admitted students

Average undergraduate grade point average: **3.75**
MCAT averages (scale: 1-15; writing test: J-T):
Composite score: **11.2**
Verbal reasoning score: **10.2**, Physical sciences score: **11.6**, Biological sciences score: **11.8**, Writing score: **Q**
Proportion with undergraduate majors in: Biological sciences: **49%**, Physical sciences: **41%**, Non-sciences: **7%**, Other health professions: **0%**, Mixed disciplines and other: **3%**
Percentage of students not coming directly from college after graduation: **59%**

Dates and details

The American Medical College Application Service (AMCAS) application is accepted.
School asks for a school-specific application as part of the admissions process.
Oldest MCAT considered for Fall 2005 entry: **2002**
Earliest application date for the 2005-2006 first-year class: **June 1, 2004**
Latest application date: **October 15, 2004**
Acceptance dates for regular application for the class entering in fall 2005:
Earliest: **November 1, 2004**

Latest: **April 30, 2005**
The school considers requests for deferred entrance.
Starting month for the class entering in 2005-2006:
September
The school has an Early Decision Plan (EDP).
A personal interview is required for admission.

Undergraduate coursework required

Medical school requires undergraduate work in these subjects: biology, organic chemistry, inorganic (general) chemistry, physics.

ADMISSIONS POLICY
(TEXT PROVIDED BY SCHOOL):

Stanford University School of Medicine is interested in candidates who have a strong humanitarian commitment and whose accomplishments show originality, creativity, and a capacity for independent, critical thinking. Enthusiasm for the basic sciences and humanities is prerequisite for admission to the school. An undergraduate major in any field is acceptable. The committee values applications from students who have tested their interest in working in the healthcare environment, in the laboratory, in activities involving the care of others, and in community services that include a working knowledge of the human condition beyond one's own socioeconomic and cultural group.

Grade-point average and Medical College Admission Test scores are important variables but do not entirely govern the process. The MCAT should be taken in April, but in no case later than the late summer of the year in which the application is submitted. Applications are not processed until the Office of Admissions receives the MCAT scores.

Minimum course requirements for admission include: biological sciences (the equivalent of one full academic year), chemistry (the equivalent of two full academic years, including organic chemistry), and physics (the equivalent of one full academic year), including laboratory work in each of these subjects. Waivers may occasionally be given. Knowledge of a modern foreign language, specifically Spanish or an Asian language, and coursework in behavioral sciences, calculus, physical chemistry, cellular biology, genetics, and, in particular, biochemistry are strongly recommended.

Foreign students must have studied for at least one year in an accredited college or university in the United States, Canada, or the United Kingdom before applying. In-state residency does not grant special consideration in the admissions process.

COSTS AND FINANCIAL AID
Financial aid phone number: **(650) 723-6958**
Tuition, 2003-2004 academic year: **$35,682**
Room and board: **$17,467**
Percentage of students receiving financial aid in 2003-04: **73%**
Percentage of students receiving: Loans: **60%**, Grants/scholarships: **61%**, Work-study aid: **5%**
Average medical school debt for the Class of 2002: **$64,877**

STUDENT BODY
Fall 2003 full-time enrollment: **463**
Men: **49%**, Women: **51%**, In-state: **46%**, Minorities: **59%**, American Indian: **1.7%**, Asian-American: **35.6%**, African-American: **5.2%**, Hispanic-American: **14.7%**, White: **39.5%**, International: **3.0%**, Unknown: **0.2%**

ACADEMIC PROGRAMS
The school's curriculum gives first-year students substantial contact with patients.
There are opportunities for first- or second-year students to work in community health clinics.
Program offerings: AIDS, drug/alcohol abuse, family medicine, geriatrics, internal medicine, pediatrics, rural medicine, women's health
Joint degrees awarded: M.D./Ph.D., M.D./M.P.H., M.D./M.S.
Total National Institutes of Health (NIH) grants awarded to the medical school and affiliated hospitals: **N/A**

CURRICULUM
(TEXT PROVIDED BY SCHOOL):
The Stanford School of Medicine stepped into the education reform spotlight in the fall of 2003 with the launch of a new curriculum aimed at instilling a lifelong passion for learning while equipping students with the tools to translate laboratory discoveries into life-enhancing therapies throughout their careers.

The new curriculum strengthens clinical training earlier in the education process, adds basic science "refreshers" during the clinical years, and requires students to participate in a scholarly concentration, or medical major, in which they can hone their research skills while developing early expertise in a topic that excites them.

Key elements of the curriculum include: in-depth study in a scholarly concentration area that will span the student's years at Stanford; better integration of the basic science and clinical portions of the curriculum; restructuring courses to focus on individual organ systems to avoid the redundancies that occur by teaching each discipline as a separate subject; and reducing weekly classroom instruction to give students more time for research and academic exploration.

A primary goal of the new curriculum is to prepare students to continue learning throughout their careers. In addition to the science coursework during the first two years of the curriculum, students will get refreshers on basic science topics during the latter two years of medical school. Students will also develop their clinical skills each week of the first two years and work with patients experiencing the disorders being studied in the classroom.

Students will be expected to devote at least 200 hours to a project in the scholarly concentration area they select. The initial scholarly concentration areas are biomedical ethics and humanities; bioengineering; biomedical informatics; immunology; public service, and community medicine; women's health; health services and policy research; and molecular and genetic medicine. Students can create their own concentration area under faculty supervision.

FACULTY PROFILE (FALL 2003)
Total teaching faculty: **838 (full-time)**, **176 (part-time)**
Of full-time faculty, those teaching in basic sciences: **11%**; in clinical programs: **89%**
Of part-time faculty, those teaching in basic sciences: **2%**; in clinical programs: **98%**
Full-time faculty/student ratio: **1.8**

SUPPORT SERVICES
The school offers students these services for dealing with stress: expanded-hour gym access, peer counseling, professional counseling, religious support, support groups.

RESIDENCY CHOICES
Most popular residency and specialty programs chosen by the 2002 and 2003 M.D. graduating classes: dermatology, emergency medicine, internal medicine, neurology, obstetrics and gynecology, pathology–anatomic and clinical, pediatrics, psychiatry, radiology–diagnostic, surgery–general.

WHERE GRADS GO
39.5%
Proportion of 2001-2003 graduates who entered primary care specialties

58.0%
Proportion of 2002-2003 graduates who accepted in-state residencies

St. Louis University

■ 1402 S. Grand Boulevard, St. Louis, MO 63104
■ Private
■ Year Founded: 1836
■ Tuition, 2003-2004: $37,850
■ Enrollment, 2003-2004: 621
■ Website: http://medschool.slu.edu
■ Specialty ranking: geriatrics: 10

3.61	AVERAGE GPA, ENTERING CLASS FALL 2003
10.0	AVERAGE MCAT, ENTERING CLASS FALL 2003
15.5%	ACCEPTANCE RATE, ENTERING CLASS FALL 2003
Unranked	2005 U.S.NEWS MEDICAL SCHOOL RANKING (RESEARCH)
Unranked	2005 U.S.NEWS MEDICAL SCHOOL RANKING (PRIMARY CARE)

ADMISSIONS
Admissions phone number: **(314) 977-9870**
Admissions email address: **slumd@slu.edu**
Application website: **N/A**
Acceptance rate: **15.5%**
In-state acceptance rate: **28.0%**
Out-of-state acceptance rate: **14.3%**
Minority acceptance rate: **12.0%**
International acceptance rate: **9.1%**

Fall 2003 applications and acceptees
	Applied	Interviewed	Accepted	Enrolled
Total:	3,120	962	483	158
In-state:	261	117	73	46
Out-of-state:	2,859	845	410	112

Profile of admitted students
Average undergraduate grade point average: **3.61**
MCAT averages (scale: 1-15; writing test: J-T):
  Composite score: **10.0**
  Verbal reasoning score: **9.8**, Physical sciences score: **9.9**,
  Biological sciences score: **10.3**, Writing score: **P**
Proportion with undergraduate majors in: Biological
  sciences: **60%**, Physical sciences: **16%**, Non-sciences:
  21%, Other health professions: **1%**, Mixed disciplines
  and other: **2%**
Percentage of students not coming directly from college
  after graduation: **34%**

Dates and details
The American Medical College Application Service
  (AMCAS) application is accepted.
School asks for a school-specific application as part of the
  admissions process.
Oldest MCAT considered for Fall 2005 entry: **2000**
Earliest application date for the 2005-2006 first-year class:
  June 1, 2004
Latest application date: **December 15, 2004**
Acceptance dates for regular application for the class
  entering in fall 2005:
  Earliest: **October 15, 2004**

Latest: **N/A**
The school considers requests for deferred entrance.
Starting month for the class entering in 2005-2006:
  August
The school has an Early Decision Plan (EDP).
A personal interview is required for admission.

Undergraduate coursework required
Medical school requires undergraduate work in these subjects: biology/zoology, English, organic chemistry, inorganic
(general) chemistry, physics, humanities.

ADMISSIONS POLICY
(TEXT PROVIDED BY SCHOOL):
St. Louis University School of Medicine is a private institution that considers applications from national and international students. The school encourages applications from
students who have achieved a high level of academic performance and who manifest in their personal lives those
human qualities compatible with a career of service to society. The university's mission statement affirms the value of
a diverse educational environment to prepare students for
life and work in a global society. To foster this mission, the
School of Medicine strives to recruit, admit, retain, and
graduate a diverse student body. Besides ethnicity, this
diversity encompasses differences based on gender, culture,
and economic circumstances.

Specific academic requirements include a minimum of
90 semester hours (135 quarter hours) in undergraduate
arts and sciences courses. Virtually all accepted applicants
complete a baccalaureate degree of at least 120 semester
hours (180 quarter hours) from an accredited college or university. In all cases, the Committee on Admissions is more
concerned with the quality of the applicant's education than
with the number of hours or years of premedical training.
Students who have received their education in a foreign
school must complete at least one academic year of coursework in an accredited North American college or university
prior to making application.

Course requirements for admission include: general biology or zoology (eight semester hours, with lab); inorganic

chemistry (eight semester hours, with lab); organic chemistry (eight semester hours, with lab); physics (eight semester hours, with lab); English (six semester hours); and other humanities and behavioral sciences (12 semester hours).

The Medical College Admission Test is required.

COSTS AND FINANCIAL AID

Financial aid phone number: **(314) 977-9840**
Tuition, 2003-2004 academic year: **$37,850**
Room and board: **$14,411**
Percentage of students receiving financial aid in 2003-04: **N/A**
Percentage of students receiving: Loans: **N/A**, Grants/scholarships: **N/A**, Work-study aid: **N/A**
Average medical school debt for the Class of 2002: **$125,434**

STUDENT BODY

Fall 2003 full-time enrollment: **621**
Men: **54%**, Women: **46%**, In-state: **41%**, Minorities: **33%**, American Indian: **0.3%**, Asian-American: **21.7%**, African-American: **8.1%**, Hispanic-American: **2.4%**, White: **63.3%**, International: **0.3%**, Unknown: **3.9%**

ACADEMIC PROGRAMS

The school's curriculum gives first-year students substantial contact with patients.
There are opportunities for first- or second-year students to work in community health clinics.
Program offerings: AIDS, drug/alcohol abuse, family medicine, geriatrics, internal medicine, pediatrics, rural medicine, women's health
Joint degrees awarded: M.D./Ph.D., M.D./M.B.A., M.D./M.P.H.
Total National Institutes of Health (NIH) grants awarded to the medical school and affiliated hospitals: **N/A**

CURRICULUM
(TEXT PROVIDED BY SCHOOL):

The M.D. degree program curriculum at St. Louis University School of Medicine has undergone extensive changes in order to adapt to the needs of the evolving healthcare environment. The goal is to prepare students for the practice of medicine in the society they will face in the new millennium. The new curriculum is the result of several years of study by committees composed of faculty and students. However, the curriculum designed to attain the M.D. degree is only one phase of a continuum of learning in the practice of medicine. It is expected that students will

pursue graduate study to further advance their skills before being able to practice without supervision.

The new curriculum offers better coordination and integration of subjects than the curriculum that was replaced. Additionally, it follows established principles of adult learning, and so contains fewer lectures, more small-group activities, earlier clinical activities, and more problem-solving exercises.

The first two years of the four-year curriculum (Phase 1 and Phase 2) are primarily devoted to the study of the fundamental sciences basic to medicine, while the last two years concentrate on the acquisition of clinical skills. Year 3 and Year 4 have been combined into one continuous period, Phase 3. This new structure enables students to pursue curricular offerings during the first half of Phase 3 that were previously unavailable, such as neurology, electives, and a family medicine requirement.

The total time of instruction in the four-year curriculum is 158 weeks.

FACULTY PROFILE (FALL 2003)

Total teaching faculty: **571 (full-time), 1,160 (part-time)**
Of full-time faculty, those teaching in basic sciences: **25%**; in clinical programs: **75%**
Of part-time faculty, those teaching in basic sciences: **3%**; in clinical programs: **97%**
Full-time faculty/student ratio: **0.9**

SUPPORT SERVICES

The school offers students these services for dealing with stress: expanded-hour gym access, peer counseling, professional counseling, religious support, support groups.

RESIDENCY CHOICES

Most popular residency and specialty programs chosen by the 2002 and 2003 M.D. graduating classes: anesthesiology, emergency medicine, family practice, internal medicine, internal medicine–pediatrics, obstetrics and gynecology, ophthalmology, pediatrics–adolescent medicine, psychiatry, radiology–diagnostic.

WHERE GRADS GO

52.0%

Proportion of 2001-2003 graduates who entered primary care specialties

27.3%

Proportion of 2002-2003 graduates who accepted in-state residencies

Stony Brook University

- Office of Admissions, Health Science Center, L4, Stony Brook, NY 11794-8434
- Public
- Year Founded: 1971
- Tuition, 2003-2004: In-state: $17,470; Out-of-state: $30,470
- Enrollment, 2003-2004: 428
- Website: http://www.hsc.sunysb.edu/som
- Specialty ranking: N/A

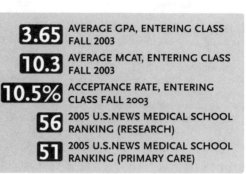

3.65	AVERAGE GPA, ENTERING CLASS FALL 2003
10.3	AVERAGE MCAT, ENTERING CLASS FALL 2003
10.5%	ACCEPTANCE RATE, ENTERING CLASS FALL 2003
56	2005 U.S.NEWS MEDICAL SCHOOL RANKING (RESEARCH)
51	2005 U.S.NEWS MEDICAL SCHOOL RANKING (PRIMARY CARE)

ADMISSIONS

Admissions phone number: **(631) 444-2113**
Admissions email address:
  somadmissions@stonybrook.edu
Application website: **http://www.hsc.sunysb.edu/som**
Acceptance rate: **10.5%**
In-state acceptance rate: **13.7%**
Out-of-state acceptance rate: **1.2%**
Minority acceptance rate: **10.4%**
International acceptance rate: **2.4%**

Fall 2003 applications and acceptees

	Applied	Interviewed	Accepted	Enrolled
Total:	2,523	564	266	101
In-state:	1,880	549	258	99
Out-of-state:	643	15	8	2

Profile of admitted students

Average undergraduate grade point average: **3.65**
MCAT averages (scale: 1-15; writing test: J-T):
  Composite score: **10.3**
  Verbal reasoning score: **10.0**, Physical sciences score: **10.0**, Biological sciences score: **11.0**, Writing score: **P**
Proportion with undergraduate majors in: Biological sciences: **41%**, Physical sciences: **29%**, Non-sciences: **30%**, Other health professions: **0%**, Mixed disciplines and other: **0%**
Percentage of students not coming directly from college after graduation: **64%**

Dates and details

The American Medical College Application Service (AMCAS) application is accepted.
School asks for a school-specific application as part of the admissions process.
Oldest MCAT considered for Fall 2005 entry: **2000**
Earliest application date for the 2005-2006 first-year class: **June 1, 2004**
Latest application date: **December 15, 2004**
Acceptance dates for regular application for the class entering in fall 2005:

Earliest: **October 15, 2004**
Latest: **N/A**
The school considers requests for deferred entrance.
Starting month for the class entering in 2005-2006: **August**
The school has an Early Decision Plan (EDP).
A personal interview is required for admission.

Undergraduate coursework required

Medical school requires undergraduate work in these subjects: biology, English, organic chemistry, inorganic (general) chemistry, physics.

ADMISSIONS POLICY

(TEXT PROVIDED BY SCHOOL):
Grades, Medical College Admission Test scores, letters of evaluation, and extracurricular and work experiences are carefully examined. Motivational and personal characteristics as indicated in the application, letters of evaluation, and a personal interview are also a major part of the admissions assessment. There is no discrimination in the admissions review and selection process on the basis of sex, race, religion, national origin, age, marital status, or handicap.

Students learn from one another as well as from their teachers, textbooks, and parents; therefore, the school attempts to acquire a class representative of a variety of backgrounds and academic interests. Indeed, given the demands on physicians in the 21st century, breadth of individual background is particularly important. Stony Brook hopes to attract a significant representation of groups that have historically been underrepresented in medicine. Applicants from foreign schools must have completed at least one year in an American college or university. Residents of New York constitute the majority of the applicants and entrants; however, out-of-state applicants will be given due consideration, particularly those to special programs, such as the Medical Scientist Training Program (M.D./Ph.D.).

Required supporting documents include official transcripts of all college work and a letter of official evaluation from the applicant's premedical adviser (or, when no adviser exists at the applicant's college, from two instructors, one of whom must be from a science field). If other individuals are in a position to provide important information, the school would be happy to receive letters from them. Personal interviews will be arranged at the initiative of the school for candidates who appear to be serious contenders for admission.

COSTS AND FINANCIAL AID

Financial aid phone number: **(631) 444-2341**
Tuition, 2003-2004 academic year: **In-state: $17,470; Out-of-state: $30,470**
Room and board: **$19,350**
Percentage of students receiving financial aid in 2003-04: **85%**
Percentage of students receiving: Loans: **83%**, Grants/scholarships: **41%**, Work-study aid: **10%**
Average medical school debt for the Class of 2002: **$107,000**

STUDENT BODY

Fall 2003 full-time enrollment: **428**
Men: **47%**, Women: **53%**, In-state: **100%**, Minorities: **41%**, American Indian: **0.2%**, Asian-American: **27.3%**, African-American: **9.8%**, Hispanic-American: **4.0%**, White: **58.6%**, International: **0.0%**, Unknown: **0.0%**

ACADEMIC PROGRAMS

The school's curriculum gives first-year students substantial contact with patients.
There are opportunities for first- or second-year students to work in community health clinics.
Program offerings: AIDS, drug/alcohol abuse, family medicine, geriatrics, internal medicine, pediatrics, women's health
Joint degrees awarded: M.D./Ph.D.
Total National Institutes of Health (NIH) grants awarded to the medical school and affiliated hospitals: **$62.5 million**

CURRICULUM

(TEXT PROVIDED BY SCHOOL):
The curriculum of the School of Medicine is designed to provide the opportunity for extensive training in the basic medical sciences and teaching in the clinical disciplines of medicine. The curriculum requires the acquisition and utilization of a variety of skills in basic and clinical sciences. The faculty has determined that a successful candidate for the M.D. degree must pass each unit of curriculum and that waiver of units of curriculum is offered only to those who because of prior experience are able to place out through examination.

The first year of the curriculum consists of integrated instruction in the basic sciences and introduction to clinical skills, human behavior, nutrition, and preventive medicine. The second-year curriculum includes microbiology, pharmacology, and an interdisciplinary course in pathophysiology of the different systems. In both the first and second years, students participate in the Introduction to Clinical Medicine and Medicine in Contemporary Society courses.

In the third year, students move to a series of clinical clerkships in medicine, surgery, pediatrics, obstetrics and gynecology, psychiatry, and family medicine, where opportunities for problem solving and patient responsibility are presented. Additional experiences are provided in radiology and emergency medicine. Clinical teaching in the Introduction to Clinical Medicine course, in the systems program, and in the clinical clerkships takes place at the University Hospital and various clinical facilities affiliated with the School of Medicine. The clerkship program is followed by selectives and electives in the fourth year. The curriculum emphasizes social issues in medicine and bioethics at each level of medical training.

FACULTY PROFILE (FALL 2003)

Total teaching faculty: **465 (full-time), 62 (part-time)**
Of full-time faculty, those teaching in basic sciences: **20%**; in clinical programs: **80%**
Of part-time faculty, those teaching in basic sciences: **2%**; in clinical programs: **98%**
Full-time faculty/student ratio: **1.1**

SUPPORT SERVICES

The school offers students these services for dealing with stress: expanded-hour gym access, peer counseling, professional counseling, religious support, support groups.

RESIDENCY CHOICES

Most popular residency and specialty programs chosen by the 2002 and 2003 M.D. graduating classes: anesthesiology, emergency medicine, internal medicine, obstetrics and gynecology, pediatrics, psychiatry, surgery–general.

WHERE GRADS GO

53.8%
Proportion of 2001-2003 graduates who entered primary care specialties

66.5%
Proportion of 2002-2003 graduates who accepted in-state residencies

SUNY–Syracuse

- 766 Irving Avenue, Syracuse, NY 13210
- Public
- Year Founded: 1834
- Tuition, 2003-2004: In-state: $17,900; Out-of-state: $30,000
- Enrollment, 2003-2004: 631
- Website: http://www.upstate.edu
- Specialty ranking: rural medicine: 20

3.64	AVERAGE GPA, ENTERING CLASS FALL 2003
9.8	AVERAGE MCAT, ENTERING CLASS FALL 2003
15.0%	ACCEPTANCE RATE, ENTERING CLASS FALL 2003
Unranked	2005 U.S.NEWS MEDICAL SCHOOL RANKING (RESEARCH)
Unranked	2005 U.S.NEWS MEDICAL SCHOOL RANKING (PRIMARY CARE)

ADMISSIONS

Admissions phone number: (315) 464-4570
Admissions email address: **admiss@upstate.edu**
Application website: **http://www.aamc.org**
Acceptance rate: 15.0%
In-state acceptance rate: 18.2%
Out-of-state acceptance rate: 7.8%
Minority acceptance rate: N/A
International acceptance rate: N/A

Fall 2003 applications and acceptees

	Applied	Interviewed	Accepted	Enrolled
Total:	2,441	720	366	152
In-state:	1,687	575	307	131
Out-of-state:	754	145	59	21

Profile of admitted students

Average undergraduate grade point average: 3.64
MCAT averages (scale: 1-15; writing test: J-T):
Composite score: 9.8
Verbal reasoning score: 9.4, Physical sciences score: 9.9,
Biological sciences score: 10.0, Writing score: P
Proportion with undergraduate majors in: Biological
sciences: 47%, Physical sciences: 16%, Non-sciences:
17%, Other health professions: 3%, Mixed disciplines
and other: 17%
Percentage of students not coming directly from college
after graduation: N/A

Dates and details

The American Medical College Application Service
(AMCAS) application is accepted.
School asks for a school-specific application as part of the
admissions process.
Oldest MCAT considered for Fall 2005 entry: 2001
Earliest application date for the 2005-2006 first-year class:
June 1, 2004
Latest application date: **November 1, 2004**
Acceptance dates for regular application for the class
entering in fall 2005:
Earliest: **October 15, 2004**

Latest: **August 25, 2004**
The school considers requests for deferred entrance.
Starting month for the class entering in 2005-2006:
August
The school has an Early Decision Plan (EDP).
A personal interview is required for admission.

Undergraduate coursework required

Medical school requires undergraduate work in these subjects: biology, biology/zoology, English, organic chemistry,
inorganic (general) chemistry, physics, general chemistry.

COSTS AND FINANCIAL AID

Financial aid phone number: (315) 464-4329
Tuition, 2003-2004 academic year: **In-state: $17,900; Out-
of-state: $30,000**
Room and board: N/A
Percentage of students receiving financial aid in 2003-04:
90%
Percentage of students receiving: Loans: 90%,
Grants/scholarships: N/A, Work-study aid: N/A
Average medical school debt for the Class of 2002:
$98,000

STUDENT BODY

Fall 2003 full-time enrollment: 631
Men: 55%, Women: 45%, In-state: 94%, Minorities: 31%,
American Indian: 0.3%, Asian-American: 23.5%,
African-American: 4.9%, Hispanic-American: 2.7%,
White: 67.7%, International: 1.0%, Unknown: 0.0%

ACADEMIC PROGRAMS

The school's curriculum gives first-year students
substantial contact with patients.
There are opportunities for first- or second-year students to
work in community health clinics.
Program offerings: AIDS, drug/alcohol abuse, family
medicine, geriatrics, internal medicine, pediatrics, rural
medicine, women's health
Joint degrees awarded: M.D./Ph.D.

Total National Institutes of Health (NIH) grants awarded to the medical school and affiliated hospitals: **N/A**

SUPPORT SERVICES

The school offers students these services for dealing with stress: professional counseling, religious support, support groups.

RESIDENCY CHOICES

Most popular residency and specialty programs chosen by the 2002 and 2003 M.D. graduating classes: emergency medicine, family practice, internal medicine, obstetrics and gynecology, orthopedic surgery, pathology–anatomic and clinical, pediatrics, psychiatry, surgery–general, transitional year.

WHERE GRADS GO

56.0%

Proportion of 2001-2003 graduates who entered primary care specialties

85.5%

Proportion of 2002-2003 graduates who accepted in-state residencies

Temple University

- 3420 N. Broad Street, MRB 102, Philadelphia, PA 19140
- Public
- Year Founded: 1901
- Tuition, 2003-2004: In-state: $30,665; Out-of-state: $37,411
- Enrollment, 2003-2004: 786
- Website: http://www.medschool.temple.edu
- Specialty ranking: N/A

3.52 AVERAGE GPA, ENTERING CLASS FALL 2003

9.7 AVERAGE MCAT, ENTERING CLASS FALL 2003

6.8% ACCEPTANCE RATE, ENTERING CLASS FALL 2003

Unranked 2005 U.S.NEWS MEDICAL SCHOOL RANKING (RESEARCH)

Unranked 2005 U.S.NEWS MEDICAL SCHOOL RANKING (PRIMARY CARE)

ADMISSIONS

Admissions phone number: (215) 707-3656
Admissions email address: **medadmissions@temple.edu**
Application website:
   **http://www.medschool.temple.edu/Admissions/
   procedures.html**
Acceptance rate: 6.8%
In-state acceptance rate: 32.4%
Out-of-state acceptance rate: 3.1%
Minority acceptance rate: 6.0%
International acceptance rate: 0.0%

Fall 2003 applications and acceptees

	Applied	Interviewed	Accepted	Enrolled
Total:	7,239	770	493	177
In-state:	913	388	296	107
Out-of-state:	6,326	382	197	70

Profile of admitted students

Average undergraduate grade point average: 3.52
MCAT averages (scale: 1-15; writing test: J-T):
   Composite score: 9.7
   Verbal reasoning score: 9.0, Physical sciences score:
   10.0, Biological sciences score: 10.0, Writing score: O
Proportion with undergraduate majors in: Biological
   sciences: 58%, Physical sciences: 19%, Non-sciences:
   18%, Other health professions: 3%, Mixed disciplines
   and other: 2%
Percentage of students not coming directly from college
   after graduation: 52%

Dates and details

The American Medical College Application Service
   (AMCAS) application is accepted.
School asks for a school-specific application as part of the
   admissions process.
Oldest MCAT considered for Fall 2005 entry: 2002
Earliest application date for the 2005-2006 first-year class:
   June 1, 2004
Latest application date: **December 15, 2004**

Acceptance dates for regular application for the class
   entering in fall 2005:
   Earliest: **October 15, 2004**
   Latest: **August 27, 2005**
The school considers requests for deferred entrance.
Starting month for the class entering in 2005-2006:
   August
The school has an Early Decision Plan (EDP).
A personal interview is required for admission.

Undergraduate coursework required

Medical school requires undergraduate work in these subjects: biology, organic chemistry, inorganic (general) chemistry, physics, humanities.

ADMISSIONS POLICY
(TEXT PROVIDED BY SCHOOL):

The Admissions Committee at Temple interviews about 20
percent of the applicants who complete their applications.
That statistic says a lot about Temple's admissions philosophy: Yes, standards are high—many applicants will be
screened out early because they don't meet the minimum
academic requirements for admission. But standards are
not rigid, and what's more, they're not purely quantitative.
An applicant's performance during the interview may
weigh just as heavily as test scores and grades, and grade
progress in college (i.e., a real improvement) could tip the
scales in an applicant's favor. In the end, many nontraditional students are admitted to Temple—older "second
career" students, minorities, and, generally, people with a
wide variety of social, ethnic, and scholastic backgrounds
that have led to the school's notable reputation for plural-
ism.

As a state-related school, Temple shows preference to residents of Pennsylvania; however, a significant percentage of
matriculants may be residents of other states. Nonresidents
with a particular interest in Temple and strong credentials
are encouraged to apply. Foreign nationals without perma-
nent-resident status are ineligible for consideration.

Once invited for interview, you will schedule a meeting
with a single faculty member of the Admissions

Committee. What does the Temple interviewer look for in an applicant? The associate dean for admissions singles out these attributes (by no means an exhaustive list): strong interpersonal skills—poise, tact, appropriate sense of humor, ability to listen and take another's point of view; self-confident; articulate; compassionate; socially conscious. After the interviewer has briefed the committee on the applicant's qualifications and personal qualities, a full vote is called. Students are notified of the decision several weeks after the interview, but not before October 15 of the year before admission.

COSTS AND FINANCIAL AID

Financial aid phone number: **(215) 707-2667**
Tuition, 2003-2004 academic year: **In-state: $30,665; Out-of-state: $37,411**
Room and board: **N/A**
Percentage of students receiving financial aid in 2003-04: **89%**
Percentage of students receiving: Loans: **66%**, Grants/scholarships: **41%**, Work-study aid: **4%**
Average medical school debt for the Class of 2002: **$129,120**

STUDENT BODY

Fall 2003 full-time enrollment: **786**
Men: **54%**, Women: **46%**, In-state: **69%**, Minorities: **38%**, American Indian: **0.3%**, Asian-American: **20.5%**, African-American: **11.8%**, Hispanic-American: **5.1%**, White: **62.3%**, International: **0.0%**, Unknown: **0.0%**

ACADEMIC PROGRAMS

The school's curriculum doesn't give first-year students substantial contact with patients.
There are opportunities for first- or second-year students to work in community health clinics.
Program offerings: AIDS, drug/alcohol abuse, family medicine, geriatrics, internal medicine, pediatrics, rural medicine, women's health
Joint degrees awarded: M.D./Ph.D., M.D./M.B.A., M.D./M.P.H.
Total National Institutes of Health (NIH) grants awarded to the medical school and affiliated hospitals: **$28.4 million**

CURRICULUM

(TEXT PROVIDED BY SCHOOL):
The curriculum of the program leading to the M.D. degree provides a traditional general professional education that prepares students for all career options in medicine.
Instruction in the basic sciences takes place in the first two years. It is designed to provide students with an understanding of the scientific concepts underlying the practice of medicine and to instill habits of lifelong learning. First-year courses in anatomy, biochemistry, and physiology provide students with core knowledge of normal structure and function. The pathology, pathophysiology, and pharmacology courses in the second year have been integrated in a systems approach designed to cover basic mechanisms of disease and available treatment methods.

A hybrid of instructional methods is used in the first biennium, including didactic lectures, self-directed learning, and evidence-based principles. Relevance to the practice of medicine is emphasized through the use of clinical case-based conferences in all basic science courses. In addition, students learn the basics of patient interviewing, physical examination skills, and clinical problem solving. Topics in professionalism, humanism, medical ethics, cultural competence, and death and dying are incorporated throughout the courses. Standardized patients are used in the teaching and assessment of clinical skills throughout the curriculum.

The clinical education program of the third year includes required clerkships in family medicine, internal medicine, pediatrics, psychiatry, surgery (with a week of anesthesiology), and obstetrics and gynecology. In the fourth year, the program includes requirements in neurology, emergency medicine, and two subinternships. Students are also required to take 20 weeks of selectives designed to allow students to pursue areas of individual interest.

Instruction and experience in patient care are provided in both ambulatory and hospital settings, with clinical sites in urban, suburban, and rural areas. The diverse settings of patient contact, including traditional hospital and intensive care units, emergency centers, and office-based medicine, ensure that students are well prepared for residency and all career options in medicine.

FACULTY PROFILE (FALL 2003)

Total teaching faculty: **377 (full-time), 80 (part-time)**
Of full-time faculty, those teaching in basic sciences: **28%**; in clinical programs: **72%**
Of part-time faculty, those teaching in basic sciences: **31%**; in clinical programs: **69%**
Full-time faculty/student ratio: **0.5**

SUPPORT SERVICES

The school offers students these services for dealing with stress: expanded-hour gym access, peer counseling, professional counseling.

RESIDENCY CHOICES

Most popular residency and specialty programs chosen by the 2002 and 2003 M.D. graduating classes: anesthesiology, emergency medicine, family practice, internal medicine, ophthalmology, orthopedic surgery, pediatrics, radiology–diagnostic, surgery–general, transitional year.

WHERE GRADS GO

43.0%
Proportion of 2001-2003 graduates who entered primary care specialties

45.0%
Proportion of 2002-2003 graduates who accepted in-state residencies

xas A&M University System

HEALTH SCIENCE CENTER

- 147 Joe H. Reynolds Medical Building, College Station, TX 77843-1114
- Public
- Year Founded: 1971
- Tuition, 2003-2004: In-state: $7,770; Out-of-state: $20,870
- Enrollment, 2003-2004: 276
- Website: http://medicine.tamu.edu
- Specialty ranking: N/A

3.65 AVERAGE GPA, ENTERING CLASS FALL 2003

8.9 AVERAGE MCAT, ENTERING CLASS FALL 2003

10.9% ACCEPTANCE RATE, ENTERING CLASS FALL 2003

Unranked 2005 U.S.NEWS MEDICAL SCHOOL RANKING (RESEARCH)

Unranked 2005 U.S.NEWS MEDICAL SCHOOL RANKING (PRIMARY CARE)

ADMISSIONS

Admissions phone number: **(979) 845-7743**
Admissions email address:
  admissions@medicine.tamu.edu
Application website: **http://www.utsystem.edu/tmdsas**
Acceptance rate: **10.9%**
In-state acceptance rate: **11.2%**
Out-of-state acceptance rate: **7.4%**
Minority acceptance rate: **15.4%**
International acceptance rate: **9.1%**

Fall 2003 applications and acceptees

	Applied	Interviewed	Accepted	Enrolled
Total:	2,233	514	243	70
In-state:	2,029	490	228	63
Out-of-state:	204	24	15	7

Profile of admitted students

Average undergraduate grade point average: **3.65**
MCAT averages (scale: 1-15; writing test: J-T):
  Composite score: **8.9**
  Verbal reasoning score: **8.3**, Physical sciences score: **9.0**,
  Biological sciences score: **9.4**, Writing score: **Q**
Proportion with undergraduate majors in: Biological
  sciences: **62%**, Physical sciences: **10%**, Non-sciences:
  11%, Other health professions: **6%**, Mixed disciplines
  and other: **11%**
Percentage of students not coming directly from college
  after graduation: **4%**

Dates and details

The American Medical College Application Service
  (AMCAS) application is not accepted.
School asks for a school-specific application as part of the
  admissions process.
Oldest MCAT considered for Fall 2005 entry: **2000**
Earliest application date for the 2005-2006 first-year class:
  May 1, 2004
Latest application date: **November 1, 2004**
Acceptance dates for regular application for the class
  entering in fall 2005:

Earliest: **February 1, 2005**
Latest: **May 31, 2005**
The school considers requests for deferred entrance.
Starting month for the class entering in 2005-2006:
  August
The school doesn't have an Early Decision Plan (EDP).
A personal interview is required for admission.

Undergraduate coursework required

Medical school requires undergraduate work in these subjects: biology, biology/zoology, English, organic chemistry,
inorganic (general) chemistry, physics, calculus.

ADMISSIONS POLICY

(TEXT PROVIDED BY SCHOOL):
The College of Medicine considers for enrollment individuals who have completed at least 90 credit hours of their
undergraduate coursework at a fully accredited college or
university in the United States or its territories. By state
mandate, enrollment of residents of states other than Texas
may not exceed 10 percent.

Applicants must demonstrate better than average ability
to master a challenging educational experience. In addition
to academic ability, successful applicants must demonstrate
the personal qualities necessary to interact with others in an
effective and compassionate manner. Most entering students have completed a baccalaureate degree before
enrolling. However, exceptional applicants may be considered with 90 semester hours of college coursework.

Each year, 80 entering students are enrolled. The following courses are required with at least a grade of C from a
fully accredited U.S. college or university and must be completed before or by the time of matriculation: general biology with labs (one year or eight semester hours), advanced
biological sciences (one year or six semester hours), general
chemistry with labs (one year or eight semester hours),
organic chemistry with labs (one year or eight semester
hours), college physics with labs (one year or eight semester
hours), calculus or math-based statistics (half a year or three
semester hours), and English (one year or six semester
hours).

Applicants are screened for interview on academic performance and intellectual capacity, dedication to service and capacity for effective interactions, special life circumstances, and other compelling factors. Such factors include involvement in community human-service activities, leadership in school or community organizations, clinical or health-related experiences, quality of personal statement, motivation for medicine as a career, supportive letters of evaluation from faculty and mentors, socioeconomic background, residing in an underserved or health professions shortage area, and experience of other cultures and the human condition, including multilingual proficiency.

COSTS AND FINANCIAL AID
Financial aid phone number: **(979) 845-8854**
Tuition, 2003-2004 academic year: **In-state: $7,770; Out-of-state: $20,870**
Room and board: **$10,500**
Percentage of students receiving financial aid in 2003-04: **83%**
Percentage of students receiving: Loans: **83%**, Grants/scholarships: **20%**, Work-study aid: **0%**
Average medical school debt for the Class of 2002: **$66,275**

STUDENT BODY
Fall 2003 full-time enrollment: **276**
Men: **49%**, Women: **51%**, In-state: **94%**, Minorities: **34%**, American Indian: **0.4%**, Asian-American: **23.2%**, African-American: **2.9%**, Hispanic-American: **8.0%**, White: **60.5%**, International: **1.1%**, Unknown: **4.0%**

ACADEMIC PROGRAMS
The school's curriculum doesn't give first-year students substantial contact with patients.
There are opportunities for first- or second-year students to work in community health clinics.
Program offerings: AIDS, drug/alcohol abuse, family medicine, geriatrics, internal medicine, pediatrics, rural medicine
Joint degrees awarded: M.D./Ph.D., M.D./M.B.A.
Total National Institutes of Health (NIH) grants awarded to the medical school and affiliated hospitals: **$13.3 million**

CURRICULUM
(TEXT PROVIDED BY SCHOOL):
The Doctor of Medicine degree requires a minimum of four years of study. Students spend their first two years at the College Station campus studying basic medical sciences. The first year, organized in blocks over 36 weeks, is designed to lead the students through an introduction to fundamental concepts in cell and molecular biology to an in-depth, systems-based overview of the normal structure and function of the human body, and finally, to an introduction to the alterations in structure and function characteristic of the disease state. The Becoming a Clinician course runs concurrently with the basic science courses throughout the first year. The

course serves as an introduction to patient care, and clinical instruction complements topics presented in the basic sciences courses.

The second year is a systems-oriented overview of pathogenesis organized in blocks over 36 weeks. Students also spend half a day each week learning fundamental clinical skills under the supervision of practicing-physician faculty members. The Becoming a Clinician II course ranges from biostatistics/epidemiology to human sexuality and clinical clerkship introductions. The ethical and social aspects of medical practice receive special emphasis.

During the third and fourth years in Temple, Texas, students receive clinical training in different patient care settings: the Central Texas Veterans' Health Care System, Scott and White Memorial Hospital and Clinic, Darnall Army Community Hospital at Fort Hood, and Driscoll Children's Hospital in Corpus Christi. Small classes permit individual attention and close working relationships between attending physician faculty and students. The third-year curriculum is structured over 51 weeks, immersing students in the traditional clerkships. The fourth-year curriculum is structured over 50 weeks and is distinguished by a four-week acting internship and its flexible schedule, which allows students 27 weeks of selective clerkships (20 weeks of which can be completed anywhere in the state or nation).

FACULTY PROFILE (FALL 2003)
Total teaching faculty: **734 (full-time), 52 (part-time)**
Of full-time faculty, those teaching in basic sciences: **11%**; in clinical programs: **89%**
Of part-time faculty, those teaching in basic sciences: **4%**; in clinical programs: **96%**
Full-time faculty/student ratio: **2.7**

SUPPORT SERVICES
The school offers students these services for dealing with stress: expanded-hour gym access, peer counseling, professional counseling, religious support, support groups.

RESIDENCY CHOICES
Most popular residency and specialty programs chosen by the 2002 and 2003 M.D. graduating classes: anesthesiology, emergency medicine, family practice, internal medicine, obstetrics and gynecology, pediatrics, radiology–diagnostic, surgery–general.

WHERE GRADS GO
39.4%
Proportion of 2001-2003 graduates who entered primary care specialties

42.0%
Proportion of 2002-2003 graduates who accepted in-state residencies

xas Tech University

HEALTH SCIENCES CENTER

- 3601 Fourth Street, Lubbock, TX 79430
- Public
- Year Founded: 1969
- Tuition, 2003-2004: In-state: $8,683; Out-of-state: $21,783
- Enrollment, 2003-2004: 515
- Website: http://www.ttuhsc.edu/SOM/admissions/default.htm
- Specialty ranking: N/A

3.63	AVERAGE GPA, ENTERING CLASS FALL 2003
9.5	AVERAGE MCAT, ENTERING CLASS FALL 2003
7.8%	ACCEPTANCE RATE, ENTERING CLASS FALL 2003
Unranked	2005 U.S.NEWS MEDICAL SCHOOL RANKING (RESEARCH)
Unranked	2005 U.S.NEWS MEDICAL SCHOOL RANKING (PRIMARY CARE)

ADMISSIONS

Admissions phone number: **(806) 743-2297**
Admissions email address: **somadm@ttuhsc.edu**
Application website: **http://www.utsystem.edu/tmdsas**
Acceptance rate: **7.8%**
In-state acceptance rate: **7.9%**
Out-of-state acceptance rate: **6.6%**
Minority acceptance rate: **6.2%**
International acceptance rate: **9.5%**

Fall 2003 applications and acceptees

	Applied	Interviewed	Accepted	Enrolled
Total:	2,202	651	172	130
In-state:	2,036	633	161	124
Out-of-state:	166	18	11	6

Profile of admitted students

Average undergraduate grade point average: **3.63**
MCAT averages (scale: 1-15; writing test: J-T):
  Composite score: **9.5**
  Verbal reasoning score: **8.9**, Physical sciences score: **9.6**,
  Biological sciences score: **9.9**, Writing score: **N/A**
Proportion with undergraduate majors in: Biological sciences: **46%**, Physical sciences: **21%**, Non-sciences: **12%**, Other health professions: **4%**, Mixed disciplines and other: **17%**
Percentage of students not coming directly from college after graduation: **48%**

Dates and details

The American Medical College Application Service (AMCAS) application is not accepted.
School asks for a school-specific application as part of the admissions process.
Oldest MCAT considered for Fall 2005 entry: **2001**
Earliest application date for the 2005-2006 first-year class:
  May 1, 2004
Latest application date: **November 1, 2004**
Acceptance dates for regular application for the class entering in fall 2005:
  Earliest: **February 1, 2005**

Latest: **November 1, 2005**
The school considers requests for deferred entrance.
Starting month for the class entering in 2005-2006:
  August
The school has an Early Decision Plan (EDP).
A personal interview is required for admission.

Undergraduate coursework required

Medical school requires undergraduate work in these subjects: biology, biology/zoology, English, organic chemistry, inorganic (general) chemistry, physics, mathematics, calculus, general chemistry.

ADMISSIONS POLICY
(TEXT PROVIDED BY SCHOOL):

At least three years of study (90 semester hours) in a U.S. or Canadian accredited college or university are required, and all prerequisite courses must be taken in a U.S. or Canadian school. A baccalaureate degree is highly desirable. Only students with superior credentials and definite evidence of maturity will be considered without a degree. Some preference is given to applicants from West Texas.

Specific course requirements have been kept at a minimum to permit maximum flexibility in the selection of well-rounded students. The prerequisite courses are: biology or zoology (12 hours), biology lab (two hours), inorganic chemistry with lab (eight hours), organic chemistry with lab (eight hours), physics with lab (eight hours), English (six hours), and calculus or math-based statistics (three hours). All graded prerequisite courses require a grade of C or better or Advanced Placement credit.

The Medical College Admission Test also is a requirement of admission. It is recommended that students take the MCAT in the spring of the year in which application will be made.

Applications are invited from qualified residents of Texas and neighboring counties of New Mexico and Oklahoma, which make up the service area of the school.

The Admissions Committee carefully reviews the applications of all individuals meeting the entrance requirements. Although evidence of high intellectual ability and a record of strong academic achievement are essential for success in the study of medicine, the committee recognizes that these are not the only qualities necessary for a physician's development. Compassion, motivation, the ability to communicate, maturity, and personal integrity also are deemed important. There is no discrimination on the basis of race, sex, creed, national origin, age, or disability.

Personal interviews are offered to candidates considered to be competitive for admission. Interviews are conducted at the Lubbock and El Paso campuses.

COSTS AND FINANCIAL AID
Financial aid phone number: **(806) 743-3025**
Tuition, 2003-2004 academic year: **In-state: $8,683; Out-of-state: $21,783**
Room and board: **$9,778**
Percentage of students receiving financial aid in 2003-04: **91%**
Percentage of students receiving: Loans: **88%**, Grants/scholarships: **63%**, Work-study aid: **0%**
Average medical school debt for the Class of 2002: **$108,149**

STUDENT BODY
Fall 2003 full-time enrollment: **515**
Men: **60%**, Women: **40%**, In-state: **95%**, Minorities: **31%**, American Indian: **0.2%**, Asian-American: **20.4%**, African-American: **1.6%**, Hispanic-American: **8.5%**, White: **66.2%**, International: **0.4%**, Unknown: **2.7%**

ACADEMIC PROGRAMS
The school's curriculum doesn't give first-year students substantial contact with patients.
There are opportunities for first- or second-year students to work in community health clinics.
Program offerings: AIDS, drug/alcohol abuse, family medicine, geriatrics, internal medicine, pediatrics
Joint degrees awarded: M.D./Ph.D., M.D./M.B.A.
Total National Institutes of Health (NIH) grants awarded to the medical school and affiliated hospitals: **$4.7 million**

CURRICULUM
(TEXT PROVIDED BY SCHOOL):
The Texas Tech University School of Medicine has a four-year curriculum focusing on basic science in years 1 and 2 and clinical clerkships in years 3 and 4. Students spend their first two years on the Lubbock campus. In years 3 and 4, students receive clinical training on one of three campuses: Lubbock, El Paso, or Amarillo.

The curriculum is currently undergoing intensive review and redesign to increase integration of basic science and clinical medicine in all four years. In 2002-2003, the dean reorganized the educational management structure of the school to facilitate this redesign and promote educational innovation. He established the Office of Curriculum,

headed by a new associate dean for curriculum and staffed by a new director for educational technology. In parallel, the role and responsibilities of the Educational Policy Committee, the primary body overseeing educational programs, have also been redefined.

The Year 1 curriculum consists of courses in anatomy, physiology, biochemistry, histology, neurosciences, and foundations for medical practice. Year 2 courses include microbiology, pathology, pharmacology, pathology, psychiatry, skills for patient assessment, assessing medical evidence, and integration and analysis. These courses place increasing focus on student-centered small-group or team learning in addition to didactic lectures.

In Year 3 there are six required clerkships: internal medicine, family medicine, pediatrics, obstetrics/gynecology, psychiatry, and surgery. The Year 4 curriculum has just been revised to include four required one-month rotations: ambulatory; critical care/emergency room; a subinternship in family medicine, internal medicine, pediatrics, or surgery; and neurology. There are four months for electives. The school is currently implementing a four-week geriatrics requirement: Two weeks will be within the neurology rotation, and two weeks will be required among either the ambulatory or the elective options. The school has embarked on a series of innovative projects to enrich the comparability of student clerkship experiences across campuses.

FACULTY PROFILE (FALL 2003)
Total teaching faculty: **431 (full-time)**, **90 (part-time)**
Of full-time faculty, those teaching in basic sciences: **15%**; in clinical programs: **85%**
Of part-time faculty, those teaching in basic sciences: **3%**; in clinical programs: **97%**
Full-time faculty/student ratio: **0.8**

SUPPORT SERVICES
The school offers students these services for dealing with stress: expanded-hour gym access, professional counseling.

RESIDENCY CHOICES
Most popular residency and specialty programs chosen by the 2002 and 2003 M.D. graduating classes: anesthesiology, emergency medicine, family practice, internal medicine, obstetrics and gynecology, pediatrics, surgery–general.

WHERE GRADS GO
47.0%
Proportion of 2001-2003 graduates who entered primary care specialties

58.0%
Proportion of 2002-2003 graduates who accepted in-state residencies

Tufts University

- 136 Harrison Avenue, Boston, MA 02111
- Private
- Year Founded: 1893
- Tuition, 2003-2004: $40,134
- Enrollment, 2003-2004: 698
- Website: http://www.tufts.edu/med
- Specialty ranking: N/A

3.52 AVERAGE GPA, ENTERING CLASS FALL 2003

10.2 AVERAGE MCAT, ENTERING CLASS FALL 2003

7.5% ACCEPTANCE RATE, ENTERING CLASS FALL 2003

40 2005 U.S.NEWS MEDICAL SCHOOL RANKING (RESEARCH)

Unranked 2005 U.S.NEWS MEDICAL SCHOOL RANKING (PRIMARY CARE)

ADMISSIONS

Admissions phone number: **(617) 636-6571**
Admissions email address: **med-admissions@tufts.edu**
Application website:
**http://www.tufts.edu/med/admissions/fyc_secondary
_app.html**
Acceptance rate: **7.5%**
In-state acceptance rate: **24.5%**
Out-of-state acceptance rate: **6.0%**
Minority acceptance rate: **8.0%**
International acceptance rate: **1.8%**

Fall 2003 applications and acceptees

	Applied	Interviewed	Accepted	Enrolled
Total:	6,526	917	491	170
In-state:	523	225	128	57
Out-of-state:	6,003	692	363	113

Profile of admitted students

Average undergraduate grade point average: **3.52**
MCAT averages (scale: 1-15; writing test: J-T):
  Composite score: **10.2**
  Verbal reasoning score: **9.9**, Physical sciences score:
  10.3, Biological sciences score: **10.5**, Writing score: **Q**
Proportion with undergraduate majors in: Biological
  sciences: **56%**, Physical sciences: **10%**, Non-sciences:
  29%, Other health professions: **0%**, Mixed disciplines
  and other: **5%**
Percentage of students not coming directly from college
  after graduation: **67%**

Dates and details

The American Medical College Application Service
  (AMCAS) application is accepted.
School asks for a school-specific application as part of the
  admissions process.
Oldest MCAT considered for Fall 2005 entry: **2002**
Earliest application date for the 2005-2006 first-year class:
  June 15, 2004
Latest application date: **November 1, 2004**

Acceptance dates for regular application for the class
  entering in fall 2005:
  Earliest: **December 1, 2004**
  Latest: **August 25, 2005**
The school considers requests for deferred entrance.
Starting month for the class entering in 2005-2006:
  August
The school has an Early Decision Plan (EDP).
A personal interview is required for admission.

Undergraduate coursework required

Medical school requires undergraduate work in these subjects: biology, organic chemistry, inorganic (general) chemistry, physics.

ADMISSIONS POLICY
(TEXT PROVIDED BY SCHOOL):

Applicants to the first-year class at Tufts University School
of Medicine must meet our course prerequisites and take
the Medical College Admission Test no later than the
August administration of the exam one calendar year prior
to enrollment.

Applicants to TUSM must first submit the online appli-
cation of the American Medical College Application Service.
The TUSM admissions office receives applications from
AMCAS from June through November.

All applicants who apply to TUSM via AMCAS are
requested to complete a secondary application (TUSM does
not disqualify any applicants at this stage) and to submit letters of recommendation and a $95 application fee. (The fee
is waived for any applicant who has received an AMCAS fee
waiver.) TUSM receives secondary applications and letters
of recommendation from July until the secondary application deadline of February 1.

Applicants who complete a secondary application are
considered for a personal interview at the Boston campus.
Interviews are required for admission and are conducted
from mid-October through the end of April.

All complete applications remain under active consideration for an interview until the end of February. All applicants

receive either an invitation to interview or a letter of regret by April 15.

The TUSM Admissions Committee meets periodically during the interview season and admits selected applicants on a rolling basis from December through May. Selected applicants are admitted from the wait list during the summer.

The selection of applicants is based not only on performance in the required premedical courses but also on the applicant's entire academic record and extracurricular experiences. Letters of recommendation and information supplied by the applicant are reviewed for indications of promise and fitness for a medical career. Preference is given to U.S. citizens and permanent residents who will receive a bachelor's degree from an American college or university prior to matriculation.

COSTS AND FINANCIAL AID

Financial aid phone number: **(617) 636-6574**
Tuition, 2003-2004 academic year: **$40,134**
Room and board: **N/A**
Percentage of students receiving financial aid in 2003-04: **79%**
Percentage of students receiving: Loans: **74%**, Grants/scholarships: **20%**, Work-study aid: **1%**
Average medical school debt for the Class of 2002: **$158,599**

STUDENT BODY

Fall 2003 full-time enrollment: **698**
Men: **52%**, Women: **48%**, In-state: **33%**, Minorities: **45%**,
American Indian: **0.4%**, Asian-American: **34.5%**,
African-American: **5.6%**, Hispanic-American: **4.4%**,
White: **50.6%**, International: **0.7%**, Unknown: **3.7%**

ACADEMIC PROGRAMS

The school's curriculum gives first-year students substantial contact with patients.

There are opportunities for first- or second-year students to work in community health clinics.

Program offerings: AIDS, drug/alcohol abuse, family medicine, geriatrics, internal medicine, pediatrics, rural medicine

Joint degrees awarded: M.D./Ph.D., M.D./M.B.A., M.D./M.P.H.

Total National Institutes of Health (NIH) grants awarded to the medical school and affiliated hospitals: **$81.8 million**

CURRICULUM

(TEXT PROVIDED BY SCHOOL):

Tufts University School of Medicine, located in Boston, has a long tradition of excellence in clinical training and provides a curriculum that balances science with the humanities and the art of medicine, while remaining a leader in curricular innovation. Our curriculum enables graduates to assume lifelong scientific, scholarly, and humanistic professional attitudes as they face the myriad challenges that confront physicians in the 21st century. At Tufts, the emphasis is on teamwork, not competition.

TUSM is known for clinical teaching. During the first and second years, a clinically integrated block system is used to teach basic sciences and pathophysiology. Hybrid teaching methods (lecture, small group, problem-based learning, standardized patient educators, patient contact, and extensive online resources) are used to accommodate a variety of learning styles and accomplish the goals of providing balanced education and training. Students explore a variety of clinical disciplines and research opportunities through an extensive electives program in years 1 and 2. During their clinical years, Tufts students complete clerkships at a wide variety of ambulatory and inpatient teaching sites. Students are offered opportunities in many varied elective experiences in all clinical areas and can participate in advanced research activities.

Tufts is recognized as having an outstanding continuous improvement system and feedback process for the curriculum, incorporating a comprehensive student and peer evaluation system.

Rapid changes in healthcare delivery, biomedical knowledge, and technology require medical students to confront a wide range of new information, practices, and issues as they proceed through their education and careers. The TUSM curriculum features the Tufts University Sciences Knowledgebase (TUSK), an award-winning comprehensive and integrated multimedia curriculum resource database; problem-based learning that emphasizes critical thinking; and clinical education within an extensive and diverse network of healthcare sites.

TUSM offers five combined degree programs and several independent master's programs.

FACULTY PROFILE (FALL 2003)

Total teaching faculty: **1,258 (full-time)**, **2,498 (part-time)**
Of full-time faculty, those teaching in basic sciences: **9%**; in clinical programs: **91%**
Of part-time faculty, those teaching in basic sciences: **5%**; in clinical programs: **95%**
Full-time faculty/student ratio: **1.8**

SUPPORT SERVICES

The school offers students these services for dealing with stress: expanded-hour gym access, peer counseling, professional counseling, religious support, support groups.

RESIDENCY CHOICES

Most popular residency and specialty programs chosen by the 2002 and 2003 M.D. graduating classes: anesthesiology, emergency medicine, family practice, internal medicine, obstetrics and gynecology, pediatrics, surgery–general.

WHERE GRADS GO

45.0%

Proportion of 2001-2003 graduates who entered primary care specialties

32.0%

Proportion of 2002-2003 graduates who accepted in-state residencies

Tulane University

- 1430 Tulane Avenue, SL67, New Orleans, LA 70112-2699
- Private
- Year Founded: 1834
- Tuition, 2003-2004: $37,086
- Enrollment, 2003-2004: 621
- Website: http://www.mcl.tulane.edu
- Specialty ranking: N/A

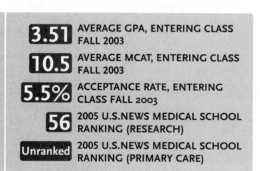

3.51 AVERAGE GPA, ENTERING CLASS FALL 2003

10.5 AVERAGE MCAT, ENTERING CLASS FALL 2003

5.5% ACCEPTANCE RATE, ENTERING CLASS FALL 2003

56 2005 U.S.NEWS MEDICAL SCHOOL RANKING (RESEARCH)

Unranked 2005 U.S.NEWS MEDICAL SCHOOL RANKING (PRIMARY CARE)

ADMISSIONS
Admissions phone number: **(504) 588-5187**
Admissions email address: **medsch@tulane.edu**
Application website:
   http://www.som.tulane.edu/admissions/application.pdf
Acceptance rate: **5.5%**
In-state acceptance rate: **11.5%**
Out-of-state acceptance rate: **5.0%**
Minority acceptance rate: **3.1%**
International acceptance rate: **4.2%**

Fall 2003 applications and acceptees
	Applied	Interviewed	Accepted	Enrolled
Total:	6,627	1,005	365	155
In-state:	539	240	62	39
Out-of-state:	6,088	765	303	116

Profile of admitted students
Average undergraduate grade point average: **3.51**
MCAT averages (scale: 1-15; writing test: J-T):
   Composite score: **10.5**
   Verbal reasoning score: **10.2**, Physical sciences score:
   10.4, Biological sciences score: **10.6**, Writing score: **P**
Proportion with undergraduate majors in: Biological
   sciences: **44%**, Physical sciences: **15%**, Non-sciences:
   24%, Other health professions: **1%**, Mixed disciplines
   and other: **16%**
Percentage of students not coming directly from college
   after graduation: **20%**

Dates and details
The American Medical College Application Service
   (AMCAS) application is accepted.
School asks for a school-specific application as part of the
   admissions process.
Oldest MCAT considered for Fall 2005 entry: **2001**
Earliest application date for the 2005-2006 first-year class:
   June 1, 2004
Latest application date: **December 15, 2004**
Acceptance dates for regular application for the class
   entering in fall 2005:

Earliest: **October 15, 2004**
Latest: **August 6, 2005**
The school considers requests for deferred entrance.
Starting month for the class entering in 2005-2006:
   August
The school has an Early Decision Plan (EDP).
A personal interview is required for admission.

Undergraduate coursework required
Medical school requires undergraduate work in these subjects: biology, English, organic chemistry, physics, general
chemistry.

ADMISSIONS POLICY
(TEXT PROVIDED BY SCHOOL):
All applications are hand screened by the associate or assistant dean for admissions. Approximately 1,000 applicants
are invited for interviews. Each applicant is interviewed by
two faculty members and a student. The Admissions
Committee meets weekly, and admissions are granted on a
rolling basis. Tulane strives for a class diverse in talents,
interests, and background.

COSTS AND FINANCIAL AID
Financial aid phone number: **(504) 585-6135**
Tuition, 2003-2004 academic year: **$37,086**
Room and board: **$8,826**
Percentage of students receiving financial aid in 2003-04:
   90%
Percentage of students receiving: Loans: **85%**,
   Grants/scholarships: **53%**, Work-study aid: **0%**
Average medical school debt for the Class of 2002:
   $122,959

STUDENT BODY
Fall 2003 full-time enrollment: **621**
Men: **56%**, Women: **44%**, In-state: **46%**, Minorities: **27%**,
   American Indian: **0.6%**, Asian-American: **15.6%**,
   African-American: **7.4%**, Hispanic-American: **3.1%**,
   White: **69.4%**, International: **1.6%**, Unknown: **2.3%**

ACADEMIC PROGRAMS

The school's curriculum gives first-year students substantial contact with patients.

There are opportunities for first- or second-year students to work in community health clinics.

Program offerings: AIDS, drug/alcohol abuse, family medicine, geriatrics, internal medicine, pediatrics, rural medicine, women's health

Joint degrees awarded: M.D./Ph.D., M.D./M.P.H., M.D./M.S.

Total National Institutes of Health (NIH) grants awarded to the medical school and affiliated hospitals: **$51.9 million**

CURRICULUM

(TEXT PROVIDED BY SCHOOL):

The first year of medical school is dedicated to normal structure function. Students also have immediate patient care through the Foundations in Medicine Program. The second year is a systems-based approach to abnormal structure function and incorporates clinical exercises and practice-based learning. The third and fourth years are a clinical continuum including required courses and electives. A standardized patient program is interwoven into the four years.

FACULTY PROFILE (FALL 2003)

Total teaching faculty: 502 **(full-time)**, 1,032 **(part-time)**
Of full-time faculty, those teaching in basic sciences: **15%**; in clinical programs: **85%**

Of part-time faculty, those teaching in basic sciences: **4%**; in clinical programs: **96%**
Full-time faculty/student ratio: **0.8**

SUPPORT SERVICES

The school offers students these services for dealing with stress: expanded-hour gym access, peer counseling, professional counseling, religious support, support groups.

RESIDENCY CHOICES

Most popular residency and specialty programs chosen by the 2002 and 2003 M.D. graduating classes: anesthesiology, emergency medicine, family practice, internal medicine, orthopedic surgery, pediatrics, psychiatry, radiology–diagnostic, surgery–general, internal medicine/pediatrics.

WHERE GRADS GO

40.0%

Proportion of 2001-2003 graduates who entered primary care specialties

22.0%

Proportion of 2002-2003 graduates who accepted in-state residencies

UMDNJ
NEW JERSEY MEDICAL SCHOOL

- 185 S. Orange Avenue, PO Box 1709, Newark, NJ 07101-1709
- Public
- Year Founded: 1954
- Tuition, 2003-2004: In-state: $22,491; Out-of-state: $33,662
- Enrollment, 2003-2004: 693
- Website: http://www.njms.umdnj.edu
- Specialty ranking: N/A

3.47 AVERAGE GPA, ENTERING CLASS FALL 2003

9.7 AVERAGE MCAT, ENTERING CLASS FALL 2003

15.0% ACCEPTANCE RATE, ENTERING CLASS FALL 2003

Unranked 2005 U.S.NEWS MEDICAL SCHOOL RANKING (RESEARCH)

Unranked 2005 U.S.NEWS MEDICAL SCHOOL RANKING (PRIMARY CARE)

ADMISSIONS

Admissions phone number: **(973) 972-4631**
Admissions email address: **njmsadmiss@umdnj.edu**
Application website: **http://www.aamc.org**
Acceptance rate: **15.0%**
In-state acceptance rate: **N/A**
Out-of-state acceptance rate: **N/A**
Minority acceptance rate: **N/A**
International acceptance rate: **N/A**

Fall 2003 applications and acceptees

	Applied	Interviewed	Accepted	Enrolled
Total:	2,940	679	440	170
In-state:	930	N/A	N/A	N/A
Out-of-state:	2,010	N/A	N/A	N/A

Profile of admitted students

Average undergraduate grade point average: **3.47**
MCAT averages (scale: 1-15; writing test: J-T):
   Composite score: **9.7**
   Verbal reasoning score: **9.3**, Physical sciences score: **9.7**, Biological sciences score: **10.1**, Writing score: **O**
Proportion with undergraduate majors in: Biological sciences: **48%**, Physical sciences: **21%**, Non-sciences: **18%**, Other health professions: **6%**, Mixed disciplines and other: **7%**
Percentage of students not coming directly from college after graduation: **19%**

Dates and details

The American Medical College Application Service (AMCAS) application is accepted.
School asks for a school-specific application as part of the admissions process.
Oldest MCAT considered for Fall 2005 entry: **2000**
Earliest application date for the 2005-2006 first-year class: **June 1, 2004**
Latest application date: **December 1, 2004**
Acceptance dates for regular application for the class entering in fall 2005:
   Earliest: **October 4, 2004**

Latest: **August 12, 2004**
The school considers requests for deferred entrance.
Starting month for the class entering in 2005-2006:
   August
The school has an Early Decision Plan (EDP).
A personal interview is required for admission.

Undergraduate coursework required

Medical school requires undergraduate work in these subjects: biology, English, organic chemistry, inorganic (general) chemistry, physics.

ADMISSIONS POLICY
(TEXT PROVIDED BY SCHOOL):

Students are selected on the basis of scholastic achievement, aptitude for the study of medicine, and personal qualifications. Since success in medicine depends on a number of related factors in a student's development, of which scholastic accomplishments are only a part, the Admissions Committee also gives consideration to the use of language, special aptitudes, mechanical skill, stamina, perseverance, and motivation.

New Jersey Medical School applies no grade-point average or Medical College Admission Test cutoff levels in its selection process. It must be remembered, however, that competition is very keen, and applicants who are high in all determinable categories often receive the highest priority for acceptance. There are no restrictions as to race, creed, gender, national origin, age, or handicap. Applications from non-New Jersey residents are encouraged. New Jersey residents do get some preference in the selection process.

COSTS AND FINANCIAL AID

Financial aid phone number: **(973) 972-7030**
Tuition, 2003-2004 academic year: **In-state: $22,491; Out-of-state: $33,662**
Room and board: **$11,140**
Percentage of students receiving financial aid in 2003-04: **88%**
Percentage of students receiving: Loans: **83%**, Grants/scholarships: **72%**, Work-study aid: **1%**

Average medical school debt for the Class of 2002: **$88,978**

STUDENT BODY

Fall 2003 full-time enrollment: **693**
Men: **54%**, Women: **46%**, In-state: **99%**, Minorities: **52%**,
American Indian: **0.1%**, Asian-American: **29.4%**,
African-American: **10.7%**, Hispanic-American: **11.7%**,
White: **47.0%**, International: **0.0%**, Unknown: **1.0%**

ACADEMIC PROGRAMS

The school's curriculum doesn't give first-year students
substantial contact with patients.
There are opportunities for first- or second-year students to
work in community health clinics.
Program offerings: AIDS, drug/alcohol abuse, family
medicine, geriatrics, internal medicine, pediatrics,
women's health
Joint degrees awarded: M.D./Ph.D., M.D./M.B.A.,
M.D./M.P.H.
Total National Institutes of Health (NIH) grants awarded to
the medical school and affiliated hospitals: **$60.4 million**

CURRICULUM

(TEXT PROVIDED BY SCHOOL):
The curriculum of the New Jersey Medical School is undergoing a major revision beginning with academic year 2003-
2004. The changes that are being implemented are derived
from the following six goals, which form the overarching
principles of the medical school: 1) mastery of clinical
knowledge with integration of basic sciences, 2) excellence
in clinical skills, 3) excellence in professionalism and
humanism, 4) commitment to the health of the community
and appreciation of social/cultural diversity, 5) dedication to
lifelong learning, and 6) development of effective skills in
education and communication.

During the first two years of the curriculum, a doctoring
course will teach students how to perform a history and
physical examination. Early contact with patients will serve
as the opportunity to begin to address the moral, ethical,
and social issues that are critical to the practice of medicine.
The doctoring course will also train students in how to utilize evidence-based medicine to provide the most comprehensive and state-of-the-art clinical care.

Science courses will use a variety of teaching techniques,
including small-group learning, lectures, and laboratory
experiences. In the clinical years, students will rotate
through all of the major disciplines in medicine, including

surgery, obstetrics/gynecology, internal medicine, pediatrics,
family medicine, psychiatry, emergency medicine, rehabilitation medicine, and neurology. The medical school utilizes
numerous teaching hospitals, including an inner-city hospital, Veterans Affairs hospital, and community hospitals, to
ensure that students are exposed to multiple inpatient settings. Each rotation also has an outpatient component,
which provides students with the opportunity to interact
with patients in the ambulatory setting.

Throughout the four years of medical school, students
may become involved in a multitude of activities. There are
numerous student-run community organizations, including
a weekly student-directed healthcare clinic. Research opportunities are plentiful, and most students spend their summer between the first and second years of medical school
involved in research projects. During the final year of medical school, faculty members help guide students in making
career decisions for postgraduate training. It is also the perfect opportunity to utilize the school's elective program to
participate in electives throughout the world.

FACULTY PROFILE (FALL 2003)

Total teaching faculty: **699 (full-time)**, **94 (part-time)**
Of full-time faculty, those teaching in basic sciences: **25%**;
in clinical programs: **50%**
Of part-time faculty, those teaching in basic sciences: **28%**;
in clinical programs: **72%**
Full-time faculty/student ratio: **1.0**

SUPPORT SERVICES

The school offers students these services for dealing with
stress: peer counseling, professional counseling.

RESIDENCY CHOICES

Most popular residency and specialty programs chosen by
the 2002 and 2003 M.D. graduating classes: family practice, internal medicine, obstetrics and gynecology, orthopedic surgery, pediatrics.

WHERE GRADS GO

39.0%

*Proportion of 2001-2003 graduates who entered primary
care specialties*

29.0%

*Proportion of 2002-2003 graduates who accepted in-state
residencies*

UMDNJ
ROBERT WOOD JOHNSON MEDICAL SCHOOL

- 675 Hoes Lane, Piscataway, NJ 08854
- Public
- Year Founded: 1961
- Tuition, 2003-2004: In-state: $22,167; Out-of-state: $33,338
- Enrollment, 2003-2004: 638
- Website: http://rwjms.umdnj.edu
- Specialty ranking: N/A

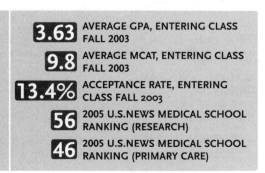

3.63 AVERAGE GPA, ENTERING CLASS FALL 2003

9.8 AVERAGE MCAT, ENTERING CLASS FALL 2003

13.4% ACCEPTANCE RATE, ENTERING CLASS FALL 2003

56 2005 U.S.NEWS MEDICAL SCHOOL RANKING (RESEARCH)

46 2005 U.S.NEWS MEDICAL SCHOOL RANKING (PRIMARY CARE)

ADMISSIONS
Admissions phone number: **(732) 235-4576**
Admissions email address: **rwjapadm@umdnj.edu**
Application website: **http://www.aamc.org**
Acceptance rate: **13.4%**
In-state acceptance rate: **31.2%**
Out-of-state acceptance rate: **2.6%**
Minority acceptance rate: **14.0%**
International acceptance rate: **0.0%**

Fall 2003 applications and acceptees

	Applied	Interviewed	Accepted	Enrolled
Total:	2,498	625	335	156
In-state:	945	469	295	137
Out-of-state:	1,553	156	40	19

Profile of admitted students
Average undergraduate grade point average: **3.63**
MCAT averages (scale: 1-15; writing test: J-T):
Composite score: **9.8**
Verbal reasoning score: **9.0**, Physical sciences score: **10.0**, Biological sciences score: **10.2**, Writing score: **P**
Proportion with undergraduate majors in: Biological sciences: **52%**, Physical sciences: **19%**, Non-sciences: **21%**, Other health professions: **5%**, Mixed disciplines and other: **3%**
Percentage of students not coming directly from college after graduation: **41%**

Dates and details
The American Medical College Application Service (AMCAS) application is accepted.
School does not ask for a school-specific application as part of the admissions process.
Oldest MCAT considered for Fall 2005 entry: **1999**
Earliest application date for the 2005-2006 first-year class: **June 1, 2004**
Latest application date: **December 1, 2004**
Acceptance dates for regular application for the class entering in fall 2005:
Earliest: **October 15, 2004**
Latest: **August 1, 2005**

The school considers requests for deferred entrance. Starting month for the class entering in 2005-2006:
August
The school has an Early Decision Plan (EDP).
A personal interview is required for admission.

Undergraduate coursework required
Medical school requires undergraduate work in these subjects: biology/zoology, English, organic chemistry, inorganic (general) chemistry, physics, mathematics.

ADMISSIONS POLICY
(TEXT PROVIDED BY SCHOOL):
Robert Wood Johnson Medical School participates in the American Medical College Application Service. All applications will be reviewed after the Admissions Committee receives Medical College Admission Test scores and letters of recommendations (a premedical advisory committee evaluation or three academic recommendations). Interviews will be arranged at the invitation of the Admissions Committee.

Applicants must be U.S. citizens or permanent residents. Preference for admission is given to New Jersey residents. However, out-of-state applicants with outstanding credentials are encouraged to apply.

Robert Wood Johnson Medical School places high value on a balanced undergraduate education. It is expected that applicants will have exposed themselves to coursework in the humanities, the behavioral sciences, and the liberal arts as well as the premedical sciences. Students with diverse backgrounds and careers are encouraged to apply.

Students in postbaccalaureate programs are encouraged to apply. The medical school has linkage agreements with several such programs.

Admission requirements include the MCAT and a minimum of three years of college, consisting of 90 semester hours of college work. The following undergraduate courses are required: two semesters of biology or zoology (with laboratory); two semesters of inorganic chemistry (with laboratory); two semesters of organic chemistry (with laboratory); two semesters of physics (with laboratory); one semester of college mathematics; and two semesters of English.

Selection criteria include academic excellence, interpersonal skills, and diversity and experiential factors, in addition to contributions in areas such as service and research.

COSTS AND FINANCIAL AID

Financial aid phone number: **(732) 235-4689**
Tuition, 2003-2004 academic year: **In-state: $22,167; Out-of-state: $33,338**
Room and board: **$10,026**
Percentage of students receiving financial aid in 2003-04: **80%**
Percentage of students receiving: Loans: **80%**, Grants/scholarships: **30%**, Work-study aid: **10%**
Average medical school debt for the Class of 2002: **$91,488**

STUDENT BODY

Fall 2003 full-time enrollment: **638**
Men: **51%**, Women: **49%**, In-state: **99%**, Minorities: **53%**, American Indian: **0.2%**, Asian-American: **33.2%**, African-American: **14.1%**, Hispanic-American: **5.3%**, White: **46.2%**, International: **0.0%**, Unknown: **0.9%**

ACADEMIC PROGRAMS

The school's curriculum gives first-year students substantial contact with patients.
There are opportunities for first- or second-year students to work in community health clinics.
Program offerings: AIDS, drug/alcohol abuse, family medicine, geriatrics, internal medicine, pediatrics, rural medicine, women's health
Joint degrees awarded: M.D./Ph.D., M.D./M.B.A., M.D./M.P.H., M.D./J.D., M.D./M.S.
Total National Institutes of Health (NIH) grants awarded to the medical school and affiliated hospitals: **$54.2 million**

CURRICULUM
(TEXT PROVIDED BY SCHOOL):

Our curriculum develops students who are competent to begin postgraduate training and become physicians who are humanitarian, compassionate, and focused on disease prevention, with the skills for self-directed, lifelong learning.

Curricular goals and competencies have been defined, and courses, clerkships, and electives have learning objectives grouped as the ASK (attitudes, skills, and knowledge) curriculum.

Goal 1 is to develop enthusiastic, self-directed learners who possess essential knowledge in basic medical sciences and clinical medicine, and have the ability to assimilate new knowledge in these disciplines. Competencies include demonstrating knowledge in basic medical sciences and clinical medicine. Attitudes include enthusiasm for learning and commitment to problem solving; self-directed, lifelong learning; and data-based decision making.

Goal 2 is to produce humanitarian physicians with high moral and ethical standards. Competencies include ethical decision making and understanding ethical complexity. Attitudes include demonstrating personal integrity and honesty, providing service.

Goal 3 is to ensure that students acquire the fundamental knowledge, skills, and attitudes necessary for a physician beginning residency training. Competencies include demonstrating attitudes, skills, and knowledge to provide quality care. Attitudes include developing professional identity and responsibility, enthusiasm for collaboration and teamwork, and sound clinical decision making.

Goal 4 is to prepare physicians who appreciate the environmental, emotional, and social aspects of health and illness and who focus on disease prevention as well as on diagnosis and cure. Competencies include taking into account the emotional, environmental, cultural, and societal aspects of health and illness and focusing on disease prevention for individuals, families, and communities. Attitudes include valuing and respecting differences and appreciating complex individuals.

The first-year curriculum includes courses in gross and developmental anatomy, cell biology/histology, biochemistry, neuroscience, immunology/microbiology, physiology, medical ethics, genetics, biostatistics, and epidemiology.

Three second-year courses are yearlong and integrated: clinical pathophysiology, pathology, and behavioral science and psychiatry. Small-group integrated cases complement instruction. Interviewing and communication skills are emphasized.

The third year includes five eight-week clerkships (family medicine, medicine, obstetrics/gynecology, pediatrics, and surgery), a six-week psychiatry clerkship, and electives. Passing a clinical skills assessment exercise is a graduation requirement.

The fourth year includes four-week required rotations in ambulatory medicine, surgery, neurology, and a subinternship, and a minimum of four electives.

FACULTY PROFILE (FALL 2003)

Total teaching faculty: **732 (full-time)**, **139 (part-time)**
Of full-time faculty, those teaching in basic sciences: **18%**; in clinical programs: **82%**
Of part-time faculty, those teaching in basic sciences: **16%**; in clinical programs: **84%**
Full-time faculty/student ratio: **1.1**

SUPPORT SERVICES

The school offers students these services for dealing with stress: peer counseling, professional counseling, religious support, support groups.

RESIDENCY CHOICES

Most popular residency and specialty programs chosen by the 2002 and 2003 M.D. graduating classes: emergency medicine, family practice, internal medicine, obstetrics and gynecology, orthopedic surgery, pediatrics, physical medicine and rehabilitation, psychiatry, radiology–diagnostic, surgery–general.

WHERE GRADS GO

45.7%
Proportion of 2001-2003 graduates who entered primary care specialties

27.0%
Proportion of 2002-2003 graduates who accepted in-state residencies

Uniformed Services University

OF THE HEALTH SCIENCES

- 4301 Jones Bridge Road, Bethesda, MD 20814
- Public
- Year Founded: 1972
- Tuition, 2003-2004: $0
- Enrollment, 2003-2004: 681
- Website: http://www.usuhs.mil
- Specialty ranking: N/A

3.53 AVERAGE GPA, ENTERING CLASS FALL 2003

9.4 AVERAGE MCAT, ENTERING CLASS FALL 2003

15.5% ACCEPTANCE RATE, ENTERING CLASS FALL 2003

Unranked 2005 U.S.NEWS MEDICAL SCHOOL RANKING (RESEARCH)

Unranked 2005 U.S.NEWS MEDICAL SCHOOL RANKING (PRIMARY CARE)

ADMISSIONS

Admissions phone number: **(800) 772-1743**
Admissions email address: **admissions@usuhs.mil**
Application website: **N/A**
Acceptance rate: **15.5%**
In-state acceptance rate: **N/A**
Out-of-state acceptance rate: **N/A**
Minority acceptance rate: **13.7%**
International acceptance rate: **N/A**

Fall 2003 applications and acceptees

	Applied	Interviewed	Accepted	Enrolled
Total:	1,686	465	262	167
In-state:	N/A	N/A	N/A	N/A
Out-of-state:	N/A	N/A	N/A	N/A

Profile of admitted students

Average undergraduate grade point average: **3.53**
MCAT averages (scale: 1-15; writing test: J-T):
Composite score: **9.4**
Verbal reasoning score: **9.2**, Physical sciences score: **9.3**, Biological sciences score: **9.7**, Writing score: **O**
Proportion with undergraduate majors in: Biological sciences: **47%**, Physical sciences: **22%**, Non-sciences: **7%**, Other health professions: **21%**, Mixed disciplines and other: **3%**
Percentage of students not coming directly from college after graduation: **60%**

Dates and details

The American Medical College Application Service (AMCAS) application is accepted.
School asks for a school-specific application as part of the admissions process.
Oldest MCAT considered for Fall 2005 entry: **2002**
Earliest application date for the 2005-2006 first-year class: **June 1, 2004**
Latest application date: **November 1, 2004**
Acceptance dates for regular application for the class entering in fall 2005:
Earliest: **October 15, 2004**

Latest: **August 1, 2004**
The school considers requests for deferred entrance.
Starting month for the class entering in 2005-2006: **June**
The school doesn't have an Early Decision Plan (EDP).
A personal interview is required for admission.

Undergraduate coursework required

Medical school requires undergraduate work in these subjects: biology, English, organic chemistry, inorganic (general) chemistry, physics, calculus.

ADMISSIONS POLICY

(TEXT PROVIDED BY SCHOOL):
The School of Medicine subscribes fully to the policy of equal educational opportunity. There are no quotas by race, sex, religion, marital status, national origin, socioeconomic background, or state of residence. There are no congressional quotas or appointments.

All applicants are judged on personal merit in terms of demonstrated aptitude, potential, and motivation for the study and practice of military medicine. Only the best-qualified, most promising candidates are selected.

Intellectual maturity, however, is an important consideration in admissions decisions. Applicants should be well-informed, knowledgeable individuals who have demonstrated competence in scholastic pursuits. They should be adept in organizing, analyzing, and synthesizing factual information. Mathematical ability and a background in the sciences—natural, physical, and social—are expected.

Applicants are strongly encouraged by the Admissions Committee to pursue some form of clinical work, e.g., emergency room, emergency medical technician, or shadowing a physician. Applicants are seldom accepted without clinical experience.

The quality of an applicant's work at the preprofessional level is of major interest to the school and is important in admissions decisions. Although grades are not the only criterion used in making decisions, college achievements are scrutinized very carefully since academic performance reflects achievement potential, interest, motivation, and self-discipline.

While extracurricular activities, community service, employment, graduate study, military service, and personal accomplishments are considered in evaluating the applicant as a total individual, these factors cannot substitute entirely for a poor academic undergraduate record.

COSTS AND FINANCIAL AID
Tuition, 2003-2004 academic year: **$0**
Average medical school debt for the Class of 2002: **$0**

STUDENT BODY
Fall 2003 full-time enrollment: **681**
Men: **70%**, Women: **30%**, In-state: **7%**, Minorities: **22%**,
   American Indian: **0.7%**, Asian-American: **14.7%**,
   African-American: **2.8%**, Hispanic-American: **4.1%**,
   White: **76.4%**, International: **0.0%**, Unknown: **1.3%**

ACADEMIC PROGRAMS
The school's curriculum gives first-year students substantial contact with patients.
There are opportunities for first- or second-year students to work in community health clinics.
Program offerings: AIDS, drug/alcohol abuse, family medicine, geriatrics, internal medicine, pediatrics
Joint degrees awarded: M.D./Ph.D.
Total National Institutes of Health (NIH) grants awarded to the medical school and affiliated hospitals: **N/A**

CURRICULUM
(TEXT PROVIDED BY SCHOOL):
The school has a four-year program culminating in the doctor of medicine degree. Each of the first three academic years is 48 weeks, and the final year runs 40 weeks. Basic science instruction predominates in the initial two academic years, with the final two years being devoted to clinical education. Basic science instruction is correlated, as appropriate, both interdisciplinarily and clinically. The integration between the clinical and basic sciences is progressive and proceeds with involvement in patient-care activities early in the curriculum, starting with the first semester of the freshman year.

While the overall program is designed to educate students to serve as providers of primary healthcare, there is sufficient flexibility to enable graduates to pursue postgraduate activities such as research. Elective courses are offered in clinical and research facilities in this country and in areas of the world where diseases rarely seen in the United States are responsible for 80 percent of the morbidity and mortality.

The curriculum also includes basic military orientation and concentration on unique aspects of military medicine. A conventional letter-grading system is employed to record student progress.

FACULTY PROFILE (FALL 2003)
Total teaching faculty: **281 (full-time)**, **2,222 (part-time)**
Of full-time faculty, those teaching in basic sciences: **50%**; in clinical programs: **50%**
Of part-time faculty, those teaching in basic sciences: **2%**; in clinical programs: **98%**
Full-time faculty/student ratio: **0.4**

SUPPORT SERVICES
The school offers students these services for dealing with stress: expanded-hour gym access, professional counseling, religious support, support groups.

RESIDENCY CHOICES
Most popular residency and specialty programs chosen by the 2002 and 2003 M.D. graduating classes: anesthesiology, emergency medicine, family practice, internal medicine, obstetrics and gynecology, orthopedic surgery, pediatrics, psychiatry, surgery–general, internal medicine/psychiatry.

WHERE GRADS GO
42.0%
Proportion of 2001-2003 graduates who entered primary care specialties

N/A
Proportion of 2002-2003 graduates who accepted in-state residencies

iversity at Buffalo–SUNY

- ■ 155 Biomedical Education Building, Buffalo, NY 14214
- ■ Public
- ■ Year Founded: 1846
- ■ Tuition, 2003-2004: In-state: $18,000; Out-of-state: $31,100
- ■ Enrollment, 2003-2004: 568
- ■ Website: http://www.smbs.buffalo.edu/ome
- ■ Specialty ranking: N/A

3.57 AVERAGE GPA, ENTERING CLASS FALL 2003

9.5 AVERAGE MCAT, ENTERING CLASS FALL 2003

17.6% ACCEPTANCE RATE, ENTERING CLASS FALL 2003

Unranked 2005 U.S.NEWS MEDICAL SCHOOL RANKING (RESEARCH)

Unranked 2005 U.S.NEWS MEDICAL SCHOOL RANKING (PRIMARY CARE)

ADMISSIONS

Admissions phone number: **(716) 829-3466**
Admissions email address: **jjrosso@acsu.buffalo.edu**
Application website: **http://www.aamc.org**
Acceptance rate: **17.6%**
In-state acceptance rate: **20.8%**
Out-of-state acceptance rate: **8.6%**
Minority acceptance rate: **N/A**
International acceptance rate: **N/A**

Fall 2003 applications and acceptees

	Applied	Interviewed	Accepted	Enrolled
Total:	2,063	464	363	135
In-state:	1,517	397	316	116
Out-of-state:	546	67	47	19

Profile of admitted students

Average undergraduate grade point average: **3.57**
MCAT averages (scale: 1-15; writing test: J-T):
  Composite score: **9.5**
  Verbal reasoning score: **9.2**, Physical sciences score: **9.6**,
  Biological sciences score: **9.8**, Writing score: **P**
Proportion with undergraduate majors in: Biological
  sciences: **47%**, Physical sciences: **26%**, Non-sciences:
  19%, Other health professions: **3%**, Mixed disciplines
  and other: **5%**
Percentage of students not coming directly from college
  after graduation: **N/A**

Dates and details

The American Medical College Application Service
  (AMCAS) application is accepted.
School asks for a school-specific application as part of the
  admissions process.
Oldest MCAT considered for Fall 2005 entry: **2001**
Earliest application date for the 2005-2006 first-year class:
  June 1, 2004
Latest application date: **November 15, 2004**
Acceptance dates for regular application for the class
  entering in fall 2005:
  Earliest: **October 15, 2004**

Latest: **August 15, 2005**
The school considers requests for deferred entrance.
Starting month for the class entering in 2005-2006:
  August
The school has an Early Decision Plan (EDP).
A personal interview is required for admission.

Undergraduate coursework required

Medical school requires undergraduate work in these subjects: biology, English, organic chemistry, inorganic (general) chemistry, physics.

ADMISSIONS POLICY
(TEXT PROVIDED BY SCHOOL):

The School of Medicine and Biomedical Sciences admits 135
students to its first-year class. Selection is based on scholastic achievement, aptitude, personal qualifications, and evidence of motivation toward medicine. These are judged
from the college record, the Medical College Admission
Test, letters of reference and evaluation, and a personal
interview.

Students with a bachelor's degree from an accredited college or university are preferred. In exceptional cases, those
with shorter preparation will be considered. In selecting a
field of undergraduate concentration, the student should be
strongly influenced by his or her real inclinations. Medicine
is a profession with many career opportunities, and the
exploration of almost any field in depth is encouraged.
Students presently matriculated in or having graduated
from another professional degree program are eligible to
apply to the first-year class only. Students presently enrolled
in an American or Canadian or other foreign medical or
osteopathic school are ineligible to apply to the first-year
class but are eligible to apply to our transfer program. All
applicants must be U.S. citizens or permanent residents
and have had two full years or 60 credit hours of higher
education in the United States or Canada.

The school encourages minorities and disadvantaged students underrepresented in the medical profession to apply
and provides educational opportunities for them. A summer
enrichment and support program is available to facilitate

student retention in medical school. It is important that students obtain a broad general education. In addition to special scientific and academic prerequisites, students should develop an educational background designed to enjoy life and its varied experiences. It is not necessary to be a science major to be admitted. In-state residency, while not required, is looked upon favorably.

COSTS AND FINANCIAL AID

Financial aid phone number: **(716) 645-2450**
Tuition, 2003-2004 academic year: **In-state: $18,000; Out-of-state: $31,100**
Room and board: **$8,000**
Percentage of students receiving financial aid in 2003-04: **81%**
Percentage of students receiving: Loans: **84%**, Grants/scholarships: **78%**, Work-study aid: **2%**
Average medical school debt for the Class of 2002: **$54,368**

STUDENT BODY

Fall 2003 full-time enrollment: **568**
Men: **47%**, Women: **53%**, In-state: **100%**, Minorities: **28%**, American Indian: **0.7%**, Asian-American: **18.1%**, African-American: **6.5%**, Hispanic-American: **2.8%**, White: **70.6%**, International: **0.0%**, Unknown: **12%**

ACADEMIC PROGRAMS

The school's curriculum gives first-year students substantial contact with patients.
There are opportunities for first- or second-year students to work in community health clinics.
Program offerings: AIDS, drug/alcohol abuse, family medicine, geriatrics, internal medicine, pediatrics, rural medicine
Joint degrees awarded: M.D./Ph.D., M.D./M.B.A., M.D./M.P.H.
Total National Institutes of Health (NIH) grants awarded to the medical school and affiliated hospitals: **$57.6 million**

CURRICULUM

(TEXT PROVIDED BY SCHOOL):

The four-year medical curriculum at the University at Buffalo begins with years 1 and 2 dominated by an organ-based, interdisciplinary core curriculum. The first-semester Foundations lecture module is designed to give all students a basic foundation of information in molecular and cell biology and epidemiology. Other modular lecture sections are dedicated to organs of interest. The modules incorporate the anatomy, histology, physiology, biochemistry, pathology, microbiology, and pharmacology and toxicology associated with the organ and its diseases. Gross anatomy is provided as a course in the first semester of study. In addition to didactic lectures, students are expected to participate in small-group, problem-based learning sessions. The students

also get practical experience in the Clinical Practice of Medicine course. In the third and fourth years, students rotate in the specialty clinical areas.

The University at Buffalo relies on a consortium of hospitals to provide training to our medical students. This association with hospitals such as Roswell Park Cancer Memorial Institute, Buffalo General Hospital, and Women's and Children's Hospital of Buffalo provides a rich source of experience for our students.

In addition to formal clinical training, students are in an atmosphere infused with exciting research. The school attracted approximately $41 million in research grants in 2003. The basic science research faculty is involved in research relating to Parkinson's disease, diabetes, obesity, drug abuse, stem cells, and cardiology, among others. The newly created Center of Excellence in Bioinformatics promises to be a world-class center for developing new drugs and therapeutic approaches involving genomics and unique protein identification. Medical students are encouraged to participate in a clinical or laboratory research experience, and there is a yearly celebration of research where the students present their findings and compete for prizes.

The University at Buffalo allows medical students to explore their talents, benefit from a talented faculty, and prepare for a rewarding and creative career.

FACULTY PROFILE (FALL 2003)

Total teaching faculty: **525 (full-time)**, **33 (part-time)**
Of full-time faculty, those teaching in basic sciences: **24%**; in clinical programs: **76%**
Of part-time faculty, those teaching in basic sciences: **18%**; in clinical programs: **82%**
Full-time faculty/student ratio: **0.9**

SUPPORT SERVICES

The school offers students these services for dealing with stress: professional counseling, religious support.

RESIDENCY CHOICES

Most popular residency and specialty programs chosen by the 2002 and 2003 M.D. graduating classes: anesthesiology, emergency medicine, family practice, internal medicine, neurology, obstetrics and gynecology, ophthalmology, pediatrics, psychiatry, radiology–diagnostic.

WHERE GRADS GO

36.0%
Proportion of 2001-2003 graduates who entered primary care specialties

52.7%
Proportion of 2002-2003 graduates who accepted in-state residencies

University of Alabama–Birmingham

■ **Medical Student Services, VH Suite 100, Birmingham, AL**
  35294-0019
■ **Public**
■ **Year Founded:** N/A
■ **Tuition, 2003-2004:** In-state: $13,055; Out-of-state: $30,827
■ **Enrollment, 2003-2004:** 692
■ **Website:** http://www.uab.edu/uasom/admissions
■ **Specialty ranking:** AIDS: 5, internal medicine: 19, women's
  health: 8

3.70	AVERAGE GPA, ENTERING CLASS FALL 2003
9.8	AVERAGE MCAT, ENTERING CLASS FALL 2003
16.7%	ACCEPTANCE RATE, ENTERING CLASS FALL 2003
25	2005 U.S.NEWS MEDICAL SCHOOL RANKING (RESEARCH)
30	2005 U.S.NEWS MEDICAL SCHOOL RANKING (PRIMARY CARE)

ADMISSIONS

Admissions phone number: **(205) 934-2330**
Admissions email address:
  admissions@uasom.meis.uab.edu
Acceptance rate: **16.7%**
In-state acceptance rate: **41.1%**
Out-of-state acceptance rate: **5.9%**
Minority acceptance rate: **13.7%**

Fall 2003 applications and acceptees

	Applied	Interviewed	Accepted	Enrolled
Total:	1,365	461	228	160
In-state:	418	292	172	144
Out-of-state:	947	169	56	16

Profile of admitted students

Average undergraduate grade point average: **3.70**
MCAT averages (scale: 1-15; writing test: J-T):
  Composite score: **9.8**
  Verbal reasoning score: **98**, Physical sciences score: **9.7**,
  Biological sciences score: **9.9**, Writing score: **N/A**
Proportion with undergraduate majors in: Biological
  sciences: **54%**, Physical sciences: **21%**, Non-sciences:
  6%, Other health professions: **13%**, Mixed disciplines
  and other: **6%**

Dates and details

The American Medical College Application Service
  (AMCAS) application is accepted.
Oldest MCAT considered for Fall 2005 entry: **2003**
Earliest application date for the 2005-2006 first-year class:
  June 1, 2004
Latest application date: **November 1, 2004**

COSTS AND FINANCIAL AID

Financial aid phone number: **(205) 934-8223**
Tuition, 2003-2004 academic year: **In-state: $13,055; Out-
  of-state: $30,827**
Room and board: **$10,340**
Percentage of students receiving financial aid in 2003-04:
  82%

Percentage of students receiving: Loans: **79%**,
  Grants/scholarships: **16%**, Work-study aid: **0%**
Average medical school debt for the Class of 2002:
  $84,040

STUDENT BODY

Fall 2003 full-time enrollment: **692**
Men: **59%**, Women: **41%**, In-state: **86%**, Minorities: **23%**,
  American Indian: **1.4%**, Asian-American: **14.5%**,
  African-American: **6.4%**, Hispanic-American: **0.6%**,
  White: **76.4%**, International: **0.4%**, Unknown: **0.3%**

ACADEMIC PROGRAMS

Program offerings: AIDS, drug/alcohol abuse, family
  medicine, geriatrics, internal medicine, pediatrics, rural
  medicine, women's health
Joint degrees awarded: M.D./Ph.D., M.D./M.P.H.
Total National Institutes of Health (NIH) grants awarded to
  the medical school and affiliated hospitals: **$210.9 million**

FACULTY PROFILE (FALL 2003)

Total teaching faculty: **1,131 (full-time), 108 (part-time)**
Of full-time faculty, those teaching in basic sciences: **21%**;
  in clinical programs: **79%**
Of part-time faculty, those teaching in basic sciences: **15%**;
  in clinical programs: **85%**
Full-time faculty/student ratio: **1.6**

WHERE GRADS GO

41.0%
*Proportion of 2001-2003 graduates who entered primary
care specialties*

46.0%
*Proportion of 2002-2003 graduates who accepted in-state
residencies*

∪niversity of Arkansas
FOR MEDICAL SCIENCES

- 4301 W. Markham, Slot 551, Little Rock, AR 72205
- Public
- **Year Founded:** 1879
- **Tuition, 2003-2004:** In-state: $12,165; Out-of-state: $23,807
- **Enrollment, 2003-2004:** 557
- **Website:** http://www.uams.edu
- **Specialty ranking:** geriatrics: 8

3.66	AVERAGE GPA, ENTERING CLASS FALL 2003
9.0	AVERAGE MCAT, ENTERING CLASS FALL 2003
22.8%	ACCEPTANCE RATE, ENTERING CLASS FALL 2003
Unranked	2005 U.S.NEWS MEDICAL SCHOOL RANKING (RESEARCH)
52	2005 U.S.NEWS MEDICAL SCHOOL RANKING (PRIMARY CARE)

ADMISSIONS
Admissions phone number: **(501) 686-5354**
Admissions email address: **southtomg@uams.edu**
Application website: **N/A**
Acceptance rate: 22.8%
In-state acceptance rate: **47.3%**
Out-of-state acceptance rate: **0.6%**
Minority acceptance rate: **22.7%**
International acceptance rate: **N/A**

Fall 2003 applications and acceptees

	Applied	Interviewed	Accepted	Enrolled
Total:	659	337	150	147
In-state:	313	309	148	145
Out-of-state:	346	28	2	2

Profile of admitted students
Average undergraduate grade point average: 3.66
MCAT averages (scale: 1-15; writing test: J-T):
   Composite score: **9.0**
   Verbal reasoning score: **9.0**, Physical sciences score: **9.0**,
   Biological sciences score: **9.0**, Writing score: **O**
Proportion with undergraduate majors in: Biological sciences: **61%**, Physical sciences: **21%**, Non-sciences: **7%**, Other health professions: **2%**, Mixed disciplines and other: **9%**
Percentage of students not coming directly from college after graduation: **24%**

Dates and details
The American Medical College Application Service (AMCAS) application is accepted.
School asks for a school-specific application as part of the admissions process.
Oldest MCAT considered for Fall 2005 entry: **2002**
Earliest application date for the 2005-2006 first-year class: **July 1, 2004**
Latest application date: **November 1, 2004**
Acceptance dates for regular application for the class entering in fall 2005:
   Earliest: **December 15, 2004**

Latest: **August 5, 2005**
The school considers requests for deferred entrance.
Starting month for the class entering in 2005-2006:
   August
The school doesn't have an Early Decision Plan (EDP).
A personal interview is required for admission.

Undergraduate coursework required
Medical school requires undergraduate work in these subjects: biology, English, organic chemistry, inorganic (general) chemistry, physics, mathematics.

COSTS AND FINANCIAL AID
Financial aid phone number: **(501) 686-5813**
Tuition, 2003-2004 academic year: **In-state: $12,165; Out-of-state: $23,807**
Room and board: **N/A**
Percentage of students receiving financial aid in 2003-04: **90%**
Percentage of students receiving: Loans: **88%**, Grants/scholarships: **44%**, Work-study aid: **1%**
Average medical school debt for the Class of 2002: **$71,537**

STUDENT BODY
Fall 2003 full-time enrollment: **557**
Men: **60%**, Women: **40%**, In-state: **99%**, Minorities: **9%**, American Indian: **1.2%**, Asian-American: **1.4%**, African-American: **6.2%**, Hispanic-American: **0.6%**, White: **90.7%**, International: **0.0%**, Unknown: **0.0%**

ACADEMIC PROGRAMS
The school's curriculum gives first-year students substantial contact with patients.
There are opportunities for first- or second-year students to work in community health clinics.
Program offerings: AIDS, drug/alcohol abuse, family medicine, geriatrics, internal medicine, pediatrics, rural medicine, women's health
Joint degrees awarded: M.D./Ph.D., M.D./M.P.H.
Total National Institutes of Health (NIH) grants awarded to the medical school and affiliated hospitals: **$44.8 million**

FACULTY PROFILE (FALL 2003)

Total teaching faculty: **826 (full-time)**, **76 (part-time)**

Of full-time faculty, those teaching in basic sciences: **12%**; in clinical programs: **88%**

Of part-time faculty, those teaching in basic sciences: **4%**; in clinical programs: **96%**

Full-time faculty/student ratio: **1.5**

SUPPORT SERVICES

The school offers students these services for dealing with stress: peer counseling, professional counseling, support groups.

RESIDENCY CHOICES

Most popular residency and specialty programs chosen by the 2002 and 2003 M.D. graduating classes: anesthesiology, family practice, internal medicine, internal medicine–pediatrics, obstetrics and gynecology, orthopedic surgery, pediatrics, psychiatry, radiology–diagnostic, surgery–general.

WHERE GRADS GO

56.0%

Proportion of 2001-2003 graduates who entered primary care specialties

53.0%

Proportion of 2002-2003 graduates who accepted in-state residencies

University of California–Davis

- 1 Shields Avenue, Davis, CA 95616
- Public
- Year Founded: 1966
- Tuition, 2003-2004: In-state: $15,882; Out-of-state: $28,127
- Enrollment, 2003-2004: 404
- Website: http://medome.ucdavis.edu
- Specialty ranking: N/A

3.62 AVERAGE GPA, ENTERING CLASS FALL 2003

10.6 AVERAGE MCAT, ENTERING CLASS FALL 2003

5.3% ACCEPTANCE RATE, ENTERING CLASS FALL 2003

49 2005 U.S.NEWS MEDICAL SCHOOL RANKING (RESEARCH)

17 2005 U.S.NEWS MEDICAL SCHOOL RANKING (PRIMARY CARE)

ADMISSIONS

Admissions phone number: **(530) 752-2717**
Admissions email address: **medadmisinfo@ucdavis.edu**
Application website: **N/A**
Acceptance rate: **5.3%**
In-state acceptance rate: **6.3%**
Out-of-state acceptance rate: **0.5%**
Minority acceptance rate: **5.7%**
International acceptance rate: **N/A**

Fall 2003 applications and acceptees

	Applied	Interviewed	Accepted	Enrolled
Total:	3,635	366	194	96
In-state:	3,014	364	191	96
Out-of-state:	621	2	3	0

Profile of admitted students

Average undergraduate grade point average: **3.62**
MCAT averages (scale: 1-15; writing test: J-T):
Composite score: **10.6**
Verbal reasoning score: **9.9**, Physical sciences score: **10.9**, Biological sciences score: **11.0**, Writing score: **P**
Proportion with undergraduate majors in: Biological sciences: **54%**, Physical sciences: **16%**, Non-sciences: **20%**, Other health professions: **0%**, Mixed disciplines and other: **10%**
Percentage of students not coming directly from college after graduation: **N/A**

Dates and details

The American Medical College Application Service (AMCAS) application is accepted.
School asks for a school-specific application as part of the admissions process.
Oldest MCAT considered for Fall 2005 entry: **2001**
Earliest application date for the 2005-2006 first-year class: **June 1, 2004**
Latest application date: **November 1, 2004**
Acceptance dates for regular application for the class entering in fall 2005:
Earliest: **October 15, 2004**

Latest: **September 1, 2005**
The school considers requests for deferred entrance.
Starting month for the class entering in 2005-2006:
September
The school doesn't have an Early Decision Plan (EDP).
A personal interview is required for admission.

Undergraduate coursework required

Medical school requires undergraduate work in these subjects: biology, English, organic chemistry, inorganic (general) chemistry, physics, molecular and cell biology, biochemistry, mathematics, general chemistry.

ADMISSIONS POLICY
(TEXT PROVIDED BY SCHOOL):

The School of Medicine seeks to attract students who are curious, motivated, and intelligent, with a view toward meeting the needs of society. The ideal student will have a demonstrated track record of achievement and leadership in an area of interest, demonstrable humanistic attitudes, and a realistic vision of the role he or she hopes to play in healthcare delivery. In their pursuit of excellence, students will have demonstrated strong interpersonal skills and ethical judgment, and have explored methods of inquiry.

The school embraces diversity in its student body. This is reflected in the school's commitment to expand opportunities in medical education for individuals from groups underrepresented in medicine as a result of social discrimination and to increase the number of physicians practicing in underserved areas. Therefore, the Admissions Committee, which is composed of individuals from a variety of cultural and professional backgrounds, evaluates each applicant in terms of the total person, carefully considering all relevant factors. These include academic credentials, with due regard to how they have been affected by disadvantage experienced by the applicant; such personal traits as character and motivation; experience in the health sciences and/or the community; career objectives; and the ability of the individual to make a positive contribution to society, the profession, and the school.

Factors considered for admission include the applicant's scholastic record, grade-point average, Medical College Admission Test performance, community service, and leadership and reports of teachers and advisers regarding intellectual capacity, motivation, and emotional stability. Characteristics that make applicants particularly attractive to the Admissions Committee are outstanding nonacademic achievements, capability for independent study, maturity, and other factors that suggest good academic and leadership potential.

A personal interview will normally be required of each applicant who is accepted. Regional interviews are not normally available. We now expect that 10 percent of our entering class will come from outside the state of California. UC Davis School of Medicine participates in the Western Interstate Commission on Higher Education Professional Student Exchange Program for applicants from certain western states that do not have a medical school.

COSTS AND FINANCIAL AID

Financial aid phone number: **(530) 752-6618**
Tuition, 2003-2004 academic year: **In-state: $15,882; Out-of-state: $28,127**
Room and board: **$10,803**
Percentage of students receiving financial aid in 2003-04: **91%**
Percentage of students receiving: Loans: **87%**, Grants/scholarships: **90%**, Work-study aid: **0%**
Average medical school debt for the Class of 2002: **$61,833**

STUDENT BODY

Fall 2003 full-time enrollment: **404**
Men: **48%**, Women: **52%**, In-state: **100%**, Minorities: **45%**,

ACADEMIC PROGRAMS

The school's curriculum gives first-year students substantial contact with patients.
There are opportunities for first- or second-year students to work in community health clinics.
Program offerings: AIDS, drug/alcohol abuse, family medicine, geriatrics, internal medicine, pediatrics, rural medicine
Joint degrees awarded: M.D./Ph.D., M.D./M.B.A., M.D./M.P.H., M.D./M.S., M.D./M.A.
Total National Institutes of Health (NIH) grants awarded to the medical school and affiliated hospitals: **$62.2 million**

CURRICULUM
(TEXT PROVIDED BY SCHOOL):
The UC Davis School of Medicine offers a four-year, comprehensive curriculum leading to a medical degree. Students are exposed to patient management at the start of their first year. The curriculum is designed to integrate basic and clinical sciences, promote active learning and critical thinking, and foster the highest standards of professionalism. The school has a strong tradition of community service by students through participation in several community clinics. The faculty also strongly encourages students to pursue research opportunities and advanced degrees. There are many new and exciting curriculum changes on the horizon for the UC Davis School of Medicine. For a detailed look at our current curriculum and updates on future changes, please visit our Web site.

FACULTY PROFILE (FALL 2003)
Total teaching faculty: **548 (full-time), 123 (part-time)**
Of full-time faculty, those teaching in basic sciences: **9%**; in clinical programs: **91%**
Of part-time faculty, those teaching in basic sciences: **7%**; in clinical programs: **93%**
Full-time faculty/student ratio: **1.4**

SUPPORT SERVICES
The school offers students these services for dealing with stress: peer counseling, professional counseling, support groups.

RESIDENCY CHOICES
Most popular residency and specialty programs chosen by the 2002 and 2003 M.D. graduating classes: family practice, internal medicine, obstetrics and gynecology, pediatrics, psychiatry, surgery–general.

WHERE GRADS GO

50.0%
Proportion of 2001-2003 graduates who entered primary care specialties

77.3%
Proportion of 2002-2003 graduates who accepted in-state residencies

University of California–Irvine

- Irvine Hall, Irvine, CA 92697-3950
- Public
- Year Founded: N/A
- Tuition, 2003-2004: In-state: $16,202; Out-of-state: $28,447
- Enrollment, 2003-2004: 390
- Website: http://www.ucihs.uci.edu/admissions
- Specialty ranking: N/A

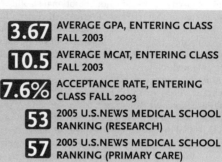

3.67 AVERAGE GPA, ENTERING CLASS FALL 2003

10.5 AVERAGE MCAT, ENTERING CLASS FALL 2003

7.6% ACCEPTANCE RATE, ENTERING CLASS FALL 2003

53 2005 U.S.NEWS MEDICAL SCHOOL RANKING (RESEARCH)

57 2005 U.S.NEWS MEDICAL SCHOOL RANKING (PRIMARY CARE)

ADMISSIONS

Admissions phone number: **(949) 824-5388**
Admissions email address: **medadmit@uci.edu**
Application website: **N/A**
Acceptance rate: **7.6%**
In-state acceptance rate: **8.6%**
Out-of-state acceptance rate: **0.2%**
Minority acceptance rate: **4.6%**
International acceptance rate: **0.0%**

Fall 2003 applications and acceptees

	Applied	Interviewed	Accepted	Enrolled
Total:	3,460	418	263	92
In-state:	3,037	417	262	91
Out-of-state:	423	1	1	1

Profile of admitted students

Average undergraduate grade point average: **3.67**
MCAT averages (scale: 1-15; writing test: J-T):
  Composite score: **10.5**
  Verbal reasoning score: **9.9**, Physical sciences score: **10.9**, Biological sciences score: **10.7**, Writing score: **Q**
Proportion with undergraduate majors in: Biological sciences: **53%**, Physical sciences: **24%**, Non-sciences: **12%**, Other health professions: **0%**, Mixed disciplines and other: **11%**
Percentage of students not coming directly from college after graduation: **N/A**

Dates and details

The American Medical College Application Service (AMCAS) application is accepted.
School asks for a school-specific application as part of the admissions process.
Oldest MCAT considered for Fall 2005 entry: **2002**
Earliest application date for the 2005-2006 first-year class: **June 1, 2004**
Latest application date: **November 1, 2004**
Acceptance dates for regular application for the class entering in fall 2005:
  Earliest: **November 15, 2004**

Latest: **September 1, 2005**
The school considers requests for deferred entrance.
Starting month for the class entering in 2005-2006:
  September
The school doesn't have an Early Decision Plan (EDP).
A personal interview is required for admission.

Undergraduate coursework required

Medical school requires undergraduate work in these subjects: biology/zoology, organic chemistry, inorganic (general) chemistry, physics, biochemistry, calculus, general chemistry.

ADMISSIONS POLICY
(TEXT PROVIDED BY SCHOOL):

The UCI College of Medicine seeks to admit students who are highly qualified to be trained in the practice of medicine and whose backgrounds, talents, and experiences contribute to a diverse student body. The Admissions Committee carefully reviews all applicants whose academic record and Medical College Admission Test scores indicate that they will be able to handle the rigorous medical school curriculum. Careful consideration is given to applicants from disadvantaged backgrounds (i.e., disadvantaged through social, cultural, and/or economic conditions). In addition to scholastic achievement, attributes deemed desirable in prospective students include leadership ability and participation in extracurricular activities, such as clinical and/or medically related research experience, as well as community service.

Information provided by the American Medical College Application Service application is used for preliminary screening. Based on decisions reached by the Admissions Committee, applicants may be sent a secondary application. Applicants receiving a secondary application are asked to submit additional materials, including a minimum of three letters of recommendation, supplemental information forms, and a nonrefundable application fee. Upon further review by the Admissions Committee, approximately 500 of those applicants receiving a secondary application will be invited to interview. Regional interviews are not available.

Preference is given to California residents and applicants who are either U.S. citizens or permanent residents. The UCI College of Medicine does not accept transfer students.

COSTS AND FINANCIAL AID

Financial aid phone number: **(949) 824-6476**
Tuition, 2003-2004 academic year: **In-state: $16,202; Out-of-state: $28,447**
Room and board: **$9,560**
Percentage of students receiving financial aid in 2003-04: **96%**
Percentage of students receiving: Loans: **85%**, Grants/scholarships: **83%**, Work-study aid: **0%**
Average medical school debt for the Class of 2002: **$79,767**

STUDENT BODY

Fall 2003 full-time enrollment: **390**
Men: **55%**, Women: **45%**, In-state: **99%**, Minorities: **38%**, American Indian: **0.0%**, Asian-American: **30.3%**, African-American: **2.1%**, Hispanic-American: **6.2%**, White: **61.5%**, International: **0.0%**, Unknown: **0.0%**

ACADEMIC PROGRAMS

The school's curriculum gives first-year students substantial contact with patients.
There are opportunities for first- or second-year students to work in community health clinics.
Program offerings: AIDS, drug/alcohol abuse, family medicine, geriatrics, internal medicine, pediatrics, rural medicine, women's health
Joint degrees awarded: M.D./Ph.D., M.D./M.B.A., M.D./M.S.
Total National Institutes of Health (NIH) grants awarded to the medical school and affiliated hospitals: **$63.6 million**

CURRICULUM

(TEXT PROVIDED BY SCHOOL):
The first two years are devoted to basic science instruction and preclinical experiences. There is a vacation period between the first and second years; students may use this time for research in place of vacation. Between the second and third years, there is a vacation period, which is typically used to prepare for Step 1 of the United States Medical Licensing Examination (USMLE).

The third year is scheduled in six eight-week blocks, with one month off during the winter. The fourth year is scheduled in two- and four-week blocks. During the clinical third and fourth years, clerkships and elective rotations are taken. The sequence of these clinical rotations is variable, based on lottery assignments.

To become eligible for the M.D. degree, each student must demonstrate mastery of the material presented in the courses and programs of the curriculum. All of the following requirements must be completed in order for a student to be recommended for graduation: achievement of a passing grade in all courses in the M.D. curriculum; successful passage of the USMLE steps 1 and 2 administered by the National Board of Medical Examiners (failure to pass either step precludes graduation, without exception); and passage of the Clinical Practice Examination near the end of the third year.

The Patient-Doctor Continuum is a four-year longitudinal, multidisciplinary, and multiple-course curriculum. The continuum begins with Patient, Doctor, and Society, a 55-hour interactive, didactic course that sets the tone and establishes the knowledge base.

The first-year course begins with supervised interviews that progressively increase in difficulty. Each student interviews a standardized patient while being observed from a monitoring room by his partner and the faculty preceptor. After four supervised practice interview sessions, students participate in six more complex, organ-based modules.

During the second year, students will spend one half day a week participating in clinical service experiences, which are designed to provide them with real patient experience and exposure to the different fields of medicine. Students are assigned a "content theme" to explore during each four-week block and meet monthly with a faculty mentor for a problem-based-learning session. Midway through their second year, students' clinical skills are tested through a practical examination.

FACULTY PROFILE (FALL 2003)

Total teaching faculty: **639 (full-time), 123 (part-time)**
Of full-time faculty, those teaching in basic sciences: **11%**; in clinical programs: **89%**
Of part-time faculty, those teaching in basic sciences: **2%**; in clinical programs: **98%**
Full-time faculty/student ratio: **1.6**

SUPPORT SERVICES

The school offers students these services for dealing with stress: expanded-hour gym access, peer counseling, professional counseling, religious support, support groups.

RESIDENCY CHOICES

Most popular residency and specialty programs chosen by the 2002 and 2003 M.D. graduating classes: anesthesiology, emergency medicine, family practice, internal medicine, obstetrics and gynecology, ophthalmology, orthopedic surgery, pediatrics, psychiatry, radiology–diagnostic.

WHERE GRADS GO

44.0%
Proportion of 2001-2003 graduates who entered primary care specialties

75.0%
Proportion of 2002-2003 graduates who accepted in-state residencies

University of California–Los Angeles

GEFFEN

- 12-138 CHS, 10833 Le Conte Avenue, Los Angeles, CA 90095
- Public
- Year Founded: 1951
- Tuition, 2003-2004: In-state: $15,173; Out-of-state: $27,418
- Enrollment, 2003-2004: 710
- Website: http://wwwmedsch.ucla.edu
- Specialty ranking: AIDS: 6, drug/alcohol abuse: 7, family medicine: 26, geriatrics: 2, internal medicine: 13, pediatrics: 15, women's health: 8

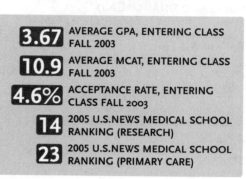

3.67 AVERAGE GPA, ENTERING CLASS FALL 2003

10.9 AVERAGE MCAT, ENTERING CLASS FALL 2003

4.6% ACCEPTANCE RATE, ENTERING CLASS FALL 2003

14 2005 U.S.NEWS MEDICAL SCHOOL RANKING (RESEARCH)

23 2005 U.S.NEWS MEDICAL SCHOOL RANKING (PRIMARY CARE)

ADMISSIONS

Admissions phone number: (310) 825-6081
Admissions email address: **somadmiss@mednet.ucla.edu**
Application website:
  http://www.medstudent.ucla.edu/admiss
Acceptance rate: 4.6%
In-state acceptance rate: 5.8%
Out-of-state acceptance rate: 2.9%
Minority acceptance rate: 5.1%
International acceptance rate: 2.0%

Fall 2003 applications and acceptees

	Applied	Interviewed	Accepted	Enrolled
Total:	5,137	728	238	121
In-state:	3,045	520	177	102
Out-of-state:	2,092	208	61	19

Profile of admitted students

Average undergraduate grade point average: 3.67
MCAT averages (scale: 1-15; writing test: J-T):
  Composite score: 10.9
  Verbal reasoning score: 9.9, Physical sciences score: 11.3, Biological sciences score: 11.5, Writing score: Q
Proportion with undergraduate majors in: Biological sciences: 51%, Physical sciences: 22%, Non-sciences: 17%, Other health professions: 1%, Mixed disciplines and other: 9%
Percentage of students not coming directly from college after graduation: 0%

Dates and details

The American Medical College Application Service (AMCAS) application is accepted.
School asks for a school-specific application as part of the admissions process.
Oldest MCAT considered for Fall 2005 entry: 2001
Earliest application date for the 2005-2006 first-year class:
  June 15, 2004
Latest application date: **November 1, 2004**
Acceptance dates for regular application for the class entering in fall 2005:

Earliest: **December 15, 2004**
  Latest: **August 8, 2005**
The school considers requests for deferred entrance.
Starting month for the class entering in 2005-2006:
  August
The school doesn't have an Early Decision Plan (EDP).
A personal interview is required for admission.

Undergraduate coursework required

Medical school requires undergraduate work in these subjects: biology, English, organic chemistry, inorganic (general) chemistry, physics, mathematics, calculus, general chemistry.

ADMISSIONS POLICY
(TEXT PROVIDED BY SCHOOL):

The David Geffen School of Medicine at UCLA seeks to admit students who embody the mission and goals of the school and will be future leaders in their communities, having distinguished careers in clinical practice, teaching, research, and public service.

The Admissions Committee gives preference to those applicants showing evidence of broad training and high achievement in their college education and possessing those traits of personality and character essential to succeeding in medicine and to providing quality, professional, and humane medical care. The committee looks for applicants who have demonstrated through coursework, school activities, community service, and research evidence of maturity, intellect, scholarship, and service to their communities and for those who are underprivileged and disadvantaged, culturally aware, and able to speak a second language, especially Spanish. We seek a student body with a broad diversity of backgrounds and interests. No preference is given to any particular undergraduate major. Final selections are made on the basis of individual qualifications and not on the basis of race, ethnicity, sex, age, sexual orientation, national origin, or disability.

Students submit their applications through the American Medical College Application Service. Applications are screened by the Admissions Committee. Students who pass this first screen are invited to submit a supplemental application, including letters of recommendation and transcripts. Successful applicants tend to have strong academic records, including firm and clear motivation for medicine. The committee looks for objective evidence that the applicant can handle the academic demands of the medical curriculum. Those judged to possess these necessary skills, knowledge, and attitudes are invited to interview.

Students interview with a faculty member and, if possible, a medical student, who are members of the Admissions Committee. Each student is given a thorough and personal review. Students are accepted each year beginning in January.

COSTS AND FINANCIAL AID

Financial aid phone number: (310) 825-4181
Tuition, 2003-2004 academic year: **In-state: $15,173; Out-of-state: $27,418**
Room and board: **$14,000**
Percentage of students receiving financial aid in 2003-04: 90%
Percentage of students receiving: Loans: 90%,
Grants/scholarships: 80%, Work-study aid: 0%
Average medical school debt for the Class of 2002: **$75,725**

STUDENT BODY

Fall 2003 full-time enrollment: 710
Men: 50%, Women: 50%, In-state: 96%, Minorities: 60%, American Indian: 0.6%, Asian-American: 33.1%, African-American: 9.7%, Hispanic-American: 16.1%, White: 36.9%, International: 0.4%, Unknown: 3.2%

ACADEMIC PROGRAMS

The school's curriculum gives first-year students substantial contact with patients.
There are opportunities for first- or second-year students to work in community health clinics.
Program offerings: AIDS, drug/alcohol abuse, family medicine, geriatrics, internal medicine, pediatrics, women's health
Joint degrees awarded: M.D./Ph.D., M.D./M.B.A., M.D./M.P.H.
Total National Institutes of Health (NIH) grants awarded to the medical school and affiliated hospitals: **$383.8 million**

CURRICULUM
(TEXT PROVIDED BY SCHOOL):
The David Geffen School of Medicine at UCLA seeks to prepare its graduates for distinguished careers in clinical practice, teaching, research, and public service. Recognizing that medical school is but one phase in a physician's education, the curriculum is designed to create an environment in which students prepare for a future in which scientific knowledge, societal values, and human needs are ever changing.

Critical competencies developed throughout the curriculum include: an enthusiasm for lifelong learning; a commitment to humanistic, compassionate, and ethical care of individuals and families; skills in effective communication; attainment of a broad and flexible base of knowledge and skills; an understanding of the scientific method and its application to clinical practice and research; a commitment to promote the community's health and well-being; ability to lead in settings of rapidly changing technology and societal needs; and a readiness to address complex societal and medical issues.

The UCLA curriculum consists of three phases. In Human Biology and Disease (Phase 1), students complete eight sequential, interdisciplinary block courses with an emphasis on the integration of basic, clinical, and social sciences. The grading system is pass/fail across all parts of the curriculum.

The Clinical Core (Phase 2) begins with a two-week foundation experience in which students prepare for working in ambulatory and hospital settings. This is followed by six core clerkships over a total of 48 weeks: inpatient medicine, ambulatory care (family medicine, internal medicine), obstetrics/gynecology, pediatrics, psychiatry/neurology, and surgery/ophthalmology. Students also participate in longitudinal courses: radiology, doctoring, and a preceptorship that allows them to work with community physicians.

Before beginning the College Phase (3), students join one of four colleges: Applied Anatomy, Acute Care, Primary Care, and Medical Sciences. Students enrolled in UCLA's joint degree programs for the M.B.A. or M.P.H. have a separate college on Healthcare Leadership.

FACULTY PROFILE (FALL 2003)
Total teaching faculty: 2,156 **(full-time)**, 218 **(part-time)**
Of full-time faculty, those teaching in basic sciences: 18%; in clinical programs: 82%
Of part-time faculty, those teaching in basic sciences: 34%; in clinical programs: 66%
Full-time faculty/student ratio: 3.0

SUPPORT SERVICES
The school offers students these services for dealing with stress: expanded-hour gym access, professional counseling, religious support, support groups.

RESIDENCY CHOICES
Most popular residency and specialty programs chosen by the 2002 and 2003 M.D. graduating classes: anesthesiology, emergency medicine, family practice, internal medicine, obstetrics and gynecology, ophthalmology, orthopedic surgery, pediatrics, radiology–diagnostic, surgery–general.

WHERE GRADS GO

45.1%
Proportion of 2001-2003 graduates who entered primary care specialties

70.7%
Proportion of 2002-2003 graduates who accepted in-state residencies

University of California–San Diego

- 9500 Gilman Drive, La Jolla, CA 92093-0602
- Public
- Year Founded: 1965
- Tuition, 2003-2004: In-state: $15,570; Out-of-state: $27,815
- Enrollment, 2003-2004: 491
- Website: http://meded.ucsd.edu/admissions
- Specialty ranking: AIDS: 9, drug/alcohol abuse: 8, internal medicine: 21

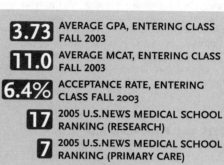

3.73 AVERAGE GPA, ENTERING CLASS FALL 2003

11.0 AVERAGE MCAT, ENTERING CLASS FALL 2003

6.4% ACCEPTANCE RATE, ENTERING CLASS FALL 2003

17 2005 U.S.NEWS MEDICAL SCHOOL RANKING (RESEARCH)

7 2005 U.S.NEWS MEDICAL SCHOOL RANKING (PRIMARY CARE)

ADMISSIONS

Admissions phone number: **(858) 534-3880**
Admissions email address: **somadmissions@ucsd.edu**
Application website: **N/A**
Acceptance rate: **6.4%**
In-state acceptance rate: **8.2%**
Out-of-state acceptance rate: **2.1%**
Minority acceptance rate: **7.3%**
International acceptance rate: **0.0%**

Fall 2003 applications and acceptees

	Applied	Interviewed	Accepted	Enrolled
Total:	4,297	521	274	121
In-state:	3,000	442	247	111
Out-of-state:	1,297	79	27	10

Profile of admitted students

Average undergraduate grade point average: **3.73**
MCAT averages (scale: 1-15; writing test: J-T):
  Composite score: **11.0**
  Verbal reasoning score: **9.9**, Physical sciences score: **11.4**, Biological sciences score: **11.6**, Writing score: **Q**
Proportion with undergraduate majors in: Biological sciences: **47%**, Physical sciences: **20%**, Non-sciences: **11%**, Other health professions: **1%**, Mixed disciplines and other: **21%**
Percentage of students not coming directly from college after graduation: **55%**

Dates and details

The American Medical College Application Service (AMCAS) application is accepted.
School asks for a school-specific application as part of the admissions process.
Oldest MCAT considered for Fall 2005 entry: **2002**
Earliest application date for the 2005-2006 first-year class: **June 1, 2004**
Latest application date: **November 1, 2004**
Acceptance dates for regular application for the class entering in fall 2005:
  Earliest: **October 15, 2004**
  Latest: **September 6, 2005**
The school considers requests for deferred entrance.
Starting month for the class entering in 2005-2006:
  September
The school doesn't have an Early Decision Plan (EDP).
A personal interview is required for admission.

Undergraduate coursework required

Medical school requires undergraduate work in these subjects: biology, organic chemistry, inorganic (general) chemistry, physics, mathematics.

ADMISSIONS POLICY

(TEXT PROVIDED BY SCHOOL):
The University of California, San Diego School of Medicine's admission requirements include a minimum of three years of college or university education, at least one year of which has to have been undertaken in the United States. Consideration is given only to applicants who are U.S. citizens or permanent residents. Preference is given to California residents unless an application is being made to the joint M.D./ Ph.D. Medical Scientist Training Program. Coursework requirements are: a year each of general/inorganic chemistry, organic chemistry, general physics, general biology, and mathematics (calculus or beyond, including statistics or computer science). Beyond the course requirements, applications are evaluated without regard to undergraduate major.

Initially, the American Medical College Application Service application is evaluated by a member of the executive committee of the school's Recruitment and Admissions Committee (RAC). The application is examined to judge each applicant's academic preparation for medical school, knowledge and interest in a medical career, and motivation. Also considered are factors such as demonstrated ability to overcome social, economic, and educational disadvantage and/or willingness to practice medicine in an underserved region or community. Selected applicants are sent a secondary application. Additional material requested includes letters of reference, a personal autobiography, and further details about a candidate's leadership activities, community service, exposure to the clinical/medical workplace, and research, as well as any extraordinary skills in sports, music, art, government, and so on.

Selected candidates are invited for a personal interview with two RAC members. Following the interview, each interviewer produces a summary of his or her impression of the candidate's suitability. The full RAC assigns each applicant a final rating. The school has a rolling admissions process. Offers of acceptance are made from October 15 to just before the beginning of the next medical school academic year.

COSTS AND FINANCIAL AID

Financial aid phone number: (858) 534-4664
Tuition, 2003-2004 academic year: **In-state: $15,570; Out-of-state: $27,815**
Room and board: **$11,134**
Percentage of students receiving financial aid in 2003-04: 86%
Percentage of students receiving: Loans: 82%, Grants/scholarships: 70%, Work-study aid: 2%
Average medical school debt for the Class of 2002: $56,094

STUDENT BODY

Fall 2003 full-time enrollment: 491
Men: 51%, Women: 49%, In-state: 98%, Minorities: 45%,
American Indian: 0.0%, Asian-American: 35.2%,
African-American: 2.0%, Hispanic-American: 7.3%,
White: 51.3%, International: 0.0%, Unknown: 4.1%

ACADEMIC PROGRAMS

The school's curriculum gives first-year students substantial contact with patients.
There are opportunities for first- or second-year students to work in community health clinics.
Program offerings: AIDS, drug/alcohol abuse, family medicine, geriatrics, internal medicine, pediatrics, rural medicine, women's health
Joint degrees awarded: M.D./Ph.D., M.D./M.P.H., M.D./M.S.
Total National Institutes of Health (NIH) grants awarded to the medical school and affiliated hospitals: **$241.9 million**

CURRICULUM

(TEXT PROVIDED BY SCHOOL):
The UCSD School of Medicine seeks to train humanistic physicians and physician-scientists who are also highly skilled practitioners, innovators, and leaders. The goal of the curriculum is to prepare physicians who are scientifically expert, clinically astute, responsive to community problems, and compassionate in patient care.

The preclinical curriculum emphasizes not only basic sciences but also medical skills. In addition to courses like biochemistry and microbiology, curricular content includes doctor-patient communication, ethics, and alternative medicine. The school capitalizes on the superb basic science

departments on UCSD's general campus. Scientists and clinicians work together in the school's clinical departments, and both are heavily involved in teaching the first two years of medical school. During those two years, students complete 227 hours of preclinical electives, which may include everything from preceptorships to learning how to take a history in Spanish, Mandarin Chinese, or sign language.

During the third year, students complete 12-week rotations in medicine and surgery, six-week rotations in psychiatry and reproductive medicine, a four-week rotation in neurology, and an eight-week pediatric experience, in addition to a yearlong clerkship in primary care. Fourth-year students may choose from several hundred electives. At least 12 weeks of direct patient care are required. Passing an examination that uses standardized patients is a graduation requirement. The fourth year also contains a 90-hour course entitled Principles to Practice, which integrates basic science principles into clinical medicine and prepares students better for residency. Students also must complete an independent study project before graduation. Students are required to pass both Step 1 and Step 2 of the U.S. Medical Licensing Examination to graduate.

Graduates are prepared to enter residencies in every surgical, medical, or hospital-based specialty offered today or to enter a career in primary-care medicine. Advanced training opportunities are available, leading to master's and Ph.D. degrees in multiple disciplines.

FACULTY PROFILE (FALL 2003)

Total teaching faculty: **785 (full-time), 20 (part-time)**
Of full-time faculty, those teaching in basic sciences: 25%; in clinical programs: 75%
Of part-time faculty, those teaching in basic sciences: 20%; in clinical programs: 80%
Full-time faculty/student ratio: **1.6**

SUPPORT SERVICES

The school offers students these services for dealing with stress: expanded-hour gym access, peer counseling, professional counseling, religious support, support groups.

RESIDENCY CHOICES

Most popular residency and specialty programs chosen by the 2002 and 2003 M.D. graduating classes: anesthesiology, emergency medicine, family practice, internal medicine, obstetrics and gynecology, orthopedic surgery, pediatrics, radiology–diagnostic, surgery–general, transitional year.

WHERE GRADS GO

	63.0%	

Proportion of 2001-2003 graduates who entered primary care specialties

	71.0%	

Proportion of 2002-2003 graduates who accepted in-state residencies

University of California–San Francisco

- 513 Parnassus Avenue, Room S224, San Francisco, CA 94143-0410
- Public
- Year Founded: 1864
- Tuition, 2003-2004: In-state: $15,977; Out-of-state: $28,222
- Enrollment, 2003-2004: 629
- Website: http://medschool.ucsf.edu/admissions
- Specialty ranking: AIDS: 1, drug/alcohol abuse: 4, family medicine: 9, geriatrics: 11, internal medicine: 3, pediatrics: 5, women's health: 3

3.76 AVERAGE GPA, ENTERING CLASS FALL 2003

11.2 AVERAGE MCAT, ENTERING CLASS FALL 2003

5.6% ACCEPTANCE RATE, ENTERING CLASS FALL 2003

6 2005 U.S.NEWS MEDICAL SCHOOL RANKING (RESEARCH)

8 2005 U.S.NEWS MEDICAL SCHOOL RANKING (PRIMARY CARE)

ADMISSIONS

Admissions phone number: **(415) 476-4044**
Admissions email address: **admissions@medsch.ucsf.edu**
Application website: **http://www.aamc.org**
Acceptance rate: **5.6%**
In-state acceptance rate: **6.8%**
Out-of-state acceptance rate: **3.9%**
Minority acceptance rate: **N/A**
International acceptance rate: **N/A**

Fall 2003 applications and acceptees

	Applied	Interviewed	Accepted	Enrolled
Total:	4,045	553	226	141
In-state:	2,352	N/A	160	115
Out-of-state:	1,693	N/A	66	26

Profile of admitted students

Average undergraduate grade point average: **3.76**
MCAT averages (scale: 1-15; writing test: J-T):
  Composite score: **11.2**
  Verbal reasoning score: **10.4**, Physical sciences score: **11.4**, Biological sciences score: **11.7**, Writing score: **Q**
Percentage of students not coming directly from college after graduation: **69%**

Dates and details

The American Medical College Application Service (AMCAS) application is accepted.
School asks for a school-specific application as part of the admissions process.
Oldest MCAT considered for Fall 2005 entry: **2002**
Earliest application date for the 2005-2006 first-year class: **June 1, 2004**
Latest application date: **November 1, 2004**
Acceptance dates for regular application for the class entering in fall 2005:
  Earliest: **December 15, 2004**
  Latest: **N/A**
The school considers requests for deferred entrance.
Starting month for the class entering in 2005-2006: **September**

The school doesn't have an Early Decision Plan (EDP). A personal interview is required for admission.

Undergraduate coursework required

Medical school requires undergraduate work in these subjects: biology/zoology, organic chemistry, inorganic (general) chemistry, physics.

ADMISSIONS POLICY

(TEXT PROVIDED BY SCHOOL):
Please refer to the University of California, San Francisco School of Medicine admissions Web site for specific details regarding policies, preferences, criteria, selection factors, and procedures.

COSTS AND FINANCIAL AID

Financial aid phone number: **(415) 476-4181**
Tuition, 2003-2004 academic year: **In-state: $15,977; Out-of-state: $28,222**
Room and board: **$14,877**
Percentage of students receiving financial aid in 2003-04: **87%**
Percentage of students receiving: Loans: **79%**, Grants/scholarships: **85%**, Work-study aid: **2%**
Average medical school debt for the Class of 2002: **$55,144**

STUDENT BODY

Fall 2003 full-time enrollment: **629**
Men: **44%**, Women: **56%**, In-state: **95%**, Minorities: **43%**, American Indian: **1.1%**, Asian-American: **28.8%**, African-American: **5.1%**, Hispanic-American: **7.3%**, White: **55.8%**, International: **0.0%**, Unknown: **1.9%**

ACADEMIC PROGRAMS

The school's curriculum gives first-year students substantial contact with patients.
There are opportunities for first- or second-year students to work in community health clinics.
Program offerings: AIDS, drug/alcohol abuse, family medicine, geriatrics, internal medicine, pediatrics, rural medicine, women's health

Joint degrees awarded: M.D./Ph.D., M.D./M.P.H., M.D./M.S.

Total National Institutes of Health (NIH) grants awarded to the medical school and affiliated hospitals: **$383.6 million**

CURRICULUM

(TEXT PROVIDED BY SCHOOL):

Inaugurated in 2001, UCSF's medical curriculum emphasizes interdisciplinary approaches and clinical case studies to prepare students for the future of healthcare delivery.

Students spend the first two years in the Essential Core curriculum in integrated block courses that weave together basic, clinical, and social sciences. Clinical cases are used extensively to motivate learners, increase retention, and enhance critical thinking. To encourage self-directed learning, formal class time is limited to 24 hours per week, allowing for enrollment in electives and research with faculty mentors. To promote collaborative and interdependent learning, half of all instructional hours occur in small groups. The electronic curriculum, iROCKET, fosters team learning through online forums and cooperative projects. Five advisory colleges, led by faculty mentors, serve as communities for student well-being and advising.

Essential Core block courses include:

Prologue: an introduction to essential anatomy, physiology, biochemistry, molecular and cell biology, epidemiology, social and behavioral science, and pharmacology.

Foundations of Patient Care: a longitudinal block spanning the entire Essential Core, covering clinical skills, professional development, and clinical reasoning.

Organ Systems: an integrated approach to cardiovascular, pulmonary, and renal systems.

Clinical Interlude: a three-day immersion in a hospital setting.

Cancer: an in-depth and innovative approach to the pathology and therapy of major human cancers, and a broad exploration of epidemiology, genetics, hematology, culture, behavioral sciences, ethics, and complementary and alternative medicine.

Brain, Mind, and Behavior: a comprehensive overview of principles in neuroscience, neurology, and psychiatry.

Infection, Inflammation, and Immunity: The first block of the second year covers microbiology, immunology, infectious disease, and public and international health.

Metabolism and Nutrition: an investigation of the gastrointestinal system, endocrinology, and metabolism, emphasizing disease prevention and nutritional health counseling.

Life Cycle: a study of the human developmental sequence, considering special topics in childhood and adolescent medicine, men's and women's health, and aging.

Integration and Consolidation: The final course of the Essential Core challenges students to review and integrate concepts through case-based study. This block also incorporates review for board exams and clerkship preparation.

The Clinical Core, the third year, comprises eight-week-long clerkships, including the following required clinical clerkships: anesthesia; family and community medicine; internal medicine; neurology; obstetrics and gynecology; pediatrics; psychiatry; surgery; and surgical specialties. Three weeklong intersessions punctuate clerkship rotations, allowing students to discuss clinical experiences and explore more fully medical ethics, health systems, advances in medical science, and clinical decision making. The Longitudinal Clinical Experience runs concurrently with the clerkships, exposing students to outpatient settings in a field of their choice one half day each week. UCSF's simulation labs aid the development and assessment of clinical and communication skills.

Advanced Studies, the fourth year, prepares students for postgraduate study and provides curricular support for projects that students undertake during training. The area of concentration, comparable to a college "minor," offers networks to connect students and faculty with similar interests, and appeals to students across clinical disciplines. The areas of concentration identified initially are: Advocacy and Community Medicine; Global and Public Health; Humanities and Medicine; Medical Education; The Healthcare System and the Physician-Leader; and The Science of Medicine and the Physician-Investigator.

FACULTY PROFILE (FALL 2003)

Total teaching faculty: 1,500 (full-time), 58 (part-time)

Of full-time faculty, those teaching in basic sciences: 11%; in clinical programs: 89%

Of part-time faculty, those teaching in basic sciences: 19%; in clinical programs: 81%

Full-time faculty/student ratio: 2.4

SUPPORT SERVICES

The school offers students these services for dealing with stress: expanded-hour gym access, professional counseling, support groups.

RESIDENCY CHOICES

Most popular residency and specialty programs chosen by the 2002 and 2003 M.D. graduating classes: anesthesiology, emergency medicine, internal medicine, obstetrics and gynecology, ophthalmology, orthopedic surgery, pediatrics, psychiatry, radiology–diagnostic.

WHERE GRADS GO

39.4%

Proportion of 2001-2003 graduates who entered primary care specialties

62.8%

Proportion of 2002-2003 graduates who accepted in-state residencies

University of Chicago

PRITZKER SCHOOL OF MEDICINE

- 924 E. 57th Street, BSLC 104, Chicago, IL 60637-5416
- Private
- Year Founded: 1927
- Tuition, 2003-2004: $32,151
- Enrollment, 2003-2004: 421
- Website: http://pritzker.bsd.uchicago.edu
- Specialty ranking: internal medicine: 15, pediatrics: 20

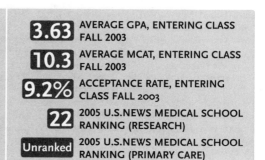

3.63 AVERAGE GPA, ENTERING CLASS FALL 2003

10.3 AVERAGE MCAT, ENTERING CLASS FALL 2003

9.2% ACCEPTANCE RATE, ENTERING CLASS FALL 2003

22 2005 U.S.NEWS MEDICAL SCHOOL RANKING (RESEARCH)

Unranked 2005 U.S.NEWS MEDICAL SCHOOL RANKING (PRIMARY CARE)

ADMISSIONS

Admissions phone number: **(773) 702-1937**
Admissions email address:
  pritzkeradmissions@bsd.uchicago.edu
Application website: **N/A**
Acceptance rate: **9.2%**
In-state acceptance rate: **15.5%**
Out-of-state acceptance rate: **8.0%**
Minority acceptance rate: **8.2%**
International acceptance rate: **3.9%**

Fall 2003 applications and acceptees

	Applied	Interviewed	Accepted	Enrolled
Total:	2,890	557	265	104
In-state:	438	124	68	41
Out-of-state:	2,452	433	197	63

Profile of admitted students

Average undergraduate grade point average: **3.63**
MCAT averages (scale: 1-15; writing test: J-T):
  Composite score: **10.3**
  Verbal reasoning score: **9.8**, Physical sciences score:
  10.4, Biological sciences score: **10.6**, Writing score: **Q**
Proportion with undergraduate majors in: Biological
  sciences: **41%**, Physical sciences: **18%**, Non-sciences:
  22%, Other health professions: **0%**, Mixed disciplines
  and other: **19%**
Percentage of students not coming directly from college
  after graduation: **N/A**

Dates and details

The American Medical College Application Service
  (AMCAS) application is accepted.
School asks for a school-specific application as part of the
  admissions process.
Oldest MCAT considered for Fall 2005 entry: **2002**
Earliest application date for the 2005-2006 first-year class:
  June 15, 2004
Latest application date: **October 15, 2004**
Acceptance dates for regular application for the class
  entering in fall 2005:

Earliest: **October 15, 2004**
Latest: **September 15, 2005**
The school considers requests for deferred entrance.
Starting month for the class entering in 2005-2006:
  September
The school has an Early Decision Plan (EDP).
A personal interview is required for admission.

Undergraduate coursework required

Medical school requires undergraduate work in these subjects: biology, organic chemistry, inorganic (general) chemistry, physics.

ADMISSIONS POLICY

(TEXT PROVIDED BY SCHOOL):
The University of Chicago Pritzker School of Medicine provides more than training in medicine. It provides an
immersion into the scholarship of a prestigious university,
where the medical school, the hospitals, and the university
share the same campus; where interdisciplinary research
and teaching are the norm, not the exception; and where
recognized experts from all disciplines contribute to the
development of young physicians in training.

Our mission is to educate our students to become
accomplished physicians who are capable of functioning as
outstanding clinicians, physician-scientists, medical educators, and clinical scholars. Pritzker graduates are known to
acquire superb skills in medical reasoning, problem solving, team building, and lifelong learning, which help them
assume leadership roles in their residency training programs and clinical practices, and as faculty in academic
medicine.

Once application materials are complete, the Committee
on Admissions reviews the candidate's entire application.
Applicants whose credentials are favorably reviewed are
invited to visit the campus for an interview day. The interviews provide the committee with an opportunity to get to
know the candidate, while the candidate has the opportunity
to ask questions and obtain insights into the university, curriculum, faculty, and student body. As part of the visit, candidates are given an orientation to Pritzker and the

University of Chicago; provided information on financial aid; given a tour of the medical center; and hosted for lunch by medical students.

Offers of admission are made solely on the basis of ability, achievement, motivation, and humanistic qualities. Successful applicants have demonstrated a passion for life-long learning, a commitment to others and to the goals of medicine, and leadership among their peers.

COSTS AND FINANCIAL AID
Financial aid phone number: **(773) 702-1938**
Tuition, 2003-2004 academic year: **$32,151**
Room and board: **$9,524**
Percentage of students receiving financial aid in 2003-04: **83%**
Percentage of students receiving: Loans: **81%**, Grants/scholarships: **72%**, Work-study aid: **0%**
Average medical school debt for the Class of 2002: **$112,170**

STUDENT BODY
Fall 2003 full-time enrollment: **421**
Men: **49%**, Women: **51%**, In-state: **38%**, Minorities: **38%**, American Indian: **0.2%**, Asian-American: **24.5%**, African-American: **11.4%**, Hispanic-American: **2.1%**, White: **59.1%**, International: **2.4%**, Unknown: **0.2%**

ACADEMIC PROGRAMS
The school's curriculum gives first-year students substantial contact with patients.
There are opportunities for first- or second-year students to work in community health clinics.
Program offerings: AIDS, drug/alcohol abuse, family medicine, geriatrics, internal medicine, pediatrics, women's health
Joint degrees awarded: M.D./Ph.D., M.D./M.B.A., M.D./J.D.
Total National Institutes of Health (NIH) grants awarded to the medical school and affiliated hospitals: **$142.9 million**

CURRICULUM
(TEXT PROVIDED BY SCHOOL):
The goal of the University of Chicago Pritzker School of Medicine is to graduate accomplished physicians who aspire to excellence as outstanding physician-scientists, medical educators, and clinical scholars. Pritzker traditionally attracts and recruits culturally diverse student leaders with strong academic backgrounds and personal accomplishments. By the time each class graduates, over 90 percent of students have explored scholarly pursuits outside the required academic program. We emphasize the importance of humanistic care and learning to think critically. Pritzker operates on a pass/fail grading system to encourage students to develop teamwork skills, discover and develop their unique talents, and promote cooperative learn-

ing through focused curricular and cocurricular activities. These medical education programs include the following:

Integration of basic science and clinical medicine across the four years of the curriculum.

Clinical experiences with patients and standardized patients beginning the first week of medical school, aided by the formative feedback provided by review of videotaped patient encounters with full-time faculty preceptors.

Summer research training allowing approximately 70 percent of the students to extend their research aptitudes before entering second-year medicine and to continue research throughout their medical education to help inculcate and disseminate the scientific basis of medicine.

A comprehensive group of required core clerkships beginning in the third year and combining ambulatory and inpatient experiences taught by full-time faculty together with highly selected house staff to promote and model clinical proficiency.

Web-based programs and instruction in academic computing and medical informatics to integrate curricular and cocurricular educational programs.

Opportunities to participate in M.D./Ph.D. and M.D./J.D. programs, master's degree programs (M.B.A., M.P.H., M.P.P.), and research "year out" experiences subscribed by a quarter of the class.

Accredited opportunities to develop scholarship of teaching as assistants in medical courses.

An extensive array of cocurricular activities that provide the arena for students to develop further their altruism, collegiality, leadership, and professionalism.

FACULTY PROFILE (FALL 2003)
Total teaching faculty: **769 (full-time)**, **212 (part-time)**
Of full-time faculty, those teaching in basic sciences: **15%**; in clinical programs: **85%**
Of part-time faculty, those teaching in basic sciences: **2%**; in clinical programs: **98%**
Full-time faculty/student ratio: **1.8**

RESIDENCY CHOICES
Most popular residency and specialty programs chosen by the 2002 and 2003 M.D. graduating classes: anesthesiology, family practice, internal medicine, orthopedic surgery, pediatrics, psychiatry, radiology–diagnostic, transitional year.

WHERE GRADS GO

50.7%
Proportion of 2001-2003 graduates who entered primary care specialties

23.5%
Proportion of 2002-2003 graduates who accepted in-state residencies

University of Cincinnati

- Office of Student Affairs and Admissions, Cincinnati, OH 45267-0552
- Public
- **Year Founded:** 1819
- **Tuition, 2003-2004:** In-state: $19,662; Out-of-state: $34,191
- **Enrollment, 2003-2004:** 620
- **Website:** http://www.med.uc.edu
- **Specialty ranking:** pediatrics: 4

3.59 AVERAGE GPA, ENTERING CLASS FALL 2003

9.9 AVERAGE MCAT, ENTERING CLASS FALL 2003

17.4% ACCEPTANCE RATE, ENTERING CLASS FALL 2003

43 2005 U.S.NEWS MEDICAL SCHOOL RANKING (RESEARCH)

Unranked 2005 U.S.NEWS MEDICAL SCHOOL RANKING (PRIMARY CARE)

ADMISSIONS

Admissions phone number: **(513) 558-7314**
Admissions email address: **comadmis@ucmail.uc.edu**
Application website: **http://comdows.uc.edu/MedOneStop**
Acceptance rate: **17.4%**
In-state acceptance rate: **30.3%**
Out-of-state acceptance rate: **9.7%**
Minority acceptance rate: **14.2%**
International acceptance rate: **0.0%**

Fall 2003 applications and acceptees

	Applied	Interviewed	Accepted	Enrolled
Total:	2,226	634	387	161
In-state:	833	390	252	122
Out-of-state:	1,393	244	135	39

Profile of admitted students

Average undergraduate grade point average: **3.59**
MCAT averages (scale: 1-15; writing test: J-T):
Composite score: **9.9**
Verbal reasoning score: **9.4**, Physical sciences score: **10.0**, Biological sciences score: **10.3**, Writing score: **O**
Proportion with undergraduate majors in: Biological sciences: **49%**, Physical sciences: **25%**, Non-sciences: **19%**, Other health professions: **0%**, Mixed disciplines and other: **7%**
Percentage of students not coming directly from college after graduation: **35%**

Dates and details

The American Medical College Application Service (AMCAS) application is accepted.
School asks for a school-specific application as part of the admissions process.
Oldest MCAT considered for Fall 2005 entry: **2002**
Earliest application date for the 2005-2006 first-year class: **June 1, 2004**
Latest application date: **December 15, 2004**
Acceptance dates for regular application for the class entering in fall 2005:
Earliest: **October 15, 2004**

Latest: **August 8, 2005**
The school considers requests for deferred entrance.
Starting month for the class entering in 2005-2006: **August**
The school has an Early Decision Plan (EDP).
A personal interview is required for admission.

ADMISSIONS POLICY

(TEXT PROVIDED BY SCHOOL):
In addition to the American Medical College Application Service application, the University of Cincinnati asks all prospective students to complete an online supplementary form. Applicants are directed to our Web site to complete this secondary process. Once the secondary application and letters of recommendation are received, the applicant will be evaluated for an interview. In addition to the online application, the Web site provides information about the progress of each applicant in the admissions process.

The Interview Day Program is designed to present a brief description of the college and student services. It will include one interview; presentations on the admissions process, the curriculum, and student services; lunch; and a tour.

Notification of final decisions will be made on or near the 15th of each month. Prior to January, acceptances may be sent on a weekly basis.

Offers of acceptance are based upon the overall evaluation of applicants' academic and personal qualities. Postbaccalaureate and graduate coursework will be considered. Personal characteristics include demonstrated motivation, maturity, coping skills, interpersonal skills, sensitivity and tolerance toward others, communication, and critical-thinking skills. Students are admitted on the basis of individual qualifications, regardless of age, sex, sexual orientation, race, color, national origin, or physical or mental disabilities.

COSTS AND FINANCIAL AID

Financial aid phone number: **(513) 558-6797**
Tuition, 2003-2004 academic year: **In-state: $19,662; Out-of-state: $34,191**

Room and board: **$14,081**
Percentage of students receiving financial aid in 2003-04:
  87%
Percentage of students receiving: Loans: **83%**,
  Grants/scholarships: **39%**, Work-study aid: **3%**
Average medical school debt for the Class of 2002:
  $98,832

STUDENT BODY
Fall 2003 full-time enrollment: **620**
Men: **60%**, Women: **40%**, In-state: **82%**, Minorities: **23%**,
  American Indian: **0.3%**, Asian-American: **15.8%**,
  African-American: **6.6%**, Hispanic-American: **0.3%**,
  White: **76.1%**, International: **0.0%**, Unknown: **0.8%**

ACADEMIC PROGRAMS
The school's curriculum gives first-year students
  substantial contact with patients.
There are opportunities for first- or second-year students to
  work in community health clinics.
Program offerings: AIDS, drug/alcohol abuse, family
  medicine, geriatrics, internal medicine, pediatrics, rural
  medicine, women's health
Joint degrees awarded: M.D./Ph.D., M.D./M.B.A.
Total National Institutes of Health (NIH) grants awarded to
  the medical school and affiliated hospitals: **$173.3 million**

CURRICULUM
(TEXT PROVIDED BY SCHOOL):
Year 1 introduces students to normal structure, function,
and development of the human body in an integrated educational program. The integration continues in Year 2 as the
students focus on the basis and mechanisms of human disease. All year 1 and 2 courses combine lectures, laboratories, clinical case discussions, and small groups to facilitate
the acquisition and application of knowledge. Students in
the first two years are also introduced to clinical skills training and clinically oriented material on human sexuality,

medical ethics, and end-of-life care through a two-year
course, Clinical Foundations of Medical Practice.
  Year 3 presents a strong core of clinical material in all the
major disciplines as well as three electives to allow students
to begin exploring career options. Year 4 contains two acting internship, a clinical neuroscience selective, a four week
primary care selective in an underserved area, and a wide
variety of electives. Away rotations are encouraged.

FACULTY PROFILE (FALL 2003)
Total teaching faculty: **1,190 (full-time)**, **112 (part-time)**
Of full-time faculty, those teaching in basic sciences: **8%**;
  in clinical programs: **92%**
Of part-time faculty, those teaching in basic sciences: **6%**;
  in clinical programs: **94%**
Full-time faculty/student ratio: **1.9**

SUPPORT SERVICES
The school offers students these services for dealing with
stress: expanded-hour gym access, peer counseling, professional counseling, support groups.

RESIDENCY CHOICES
Most popular residency and specialty programs chosen by
the 2002 and 2003 M.D. graduating classes: anesthesiology,
emergency medicine, family practice, internal medicine,
obstetrics and gynecology, orthopedic surgery, pediatrics,
psychiatry, radiology–diagnostic, surgery–general.

WHERE GRADS GO

40.0%
*Proportion of 2001-2003 graduates who entered primary
care specialties*

46.0%
*Proportion of 2002-2003 graduates who accepted in-state
residencies*

University of Colorado

HEALTH SCIENCES CENTER

- 4200 E. Ninth Avenue, Box C290, Denver, CO 80262
- Public
- Year Founded: 1883
- Tuition, 2003-2004: In-state: $15,748; Out-of-state: $67,415
- Enrollment, 2003-2004: 526
- Website: http://www.uchsc.edu/sm/sm/mddgree.htm
- Specialty ranking: AIDS: 11, drug/alcohol abuse: 13, family medicine: 5, internal medicine: 20, pediatrics: 11, rural medicine: 24

3.71 AVERAGE GPA, ENTERING CLASS FALL 2003

10.1 AVERAGE MCAT, ENTERING CLASS FALL 2003

10.2% ACCEPTANCE RATE, ENTERING CLASS FALL 2003

31 2005 U.S.NEWS MEDICAL SCHOOL RANKING (RESEARCH)

9 2005 U.S.NEWS MEDICAL SCHOOL RANKING (PRIMARY CARE)

ADMISSIONS

Admissions phone number: **(303) 315-7361**
Admissions email address: **somadmin@uchsc.edu**
Application website: **http://www.aamc.org**
Acceptance rate: **10.2%**
In-state acceptance rate: **22.9%**
Out-of-state acceptance rate: **5.7%**
Minority acceptance rate: **5.9%**
International acceptance rate: **6.3%**

Fall 2003 applications and acceptees

	Applied	Interviewed	Accepted	Enrolled
Total:	2,382	578	243	132
In-state:	630	341	144	107
Out-of-state:	1,752	237	99	25

Profile of admitted students

Average undergraduate grade point average: **3.71**
MCAT averages (scale: 1-15; writing test: J-T):
  Composite score: **10.1**
  Verbal reasoning score: **10.1**, Physical sciences score: **10.1**, Biological sciences score: **10.1**, Writing score: **Q**
Proportion with undergraduate majors in: Biological sciences: **51%**, Physical sciences: **20%**, Non-sciences: **9%**, Other health professions: **2%**, Mixed disciplines and other: **18%**
Percentage of students not coming directly from college after graduation: **26%**

Dates and details

The American Medical College Application Service (AMCAS) application is accepted.
School asks for a school-specific application as part of the admissions process.
Oldest MCAT considered for Fall 2005 entry: **2002**
Earliest application date for the 2005-2006 first-year class: **June 15, 2004**
Latest application date: **November 1, 2004**
Acceptance dates for regular application for the class entering in fall 2005:
  Earliest: **October 16, 2004**

Latest: **March 20, 2005**
The school considers requests for deferred entrance.
Starting month for the class entering in 2005-2006:
  August
The school doesn't have an Early Decision Plan (EDP).
A personal interview is required for admission.

Undergraduate coursework required

Medical school requires undergraduate work in these subjects: biology, English, organic chemistry, inorganic (general) chemistry, physics, mathematics.

ADMISSIONS POLICY

(TEXT PROVIDED BY SCHOOL):

Places are offered to the applicants who appear to the Admissions Committee to be the most highly qualified in terms of academic and intellectual achievement, character, motivation, maturity, service, and emotional stability. For this assessment, college grades, Medical College Admission Test scores, letters of recommendation, and personal interviews are used. Interviews are arranged for applicants who have a good chance of being accepted, and no applicant will be accepted without a personal interview.

Of the 132 places in each class, approximately 80 percent will be awarded to Colorado residents. Thereafter, preference will be given to applicants from certain western states participating in the Western Interstate Commission on Higher Education program and to applicants from other states who have high grade-point averages and MCAT scores.

A variety of undergraduate majors are considered acceptable. No special preference is given to science majors over nonscience majors. However, demonstration of outstanding performance in the required science courses is essential. Accepted students for the 2003 entering class had the following statistics: mean GPA, 3.71; mean MCAT, 10.1; and mean age, 24 years.

The University of Colorado encourages applications from qualified diverse student groups. Acceptance is determined by the Admissions Committee and is based on the same type of criteria that apply to all other applicants. The committee carefully considers the student's social, economic, and educational background.

COSTS AND FINANCIAL AID

Financial aid phone number: **(303) 315-5621**

Tuition, 2003-2004 academic year: **In-state: $15,748; Out-of-state: $67,415**

Room and board: **$11,160**

Percentage of students receiving financial aid in 2003-04: **93%**

Percentage of students receiving: Loans: **87%**, Grants/scholarships: **69%**, Work-study aid: **4%**

Average medical school debt for the Class of 2002: **$89,892**

STUDENT BODY

Fall 2003 full-time enrollment: **526**

Men: **53%**, Women: **47%**, In-state: **94%**, Minorities: **20%**, American Indian: **0.6%**, Asian-American: **8.0%**, African-American: **4.2%**, Hispanic-American: **68%**, White: **80.2%**, International: **0.2%**, Unknown: **0.0%**

ACADEMIC PROGRAMS

The school's curriculum gives first-year students substantial contact with patients.

There are opportunities for first- or second-year students to work in community health clinics.

Program offerings: AIDS, drug/alcohol abuse, family medicine, geriatrics, internal medicine, pediatrics, rural medicine

Joint degrees awarded: M.D./Ph.D., M.D./M.B.A., M.D./M.P.H.

Total National Institutes of Health (NIH) grants awarded to the medical school and affiliated hospitals: **N/A**

CURRICULUM

(TEXT PROVIDED BY SCHOOL):

The curriculum of the University of Colorado School of Medicine is designed to provide scientific and clinical backgrounds to prepare graduates for the practice of medicine.

Most of the basic science courses are taught during the first two years. The freshman year includes basic cardiac life support, biochemistry (including nutrition), ethics in medicine, medical biophysics and genetics, neurobiology, physiology, and an integrated anatomy that includes cell biology, microanatomy, and embryology. The sophomore year includes clinical neurosciences, clinical epidemiology/biostatistics, pathology, immunology, microbiology, and psychiatry (human behavior). Pharmacology and pathophysiology are integrated with the other courses. The junior year includes core clerkships of family medicine, medicine, neurology, obstetrics and gynecology, pediatrics, psychiatry, surgery, and surgical subspecialties. Area Health Education Center (AHEC) rotations throughout Colorado are utilized for additional sites for most clerkships. The senior year consists almost entirely of 28 weeks of electives, which must include one four-week subinternship.

Over the past decade, several innovations have been added. Foundations of Doctoring is a three-year curriculum that includes ambulatory preceptor experience in all three years, a physical examination program, an extensive communication curriculum, and six hidden curriculum sessions. In the first year, orientation is offered as well as an ethics course involving other health professions students.

A simulation center using standardized patients is utilized for both teaching and evaluation of students' knowledge, skills, and attitudes. Gynecologic and urologic associates teach students the breast, pelvic, male genital, rectal, and prostate examinations. Students planning a career in academic medicine participate in the Medical Scientist Training Program, which results in both M.D. and Ph.D. degrees.

The school is planning to implement a new curriculum for the class entering in 2005. It will be an integrated block curriculum including basic sciences, clinical sciences, and threads such as humanities and ethics. Phase 1 of the essential core will be 39 weeks of interdisciplinary integrated block courses followed by 10 weeks of summer for vacation, AHEC preceptor rotations, or sponsored research. Phase 2 of the essential core will be 28 weeks of interdisciplinary integrated block courses. The clinical core (Phase 3) will begin in March of the second year and consist of required clerkships and intercession to address basic sciences and content gaps. This will be followed by advanced studies (Phase 4) including elective rotations, research, and a capstone project.

FACULTY PROFILE (FALL 2003)

Total teaching faculty: **1,311 (full-time)**, **115 (part-time)**

Of full-time faculty, those teaching in basic sciences: **15%**; in clinical programs: **85%**

Of part-time faculty, those teaching in basic sciences: **25%**; in clinical programs: **75%**

Full-time faculty/student ratio: **2.5**

SUPPORT SERVICES

The school offers students these services for dealing with stress: peer counseling, professional counseling, support groups.

RESIDENCY CHOICES

Most popular residency and specialty programs chosen by the 2002 and 2003 M.D. graduating classes: anesthesiology, emergency medicine, family practice, internal medicine, neurological surgery, obstetrics and gynecology, pediatrics, psychiatry, radiology–diagnostic, surgery–general.

WHERE GRADS GO

43.7%

Proportion of 2001-2003 graduates who entered primary care specialties

46.0%

Proportion of 2002-2003 graduates who accepted in-state residencies

University of Connecticut

- 263 Farmington Avenue, Farmington, CT 06030
- Public
- Year Founded: 1961
- Tuition, 2003-2004: In-state: $17,040; Out-of-state: $32,340
- Enrollment, 2003-2004: 309
- Website: http://medicine.uchc.edu
- Specialty ranking: geriatrics: 19

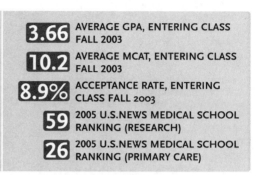

3.66 AVERAGE GPA, ENTERING CLASS FALL 2003

10.2 AVERAGE MCAT, ENTERING CLASS FALL 2003

8.9% ACCEPTANCE RATE, ENTERING CLASS FALL 2003

59 2005 U.S.NEWS MEDICAL SCHOOL RANKING (RESEARCH)

26 2005 U.S.NEWS MEDICAL SCHOOL RANKING (PRIMARY CARE)

ADMISSIONS
Admissions phone number: **(860) 679-3874**
Admissions email address: **sanford@ns01.uchc.edu**
Application website: **N/A**
Acceptance rate: **8.9%**
In-state acceptance rate: **30.9%**
Out-of-state acceptance rate: **4.9%**
Minority acceptance rate: **N/A**
International acceptance rate: **N/A**

Fall 2003 applications and acceptees

	Applied	Interviewed	Accepted	Enrolled
Total:	2,208	380	196	74
In-state:	340	210	105	53
Out-of-state:	1,868	170	91	21

Profile of admitted students
Average undergraduate grade point average: **3.66**
MCAT averages (scale: 1-15; writing test: J-T):
  Composite score: **10.2**
  Verbal reasoning score: **9.7**, Physical sciences score: **10.2**, Biological sciences score: **10.6**, Writing score: **Q**
Proportion with undergraduate majors in: Biological sciences: **53%**, Physical sciences: **28%**, Non-sciences: **9%**, Other health professions: **1%**, Mixed disciplines and other: **9%**
Percentage of students not coming directly from college after graduation: **39%**

Dates and details
The American Medical College Application Service (AMCAS) application is accepted.
School asks for a school-specific application as part of the admissions process.
Oldest MCAT considered for Fall 2005 entry: **2001**
Earliest application date for the 2005-2006 first-year class: **June 15, 2004**
Latest application date: **December 15, 2004**
Acceptance dates for regular application for the class entering in fall 2005:
  Earliest: **October 15, 2004**

Latest: **August 1, 2005**
The school considers requests for deferred entrance.
Starting month for the class entering in 2005-2006:
  August
The school has an Early Decision Plan (EDP).
A personal interview is required for admission.

Undergraduate coursework required
Medical school requires undergraduate work in these subjects: biology, biology/zoology, English, organic chemistry, inorganic (general) chemistry, physics, general chemistry.

ADMISSIONS POLICY
(TEXT PROVIDED BY SCHOOL):
The curriculum plan for medical students is based on a multidepartmental approach. Basic medical sciences are taught from an organ-system approach. Normal structure/function is presented first, followed by pathophysiology and therapeutic approaches. Patient contact begins in Year 1 as part of the clinical medicine course. Students learn medical history taking, physical diagnosis, and various other aspects of the physician-patient relationship. In addition, students participate in a longitudinal ambulatory clinical experience throughout all four years. In the third year, the students rotate through ambulatory and in-patient activities in each of the major clinical disciplines. In the fourth-year, students complete clinical rotations in emergent and urgent care and have five months of electives. To aid individual development, students are assigned significant amounts of free time during the first two years and a wide choice of elective subjects in the clinical years. The NBME examinations are required of all students. The grading system is strictly pass/fail; there are no class rank scales or class standing. The third year grading system is honors and pass/fail.

COSTS AND FINANCIAL AID
Financial aid phone number: **(860) 679-3574**
Tuition, 2003-2004 academic year: **In-state: $17,040; Out-of-state: $32,340**
Room and board: **N/A**

Percentage of students receiving financial aid in 2003-04: 95%

Percentage of students receiving: Loans: **90%**, Grants/scholarships: **45%**, Work-study aid: **0%**

Average medical school debt for the Class of 2002: **$64,000**

STUDENT BODY

Fall 2003 full-time enrollment: **309**

Men: **42%**, Women: **58%**, In-state: **92%**, Minorities: **27%**, American Indian: **0.3%**, Asian-American: **12.9%**, African-American: **11.0%**, Hispanic-American: **2.9%**, White: **69.3%**, International: **1.3%**, Unknown: **2.3%**

ACADEMIC PROGRAMS

The school's curriculum gives first-year students substantial contact with patients.

There are opportunities for first- or second-year students to work in community health clinics.

Program offerings: AIDS, drug/alcohol abuse, family medicine, geriatrics, internal medicine, pediatrics, women's health

Joint degrees awarded: M.D./Ph.D., M.D./M.B.A., M.D./M.P.H.

Total National Institutes of Health (NIH) grants awarded to the medical school and affiliated hospitals: **N/A**

CURRICULUM

(TEXT PROVIDED BY SCHOOL):

The curriculum plan for medical students is based on a multidepartmental approach. Basic medical sciences are taught from an organ-system approach. Normal structure/function is presented first, followed by pathophysiology and therapeutic approaches.

Patient contact begins in Year 1 as part of the clinical medicine course. Students learn medical history taking, physical diagnosis, and various other aspects of the physician-patient relationship. In addition, students participate in a longitudinal ambulatory clinical experience throughout all four years. In the third year, students rotate through ambulatory and inpatient activities in each of the major clinical

disciplines. In the fourth year, students complete clinical rotations in emergent and urgent care and have five months of electives. To aid individual development, students are assigned significant amounts of free time during the first two years and a wide choice of elective subjects in the clinical years.

The National Board of Medical Examiners examinations are required of all students. The grading system is strictly pass/fail; there are no class rank scales or class standing. The third-year grading system is honors and pass/fail.

FACULTY PROFILE (FALL 2003)

Total teaching faculty: **409 (full-time)**, **98 (part-time)**

Of full-time faculty, those teaching in basic sciences: **31%**; in clinical programs: **69%**

Of part-time faculty, those teaching in basic sciences: **18%**; in clinical programs: **82%**

Full-time faculty/student ratio: **1.3**

SUPPORT SERVICES

The school offers students these services for dealing with stress: peer counseling, professional counseling, support groups.

RESIDENCY CHOICES

Most popular residency and specialty programs chosen by the 2002 and 2003 M.D. graduating classes: anesthesiology, emergency medicine, family practice, internal medicine, obstetrics and gynecology, otolaryngology, pediatrics, psychiatry, radiology–diagnostic, surgery–general.

WHERE GRADS GO

52.0%

Proportion of 2001-2003 graduates who entered primary care specialties

31.0%

Proportion of 2002-2003 graduates who accepted in-state residencies

University of Florida

- Box 100215 UFHSC, Gainesville, FL 32610-0215
- Public
- Year Founded: 1956
- Tuition, 2003-2004: In-state: $15,741; Out-of-state: $41,897
- Enrollment, 2003-2004: 459
- Website: http://www.med.ufl.edu/oea/admiss
- Specialty ranking: N/A

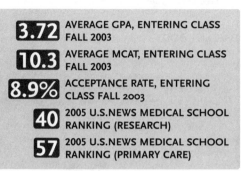

3.72 AVERAGE GPA, ENTERING CLASS FALL 2003

10.3 AVERAGE MCAT, ENTERING CLASS FALL 2003

8.9% ACCEPTANCE RATE, ENTERING CLASS FALL 2003

40 2005 U.S.NEWS MEDICAL SCHOOL RANKING (RESEARCH)

57 2005 U.S.NEWS MEDICAL SCHOOL RANKING (PRIMARY CARE)

ADMISSIONS

Admissions phone number: (352) 392-4569
Admissions email address: robyn@dean.med.ufl.edu
Application website: N/A
Acceptance rate: 8.9%
In-state acceptance rate: 14.7%
Out-of-state acceptance rate: 0.9%
Minority acceptance rate: 22.2%
International acceptance rate: 0.0%

Fall 2003 applications and acceptees

	Applied	Interviewed	Accepted	Enrolled
Total:	2,003	302	179	116
In-state:	1,160	293	171	113
Out-of-state:	843	9	8	3

Profile of admitted students

Average undergraduate grade point average: 3.72
MCAT averages (scale: 1-15; writing test: J-T):
Composite score: 10.3
Verbal reasoning score: 9.7, Physical sciences score: 10.7, Biological sciences score: 10.5, Writing score: O
Proportion with undergraduate majors in: Biological sciences: 24%, Physical sciences: 29%, Non-sciences: 22%, Other health professions: 1%, Mixed disciplines and other: 24%
Percentage of students not coming directly from college after graduation: 53%

Dates and details

The American Medical College Application Service (AMCAS) application is accepted.
School asks for a school-specific application as part of the admissions process.
Oldest MCAT considered for Fall 2005 entry: 2002
Earliest application date for the 2005-2006 first-year class: June 2, 2004
Latest application date: December 1, 2004
Acceptance dates for regular application for the class entering in fall 2005:
Earliest: October 15, 2004

Latest: August 11, 2005
The school considers requests for deferred entrance.
Starting month for the class entering in 2005-2006:
August
The school doesn't have an Early Decision Plan (EDP).
A personal interview is required for admission.

Undergraduate coursework required

Medical school requires undergraduate work in these subjects: biology, organic chemistry, inorganic (general) chemistry, physics, biochemistry, general chemistry.

ADMISSIONS POLICY
(TEXT PROVIDED BY SCHOOL):

Admission to the University of Florida College of Medicine is highly competitive. The college seeks students who demonstrate personal and intellectual characteristics essential for physicians. The college offers 108 positions through the regular admissions process.

Applicants are appraised on the basis of personal attributes, academic record, evaluation of past activities, the Medical College Admission Test, and letters of recommendation. The college does not discriminate on the basis of race, gender, age, disability, creed, or national origin. The college welcomes applications from minorities and from persons who demonstrate a commitment to underserved populations.

Applicants must be U.S. citizens or permanent residents. They must receive a bachelor's degree or its equivalent from a Council on Higher Education-accredited institution prior to matriculation to the college. Preference is given to Florida residents.

It is not necessary for applicants to pursue an undergraduate major in the sciences, but prior to matriculation applicants must complete eight semester hours each of general chemistry, general physics, and biological sciences and four hours each of organic chemistry and biochemistry. All courses must include a laboratory section.

The MCAT is required. It must be taken within three years prior to matriculation and before the application deadline.

There is no minimum MCAT score or grade-point average required of applicants.

The application deadline is December 1. Applicants submit an initial application to the American Medical College Application Service. The college's Medical Selection Committee invites competitive applicants to submit a second application directly to the college. After review of the second application, MCAT scores, and letters of recommendation, some applicants are invited for interviews. Interviews, required for admission to the college, are conducted from mid-August through March. The committee makes a recommendation regarding the applicant. With the dean's approval, the committee's chairman or chairwoman makes the final determination of each applicant's status.

COSTS AND FINANCIAL AID
Financial aid phone number: (352) 392-7800
Tuition, 2003-2004 academic year: **In-state: $15,741; Out-of-state: $41,897**
Room and board: **$7,816**
Percentage of students receiving financial aid in 2003-04: 88%
Percentage of students receiving: Loans: 82%, Grants/scholarships: 87%, Work-study aid: 0%
Average medical school debt for the Class of 2002: $86,000

STUDENT BODY
Fall 2003 full-time enrollment: 459
Men: 50%, Women: 50%, In-state: 96%, Minorities: 37%, American Indian: 1.1%, Asian-American: 19.4%, African-American: 7.8%, Hispanic-American: 8.7%, White: 61.2%, International: 0.0%, Unknown: 1.7%

ACADEMIC PROGRAMS
The school's curriculum gives first-year students substantial contact with patients.
There are opportunities for first- or second-year students to work in community health clinics.
Program offerings: AIDS, drug/alcohol abuse, family medicine, geriatrics, internal medicine, pediatrics, rural medicine, women's health
Joint degrees awarded: M.D./Ph.D., M.D./M.B.A., M.D./J.D.
Total National Institutes of Health (NIH) grants awarded to the medical school and affiliated hospitals: **N/A**

CURRICULUM
(TEXT PROVIDED BY SCHOOL):
Our curriculum is based on 12 educational principles and focuses on the development and assessment of competencies. We strive to provide a general professional education.

Each course and clerkship develops learning objectives tied to specific competencies. Feedback is provided to students as they proceed. We emphasize the competency category of professionalism because it is crucial to our students' success.

Our first year includes traditional basic science courses. The Essentials of Patient Care course provides an early introduction to such clinical skills as the medical history and physical examination. These are taught in the state-of-the-art Harrell Assessment and Development Center using our nationally recognized standardized patient program.

At the end of the first semester, each student is placed with a practicing physician for two weeks at sites throughout Florida. All first-year students also participate in a year-long interdisciplinary family health course, during which they visit volunteer families in their homes.

Second-year coursework includes pathology, immunology and medical microbiology, pharmacology, oncology, courses in medical ethics and evidence-based medicine, and continuance of Essentials of Patient Care. At four points during their training, students must pass a performance-based examination assessing clinical skills. All students must pass the National Board of Medical Examiners Step 1 test to proceed to their clinical years.

Our third year includes core clerkships in internal medicine, surgery, pediatrics, obstetrics and gynecology, psychiatry, family medicine, geriatrics, and neurology. Additional required clerkships in the fourth year include emergency medicine and anesthesiology, and students must do a subinternship in internal medicine, family medicine, or pediatrics. Much of the fourth year is elective time, to allow students to prepare for residency training.

We have two major clinical locations: Gainesville, including both Shands at the University of Florida and the Veterans Affairs Medical Center; and our urban campus location in Jacksonville at University Hospital.

FACULTY PROFILE (FALL 2003)
Total teaching faculty: **1,068 (full-time), 109 (part-time)**
Of full-time faculty, those teaching in basic sciences: 14%; in clinical programs: 86%
Of part-time faculty, those teaching in basic sciences: 7%; in clinical programs: 93%
Full-time faculty/student ratio: 2.3

SUPPORT SERVICES
The school offers students these services for dealing with stress: expanded-hour gym access, peer counseling, professional counseling, religious support, support groups.

RESIDENCY CHOICES
Most popular residency and specialty programs chosen by the 2002 and 2003 M.D. graduating classes: anesthesiology, family practice, family practice–sports medicine, internal medicine, internal medicine–pediatrics, obstetrics and gynecology, orthopedic surgery, pediatrics, radiology–diagnostic, surgery–general, internal medicine/dermatology.

WHERE GRADS GO
44.2%
Proportion of 2001-2003 graduates who entered primary care specialties

53.1%
Proportion of 2002-2003 graduates who accepted in-state residencies

University of Illinois—Chicago

- 1853 W. Polk Street, M/C 784, Chicago, IL 60612
- Public
- Year Founded: 1887
- Tuition, 2003-2004: In-state: $22,780; Out-of-state: $50,216
- Enrollment, 2003-2004: 1,375
- Website: http://www.uic.edu/depts/mcam
- Specialty ranking: N/A

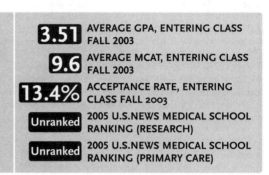

3.51 AVERAGE GPA, ENTERING CLASS FALL 2003

9.6 AVERAGE MCAT, ENTERING CLASS FALL 2003

13.4% ACCEPTANCE RATE, ENTERING CLASS FALL 2003

Unranked 2005 U.S.NEWS MEDICAL SCHOOL RANKING (RESEARCH)

Unranked 2005 U.S.NEWS MEDICAL SCHOOL RANKING (PRIMARY CARE)

ADMISSIONS

Admissions phone number: **(312) 996-5635**
Admissions email address: **medadmit@uic.edu**
Application website: **http://www.aamc.org**
Acceptance rate: **13.4%**
In-state acceptance rate: **31.2%**
Out-of-state acceptance rate: **4.7%**
Minority acceptance rate: **14.3%**
International acceptance rate: **N/A**

Fall 2003 applications and acceptees

	Applied	Interviewed	Accepted	Enrolled
Total:	4,478	912	601	313
In-state:	1,478	623	461	254
Out-of-state:	3,000	289	140	59

Profile of admitted students

Average undergraduate grade point average: **3.51**
MCAT averages (scale: 1-15; writing test: J-T):
  Composite score: **9.6**
  Verbal reasoning score: **N/A**, Physical sciences score: **N/A**, Biological sciences score: **N/A**, Writing score: **N/A**
Proportion with undergraduate majors in: Biological sciences: **48%**, Physical sciences: **12%**, Non-sciences: **8%**, Other health professions: **5%**, Mixed disciplines and other: **27%**
Percentage of students not coming directly from college after graduation: **27%**

Dates and details

The American Medical College Application Service (AMCAS) application is accepted.
School asks for a school-specific application as part of the admissions process.
Oldest MCAT considered for Fall 2005 entry: **2002**
Earliest application date for the 2005-2006 first-year class: **June 1, 2004**
Latest application date: **December 15, 2004**
Acceptance dates for regular application for the class entering in fall 2005:
  Earliest: **October 2, 2004**

Latest: **August 15, 2005**
The school considers requests for deferred entrance.
Starting month for the class entering in 2005-2006:
  August
The school has an Early Decision Plan (EDP).
A personal interview is required for admission.

Undergraduate coursework required

Medical school requires undergraduate work in these subjects: biology, organic chemistry, inorganic (general) chemistry, physics, behavioral science, social sciences, general chemistry.

ADMISSIONS POLICY

(TEXT PROVIDED BY SCHOOL):
The UIC College of Medicine selects applicants who, in the judgment of the Committee on Admissions, demonstrate the qualities that are necessary for the successful study and practice of medicine and that best meet the needs of the citizenry of Illinois. These qualities include academic achievement, good communication skills, emotional stability, maturity, integrity, diversity of interests, leadership, and motivation. The committee considers the quality of all academic accomplishments of each applicant, including achievement in advanced projects, as well as the work and extracurricular experiences that demonstrate the applicant's initiative and creativity.

COSTS AND FINANCIAL AID

Financial aid phone number: **(312) 413-0127**
Tuition, 2003-2004 academic year: **In-state: $22,780; Out-of-state: $50,216**
Room and board: **$10,850**
Percentage of students receiving financial aid in 2003-04: **N/A**
Percentage of students receiving: Loans: **N/A**, Grants/scholarships: **N/A**, Work-study aid: **N/A**
Average medical school debt for the Class of 2002: **$101,295**

STUDENT BODY

Fall 2003 full-time enrollment: 1,375

Men: 56%, Women: 44%, In-state: 83%, Minorities: 51%,
  American Indian: 0.5%, Asian-American: 33.5%,
  African-American: 8.2%, Hispanic-American: 9.5%,
  White: 46.0%, International: 0.0%, Unknown: 2.4%

ACADEMIC PROGRAMS

The school's curriculum gives first-year students
  substantial contact with patients.

There are opportunities for first- or second-year students to
  work in community health clinics.

Program offerings: AIDS, drug/alcohol abuse, family
  medicine, geriatrics, internal medicine, pediatrics, rural
  medicine, women's health

Joint degrees awarded: M.D./Ph.D., M.D./M.B.A.,
  M.D./M.P.H., M.D./M.H.I., M.D./J.D., M.D./M.S.W.,
  M.D./M.S., M.D./M.A., M.D./M.H.A.

Total National Institutes of Health (NIH) grants awarded to
  the medical school and affiliated hospitals: N/A

CURRICULUM

(TEXT PROVIDED BY SCHOOL):

The College of Medicine curriculum is designed to serve a
variety of career choices. The educational program allows
students to prepare for careers in medical practice, research,
teaching, community medicine, medical administration,
and other fields. The programs are diversified through relationships with many hospitals and other institutions, allowing for a wide range of learning opportunities in a variety of
medical practice settings.

The curriculum is supported by a sound advising system
and useful independent study aids. While all of these features are available in the curriculum, a student may seek
even greater curricular independence through the College
of Medicine at Chicago's Independent Study Program. The
curriculum includes a wide variety of programs and
courses. In addition to programs offered by the UIC College
of Medicine at Chicago, there are opportunities available at
other clinical sites.

The curriculum creates an environment for learning in
which students will develop the willingness and competence to promote and contribute to improved healthcare and
become responsible for their own continuing education
and, thereby, become able to cope with the ever changing
demands on physicians.

The learning environment is sufficiently flexible to allow
for differences in student backgrounds, learning rates, and
career goals. Proper emphasis is placed on the development
of the attitudes necessary for effective interaction with individual patients, with health-professional colleagues, and
with society at large. The curriculum stresses rational decision making and clinical problem solving based on an
understanding of the basic biological, physical, and behavioral sciences; thus the integration of basic and clinical sciences is emphasized throughout the program.

FACULTY PROFILE (FALL 2003)

Total teaching faculty: 786 (full-time), 475 (part-time)

Of full-time faculty, those teaching in basic sciences: 26%;
  in clinical programs: 74%

Of part-time faculty, those teaching in basic sciences: 4%;
  in clinical programs: 96%

Full-time faculty/student ratio: 0.6

SUPPORT SERVICES

The school offers students these services for dealing with
stress: expanded-hour gym access, peer counseling, professional counseling, religious support, support groups.

RESIDENCY CHOICES

Most popular residency and specialty programs chosen by
the 2002 and 2003 M.D. graduating classes: anesthesiology, emergency medicine, family practice, internal medicine, internal medicine–pediatrics, obstetrics and
gynecology, pediatrics, psychiatry, radiology–diagnostic,
surgery–general.

University of Iowa

ROY J. AND LUCILLE A. CARVER

- **200 CMAB, Iowa City, IA 52242-1101**
- **Public**
- **Year Founded:** N/A
- **Tuition, 2003-2004:** In-state: $19,310; Out-of-state: $37,778
- **Enrollment, 2003-2004:** 583
- **Website:** http://www.medicine.uiowa.edu
- **Specialty ranking:** internal medicine: 26, pediatrics: 22, rural medicine: 13

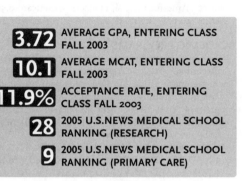

3.72	AVERAGE GPA, ENTERING CLASS FALL 2003
10.1	AVERAGE MCAT, ENTERING CLASS FALL 2003
11.9%	ACCEPTANCE RATE, ENTERING CLASS FALL 2003
28	2005 U.S.NEWS MEDICAL SCHOOL RANKING (RESEARCH)
9	2005 U.S.NEWS MEDICAL SCHOOL RANKING (PRIMARY CARE)

ADMISSIONS

Admissions phone number: **(319) 335-8052**
Admissions email address: **medical-admissions @uiowa.edu**
Application website:
http://www.medicine.uiowa.edu/osac/admissions
Acceptance rate: **11.9%**
In-state acceptance rate: **39.4%**
Out-of-state acceptance rate: **7.4%**
Minority acceptance rate: **N/A**
International acceptance rate: **N/A**

Fall 2003 applications and acceptees

	Applied	Interviewed	Accepted	Enrolled
Total:	2,326	547	277	142
In-state:	325	243	128	97
Out-of-state:	2,001	304	149	45

Profile of admitted students

Average undergraduate grade point average: **3.72**
MCAT averages (scale: 1-15; writing test: J-T):
Composite score: **10.1**
Verbal reasoning score: **9.9**, Physical sciences score: **10.0**, Biological sciences score: **10.3**, Writing score: **P**
Proportion with undergraduate majors in: Biological sciences: **54%**, Physical sciences: **19%**, Non-sciences: **14%**, Other health professions: **1%**, Mixed disciplines and other: **12%**
Percentage of students not coming directly from college after graduation: **13%**

Dates and details

The American Medical College Application Service (AMCAS) application is accepted.
School asks for a school-specific application as part of the admissions process.
Oldest MCAT considered for Fall 2005 entry: **1999**
Earliest application date for the 2005-2006 first-year class:
June 1, 2004
Latest application date: **November 1, 2004**

Acceptance dates for regular application for the class entering in fall 2005:
Earliest: **October 15, 2004**
Latest: **August 17, 2005**
The school considers requests for deferred entrance.
Starting month for the class entering in 2005-2006:
August
The school has an Early Decision Plan (EDP).
A personal interview is required for admission.

Undergraduate coursework required

Medical school requires undergraduate work in these subjects: biology, organic chemistry, inorganic (general) chemistry, physics, mathematics.

ADMISSIONS POLICY

(TEXT PROVIDED BY SCHOOL):
The Carver College of Medicine Admissions Committee selects students it considers best qualified for the study and practice of medicine from applicants who meet the basic requirements. Preference is given to applicants with high scholastic standing who are residents of Iowa. Consideration also is given to outstanding nonresidents.

Residency is determined by the university registrar in accordance with rules adopted by the Iowa Board of Regents. Nonresidents usually can obtain Iowa residency if they are enrolled as a half-time (or less) student for 12 consecutive months and are not claimed on tax forms in another state.

In addition to an on-campus interview, selection of applicants is based on a thorough review of all application materials, including the American Medical College Application Service application, a secondary application, and letters of reference. Academic promise is measured best by past performance (as indicated by grade-point average) in combination with scores on the Medical College Admission Test. Personal characteristics important in the practice of medicine, moral character, a commitment to service, and enriching qualities are all considered in the process of an application appraisal.

Admission is on the basis of individual qualifications, and applicants are not discriminated against on the basis of age, sex, race, disability, religion, sexual orientation, national origin, or marital status. The Carver College of Medicine is firmly committed to admitting a diverse student body.

COSTS AND FINANCIAL AID
Financial aid phone number: **(319) 335-8059**
Tuition, 2003-2004 academic year: **In-state: $19,310; Out-of-state: $37,778**
Room and board: **$5,940**
Percentage of students receiving financial aid in 2003-04: **96%**
Percentage of students receiving: Loans: **90%**, Grants/scholarships: **60%**, Work-study aid: **1%**
Average medical school debt for the Class of 2002: **$89,815**

STUDENT BODY
Fall 2003 full-time enrollment: **583**
Men: **54%**, Women: **46%**, In-state: **72%**, Minorities: **20%**, American Indian: **0.7%**, Asian-American: **6.5%**, African-American: **3.9%**, Hispanic-American: **57%**, White: **80.4%**, International: **0.0%**, Unknown: **2.7%**

ACADEMIC PROGRAMS
The school's curriculum gives first-year students substantial contact with patients.
There are opportunities for first- or second-year students to work in community health clinics.
Program offerings: AIDS, drug/alcohol abuse, family medicine, geriatrics, internal medicine, pediatrics, rural medicine
Joint degrees awarded: M.D./Ph.D., M.D./M.B.A., M.D./M.P.H., M.D./J.D.

Total National Institutes of Health (NIH) grants awarded to the medical school and affiliated hospitals: **$136.1 million**

FACULTY PROFILE (FALL 2003)
Total teaching faculty: **794 (full-time)**, **603 (part-time)**
Of full-time faculty, those teaching in basic sciences: **12%**; in clinical programs: **88%**
Of part-time faculty, those teaching in basic sciences: **0%**; in clinical programs: **100%**
Full-time faculty/student ratio: **1.4**

SUPPORT SERVICES
The school offers students these services for dealing with stress: peer counseling, professional counseling, support groups.

RESIDENCY CHOICES
Most popular residency and specialty programs chosen by the 2002 and 2003 M.D. graduating classes: anesthesiology, emergency medicine, family practice, internal medicine, obstetrics and gynecology, orthopedic surgery, pediatrics, psychiatry, surgery–general, transitional year.

WHERE GRADS GO
47.3%
Proportion of 2001-2003 graduates who entered primary care specialties

34.0%
Proportion of 2002-2003 graduates who accepted in-state residencies

University of Kansas Medical Center

- 3901 Rainbow Boulevard, Kansas City, KS 66160
- Public
- Year Founded: 1905
- Tuition, 2003-2004: In-state: $14,961; Out-of-state: $29,492
- Enrollment, 2003-2004: 707
- Website: http://www.kumc.edu/som/som.html
- Specialty ranking: rural medicine: 25

3.63 AVERAGE GPA, ENTERING CLASS FALL 2003

9.3 AVERAGE MCAT, ENTERING CLASS FALL 2003

18.7% ACCEPTANCE RATE, ENTERING CLASS FALL 2003

Unranked 2005 U.S.NEWS MEDICAL SCHOOL RANKING (RESEARCH)

Unranked 2005 U.S.NEWS MEDICAL SCHOOL RANKING (PRIMARY CARE)

ADMISSIONS

Admissions phone number: **(913) 588-5283**
Admissions email address: **smccurdy@kumc.edu**
Application website:
  http://www.kumc.edu/studentcenter/regacademic.html
Acceptance rate: **18.7%**
In-state acceptance rate: **43.8%**
Out-of-state acceptance rate: **6.9%**
Minority acceptance rate: **17.6%**
International acceptance rate: **0.0%**

Fall 2003 applications and acceptees

	Applied	Interviewed	Accepted	Enrolled
Total:	1,293	398	242	175
In-state:	413	297	181	153
Out-of-state:	880	101	61	22

Profile of admitted students

Average undergraduate grade point average: **3.63**
MCAT averages (scale: 1-15; writing test: J-T):
  Composite score: **9.3**
  Verbal reasoning score: **9.2**, Physical sciences score: **9.1**,
  Biological sciences score: **9.5**, Writing score: **N/A**
Proportion with undergraduate majors in: Biological
  sciences: **49%**, Physical sciences: **22%**, Non-sciences:
  11%, Other health professions: **4%**, Mixed disciplines
  and other: **14%**
Percentage of students not coming directly from college
  after graduation: **53%**

Dates and details

The American Medical College Application Service
  (AMCAS) application is accepted.
School does not ask for a school-specific application as part
  of the admissions process.
Oldest MCAT considered for Fall 2005 entry: **2002**
Earliest application date for the 2005-2006 first-year class:
  June 1, 2004
Latest application date: **October 15, 2004**
Acceptance dates for regular application for the class
  entering in fall 2005:

Earliest: **February 1, 2005**
Latest: **February 28, 2005**
The school considers requests for deferred entrance.
Starting month for the class entering in 2005-2006: **July**
The school has an Early Decision Plan (EDP).
A personal interview is required for admission.

Undergraduate coursework required

Medical school requires undergraduate work in these subjects: biology, English, organic chemistry, inorganic (general) chemistry, physics, general chemistry.

ADMISSIONS POLICY
(TEXT PROVIDED BY SCHOOL):

Applicants must have earned a bachelor's degree by the time of enrollment in the University of Kansas School of Medicine. While this degree may be in any discipline and earned at any accredited institution, the following courses are required of all applicants: general biology, inorganic (general) chemistry, organic chemistry, and general physics, each a one-year course with lab; and one year of English or sufficient credit for a liberal arts degree. Science courses taken to meet prerequisites should be one-year sequential courses intended for students majoring in the sciences. Applicants are expected to take coursework that demonstrates the requisite intellectual discipline and analytical and problem-solving skills necessary to succeed in medical school.

Applicants are encouraged to select courses, within their major and outside, that they find stimulating and that fulfill requirements for the baccalaureate degree. While not required, statistics, biochemistry, and upper-level biology courses are helpful in providing additional preparation for the medical school curriculum. Students are strongly advised to balance their work in the natural sciences with the following disciplines: anthropology, communications, computer science, economics, ethics, family life studies, fine arts, human development, literature, philosophy, psychology, and sociology. A broad understanding of healthcare and medicine is also expected. Work and/or volunteer experiences (including physician shadowing), in settings such as healthcare agencies, hospitals, and physician offices, are strongly recommended.

COSTS AND FINANCIAL AID
Financial aid phone number: **(913) 588-5170**
Tuition, 2003-2004 academic year: **In-state: $14,961; Out-of-state: $29,492**
Room and board: **$20,076**
Percentage of students receiving financial aid in 2003-04: **95%**
Percentage of students receiving: Loans: **88%**, Grants/scholarships: **84%**, Work-study aid: **0%**
Average medical school debt for the Class of 2002: **$78,915**

STUDENT BODY
Fall 2003 full-time enrollment: **707**
Men: **55%**, Women: **45%**, In-state: **90%**, Minorities: **21%**, American Indian: **1.1%**, Asian-American: **10.5%**, African-American: **5.9%**, Hispanic-American: **3.5%**, White: **75.7%**, International: **0.0%**, Unknown: **3.3%**

ACADEMIC PROGRAMS
The school's curriculum doesn't give first-year students substantial contact with patients.
There are opportunities for first- or second-year students to work in community health clinics.
Program offerings: AIDS, drug/alcohol abuse, family medicine, geriatrics, internal medicine, pediatrics, rural medicine
Joint degrees awarded: M.D./Ph.D.
Total National Institutes of Health (NIH) grants awarded to the medical school and affiliated hospitals: **$36.4 million**

CURRICULUM
(TEXT PROVIDED BY SCHOOL):
Faculty from the basic and clinical sciences collaborate to present a curriculum that integrates normal human structure and function along with alterations caused by disease and illness. Clinical experiences in all four years of the curriculum reinforce the biomedical sciences as well as provide students with opportunities to learn the necessary principles of patient assessment, preventive and behavioral medicine,

public health, and medical ethics. Clinical training is also conducted in community and ambulatory settings, including sites in rural Kansas communities.

A variety of teaching methods, such as computer-assisted, small-group, and case-based instruction, are used to enhance problem-solving skills and encourage lifelong learning. By using a generalist approach that emphasizes the evaluation of patients with undifferentiated problems, the school's curriculum identifies the knowledge, skills, attitudes, and behaviors required of all medical graduates, regardless of specialty choice.

FACULTY PROFILE (FALL 2003)
Total teaching faculty: **475 (full-time), 110 (part-time)**
Of full-time faculty, those teaching in basic sciences: **29%**; in clinical programs: **71%**
Of part-time faculty, those teaching in basic sciences: **9%**; in clinical programs: **91%**
Full-time faculty/student ratio: **0.7**

SUPPORT SERVICES
The school offers students these services for dealing with stress: expanded-hour gym access, professional counseling, religious support, support groups.

RESIDENCY CHOICES
Most popular residency and specialty programs chosen by the 2002 and 2003 M.D. graduating classes: anesthesiology, emergency medicine, family practice, internal medicine, obstetrics and gynecology, orthopedic surgery, pediatrics, radiology–diagnostic, surgery–general, internal medicine/pediatrics.

WHERE GRADS GO

42.0%			

Proportion of 2001-2003 graduates who entered primary care specialties

36.0%			

Proportion of 2002-2003 graduates who accepted in-state residencies

University of Kentucky

■ Chandler Medical Center, 800 Rose Street, Lexington, KY
40536
■ Public
■ Year Founded: 1956
■ Tuition, 2003-2004: In-state: $14,270; Out-of-state: $32,662
■ Enrollment, 2003-2004: 382
■ Website: http://www.mc.uky.edu/medicine
■ Specialty ranking: rural medicine: 20

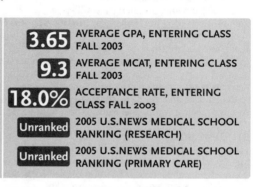

3.65 AVERAGE GPA, ENTERING CLASS FALL 2003

9.3 AVERAGE MCAT, ENTERING CLASS FALL 2003

18.0% ACCEPTANCE RATE, ENTERING CLASS FALL 2003

Unranked 2005 U.S.NEWS MEDICAL SCHOOL RANKING (RESEARCH)

Unranked 2005 U.S.NEWS MEDICAL SCHOOL RANKING (PRIMARY CARE)

ADMISSIONS

Admissions phone number: (859) 323-6161
Admissions email address: kymedap@uky.edu
Application website: http://www.aamc.org
Acceptance rate: 18.0%
In-state acceptance rate: 36.3%
Out-of-state acceptance rate: 4.4%
Minority acceptance rate: N/A
International acceptance rate: N/A

Fall 2003 applications and acceptees

	Applied	Interviewed	Accepted	Enrolled
Total:	941	308	169	95
In-state:	400	242	145	88
Out-of-state:	541	66	24	7

Profile of admitted students

Average undergraduate grade point average: 3.65
MCAT averages (scale: 1-15; writing test: J-T):
  Composite score: 9.3
  Verbal reasoning score: 9.3, Physical sciences score: 9.1,
  Biological sciences score: 9.6, Writing score: O
Proportion with undergraduate majors in: Biological
  sciences: 64%, Physical sciences: 13%, Non-sciences:
  15%, Other health professions: 4%, Mixed disciplines
  and other: 4%
Percentage of students not coming directly from college
  after graduation: 62%

Dates and details

The American Medical College Application Service
  (AMCAS) application is accepted.
School asks for a school-specific application as part of the
  admissions process.
Oldest MCAT considered for Fall 2005 entry: 2002
Earliest application date for the 2005-2006 first-year class:
  June 1, 2004
Latest application date: November 1, 2004
Acceptance dates for regular application for the class
  entering in fall 2005:
  Earliest: October 15, 2004

Latest: N/A
The school considers requests for deferred entrance.
Starting month for the class entering in 2005-2006:
  August
The school has an Early Decision Plan (EDP).
A personal interview is required for admission.

Undergraduate coursework required

Medical school requires undergraduate work in these subjects: biology, English, organic chemistry, inorganic (general) chemistry, physics.

ADMISSIONS POLICY

(TEXT PROVIDED BY SCHOOL):

Several factors are considered by the College of Medicine in
the evaluation of candidates for admission: cumulative science grade-point average, cumulative nonscience grade-
point average, Medical College Admission Test
performance, humanitarian or service activities, premedical
references and evaluations, interpersonal or group accomplishments, and special characteristics, including residence
in a physician-shortage area. Preference is also given to residents of the state of Kentucky.

COSTS AND FINANCIAL AID

Financial aid phone number: (859) 323-6271
Tuition, 2003-2004 academic year: In-state: $14,270; Out-
  of-state: $32,662
Room and board: $666
Percentage of students receiving financial aid in 2003-04:
  96%
Percentage of students receiving: Loans: 83%,
  Grants/scholarships: 62%, Work-study aid: 7%
Average medical school debt for the Class of 2002:
  $82,828

STUDENT BODY

Fall 2003 full-time enrollment: 382
Men: 56%, Women: 44%, In-state: 95%, Minorities: 12%,
  American Indian: 0.0%, Asian-American: 6.3%,

African-American: 4.5%, Hispanic-American: 03%, White: 87.7%, International: 1.3%, Unknown: 0.0%

ACADEMIC PROGRAMS

The school's curriculum gives first-year students substantial contact with patients.

There are opportunities for first- or second-year students to work in community health clinics.

Program offerings: AIDS, drug/alcohol abuse, family medicine, geriatrics, internal medicine, pediatrics, rural medicine, women's health

Joint degrees awarded: M.D./Ph.D., M.D./M.B.A., M.D./M.P.H.

Total National Institutes of Health (NIH) grants awarded to the medical school and affiliated hospitals: N/A

CURRICULUM
(TEXT PROVIDED BY SCHOOL):

The required course of study at the University of Kentucky College of Medicine provides an excellent foundation in medical science. The goal of undergraduate education is to train physicians who are altruistic, knowledgeable, skillful, and dutiful. The Kentucky medical curriculum relates those scientific principles and concepts to the prevention of disease and to the delivery of cutting-edge, compassionate medical care. Because students with diverse backgrounds and interests embark upon a variety of medical careers, the curriculum provides the basic knowledge and skills essential for further professional development. We prepare our graduates to pursue careers in all areas of medicine, including primary care, academic medicine, biomedical research, and the practice of medicine in specialized fields. The curriculum is designed to be adapted to anticipated changes in medical practice and in the medical needs of our society.

The curriculum emphasizes early clinical experiences, integration of the basic and clinical sciences, preventive medicine and cost-containment measures, teaching in ambulatory clinic settings, and primary care. In addition, it provides experiences in emergency medicine, geriatrics, and clinical pharmacology. This curriculum uses many learning methods, including standardized patients, clinical training models, computer-assisted instruction, problem-based learning, small-group tutorials, and interactive lectures and laboratory exercises.

The first two years of study introduce students to the technical language, principles, and methods of investigation in the primary disciplines of biomedical science. Normal and abnormal functions of the body as they relate to health and disease are studied. The module block structure of the curriculum provides an intensive, concentrated exposure to each content area. Additionally, standardized patients are instrumental in the college's Clinical Performance Examination Project. The UK College of Medicine was one of the first medical schools to require all students to complete a multistation clinical performance examination prior to graduation. This program has received national and international attention.

The third-year curriculum provides the student with broad exposure to the principal medical disciplines. The year balances the need for adequate exposure to and involvement in patient care with the time needed for study and assimilation of information. The clinical casework integrates related medical disciplines so that students can appreciate the broad medical and social problems that many patients encounter. Student learning occurs in hospital facilities and ambulatory settings. The third-year clerkships include primary care, medical and surgical care, clinical neurosciences, and women's, maternal, and child health. An elective period at the end of the third year allows interested students to experience a specialty about which they wish to learn more, to spend an extra research period, or to take a vacation.

The fourth year of study is designed to allow students to further develop and demonstrate their clinical skills on the required acting internships. Students complete two four-week acting internships, one in a medical discipline and one in a surgical discipline. Students also complete a required four-week rotation in emergency medicine. Students also complete 12 weeks of elective rotations at the University of Kentucky or at another approved site. In the spring of the fourth year, all students return to campus for clinical pharmacology and anesthesiology. Before graduation, students complete the Dean's Colloquium. This capstone learning experience focuses on interprofessional relationships, updates in primary care and clinical research, medical jurisprudence, healthcare systems, and issues of managed care.

FACULTY PROFILE (FALL 2003)

Total teaching faculty: 604 (full-time), 178 (part-time)

Of full-time faculty, those teaching in basic sciences: 24%; in clinical programs: 76%

Of part-time faculty, those teaching in basic sciences: 9%; in clinical programs: 91%

Full-time faculty/student ratio: 1.6

SUPPORT SERVICES

The school offers students these services for dealing with stress: expanded-hour gym access, professional counseling.

RESIDENCY CHOICES

Most popular residency and specialty programs chosen by the 2002 and 2003 M.D. graduating classes: emergency medicine, family practice, internal medicine, internal medicine–pediatrics, obstetrics and gynecology, orthopedic surgery, pediatrics, psychiatry, surgery–general.

WHERE GRADS GO

46.0%
Proportion of 2001-2003 graduates who entered primary care specialties

33.0%
Proportion of 2002-2003 graduates who accepted in-state residencies

University of Louisville

- Abell Administration Center, H.S.C., Louisville, KY 40202
- Public
- Year Founded: 1876
- Tuition, 2003-2004: In-state: $15,204; Out-of-state: $36,922
- Enrollment, 2003-2004: 588
- Website: http://www.louisville.edu
- Specialty ranking: N/A

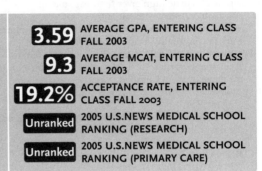

3.59 AVERAGE GPA, ENTERING CLASS FALL 2003

9.3 AVERAGE MCAT, ENTERING CLASS FALL 2003

19.2% ACCEPTANCE RATE, ENTERING CLASS FALL 2003

Unranked 2005 U.S.NEWS MEDICAL SCHOOL RANKING (RESEARCH)

Unranked 2005 U.S.NEWS MEDICAL SCHOOL RANKING (PRIMARY CARE)

ADMISSIONS

Admissions phone number: **(502) 852-5193**
Admissions email address: **medadm@louisville.edu**
Application website: **http://www.aamc.org**
Acceptance rate: **19.2%**
In-state acceptance rate: **44.8%**
Out-of-state acceptance rate: **8.1%**
Minority acceptance rate: **11.9%**
International acceptance rate: **N/A**

Fall 2003 applications and acceptees

	Applied	Interviewed	Accepted	Enrolled
Total:	1,311	290	252	149
In-state:	397	211	178	123
Out-of-state:	914	79	74	26

Profile of admitted students

Average undergraduate grade point average: **3.59**
MCAT averages (scale: 1-15; writing test: J-T):
   Composite score: **9.3**
   Verbal reasoning score: **9.3**, Physical sciences score: **9.2**,
   Biological sciences score: **9.5**, Writing score: **O**
Proportion with undergraduate majors in: Biological
   sciences: **53%**, Physical sciences: **24%**, Non-sciences: **5%**,
   Other health professions: **3%**, Mixed disciplines and
   other: **15%**
Percentage of students not coming directly from college
   after graduation: **5%**

Dates and details

The American Medical College Application Service
   (AMCAS) application is accepted.
School asks for a school-specific application as part of the
   admissions process.
Oldest MCAT considered for Fall 2005 entry: **2002**
Earliest application date for the 2005-2006 first-year class:
   June 1, 2004
Latest application date: **November 1, 2004**
Acceptance dates for regular application for the class
   entering in fall 2005:
   Earliest: **October 15, 2004**

Latest: **April 30, 2005**
The school considers requests for deferred entrance.
Starting month for the class entering in 2005-2006:
   August
The school has an Early Decision Plan (EDP).
A personal interview is required for admission.

Undergraduate coursework required

Medical school requires undergraduate work in these subjects: biology, English, organic chemistry, inorganic (general) chemistry, physics, mathematics, calculus, general
chemistry.

ADMISSIONS POLICY

(TEXT PROVIDED BY SCHOOL):

Because the University of Louisville is a state institution,
the School of Medicine gives preference to qualified residents of Kentucky. Applicants are selected on the basis of
their individual merits without bias concerning sex, race,
creed, national origin, age, or handicap. Applicants are chosen on the basis of intellect, integrity, maturity, and the ability to interact with sensitivity toward others. In the selection
of applicants, consideration is given to the past academic
record, evaluation of college preprofessional committees or
faculty letters of recommendations, extracurricular activities, and personal interviews. The interviews are given considerable weight and are held at the medical school.

COSTS AND FINANCIAL AID

Financial aid phone number: **(502) 852-5187**
Tuition, 2003-2004 academic year: **In-state: $15,204; Out-
   of-state: $36,922**
Room and board: **$6,672**
Percentage of students receiving financial aid in 2003-04:
   88%
Percentage of students receiving: Loans: **80%**,
   Grants/scholarships: **39%**, Work-study aid: **0%**
Average medical school debt for the Class of 2002: **$83,356**

STUDENT BODY

Fall 2003 full-time enrollment: **588**

Men: 50%, Women: 50%, In-state: 87%, Minorities: 17%, American Indian: 0.0%, Asian-American: 8.2%, African-American: 7.8%, Hispanic-American: 09%, White: 83.2%, International: 0.0%, Unknown: 0.0%

ACADEMIC PROGRAMS

The school's curriculum doesn't give first-year students substantial contact with patients.

There are opportunities for first- or second-year students to work in community health clinics.

Program offerings: family medicine, geriatrics, internal medicine, pediatrics, rural medicine, women's health

Joint degrees awarded: M.D./Ph.D., M.D./M.P.H.

Total National Institutes of Health (NIH) grants awarded to the medical school and affiliated hospitals: **$29.2 million**

CURRICULUM

(TEXT PROVIDED BY SCHOOL):

The University of Louisville School of Medicine is committed to training physicians who are humanitarian and patient-centered and who will meet the diverse healthcare needs of Kentucky's citizens throughout the 21st century. This curriculum for the 21st century is being developed to provide comprehensive exposure to the fundamental aspects of medicine while retaining sufficient flexibility for effective development of a student's individual abilities and interests.

Four overarching goals drive the design, development, implementation, and evaluation of the new curriculum: integration of basic and clinical sciences, both within and across courses and clinical rotations; expanded use of non-lecture teaching and learning modalities such as directed self-learning, small-group activities, and case-based learning; expanded use of technology to support teaching and learning, such as personal digital assistants, course and clerkship Web sites, and patient simulations; and development of course and clerkship learning objectives that support the goals of the "Educational Objectives for the Undergraduate Medical Education Program." Students are also exposed to state-of-the-art educational technology in the Patient Simulation Center and the standardized patient clinic. Upon entry, all students receive a PDA to support their educational experiences.

In 2001, the School of Medicine developed the "Educational Objectives for the Undergraduate Medical Education Program." The document highlights 10 critical themes (areas of proficiency) and approximately 85 specific program objectives, which represent the knowledge, attitudes, and skills that students must master before they graduate. The themes are: professionalism; clinical skills; communication; ethics, morals, and judgment; information management and critical thinking; medical economics and healthcare delivery systems; personal knowledge, self-knowledge, and lifelong learning; scientific foundations of clinical practice; public health, social, cultural,

and community contexts of healthcare; and problem solving and clinical decision making.

The primary goal of the new curriculum is to provide each student with the basic knowledge, skills, and behaviors or attitudes considered essential to all 21st-century physicians. The basic science years, the first two years of the curriculum, are designed to provide an interdisciplinary approach to medicine through the use of clinical correlations and problem-solving experiences. The inclusion of biopsychosocial aspects of medicine, as well as clinical diagnostic skills and practical experience in the physician-patient relationship, provides an effective introduction to what it means to be a physician. Second-year students are also required to take at least two electives. An Advanced Cardiac Life Support course must also be taken in late June before the third year starts.

The clinical years, years 3 and 4, consist of several clinical clerkships and electives that expose students to all of the major clinical fields of medicine, utilizing multiple hospital-based and outpatient sites. Students also complete rotations at urban or rural Area Health Education Centers located throughout the state. A unique program allows a small number of students to complete their clinical training at an off-campus training site in Madisonville, Ky.

FACULTY PROFILE (FALL 2003)

Total teaching faculty: **602 (full-time), 79 (part-time)**

Of full-time faculty, those teaching in basic sciences: **14%**; in clinical programs: **86%**

Of part-time faculty, those teaching in basic sciences: **20%**; in clinical programs: **80%**

Full-time faculty/student ratio: **1.0**

SUPPORT SERVICES

The school offers students these services for dealing with stress: expanded-hour gym access, peer counseling, professional counseling, support groups.

RESIDENCY CHOICES

Most popular residency and specialty programs chosen by the 2002 and 2003 M.D. graduating classes: anesthesiology, family practice, internal medicine, obstetrics and gynecology, orthopedic surgery, pediatrics, psychiatry, radiology–diagnostic, surgery–general.

WHERE GRADS GO

46.0%

Proportion of 2001-2003 graduates who entered primary care specialties

45.0%

Proportion of 2002-2003 graduates who accepted in-state residencies

University of Maryland

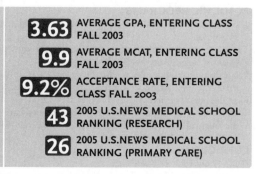

- 655 W. Baltimore Street, Room 14-029, Baltimore, MD 21201-1559
- Public
- Year Founded: 1807
- Tuition, 2003-2004: In-state: $18,258; Out-of-state: $33,323
- Enrollment, 2003-2004: 585
- Website: http://medschool.umaryland.edu
- Specialty ranking: AIDS: 21

3.63 AVERAGE GPA, ENTERING CLASS FALL 2003

9.9 AVERAGE MCAT, ENTERING CLASS FALL 2003

9.2% ACCEPTANCE RATE, ENTERING CLASS FALL 2003

43 2005 U.S.NEWS MEDICAL SCHOOL RANKING (RESEARCH)

26 2005 U.S.NEWS MEDICAL SCHOOL RANKING (PRIMARY CARE)

ADMISSIONS

Admissions phone number: **(410) 706-7478**
Admissions email address: **mfoxwell@som.umaryland.edu**
Application website: **N/A**
Acceptance rate: **9.2%**
In-state acceptance rate: **26.0%**
Out-of-state acceptance rate: **4.5%**
Minority acceptance rate: **8.5%**
International acceptance rate: **1.4%**

Fall 2003 applications and acceptees

	Applied	Interviewed	Accepted	Enrolled
Total:	3,258	520	301	150
In-state:	722	301	188	112
Out-of-state:	2,536	219	113	38

Profile of admitted students

Average undergraduate grade point average: **3.63**
MCAT averages (scale: 1-15; writing test: J-T):
Composite score: **9.9**
Verbal reasoning score: **97**, Physical sciences score: **9.8**,
Biological sciences score: **10.2**, Writing score: **P**
Proportion with undergraduate majors in: Biological sciences: **52%**, Physical sciences: **16%**, Non-sciences: **20%**, Other health professions: **2%**, Mixed disciplines and other: **10%**
Percentage of students not coming directly from college after graduation: **30%**

Dates and details

The American Medical College Application Service (AMCAS) application is accepted.
School asks for a school-specific application as part of the admissions process.
Oldest MCAT considered for Fall 2005 entry: **2001**
Earliest application date for the 2005-2006 first-year class: **June 1, 2004**
Latest application date: **November 1, 2004**
Acceptance dates for regular application for the class entering in fall 2005:
Earliest: **October 15, 2004**

Latest: **N/A**
The school considers requests for deferred entrance.
Starting month for the class entering in 2005-2006:
August
The school has an Early Decision Plan (EDP).
A personal interview is required for admission.

Undergraduate coursework required

Medical school requires undergraduate work in these subjects: biology/zoology, English, organic chemistry, inorganic (general) chemistry, physics.

ADMISSIONS POLICY

(TEXT PROVIDED BY SCHOOL):

The University of Maryland School of Medicine can consider for admission only those students who are citizens or permanent residents of the United States and Canada. As a state-assisted medical school, the University of Maryland does give preference in the selection process to residents of Maryland. However, a significant number of nonresident applicants are accepted to enter each freshman class. The school welcomes applications from individuals throughout the United States. Diversity is highly valued in the educational process, and applications are encouraged from individuals from nontraditional and disadvantaged backgrounds.

The criteria for admission are closely allied to the school's academic mission and goals. The School of Medicine will admit only those individuals who have documented that they possess the ability to successfully complete the academically rigorous curriculum and the personal characteristics that we would all like to see in our own physicians. Academic excellence is expected. The Committee on Admissions seeks out evidence of the following qualities in an applicant's personal statement, extracurricular activities and life experiences, and letters of recommendation: maturity, character and integrity, good judgment, empathy and concern for others, intellectual curiosity, appropriate motivation for a career in medicine, leadership skills, and commitment to excellence.

Applications may be rejected from both residents and nonresidents without an interview. Applicants with competitive academic credentials and the personal characteristics noted above may be invited to interview. Interviewers are trained to evaluate an applicant's maturity, level of competence, intellectual curiosity, adequacy of support systems, communication skills, motivation for medicine, and professional bearing. The interview evaluations are the last important factor considered by members of the Committee on Admissions in its deliberations regarding each applicant's candidacy.

COSTS AND FINANCIAL AID

Financial aid phone number: **(410) 706-7347**
Tuition, 2003-2004 academic year: **In-state: $18,258; Out-of-state: $33,323**
Room and board: **$15,450**
Percentage of students receiving financial aid in 2003-04: **88%**
Percentage of students receiving: Loans: **86%**, Grants/scholarships: **77%**, Work-study aid: **1%**
Average medical school debt for the Class of 2002: **$97,000**

STUDENT BODY

Fall 2003 full-time enrollment: **585**
Men: **43%**, Women: **57%**, In-state: **85%**, Minorities: **36%**, American Indian: **0.0%**, Asian-American: **22.9%**, African-American: **11.6%**, Hispanic-American: **1.0%**, White: **60.3%**, International: **0.0%**, Unknown: **4.1%**

ACADEMIC PROGRAMS

The school's curriculum gives first-year students substantial contact with patients.
There are opportunities for first- or second-year students to work in community health clinics.
Program offerings: AIDS, drug/alcohol abuse, family medicine, geriatrics, internal medicine, pediatrics, rural medicine
Joint degrees awarded: M.D./Ph.D., M.D./M.S.
Total National Institutes of Health (NIH) grants awarded to the medical school and affiliated hospitals: **N/A**

CURRICULUM

(TEXT PROVIDED BY SCHOOL):
Complex changes in American medicine forced dramatic changes in medical education in the 1990s, and the volume of emerging scientific information compounded the need for reforms. The University of Maryland introduced a dramatically revised curriculum in 1994. As partners in their education, students at Maryland now prepare for a lifetime of learning.

The basic sciences during the first two years of medical school have been integrated and taught as systems, using interdisciplinary teaching with both basic- and clinical-science faculty. Problem-based learning has been implemented throughout the basic-science years. Contact hours have been reduced, with an emphasis on independent study with the availability of mentors and learning resources. The University of Maryland was one of the first schools in the nation to make innovative information-technology training part of the required curriculum. The Practice of Medicine course begins at the inception of the freshman year and continues throughout the first two years. It is dedicated to instruction in interviewing, physical examination, intimate human behavior, biomedical ethics, and the dynamics of ambulatory care. Much of this experience will be off-site in clinical settings.

The clinical clerkships during the last two years of medical school include a mandatory ambulatory month in family medicine, an emphasis on ambulatory teaching in all other disciplines, and a longitudinal half-day experience in a clinical setting, in which the student will have the experience of continuity of care for patients and families.

FACULTY PROFILE (FALL 2003)

Total teaching faculty: **1,014 (full-time)**, **198 (part-time)**
Of full-time faculty, those teaching in basic sciences: **13%**; in clinical programs: **87%**
Of part-time faculty, those teaching in basic sciences: **3%**; in clinical programs: **97%**
Full-time faculty/student ratio: **1.7**

SUPPORT SERVICES

The school offers students these services for dealing with stress: expanded-hour gym access, peer counseling, professional counseling, support groups.

RESIDENCY CHOICES

Most popular residency and specialty programs chosen by the 2002 and 2003 M.D. graduating classes: emergency medicine, family practice, internal medicine, pediatrics.

WHERE GRADS GO

55.0%
Proportion of 2001-2003 graduates who entered primary care specialties

56.5%
Proportion of 2002-2003 graduates who accepted in-state residencies

University of Massachusetts–Worcester

- 55 Lake Avenue N, Worcester, MA 01655
- Public
- **Year Founded:** 1970
- **Tuition, 2003-2004:** $13,102
- **Enrollment, 2003-2004:** 425
- **Website:** http://www.umassmed.edu
- **Specialty ranking:** family medicine: 19

3.60 AVERAGE GPA, ENTERING CLASS FALL 2003

10.3 AVERAGE MCAT, ENTERING CLASS FALL 2003

24.8% ACCEPTANCE RATE, ENTERING CLASS FALL 2003

53 2005 U.S.NEWS MEDICAL SCHOOL RANKING (RESEARCH)

3 2005 U.S.NEWS MEDICAL SCHOOL RANKING (PRIMARY CARE)

ADMISSIONS

Admissions phone number: **(508) 856-2323**
Admissions email address: **admissions@umassmed.edu**
Application website: **http://www.aamc.org**
Acceptance rate: **24.8%**
In-state acceptance rate: **24.8%**
Out-of-state acceptance rate: **N/A**
Minority acceptance rate: **N/A**
International acceptance rate: **N/A**

Fall 2003 applications and acceptees

	Applied	Interviewed	Accepted	Enrolled
Total:	621	349	154	100
In-state:	621	349	154	100
Out-of-state:	0	0	0	0

Profile of admitted students

Average undergraduate grade point average: **3.60**
MCAT averages (scale: 1-15; writing test: J-T):
  Composite score: **10.3**
  Verbal reasoning score: **10.4**, Physical sciences score: **10.0**, Biological sciences score: **10.5**, Writing score: **Q**
Proportion with undergraduate majors in: Biological sciences: **39%**, Physical sciences: **19%**, Non-sciences: **16%**, Other health professions: **1%**, Mixed disciplines and other: **25%**
Percentage of students not coming directly from college after graduation: **35%**

Dates and details

The American Medical College Application Service (AMCAS) application is accepted.
School asks for a school-specific application as part of the admissions process.
Oldest MCAT considered for Fall 2005 entry: **2001**
Earliest application date for the 2005-2006 first-year class: **June 15, 2004**
Latest application date: **November 1, 2004**
Acceptance dates for regular application for the class entering in fall 2005:
  Earliest: **November 1, 2004**

Latest: **August 1, 2005**
The school considers requests for deferred entrance.
Starting month for the class entering in 2005-2006:
  August
The school has an Early Decision Plan (EDP).
A personal interview is required for admission.

Undergraduate coursework required

Medical school requires undergraduate work in these subjects: biology, biology/zoology, English, organic chemistry, inorganic (general) chemistry, physics.

ADMISSIONS POLICY

(TEXT PROVIDED BY SCHOOL):
The admissions process promotes the UMMS mission by selecting those qualified residents of Massachusetts who will best serve the commonwealth's healthcare needs through medical practice, public service, education, and research, as stated in our educational goals and objectives: 'the training of physicians in the full range of medical disciplines with emphasis on practice in the primary-care specialties, in the public sector, and in underserved areas of Massachusetts.'

An Admissions Committee determines selection. Factors considered include: residency in Massachusetts (application to the Ph.D./M.D. program is not restricted to Massachusetts residents); a baccalaureate degree and prior academic performance (grade-point average); performance on the Medical College Admission Test; service activities that indicate an ability to work with people in a helping role; diversity of experience; extracurricular accomplishments; oral communication and interpersonal skills; written communication skills; achievement in scientific research and/or medically related service; evidence of motivation and preparedness for medicine; and essential attributes and values for physicians, including honesty, altruism, compassion, flexibility, maturity, intellectual curiosity, self-awareness, and ability for self-directed learning and work as team member.

The following coursework is required within the past four years: one year of biology or zoology, with lab; one year of both inorganic and organic chemistry, each with lab; one year of general physics, with lab; and English.

The committee reviews applications only when complete, as follows: the American Medical College Application Service and UMMS supplemental applications, including additional written materials; official transcript; letters of recommendation; MCAT within three years prior to application; notarized Proof of Massachusetts Residency Form; and nonrefundable application fee. Selected applicants receive two one-on-one interviews.

The final admissions decision is by vote of the entire committee. Applicants with disadvantaged status who do not otherwise meet the criteria for admission, but who show significant academic promise, may enter the UMMS postbaccalaureate program. If academically successful, they are encouraged to reapply to the medical school.

COSTS AND FINANCIAL AID

Financial aid phone number: **(508) 856-2265**
Tuition, 2003-2004 academic year: **$13,102**
Room and board: **$11,350**
Percentage of students receiving financial aid in 2003-04: **97%**
Percentage of students receiving: Loans: **95%**, Grants/scholarships: **36%**, Work-study aid: **0%**
Average medical school debt for the Class of 2002: **$93,110**

STUDENT BODY

Fall 2003 full-time enrollment: **425**
Men: **48%**, Women: **52%**, In-state: **100%**, Minorities: **20%**,
   American Indian: **0.7%**, Asian-American: **14.4%**,
   African-American: **2.6%**, Hispanic-American: **1.9%**,
   White: **79.8%**, International: **0.0%**, Unknown: **0.7%**

ACADEMIC PROGRAMS

The school's curriculum gives first-year students substantial contact with patients.
There are opportunities for first- or second-year students to work in community health clinics.
Program offerings: AIDS, drug/alcohol abuse, family medicine, geriatrics, internal medicine, pediatrics, rural medicine, women's health
Joint degrees awarded: M.D./Ph.D.
Total National Institutes of Health (NIH) grants awarded to the medical school and affiliated hospitals: **N/A**

CURRICULUM

(TEXT PROVIDED BY SCHOOL):
Our curriculum teaches core knowledge, skills, attitudes, and values, as the foundation for training the "undifferentiated" physician. Given this emphasis on preparing students for the generalist specialties, UMMS successfully meets its goal of 50 percent of graduates entering primary care fields. However, our students leave UMMS with an outstanding preparation for all medical specialties.

Our curriculum emphasizes early patient-care exposure from Day 1; strong clinical skills development; student activism in community service and advocacy; and lifelong learning skills. Our educational philosophy values partnership with students in teaching and learning; respect and dignity in the doctor-patient and student-learner relationship; and a milieu of collegiality, collaboration, and diversity.

The years 1 and 2 curriculum provides a strong foundation in the medical sciences; a focus on health and wellness as well as disease states; and early exposure to patient care and development of clinical skills through a longitudinal preceptorship program that spans both years. The basic science courses emphasize problem solving, cross-disciplinary teaching, interactive small-group learning, and technology-based teaching. Introductory clinical skills, medical ethics, communications, physical diagnosis, and the doctor-patient relationship are taught across both years in the Physician, Patient, and Society course.

The third year begins with a comprehensive orientation that serves as a transition to the six required clerkships: medicine, surgery, pediatrics, obstetrics /gynecology, psychiatry, and family medicine. A total of 13 weeks are devoted to primary care with placements in office-based practices across the state. Each clerkship features a robust core curriculum and the extensive use of standardized patients to teach and assess clinical skills. At the end of year 3, all students must complete a comprehensive exam of core clinical skills.

Year 4 includes required rotations in neurology and a subinternship, with 24 weeks of elective opportunity.

FACULTY PROFILE (FALL 2003)

Total teaching faculty: **839 (full-time)**, **72 (part-time)**
Of full-time faculty, those teaching in basic sciences: **27%**; in clinical programs: **73%**
Of part-time faculty, those teaching in basic sciences: **14%**; in clinical programs: **86%**
Full-time faculty/student ratio: **2.0**

SUPPORT SERVICES

The school offers students these services for dealing with stress: expanded-hour gym access, peer counseling, professional counseling, religious support, support groups.

RESIDENCY CHOICES

Most popular residency and specialty programs chosen by the 2002 and 2003 M.D. graduating classes: emergency medicine, family practice, internal medicine, neurology, obstetrics and gynecology, orthopedic surgery, pediatrics, psychiatry, radiology–diagnostic, surgery–general.

WHERE GRADS GO

64.0%
Proportion of 2001-2003 graduates who entered primary care specialties

55.4%
Proportion of 2002-2003 graduates who accepted in-state residencies

University of Miami

- 1600 N.W. 10th Avenue, Miami, FL 33136
- Private
- Year Founded: 1952
- Tuition, 2003-2004: $28,190
- Enrollment, 2003-2004: 605
- Website: http://www.miami.edu/medical-admissions
- Specialty ranking: AIDS: 19

3.70 AVERAGE GPA, ENTERING CLASS FALL 2003

9.7 AVERAGE MCAT, ENTERING CLASS FALL 2003

10.3% ACCEPTANCE RATE, ENTERING CLASS FALL 2003

50 2005 U.S.NEWS MEDICAL SCHOOL RANKING (RESEARCH)

Unranked 2005 U.S.NEWS MEDICAL SCHOOL RANKING (PRIMARY CARE)

ADMISSIONS

Admissions phone number: **(305) 243-6791**
Admissions email address: **med.admissions@miami.edu**
Application website: **N/A**
Acceptance rate: **10.3%**
In-state acceptance rate: **15.9%**
Out-of-state acceptance rate: **5.8%**
Minority acceptance rate: **7.4%**
International acceptance rate: **N/A**

Fall 2003 applications and acceptees

	Applied	Interviewed	Accepted	Enrolled
Total:	2,623	325	271	141
In-state:	1,183	225	188	106
Out-of-state:	1,440	100	83	35

Profile of admitted students

Average undergraduate grade point average: **3.70**
MCAT averages (scale: 1-15; writing test: J-T):
Composite score: **9.7**
Verbal reasoning score: **9.5**, Physical sciences score: **9.3**, Biological sciences score: **10.3**, Writing score: **P**
Proportion with undergraduate majors in: Biological sciences: **65%**, Physical sciences: **15%**, Non-sciences: **10%**, Other health professions: **4%**, Mixed disciplines and other: **6%**
Percentage of students not coming directly from college after graduation: **32%**

Dates and details

The American Medical College Application Service (AMCAS) application is accepted.
School asks for a school-specific application as part of the admissions process.
Oldest MCAT considered for Fall 2005 entry: **2001**
Earliest application date for the 2005-2006 first-year class: **June 1, 2004**
Latest application date: **December 15, 2004**
Acceptance dates for regular application for the class entering in fall 2005:
Earliest: **October 15, 2004**

Latest: **August 8, 2005**
The school doesn't consider requests for deferred entrance.
Starting month for the class entering in 2005-2006:
August
The school doesn't have an Early Decision Plan (EDP).
A personal interview is required for admission.

Undergraduate coursework required

Medical school requires undergraduate work in these subjects: biology/zoology, English, organic chemistry, inorganic (general) chemistry, physics.

ADMISSIONS POLICY

(TEXT PROVIDED BY SCHOOL):

The University of Miami School of Medicine participates in the American Medical College Application Service and accepts applications only from U.S. citizens and permanent residents. Although Florida residents are given preference in all admissions decisions, the School of Medicine has made a commitment to enroll up to 35 exceptionally qualified non-Floridians in each first-year class.

To receive a secondary application, Florida residents must have a 3.2 or higher undergraduate cumulative grade-point average or a postbaccalaureate or graduate GPA of at least 3.5 (minimum of 15 credits). Non-Floridians must have a cumulative undergraduate GPA of at least 3.6 to receive a secondary.

Factors used by the admissions committee to rate all completed paper applications include: quality of undergraduate education and preparedness to study medicine, Medical College Admission Test scores, diversity of life experiences, meaningfulness of direct patient contact experiences, writing ability, and quality of letters of recommendation.

Applicants with the highest ratings are invited for an interview, which is an integral part of the selection process. Interviews are arranged only at the initiative of the Office of Admissions and are held on the medical campus. Some of the factors evaluated at the time of interview are: maturity, knowledge about the profession of medicine, interpersonal skill level, depth and source of motivation to study medicine, and desire to serve others. Applicants' files are reviewed without regard to race, creed, sex, national origin, age, or handicap.

COSTS AND FINANCIAL AID
Financial aid phone number: **(305) 243-6211**
Tuition, 2003-2004 academic year: **$28,190**
Room and board: **$21,690**
Percentage of students receiving financial aid in 2003-04: **80%**
Percentage of students receiving: Loans: **76%**, Grants/scholarships: **20%**, Work-study aid: **0%**
Average medical school debt for the Class of 2002: **$144,000**

STUDENT BODY
Fall 2003 full-time enrollment: **605**
Men: **49%**, Women: **51%**, In-state: **81%**, Minorities: **41%**, American Indian: **0.2%**, Asian-American: **17.0%**, African-American: **5.6%**, Hispanic-American: **18.3%**, White: **58.3%**, International: **0.0%**, Unknown: **0.5%**

ACADEMIC PROGRAMS
The school's curriculum gives first-year students substantial contact with patients.
There are opportunities for first- or second-year students to work in community health clinics.
Program offerings: AIDS, drug/alcohol abuse, family medicine, geriatrics, internal medicine, pediatrics, rural medicine, women's health
Joint degrees awarded: M.D./Ph.D., M.D./M.P.H.
Total National Institutes of Health (NIH) grants awarded to the medical school and affiliated hospitals: **$75.9 million**

CURRICULUM
(TEXT PROVIDED BY SCHOOL):
The University of Miami School of Medicine launched a new medical curriculum in 2001 with the entering class of 2005. It is now in its third year. The curriculum was developed to integrate the teaching of the health sciences at three levels: among the basic sciences; among the basic and clinical sciences; and between the study of normal structure and function and abnormal structure and function. Basic science concepts are introduced and assimilated in the context of common disease processes and clinical relevance. Also included in the curriculum were the nontraditional areas of medicine that are necessary for physicians to practice in today's healthcare system. Physicians must have knowledge of cultural diversity, public-health issues, healthcare delivery systems, professionalism, and population medicine, to name a few of these content areas. Professional qualities, attitudes, and behaviors are evaluated in addition to knowledge acquisition.

Another driving force in the curricular change was to incorporate modern educational methodologies. Lecture-based teaching would be decreased while small-group learning with clinical cases, with and without explicit learning objectives, would be encouraged. Web-based resources and distance-learning facilities are used.

The curriculum is divided into sequential blocks. In the first block (21 weeks), the fundamental building blocks of the basic sciences are taught. The second block is the organ-system modules (47 weeks), in which the basic and clinical sciences of the particular organ system are taught. This section is followed by a transitional block (nine weeks) where students are prepared to enter the clinical clerkships. The clinical years (84 weeks) have been combined so that students can explore areas of clinical medicine and research that interest them before completion of their core clinical clerkships. New clinical electives are being added in such areas as women's health, genetic medicine, international health, public health, child care, community service, and healthcare administration. Clinical experiences at the subinternship level in medicine and surgery specialties are required for graduation.

FACULTY PROFILE (FALL 2003)
Total teaching faculty: **1,138 (full-time), 3 (part-time)**
Of full-time faculty, those teaching in basic sciences: **37%**; in clinical programs: **63%**
Of part-time faculty, those teaching in basic sciences: **100%**; in clinical programs: **0%**
Full-time faculty/student ratio: **1.9**

SUPPORT SERVICES
The school offers students these services for dealing with stress: expanded-hour gym access, professional counseling.

RESIDENCY CHOICES
Most popular residency and specialty programs chosen by the 2002 and 2003 M.D. graduating classes: dermatology, emergency medicine, family practice, internal medicine, neurology, obstetrics and gynecology, ophthalmology, otolaryngology, pediatrics, surgery–general.

WHERE GRADS GO
47.0%
Proportion of 2001-2003 graduates who entered primary care specialties

44.2%
Proportion of 2002-2003 graduates who accepted in-state residencies

University of Michigan–Ann Arbor

- 1301 Catherine Road, Ann Arbor, MI 48109-0624
- Public
- Year Founded: 1848
- Tuition, 2003-2004: In-state: $20,525; Out-of-state: $31,525
- Enrollment, 2003-2004: 670
- Website: http://www.med.umich.edu/medschool
- Specialty ranking: AIDS: 22, drug/alcohol abuse: 11, family medicine: 5, geriatrics: 5, internal medicine: 8, pediatrics: 14, women's health: 5

3.75	AVERAGE GPA, ENTERING CLASS FALL 2003
11.5	AVERAGE MCAT, ENTERING CLASS FALL 2003
8.5%	ACCEPTANCE RATE, ENTERING CLASS FALL 2003
7	2005 U.S.NEWS MEDICAL SCHOOL RANKING (RESEARCH)
23	2005 U.S.NEWS MEDICAL SCHOOL RANKING (PRIMARY CARE)

ADMISSIONS

Admissions phone number: **(734) 764-6317**
Admissions email address: **umichmedadmiss@umich.edu**
Application website: **N/A**
Acceptance rate: **8.5%**
In-state acceptance rate: **12.3%**
Out-of-state acceptance rate: **7.7%**
Minority acceptance rate: **9.1%**
International acceptance rate: **N/A**

Fall 2003 applications and acceptees

	Applied	Interviewed	Accepted	Enrolled
Total:	4,767	672	403	170
In-state:	815	180	100	77
Out-of-state:	3,952	492	303	93

Profile of admitted students

Average undergraduate grade point average: **3.75**
MCAT averages (scale: 1-15; writing test: J-T):
  Composite score: **11.5**
  Verbal reasoning score: **10.7**, Physical sciences score: **12.0**, Biological sciences score: **11.9**, Writing score: **R**
Proportion with undergraduate majors in: Biological sciences: **37%**, Physical sciences: **24%**, Non-sciences: **15%**, Other health professions: **0%**, Mixed disciplines and other: **24%**
Percentage of students not coming directly from college after graduation: **44%**

Dates and details

The American Medical College Application Service (AMCAS) application is accepted.
School asks for a school-specific application as part of the admissions process.
Oldest MCAT considered for Fall 2005 entry: **2000**
Earliest application date for the 2005-2006 first-year class: **June 1, 2004**
Latest application date: **November 15, 2004**
Acceptance dates for regular application for the class entering in fall 2005:
  Earliest: **October 15, 2004**

Latest: **N/A**
The school considers requests for deferred entrance.
Starting month for the class entering in 2005-2006:
  August
The school doesn't have an Early Decision Plan (EDP).
A personal interview is required for admission.

Undergraduate coursework required

Medical school requires undergraduate work in these subjects: biology, English, organic chemistry, inorganic (general) chemistry, physics, biochemistry, humanities.

ADMISSIONS POLICY

(TEXT PROVIDED BY SCHOOL):
Applicants to the Medical School are screened for academic and personal characteristics that predict success in the curriculum and as a future physician. Of the approximately 4,800 applicants in 2003, 670 received interviews. The class size is 170.

The Admissions Committee, composed of student and faculty volunteers, is charged with conducting interviews and evaluating candidates. Each applicant has three one-on-one interviews with a committee member. Selection criteria currently in use by this committee include quality of education, knowledge of medicine, research activities, service to others, life experiences and extracurricular activities, leadership roles, letters of reference, communication skills, and overall attributes.

An Admissions Executive Committee, appointed by the dean from the pool of experienced interviewers, meets regularly to give final ranking scores to all applicants after the interviews. The assistant dean of admissions chairs this committee and directs the admissions program. An effort is made to balance the class for variety and diversity, including gender, age, ethnic/racial groups, academic backgrounds, career interests, and state or country of origin. In recent years, about half of the entering class has consisted of residents of the state of Michigan.

COSTS AND FINANCIAL AID

Financial aid phone number: **(734) 763-4147**

Tuition, 2003-2004 academic year: **In-state: $20,525; Out-of-state: $31,525**

Room and board: **$20,322**

Percentage of students receiving financial aid in 2003-04: **86%**

Percentage of students receiving: Loans: **74%**, Grants/scholarships: **56%**, Work-study aid: **0%**

Average medical school debt for the Class of 2002: **$92,285**

STUDENT BODY

Fall 2003 full-time enrollment: **670**

Men: **56%**, Women: **44%**, In-state: **50%**, Minorities: **43%**, American Indian: **0.6%**, Asian-American: **27.3%**, African-American: **9.9%**, Hispanic-American: **5.1%**, White: **54.5%**, International: **0.0%**, Unknown: **2.7%**

ACADEMIC PROGRAMS

The school's curriculum gives first-year students substantial contact with patients.

There are opportunities for first- or second-year students to work in community health clinics.

Program offerings: AIDS, drug/alcohol abuse, family medicine, geriatrics, internal medicine, pediatrics, rural medicine, women's health

Joint degrees awarded: M.D./Ph.D., M.D./M.B.A., M.D./M.P.H.

Total National Institutes of Health (NIH) grants awarded to the medical school and affiliated hospitals: **$287.1 million**

CURRICULUM

(TEXT PROVIDED BY SCHOOL):

The University of Michigan Medical School's curriculum provides students with the opportunity to develop the knowledge, skills, attitudes, and behaviors for entry into all fields of graduate medical education and to assume leadership roles in the areas of clinical medicine, research, and teaching.

The first-year curriculum is interdisciplinary, with basic sciences presented in an organ-system format, covering the normal cell and organ systems, immunology, and infectious diseases. As appropriate, material is presented in a clinical context and supported by patient cases. An introductory Patients & Populations course provides students with a foundation in genetics and disease, and equips them with the knowledge and skills to construct clinical questions, conduct literature searches, and evaluate evidence. The second-year curriculum continues to be interdisciplinary and organ-system based, covering the abnormal organ systems.

Within most of the organ-systems sequences, a longitudinal patient case is introduced and discussed in small groups with clinical faculty facilitators. Each case includes personal, cultural, and medical information and is accompanied by specific questions and problems to augment learning and help students understand how patients and families experience illness.

Students begin the two-year Family-Centered Experience early in the first year. Pairs of students are assigned to families that have been recruited to help them understand how health changes, chronic conditions, and serious illnesses affect patients and those close to them. Students explore connections between healthcare and culture, health beliefs, age, gender, and support systems. They also learn about rapport between patients and their physicians.

Clinical Foundations in Medicine modules are scheduled during breaks between the sequences in years 1 and 2 to allow students to focus on development of clinical and communication skills.

Third- and fourth-year clinical clerkships are discipline based and include both inpatient and ambulatory experiences. Throughout the third year, students assume increasing responsibility for patient care under faculty supervision. Required clerkships include internal medicine, surgery, obstetrics/gynecology/women's health, pediatrics, family medicine, neurology, and psychiatry. Weekly Seminars in Medicine provide learning in more complex clinical contexts. Emergency medicine, subinternship, advanced medical therapeutics, and intensive care unit rotations are required fourth-year experiences, complemented by up to seven months of elective clerkships.

Standardized patient instructors are an integral learning and assessment tool across the four-year curriculum. Comprehensive clinical assessments at the end of the second year and after completion of the required clinical clerkships assure that all students graduate with the necessary communication and clinical skills to succeed as first-year residents.

FACULTY PROFILE (FALL 2003)

Total teaching faculty: **1,700 (full-time), 536 (part-time)**

Of full-time faculty, those teaching in basic sciences: **10%**; in clinical programs: **90%**

Of part-time faculty, those teaching in basic sciences: **6%**; in clinical programs: **94%**

Full-time faculty/student ratio: **2.5**

SUPPORT SERVICES

The school offers students these services for dealing with stress: expanded-hour gym access, peer counseling, professional counseling, support groups.

RESIDENCY CHOICES

Most popular residency and specialty programs chosen by the 2002 and 2003 M.D. graduating classes: anesthesiology, emergency medicine, family practice, internal medicine, obstetrics and gynecology, ophthalmology, orthopedic surgery, pediatrics, radiology–diagnostic, surgery–general.

WHERE GRADS GO

34.6%

Proportion of 2001-2003 graduates who entered primary care specialties

43.6%

Proportion of 2002-2003 graduates who accepted in-state residencies

University of Minnesota–Duluth

- 1035 University Drive, Duluth, MN 55812-3031
- Public
- **Year Founded:** 1969
- **Tuition, 2003-2004:** In-state: $27,096; Out-of-state: $48,604
- **Enrollment, 2003-2004:** 112
- **Website:** http://penguin.d.umn.edu
- **Specialty ranking:** rural medicine: 7

3.67	AVERAGE GPA, ENTERING CLASS FALL 2003
9.3	AVERAGE MCAT, ENTERING CLASS FALL 2003
17.0%	ACCEPTANCE RATE, ENTERING CLASS FALL 2003
Unranked	2005 U.S.NEWS MEDICAL SCHOOL RANKING (RESEARCH)
5	2005 U.S.NEWS MEDICAL SCHOOL RANKING (PRIMARY CARE)

ADMISSIONS

Admissions phone number: **(218) 726-8511**
Admissions email address: **medadmis@d.umn.edu**
Application website: **N/A**
Acceptance rate: **17.0%**
In-state acceptance rate: **18.5%**
Out-of-state acceptance rate: **7.8%**
Minority acceptance rate: **10.5%**
International acceptance rate: **7.1%**

Fall 2003 applications and acceptees

	Applied	Interviewed	Accepted	Enrolled
Total:	458	139	78	53
In-state:	394	126	73	52
Out-of-state:	64	13	5	1

Profile of admitted students

Average undergraduate grade point average: **3.67**
MCAT averages (scale: 1-15; writing test: J-T):
  Composite score: **9.3**
  Verbal reasoning score: **8.9**, Physical sciences score: **9.4**,
  Biological sciences score: **9.6**, Writing score: **Q**
Proportion with undergraduate majors in: Biological
  sciences: **66%**, Physical sciences: **8%**, Non-sciences: **9%**,
  Other health professions: **4%**, Mixed disciplines and
  other: **13%**
Percentage of students not coming directly from college
  after graduation: **60%**

Dates and details

The American Medical College Application Service
  (AMCAS) application is accepted.
School asks for a school-specific application as part of the
  admissions process.
Oldest MCAT considered for Fall 2005 entry: **2001**
Earliest application date for the 2005-2006 first-year class:
  June 1, 2004
Latest application date: **November 15, 2004**
Acceptance dates for regular application for the class
  entering in fall 2005:
  Earliest: **October 1, 2004**

Latest: **August 31, 2005**
The school considers requests for deferred entrance.
Starting month for the class entering in 2005-2006:
  August
The school has an Early Decision Plan (EDP).
A personal interview is required for admission.

Undergraduate coursework required

Medical school requires undergraduate work in these subjects: biology, English, organic chemistry, inorganic (general) chemistry, physics, biochemistry, humanities,
mathematics, behavioral science, demonstration of writing
skills, calculus, social sciences, general chemistry.

ADMISSIONS POLICY
(TEXT PROVIDED BY SCHOOL):

The School of Medicine receives applications from the
American Medical College Application Service and screens
them for residency requirements and minimum grade-
point average and Medical College Admission Test scores.
Applicants who pass the initial screening complete a supplemental application. Competitive applicants are invited to
be interviewed by two members of the Committee on
Admissions. Each interviewer submits a form evaluating
the applicant's qualifications relating to the interview. Prior
to each committee meeting, members review applicants'
files and submit a nonbinding vote of accept, hold, or reject.
Votes are tallied and presented for committee members'
information. The committee meets during the last week in
September to review early-decision applications and approximately once a week from mid-October until mid-April for
regular pool applications. Some 10 to 12 applicants are
reviewed per meeting and either accepted, put on an alternate list, or rejected.

The committee seeks applicants whose personal and
background traits and career objectives indicate a high
potential for becoming a family physician or other primary-
care specialist in a small town or nonurban setting; who are
academically qualified to accomplish the work necessary to
progress through the medical school curriculum; and who
demonstrate maturity, compassion, excellent interpersonal

communication skills, and a strong motivation for a career in medicine. Priority consideration is given to applicants who are Minnesota residents and who wish to become family practice or other primary-care physicians in a rural setting. Applicants from other states and the Canadian province of Manitoba who demonstrate a high potential and motivation for practicing medicine in Minnesota will also be considered for admission.

The University of Minnesota is committed to providing equal opportunity to students who are from groups that are underrepresented in medicine or from educationally disadvantaged backgrounds. Transfer students are not admitted. Applicants must be U.S. citizens or have permanent resident status and must have completed all requirements for a baccalaureate degree by the time of possible matriculation.

COSTS AND FINANCIAL AID
Financial aid phone number: **(218) 726-8000**
Tuition, 2003-2004 academic year: **In-state: $27,096; Out-of-state: $48,604**
Room and board: **$12,603**
Percentage of students receiving financial aid in 2003-04: **98%**
Percentage of students receiving: Loans: **97%**, Grants/scholarships: **55%**, Work-study aid: **0%**
Average medical school debt for the Class of 2002: **$91,845**

STUDENT BODY
Fall 2003 full-time enrollment: **112**
Men: **53%**, Women: **47%**, In-state: **91%**, Minorities: **16%**, American Indian: **8.0%**, Asian-American: **6.3%**, African-American: **0.9%**, Hispanic-American: **0.9%**, White: **83.9%**, International: **0.0%**, Unknown: **0.0%**

ACADEMIC PROGRAMS
The school's curriculum gives first-year students substantial contact with patients.
There are opportunities for first- or second-year students to work in community health clinics.
Program offerings: family medicine, internal medicine, pediatrics, rural medicine
Joint degrees awarded: M.D./M.P.H.
Total National Institutes of Health (NIH) grants awarded to the medical school and affiliated hospitals: **N/A**

CURRICULUM
(TEXT PROVIDED BY SCHOOL):
The first-year curriculum includes presentations in applied anatomy, clinical pathology conferences, an introduction to rural primary-care medicine, coursework in the clinical and behavioral sciences, and the following integrated courses: principles of basic medical science, histopathology, hematopoiesis and host defenses, dermatology and the musculoskeletal system, and the nervous system. This coursework is correlated with the appropriate clinical examples and incorporates the latest features of computerized and laser disk instruction.

During the second year, clinical material is again correlated with the basic science presentations in the following integrated courses: the gastrointestinal hepatobiliary system, respiratory medicine, fluids and electrolytes, the cardiovascular system, the endocrine and reproductive systems, and integrated clinical medicine. Additional courses in the behavioral sciences are offered in the second year (behavioral medicine, medical social psychology, and psycho-social-spiritual aspects of life-threatening illness) as well as ongoing clinical pathology conferences and a medicine epidemiology and biometrics course. During this year, the student spends more time in clinical settings and receives more intensive instruction in clinical medicine.

During both years of study, students participate in the Family Practice Preceptorship Program. In the first year, each student is assigned to a family practitioner within the immediate geographic area and is introduced to medicine as practiced in its actual setting. The preceptorship during the second year involves the student with physicians who practice in nonurban areas of northern Minnesota and Wisconsin.

Following the successful completion of all coursework in the first two years of medical school and the successful completion of Step 1 of the U.S. Medical Licensing Examination, students transfer on a noncompetitive basis to the University of Minnesota Medical School for completion of the final two years of undergraduate medical education.

FACULTY PROFILE (FALL 2003)
Total teaching faculty: **40 (full-time)**, **3 (part-time)**
Of full-time faculty, those teaching in basic sciences: **85%**; in clinical programs: **15%**
Of part-time faculty, those teaching in basic sciences: **33%**; in clinical programs: **67%**
Full-time faculty/student ratio: **0.4**

SUPPORT SERVICES
The school offers students these services for dealing with stress: peer counseling, professional counseling, support groups.

RESIDENCY CHOICES
Most popular residency and specialty programs chosen by the 2002 and 2003 M.D. graduating classes: emergency medicine, family practice, internal medicine, internal medicine–pediatrics, obstetrics and gynecology, orthopedic surgery, pathology–anatomic and clinical, pediatrics, radiology–diagnostic, surgery–general.

WHERE GRADS GO

66.9%
Proportion of 2001-2003 graduates who entered primary care specialties

60.2%
Proportion of 2002-2003 graduates who accepted in-state residencies

University of Minnesota–Twin Cities

- 420 Delaware Street SE, MMC 293, Minneapolis, MN 55455
- Public
- Year Founded: 1851
- Tuition, 2003-2004: In-state: $25,266; Out-of-state: $33,647
- Enrollment, 2003-2004: 820
- Website: http://www.meded.umn.edu
- Specialty ranking: family medicine: 12, rural medicine: 17

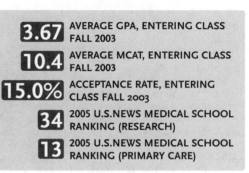

3.67	AVERAGE GPA, ENTERING CLASS FALL 2003
10.4	AVERAGE MCAT, ENTERING CLASS FALL 2003
15.0%	ACCEPTANCE RATE, ENTERING CLASS FALL 2003
34	2005 U.S.NEWS MEDICAL SCHOOL RANKING (RESEARCH)
13	2005 U.S.NEWS MEDICAL SCHOOL RANKING (PRIMARY CARE)

ADMISSIONS

Admissions phone number: **(612) 625-7977**
Admissions email address: **meded@umn.edu**
Application website: **N/A**
Acceptance rate: **15.0%**
In-state acceptance rate: **28.9%**
Out-of-state acceptance rate: **9.3%**
Minority acceptance rate: **17.9%**
International acceptance rate: **11.7%**

Fall 2003 applications and acceptees

	Applied	Interviewed	Accepted	Enrolled
Total:	1,987	678	299	165
In-state:	581	401	168	110
Out-of-state:	1,406	277	131	55

Profile of admitted students

Average undergraduate grade point average: 3.67
MCAT averages (scale: 1-15; writing test: J-T):
 Composite score: **10.4**
 Verbal reasoning score: **10.0**, Physical sciences score:
 10.3, Biological sciences score: **10.8**, Writing score: **P**
Proportion with undergraduate majors in: Biological
 sciences: **28%**, Physical sciences: **12%**, Non-sciences:
 10%, Other health professions: **1%**, Mixed disciplines
 and other: **49%**
Percentage of students not coming directly from college
 after graduation: **60%**

Dates and details

The American Medical College Application Service
 (AMCAS) application is accepted.
School asks for a school-specific application as part of the
 admissions process.
Oldest MCAT considered for Fall 2005 entry: **2001**
Earliest application date for the 2005-2006 first-year class:
 June 1, 2004
Latest application date: **November 15, 2004**
Acceptance dates for regular application for the class
 entering in fall 2005:
 Earliest: **October 15, 2004**

Latest: **May 15, 2005**
The school considers requests for deferred entrance.
Starting month for the class entering in 2005-2006:
 August
The school has an Early Decision Plan (EDP).
A personal interview is required for admission.

Undergraduate coursework required

Medical school requires undergraduate work in these subjects: biology, English, organic chemistry, inorganic (general) chemistry, physics, biochemistry, humanities,
mathematics, behavioral science, calculus, social sciences.

ADMISSIONS POLICY

(TEXT PROVIDED BY SCHOOL):

Early Decision Program applications: The Admissions
Committee reviews EDP applications and makes a decision
in late September. The committee may place an application
not accepted through EDP in the regular application pool
for future consideration or reject the application from any
further consideration.
 Regular applications: Applications submitted under this
process are the majority and are submitted to the American
Medical College Application Service between June 1 and
November 15 each year.
 Step 1 review: The application is screened by Admissions
Committee members. If the applicant passes the Step 1
review, he or she is sent a supplemental application, specific
to the University of Minnesota Medical School. It includes
requests for supplemental information, a short personal
essay, letters of recommendation, verification of prerequisite courses, a recent photo, and a $75 application fee.
Applicants who have been granted a fee waiver by AMCAS
are eligible to have the application fee waived.
 Step 2 review: Two Admissions Committee members
independently review the candidate's supplemental application and file. An interview is scheduled for each applicant
who passes the Step 2 review.
 Step 3 review: After the interview, the applicant's file is
complete. Two members of the Admissions Committee
then independently review the applicant file and assign a

numerical rating that places the applicant's file into one of three categories (accept, reject, or committee review).

Final review: The file is brought before the Admissions Committee for a final decision. The committee utilizes an Olympic-style rating system by which, after each member gives the candidate a numerical rating, the high and low votes are discarded and an average is calculated. This number establishes the final rating of the candidate and determines the final decision: accept, wait list, or reject. Applicants are informed of the final decision no later than May 15.

COSTS AND FINANCIAL AID
Financial aid phone number: **(612) 625-4998**
Tuition, 2003-2004 academic year: **In-state: $25,266; Out-of-state: $33,647**
Room and board: **$11,090**
Percentage of students receiving financial aid in 2003-04: 92%
Percentage of students receiving: Loans: **90%**, Grants/scholarships: **86%**, Work-study aid: **1%**
Average medical school debt for the Class of 2002: **$91,845**

STUDENT BODY
Fall 2003 full-time enrollment: **820**
Men: **52%**, Women: **48%**, In-state: **77%**, Minorities: **18%**, American Indian: **2.2%**, Asian-American: **11.6%**, African-American: **1.6%**, Hispanic-American: **2.6%**, White: **80.6%**, International: **1.5%**, Unknown: **0.0%**

ACADEMIC PROGRAMS
The school's curriculum gives first-year students substantial contact with patients.

There are opportunities for first- or second-year students to work in community health clinics.

Program offerings: AIDS, drug/alcohol abuse, family medicine, geriatrics, internal medicine, pediatrics, rural medicine, women's health

Joint degrees awarded: M.D./Ph.D., M.D./M.B.A., M.D./M.P.H., M.D./M.H.I., M.D./J.D.

Total National Institutes of Health (NIH) grants awarded to the medical school and affiliated hospitals: **$140.1 million**

CURRICULUM
(TEXT PROVIDED BY SCHOOL):
The University of Minnesota Medical School's educational mission is to graduate physicians who will serve the health needs of Minnesota, the nation, and the world through excellence in clinical medicine, research, education, and healthcare leadership. The curriculum is designed to provide sound training in modern human biology and to help students master the competencies required to enter graduate medical education in any of the medical specialties. It is also considered the first step in an educational continuum that extends through postgraduate training and continuing

medical education. Our curriculum emphasizes the concept of the student as an independent learner.

The course of study for the M.D. degree requires completion of 152 weeks of academic work: Year 1 begins in August and is 43 weeks long. It includes discipline-based courses in basic medical sciences and behavioral science as well as introductory experiences with patients. Year 2 begins in September and is 33 weeks long. It includes departmental and interdepartmental courses organized along organ system lines, as well as more advanced patient experiences. Years 3 and 4 include 76 weeks of required and elective clerkships.

Before beginning years 3 and 4, students select a faculty adviser. Each student plans his or her own two-year schedule, which includes 52 weeks of required clinical courses: 12 weeks of internal medicine; six weeks each of surgery, obstetrics/gynecology, pediatrics, and psychiatry; four weeks of neurology; four weeks in surgical specialties; and an eight-week ambulatory care experience, with four weeks in family practice and four weeks in general medicine, general pediatrics, or geriatrics. The balance of the program includes 24 weeks of electives and 26 weeks of free time.

Students must pass the U.S. Medical Licensing Examination Step 1 to continue full-time work in Year 3 and must pass USMLE Step 2 to receive the M.D. degree.

FACULTY PROFILE (FALL 2003)
Total teaching faculty: **1,264 (full-time), 124 (part-time)**
Of full-time faculty, those teaching in basic sciences: **12%**; in clinical programs: **88%**
Of part-time faculty, those teaching in basic sciences: **17%**; in clinical programs: **83%**
Full-time faculty/student ratio: **1.5**

SUPPORT SERVICES
The school offers students these services for dealing with stress: peer counseling, professional counseling, support groups.

RESIDENCY CHOICES
Most popular residency and specialty programs chosen by the 2002 and 2003 M.D. graduating classes: anesthesiology, emergency medicine, family practice, internal medicine, obstetrics and gynecology, orthopedic surgery, pediatrics, radiology–diagnostic, surgery–general, internal medicine/pediatrics.

WHERE GRADS GO
52.9%
Proportion of 2001-2003 graduates who entered primary care specialties

59.6%
Proportion of 2002-2003 graduates who accepted in-state residencies

University of Mississippi

- 2500 N. State Street, Jackson, MS 39216-4505
- Public
- Year Founded: 1903
- Tuition, 2003-2004: In-state: $6,715; Out-of-state: $12,830
- Enrollment, 2003-2004: 394
- Website: http://www.umc.edu
- Specialty ranking: N/A

3.71	AVERAGE GPA, ENTERING CLASS FALL 2003
9.3	AVERAGE MCAT, ENTERING CLASS FALL 2003
50.2%	ACCEPTANCE RATE, ENTERING CLASS FALL 2003
Unranked	2005 U.S.NEWS MEDICAL SCHOOL RANKING (RESEARCH)
52	2005 U.S.NEWS MEDICAL SCHOOL RANKING (PRIMARY CARE)

ADMISSIONS

Admissions phone number: **(601) 984-5010**
Admissions email address: **N/A**
Application website: **N/A**
Acceptance rate: **50.2%**
In-state acceptance rate: **50.2%**
Out-of-state acceptance rate: **N/A**
Minority acceptance rate: **38.0%**
International acceptance rate: **N/A**

Fall 2003 applications and acceptees

	Applied	Interviewed	Accepted	Enrolled
Total:	239	159	120	100
In-state:	239	159	120	100
Out-of-state:	0	0	0	0

Profile of admitted students

Average undergraduate grade point average: **3.71**
MCAT averages (scale: 1-15; writing test: J-T):
  Composite score: **9.3**
  Verbal reasoning score: **9.6**, Physical sciences score: **8.9**,
  Biological sciences score: **9.5**, Writing score: **N/A**
Proportion with undergraduate majors in: Biological
  sciences: **48%**, Physical sciences: **32%**, Non-sciences:
  10%, Other health professions: **3%**, Mixed disciplines
  and other: **7%**
Percentage of students not coming directly from college
  after graduation: **0%**

Dates and details

The American Medical College Application Service
  (AMCAS) application is accepted.
School asks for a school-specific application as part of the
  admissions process.
Oldest MCAT considered for Fall 2005 entry: **N/A**
Earliest application date for the 2005-2006 first-year class:
  June 1, 2004
Latest application date: **October 15, 2004**
Acceptance dates for regular application for the class
  entering in fall 2005:
  Earliest: **October 15, 2004**

Latest: **March 15, 2005**
The school considers requests for deferred entrance.
Starting month for the class entering in 2005-2006:
  August
The school has an Early Decision Plan (EDP).
A personal interview is required for admission.

Undergraduate coursework required

Medical school requires undergraduate work in these subjects: biology, biology/zoology, English, organic chemistry,
inorganic (general) chemistry, physics, humanities, general
chemistry.

ADMISSIONS POLICY

(TEXT PROVIDED BY SCHOOL):
The medical school Admissions Committee reviews the
entire file for every interviewed applicant. Committee deliberations include a discussion of an applicant's complete academic record; all Medical College Admission Test scores;
interviews; evaluations of noncognitive variables; other
nonacademic and professional attributes; letters of evaluation; part- and full-time employment, particularly while
enrolled in school; and educational and socioeconomic
disadvantages.

COSTS AND FINANCIAL AID

Financial aid phone number: **(601) 984-1117**
Tuition, 2003-2004 academic year: **In-state: $6,715; Out-of-
  state: $12,830**
Room and board: **$8,755**
Percentage of students receiving financial aid in 2003-04:
  89%
Percentage of students receiving: Loans: **89%**,
  Grants/scholarships: **61%**, Work-study aid: **0%**
Average medical school debt for the Class of 2002: **$76,145**

STUDENT BODY

Fall 2003 full-time enrollment: **394**
Men: **61%**, Women: **39%**, In-state: **100%**, Minorities: **11%**,
  American Indian: **0.3%**, Asian-American: **4.3%**,

African-American: **6.3%**, Hispanic-American: **0.3%**, White: **88.8%**, International: **0.0%**, Unknown: **0.0%**

ACADEMIC PROGRAMS

The school's curriculum doesn't give first-year students substantial contact with patients.

There are opportunities for first- or second-year students to work in community health clinics.

Program offerings: AIDS, drug/alcohol abuse, family medicine, geriatrics, internal medicine, pediatrics, rural medicine

Joint degrees awarded: M.D./Ph.D.

Total National Institutes of Health (NIH) grants awarded to the medical school and affiliated hospitals: **$13.5 million**

CURRICULUM

(TEXT PROVIDED BY SCHOOL):

The curriculum in medicine consists of four academic sessions. The first two years consist of academic sessions 36 weeks in length, divided into three 12-week periods. During the first two years, students learn the basic sciences. The third year consists of a 48-week session arranged in six- and 12-week academic periods. The students rotate through the major clinical disciplines. The fourth year consists of eight required calendar- month blocks, which may be taken anytime during the 11 months from July through May.

FACULTY PROFILE (FALL 2003)

Total teaching faculty: **496 (full-time)**, **93 (part-time)**

Of full-time faculty, those teaching in basic sciences: **20%**; in clinical programs: **80%**

Of part-time faculty, those teaching in basic sciences: **9%**; in clinical programs: **91%**

Full-time faculty/student ratio: **1.3**

SUPPORT SERVICES

The school offers students these services for dealing with stress: expanded-hour gym access, peer counseling, professional counseling, religious support, support groups.

RESIDENCY CHOICES

Most popular residency and specialty programs chosen by the 2002 and 2003 M.D. graduating classes: family practice, internal medicine, obstetrics and gynecology, orthopedic surgery, pathology–anatomic and clinical, pediatrics, psychiatry, surgery–general, urology, internal medicine/pediatrics.

WHERE GRADS GO

61.0%

Proportion of 2001-2003 graduates who entered primary care specialties

46.0%

Proportion of 2002-2003 graduates who accepted in-state residencies

University of Missouri–Columbia

- 1 Hospital Drive, Columbia, MO 65212
- Public
- **Year Founded:** 1872
- **Tuition, 2003-2004:** In-state: $19,572; Out-of-state: $38,198
- **Enrollment, 2003-2004:** 371
- **Website:** http://www.muhealth.org/~medicine
- **Specialty ranking:** family medicine: 2, rural medicine: 10

3.72 AVERAGE GPA, ENTERING CLASS FALL 2003

9.6 AVERAGE MCAT, ENTERING CLASS FALL 2003

16.7% ACCEPTANCE RATE, ENTERING CLASS FALL 2003

Unranked 2005 U.S.NEWS MEDICAL SCHOOL RANKING (RESEARCH)

9 2005 U.S.NEWS MEDICAL SCHOOL RANKING (PRIMARY CARE)

ADMISSIONS

Admissions phone number: **(573) 882-9219**
Admissions email address: **nolkej@health.missouri.edu**
Application website: **N/A**
Acceptance rate: **16.7%**
In-state acceptance rate: **29.8%**
Out-of-state acceptance rate: **4.8%**
Minority acceptance rate: **10.3%**
International acceptance rate: **N/A**

Fall 2003 applications and acceptees

	Applied	Interviewed	Accepted	Enrolled
Total:	822	251	137	96
In-state:	389	207	116	92
Out-of-state:	433	44	21	4

Profile of admitted students

Average undergraduate grade point average: **3.72**
MCAT averages (scale: 1-15; writing test: J-T):
  Composite score: **9.6**
  Verbal reasoning score: **9.4**, Physical sciences score: **9.4**, Biological sciences score: **9.9**, Writing score: **O**
Proportion with undergraduate majors in: Biological sciences: **56%**, Physical sciences: **20%**, Non-sciences: **21%**, Other health professions: **1%**, Mixed disciplines and other: **2%**
Percentage of students not coming directly from college after graduation: **16%**

Dates and details

The American Medical College Application Service (AMCAS) application is accepted.
School asks for a school-specific application as part of the admissions process.
Oldest MCAT considered for Fall 2005 entry: **1998**
Earliest application date for the 2005-2006 first-year class: **June 1, 2004**
Latest application date: **November 1, 2004**
Acceptance dates for regular application for the class entering in fall 2005:
  Earliest: **November 15, 2004**

Latest: **March 15, 2004**
The school considers requests for deferred entrance.
Starting month for the class entering in 2005-2006:
  August
The school has an Early Decision Plan (EDP).
A personal interview is required for admission.

Undergraduate coursework required

Medical school requires undergraduate work in these subjects: biology, English, organic chemistry, inorganic (general) chemistry, physics, mathematics, demonstration of writing skills, general chemistry.

ADMISSIONS POLICY

(TEXT PROVIDED BY SCHOOL):

Applicants must have completed at least 90 semester hours (not including physical education and military science) at a recognized college or university. Required coursework includes: English composition or writing intensive (two semesters); college-level mathematics (one semester); general biology with lab (eight hours); general chemistry with lab (eight hours); organic chemistry with lab (eight hours); and general physics with lab (eight hours).

One or two courses in biochemistry are strongly recommended, and one or two additional biology or chemistry courses are recommended. Only those courses required for science majors are acceptable; introductory survey science courses are not.

The Medical College Admission Test is required.

COSTS AND FINANCIAL AID

Financial aid phone number: **(573) 882-2923**
Tuition, 2003-2004 academic year: **In-state: $19,572; Out-of-state: $38,198**
Room and board: **$8,027**
Percentage of students receiving financial aid in 2003-04: **95%**
Percentage of students receiving: Loans: **95%**, Grants/scholarships: **43%**, Work-study aid: **0%**
Average medical school debt for the Class of 2002: **$96,200**

STUDENT BODY
Fall 2003 full-time enrollment: 371
Men: 53%, Women: 47%, In-state: 98%, Minorities: 17%,

ACADEMIC PROGRAMS
The school's curriculum gives first-year students
  substantial contact with patients.
There are opportunities for first- or second-year students to
  work in community health clinics.
Program offerings: AIDS, drug/alcohol abuse, family
  medicine, geriatrics, internal medicine, pediatrics, rural
  medicine
Joint degrees awarded: M.D./Ph.D., M.D./M.S.
Total National Institutes of Health (NIH) grants awarded to
  the medical school and affiliated hospitals: **$7.6 million**

CURRICULUM
(TEXT PROVIDED BY SCHOOL):
Each year, 96 first-year slots are available. The School of
Medicine is a pioneer in the style of medical education that
emphasizes problem solving, self-directed learning, and
early clinical experience. In addition, the Bryant Scholars
Program and the Rural Track Program offered through the
school give students an opportunity to gain education and
experience practicing medicine in a rural area.

The faculty joins 350 residents in more than 60 specialties and subspecialities to supervise patient care and student teaching. The school provides postgraduate medical
training in virtually all specialties and subspecialties.

As part of the Health Sciences Center, the school continues to revolutionize medicine by exploring innovative ways
to deliver healthcare to the residents of Missouri. Its faculty
and administrators are leading a major initiative that allows
rural physicians and their patients to consult with Health
Sciences Center specialists via telemedicine technology.

FACULTY PROFILE (FALL 2003)
Total teaching faculty: **328 (full-time)**, **91 (part-time)**
Of full-time faculty, those teaching in basic sciences: **26%**;
  in clinical programs: **74%**
Of part-time faculty, those teaching in basic sciences: **12%**;
  in clinical programs: **88%**
Full-time faculty/student ratio: **0.9**

SUPPORT SERVICES
The school offers students these services for dealing with
stress: peer counseling, professional counseling, support
groups.

RESIDENCY CHOICES
Most popular residency and specialty programs chosen by
the 2002 and 2003 M.D. graduating classes: emergency
medicine, family practice, internal medicine, obstetrics and
gynecology, pediatrics.

WHERE GRADS GO

56.1%
*Proportion of 2001-2003 graduates who entered primary
care specialties*

36.0%
*Proportion of 2002-2003 graduates who accepted in-state
residencies*

University of Nebraska

COLLEGE OF MEDICINE

- 986585 Nebraska Medical Center, Omaha, NE 68198-6585
- Public
- **Year Founded:** N/A
- **Tuition, 2003-2004:** In-state: $18,450; Out-of-state: $40,829
- **Enrollment, 2003-2004:** 472
- **Website:** http://www.unmc.edu/UNCOM
- **Specialty ranking:** rural medicine: 13

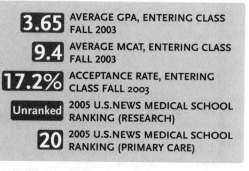

3.65 AVERAGE GPA, ENTERING CLASS FALL 2003

9.4 AVERAGE MCAT, ENTERING CLASS FALL 2003

17.2% ACCEPTANCE RATE, ENTERING CLASS FALL 2003

Unranked 2005 U.S.NEWS MEDICAL SCHOOL RANKING (RESEARCH)

20 2005 U.S.NEWS MEDICAL SCHOOL RANKING (PRIMARY CARE)

ADMISSIONS
Admissions phone number: **(402) 559-2259**
Admissions email address: **grrogers@unmc.edu**
Application website: **N/A**
Acceptance rate: **17.2%**
In-state acceptance rate: **46.1%**
Out-of-state acceptance rate: **6.2%**
Minority acceptance rate: **7.6%**
International acceptance rate: **0.0%**

Fall 2003 applications and acceptees

	Applied	Interviewed	Accepted	Enrolled
Total:	980	353	169	118
In-state:	271	244	125	104
Out-of-state:	709	109	44	14

Profile of admitted students
Average undergraduate grade point average: **3.65**
MCAT averages (scale: 1-15; writing test: J-T):
Composite score: **9.4**
Verbal reasoning score: **9.1**, Physical sciences score: **9.3**, Biological sciences score: **9.7**, Writing score: **N/A**
Proportion with undergraduate majors in: Biological sciences: **55%**, Physical sciences: **21%**, Non-sciences: **14%**, Other health professions: **5%**, Mixed disciplines and other: **5%**
Percentage of students not coming directly from college after graduation: **N/A**

Dates and details
The American Medical College Application Service (AMCAS) application is accepted.
School asks for a school-specific application as part of the admissions process.
Oldest MCAT considered for Fall 2005 entry: **2002**
Earliest application date for the 2005-2006 first-year class: **June 1, 2004**
Latest application date: **November 1, 2004**
Acceptance dates for regular application for the class entering in fall 2005:
Earliest: **December 15, 2004**

Latest: **March 15, 2005**
The school doesn't consider requests for deferred entrance.
Starting month for the class entering in 2005-2006:
August
The school has an Early Decision Plan (EDP).
A personal interview is required for admission.

Undergraduate coursework required
Medical school requires undergraduate work in these subjects: biology, English, organic chemistry, inorganic (general) chemistry, physics, biochemistry, humanities, calculus, general chemistry.

COSTS AND FINANCIAL AID
Financial aid phone number: **(402) 559-4199**
Tuition, 2003-2004 academic year: **In-state: $18,450; Out-of-state: $40,829**
Room and board: **$13,500**
Percentage of students receiving financial aid in 2003-04: **98%**
Percentage of students receiving: Loans: **90%**, Grants/scholarships: **62%**, Work-study aid: **0%**
Average medical school debt for the Class of 2002: **$92,917**

STUDENT BODY
Fall 2003 full-time enrollment: **472**
Men: **62%**, Women: **38%**, In-state: **89%**, Minorities: **10%**, American Indian: **0.2%**, Asian-American: **6.1%**, African-American: **2.8%**, Hispanic-American: **11%**, White: **89.4%**, International: **0.0%**, Unknown: **0.4%**

ACADEMIC PROGRAMS
The school's curriculum gives first-year students substantial contact with patients.
There are opportunities for first- or second-year students to work in community health clinics.
Program offerings: AIDS, drug/alcohol abuse, family medicine, geriatrics, internal medicine, pediatrics, rural medicine
Joint degrees awarded: M.D./Ph.D.

Total National Institutes of Health (NIH) grants awarded to the medical school and affiliated hospitals: **$27.3 million**

FACULTY PROFILE (FALL 2003)
Total teaching faculty: **516 (full-time), 114 (part-time)**
Of full-time faculty, those teaching in basic sciences: **14%**; in clinical programs: **86%**
Of part-time faculty, those teaching in basic sciences: **5%**; in clinical programs: **95%**
Full-time faculty/student ratio: **1.1**

SUPPORT SERVICES
The school offers students these services for dealing with stress: expanded-hour gym access, professional counseling, religious support, support groups.

RESIDENCY CHOICES
Most popular residency and specialty programs chosen by the 2002 and 2003 M.D. graduating classes: anesthesiology, emergency medicine, family practice, internal medicine, obstetrics and gynecology, pathology–anatomic and clinical, pediatrics, psychiatry, radiology–diagnostic.

WHERE GRADS GO

60.0%
Proportion of 2001-2003 graduates who entered primary care specialties

36.0%
Proportion of 2002-2003 graduates who accepted in-state residencies

University of New Mexico

- Basic Medical Sciences Building, Room 107, Albuquerque, NM 87131
- Public
- Year Founded: 1964
- Tuition, 2003-2004: In-state: $12,122; Out-of-state: $31,558
- Enrollment, 2003-2004: 304
- Website: http://hsc.unm.edu/som
- Specialty ranking: family medicine: 10, rural medicine: 2

3.53 AVERAGE GPA, ENTERING CLASS FALL 2003

9.4 AVERAGE MCAT, ENTERING CLASS FALL 2003

17.1% ACCEPTANCE RATE, ENTERING CLASS FALL 2003

Unranked 2005 U.S.NEWS MEDICAL SCHOOL RANKING (RESEARCH)

12 2005 U.S.NEWS MEDICAL SCHOOL RANKING (PRIMARY CARE)

ADMISSIONS

Admissions phone number: **(505) 272-4766**
Admissions email address: **mballejos@salud.unm.edu**
Application website: **http://hsc.unm.edu/som/admissions**
Acceptance rate: **17.1%**
In-state acceptance rate: **37.5%**
Out-of-state acceptance rate: **1.8%**
Minority acceptance rate: **N/A**
International acceptance rate: **N/A**

Fall 2003 applications and acceptees

	Applied	Interviewed	Accepted	Enrolled
Total:	578	267	99	75
In-state:	248	241	93	72
Out-of-state:	330	26	6	3

Profile of admitted students

Average undergraduate grade point average: **3.53**
MCAT averages (scale: 1-15; writing test: J-T):
  Composite score: **9.4**
  Verbal reasoning score: **9.5**, Physical sciences score: **9.0**, Biological sciences score: **9.7**, Writing score: **P**
Proportion with undergraduate majors in: Biological sciences: **55%**, Physical sciences: **9%**, Non-sciences: **16%**, Other health professions: **7%**, Mixed disciplines and other: **13%**
Percentage of students not coming directly from college after graduation: **17%**

Dates and details

The American Medical College Application Service (AMCAS) application is accepted.
School asks for a school-specific application as part of the admissions process.
Oldest MCAT considered for Fall 2005 entry: **2001**
Earliest application date for the 2005-2006 first-year class: **June 1, 2004**
Latest application date: **November 15, 2004**
Acceptance dates for regular application for the class entering in fall 2005:
  Earliest: **October 1, 2004**

Latest: **March 15, 2004**
The school considers requests for deferred entrance.
Starting month for the class entering in 2005-2006: **August**
The school has an Early Decision Plan (EDP).
A personal interview is required for admission.

Undergraduate coursework required

Medical school requires undergraduate work in these subjects: biology/zoology, organic chemistry, inorganic (general) chemistry, biochemistry, general chemistry.

ADMISSIONS POLICY
(TEXT PROVIDED BY SCHOOL):

In general, the Committee on Admissions at the University of New Mexico School of Medicine bases the selection of students on academic achievement, motivation for the study of medicine, problem-solving ability, self-appraisal, ability to relate to people, maturity, breadth of interests and achievements, professional goals, and likelihood of serving the healthcare needs of the state following postgraduate training. Information that is essential in the decision-making process is gleaned from the application form, letters of recommendation, and two interviews with committee members. Committee members make the final acceptance decisions.

The state has unique problems in the delivery of healthcare, particularly in the distribution of healthcare personnel. The medical school feels obliged to help meet the state's physician manpower needs by selecting students who are likely to train in specialty areas of current need and remain in or return to the areas in New Mexico that are medically underserved.

As a state-supported institution in a state where healthcare needs are great, the medical school feels strongly that most of the accepted applicants should be residents of New Mexico. The school acknowledges a secondary obligation to students from Montana and Wyoming, states without medical schools, through participation in the Western Interstate Commission on Higher Education program, and will continue to accept one or two of these students each year. All nonresident applicants, including those from Montana and Wyoming, must apply during the Early Decision Program. During the past several years, more than 95 percent of accepted students have been New Mexico residents.

The school strives to achieve diversity among faculty, staff, and student body, including maintaining a critical mass of both Hispanic and Native American students. A diverse student body promotes cross-racial understanding, creates a richer learning experience, and better prepares our students to serve the communities of New Mexico.

COSTS AND FINANCIAL AID

Financial aid phone number: **(505) 272-8008**
Tuition, 2003-2004 academic year: **In-state: $12,122; Out-of-state: $31,558**
Room and board: **$7,905**
Percentage of students receiving financial aid in 2003-04: **85%**
Percentage of students receiving: Loans: **84%**, Grants/scholarships: **83%**, Work-study aid: **0%**
Average medical school debt for the Class of 2002: **$70,780**

STUDENT BODY

Fall 2003 full-time enrollment: **304**
Men: **42%**, Women: **58%**, In-state: **98%**, Minorities: **38%**, American Indian: **4.3%**, Asian-American: **6.9%**, African-American: **1.0%**, Hispanic-American: **26.3%**, White: **60.9%**, International: **0.0%**, Unknown: **0.7%**

ACADEMIC PROGRAMS

The school's curriculum gives first-year students substantial contact with patients.
There are opportunities for first- or second-year students to work in community health clinics.
Program offerings: AIDS, drug/alcohol abuse, family medicine, geriatrics, internal medicine, pediatrics, rural medicine, women's health
Joint degrees awarded: M.D./Ph.D.
Total National Institutes of Health (NIH) grants awarded to the medical school and affiliated hospitals: **$49.6 million**

CURRICULUM

(TEXT PROVIDED BY SCHOOL):
The primary goal of the School of Medicine is to produce competent, humanistic physicians capable of pursuing a complete spectrum of medical careers. The educational program strives to imbue the medical student with a deep concern for continuing intellectual growth that will lead to a lifelong commitment to self-education. UNM seeks to recruit and retain educationally disadvantaged New Mexicans in healthcare professions.

Unique aspects of the UNM School of Medicine include problem-based and student-centered learning; early clinical skills learning coupled with sustained, community-based learning; the incorporation of a population and behavioral perspective into the clinical years; peer teaching; computer-

assisted instruction; and biweekly seminars on professional responsibility. The curriculum also addresses the historically unmet as well as changing healthcare needs of New Mexico's population.

Integration of learning throughout the four years includes consideration of normal and abnormal; biology, behavior, and population; primary and tertiary care; and urban and rural community experiences. The curriculum consists of three phases:

Phase 1 (18 months) is organized around organ systems, each incorporating three perspectives: biologic, behavioral, and population. Hands-on medical skills are gained through weekly clinical skills and laboratory sessions. Students have the opportunity to apply these skills in a weekly continuity clinic. At the end of the first academic year, students participate in an in-depth Practical Immersion Experience in a professional setting in either a rural or urban community.

In Phase 2 (12 months), students spend half of their time in an ambulatory setting and half on inpatient services. This phase features continued reinforcement of basic and clinical science integration and development of basic science learning resources for use on clinical services.

Phase 3 (15 months) features more hospital-based clinical experiences in which the student has progressive responsibility for patient care under the supervision of house staff and faculty. One month is spent working with a practicing physician.

FACULTY PROFILE (FALL 2003)

Total teaching faculty: **636 (full-time)**, **116 (part-time)**
Of full-time faculty, those teaching in basic sciences: **11%**; in clinical programs: **89%**
Of part-time faculty, those teaching in basic sciences: **6%**; in clinical programs: **94%**
Full-time faculty/student ratio: **2.1**

SUPPORT SERVICES

The school offers students these services for dealing with stress: expanded-hour gym access, peer counseling, professional counseling, support groups.

RESIDENCY CHOICES

Most popular residency and specialty programs chosen by the 2002 and 2003 M.D. graduating classes: anesthesiology, emergency medicine, family practice, internal medicine, neurology, obstetrics and gynecology, orthopedic surgery, pediatrics, psychiatry, surgery–general.

WHERE GRADS GO

56.4%
Proportion of 2001-2003 graduates who entered primary care specialties

29.3%
Proportion of 2002-2003 graduates who accepted in-state residencies

University of North Carolina–Chapel Hill

- CB #7000, 125 MacNider Building, Chapel Hill, NC 27599-7000
- Public
- Year Founded: 1879
- Tuition, 2003-2004: In-state: $8,495; Out-of-state: $34,111
- Enrollment, 2003-2004: 653
- Website: http://www.med.unc.edu/admit
- Specialty ranking: AIDS: 11, drug/alcohol abuse: 18, family medicine: 5, geriatrics: 17, internal medicine: 16, pediatrics: 18, rural medicine: 5, women's health: 6

3.65 AVERAGE GPA, ENTERING CLASS FALL 2003

10.4 AVERAGE MCAT, ENTERING CLASS FALL 2003

7.5% ACCEPTANCE RATE, ENTERING CLASS FALL 2003

20 2005 U.S.NEWS MEDICAL SCHOOL RANKING (RESEARCH)

5 2005 U.S.NEWS MEDICAL SCHOOL RANKING (PRIMARY CARE)

ADMISSIONS
Admissions phone number: (919) 962-8331
Admissions email address: admissions@med.unc.edu
Application website: N/A
Acceptance rate: 7.5%
In-state acceptance rate: 23.8%
Out-of-state acceptance rate: 1.9%
Minority acceptance rate: 7.2%
International acceptance rate: 0.0%

Fall 2003 applications and acceptees
	Applied	Interviewed	Accepted	Enrolled
Total:	2,964	527	223	160
In-state:	760	436	181	140
Out-of-state:	2,204	91	42	20

Profile of admitted students
Average undergraduate grade point average: 3.65
MCAT averages (scale: 1-15; writing test: J-T):
Composite score: 10.4
Verbal reasoning score: 10.2, Physical sciences score: 10.5, Biological sciences score: 10.6, Writing score: O
Proportion with undergraduate majors in: Biological sciences: 64%, Physical sciences: 7%, Non-sciences: 18%, Other health professions: 4%, Mixed disciplines and other: 7%
Percentage of students not coming directly from college after graduation: 61%

Dates and details
The American Medical College Application Service (AMCAS) application is accepted.
School asks for a school-specific application as part of the admissions process.
Oldest MCAT considered for Fall 2005 entry: 2000
Earliest application date for the 2005-2006 first-year class: June 1, 2004
Latest application date: November 15, 2004
Acceptance dates for regular application for the class entering in fall 2005:
Earliest: October 15, 2004

Latest: August 15, 2005
The school considers requests for deferred entrance.
Starting month for the class entering in 2005-2006:
August
The school has an Early Decision Plan (EDP).
A personal interview is required for admission.

Undergraduate coursework required
Medical school requires undergraduate work in these subjects: biology, English, organic chemistry, inorganic (general) chemistry, physics, general chemistry.

ADMISSIONS POLICY
(TEXT PROVIDED BY SCHOOL):
The Committee on Admissions evaluates the qualifications of all applicants to select those with the greatest potential for accomplishment in one of the many careers open to medical graduates. Preference is given to North Carolina residents. The University of North Carolina does not discriminate on the basis of race, national origin, religion, sex, age, or handicap.

The American Medical College Application Service application is used for initial screening. Qualified North Carolina applicants and selected nonresidents are sent a supplementary application. Following receipt of the supplementary application, applicants are invited for an interview. In making its final selections from the group of qualified applicants, the committee considers evidence of each candidate's motivation, maturity, leadership, integrity, and a variety of other personal qualifications and accomplishments in addition to the scholastic record. All information available about each applicant is considered without assigning priority to any single factor. No special admission tracks or quotas are applied among applicants. The undergraduate major is not an important consideration, but excellence in the chosen field is expected. Previously rejected applicants are considered without prejudice, but reapplications are compared with those previously submitted to assess changes in the applicant's qualifications.

COSTS AND FINANCIAL AID

Financial aid phone number: **(919) 962-6117**

Tuition, 2003-2004 academic year: **In-state: $8,495; Out-of-state: $34,111**

Room and board: **$24,666**

Percentage of students receiving financial aid in 2003-04: **83%**

Percentage of students receiving: Loans: **76%**, Grants/scholarships: **72%**, Work-study aid: **0%**

Average medical school debt for the Class of 2002: **$66,386**

STUDENT BODY

Fall 2003 full-time enrollment: **653**

Men: **48%**, Women: **52%**, In-state: **94%**, Minorities: **27%**, American Indian: **1.7%**, Asian-American: **12.4%**, African-American: **11.8%**, Hispanic-American: **1.1%**, White: **72.7%**, International: **0.0%**, Unknown: **0.3%**

ACADEMIC PROGRAMS

The school's curriculum gives first-year students substantial contact with patients.

There are opportunities for first- or second-year students to work in community health clinics.

Program offerings: AIDS, drug/alcohol abuse, family medicine, geriatrics, internal medicine, pediatrics, rural medicine, women's health

Joint degrees awarded: M.D./Ph.D.

Total National Institutes of Health (NIH) grants awarded to the medical school and affiliated hospitals: **$209.9 million**

CURRICULUM

(TEXT PROVIDED BY SCHOOL):

The curriculum encompasses 144 weeks of instruction, preparing students for career options through a comprehensive set of learning experiences. Students are taught fundamental principles and skills of medicine and underlying scientific foundations, with an emphasis on developing critical thinking and medical problem-solving skills. The curriculum is traditional, with two years devoted primarily to basic science and two years to clinical education; students acquire clinical skills in the first two years through a longitudinal, comprehensive course. Lecture is the predominant teaching method used in the first two years, although the number of hours in lecture has decreased.

The School of Medicine continues to increase the number of small-group/independent learning activities to strengthen students' self-directed learning and critical-thinking skills. Independent projects require students to gather information. Courses use a variety of strategies, e.g., adding online exercises, writing assignments, and readings to prepare for in-class application exercises. The first-year two-day workshop, Where Basic Science Meets the Clinical World: A Woman With Breast Cancer, provides students with the opportunity to study an issue in depth.

Our use of community-based clinical education sites across the state is one of the most notable and unique strengths of our curriculum. The curriculum includes all required content areas. Students study the required basic sciences of anatomy, biochemistry, genetics, physiology, microbiology, immunology, pathology, pharmacology and therapeutics, and preventive medicine. Courses address knowledge of basic science principles, introduce relevant new biomedical research discoveries, and discuss the socio-cultural dimensions of health and illness. Students learn in practices ranging from academic referral centers to rural primary care. Longitudinal programs cover prevention and geriatrics. Emergency medicine and clinical pathology are taught both in discrete courses and via integration of content in other required courses. Diagnostic imaging and radiology content has been strengthened.

The third year has 12 weeks of medicine, six weeks of obstetrics/gynecology, six weeks of psychiatry, eight weeks of surgery, eight weeks of pediatrics, six weeks of family medicine, and one week of fundamentals of acute care. During family medicine, each student will work on a one-to-one basis with a primary-care physician. All students will learn and practice clinical reasoning and decision-making skills.

Senior elective courses are available, allowing students to explore areas of individual interest and need. Students must take at least three four-week electives. On ambulatory rotations, teaching is built around teachable moments found in the course of the workday.

FACULTY PROFILE (FALL 2003)

Total teaching faculty: **1,193 (full-time)**, **129 (part-time)**

Of full-time faculty, those teaching in basic sciences: **17%**; in clinical programs: **83%**

Of part-time faculty, those teaching in basic sciences: **16%**; in clinical programs: **84%**

Full-time faculty/student ratio: **1.8**

SUPPORT SERVICES

The school offers students these services for dealing with stress: peer counseling, professional counseling.

RESIDENCY CHOICES

Most popular residency and specialty programs chosen by the 2002 and 2003 M.D. graduating classes: anesthesiology, emergency medicine, family practice, internal medicine, obstetrics and gynecology, orthopedic surgery, pediatrics, psychiatry, radiology–diagnostic, surgery–general.

WHERE GRADS GO

47.0%
Proportion of 2001-2003 graduates who entered primary care specialties

32.0%
Proportion of 2002-2003 graduates who accepted in-state residencies

University of North Dakota

- 501 N. Columbia Road, Box 9037, Grand Forks, ND 58202-9037
- Public
- Year Founded: 1905
- Tuition, 2003-2004: In-state: $16,383; Out-of-state: $42,003
- Enrollment, 2003-2004: 226
- Website: http://www.med.und.nodak.edu
- Specialty ranking: rural medicine: 5

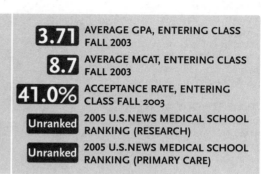

3.71 AVERAGE GPA, ENTERING CLASS FALL 2003

8.7 AVERAGE MCAT, ENTERING CLASS FALL 2003

41.0% ACCEPTANCE RATE, ENTERING CLASS FALL 2003

Unranked 2005 U.S.NEWS MEDICAL SCHOOL RANKING (RESEARCH)

Unranked 2005 U.S.NEWS MEDICAL SCHOOL RANKING (PRIMARY CARE)

ADMISSIONS

Admissions phone number: **(701) 777-4221**
Admissions email address: **jdheit@medicine.nodak.edu**
Application website:
　http://www.med.und.nodak.edu/admissions.html
Acceptance rate: **41.0%**
In-state acceptance rate: **46.9%**
Out-of-state acceptance rate: **32.7%**
Minority acceptance rate: **63.6%**
International acceptance rate: **N/A**

Fall 2003 applications and acceptees

	Applied	Interviewed	Accepted	Enrolled
Total:	249	146	102	61
In-state:	145	99	68	47
Out-of-state:	104	47	34	14

Profile of admitted students

Average undergraduate grade point average: **3.71**
MCAT averages (scale: 1-15; writing test: J-T):
　Composite score: **8.7**
　Verbal reasoning score: **8.6**, Physical sciences score: **8.4**,
　Biological sciences score: **9.0**, Writing score: **N/A**
Proportion with undergraduate majors in: Biological sciences: **51%**, Physical sciences: **18%**, Non-sciences: **12%**, Other health professions: **13%**, Mixed disciplines and other: **7%**
Percentage of students not coming directly from college after graduation: **36%**

Dates and details

The American Medical College Application Service (AMCAS) application is not accepted.
School does not ask for a school-specific application as part of the admissions process.
Oldest MCAT considered for Fall 2005 entry: **2001**
Earliest application date for the 2005-2006 first-year class: **July 1, 2004**
Latest application date: **November 1, 2004**
Acceptance dates for regular application for the class entering in fall 2005:

Earliest: **January 15, 2005**
Latest: **August 1, 2005**
The school considers requests for deferred entrance.
Starting month for the class entering in 2005-2006: **August**
The school doesn't have an Early Decision Plan (EDP).
A personal interview is required for admission.

Undergraduate coursework required

Medical school requires undergraduate work in these subjects: biology/zoology, English, organic chemistry, inorganic (general) chemistry, physics, mathematics, behavioral science, general chemistry.

ADMISSIONS POLICY

(TEXT PROVIDED BY SCHOOL):
It is the university's policy that there shall be no discrimination in admissions based on race, religion, age, creed, color, sex, disability, sexual orientation, national origin, marital status, veteran status, or political belief or affiliation. Preference in admission is given to residents of North Dakota. A resident is any applicant who has lived in North Dakota for 12 months prior to November 1 of the year of application and who is a U.S. citizen or legal permanent resident. Applicants certified by the Western Interstate Commission on Higher Education receive equal preference for up to six positions in each entering class. Residents of Minnesota also are considered for admission on a limited basis. Enrolled members of federally recognized tribes, regardless of state of residency, may apply through the school's INMED Program.

Application forms may be submitted either electronically or in paper format, no later than November 1. The school does not use the American Medical College Application Service. The completed application folder consists of the application form, a personal statement, four letters of recommendation, Medical College Admission Test scores, official academic transcripts, and a $50 nonrefundable application fee. Prior to admission, a minimum of 90 semester hours of credit from an approved college or university must be completed. Preference is given to applicants who will have completed an undergraduate degree and who are broadly educated in the sciences and humanities. A minimum cumulative and science grade-point average of 3.0 is expected. Applicants favorably considered for admission are invited for personal interviews with the Committee on Admissions. In addition to high academic achievement, selection is based on a number of factors, including qualities such as motivation and commitment to a medical career, empathy and compassion in interpersonal relationships, maturity and flexibility in dealing with problems, and the ability to work with others.

COSTS AND FINANCIAL AID

Financial aid phone number: **(701) 777-2849**
Tuition, 2003-2004 academic year: **In-state: $16,383; Out-of-state: $42,003**
Room and board: **$8,704**
Percentage of students receiving financial aid in 2003-04: **99%**
Percentage of students receiving: Loans: **98%**, Grants/scholarships: **57%**, Work-study aid: **0%**
Average medical school debt for the Class of 2002: **$98,670**

STUDENT BODY

Fall 2003 full-time enrollment: **226**
Men: **49%**, Women: **51%**, In-state: **81%**, Minorities: **11%**, American Indian: **9.7%**, Asian-American: **0.9%**, African-American: **0.0%**, Hispanic-American: **04%**, White: **88.9%**, International: **0.0%**, Unknown: **N/A**

ACADEMIC PROGRAMS

The school's curriculum gives first-year students substantial contact with patients.
There aren't opportunities for first- or second-year students to work in community health clinics.
Program offerings: AIDS, drug/alcohol abuse, family medicine, geriatrics, internal medicine, pediatrics, rural medicine, women's health
Joint degrees awarded: M.D./Ph.D., M.D./M.P.H., M.D./M.S.
Total National Institutes of Health (NIH) grants awarded to the medical school and affiliated hospitals: **N/A**

CURRICULUM

(TEXT PROVIDED BY SCHOOL):
The University of North Dakota School of Medicine and Health Sciences is a university-based, community-integrated medical education program. Students spend the initial two years attending classes at the main campus in Grand Forks. The third year is taken at one of three regional campuses in Bismarck, Fargo, or Grand Forks. Minot is added as one of four area campuses for completion of the senior year.
The curriculum for years 1 and 2 is organized in eight 10-week blocks. Using an interdisciplinary approach, Block 1 presents the basic foundation for understanding the func-

tional biology of cells and tissue. An organ-system approach is utilized for the remainder of the first year (blocks 2-4). Blocks 5-8, the second-year curriculum, stress pathobiology. The teaching of foundational clinical sciences also occurs on a continuing basis. The curriculum is presented through lectures and small-group sessions. Within a patient-centered learning format, the small-group sessions are designed to facilitate the integration of basic sciences with clinically relevant cases. To be successful, students must synthesize large amounts of information, effectively apply science concepts to clinical problems, and integrate concepts across disciplines.
The third year consists of six core clerkships of eight weeks' duration and a two-hour, didactic community medicine and epidemiology course. The clerkships include internal medicine, surgery, obstetrics and gynecology, pediatrics, psychiatry, and family medicine. A limited number of students also may complete 28 weeks of the third year in a rural community through the Rural Opportunities in Medical Education program. The fourth year consists of two acting internships of four weeks each, one in medicine and the other in surgery; six electives of four weeks each; and a final one-week transitional classroom activity.
The school utilizes a grading system of satisfactory/unsatisfactory only for the first year; the system changes to honors/satisfactory/unsatisfactory for the final three years.

FACULTY PROFILE (FALL 2003)

Total teaching faculty: **138 (full-time)**, **1,154 (part-time)**
Of full-time faculty, those teaching in basic sciences: **51%**; in clinical programs: **49%**
Of part-time faculty, those teaching in basic sciences: **1%**; in clinical programs: **99%**
Full-time faculty/student ratio: **0.6**

SUPPORT SERVICES

The school offers students these services for dealing with stress: expanded-hour gym access, professional counseling, religious support, support groups.

RESIDENCY CHOICES

Most popular residency and specialty programs chosen by the 2002 and 2003 M.D. graduating classes: anesthesiology, emergency medicine, family practice, internal medicine, neurology, obstetrics and gynecology, pediatrics, psychiatry, radiology–diagnostic, surgery–general.

WHERE GRADS GO

36.1%
Proportion of 2001-2003 graduates who entered primary care specialties

23.6%
Proportion of 2002-2003 graduates who accepted in-state residencies

University of Oklahoma

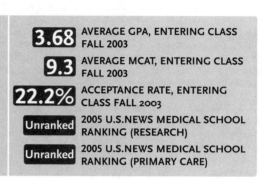

- PO Box 26901, BMSB 357, Oklahoma City, OK 73190
- Public
- Year Founded: 1900
- Tuition, 2003-2004: In-state: $15,136; Out-of-state: $35,513
- Enrollment, 2003-2004: 585
- Website: http://www.medicine.ouhsc.edu
- Specialty ranking: N/A

3.68 AVERAGE GPA, ENTERING CLASS FALL 2003

9.3 AVERAGE MCAT, ENTERING CLASS FALL 2003

22.2% ACCEPTANCE RATE, ENTERING CLASS FALL 2003

Unranked 2005 U.S.NEWS MEDICAL SCHOOL RANKING (RESEARCH)

Unranked 2005 U.S.NEWS MEDICAL SCHOOL RANKING (PRIMARY CARE)

ADMISSIONS

Admissions phone number: **(405) 271-2331**
Admissions email address: **adminmed@ouhsc.edu**
Application website: **N/A**
Acceptance rate: **22.2%**
In-state acceptance rate: **53.1%**
Out-of-state acceptance rate: **4.5%**
Minority acceptance rate: **14.9%**
International acceptance rate: **N/A**

Fall 2003 applications and acceptees

	Applied	Interviewed	Accepted	Enrolled
Total:	848	242	188	142
In-state:	309	210	164	135
Out-of-state:	539	32	24	7

Profile of admitted students

Average undergraduate grade point average: **3.68**
MCAT averages (scale: 1-15; writing test: J-T):
   Composite score: **9.3**
   Verbal reasoning score: **9.2**, Physical sciences score: **9.1**,
   Biological sciences score: **9.6**, Writing score: **O**
Proportion with undergraduate majors in: Biological
   sciences: **51%**, Physical sciences: **24%**, Non-sciences:
   11%, Other health professions: **4%**, Mixed disciplines
   and other: **10%**
Percentage of students not coming directly from college
   after graduation: **N/A**

Dates and details

The American Medical College Application Service
   (AMCAS) application is accepted.
School does not ask for a school-specific application as part
   of the admissions process.
Oldest MCAT considered for Fall 2005 entry: **1991**
Earliest application date for the 2005-2006 first-year class:
   June 15, 2004
Latest application date: **October 15, 2004**
Acceptance dates for regular application for the class
   entering in fall 2005:
   Earliest: **December 1, 2004**

Latest: **May 15, 2005**
The school doesn't consider requests for deferred entrance.
Starting month for the class entering in 2005-2006:
   August
The school doesn't have an Early Decision Plan (EDP).
A personal interview is required for admission.

Undergraduate coursework required

Medical school requires undergraduate work in these subjects: biology/zoology, English, organic chemistry, inorganic (general) chemistry, physics, humanities, social sciences, general chemistry.

ADMISSIONS POLICY
(TEXT PROVIDED BY SCHOOL):

The University of Oklahoma College of Medicine participates in the American Medical College Application Service. Applicants to the M.D. program begin the online application process during the spring or summer, a year in advance of when they wish to be admitted.

As a general rule, the College of Medicine will consider applicants with 90 or more hours of college work. No particular major is given preference, but the applicant must understand and be able to utilize scientific information. A broad education is encouraged. A letter grade of C or better is required in all prerequisite courses. Pass/fail grading, Advanced Placement, and College Level Examination Program courses are accepted if a subsequent higher course is taken for a grade.

Preference in admission is given to Oklahoma residents. Only nonresidents with superior academic records and ties to the state should apply.

All applicants are required to take the Medical College Admission Test. Eligible applicants to the College of Medicine are those students with a grade-point average of 3.0 or better and a MCAT average score of 7.0 or better. Applicants must be U.S. citizens or hold a permanent visa.

All applicants selected for final consideration will be interviewed between December and February. The College of Medicine endeavors to have a class selected by March 1.

Approximately 150 students are admitted to the first-year class, at least 85 percent from within Oklahoma.

Admissions decisions are based on an applicant's indications and probabilities of successfully completing medical school, intellectual ability, academic achievement, character, motivation, and maturity. The assessment utilizes college grades, MCAT scores, letters of recommendation, personal statements, and interview results.

Intellectual ability and academic achievement alone are not sufficient to assure the professional development and commitment required of a physician. Traits of personality, maturity, and character also are necessary.

COSTS AND FINANCIAL AID

Financial aid phone number: **(405) 271-2118**
Tuition, 2003-2004 academic year: **In-state: $15,136; Out-of-state: $35,513**
Room and board: **N/A**
Percentage of students receiving financial aid in 2003-04: **92%**
Percentage of students receiving: Loans: **90%**, Grants/scholarships: **51%**, Work-study aid: **0%**
Average medical school debt for the Class of 2002: **$105,315**

STUDENT BODY

Fall 2003 full-time enrollment: **585**
Men: **58%**, Women: **42%**, In-state: **96%**, Minorities: **23%**, American Indian: **6.8%**, Asian-American: **14.4%**, African-American: **0.9%**, Hispanic-American: **2.4%**, White: **57.6%**, International: **0.0%**, Unknown: **17.9%**

ACADEMIC PROGRAMS

The school's curriculum gives first-year students substantial contact with patients.
There are opportunities for first- or second-year students to work in community health clinics.
Program offerings: AIDS, drug/alcohol abuse, family medicine, geriatrics, internal medicine, pediatrics, rural medicine, women's health
Joint degrees awarded: M.D./Ph.D., M.D./M.P.H., M.D./M.S., M.D./M.H.A.
Total National Institutes of Health (NIH) grants awarded to the medical school and affiliated hospitals: **N/A**

CURRICULUM

(TEXT PROVIDED BY SCHOOL):
The curriculum is designed to provide an integrated overview of human biology and behavior. Classroom and laboratory studies are complemented with clinical demonstrations and case studies, problem- and team-based learning, and an extensive online curriculum called Hippocrates. Patient contact is a major component of each of the four years of medical school, beginning with simulated patients and extending to hospital and ambulatory settings.

Students are required to pass Step 1 of the U.S. Medical Licensing Examination prior to beginning third-year clinical rotations. Students must take the USMLE Step 2 examination during the fourth year and report scores. All basic science courses are conducted on the campus of the Health Sciences Center in Oklahoma City. Up to 25 percent of the class choose to undertake clinical training at the College of Medicine-Tulsa.

First-year courses focus on knowledge of structure and function of human biology, critical thinking skills, and the management of medical information. Second-year courses address the pathophysiology of diseases and form a bridge into the clinical portion of the curriculum. A significant feature of this curriculum is early exposure to patients in the two Principles of Clinical Medicine courses. Students learn interviewing skills on actual and simulated patients, and work with local physicians and clinical faculty throughout the entire first and second years. Faculty members recognize the importance of self-directed learning, small-group discussion sessions, independent learning modules, computer-assisted instruction, and integrated medical problem solving.

In the third year, all students are required to take core clerkships in family medicine, geriatrics, internal medicine, neuroscience, obstetrics/gynecology, pediatrics, psychiatry, and surgery. Fourth-year students have a required ambulatory care experience, a rural preceptorship under the guidance of an Oklahoma physician, and six months of clinical electives. Over the past 10 years, 49 percent of our students selected primary-care disciplines, and 50 percent remained in Oklahoma for residency.

FACULTY PROFILE (FALL 2003)

Total teaching faculty: **656 (full-time)**, **135 (part-time)**
Of full-time faculty, those teaching in basic sciences: **19%**; in clinical programs: **81%**
Of part-time faculty, those teaching in basic sciences: **4%**; in clinical programs: **96%**
Full-time faculty/student ratio: **1.1**

SUPPORT SERVICES

The school offers students these services for dealing with stress: professional counseling.

RESIDENCY CHOICES

Most popular residency and specialty programs chosen by the 2002 and 2003 M.D. graduating classes: family practice, internal medicine, pediatrics, radiology–diagnostic, surgery–general.

WHERE GRADS GO

46.8%
Proportion of 2001-2003 graduates who entered primary care specialties

39.5%
Proportion of 2002-2003 graduates who accepted in-state residencies

University of Pennsylvania

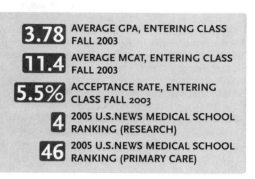

- 295 John Morgan Building, 3620 Hamilton Walk, Philadelphia, PA 19104-6055
- Private
- Year Founded: 1765
- Tuition, 2003-2004: $36,514
- Enrollment, 2003-2004: 603
- Website: http://www.med.upenn.edu
- Specialty ranking: AIDS: 11, drug/alcohol abuse: 6, geriatrics: 13, internal medicine: 6, pediatrics: 3, women's health: 2

3.78 AVERAGE GPA, ENTERING CLASS FALL 2003

11.4 AVERAGE MCAT, ENTERING CLASS FALL 2003

5.5% ACCEPTANCE RATE, ENTERING CLASS FALL 2003

4 2005 U.S.NEWS MEDICAL SCHOOL RANKING (RESEARCH)

46 2005 U.S.NEWS MEDICAL SCHOOL RANKING (PRIMARY CARE)

ADMISSIONS

Admissions phone number: (215) 898-8001
Admissions email address: admiss@mail.med.upenn.edu
Application website:
   http://www.med.upenn.edu/admiss/applications.html
Acceptance rate: 5.5%
In-state acceptance rate: 12.0%
Out-of-state acceptance rate: 4.7%
Minority acceptance rate: 5.0%
International acceptance rate: 3.0%

Fall 2003 applications and acceptees

	Applied	Interviewed	Accepted	Enrolled
Total:	4,423	816	245	147
In-state:	534	118	64	46
Out-of-state:	3,889	698	181	101

Profile of admitted students

Average undergraduate grade point average: 3.78
MCAT averages (scale: 1-15; writing test: J-T):
   Composite score: 11.4
   Verbal reasoning score: 10.8, Physical sciences score: 11.7, Biological sciences score: 11.7, Writing score: Q
Proportion with undergraduate majors in: Biological sciences: 15%, Physical sciences: 41%, Non-sciences: 36%, Other health professions: 0%, Mixed disciplines and other: 8%
Percentage of students not coming directly from college after graduation: 25%

Dates and details

The American Medical College Application Service (AMCAS) application is accepted.
School asks for a school-specific application as part of the admissions process.
Oldest MCAT considered for Fall 2005 entry: 2001
Earliest application date for the 2005-2006 first-year class: June 1, 2004
Latest application date: October 15, 2004
Acceptance dates for regular application for the class entering in fall 2005:

Earliest: March 1, 2005
Latest: August 15, 2005
The school considers requests for deferred entrance.
Starting month for the class entering in 2005-2006:
   August
The school has an Early Decision Plan (EDP).
A personal interview is required for admission.

Undergraduate coursework required

Medical school requires undergraduate work in these subjects: biology, English, physics, mathematics, general chemistry.

ADMISSIONS POLICY

(TEXT PROVIDED BY SCHOOL):
The University of Pennsylvania School of Medicine selects students based on academic and personal excellence. In accordance with the mission of the school, diversity is valued in the selection process, recognizing that such differences enhance learning and enrich all members of the school community.

Academic excellence is measured by the academic performance of the student, the rigorousness of the courses taken, the school attended, intellectual curiosity, and national testing measures, such as the Medical College Admission Test. In addition, the Committee on Admissions takes into account the student's record of activity in extracurricular college and community affairs, special talents or abilities, employment, and other life experiences. Sustained contributions to organizations, communities, research, and activities over time indicate a commitment and in-depth involvement. Leadership is strongly considered and encouraged.

Personal excellence is evidenced by behavior associated with extracurricular activities and accomplishments, life experiences, personal insight, and maturity. These characteristics are corroborated by letters of recommendation from faculty, premedical advisers, and others. Selection characteristics prized by the school are integrity, respect for and concern about others, inner strength, personal effectiveness and communication, compassion, and desire to make a contribution in healthcare.

COSTS AND FINANCIAL AID

Financial aid phone number: **(215) 573-3423**
Tuition, 2003-2004 academic year: **$36,514**
Room and board: **$15,005**
Percentage of students receiving financial aid in 2003-04:
  85%
Percentage of students receiving: Loans: **65%**,
  Grants/scholarships: **66%**, Work-study aid: **3%**
Average medical school debt for the Class of 2002:
  $101,400

STUDENT BODY

Fall 2003 full-time enrollment: **603**
Men: **52%**, Women: **48%**, In-state: **28%**, Minorities: **38%**,
  American Indian: **0.3%**, Asian-American: **20.9%**,
  African-American: **8.5%**, Hispanic-American: **8.5%**,
  White: **60.5%**, International: **1.0%**, Unknown: **0.3%**

ACADEMIC PROGRAMS

The school's curriculum gives first-year students
  substantial contact with patients.
There are opportunities for first- or second-year students to
  work in community health clinics.
Program offerings: AIDS, drug/alcohol abuse, family
  medicine, geriatrics, internal medicine, pediatrics, rural
  medicine, women's health
Joint degrees awarded: M.D./Ph.D., M.D./M.B.A.,
  M.D./M.P.H., M.D./J.D., M.D./M.S., M.D./M.A.
Total National Institutes of Health (NIH) grants awarded to
  the medical school and affiliated hospitals: **$462.5 million**

CURRICULUM
(TEXT PROVIDED BY SCHOOL):

The four-year curriculum is built on three themes: science
of medicine; technology and practice of medicine; and professionalism and humanism. It is designed with flexibility
to participate in other graduate programs offered at the
University of Pennsylvania and School of Medicine.

Module 1 is a four-month module divided into four
blocks: Developmental and Molecular Biology
(genetics/embryology); Cell Physiology and Metabolism;
Human Body, Structure and Function (histology and gross
anatomy); and Host Defenses (immunology, pharmacology,
and microbiology). Module 1 gives students the foundation
of basic sciences necessary to enter a series of organ-system
blocks, where basic sciences are integrated across each
organ system. This module is pass/fail, and all students
must successfully complete each component.

Module 2, Integrative Systems and Diseases, which
begins in January of Year 1, is composed of organ systems
and disease blocks. Topics are organized by organ systems
in the following structure: Normal Development (anatomy,
embryology, histology); Normal Processes (physiology);
Abnormal Processes (pathophysiology, pathology);
Therapeutics and Disease Management (pharmacology,
pathophysiology); Epidemiology/Evidence-Based Medicine;
and Prevention and Nutrition.

Module 3, Technology and Practice of Medicine, spans
modules 1 and 2, and concludes upon the start of Module 4,
Core Clerkships. This program is designed to achieve a level
of competency across epidemiology and biostatistics, decision making, economics of healthcare, population-based
medicine, and the basics of clinical medicine.

Upon successful completion of modules 1, 2, 3, and part
of 6, all students enter the required clerkships known as
Module 4. Module 4 begins in January of the second year
and is composed of 48 weeks of required clinical clerkships,
ending in December of the third year. All students must
complete all of the core clerkships before moving on to
Module 5. The clerkships are divided into four cross-disciplinary experiences of three months each: internal medi-
cine/family medicine; obstetrics/gynecology/pediatrics;
surgery/anesthesia/emergency medicine; and
psychiatry/neurology and clinical specialties, orthopedics,
otorhinolaryngology, and ophthalmology.

Module 5 begins in January of the third year and is the
final 16 months of medical school. All students completing a
four-year M.D. degree are required to complete six additional
electives; a subinternship in either general medicine or general pediatrics; 12 weeks of a scholarly pursuit with a mentor,
and four weeks of the Frontiers in Medical Science courses.

Module 6, Professionalism and Humanism, runs concurrently throughout the curriculum and covers topics on
bioethics, multiculturalism, spirituality, research ethics, and
confidentiality.

FACULTY PROFILE (FALL 2003)

Total teaching faculty: **1,997 (full-time)**, **1,238 (part-time)**
Of full-time faculty, those teaching in basic sciences: **10%**;
  in clinical programs: **90%**
Of part-time faculty, those teaching in basic sciences: **9%**;
  in clinical programs: **91%**
Full-time faculty/student ratio: **3.3**

SUPPORT SERVICES

The school offers students these services for dealing with
stress: peer counseling, professional counseling, support
groups.

RESIDENCY CHOICES

Most popular residency and specialty programs chosen by
the 2002 and 2003 M.D. graduating classes: dermatology,
emergency medicine, internal medicine, ophthalmology,
orthopedic surgery, pediatrics, psychiatry, radiology–diagnostic, surgery–general.

WHERE GRADS GO

37.0%
*Proportion of 2001-2003 graduates who entered primary
care specialties*

38.5%
*Proportion of 2002-2003 graduates who accepted in-state
residencies*

University of Pittsburgh

- 401 Scaife Hall, Pittsburgh, PA 15261
- Public
- Year Founded: 1886
- Tuition, 2003-2004: In-state: $30,644; Out-of-state: $36,436
- Enrollment, 2003-2004: 586
- Website: http://www.medschool.pitt.edu
- Specialty ranking: pediatrics: 19, women's health: 6

3.70 AVERAGE GPA, ENTERING CLASS FALL 2003

10.9 AVERAGE MCAT, ENTERING CLASS FALL 2003

9.9% ACCEPTANCE RATE, ENTERING CLASS FALL 2003

15 2005 U.S.NEWS MEDICAL SCHOOL RANKING (RESEARCH)

31 2005 U.S.NEWS MEDICAL SCHOOL RANKING (PRIMARY CARE)

ADMISSIONS

Admissions phone number: **(412) 648-9891**
Admissions email address:
admissions@medschool.pitt.edu
Application website: **http://www.medschool.pitt.edu**
Acceptance rate: **9.9%**
In-state acceptance rate: **14.1%**
Out-of-state acceptance rate: **9.1%**
Minority acceptance rate: **9.3%**
International acceptance rate: **N/A**

Fall 2003 applications and acceptees

	Applied	Interviewed	Accepted	Enrolled
Total:	4,842	918	481	145
In-state:	775	196	109	52
Out-of-state:	4,067	722	372	93

Profile of admitted students

Average undergraduate grade point average: **3.70**
MCAT averages (scale: 1-15; writing test: J-T):
  Composite score: **10.9**
  Verbal reasoning score: **10.4**, Physical sciences score:
  11.0, Biological sciences score: **11.2**, Writing score: **P**
Proportion with undergraduate majors in: Biological
  sciences: **50%**, Physical sciences: **22%**, Non-sciences:
  15%, Other health professions: **0%**, Mixed disciplines
  and other: **13%**
Percentage of students not coming directly from college
  after graduation: **43%**

Dates and details

The American Medical College Application Service
  (AMCAS) application is accepted.
School asks for a school-specific application as part of the
  admissions process.
Oldest MCAT considered for Fall 2005 entry: **2001**
Earliest application date for the 2005-2006 first-year class:
  June 1, 2004
Latest application date: **December 1, 2004**
Acceptance dates for regular application for the class
  entering in fall 2005:

Earliest: **March 1, 2005**
Latest: **August 8, 2005**
The school considers requests for deferred entrance.
Starting month for the class entering in 2005-2006:
  August
The school doesn't have an Early Decision Plan (EDP).
A personal interview is required for admission.

Undergraduate coursework required

Medical school requires undergraduate work in these subjects: biology, English, organic chemistry, inorganic (general) chemistry, physics, general chemistry.

ADMISSIONS POLICY
(TEXT PROVIDED BY SCHOOL):

We are an American Medical College Application Service
school. AMCAS forwards to us the applicant's academic
credentials. Our supplemental application is sent to competitive applicants and asks for three academic letters of recommendation or a committee letter; the student must also
answer questions in essay form. (Applicants who request a
supplemental application, after having received our letter
denying it, are allowed to apply.)

The applicant is interviewed by a faculty member and a
first- or second-year medical student. No applicant is admitted without an interview. Both interview reports and the
remainder of the applicant's credentials are brought before
the Admissions Committee. Each committee member ranks
the applicant on a scale of 1.0 (low) to 4.0 (high) in steps of
a tenth. During the last week of February, the Admissions
Committee decides on which ranks get admitted, rejected,
or placed on the waiting list. We do not use rolling admissions until after the last week in February.

The Admissions Committee seeks to admit a diverse,
intellectually competent student body. Intellectual competence is judged not only by numerical academic criteria but
also on the basis of recommendation letters. Applicants
should have some medical exposure to test their decision to
enter medicine. Extracurricular activities are weighted heavily. We seek to admit students who have evidenced longtime
dedication to some praiseworthy activity. This may be

sports, research, a community activity, or an artistic endeavor. During the interview, the applicant must communicate his or her motivation to enter medicine and establish a relationship with the interviewer. We seek to admit well-rounded applicants, and this facet of an individual's persona should be evident during the interview. In addition, a broad education is a major plus in consideration of the applicant's credentials.

COSTS AND FINANCIAL AID

Financial aid phone number: **(412) 648-9891**

Tuition, 2003-2004 academic year: **In-state: $30,644; Out-of-state: $36,436**

Room and board: **$14,560**

Percentage of students receiving financial aid in 2003-04: **85%**

Percentage of students receiving: Loans: **81%**, Grants/scholarships: **48%**, Work-study aid: **0%**

Average medical school debt for the Class of 2002: **$117,704**

STUDENT BODY

Fall 2003 full-time enrollment: **586**

Men: **52%**, Women: **48%**, In-state: **41%**, Minorities: **32%**, American Indian: **0.0%**, Asian-American: **21.8%**, African-American: **8.5%**, Hispanic-American: **2.0%**, White: **67.6%**, International: **0.0%**, Unknown: **0.0%**

ACADEMIC PROGRAMS

The school's curriculum gives first-year students substantial contact with patients.

There are opportunities for first- or second-year students to work in community health clinics.

Program offerings: AIDS, drug/alcohol abuse, family medicine, geriatrics, internal medicine, pediatrics, rural medicine, women's health

Joint degrees awarded: M.D./Ph.D., M.D./M.P.H., M.D./M.A.

Total National Institutes of Health (NIH) grants awarded to the medical school and affiliated hospitals: **$293.7 million**

CURRICULUM

(TEXT PROVIDED BY SCHOOL):

The Patient of Today and the Medicine of Tomorrow describes the curriculum at the University of Pittsburgh School of Medicine. The patient focus begins on Day 1, in the Introduction to Being a Physician course. Students interview patients and visit community settings to develop an early understanding of their role as medical professionals.

Patient interviewing and physical diagnosis courses follow, along with exercises examining physician life: in society, in ethical settings, and at the patient bedside. Throughout the first two years, students apply their new skills in local practices and hospitals, one afternoon per week.

Foundations for mastery of the Medicine of Tomorrow begin with the basic science block that runs through three fourths of the first year. This block provides the language and concepts that underlie the scientific basis of medical practice.

Organ system courses integrate physiology, pathophysiology, pharmacology, and introduction to medicine for the major organ systems. Students continually focus on the patient with concurrent courses in the patient care and patient-doctor relationship blocks.

A unique Clinical Scientist Training Program prepares students for a career in academic medicine. Others opt to participate in area of concentration (AOC) programs. AOCs are offered in disabilities medicine, medical humanities, service learning (underserved populations), geriatrics, women's health, informatics, global health, and biomedical research. Since 1983, our Medical Scientist Training Program has offered the M.D./Ph.D.

During the first two years, mentored student groups engage in problem-based learning (PBL) exercises based on clinical cases. The PBL learning experience culminates in the Integrated Case Studies course at the end of Year 2, which serves as a bridge to patient care responsibilities during Year 3.

All third-year students take clerkships in adult inpatient medicine, clinical neurosciences, ambulatory care, surgical subspecialties, obstetrics and gynecology, pediatrics, surgery and perioperative care, and family medicine. In Year 4, students enjoy a wide range of elective options.

FACULTY PROFILE (FALL 2003)

Total teaching faculty: **1,734 (full-time)**, **49 (part-time)**

Of full-time faculty, those teaching in basic sciences: **8%**; in clinical programs: **92%**

Of part-time faculty, those teaching in basic sciences: **2%**; in clinical programs: **98%**

Full-time faculty/student ratio: **3.0**

SUPPORT SERVICES

The school offers students these services for dealing with stress: expanded-hour gym access, peer counseling, professional counseling, support groups.

RESIDENCY CHOICES

Most popular residency and specialty programs chosen by the 2002 and 2003 M.D. graduating classes: anesthesiology, emergency medicine, family practice, internal medicine, obstetrics and gynecology, orthopedic surgery, otolaryngology, pediatrics, radiology–diagnostic, surgery–general.

WHERE GRADS GO

42.0%

Proportion of 2001-2003 graduates who entered primary care specialties

43.0%

Proportion of 2002-2003 graduates who accepted in-state residencies

University of Rochester

■ 601 Elmwood Avenue, Box 706, Rochester, NY 14642
■ Private
■ Year Founded: 1925
■ Tuition, 2003-2004: $34,317
■ Enrollment, 2003-2004: 433
■ Website: http://www.urmc.rochester.edu/smd
■ Specialty ranking: family medicine: 22, geriatrics: 13

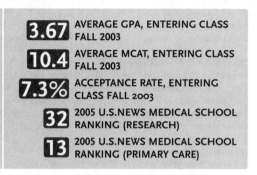

3.67 AVERAGE GPA, ENTERING CLASS FALL 2003

10.4 AVERAGE MCAT, ENTERING CLASS FALL 2003

7.3% ACCEPTANCE RATE, ENTERING CLASS FALL 2003

32 2005 U.S.NEWS MEDICAL SCHOOL RANKING (RESEARCH)

13 2005 U.S.NEWS MEDICAL SCHOOL RANKING (PRIMARY CARE)

ADMISSIONS

Admissions phone number: **(585) 275-4539**
Admissions email address:
  mdadmish@urmc.rochester.edu
Application website:
  **http://www.urmc.rochester.edu/smd/admiss/
  secondaryapp.html**
Acceptance rate: **7.3%**
In-state acceptance rate: **7.9%**
Out-of-state acceptance rate: **7.0%**
Minority acceptance rate: **8.0%**
International acceptance rate: **N/A**

Fall 2003 applications and acceptees

	Applied	Interviewed	Accepted	Enrolled
Total:	3,434	656	250	100
In-state:	920	211	73	42
Out-of-state:	2,514	445	177	58

Profile of admitted students

Average undergraduate grade point average: **3.67**
MCAT averages (scale: 1-15; writing test: J-T):
  Composite score: **10.4**
  Verbal reasoning score: **10.1**, Physical sciences score:
  10.5, Biological sciences score: **10.6**, Writing score: **Q**
Proportion with undergraduate majors in: Biological
  sciences: **54%**, Physical sciences: **13%**, Non-sciences:
  26%, Other health professions: **1%**, Mixed disciplines
  and other: **6%**
Percentage of students not coming directly from college
  after graduation: **66%**

Dates and details

The American Medical College Application Service
  (AMCAS) application is accepted.
School asks for a school-specific application as part of the
  admissions process.
Oldest MCAT considered for Fall 2005 entry: **2001**
Earliest application date for the 2005-2006 first-year class:
  June 1, 2004
Latest application date: **October 15, 2004**

Acceptance dates for regular application for the class
  entering in fall 2005:
  Earliest: **November 1, 2005**
  Latest: **August 8, 2006**
The school considers requests for deferred entrance.
Starting month for the class entering in 2005-2006:
  August
The school doesn't have an Early Decision Plan (EDP).
A personal interview is required for admission.

Undergraduate coursework required

Medical school requires undergraduate work in these subjects: biology, English, organic chemistry, inorganic (general) chemistry, physics, humanities, general chemistry.

ADMISSIONS POLICY
(TEXT PROVIDED BY SCHOOL):

A strong academic record and good scores on the Medical
College Admission Test are necessary but not sufficient criteria for admission. The Admissions Committee looks for
evidence of scholarship and research, service to the community, clinical volunteer experiences, leadership abilities,
integrity, maturity, and excellent interpersonal skills.
Rochester seeks students who value human diversity,
exhibit a love of learning, have an appreciation of the science and art of medicine, and are called to serve others.
  Applications are reviewed by the committee beginning in
July. Selected applicants are granted interviews at the medical center from September to the middle of March.
Acceptances are mailed out in late October and continue on
a rolling basis until the class is filled.

COSTS AND FINANCIAL AID

Financial aid phone number: **(585) 275-4523**
Tuition, 2003-2004 academic year: **$34,317**
Room and board: **$14,500**
Percentage of students receiving financial aid in 2003-04:
  95%
Percentage of students receiving: Loans: **89%**,
  Grants/scholarships: **45%**, Work-study aid: **20%**

Average medical school debt for the Class of 2002:
$103,809

STUDENT BODY
Fall 2003 full-time enrollment: 433
Men: 46%, Women: 54%, In-state: 48%, Minorities: 33%,
    American Indian: 0.2%, Asian-American: 19.4%,
    African-American: 9.5%, Hispanic-American: 4.4%,
    White: 64.9%, International: 0.0%, Unknown: 1.6%

ACADEMIC PROGRAMS
The school's curriculum gives first-year students
    substantial contact with patients.
There are opportunities for first- or second-year students to
    work in community health clinics.
Program offerings: AIDS, drug/alcohol abuse, family
    medicine, geriatrics, internal medicine, pediatrics, rural
    medicine
Joint degrees awarded: M.D./Ph.D., M.D./M.B.A.,
    M.D./M.S.
Total National Institutes of Health (NIH) grants awarded to
    the medical school and affiliated hospitals: $130.9 million

CURRICULUM
(TEXT PROVIDED BY SCHOOL):
The Rochester Double Helix Curriculum captures the integrated strands of basic science and clinical medicine as they
are woven throughout the four-year curriculum. Each element of the curriculum strengthens Rochester's biopsychosocial tradition by fostering knowledge, skills, attitudes,
and behaviors of the physician/scientist/humanist, by combining cutting-edge, evidence-based medical science with
the relationship-centered art that is medicine's distinctive
trademark.
    The Rochester curriculum is uniquely designed to train
lifelong learners of medicine. Special emphasis is placed on
skills acquisition and use. Sensitivity to the world of the
patient is encompassed in the biopsychosocial integration of
the curriculum and the learning experience. By ensuring
adequate and early electivity for students to enhance their
special interests, the Double Helix Curriculum generates a
knowledge base characterized by depth, breadth, rigor, and
flexibility.
    Every course is interdisciplinary; basic sciences are inte-
grated with one another, and basic and clinical sciences are
woven together as the strands of the Double Helix
Curriculum throughout the four years. Unlike the early
clinical exposure of any other school, the clinical skills training from Day 1 leads not to shadowing experiences in clinics but to the start of real clinical work as part of the
healthcare team while still in the first year.
    Every course has learning objectives, a plan for enabling
students to meet those objectives, and appropriate assessment instruments to ensure that students have met the
objectives. Emphasis is on integrated exams and evaluation
formats that assess preparation, participation, critical-thinking skills, knowledge application to problem solving, and
professionalism. We expect students to treat the educational
enterprise with the same seriousness of purpose with which
we all treat patient care and research, and participation in

course/clerkship assessment for continuous improvement
of the curriculum is expected.
    Emphasis is on active student learning through the
schoolwide use of multidisciplinary, problem-based learning
(PBL) cases in all courses. Interdepartmental, multidisciplinary faculty teams direct major curricular blocks, which
usually include three two-hour PBL tutorials per week, lectures, labs, and conferences.
    Small-group sessions consist of PBL, laboratories, confer-
ences, seminars, and computer-assisted learning, while adequate time for self-study is provided by keeping two
afternoons per week free of curricular activities.
    Clinical exposure begins during the first week of medical
school. Students complete their introduction to clinical
medicine in the fall of Year 1 and then participate in the
ambulatory care clerkship beginning their first spring
semester. This experience, unlike any other in the country,
includes the ambulatory components of family medicine,
pediatrics, internal medicine, women's health, and ambulatory surgery, and is completed by the end of the second year.
    Year 3 inpatient clerkships focus on acute-care experi-
ences in adult medicine (internal medicine and surgery),
women's and children's health (pediatrics and
obstetrics/gynecology), mind/brain/behavior (neurology
and psychiatry), and urgent/emergent care.
    Fourth-year students can choose from a wide variety of
clinical electives. They also participate in the Community
Health Improvement Clerkship and subinternship.

FACULTY PROFILE (FALL 2003)
Total teaching faculty: 1,201 (full-time), 1,235 (part-time)
Of full-time faculty, those teaching in basic sciences: 19%;
    in clinical programs: 81%
Of part-time faculty, those teaching in basic sciences: 1%;
    in clinical programs: 99%
Full-time faculty/student ratio: 2.8

SUPPORT SERVICES
The school offers students these services for dealing with
stress: expanded-hour gym access, peer counseling, professional counseling, religious support, support groups.

RESIDENCY CHOICES
Most popular residency and specialty programs chosen by the
2002 and 2003 M.D. graduating classes: anesthesiology, internal medicine, internal medicine–pediatrics, neurology, obstetrics and gynecology, ophthalmology, pediatrics, psychiatry.

WHERE GRADS GO
42.0%
*Proportion of 2001-2003 graduates who entered primary
care specialties*

40.2%
*Proportion of 2002-2003 graduates who accepted in-state
residencies*

University of South Carolina

- **School of Medicine, Columbia, SC 29208**
- **Public**
- **Year Founded:** N/A
- **Tuition, 2003-2004:** In-state: $16,950; Out-of-state: $48,920
- **Enrollment, 2003-2004:** 297
- **Website:** http://www.med.sc.edu
- **Specialty ranking:** N/A

3.56	AVERAGE GPA, ENTERING CLASS FALL 2003
9.1	AVERAGE MCAT, ENTERING CLASS FALL 2003
12.7%	ACCEPTANCE RATE, ENTERING CLASS FALL 2003
Unranked	2005 U.S.NEWS MEDICAL SCHOOL RANKING (RESEARCH)
Unranked	2005 U.S.NEWS MEDICAL SCHOOL RANKING (PRIMARY CARE)

ADMISSIONS

Admissions phone number: **(803) 733-3325**
Admissions email address: **mills@med.sc.edu**
Application website: **N/A**
Acceptance rate: **12.7%**
In-state acceptance rate: **34.3%**
Out-of-state acceptance rate: **2.7%**
Minority acceptance rate: **7.8%**
International acceptance rate: **N/A**

Fall 2003 applications and acceptees

	Applied	Interviewed	Accepted	Enrolled
Total:	1,047	287	133	80
In-state:	332	215	114	70
Out-of-state:	715	72	19	10

Profile of admitted students

Average undergraduate grade point average: **3.56**
MCAT averages (scale: 1-15; writing test: J-T):
  Composite score: **9.1**
  Verbal reasoning score: **9.0**, Physical sciences score: **9.0**, Biological sciences score: **9.0**, Writing score: **O**
Proportion with undergraduate majors in: Biological sciences: **49%**, Physical sciences: **20%**, Non-sciences: **15%**, Other health professions: **3%**, Mixed disciplines and other: **14%**
Percentage of students not coming directly from college after graduation: **15%**

Dates and details

The American Medical College Application Service (AMCAS) application is accepted.
School asks for a school-specific application as part of the admissions process.
Oldest MCAT considered for Fall 2005 entry: **2000**
Earliest application date for the 2005-2006 first-year class: **June 1, 2004**
Latest application date: **December 1, 2004**
Acceptance dates for regular application for the class entering in fall 2005:
  Earliest: **October 15, 2004**

Latest: **August 1, 2005**
The school considers requests for deferred entrance.
Starting month for the class entering in 2005-2006:
  August
The school has an Early Decision Plan (EDP).
A personal interview is required for admission.

Undergraduate coursework required

Medical school requires undergraduate work in these subjects: biology/zoology, English, organic chemistry, inorganic (general) chemistry, physics, mathematics.

ADMISSIONS POLICY
(TEXT PROVIDED BY SCHOOL):

Applicants admitted to the University of South Carolina School of Medicine are selected by an Admissions Committee composed of members of the basic science and clinical science faculties of the School of Medicine, university faculty, medical students, and area clinicians. In making selections from each year's group of applicants, members of the Admissions Committee recognize that they are selecting future physicians. The admissions procedure is therefore an effort to select applicants who possess the individual characteristics required for both the study and the practice of medicine.

The Admissions Committee considers all aspects of a prospective student's application in the decision-making process. The selection criteria for admission are weighted as one third for the Medical College Admission Test score and grade-point average, one third for letters of recommendation and work/volunteer experiences, and one third for interviews and personal attributes.

COSTS AND FINANCIAL AID

Financial aid phone number: **(803) 733-3135**
Tuition, 2003-2004 academic year: **In-state: $16,950; Out-of-state: $48,920**
Room and board: **$10,050**
Percentage of students receiving financial aid in 2003-04: **93%**

Percentage of students receiving: Loans: **90%**, Grants/scholarships: **55%**, Work-study aid: **0%**
Average medical school debt for the Class of 2002: **$72,728**

STUDENT BODY

Fall 2003 full-time enrollment: **297**
Men: **53%**, Women: **47%**, In-state: **95%**, Minorities: **20%**, American Indian: **0.0%**, Asian-American: **11.4%**, African-American: **8.1%**, Hispanic-American: **0.0%**, White: **80.5%**, International: **0.0%**, Unknown: **0.0%**

ACADEMIC PROGRAMS

The school's curriculum doesn't give first-year students substantial contact with patients.
There are opportunities for first- or second-year students to work in community health clinics.
Program offerings: family medicine, geriatrics, internal medicine, pediatrics, rural medicine
Joint degrees awarded: M.D./Ph.D., M.D./M.P.H.
Total National Institutes of Health (NIH) grants awarded to the medical school and affiliated hospitals: **$4.6 million**

CURRICULUM

(TEXT PROVIDED BY SCHOOL):
Basic sciences: During the first two years of medical education, students study a core curriculum of basic sciences and clinical disciplines necessary for an understanding of the structure and function of human systems. During Year 1, students gain a basic understanding of normal structure, function, and development. During Year 2, emphasis is placed on pathology and general therapeutic principles. Throughout the first two years, clinical correlations to basic science material are integral components of the curriculum, as is the four-semester Introduction to Clinical Medicine course continuum. Interdisciplinary material on nutrition, substance abuse, human values, genetics, and geriatrics is also presented in vertical curricula over four years. The Introduction to Clinical Medicine course and correlations provide students with the background and skills to prepare them for clinical clerkships in the third and fourth years. Introduction to Clinical Medicine courses also emphasize active, independent, and cooperative learning in a small-group format and include components devoted to problem-based learning.

Clinical clerkships: Clerkship experiences in the third year include rotations of eight weeks each in medicine, surgery, obstetrics and gynecology, psychiatry, family medicine, and pediatrics. Year 4 includes required rotations of four weeks each in neurology, surgery, medicine, and an acting internship. Also required is "capstone month," a multidisciplinary four-week rotation that concludes the process of undergraduate medical education and prepares students for the transition to residency training and clinical practice. The remainder of the fourth year is devoted to a selective/elective program, which allows for flexibility and the pursuit of individual interests. Students actively participate in the clinical setting, where emphasis is placed on the correlation of basic science and clinical material. This correlation is further nurtured by small tutorial seminars, lectures, and group discussions.

FACULTY PROFILE (FALL 2003)

Total teaching faculty: **216 (full-time)**, **15 (part-time)**
Of full-time faculty, those teaching in basic sciences: **25%**; in clinical programs: **75%**
Of part-time faculty, those teaching in basic sciences: **13%**; in clinical programs: **87%**
Full-time faculty/student ratio: **0.7**

SUPPORT SERVICES

The school offers students these services for dealing with stress: professional counseling.

RESIDENCY CHOICES

Most popular residency and specialty programs chosen by the 2002 and 2003 M.D. graduating classes: emergency medicine, family practice, internal medicine, obstetrics and gynecology, orthopedic surgery, pediatrics, psychiatry, radiology–diagnostic, surgery–general, transitional year.

WHERE GRADS GO

51.0%
Proportion of 2001-2003 graduates who entered primary care specialties

40.6%
Proportion of 2002-2003 graduates who accepted in-state residencies

University of South Dakota

- 1400 W. 22nd Street, Sioux Falls, SD 57105
- Public
- Year Founded: 1907
- Tuition, 2003-2004: In-state: $17,697; Out-of-state: $35,136
- Enrollment, 2003-2004: 206
- Website: http://med.usd.edu/md
- Specialty ranking: rural medicine: 10

3.62 AVERAGE GPA, ENTERING CLASS FALL 2003

8.9 AVERAGE MCAT, ENTERING CLASS FALL 2003

16.9% ACCEPTANCE RATE, ENTERING CLASS FALL 2003

Unranked 2005 U.S.NEWS MEDICAL SCHOOL RANKING (RESEARCH)

Unranked 2005 U.S.NEWS MEDICAL SCHOOL RANKING (PRIMARY CARE)

ADMISSIONS

Admissions phone number: **(605) 677-6886**
Admissions email address: **usdsmsa@usd.edu**
Application website: **N/A**
Acceptance rate: **16.9%**
In-state acceptance rate: **54.7%**
Out-of-state acceptance rate: **4.1%**
Minority acceptance rate: **6.2%**
International acceptance rate: **N/A**

Fall 2003 applications and acceptees

	Applied	Interviewed	Accepted	Enrolled
Total:	421	117	71	50
In-state:	106	97	58	44
Out-of-state:	315	20	13	6

Profile of admitted students

Average undergraduate grade point average: **3.62**
MCAT averages (scale: 1-15; writing test: J-T):
  Composite score: **8.9**
  Verbal reasoning score: **9.2**, Physical sciences score: **8.6**, Biological sciences score: **8.8**, Writing score: **O**
Proportion with undergraduate majors in: Biological sciences: **73%**, Physical sciences: **7%**, Non-sciences: **7%**, Other health professions: **0%**, Mixed disciplines and other: **13%**
Percentage of students not coming directly from college after graduation: **44%**

Dates and details

The American Medical College Application Service (AMCAS) application is accepted.
School asks for a school-specific application as part of the admissions process.
Oldest MCAT considered for Fall 2005 entry: **2002**
Earliest application date for the 2005-2006 first-year class: **June 1, 2004**
Latest application date: **November 15, 2004**
Acceptance dates for regular application for the class entering in fall 2005:
  Earliest: **December 10, 2004**

Latest: **March 31, 2005**
The school considers requests for deferred entrance.
Starting month for the class entering in 2005-2006:
  August
The school doesn't have an Early Decision Plan (EDP).
A personal interview is required for admission.

Undergraduate coursework required

Medical school requires undergraduate work in these subjects: biology, organic chemistry, inorganic (general) chemistry, physics, mathematics.

ADMISSIONS POLICY

(TEXT PROVIDED BY SCHOOL):

Only applicants who have earned at least 64 semester credits of college coursework will be considered for admission. Prior to acceptance, applicants must have taken the Medical College Admission Test (MCAT). Prior to matriculation, applicants must have submitted transcripts of all college credits earned, indicating at least 90 semester credit hours or, preferably, a baccalaureate degree from an accredited institution.

In preparation for medical school, students are strongly encouraged to obtain a broad background in the natural and social sciences and the humanities; in addition, good oral and written communication skills are considered essential. However, selection of majors and other coursework at the baccalaureate level should be on the basis of the student's own interest. No single field is given preference in the selection process. The School of Medicine expects courses in English (especially literature and composition), the social and behavioral sciences, and the humanities to be included in the requirement for completion of the baccalaureate degree.

In addition, the faculty of the School of Medicine requires that students preparing for admission to the school obtain appropriate background (usually one year each), including laboratory experience, in the following areas: biology, general (inorganic) chemistry, organic chemistry, mathematics, and physics. If Advanced Placement or College Level Examination Program credits are on the college transcript, these may be accepted as a fulfillment of a pre-requisite providing that there is evidence of proficiency in the subject. Examples of proficiency may be successful completion of a more advanced course in that field or a strong MCAT score. Required courses should be the same as those required of majors in each area. Correspondence courses are not considered acceptable substitutes.

All residents of South Dakota are offered an interview, and a select few applicants with strong ties to the state are also invited to interview. Transfers may be considered from students who are currently in good standing at a Liaison Committee on Medical Education-accredited medical school.

COSTS AND FINANCIAL AID

Financial aid phone number: **(605) 677-5112**
Tuition, 2003-2004 academic year: **In-state: $17,697; Out-of-state: $35,136**
Room and board: **$16,480**
Percentage of students receiving financial aid in 2003-04: 98%
Percentage of students receiving: Loans: **91%**, Grants/scholarships: **67%**, Work-study aid: **0%**
Average medical school debt for the Class of 2002: **$103,442**

STUDENT BODY

Fall 2003 full-time enrollment: 206
Men: 57%, Women: 43%, In-state: 98%, Minorities: 4%, American Indian: 2.4%, Asian-American: 1.5%, African-American: 0.0%, Hispanic-American: 0.0%, White: 94.7%, International: 0.0%, Unknown: 1.5%

ACADEMIC PROGRAMS

The school's curriculum gives first-year students substantial contact with patients.
There are opportunities for first- or second-year students to work in community health clinics.
Program offerings: AIDS, drug/alcohol abuse, family medicine, geriatrics, internal medicine, pediatrics, rural medicine
Joint degrees awarded: N/A
Total National Institutes of Health (NIH) grants awarded to the medical school and affiliated hospitals: **$8.5 million**

CURRICULUM

(TEXT PROVIDED BY SCHOOL):
A thorough knowledge of the basic biomedical sciences is emphasized during the first two years. These include anatomy, biochemistry, histology, neuroscience, physiology, microbiology, pharmacology, and pathology. In addition, the students receive clinical instruction in courses called Introduction to Clinical Medicine that are taught throughout both years. The second year is capped with a one-month family medicine preceptorship.

The junior year in Sioux Falls or Rapid City consists of six major clerkships taught in pairs during three blocks of 16 weeks: family medicine and internal medicine, surgery and psychiatry, obstetrics/gynecology and pediatrics. The junior year in Yankton is ambulatory based, emphasizing continuity of care, and students rotate through all clerkships for the entire year.

Clerkships in emergency medicine, family medicine, and several surgery subspecialties are required in the senior year, with a variety of other clerkships available on an elective basis. Primary-care medicine is emphasized in all four years of the curriculum. Longitudinal, ambulatory care clinical experience is part of the curriculum at all three clinical training sites.

FACULTY PROFILE (FALL 2003)

Total teaching faculty: **206 (full-time), 603 (part-time)**
Of full-time faculty, those teaching in basic sciences: **16%**; in clinical programs: **84%**
Of part-time faculty, those teaching in basic sciences: **0%**; in clinical programs: **100%**
Full-time faculty/student ratio: **1.0**

SUPPORT SERVICES

The school offers students these services for dealing with stress: professional counseling.

RESIDENCY CHOICES

Most popular residency and specialty programs chosen by the 2002 and 2003 M.D. graduating classes: anesthesiology, emergency medicine, family practice, internal medicine, obstetrics and gynecology, pediatrics, psychiatry, radiology–diagnostic, surgery–general, transitional year.

WHERE GRADS GO

42.3%
Proportion of 2001-2003 graduates who entered primary care specialties

31.0%
Proportion of 2002-2003 graduates who accepted in-state residencies

University of Southern California

KECK SCHOOL OF MEDICINE

- 1975 Zonal Avenue, KAM 500, Los Angeles, CA 90033
- Private
- Year Founded: 1895
- Tuition, 2003-2004: $37,076
- Enrollment, 2003-2004: 660
- Website: http://www.usc.edu/keck
- Specialty ranking: N/A

3.62	AVERAGE GPA, ENTERING CLASS FALL 2003
10.8	AVERAGE MCAT, ENTERING CLASS FALL 2003
7.9%	ACCEPTANCE RATE, ENTERING CLASS FALL 2003
32	2005 U.S.NEWS MEDICAL SCHOOL RANKING (RESEARCH)
46	2005 U.S.NEWS MEDICAL SCHOOL RANKING (PRIMARY CARE)

ADMISSIONS

Admissions phone number: **(323) 442-2552**
Admissions email address: **medadmit@hsc.usc.edu**
Application website: **N/A**
Acceptance rate: **7.9%**
In-state acceptance rate: **9.9%**
Out-of-state acceptance rate: **4.6%**
Minority acceptance rate: **6.9%**
International acceptance rate: **3.2%**

Fall 2003 applications and acceptees

	Applied	Interviewed	Accepted	Enrolled
Total:	4,656	526	370	160
In-state:	2,924	388	290	131
Out-of-state:	1,732	138	80	29

Profile of admitted students

Average undergraduate grade point average: **3.62**
MCAT averages (scale: 1-15; writing test: J-T):
    Composite score: **10.8**
    Verbal reasoning score: **10.1**, Physical sciences score: **11.0**, Biological sciences score: **11.3**, Writing score: **P**
Proportion with undergraduate majors in: Biological sciences: **59%**, Physical sciences: **24%**, Non-sciences: **11%**, Other health professions: **1%**, Mixed disciplines and other: **5%**
Percentage of students not coming directly from college after graduation: **59%**

Dates and details

The American Medical College Application Service (AMCAS) application is accepted.
School asks for a school-specific application as part of the admissions process.
Oldest MCAT considered for Fall 2005 entry: **2002**
Earliest application date for the 2005-2006 first-year class: **June 15, 2004**
Latest application date: **November 1, 2004**
Acceptance dates for regular application for the class entering in fall 2005:
    Earliest: **October 15, 2004**

Latest: **August 20, 2005**
The school considers requests for deferred entrance.
Starting month for the class entering in 2005-2006:
    August
The school has an Early Decision Plan (EDP).
A personal interview is required for admission.

Undergraduate coursework required

Medical school requires undergraduate work in these subjects: biology, organic chemistry, inorganic (general) chemistry, physics, molecular and cell biology, biochemistry, humanities, social sciences, general chemistry.

ADMISSIONS POLICY

(TEXT PROVIDED BY SCHOOL):

The Keck School of Medicine of the University of Southern California's Admissions Committee is committed to recruiting a diverse group of accomplished and promising students to its M.D. programs through its unique admissions process, which has earned the school recognition as a 'model medical school' from the American Medical Student Association.

Each year there are many more qualified candidates than there are positions available. For example, more than 4,400 individuals applied for the 160 positions in the 2002 entering class. The B.A./M.D. and early-decision programs provide additional options for those interested in earning medical degrees.

Undergraduate students must meet course requirements and take the Medical College Admission Test well before the application process begins. In general, applications must be received between June 1 and November 1 for admission in August of the following year.

All applicants to the M.D. program must have completed a minimum of four full years or 120 semester hours of academic work at an accredited college or university at the time of matriculation. Applicants are strongly encouraged to have their basic science requirements completed at the time of application.

The Admissions Committee views the personal attributes of each medical school applicant holistically. The following factors influence admission decisions: college grade-point average; MCAT scores; personal characteristics, such as communication skills, compassion, and empathy; history of leadership, civic service, and commitment to social justice; and interest in teaching, research, or providing patient care to underserved populations.

The Keck School encourages applications from all qualified students. USC does not discriminate against students or applicants for admission on the basis of race, color, ancestry, religion, sexual orientation, national origin, age, marital status, or status as a disabled veteran. An otherwise qualified individual shall not be excluded solely by reason of his or her physical handicap or medical condition.

COSTS AND FINANCIAL AID

Financial aid phone number: (323) 442-1016
Tuition, 2003-2004 academic year: $37,076
Room and board: $9,802
Percentage of students receiving financial aid in 2003-04: 88%
Percentage of students receiving: Loans: 87%, Grants/scholarships: 37%, Work-study aid: 0%
Average medical school debt for the Class of 2002: $109,300

STUDENT BODY

Fall 2003 full-time enrollment: 660
Men: 54%, Women: 46%, In-state: 85%, Minorities: 48%, American Indian: 0.8%, Asian-American: 33.2%, African-American: 4.8%, Hispanic-American: 9.2%, White: 46.5%, International: 2.0%, Unknown: 3.5%

ACADEMIC PROGRAMS

The school's curriculum gives first-year students substantial contact with patients.
There are opportunities for first- or second-year students to work in community health clinics.
Program offerings: AIDS, drug/alcohol abuse, family medicine, geriatrics, internal medicine, pediatrics, rural medicine, women's health
Joint degrees awarded: M.D./Ph.D., M.D./M.B.A., M.D./M.P.H., M.D./M.S.W., M.D./M.S., M.D./M.H.A.
Total National Institutes of Health (NIH) grants awarded to the medical school and affiliated hospitals: $166.4 million

CURRICULUM

(TEXT PROVIDED BY SCHOOL):
The Keck School of Medicine launched a major revision of its four-year curriculum in 2001, and the class of 2005 will be the first to complete this entirely new course of study. The new curriculum is designed to enhance students' understanding of the basic sciences and their relevance to clinical medicine. New educational methodology improves students' problem-solving and independent study skills.

In years 1 and 2 of the new curriculum, the teaching and learning of basic and clinical sciences are fully integrated. The curriculum begins with 19 weeks of Core Principles of Health and Disease, followed by 49 weeks of organ system study, and ending with a nine-week integrated case study section. Cadaver dissection remains a teaching tool.

Systems, such as the cardiovascular system, are presented in a case-centered format with the integration of small-group learning sessions. The curriculum is also organized around a new student "practice profile," a series of patient cases representing an idealized general clinical practice. In Professionalism and the Practice of Medicine, students meet weekly with faculty mentors in small groups. The second year concludes with the integrated cases section, in which students in small groups study more-complex cases.

The Introduction to Clinical Medicine program expresses the curriculum's strongly patient-centered orientation. Students are involved in patient care from Day 1. Throughout the first two years, students interact with patients at the Los Angeles County/USC Medical Center and other hospitals. A group of five or six students spends from four to eight hours each week with an instructor from the clinical faculty, who remains with the group for one to two years.

During the required third- and fourth-year clerkships, the students' assumption of clinical responsibility increases. In the fourth-year Internal Medicine II clerkship, students are assigned responsibility equivalent to that of first-year graduate residents.

FACULTY PROFILE (FALL 2003)

Total teaching faculty: 1,190 (full-time), 34 (part-time)
Of full-time faculty, those teaching in basic sciences: 11%; in clinical programs: 89%
Of part-time faculty, those teaching in basic sciences: 9%; in clinical programs: 91%
Full-time faculty/student ratio: 1.8

SUPPORT SERVICES

The school offers students these services for dealing with stress: expanded-hour gym access, peer counseling, professional counseling, religious support, support groups.

RESIDENCY CHOICES

Most popular residency and specialty programs chosen by the 2002 and 2003 M.D. graduating classes: emergency medicine, internal medicine, neurology, obstetrics and gynecology, orthopedic surgery, pediatrics, psychiatry, radiology–diagnostic, surgery–general, transitional year.

WHERE GRADS GO

49.0%
Proportion of 2001-2003 graduates who entered primary care specialties

87.0%
Proportion of 2002-2003 graduates who accepted in-state residencies

University of South Florida

- 12901 Bruce B. Downs Boulevard, Box 3, Tampa, FL 33612
- Public
- **Year Founded:** 1965
- **Tuition, 2003-2004:** In-state: $15,705; Out-of-state: $44,955
- **Enrollment, 2003-2004:** 416
- **Website:** http://www.hsc.usf.edu/medicine
- **Specialty ranking:** N/A

3.66	AVERAGE GPA, ENTERING CLASS FALL 2003
9.8	AVERAGE MCAT, ENTERING CLASS FALL 2003
7.3%	ACCEPTANCE RATE, ENTERING CLASS FALL 2003
Unranked	2005 U.S.NEWS MEDICAL SCHOOL RANKING (RESEARCH)
Unranked	2005 U.S.NEWS MEDICAL SCHOOL RANKING (PRIMARY CARE)

ADMISSIONS

Admissions phone number: **(813) 974-2229**
Admissions email address: **md-admissions
 @lyris.hsc.usf.edu**
Application website: **N/A**
Acceptance rate: **7.3%**
In-state acceptance rate: **9.3%**
Out-of-state acceptance rate: **0.0%**
Minority acceptance rate: **7.6%**
International acceptance rate: **N/A**

Fall 2003 applications and acceptees

	Applied	Interviewed	Accepted	Enrolled
Total:	1,585	361	115	115
In-state:	1,239	361	115	115
Out-of-state:	346	0	0	0

Profile of admitted students

Average undergraduate grade point average: **3.66**
MCAT averages (scale: 1-15; writing test: J-T):
 Composite score: **9.8**
 Verbal reasoning score: **9.6**, Physical sciences score: **9.9**,
 Biological sciences score: **10.1**, Writing score: **N/A**

Dates and details

The American Medical College Application Service
 (AMCAS) application is accepted.
School asks for a school-specific application as part of the
 admissions process.
Oldest MCAT considered for Fall 2005 entry: **N/A**
Earliest application date for the 2005-2006 first-year class:
 June 1, 2004
Latest application date: **December 1, 2004**
Acceptance dates for regular application for the class
 entering in fall 2005:
 Earliest: **N/A**
 Latest: **N/A**
The school considers requests for deferred entrance.
Starting month for the class entering in 2005-2006:
 August
The school has an Early Decision Plan (EDP).

A personal interview is required for admission.

Undergraduate coursework required

Medical school requires undergraduate work in these subjects: biology, English, organic chemistry, inorganic (general) chemistry, physics, mathematics, general chemistry.

ADMISSIONS POLICY
(TEXT PROVIDED BY SCHOOL):

The school traditionally accepts Florida students only, but
we are now able to take a limited number of superior, out-
of-state applicants.

COSTS AND FINANCIAL AID

Financial aid phone number: **(813) 974-2068**
Tuition, 2003-2004 academic year: **In-state: $15,705; Out-
 of-state: $44,955**
Room and board: **$8,690**
Percentage of students receiving financial aid in 2003-04:
 85%
Percentage of students receiving: Loans: **80%**,
 Grants/scholarships: **40%**, Work-study aid: **0%**
Average medical school debt for the Class of 2002:
 $84,776

STUDENT BODY

Fall 2003 full-time enrollment: **416**
Men: **53%**, Women: **47%**, In-state: **100%**, Minorities: **32%**,
 American Indian: **2.2%**, Asian-American: **15.5%**,
 African-American: **6.0%**, Hispanic-American: **8.5%**,
 White: **67.9%**, International: **N/A**, Unknown: **0.0%**

ACADEMIC PROGRAMS

The school's curriculum gives first-year students
 substantial contact with patients.
There are opportunities for first- or second-year students to
 work in community health clinics.
Program offerings: AIDS, drug/alcohol abuse, family
 medicine, geriatrics, internal medicine, pediatrics, rural
 medicine, women's health
Joint degrees awarded: M.D./Ph.D., M.D./M.P.H.

Total National Institutes of Health (NIH) grants awarded to the medical school and affiliated hospitals: **$30.9 million**

CURRICULUM
(TEXT PROVIDED BY SCHOOL):
The curriculum is highly integrated with clinical care, skills testing, and medical professionalism.

FACULTY PROFILE (FALL 2003)
Total teaching faculty: **493 (full-time)**, **35 (part-time)**
Of full-time faculty, those teaching in basic sciences: **29%**; in clinical programs: **71%**
Of part-time faculty, those teaching in basic sciences: **23%**; in clinical programs: **77%**
Full-time faculty/student ratio: **1.2**

SUPPORT SERVICES
The school offers students these services for dealing with stress: professional counseling, support groups.

RESIDENCY CHOICES
Most popular residency and specialty programs chosen by the 2002 and 2003 M.D. graduating classes: anesthesiology, family practice, internal medicine, obstetrics and gynecology, ophthalmology, pathology–anatomic and clinical, pediatrics, psychiatry, radiology–diagnostic, surgery–general.

WHERE GRADS GO

36.4%
Proportion of 2001-2003 graduates who entered primary care specialties

46.4%
Proportion of 2002-2003 graduates who accepted in-state residencies

University of Texas

HEALTH SCIENCE CENTER–HOUSTON

- 6431 Fannin, MSB 1.126, Houston, TX 77030
- Public
- Year Founded: 1969
- Tuition, 2003-2004: In-state: $9,480; Out-of-state: $22,580
- Enrollment, 2003-2004: 837
- Website: http://www.med.uth.tmc.edu
- Specialty ranking: N/A

3.64 AVERAGE GPA, ENTERING CLASS FALL 2003

9.6 AVERAGE MCAT, ENTERING CLASS FALL 2003

9.4% ACCEPTANCE RATE, ENTERING CLASS FALL 2003

53 2005 U.S.NEWS MEDICAL SCHOOL RANKING (RESEARCH)

Unranked 2005 U.S.NEWS MEDICAL SCHOOL RANKING (PRIMARY CARE)

ADMISSIONS

Admissions phone number: **(713) 500-5116**
Admissions email address: **msadmissions@uth.tmc.edu**
Application website: **http://www.utsystem.edu/tmdsas**
Acceptance rate: **9.4%**
In-state acceptance rate: **10.1%**
Out-of-state acceptance rate: **5.0%**
Minority acceptance rate: **6.1%**
International acceptance rate: **9.7%**

Fall 2003 applications and acceptees

	Applied	Interviewed	Accepted	Enrolled
Total:	2,756	1,140	260	202
In-state:	2,378	1,090	241	194
Out-of-state:	378	50	19	8

Profile of admitted students

Average undergraduate grade point average: **3.64**
MCAT averages (scale: 1-15; writing test: J-T):
  Composite score: **9.6**
  Verbal reasoning score: **9.5**, Physical sciences score: **9.5**,
  Biological sciences score: **9.7**, Writing score: **P**
Percentage of students not coming directly from college
  after graduation: **N/A**

Dates and details

The American Medical College Application Service
  (AMCAS) application is not accepted.
School asks for a school-specific application as part of the
  admissions process.
Oldest MCAT considered for Fall 2005 entry: **2000**
Earliest application date for the 2005-2006 first-year class:
  May 1, 2004
Latest application date: **November 1, 2004**
Acceptance dates for regular application for the class
  entering in fall 2005:
  Earliest: **February 1, 2005**
  Latest: **August 18, 2005**
The school doesn't consider requests for deferred entrance.
Starting month for the class entering in 2005-2006:
  August

The school doesn't have an Early Decision Plan (EDP).
A personal interview is required for admission.

Undergraduate coursework required

Medical school requires undergraduate work in these subjects: biology, English, organic chemistry, inorganic (general) chemistry, physics, calculus.

ADMISSIONS POLICY
(TEXT PROVIDED BY SCHOOL):

The UTHSC-H Medical School, in conformity with the purpose assigned it by the Texas Legislature and its mission statement, selects the best-qualified students for its entering class who demonstrate a potential to become competent and caring physicians and who will serve the needs of the state of Texas. The Admissions Committee considers the totality of each application and gives importance to these factors: intellectual capacity, interpersonal and communication skills, breadth and depth of premedical educational experience, potential for service to the state of Texas, motivation, and integrity.

Evidence of scholarly interest and achievement in some branch of academic endeavor must be demonstrated. A liberal arts education is an excellent basis for a medical career. Accordingly, applicants may have majored in such areas as classics, languages, history, English literature, belles-lettres, music, or philosophy, provided the specific scientific requirements listed below are fulfilled. Because the study of medicine is based upon science, majors in the scientific disciplines are satisfactory. Technological, vocational (e.g., pharmacy), engineering, or business courses of study are not viewed as favorably as those providing a broad educational background.

Students must complete at least 90 undergraduate credit hours at a U.S. or Canadian university, including the following specific premedical credits: English (one year); biology (two years, as required of science majors and including lab); mathematics (one half year of college calculus); physics (one year, as required of science majors and including lab); and chemistry (one year of general chemistry and one year of organic chemistry, both as required of science majors and including lab).

Although the minimum requirement for admission is 90 undergraduate semester hours, preference is given to students who obtain a baccalaureate degree prior to admission to medical school.

The medical and dental schools of the University of Texas System are authorized to accept only a limited number of non-Texas residents. Nonresident students who do not have outstanding qualifications and students who have been dismissed or who have withdrawn from a medical school are not encouraged to apply. Application is made through the Texas Medical and Dental Schools Application Service.

COSTS AND FINANCIAL AID

Financial aid phone number: **(713) 500-3860**
Tuition, 2003-2004 academic year: **In-state: $9,480; Out-of-state: $22,580**
Room and board: **$12,410**
Percentage of students receiving financial aid in 2003-04: **92%**
Percentage of students receiving: Loans: **92%**, Grants/scholarships: **40%**, Work-study aid: **0%**
Average medical school debt for the Class of 2002: **$73,975**

STUDENT BODY

Fall 2003 full-time enrollment: **837**
Men: **52%**, Women: **48%**, In-state: **96%**, Minorities: **28%**, American Indian: **0.4%**, Asian-American: **11.9%**, African-American: **3.0%**, Hispanic-American: **13.0%**, White: **69.7%**, International: **0.4%**, Unknown: **1.7%**

ACADEMIC PROGRAMS

The school's curriculum gives first-year students substantial contact with patients.
There are opportunities for first- or second-year students to work in community health clinics.
Program offerings: AIDS, family medicine, geriatrics, internal medicine, pediatrics, rural medicine, women's health
Joint degrees awarded: M.D./Ph.D., M.D./M.P.H.
Total National Institutes of Health (NIH) grants awarded to the medical school and affiliated hospitals: **$60.5 million**

CURRICULUM

(TEXT PROVIDED BY SCHOOL):
The basic four-year program outlined below is required for the M.D. degree. Variations and adjustments may be made as the Curriculum Committee deems necessary.

Basic sciences: The first academic year includes 18 weeks of required courses in the fall semester, including biochemistry, developmental anatomy, gross anatomy, histology, and introduction to clinical medicine (which is continued in the spring semester). The 19-week spring term also includes immunology, microbiology, neuroscience, and physiology.

Year 2 also is divided into an 18-week fall semester and a 19-week spring semester. Required courses include behavioral sciences, genetics, fundamentals of clinical medicine (with problem-based learning), pathology, physical diagnosis, reproductive biology, radiology (one week), and technical skills.

Clinical sciences: The third academic year begins the first week of July and lasts 48 weeks. It is divided into two 24-week rotation periods with four weeks of vacation. Required clerkships include medicine (12 weeks), obstetrics/gynecology (eight weeks), pediatrics (eight weeks), psychiatry (eight weeks), surgery (eight weeks), and family practice (four weeks). Year 4 begins in July and lasts 11 months. It includes required clerkships in family practice, medicine, neurology, and surgery; a minimum of five one-month electives; and two months for vacation or additional electives.

The Medical School's elective and preceptorship programs in the fourth year permit students to seek clinical opportunities away from Houston, ranging from family practice in rural communities to experiences in the most sophisticated settings requiring advanced technology. International clinical and research electives also are available. The school is fortunate regarding the wealth of clinical opportunities available to its students.

FACULTY PROFILE (FALL 2003)

Total teaching faculty: **807 (full-time)**, **123 (part-time)**
Of full-time faculty, those teaching in basic sciences: **12%**; in clinical programs: **88%**
Of part-time faculty, those teaching in basic sciences: **2%**; in clinical programs: **98%**
Full-time faculty/student ratio: **1.0**

SUPPORT SERVICES

The school offers students these services for dealing with stress: expanded-hour gym access, peer counseling, professional counseling, religious support, support groups.

RESIDENCY CHOICES

Most popular residency and specialty programs chosen by the 2002 and 2003 M.D. graduating classes: anesthesiology, emergency medicine, family practice, internal medicine, obstetrics and gynecology, orthopedic surgery, pediatrics, radiology–diagnostic, surgery–general, internal medicine/pediatrics.

WHERE GRADS GO

37.8%
Proportion of 2001-2003 graduates who entered primary care specialties

52.7%
Proportion of 2002-2003 graduates who accepted in-state residencies

Univ. of Texas Medical Branch—Galveston

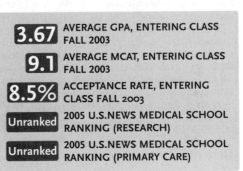

- 301 University Boulevard, Galveston, TX 77555-0133
- Public
- Year Founded: N/A
- Tuition, 2003-2004: In-state: $8,076; Out-of-state: $21,176
- Enrollment, 2003-2004: 820
- Website: http://www.utmb.edu
- Specialty ranking: N/A

3.67 AVERAGE GPA, ENTERING CLASS FALL 2003

9.1 AVERAGE MCAT, ENTERING CLASS FALL 2003

8.5% ACCEPTANCE RATE, ENTERING CLASS FALL 2003

Unranked 2005 U.S.NEWS MEDICAL SCHOOL RANKING (RESEARCH)

Unranked 2005 U.S.NEWS MEDICAL SCHOOL RANKING (PRIMARY CARE)

ADMISSIONS

Admissions phone number: **(409) 772-3517**
Admissions email address: **lauthoma@utmb.edu**
Application website:
   https://www2.utmb.edu/utmbapp/app_options.htm
Acceptance rate: **8.5%**
In-state acceptance rate: **9.0%**
Out-of-state acceptance rate: **4.9%**
Minority acceptance rate: **8.2%**
International acceptance rate: **3.8%**

Fall 2003 applications and acceptees

	Applied	Interviewed	Accepted	Enrolled
Total:	2,707	981	231	205
In-state:	2,378	876	215	195
Out-of-state:	329	105	16	10

Profile of admitted students

Average undergraduate grade point average: **3.67**
MCAT averages (scale: 1-15; writing test: J-T):
   Composite score: **9.1**
   Verbal reasoning score: **8.7**, Physical sciences score: **9.1**,
   Biological sciences score: **9.5**, Writing score: **N/A**
Proportion with undergraduate majors in: Biological
   sciences: **57%**, Physical sciences: **16%**, Non-sciences:
   10%, Other health professions: **2%**, Mixed disciplines
   and other: **15%**
Percentage of students not coming directly from college
   after graduation: **N/A**

Dates and details

The American Medical College Application Service
   (AMCAS) application is not accepted.
School does not ask for a school-specific application as part
   of the admissions process.
Oldest MCAT considered for Fall 2005 entry: **2001**
Earliest application date for the 2005-2006 first-year class:
   May 1, 2004
Latest application date: **November 1, 2004**
Acceptance dates for regular application for the class
   entering in fall 2005:

Earliest: **February 1, 2005**
Latest: **August 23, 2005**
The school considers requests for deferred entrance.
Starting month for the class entering in 2005-2006: **N/A**
The school doesn't have an Early Decision Plan (EDP).
A personal interview is required for admission.

Undergraduate coursework required

Medical school requires undergraduate work in these subjects: biology, English, organic chemistry, inorganic (general) chemistry, physics, calculus, general chemistry.

COSTS AND FINANCIAL AID

Financial aid phone number: **(409) 772-4955**
Tuition, 2003-2004 academic year: **In-state: $8,076; Out-
   of-state: $21,176**
Room and board: **N/A**
Percentage of students receiving financial aid in 2003-04:
   83%
Percentage of students receiving: Loans: **81%**,
   Grants/scholarships: **34%**, Work-study aid: **5%**
Average medical school debt for the Class of 2002: **$77,525**

STUDENT BODY

Fall 2003 full-time enrollment: **820**
Men: **52%**, Women: **48%**, In-state: **95%**, Minorities: **42%**,
   American Indian: **0.4%**, Asian-American: **17.3%**,
   African-American: **7.6%**, Hispanic-American: **16.8%**,
   White: **53.7%**, International: **0.6%**, Unknown: **3.7%**

ACADEMIC PROGRAMS

The school's curriculum gives first-year students
   substantial contact with patients.
There are opportunities for first- or second-year students to
   work in community health clinics.
Program offerings: family medicine, geriatrics, internal
   medicine, pediatrics, rural medicine, women's health
Joint degrees awarded: M.D./Ph.D.
Total National Institutes of Health (NIH) grants awarded to
   the medical school and affiliated hospitals: **N/A**

CURRICULUM

(TEXT PROVIDED BY SCHOOL):

The University of Texas Medical Branch School of Medicine, oldest in the state of Texas, has as its mission to provide innovative teaching, scholarly scientific investigation, and state-of-the-art patient care in a learning environment to better the health of Texas. UTMB is the alma mater of more physicians practicing in the state than any other medical school. Its role as a referral hospital for many counties throughout the state provides unparalleled depth and breadth of clinical experiences for UTMB students.

The Integrated Medical Curriculum (IMC) is a four-year program that emphasizes continuous integration of basic medical sciences with clinical medicine, early clinical skills and clinical experiences, and professionalism. UTMB instituted the first half of the IMC in 1998. In this student-centered curriculum, which utilizes small-group, problem-based learning, computer-assisted instruction, lectures, and labs, the basic medical sciences are learned in clinical contexts. Beyond knowledge acquisition, the IMC emphasizes the development of skills in problem solving, clinical data gathering and decision making, independent study, and lifelong learning. Its organ-system-based approach and clinical science contexts promote basic science integration across disciplines. Performance of UTMB students on the National Board of Medical Examiners Step 1 exam speaks to their mastery of basic science: a 96 percent pass rate and mean score of 223, both well above national averages.

Through all four years of the IMC, there is a heavy emphasis on the acquisition and refinement of clinical skills. Students work with standardized patients, or SPs, lay people trained to portray patients, beginning the first week of medical school to learn medical interview and physical examination techniques. Following this rapid development of fundamental skills, students begin seeing patients in physicians' offices in the fall of their first year. They continue to participate in progressively more advanced clinical experiences on and off campus during the first two years. Learning and assessment exercises with SPs continue through all four years. UTMB students participate in eight graded and numerous ungraded SP exercises during the curriculum—far more than most medical schools—giving students ample preparation and practice for the new SP-based Clinical Skills Examination that is now required for medical licensure in all 50 states. The increasing use of technology-based medical simulations and the development of new simulators here provide UTMB students with a truly state-of-the-art medical education.

The third and fourth years of the IMC, revised in 2003, are centered on ambulatory and inpatient experiences in emergency medicine, family medicine, internal medicine, neurology, obstetrics/gynecology, pediatrics, psychiatry, and surgery. A unique feature of the third-year curriculum is an elective month, which allows students to expand their experience in a primary-care field or to explore potential career interests in a medical specialty before beginning the residency application process early in their fourth year. The fourth year also includes an acting internship, community-based ambulatory medicine, and a scholarly project in which a basic science or medical humanities topic is explored in depth.

Because of their large referral base, the UTMB hospitals and clinics treat large numbers of patients with a remarkable range of conditions. Additional opportunities exist for off-campus experiences. A growing collaboration with Brackenridge Hospital in Austin provides many third- and fourth-year students the option to take some or all of their required rotations in the Austin area. An extensive network of international relationships, stemming from UTMB students' past experiences and the institution's international reputation in medical education, afford a wide variety of experiences for interested students.

FACULTY PROFILE (FALL 2003)

Total teaching faculty: **897 (full-time)**, **81 (part-time)**

Of full-time faculty, those teaching in basic sciences: **17%**; in clinical programs: **83%**

Of part-time faculty, those teaching in basic sciences: **7%**; in clinical programs: **93%**

Full-time faculty/student ratio: **1.1**

SUPPORT SERVICES

The school offers students these services for dealing with stress: expanded-hour gym access, professional counseling.

RESIDENCY CHOICES

Most popular residency and specialty programs chosen by the 2002 and 2003 M.D. graduating classes: anesthesiology, emergency medicine, family practice, internal medicine, obstetrics and gynecology, pediatrics, psychiatry, radiology–diagnostic, surgery–general, transitional year.

University of Texas

SOUTHWESTERN MEDICAL CENTER–DALLAS

- 5323 Harry Hines Boulevard, Dallas, TX 75390
- Public
- Year Founded: 1943
- Tuition, 2003-2004: In-state: $8,932; Out-of-state: $22,032
- Enrollment, 2003-2004: 869
- Website: http://www.utsouthwestern.edu
- Specialty ranking: internal medicine: 10, women's health: 15

3.75 AVERAGE GPA, ENTERING CLASS FALL 2003

10.6 AVERAGE MCAT, ENTERING CLASS FALL 2003

14.9% ACCEPTANCE RATE, ENTERING CLASS FALL 2003

17 2005 U.S.NEWS MEDICAL SCHOOL RANKING (RESEARCH)

36 2005 U.S.NEWS MEDICAL SCHOOL RANKING (PRIMARY CARE)

ADMISSIONS

Admissions phone number: **(214) 648-5617**
Admissions email address:
   admissions@utsouthwestern.edu
Application website:
   http://www.utsouthwestern.edu/medapp
Acceptance rate: **14.9%**
In-state acceptance rate: **15.6%**
Out-of-state acceptance rate: **11.0%**
Minority acceptance rate: **15.0%**
International acceptance rate: **13.9%**

Fall 2003 applications and acceptees

	Applied	Interviewed	Accepted	Enrolled
Total:	2,630	643	391	218
In-state:	2,231	574	347	195
Out-of-state:	399	69	44	23

Profile of admitted students

Average undergraduate grade point average: **3.75**
MCAT averages (scale: 1-15; writing test: J-T):
   Composite score: **10.6**
   Verbal reasoning score: **10.1**, Physical sciences score: **10.8**, Biological sciences score: **11.0**, Writing score: **P**
Proportion with undergraduate majors in: Biological sciences: **48%**, Physical sciences: **30%**, Non-sciences: **11%**, Other health professions: **1%**, Mixed disciplines and other: **10%**
Percentage of students not coming directly from college after graduation: **15%**

Dates and details

The American Medical College Application Service (AMCAS) application is not accepted.
School asks for a school-specific application as part of the admissions process.
Oldest MCAT considered for Fall 2005 entry: **2000**
Earliest application date for the 2005-2006 first-year class:
   May 1, 2004
Latest application date: **November 1, 2004**

Acceptance dates for regular application for the class entering in fall 2005:
   Earliest: **February 1, 2005**
   Latest: **August 15, 2005**
The school considers requests for deferred entrance.
Starting month for the class entering in 2005-2006:
   August
The school doesn't have an Early Decision Plan (EDP).
A personal interview is required for admission.

Undergraduate coursework required

Medical school requires undergraduate work in these subjects: biology/zoology, English, organic chemistry, inorganic (general) chemistry, physics, calculus.

ADMISSIONS POLICY
(TEXT PROVIDED BY SCHOOL):

UT Southwestern encourages application from all interested individuals. Application is made through the Texas Medical and Dental Schools Application Service between May 1 and November 1 each year for enrollment into the following year's entering class. Application to the combined M.D./Ph.D. program is made through the American Medical College Application Service.

The Admissions Committee considers all of the following in evaluating each applicant's acceptability: academic performance in college as reflected in the undergraduate grade-point average; the rigor of the undergraduate curriculum; scores from the Medical College Admission Test (MCAT); recommendation letters from the college premedical committee or faculty; research experience; extracurricular activities; socioeconomic background; any time spent in outside employment; personal integrity and compassion for others; the ability to communicate in English; other personal qualities and individual factors, such as leadership, self-appraisal, determination, social/family support, and maturity/coping capabilities; and motivation for a career in medicine.

In addition, applicants are evaluated with regard to the mission of Southwestern Medical School, which emphasizes the importance of training primary-care physicians, educating doctors who will practice in medically underserved areas of Texas, and preparing physician-scientists who seek careers in academic medicine or research.

A personal interview is required and is initiated by invitation from the Admissions Committee. The committee invites applicants to interview who have excellent academic qualifications as reflected by their GPAs and MCAT scores or who demonstrate convincing evidence of commitment to an area of medicine emphasized in the mission of Southwestern Medical School and who have an academic background that indicates the potential for success in achieving the M.D. degree. Interviews are conducted between September and mid-January each year. Applicants are notified of admission decisions on February 1.

COSTS AND FINANCIAL AID

Financial aid phone number: **(214) 648-3611**
Tuition, 2003-2004 academic year: **In-state: $8,932; Out-of-state: $22,032**
Room and board: **$17,770**
Percentage of students receiving financial aid in 2003-04: **88%**
Percentage of students receiving: Loans: **80%**, Grants/scholarships: **67%**, Work-study aid: **6%**
Average medical school debt for the Class of 2002: **$69,600**

STUDENT BODY

Fall 2003 full-time enrollment: **869**
Men: **56%**, Women: **44%**, In-state: **88%**, Minorities: **44%**, American Indian: **0.2%**, Asian-American: **26.5%**, African-American: **6.2%**, Hispanic-American: **11.0%**, White: **52.6%**, International: **0.5%**, Unknown: **3.0%**

ACADEMIC PROGRAMS

The school's curriculum gives first-year students substantial contact with patients.
There are opportunities for first- or second-year students to work in community health clinics.
Program offerings: AIDS, drug/alcohol abuse, family medicine, geriatrics, internal medicine, pediatrics, rural medicine, women's health
Joint degrees awarded: M.D./Ph.D., M.D./M.B.A., M.D./M.P.H.
Total National Institutes of Health (NIH) grants awarded to the medical school and affiliated hospitals: **N/A**

CURRICULUM

(TEXT PROVIDED BY SCHOOL):
The mission of Southwestern Medical School is to produce physicians and scientists who will be inspired to maintain lifelong medical scholarship and who will apply the knowledge gained in a responsible and humanistic manner to the care of patients.

The first year begins with a study of the normal human body and its processes. In the fall, biochemistry, genetics, and anatomy build the foundation concepts of macromolecular and cellular interactions within tissues. An introduction to clinical ethics in medicine is provided as well. The spring term is composed of interdisciplinary courses in neuroscience and physiology as well as cell biology, human behavior and psychopathology, embryology, and endocrinology. A program of preclinical electives in humanities and related topics complements the required courses. Available summer programs include research opportunities and preceptorships in family and internal medicine, pediatrics, and psychiatry. Some students continue with research experience full time as members of the Medical Scientist Training Program (M.D./Ph.D.).

The second year offers study of disease processes and the approach to affect those processes therapeutically. The material includes immunology and medical microbiology, pathology, clinical medicine, and pharmacology. Contact with patients begins early in the second year. After completion of the second year, students undertake Step 1 of the U.S. Medical Licensing Examination.

The third and fourth years offer intense clinical experiences involving the student in direct patient care. The third year offers rotations of eight weeks each in surgery and pediatrics, six weeks each in psychiatry and obstetrics, four weeks in family practice, 12 weeks in internal medicine, and a four-week flexible period. After the third year, students undertake both the clinical knowledge and clinical skills components of the USMLE.

The fourth year consists of eight individual four-week clinical rotations, including four electives and four mandatory rotations in neurology, an internal medicine subinternship, ambulatory medicine, and acute care.

FACULTY PROFILE (FALL 2003)

Total teaching faculty: **1,290 (full-time)**, **175 (part-time)**
Of full-time faculty, those teaching in basic sciences: **18%**; in clinical programs: **82%**
Of part-time faculty, those teaching in basic sciences: **5%**; in clinical programs: **95%**
Full-time faculty/student ratio: **1.5**

SUPPORT SERVICES

The school offers students these services for dealing with stress: expanded-hour gym access, professional counseling, support groups.

RESIDENCY CHOICES

Most popular residency and specialty programs chosen by the 2002 and 2003 M.D. graduating classes: anesthesiology, emergency medicine, family practice, internal medicine, obstetrics and gynecology, pediatrics, radiology–diagnostic, surgery–general.

WHERE GRADS GO

42.0%
Proportion of 2001-2003 graduates who entered primary care specialties

56.0%
Proportion of 2002-2003 graduates who accepted in-state residencies

University of Utah

■ 175 N. Medical Drive E, Salt Lake City, UT 84132-2101
■ Public
■ Year Founded: 1941
■ Tuition, 2003-2004: In-state: $13,886; Out-of-state: $25,762
■ Enrollment, 2003-2004: 410
■ Website: http://www.med.utah.edu/som
■ Specialty ranking: family medicine: 22

3.63	AVERAGE GPA, ENTERING CLASS FALL 2003
9.6	AVERAGE MCAT, ENTERING CLASS FALL 2003
12.1%	ACCEPTANCE RATE, ENTERING CLASS FALL 2003
48	2005 U.S.NEWS MEDICAL SCHOOL RANKING (RESEARCH)
31	2005 U.S.NEWS MEDICAL SCHOOL RANKING (PRIMARY CARE)

ADMISSIONS

Admissions phone number: (801) 581-7498
Admissions email address:
   deans.admissions@hsc.utah.edu
Application website: N/A
Acceptance rate: 12.1%
In-state acceptance rate: 22.9%
Out-of-state acceptance rate: 6.4%
Minority acceptance rate: 10.6%
International acceptance rate: 7.8%

Fall 2003 applications and acceptees

	Applied	Interviewed	Accepted	Enrolled
Total:	1,112	363	135	102
In-state:	388	265	89	77
Out-of-state:	724	98	46	25

Profile of admitted students

Average undergraduate grade point average: 3.63
MCAT averages (scale: 1-15; writing test: J-T):
   Composite score: 9.6
   Verbal reasoning score: 9.4, Physical sciences score: 9.4,
   Biological sciences score: 9.9, Writing score: O
Proportion with undergraduate majors in: Biological
   sciences: 48%, Physical sciences: 12%, Non-sciences:
   13%, Other health professions: 9%, Mixed disciplines
   and other: 18%
Percentage of students not coming directly from college
   after graduation: 29%

Dates and details

The American Medical College Application Service
   (AMCAS) application is accepted.
School asks for a school-specific application as part of the
   admissions process.
Oldest MCAT considered for Fall 2005 entry: 2002
Earliest application date for the 2005-2006 first-year class:
   June 1, 2004
Latest application date: November 1, 2004
Acceptance dates for regular application for the class
   entering in fall 2005:

Earliest: October 15, 2004
Latest: N/A
The school doesn't consider requests for deferred entrance.
Starting month for the class entering in 2005-2006:
   August
The school doesn't have an Early Decision Plan (EDP).
A personal interview is required for admission.

Undergraduate coursework required

Medical school requires undergraduate work in these subjects: biology, English, organic chemistry, inorganic (general) chemistry, physics, molecular and cell biology,
biochemistry, humanities, social sciences.

ADMISSIONS POLICY
(TEXT PROVIDED BY SCHOOL):

Our goal is to select the most capable students to attend our
school and to have a balanced but heterogeneous group that
will excel in both the art and sciences of medicine. A
diverse student body promotes an atmosphere of creativity,
experimentation, and discussion that is conducive to learning. Exposure to a variety of perspectives and experiences
prepares students to care for patients in all walks of life.

Considered individually, age, color, gender, sexual orientation, race, national origin, religion, status as a Vietnam or
disabled veteran, or other disability are not determinants of
diversity and are not identified as unique characteristics
during the admissions process.

We evaluate applications in the eight areas listed below.
Applicants must achieve at least the minimum level of performance in all eight areas and be average or better in five
out of the eight areas to proceed in the admissions process.

Grade-point average: Applicants with a science, nonscience, or overall GPA below 3.0 will not be considered.

Medical College Admission Test: The minimum acceptable score for each section of the MCAT examination is 7.

Physician shadowing: Applicants should spend enough
time with a physician to understand the challenges,
demands, and lifestyle of a doctor.

Patient exposure: Applicants should be comfortable working with people who are ill.

Leadership ability: Dedication, determination, ability to make decisions, and a willingness to contribute to the welfare of others are indicators of one's ability to succeed in medicine.

Extracurricular activities: How applicants deal with the demands of their lives outside of the classroom helps predict how well they may deal with stressful situations and handle the demands of medical school.

Community/volunteer service: Applicants should demonstrate a commitment to the community.

Research: Participation in research activities is important preparation for medical school.

COSTS AND FINANCIAL AID
Financial aid phone number: **(801) 581-6474**
Tuition, 2003-2004 academic year: **In-state: $13,886; Out-of-state: $25,762**
Room and board: **$8,352**
Percentage of students receiving financial aid in 2003-04: **86%**
Percentage of students receiving: Loans: **86%**, Grants/scholarships: **32%**, Work-study aid: **0%**
Average medical school debt for the Class of 2002: **$85,198**

STUDENT BODY
Fall 2003 full-time enrollment: **410**
Men: **60%**, Women: **40%**, In-state: **77%**, Minorities: **16%**

ACADEMIC PROGRAMS
The school's curriculum doesn't give first-year students substantial contact with patients.
There are opportunities for first- or second-year students to work in community health clinics.
Program offerings: family medicine, geriatrics, internal medicine, pediatrics
Joint degrees awarded: M.D./Ph.D.
Total National Institutes of Health (NIH) grants awarded to the medical school and affiliated hospitals: **$74.2 million**

CURRICULUM
(TEXT PROVIDED BY SCHOOL):
The four years of medical education constitute but a brief introduction to a broad, deep, and rapidly changing discipline. The mastery of medical knowledge and technical skills requires lifelong self-education.

The curriculum is designed to provide students with the knowledge, skills, and attitudes necessary to practice medicine. Students spend the first two years in the sciences basic to medicine, including anatomy, biochemistry, physiology, microbiology, genetics, pharmacology, pathology, and behavioral science. Concepts and skills necessary to manage clinical illness, to understand the social issues in medicine, and to be well grounded in the ethics of medical practice are introduced early and explored in depth as the curriculum progresses. Emphasis is placed on prevention, diagnosis,

and management of disease states and in the systematic application of these concepts to organ-specific diseases.

The first year includes courses in gross anatomy, embryology, histology, biochemistry, human genetics, medical immunology, medical microbiology, pathology, pharmacology, physical diagnosis, physiology, psychiatry, the science of medicine, social medicine, and the doctor-patient relationship.

During the second year, the aim is to integrate basic scientific facts with specific diseases and clinical problems. A multidisciplinary course, organized by specific organ systems, emphasizes pathophysiologic processes, clinical manifestations, and treatment.

In the third year, emphasis is on the integration of basic science knowledge with clinical, ethical, diagnostic, and problem-solving skills. Clinical clerkships, during which students learn patient management as members of the healthcare team, include family practice, internal medicine, obstetrics and gynecology, pediatrics, psychiatry, and surgery. The Topics of Medicine course reviews a series of simulated patients with common medical problems seen in ambulatory medicine. Students are also required to complete a four-week clinical neurology clerkship before graduation.

Seniors must complete a minimum of 36 weeks of credit, including a medical ethics course, a hospital-based subinternship, a public-health project, and clinical electives.

FACULTY PROFILE (FALL 2003)
Total teaching faculty: **904 (full-time)**, **231 (part-time)**
Of full-time faculty, those teaching in basic sciences: **10%**; in clinical programs: **90%**
Of part-time faculty, those teaching in basic sciences: **10%**; in clinical programs: **90%**
Full-time faculty/student ratio: **2.2**

SUPPORT SERVICES
The school offers students these services for dealing with stress: peer counseling, professional counseling, support groups.

RESIDENCY CHOICES
Most popular residency and specialty programs chosen by the 2002 and 2003 M.D. graduating classes: family practice, internal medicine.

WHERE GRADS GO

41.7%
Proportion of 2001-2003 graduates who entered primary care specialties

28.1%
Proportion of 2002-2003 graduates who accepted in-state residencies

iversity of Vermont

■ E-126 Given Building, 89 Beaumont Avenue, Burlington, VT
  05405
■ Public
■ **Year Founded:** 1822
■ **Tuition, 2003-2004:** In-state: $23,281; Out-of-state: $40,001
■ **Enrollment, 2003-2004:** 400
■ **Website:** http://www.med.uvm.edu
■ **Specialty ranking:** family medicine: 26, rural medicine: 25

3.40 AVERAGE GPA, ENTERING CLASS FALL 2003

9.2 AVERAGE MCAT, ENTERING CLASS FALL 2003

6.1% ACCEPTANCE RATE, ENTERING CLASS FALL 2003

Unranked 2005 U.S.NEWS MEDICAL SCHOOL RANKING (RESEARCH)

16 2005 U.S.NEWS MEDICAL SCHOOL RANKING (PRIMARY CARE)

ADMISSIONS
Admissions phone number: **(802) 656-2154**
Admissions email address: **medadmissions@uvm.edu**
Application website: **http://www.aamc.org**
Acceptance rate: **6.1%**
In-state acceptance rate: **50.0%**
Out-of-state acceptance rate: **5.4%**
Minority acceptance rate: **3.1%**
International acceptance rate: **12.8%**

Fall 2003 applications and acceptees
	Applied	Interviewed	Accepted	Enrolled
Total:	3,481	504	214	100
In-state:	62	36	31	28
Out-of-state:	3,419	468	183	72

Profile of admitted students
Average undergraduate grade point average: **3.40**
MCAT averages (scale: 1-15; writing test: J-T):
  Composite score: **9.2**
  Verbal reasoning score: **9.2**, Physical sciences score: **9.0**,
  Biological sciences score: **9.5**, Writing score: **Q**
Proportion with undergraduate majors in: Biological
  sciences: **49%**, Physical sciences: **21%**, Non-sciences:
  20%, Other health professions: **3%**, Mixed disciplines
  and other: **7%**
Percentage of students not coming directly from college
  after graduation: **67%**

Dates and details
The American Medical College Application Service
  (AMCAS) application is accepted.
School asks for a school-specific application as part of the
  admissions process.
Oldest MCAT considered for Fall 2005 entry: **2001**
Earliest application date for the 2005-2006 first-year class:
  June 1, 2004
Latest application date: **November 1, 2004**
Acceptance dates for regular application for the class
  entering in fall 2005:
  Earliest: **October 15, 2004**

Latest: **N/A**
The school considers requests for deferred entrance.
Starting month for the class entering in 2005-2006:
  August
The school has an Early Decision Plan (EDP).
A personal interview is required for admission.

Undergraduate coursework required
Medical school requires undergraduate work in these subjects: biology, organic chemistry, inorganic (general) chemistry, physics, general chemistry.

ADMISSIONS POLICY
(TEXT PROVIDED BY SCHOOL):
Applicants must have completed at least three years of
undergraduate study at a U.S. or Canadian institution
accredited by the National Committee of Regional
Accrediting Agencies. The baccalaureate degree is strongly
encouraged. An applicant's undergraduate studies must
include one year or eight credits each of biology, physics,
general chemistry, and organic chemistry. One year of laboratory must be included with each of these prerequisites. In
addition, we recommend one course in biochemistry or
molecular genetics be taken. The required courses should
be completed at the time of application. If they are not,
detailed plans for completion by the end of the spring
semester for the entering year must be listed on the transcript portion of the American Medical College Application
Service (AMCAS) application. High school Advanced
Placement courses will be accepted only if credit appears on
the college transcript and subsequently appears on the
AMCAS transcript portion of the application.
  We encourage students who have a broad and balanced
educational background during their undergraduate years.
In addition to prerequisite courses in the sciences, recommended areas of study include literature, mathematics,
behavioral sciences, history, philosophy, and the arts.
College work must demonstrate intellectual drive, independent thinking, curiosity, and self-discipline.
  A career in medicine calls for excellent oral and written
communication skills. Applicants should seek out

opportunities to develop such skills during their college years. Successful applicants often have a history of service to community.

COSTS AND FINANCIAL AID
Financial aid phone number: **(802) 656-8293**
Tuition, 2003-2004 academic year: **In-state: $23,281; Out-of-state: $40,001**
Room and board: **$10,280**
Percentage of students receiving financial aid in 2003-04: **91%**
Percentage of students receiving: Loans: **84%,** Grants/scholarships: **62%,** Work-study aid: **0%**
Average medical school debt for the Class of 2002: **$142,000**

STUDENT BODY
Fall 2003 full-time enrollment: **400**
Men: **40%,** Women: **60%,** In-state: **29%,** Minorities: **19%,** American Indian: **0.3%,** Asian-American: **16.8%,** African-American: **0.5%,** Hispanic-American: **0.3%,** White: **78.5%,** International: **1.0%,** Unknown: **2.8%**

ACADEMIC PROGRAMS
The school's curriculum gives first-year students substantial contact with patients.
There are opportunities for first- or second-year students to work in community health clinics.
Program offerings: AIDS, drug/alcohol abuse, family medicine, geriatrics, internal medicine, pediatrics, rural medicine, women's health
Joint degrees awarded: M.D./Ph.D.
Total National Institutes of Health (NIH) grants awarded to the medical school and affiliated hospitals: **N/A**

CURRICULUM
(TEXT PROVIDED BY SCHOOL):
For the past seven years, our school has been in the process of self-examination and curriculum reform as we worked to design a new curriculum that will provide the knowledge, skills, and attributes needed for a physician in the 21st century. The Vermont Integrated Curriculum (VIC) was fully implemented in the fall of 2003. VIC will integrate sciences and clinical medicine from the beginning of medical school, provide continuous assessment of student competency, and foster the skills needed to engage in "education" throughout a lifetime. Instruction in the art and science of medicine is woven throughout the VIC with a focus on patients, families, and communities.

The VIC progresses through three phases—from the study of the basic foundations of medicine, both clinical and basic science, to applications in clinical clerkships to senior scholarship and supervised patient management in an "advanced integration" fourth-year experience.

Integrated comprehensive examinations are administered at the end of the first year, the end of the foundations phase, the closing of clinical clerkships, and after completion of two acting internships.

Foundations studies are organized into three phases: fundamentals, systems integration, and convergence. These present a progression from basic vocabulary, concepts, and methods to relationships of organ systems in health and disease to complex presentations of pathophysiology. Principles of professionalism are integrated throughout this phase through weekly Medical Student Leadership Groups.

The clinical clerkship year is composed of three 15-week segments of departmentally based clinical experience and didactic programs, three one-week blocks of bridge clerkship, and a final performance examination before students are allowed to move into advanced integration.

Each student must complete two months of acting internships at a teaching hospital, including one in internal medicine. In addition, students must complete a four-week elective in emergency medicine. In a two-week teaching practicum, fourth-year students help to teach first-year students under faculty supervision.

The goal of our new curriculum is to integrate the ever expanding universe of knowledge with a desire for continued lifelong learning. Students will be measured both in and between courses to ensure their competency in mastering well-defined learning objectives through an extensive program of assessment involving the use of standardized patients in addition to standard examination formats.

FACULTY PROFILE (FALL 2003)
Total teaching faculty: **398 (full-time),** 1,325 **(part-time)**
Of full-time faculty, those teaching in basic sciences: **30%;** in clinical programs: **70%**
Of part-time faculty, those teaching in basic sciences: **4%;** in clinical programs: **96%**
Full-time faculty/student ratio: **1.0**

SUPPORT SERVICES
The school offers students these services for dealing with stress: expanded-hour gym access, peer counseling, professional counseling, religious support, support groups.

RESIDENCY CHOICES
Most popular residency and specialty programs chosen by the 2002 and 2003 M.D. graduating classes: anesthesiology, emergency medicine, family practice, internal medicine, obstetrics and gynecology, pediatrics, psychiatry, radiology–diagnostic, surgery–general.

WHERE GRADS GO
57.2%
Proportion of 2001-2003 graduates who entered primary care specialties

18.2%
Proportion of 2002-2003 graduates who accepted in-state residencies

University of Virginia

- PO Box 800793, McKim Hall, Health System, Charlottesville, VA 22908-0793
- Public
- Year Founded: 1819
- Tuition, 2003-2004: In-state: $22,486; Out-of-state: $34,486
- Enrollment, 2003-2004: 552
- Website: http://www.med.virginia.edu
- Specialty ranking: family medicine: 26, internal medicine: 26

3.70 AVERAGE GPA, ENTERING CLASS FALL 2003

10.7 AVERAGE MCAT, ENTERING CLASS FALL 2003

9.0% ACCEPTANCE RATE, ENTERING CLASS FALL 2003

25 2005 U.S.NEWS MEDICAL SCHOOL RANKING (RESEARCH)

31 2005 U.S.NEWS MEDICAL SCHOOL RANKING (PRIMARY CARE)

ADMISSIONS

Admissions phone number: **(434) 924-5571**
Admissions email address: **medsch-adm@virginia.edu**
Application website: **N/A**
Acceptance rate: **9.0%**
In-state acceptance rate: **20.7%**
Out-of-state acceptance rate: **6.1%**
Minority acceptance rate: **8.4%**
International acceptance rate: **N/A**

Fall 2003 applications and acceptees

	Applied	Interviewed	Accepted	Enrolled
Total:	3,577	502	321	140
In-state:	711	205	147	92
Out-of-state:	2,866	297	174	48

Profile of admitted students

Average undergraduate grade point average: **3.70**
MCAT averages (scale: 1-15; writing test: J-T):
   Composite score: **10.7**
   Verbal reasoning score: **10.3**, Physical sciences score: **10.9**, Biological sciences score: **10.8**, Writing score: **P**
Proportion with undergraduate majors in: Biological sciences: **46%**, Physical sciences: **24%**, Non-sciences: **17%**, Other health professions: **1%**, Mixed disciplines and other: **12%**
Percentage of students not coming directly from college after graduation: **55%**

Dates and details

The American Medical College Application Service (AMCAS) application is accepted.
School asks for a school-specific application as part of the admissions process.
Oldest MCAT considered for Fall 2005 entry: **2002**
Earliest application date for the 2005-2006 first-year class: **June 1, 2004**
Latest application date: **November 1, 2004**
Acceptance dates for regular application for the class entering in fall 2005:
   Earliest: **October 15, 2004**

Latest: **August 17, 2005**
The school considers requests for deferred entrance.
Starting month for the class entering in 2005-2006:
   August
The school doesn't have an Early Decision Plan (EDP).
A personal interview is required for admission.

Undergraduate coursework required

Medical school requires undergraduate work in these subjects: biology, organic chemistry, inorganic (general) chemistry, physics.

ADMISSIONS POLICY
(TEXT PROVIDED BY SCHOOL):

The Admissions Committee of the University of Virginia School of Medicine, in selecting medical school matriculants, places high value on academic excellence; diversity of culture, ethnicity, and experience; human compassion; and strong interpersonal skills. Preference is given to Virginia residents, with approximately 65 percent of the class having Virginia residence.

The school participates in the American Medical College Application Service. The deadline for receiving AMCAS applications is November 1 of the year prior to enrollment. However, because the University of Virginia utilizes a rolling admission process, it is in the best interest of the applicant to apply as early as possible. After submitting the AMCAS application, applicants will be directed to the University of Virginia School of Medicine's Web-based supplemental application. A $75 nonrefundable processing fee must accompany the supplemental application. Applicants who have been granted an AMCAS fee waiver will also be granted a supplemental application fee waiver.

A select group of applicants will be invited to the School of Medicine for interviews with members of the Admissions Committee. Students are selected and notified of their acceptance on a rolling admissions basis after October 15 until the class is filled. Applicants generally receive notice of their admission status the week following their interview.

All applicants must have completed a minimum of 90 semester hours of coursework in an accredited U.S. or Canadian college or university. The following college science courses must be completed prior to matriculation: one year each of biology, general chemistry, organic chemistry, and physics, all with lab. Biochemistry may be substituted for the second semester of organic chemistry. These courses should not be taken pass/fail, credit/no credit, or through a long-distance learning program. The Medical College Admission Test is required of all applicants.

COSTS AND FINANCIAL AID
Financial aid phone number: **(434) 924-0033**
Tuition, 2003-2004 academic year: **In-state: $22,486; Out-of-state: $34,486**
Room and board: **$13,812**
Percentage of students receiving financial aid in 2003-04: **89%**
Percentage of students receiving: Loans: **80%**, Grants/scholarships: **68%**, Work-study aid: **0%**
Average medical school debt for the Class of 2002: **$70,367**

STUDENT BODY
Fall 2003 full-time enrollment: **552**
Men: **52%**, Women: **48%**, In-state: **68%**, Minorities: **27%**, American Indian: **0.0%**, Asian-American: **19.7%**, African-American: **6.0%**, Hispanic-American: **0.9%**, White: **71.7%**, International: **0.0%**, Unknown: **1.6%**

ACADEMIC PROGRAMS
The school's curriculum gives first-year students substantial contact with patients.
There are opportunities for first- or second-year students to work in community health clinics.
Program offerings: AIDS, drug/alcohol abuse, family medicine, geriatrics, internal medicine, pediatrics, rural medicine, women's health
Joint degrees awarded: M.D./Ph.D., M.D./M.P.H., M.D./M.S., M.D./M.A.
Total National Institutes of Health (NIH) grants awarded to the medical school and affiliated hospitals: **N/A**

CURRICULUM
(TEXT PROVIDED BY SCHOOL):
At the University of Virginia art and science are blended in medical education. Our mission is to confer scientific knowledge and skill and to convey an appreciation of the interpersonal qualities of comfort, care, and understanding essential for a complete physician-patient relationship. Thus, the Practice of Medicine course introduces and integrates the patient interview and the physical exam with ethics and links with the basic sciences. Two fundamental components of our educational philosophy are, first, that principles of problem understanding and management are more important than retention of isolated facts and, second, that learning is facilitated by the presence of the patient.

At the center of the curriculum are the patient, the science of medicine, and the physician's role in improving the health of individuals and communities. Patient contact begins early in the first year and increases throughout the four years. The curriculum is a balance of lecture, problem-based small-group, laboratory, hospital, and community-based clinical experience.

In the first year, students develop an understanding of normal human biology, the scientific core of the physician's knowledge base. This is integrated with clinical applications in the Practice of Medicine-1 course, where groups of six students learn from problem-based clinical cases.

The coordinating theme of the second year is provided by the problem-based course Practice of Medicine-2. Clinical cases are solved in small-group tutorials led by physicians. Students also develop their skills in taking medical histories and conducting physical exams.

In the third year, students take clerkships in medicine, ambulatory internal medicine, surgery, pediatrics, family medicine, psychiatry, and obstetrics and gynecology. Teaching is related to the patient on rounds and in lectures and small-group discussions.

The electives program in the fourth year allows students to pursue their own interests. Under the guidance of a faculty adviser, students choose clinical rotations, basic science and humanities courses, and research activities.

FACULTY PROFILE (FALL 2003)
Total teaching faculty: **850 (full-time)**, **101 (part-time)**
Of full-time faculty, those teaching in basic sciences: **25%**; in clinical programs: **75%**
Of part-time faculty, those teaching in basic sciences: **16%**; in clinical programs: **84%**
Full-time faculty/student ratio: **1.5**

SUPPORT SERVICES
The school offers students these services for dealing with stress: expanded-hour gym access, peer counseling, professional counseling, religious support, support groups.

RESIDENCY CHOICES
Most popular residency and specialty programs chosen by the 2002 and 2003 M.D. graduating classes: anesthesiology, emergency medicine, family practice, internal medicine, obstetrics and gynecology, orthopedic surgery, pediatrics, psychiatry, radiology–diagnostic, surgery–general.

WHERE GRADS GO
42.0%
Proportion of 2001-2003 graduates who entered primary care specialties

23.0%
Proportion of 2002-2003 graduates who accepted in-state residencies

University of Washington

- School of Medicine, Box 356340, Seattle, WA 98195
- Public
- **Year Founded:** 1946
- **Tuition, 2003-2004:** In-state: $12,848; Out-of-state: $29,788
- **Enrollment, 2003-2004:** 790
- **Website:** http://www.uwmedicine.org
- **Specialty ranking:** AIDS: 4, drug/alcohol abuse: 16, family medicine: 1, geriatrics: 7, internal medicine: 5, pediatrics: 9, rural medicine: 1, women's health: 10

3.69	AVERAGE GPA, ENTERING CLASS FALL 2003
10.4	AVERAGE MCAT, ENTERING CLASS FALL 2003
8.1%	ACCEPTANCE RATE, ENTERING CLASS FALL 2003
10	2005 U.S.NEWS MEDICAL SCHOOL RANKING (RESEARCH)
1	2005 U.S.NEWS MEDICAL SCHOOL RANKING (PRIMARY CARE)

ADMISSIONS

Admissions phone number: **(206) 543-7212**
Admissions email address: **askuwsom@u.washington.edu**
Application website: **N/A**
Acceptance rate: **8.1%**
In-state acceptance rate: **20.6%**
Out-of-state acceptance rate: **1.9%**
Minority acceptance rate: **3.5%**
International acceptance rate: **N/A**

Fall 2003 applications and acceptees

	Applied	Interviewed	Accepted	Enrolled
Total:	2,905	750	235	178
In-state:	963	671	198	165
Out-of-state:	1,942	79	37	13

Profile of admitted students

Average undergraduate grade point average: **3.69**
MCAT averages (scale: 1-15; writing test: J-T):
Composite score: **10.4**
Verbal reasoning score: **10.0,** Physical sciences score: **10.3,** Biological sciences score: **10.8,** Writing score: **P**
Proportion with undergraduate majors in: Biological sciences: **54%,** Physical sciences: **23%,** Non-sciences: **15%,** Other health professions: **0%,** Mixed disciplines and other: **8%**
Percentage of students not coming directly from college after graduation: **20%**

Dates and details

The American Medical College Application Service (AMCAS) application is accepted.
School asks for a school-specific application as part of the admissions process.
Oldest MCAT considered for Fall 2005 entry: **2002**
Earliest application date for the 2005-2006 first-year class: **June 1, 2004**
Latest application date: **November 1, 2004**
Acceptance dates for regular application for the class entering in fall 2005:
Earliest: **November 15, 2004**

Latest: **April 1, 2005**
The school considers requests for deferred entrance.
Starting month for the class entering in 2005-2006:
September
The school doesn't have an Early Decision Plan (EDP).
A personal interview is required for admission.

Undergraduate coursework required

Medical school requires undergraduate work in these subjects: biology, inorganic (general) chemistry, physics.

ADMISSIONS POLICY

(TEXT PROVIDED BY SCHOOL):
Residents from the states of Washington, Wyoming, Alaska, Montana, and Idaho are eligible to apply. Proof of residency is required. Residents from outside the region who come from disadvantaged backgrounds and/or who have demonstrated a commitment to serving underserved populations will be considered. Individuals with a demonstrated interest in research may apply for the M.D./Ph.D. program regardless of residency.

Candidates for admission are considered on the basis of academic performance, motivation, maturity, personal integrity, and demonstrated humanitarian qualities. Knowledge of the needs of individuals and society and an awareness of healthcare delivery systems are expected, and direct exposure is desired. Extenuating circumstances in an applicant's background are evaluated as they relate to selection factors.

The premedical course requirements should be completed by the time of application and must be completed by matriculation. These requirements include a total of 32 semester hours or 48 quarter hours in undergraduate science courses divided as follows: biology, eight semester hours or 12 quarter hours; chemistry, 12 semester/18 quarter hours, which can be satisfied by taking any combination of inorganic, organic, biochemistry, or molecular biology courses; physics, four semester/six quarter hours; and open science subjects, eight semester/12 quarter hours in the previously mentioned study areas. Biochemistry is strongly suggested for entering students.

All candidates must demonstrate substantial ability in their field; be proficient in English; be able to use basic mathematics; and have an understanding of personal computing and information technologies.

COSTS AND FINANCIAL AID
Financial aid phone number: **(206) 685-9229**
Tuition, 2003-2004 academic year: **In-state: $12,848; Out-of-state: $29,788**
Room and board: **$11,862**
Percentage of students receiving financial aid in 2003-04: **91%**
Percentage of students receiving: Loans: **85%**, Grants/scholarships: **60%**, Work-study aid: **0%**
Average medical school debt for the Class of 2002: **$79,005**

STUDENT BODY
Fall 2003 full-time enrollment: **790**
Men: **48%**, Women: **52%**, In-state: **89%**, Minorities: **22%**, American Indian: **1.4%**, Asian-American: **14.4%**, African-American: **2.0%**, Hispanic-American: **3.9%**, White: **75.8%**, International: **0.0%**, Unknown: **2.4%**

ACADEMIC PROGRAMS
The school's curriculum gives first-year students substantial contact with patients.
There are opportunities for first- or second-year students to work in community health clinics.
Program offerings: AIDS, drug/alcohol abuse, family medicine, geriatrics, internal medicine, pediatrics, rural medicine, women's health
Joint degrees awarded: M.D./Ph.D., M.D./M.P.H.
Total National Institutes of Health (NIH) grants awarded to the medical school and affiliated hospitals: **$488.5 million**

CURRICULUM
(TEXT PROVIDED BY SCHOOL):
All students are assigned to one of five colleges and to a faculty mentor within their college with whom they interact throughout their medical education.
In the first year, students receive instruction in courses taught from specific departments or disciplines and from an organ systems approach. Biochemistry, physiology, pathology, immunology, behavioral sciences, microbiology, and anatomy and embryology are introduced. Critical reading, informatics, and evidence-based medicine are also introduced. Students begin instruction in interviewing skills, history-taking and recording techniques, and the physical examination.
The second year continues the organ systems teaching method and adds two discipline-based courses from pharmacology. Students have a weekly opportunity to learn clinical skills at the bedside, working in small groups with their college mentors.

The third and fourth years consist of required and elective clinical clerkships. Required clerkships are in family medicine, internal medicine, obstetrics and gynecology, pediatrics, psychiatry, and surgery. Rehabilitation medicine, emergency medicine, neurology, and an additional four-week selective in surgery or a surgical subspecialty are also required.
Because the UW School of Medicine serves as a regional school for the states of Washington, Wyoming, Alaska, Montana, and Idaho and because of the value of seeing healthcare delivered in different settings, all students take at least one or two clerkships outside of the Seattle area. Most clinical electives are taken in the fourth year. Typically, fourth-year schedules permit advanced coursework in preparation for assuming patient-care responsibilities in residency training.
Students must also complete a continuity curriculum and required preceptorship; four nonclinical selective credits; 32 elective credits (16 weeks); a two-week "capstone course" held in the fourth year, focusing on refresher topics and preresidency skills; and a study in medical sciences. Each student participates in the objective structured clinical examination at the end of the second year and the beginning of the fourth year.

FACULTY PROFILE (FALL 2003)
Total teaching faculty: **1,858 (full-time)**, **252 (part-time)**
Of full-time faculty, those teaching in basic sciences: **17%**; in clinical programs: **83%**
Of part-time faculty, those teaching in basic sciences: **14%**; in clinical programs: **86%**
Full-time faculty/student ratio: **2.4**

SUPPORT SERVICES
The school offers students these services for dealing with stress: expanded-hour gym access, peer counseling, professional counseling, support groups.

RESIDENCY CHOICES
Most popular residency and specialty programs chosen by the 2002 and 2003 M.D. graduating classes: anesthesiology, emergency medicine, family practice, internal medicine, pediatrics, psychiatry, surgery–general.

WHERE GRADS GO
50.0%
Proportion of 2001-2003 graduates who entered primary care specialties

44.8%
Proportion of 2002-2003 graduates who accepted in-state residencies

University of Wisconsin–Madison

- 1300 University Avenue, Madison, WI 53706
- Public
- Year Founded: 1848
- Tuition, 2003-2004: In-state: $21,728; Out-of-state: $32,852
- Enrollment, 2003-2004: 598
- Website: http://www.med.wisc.edu/Education/Programs/MD/Admissions
- Specialty ranking: family medicine: 4, rural medicine: 25, women's health: 19

3.74 AVERAGE GPA, ENTERING CLASS FALL 2003

10.4 AVERAGE MCAT, ENTERING CLASS FALL 2003

12.1% ACCEPTANCE RATE, ENTERING CLASS FALL 2003

25 2005 U.S.NEWS MEDICAL SCHOOL RANKING (RESEARCH)

3 2005 U.S.NEWS MEDICAL SCHOOL RANKING (PRIMARY CARE)

ADMISSIONS

Admissions phone number: **(608) 265-6344**
Admissions email address: **eamenzer@wisc.edu**
Application website:
   http://www.med.wisc.edu/Education/Programs/MD/Admissions/Process.asp
Acceptance rate: **12.1%**
In-state acceptance rate: **34.2%**
Out-of-state acceptance rate: **3.8%**
Minority acceptance rate: **10.1%**
International acceptance rate: **100.0%**

Fall 2003 applications and acceptees

	Applied	Interviewed	Accepted	Enrolled
Total:	1,902	652	230	150
In-state:	518	434	177	130
Out-of-state:	1,384	218	53	20

Profile of admitted students

Average undergraduate grade point average: **3.74**
MCAT averages (scale: 1-15; writing test: J-T):
   Composite score: **10.4**
   Verbal reasoning score: **10.0**, Physical sciences score: **9.8**, Biological sciences score: **10.3**, Writing score: **P**
Proportion with undergraduate majors in: Biological sciences: **56%**, Physical sciences: **17%**, Non-sciences: **24%**, Other health professions: **3%**, Mixed disciplines and other: **N/A**
Percentage of students not coming directly from college after graduation: **27%**

Dates and details

The American Medical College Application Service (AMCAS) application is accepted.
School asks for a school-specific application as part of the admissions process.
Oldest MCAT considered for Fall 2005 entry: **2000**
Earliest application date for the 2005-2006 first-year class: **June 1, 2004**
Latest application date: **October 15, 2004**

Acceptance dates for regular application for the class entering in fall 2005:
   Earliest: **October 15, 2004**
   Latest: **August 15, 2005**
The school considers requests for deferred entrance.
Starting month for the class entering in 2005-2006: **August**
The school has an Early Decision Plan (EDP).
A personal interview is required for admission.

Undergraduate coursework required
Medical school requires undergraduate work in these subjects: biology, biology/zoology, English, organic chemistry, inorganic (general) chemistry, physics, mathematics, demonstration of writing skills, general chemistry.

ADMISSIONS POLICY

(TEXT PROVIDED BY SCHOOL):
The Admissions Committee attempts to select a class in which all members have a level of past academic performance that predicts the student's academic success in medical school; personal characteristics that will enable the student to provide sympathetic and intelligent patient care; and an interest in others as might be demonstrated by community service, extracurricular activities, and/or leadership.

In the selection of candidates for admission, the committee considers undergraduate and graduate academic performance and Medical College Admission Test scores; extracurricular activities; the applicant's employment record; the personal, educational, and socioeconomic background of the applicant and the response of the applicant to any challenges; the applicant's character with reference to honesty and integrity, empathy, maturity, leadership, self-discipline, and emotional stability; the ability of the applicant to communicate and relate well with others; motivation to pursue a career in medicine; and the interest and suitability of the applicant for special programs and/or future specific careers.

Furthermore, in the interests of both enriching the educational environment for all students and better meeting the future medical, educational, and scientific needs of society, the committee makes a special effort to select a class whose members represent a broad range of diverse life experiences, backgrounds, and interests. This diversity may include ethnic or racial background; socioeconomic background; educational background; regional and geographic background; interests and/or aptitudes for different medical careers; and other cultural experiences.

It is the responsibility of the faculty and students who serve on the Admissions Committee to select the entering class. Our admissions policy does not allow the dean or anyone else to grant special consideration for applicants to the University of Wisconsin Medical School. It is the goal of the Admissions Committee to seek students capable of benefiting from the educational opportunities available at the University of Wisconsin-Madison and who give evidence that they will contribute to meeting the healthcare needs of the people of the state of Wisconsin and the nation.

Preference is given to residents of Wisconsin.

COSTS AND FINANCIAL AID

Financial aid phone number: **(608) 262-3060**
Tuition, 2003-2004 academic year: **In-state: $21,728; Out-of-state: $32,852**
Room and board: **$12,705**
Percentage of students receiving financial aid in 2003-04: **85%**
Percentage of students receiving: Loans: **85%**, Grants/scholarships: **25%**, Work-study aid: **0%**
Average medical school debt for the Class of 2002: **$110,000**

STUDENT BODY

Fall 2003 full-time enrollment: **598**
Men: **45%**, Women: **55%**, In-state: **88%**, Minorities: **22%**,

ACADEMIC PROGRAMS

The school's curriculum gives first-year students substantial contact with patients.
There are opportunities for first- or second-year students to work in community health clinics.
Program offerings: AIDS, drug/alcohol abuse, family medicine, geriatrics, internal medicine, pediatrics, rural medicine, women's health
Joint degrees awarded: M.D./Ph.D.
Total National Institutes of Health (NIH) grants awarded to the medical school and affiliated hospitals; **$166.0 million**

CURRICULUM

(TEXT PROVIDED BY SCHOOL):
The University of Wisconsin medical curriculum emphasizes the acquisition of core doctoring skills in a humane and nurturing environment. Students spend time in doctors' offices from the first month of medical school and continue to build their doctoring skills throughout the four years of medical school through a core curriculum component, which is interdisciplinary and longitudinal.

In the first year, the core curriculum is a cohesive series of courses designed to build a firm base in the sciences fundamental to clinical medicine through courses that focus on the functional, morphological, molecular, metabolic, pathologic, and developmental principles of the human body. In the second year, the courses emphasize organ systems, mechanisms of disease and abnormalities, and therapeutic intervention. Throughout the first two years, a mixture of didactic, small-group, standardized-patient, and clinical experiences help to provide a lively and varied medical education.

Beginning in the third year, clerkships expose students to a wide variety of clinical settings, including outpatient, inpatient, community-based, rural, and inner city. Our 'statewide campus' includes clinical training sites in nine communities throughout Wisconsin, with principal locations in Madison, La Crosse, Marshfield, and Milwaukee as well as at 34 preceptor sites and the Area Health Education Centers.

Students emerging from their clinical years at the UW Medical School do very well in competing for residencies, and residency supervisors rate our graduates very highly. Our graduates also look back on their medical education and rate it favorably in preparing them for residency.

FACULTY PROFILE (FALL 2003)

Total teaching faculty: **1,189 (full-time), N/A (part-time)**
Of full-time faculty, those teaching in basic sciences: **14%**; in clinical programs: **86%**
Of part-time faculty, those teaching in basic sciences: **N/A**; in clinical programs: **N/A**
Full-time faculty/student ratio: **2.0**

SUPPORT SERVICES

The school offers students these services for dealing with stress: expanded-hour gym access, professional counseling, support groups.

RESIDENCY CHOICES

Most popular residency and specialty programs chosen by the 2002 and 2003 M.D. graduating classes: anesthesiology, emergency medicine, family practice, internal medicine, obstetrics and gynecology, pediatrics, physical medicine and rehabilitation, psychiatry, radiology–diagnostic, surgery–general.

WHERE GRADS GO

55.0%
Proportion of 2001-2003 graduates who entered primary care specialties

34.0%
Proportion of 2002-2003 graduates who accepted in-state residencies

Vanderbilt University

- 21st Avenue S. at Garland Avenue, Nashville, TN 37232-2104
- Private
- Year Founded: 1875
- Tuition, 2003-2004: $32,157
- Enrollment, 2003-2004: 416
- Website: http://www.mc.vanderbilt.edu/medschool
- Specialty ranking: internal medicine: 17

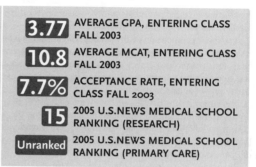

3.77 AVERAGE GPA, ENTERING CLASS FALL 2003

10.8 AVERAGE MCAT, ENTERING CLASS FALL 2003

7.7% ACCEPTANCE RATE, ENTERING CLASS FALL 2003

15 2005 U.S.NEWS MEDICAL SCHOOL RANKING (RESEARCH)

Unranked 2005 U.S.NEWS MEDICAL SCHOOL RANKING (PRIMARY CARE)

ADMISSIONS

Admissions phone number: **(615) 322-2145**
Admissions email address: **N/A**
Application website:
   **http://www.mc.vanderbilt.edu/medschool/admissions/
   online_app.php**
Acceptance rate: **7.7%**
In-state acceptance rate: **9.2%**
Out-of-state acceptance rate: **7.6%**
Minority acceptance rate: **9.7%**
International acceptance rate: **6.7%**

Fall 2003 applications and acceptees

	Applied	Interviewed	Accepted	Enrolled
Total:	3,507	895	270	104
In-state:	240	52	22	16
Out-of-state:	3,267	843	248	88

Profile of admitted students

Average undergraduate grade point average: **3.77**
MCAT averages (scale: 1-15; writing test: J-T):
   Composite score: **10.8**
   Verbal reasoning score: **10.2**, Physical sciences score:
   11.0, Biological sciences score: **11.1**, Writing score: **Q**
Proportion with undergraduate majors in: Biological
   sciences: **41%**, Physical sciences: **35%**, Non-sciences:
   23%, Other health professions: **0%**, Mixed disciplines
   and other: **1%**
Percentage of students not coming directly from college
   after graduation: **35%**

Dates and details

The American Medical College Application Service
   (AMCAS) application is accepted.
School asks for a school-specific application as part of the
   admissions process.
Oldest MCAT considered for Fall 2005 entry: **2001**
Earliest application date for the 2005-2006 first-year class:
   June 1, 2004
Latest application date: **October 15, 2004**

Acceptance dates for regular application for the class
   entering in fall 2005:
   Earliest: **October 15, 2004**
   Latest: **N/A**
The school considers requests for deferred entrance.
Starting month for the class entering in 2005-2006:
   August
The school has an Early Decision Plan (EDP).
A personal interview is required for admission.

Undergraduate coursework required

Medical school requires undergraduate work in these subjects: biology, English, organic chemistry, inorganic (general) chemistry, physics.

ADMISSIONS POLICY
(TEXT PROVIDED BY SCHOOL):

Admission to Vanderbilt University Medical School is a staged process. Applications are invited without regard to race, sex, creed, national origin, or state of residence. Applicants must possess sufficient intellectual ability, emotional stability, and sensory and motor functions to meet the academic requirements of the School of Medicine without fundamental alteration in the nature of its program.

The initial stage involves review made from material provided to the American Medical College Application Service. Competitive strength of credentials reflecting preparation for medical studies, motivation, personal qualities, and educational background as relate to a career in medicine is evaluated by the Admissions Committee. Selected candidates are asked to file a secondary application, which consists of three specific additional essays along with a $50 application fee. This second stage also involves a single, one-on-one personal interview conducted on the Vanderbilt campus by a faculty member.

When all relevant admission materials are completed, each candidate will be assigned for detailed scrutiny by three members of the Admissions Committee. The three advocating reviewers will present to the entire committee the credentials for the given applicant along with the suggested action, with numerical scores based on the National

Institutes of Health grant review process. Scores range from 1 to 5, with 1-1.5 scores needed for immediate admission, scores between 1.5 and 4.0 for waiting-list placement, and scores of 4 and above for rejection.

Admission Committee meetings are held weekly from the fall to the beginning of April, at which time a rolling admissions process begins. Approximately 250 immediate admissions are offered for the 104 places. A Second Visit Weekend is held for students holding admission places in early spring. After the May 15 decision date for students, successful applicants from the waiting list are notified.

In evaluating candidates, no specific categories of applicant are identified; there is no point system for any categories. Rather, there is a holistic review of academic performance and nonacademic factors, such as patient care experiences, research experiences, extracurricular involvement, leadership roles, sports activities, relationship to the medical school, applicants from underserved populations, and applicants who would enhance the diversity of the class toward improved education in the broadest sense. Approximately 10 positions in the medical school are reserved for the Medical Scientist Training Program. Additionally, places are available for early decision applicants and for Vanderbilt undergraduate students who apply at two early time points.

COSTS AND FINANCIAL AID

Financial aid phone number: **(615) 343-6310**
Tuition, 2003-2004 academic year: **$32,157**
Room and board: **$8,280**
Percentage of students receiving financial aid in 2003-04: **86%**
Percentage of students receiving: Loans: **73%**, Grants/scholarships: **54%**, Work-study aid: **N/A**
Average medical school debt for the Class of 2002: **$83,100**

STUDENT BODY

Fall 2003 full-time enrollment: **416**
Men: **53%**, Women: **47%**, In-state: **14%**, Minorities: **28%**, American Indian: **1.4%**, Asian-American: **21.4%**, African-American: **3.4%**, Hispanic-American: **1.7%**, White: **66.3%**, International: **4.1%**, Unknown: **1.7%**

ACADEMIC PROGRAMS

The school's curriculum doesn't give first-year students substantial contact with patients.
There are opportunities for first- or second-year students to work in community health clinics.
Program offerings: AIDS, drug/alcohol abuse, family medicine, geriatrics, internal medicine, pediatrics, rural medicine, women's health
Joint degrees awarded: M.D./Ph.D., M.D./M.B.A., M.D./M.P.H., M.D./J.D., M.D./M.S.
Total National Institutes of Health (NIH) grants awarded to the medical school and affiliated hospitals: **$220.6 million**

CURRICULUM
(TEXT PROVIDED BY SCHOOL):

During the first two years of medical school, Vanderbilt requires that students take at least seven electives. Beginning with the 2003-2004 academic year, all first-year students take at least one elective that provides exposure to clinical patient care. Prior to this year, the majority of students chose to take a clinical elective even without that requirement. Students will also use their elective time to perform independent research and to learn about the ethical, legal, social, and historical context of medicine. The overall effect of the elective program is to enrich the educational experience of the preclinical years.

During the third year, all students are required to take their six core clinical clerkships at Vanderbilt or its affiliated hospitals. During the fourth year, students are required to take eight four-week rotations. These include emergency medicine, primary care, a medicine subinternship, a surgical subinternship, and four electives. Many students will take electives at other institutions, and many seek international elective experience. Students are encouraged to consider additional scholarly and educational opportunities. Through the Medical Scholars program, students may take a year's leave of absence to pursue independent research. Also offered are numerous joint degree opportunities, including the M.D./M.B.A. and the M.D./Ph.D. in biomedical research.

FACULTY PROFILE (FALL 2003)

Total teaching faculty: **1,377 (full-time)**, **961 (part-time)**
Of full-time faculty, those teaching in basic sciences: **22%**; in clinical programs: **78%**
Of part-time faculty, those teaching in basic sciences: **5%**; in clinical programs: **95%**
Full-time faculty/student ratio: **3.3**

SUPPORT SERVICES

The school offers students these services for dealing with stress: expanded-hour gym access, peer counseling, professional counseling, religious support, support groups.

RESIDENCY CHOICES

Most popular residency and specialty programs chosen by the 2002 and 2003 M.D. graduating classes: anesthesiology, emergency medicine, internal medicine, obstetrics and gynecology, ophthalmology, orthopedic surgery, pediatrics, psychiatry, radiology–diagnostic, urology.

WHERE GRADS GO

26.0%
Proportion of 2001-2003 graduates who entered primary care specialties

34.0%
Proportion of 2002-2003 graduates who accepted in-state residencies

Virginia Commonwealth University

MEDICAL COLLEGE OF VIRGINIA

■ PO Box 980565, Richmond, VA 23298-0565
■ Public
■ Year Founded: 1838
■ Tuition, 2003-2004: In-state: $20,023; Out-of-state: $35,851
■ Enrollment, 2003-2004: 716
■ Website: http://www.medschool.vcu.edu
■ Specialty ranking: N/A

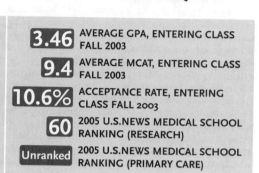

3.46	AVERAGE GPA, ENTERING CLASS FALL 2003
9.4	AVERAGE MCAT, ENTERING CLASS FALL 2003
10.6%	ACCEPTANCE RATE, ENTERING CLASS FALL 2003
60	2005 U.S.NEWS MEDICAL SCHOOL RANKING (RESEARCH)
Unranked	2005 U.S.NEWS MEDICAL SCHOOL RANKING (PRIMARY CARE)

ADMISSIONS

Admissions phone number: **(804) 828-9629**
Admissions email address: **somume@hsc.vcu.edu**
Application website: **http://www.admissions.som.vcu.edu**
Acceptance rate: **10.6%**
In-state acceptance rate: **25.6%**
Out-of-state acceptance rate: **6.8%**
Minority acceptance rate: **9.5%**
International acceptance rate: **N/A**

Fall 2003 applications and acceptees

	Applied	Interviewed	Accepted	Enrolled
Total:	3,909	629	413	184
In-state:	790	296	202	100
Out-of-state:	3,119	333	211	84

Profile of admitted students

Average undergraduate grade point average: **3.46**
MCAT averages (scale: 1-15; writing test: J-T):
Composite score: **9.4**
Verbal reasoning score: **9.1**, Physical sciences score: **9.4**,
Biological sciences score: **9.8**, Writing score: **N**
Proportion with undergraduate majors in: Biological
sciences: **47%**, Physical sciences: **24%**, Non-sciences:
29%, Other health professions: **0%**, Mixed disciplines
and other: **0%**
Percentage of students not coming directly from college
after graduation: **45%**

Dates and details

The American Medical College Application Service
(AMCAS) application is accepted.
School asks for a school-specific application as part of the
admissions process.
Oldest MCAT considered for Fall 2005 entry: **2002**
Earliest application date for the 2005-2006 first-year class:
June 1, 2004
Latest application date: **November 15, 2004**
Acceptance dates for regular application for the class
entering in fall 2005:
Earliest: **October 15, 2004**

Latest: **August 10, 2005**
The school considers requests for deferred entrance.
Starting month for the class entering in 2005-2006:
August
The school has an Early Decision Plan (EDP).
A personal interview is required for admission.

Undergraduate coursework required

Medical school requires undergraduate work in these subjects: biology, biology/zoology, English, organic chemistry, physics, mathematics, demonstration of writing skills, general chemistry.

ADMISSIONS POLICY

(TEXT PROVIDED BY SCHOOL):
Applicants are selected on the basis of their potential as prospective physicians as well as students of medicine. Attributes of character, personality factors, academic skills, and exposure to medicine are considered along with academic performance, grade-point average, Medical College Admission Test scores, letters of recommendation, and personal interviews at the School of Medicine.

The school gives preference to bona fide residents of the Commonwealth of Virginia and does not discriminate on the basis of age, race, sex, creed, national origin, or handicap. Foreign nationals must be permanent residents at the time of application.

COSTS AND FINANCIAL AID

Financial aid phone number: **(804) 828-4006**
Tuition, 2003-2004 academic year: **In-state: $20,023; Out-of-state: $35,851**
Room and board: **$8,680**
Percentage of students receiving financial aid in 2003-04: **87%**
Percentage of students receiving: Loans: **84%**, Grants/scholarships: **46%**, Work-study aid: **0%**
Average medical school debt for the Class of 2002: **$98,661**

STUDENT BODY

Fall 2003 full-time enrollment: **716**

Men: **50%**, Women: **50%**, In-state: **64%**, Minorities: **34%**,
American Indian: **0.1%**, Asian-American: **25.6%**,
African-American: **7.1%**, Hispanic-American: **1.0%**,
White: **63.1%**, International: **0.0%**, Unknown: **3.1%**

ACADEMIC PROGRAMS

The school's curriculum gives first-year students
substantial contact with patients.

There are opportunities for first- or second-year students to
work in community health clinics.

Program offerings: AIDS, drug/alcohol abuse, family
medicine, geriatrics, internal medicine, pediatrics, rural
medicine, women's health

Joint degrees awarded: M.D./Ph.D., M.D./M.P.H.,
M.D./M.H.A.

Total National Institutes of Health (NIH) grants awarded to
the medical school and affiliated hospitals: **N/A**

CURRICULUM
(TEXT PROVIDED BY SCHOOL):

The first year is spent studying normal structure and function in a traditional discipline format. The second year
emphasizes pathogenesis of disease manifestations, and
principles of management are discussed in each of the
major body systems. There is a longitudinal experience in
clinical medicine for first- and second-year students.
Students spend two afternoons per month in a small group
learning the fundamentals of clinical medicine. This is supplemental by a clinical experience in the office of a primary-
care physician two afternoons per month. This unique
clinical experience is integrated with the basic science curriculum in a way that enhances and enriches the student's
learning. There is a computer lab with over 40 workstations
and a full array of commercial and in-house, faculty-devel-
oped educational software.

In the third year, the clinical rotations are at the university and Veterans Affairs hospitals, with ambulatory care
rotations at nonuniversity primary-care sites. Computer
educational workstations, distributed throughout the hospitals and clinics, give students access to the university library
databases, expert decision support systems, and educational
software programs.

During the fourth year, the student may choose from a
wide variety of electives both at the university and throughout the United States. In addition, there are elective programs serving the first and second years.

FACULTY PROFILE (FALL 2003)

Total teaching faculty: **706 (full-time)**, **91 (part-time)**
Of full-time faculty, those teaching in basic sciences: **22%**;
in clinical programs: **78%**
Of part-time faculty, those teaching in basic sciences: **25%**;
in clinical programs: **75%**
Full-time faculty/student ratio: **1.0**

SUPPORT SERVICES

The school offers students these services for dealing with
stress: expanded-hour gym access, professional counseling.

RESIDENCY CHOICES

Most popular residency and specialty programs chosen by
the 2002 and 2003 M.D. graduating classes: emergency
medicine, family practice, internal medicine, obstetrics and
gynecology, orthopedic surgery, pediatrics, radiology–diagnostic, surgery–general, transitional year, internal medi-
cine/pediatrics.

WHERE GRADS GO

45.0%			

Proportion of 2001-2003 graduates who entered primary
care specialties

34.0%			

Proportion of 2002-2003 graduates who accepted in-state
residencies

Wake Forest University

- **Medical Center Boulevard, Winston-Salem, NC 27157**
- **Private**
- **Year Founded:** 1941
- **Tuition, 2003-2004:** $32,056
- **Enrollment, 2003-2004:** 438
- **Website:** http://www.wfubmc.edu
- **Specialty ranking:** geriatrics: 12

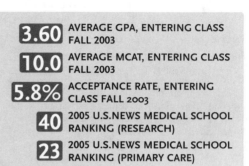

3.60 AVERAGE GPA, ENTERING CLASS FALL 2003

10.0 AVERAGE MCAT, ENTERING CLASS FALL 2003

5.8% ACCEPTANCE RATE, ENTERING CLASS FALL 2003

40 2005 U.S.NEWS MEDICAL SCHOOL RANKING (RESEARCH)

23 2005 U.S.NEWS MEDICAL SCHOOL RANKING (PRIMARY CARE)

ADMISSIONS

Admissions phone number: **(336) 716-4264**
Admissions email address: **medadmit@wfubmc.edu**
Application website: **http://www.aamc.org**
Acceptance rate: **5.8%**
In-state acceptance rate: **16.6%**
Out-of-state acceptance rate: **4.4%**
Minority acceptance rate: **N/A**
International acceptance rate: **N/A**

Fall 2003 applications and acceptees

	Applied	Interviewed	Accepted	Enrolled
Total:	5,152	572	297	108
In-state:	580	155	96	40
Out-of-state:	4,572	417	201	68

Profile of admitted students

Average undergraduate grade point average: **3.60**
MCAT averages (scale: 1-15; writing test: J-T):
  Composite score: **10.0**
  Verbal reasoning score: **10.0**, Physical sciences score: **10.0**, Biological sciences score: **10.0**, Writing score: **P**
Proportion with undergraduate majors in: Biological sciences: **51%**, Physical sciences: **24%**, Non-sciences: **14%**, Other health professions: **1%**, Mixed disciplines and other: **10%**
Percentage of students not coming directly from college after graduation: **51%**

Dates and details

The American Medical College Application Service (AMCAS) application is accepted.
School asks for a school-specific application as part of the admissions process.
Oldest MCAT considered for Fall 2005 entry: **2001**
Earliest application date for the 2005-2006 first-year class: **June 15, 2004**
Latest application date: **November 1, 2004**
Acceptance dates for regular application for the class entering in fall 2005:
  Earliest: **October 15, 2004**

Latest: **August 1, 2005**
The school considers requests for deferred entrance.
Starting month for the class entering in 2005-2006:
  August
The school has an Early Decision Plan (EDP).
A personal interview is required for admission.

Undergraduate coursework required

Medical school requires undergraduate work in these subjects: biology, biology/zoology, organic chemistry, inorganic (general) chemistry, physics, general chemistry.

ADMISSIONS POLICY
(TEXT PROVIDED BY SCHOOL):

Medical College Admission Test scores and grade-point average are considered, and personal qualities are assessed in the interviews.
  A national pool of applicants is considered, so state of residence is inconsequential.

COSTS AND FINANCIAL AID

Financial aid phone number: **(336) 716-2889**
Tuition, 2003-2004 academic year: **$32,056**
Room and board: **$13,046**
Percentage of students receiving financial aid in 2003-04: **87%**
Percentage of students receiving: Loans: **82%**, Grants/scholarships: **69%**, Work-study aid: **0%**
Average medical school debt for the Class of 2002: **$126,061**

STUDENT BODY

Fall 2003 full-time enrollment: **438**
Men: **60%**, Women: **40%**, In-state: **41%**, Minorities: **32%**, American Indian: **0.2%**, Asian-American: **17.1%**, African-American: **10.7%**, Hispanic-American: **3.9%**, White: **65.1%**, International: **3.0%**, Unknown: **0.0%**

ACADEMIC PROGRAMS

The school's curriculum gives first-year students substantial contact with patients.

There are opportunities for first- or second-year students to work in community health clinics.

Program offerings: AIDS, drug/alcohol abuse, family medicine, geriatrics, internal medicine, pediatrics, rural medicine, women's health

Joint degrees awarded: M.D./Ph.D., M.D./M.B.A., M.D./M.S., M.D./M.A.

Total National Institutes of Health (NIH) grants awarded to the medical school and affiliated hospitals: **N/A**

CURRICULUM
(TEXT PROVIDED BY SCHOOL):

The curriculum, Prescription for Excellence: A Physician's Pathway to Lifelong Learning, is organized to meet the goals of the undergraduate medical education program: the development of proficiency in self-directed learning and lifelong learning skills, and the acquisition of appropriate core biomedical science knowledge, clinical skills, problem-solving/clinical reasoning skills, interviewing and communication skills, information management skills, and professional attitudes and behavior.

Students study the basic and clinical sciences in an integrated fashion across the five phases of the four-year curriculum, utilizing a variety of educational methods including small-group, problem-based learning. Community-based clinical experiences in the first year, as well as a focus on general population health, are hallmarks of the curriculum. Humanistic and professionalism issues are addressed longitudinally across the curriculum in formats designed to provide students with a clear understanding of the role and responsibilities of physicians within society. Information technology has been integrated into the curriculum, and all incoming students are provided with a laptop computer.

Phase 1 serves as the foundation for the remainder of the curriculum and consists of seven courses: Human Structure and Development, Cellular and Subcellular Processes, Basic and Clinical Science Problems I, Foundations of Clinical Medicine I (FCM), Medicine as a Profession I (MAAP), Population Health and Epidemiology/Evidence Based Medicine, and Community Practice Experience(CPE).

Phase 2 is composed of five courses. Systems Pathophysiology begins in Phase 2, with the remaining four courses (Basic and Clinical Science Problems, FCM, MAAP, and CPE) being continuations of courses begun in Phase 1. The Systems Pathophysiology course is intended to be an introduction to clinical medicine—integrating basic science with clinical material built around nine organ-based topics: infectious disease/microbiology, hematology/lymph, endocrinology/reproduction, cardiovascular, pulmonary, renal, nervous system, digestive diseases/nutrition, and integument and musculoskeletal.

Phase 3 is composed of three 16-week blocks; approximately one third of the class is assigned to each block at any given time. Core clinical clerkships include: inpatient internal medicine, ambulatory internal medicine, surgery, obstetrics/gynecology/women's health, pediatrics, psychiatry, neurology/rehabilitation, and family medicine. There are also one-week clerkships in anesthesiology and radiology.

Phase 4 consists of 10 four-week blocks (four required, six elective) and four weeks of vacation. Numerous elective opportunities are available intramurally and externally at approved institutions. Students have the opportunity to participate in electives in foreign countries; the medical school maintains formal affiliation agreements with a number of medical schools. The four required clerkship months are advanced inpatient management (AIM) clerkships (students complete two monthlong AIM clerkships selected from two separate disciplines: surgery, psychiatry, family medicine, obstetrics and gynecology, internal medicine, and pediatrics), emergency medicine, and intensive care. The primary goal of these clerkship experiences is the development of students' abilities in complete patient management. Students are actively involved in all aspects of patient care.

Phase 5 is a five-week capstone experience for students and includes small-group problem-based learning, journal clubs, medical Spanish, and a series of basic and clinical science lectures, aimed at enhancing the abilities and preparing the soon-to-graduate student for the challenges of residency and beyond.

FACULTY PROFILE (FALL 2003)
Total teaching faculty: **819 (full-time)**, **526 (part-time)**

Of full-time faculty, those teaching in basic sciences: **27%**; in clinical programs: **73%**

Of part-time faculty, those teaching in basic sciences: **11%**; in clinical programs: **89%**

Full-time faculty/student ratio: **1.9**

SUPPORT SERVICES
The school offers students these services for dealing with stress: professional counseling, religious support.

RESIDENCY CHOICES
Most popular residency and specialty programs chosen by the 2002 and 2003 M.D. graduating classes: anesthesiology, emergency medicine, family practice, internal medicine, pediatrics, surgery–general.

WHERE GRADS GO

50.0%

Proportion of 2001-2003 graduates who entered primary care specialties

28.0%

Proportion of 2002-2003 graduates who accepted in-state residencies

---

Washington University in St. Louis

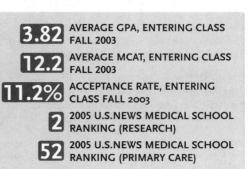

- 660 S. Euclid Avenue, St. Louis, MO 63110
- Private
- **Year Founded:** 1891
- **Tuition, 2003-2004:** $37,032
- **Enrollment, 2003-2004:** 579
- **Website:** http://medschool.wustl.edu
- **Specialty ranking:** AIDS: 17, drug/alcohol abuse: 8, geriatrics: 15, internal medicine: 7, pediatrics: 7, women's health: 15

3.82 AVERAGE GPA, ENTERING CLASS FALL 2003

12.2 AVERAGE MCAT, ENTERING CLASS FALL 2003

11.2% ACCEPTANCE RATE, ENTERING CLASS FALL 2003

2 2005 U.S.NEWS MEDICAL SCHOOL RANKING (RESEARCH)

52 2005 U.S.NEWS MEDICAL SCHOOL RANKING (PRIMARY CARE)

ADMISSIONS

Admissions phone number: **(314) 362-6858**
Admissions email address: **wumscoa@msnotes.wustl.edu**
Application website:
http://medschool.wustl.edu/admissions
Acceptance rate: **11.2%**
In-state acceptance rate: **13.9%**
Out-of-state acceptance rate: **11.1%**
Minority acceptance rate: **12.4%**
International acceptance rate: **11.9%**

Fall 2003 applications and acceptees

	Applied	Interviewed	Accepted	Enrolled
Total:	2,998	1,085	337	122
In-state:	151	52	21	15
Out-of-state:	2,847	1,033	316	107

Profile of admitted students

Average undergraduate grade point average: **3.82**
MCAT averages (scale: 1-15; writing test: J-T):
Composite score: **12.2**
Verbal reasoning score: **11.3**, Physical sciences score: **12.6**, Biological sciences score: **12.5**, Writing score: **Q**
Proportion with undergraduate majors in: Biological sciences: **44%**, Physical sciences: **32%**, Non-sciences: **8%**, Other health professions: **0%**, Mixed disciplines and other: **16%**
Percentage of students not coming directly from college after graduation: **40%**

Dates and details

The American Medical College Application Service (AMCAS) application is accepted.
School asks for a school-specific application as part of the admissions process.
Oldest MCAT considered for Fall 2005 entry: **2002**
Earliest application date for the 2005-2006 first-year class: **June 1, 2004**
Latest application date: **December 1, 2004**
Acceptance dates for regular application for the class entering in fall 2005:

Earliest: **November 15, 2004**
Latest: **N/A**
The school considers requests for deferred entrance.
Starting month for the class entering in 2005-2006: **August**
The school doesn't have an Early Decision Plan (EDP).
A personal interview is required for admission.

Undergraduate coursework required

Medical school requires undergraduate work in these subjects: biology, organic chemistry, inorganic (general) chemistry, physics, calculus, general chemistry.

ADMISSIONS POLICY
(TEXT PROVIDED BY SCHOOL):

Washington University School of Medicine seeks to enroll bright, energetic, compassionate students who want to learn to practice medicine at the edge of what is known. The recruitment and selection process seeks to identify people who are personally and academically accomplished and who are energized by interacting with others and improving their well-being. Applications are especially encouraged from women and members of underrepresented minority groups as well as those with diverse life experiences and backgrounds.

Once students are enrolled, the school supports them wholeheartedly. This includes robust financial aid, outstanding learning facilities, and world-renowned and accessible faculty plus a multitude of opportunities for research, community service, and leadership experience.

The coursework required for admission includes one year each of biology, general (inorganic) chemistry, organic chemistry, physics, and mathematics through differential calculus. Applicants must present evidence of superior intellectual ability and scholastic achievement in addition to evidence of superior character and integrity that justify the trust their colleagues, patients, and society will place in them. Although many applicants have majored in science, engineering, or mathematics, those who have majored in humanities or social science are equally welcome.

The application process starts with designating Washington University School of Medicine on the online American Medical College Application Service. Candidates are then invited to complete a secondary online application.

Applications are evaluated based on the applicant's entire undergraduate and, where applicable, graduate academic record. Items scrutinized include rigor of the curriculum, grades, Medical College Admission Test scores, recommendation letters, extracurricular activities, life experiences, and AMCAS essay.

Selected applicants are invited to visit St. Louis to tour the medical center, meet medical students, and interview with a member of the Committee on Admissions. Interviews focus on communication skills, accomplishments, avocations, and interests plus the applicant's motivation for deciding to study medicine.

COSTS AND FINANCIAL AID

Financial aid phone number: **(314) 362-6845**
Tuition, 2003-2004 academic year: **$37,032**
Room and board: **$8,256**
Percentage of students receiving financial aid in 2003-04: **80%**
Percentage of students receiving: Loans: **57%**, Grants/scholarships: **63%**, Work-study aid: **0%**
Average medical school debt for the Class of 2002: **$85,122**

STUDENT BODY

Fall 2003 full-time enrollment: **579**
Men: **55%**, Women: **45%**, In-state: **8%**, Minorities: **34%**, American Indian: **0.5%**, Asian-American: **24.0%**, African-American: **4.0%**, Hispanic-American: **2.2%**, White: **57.3%**, International: **4.5%**, Unknown: **7.4%**

ACADEMIC PROGRAMS

The school's curriculum gives first-year students substantial contact with patients.
There are opportunities for first- or second-year students to work in community health clinics.
Program offerings: AIDS, drug/alcohol abuse, family medicine, geriatrics, internal medicine, pediatrics, rural medicine
Joint degrees awarded: M.D./Ph.D., M.D./M.A.
Total National Institutes of Health (NIH) grants awarded to the medical school and affiliated hospitals: **$373.1 million**

CURRICULUM

(TEXT PROVIDED BY SCHOOL):
The first-year curriculum focuses on the acquisition of a core knowledge of human biology, as well as on an introduction to the essentials of good patient care. Diversity among matriculants in undergraduate background, and in approaches to learning, is recognized and fostered. Courses are graded pass/fail, and a variety of didactic means are made available, including lectures, small groups, extensive course syllabi, clinical correlations, and a Lotus Notes computerized curriculum database. The Practice of Medicine I uses regular patient interactions and integrative cases to teach students to skillfully interview and examine patients,

as well as the fundamentals of bioethics, health promotion/disease prevention, biostatistics, and epidemiology.

The second-year curriculum is focused on human pathophysiology and pathology. Through lectures, small-group discussions, laboratory exercises, and independent study, students acquire broad, detailed knowledge of mechanisms of disease pathogenesis, clinopathological relationships, and fundamental principles of therapy. The Practice of Medicine II continues students' introduction to the fundamentals of patient care, and emphasizes organizing and interpreting clinical information.

The overall goal of the third year is implementation of fundamental interactive clinical skills necessary for the practice of medicine at the highest possible level of excellence. Students achieve this goal by participating in intensive, closely supervised training experiences in the core clinical clerkships involving inpatient and ambulatory settings and interactions with patients who present a spectrum of emergent, urgent, routine, and chronic clinical problems. Through these experiences, students exhibit growth and maturation in their abilities to take medical histories, perform complete physical examinations, synthesize findings into a diagnosis, formulate treatment plans, and document and present information in a concise, logical, and organized fashion.

The overall goals of the fourth year are to consolidate, enhance, and refine the basic clinical skills developed during the clinical clerkships and to explore specialty areas within the field of medicine.

FACULTY PROFILE (FALL 2003)

Total teaching faculty: **1,396 (full-time)**, **79 (part-time)**
Of full-time faculty, those teaching in basic sciences: **11%**; in clinical programs: **89%**
Of part-time faculty, those teaching in basic sciences: **3%**; in clinical programs: **97%**
Full-time faculty/student ratio: **2.4**

SUPPORT SERVICES

The school offers students these services for dealing with stress: peer counseling, professional counseling, religious support, support groups.

RESIDENCY CHOICES

Most popular residency and specialty programs chosen by the 2002 and 2003 M.D. graduating classes: anesthesiology, dermatology, emergency medicine, internal medicine, ophthalmology, orthopedic surgery, pediatrics, radiology–diagnostic, surgery–general.

WHERE GRADS GO

35.8%
Proportion of 2001-2003 graduates who entered primary care specialties

32.2%
Proportion of 2002-2003 graduates who accepted in-state residencies

Wayne State University

- 540 E. Canfield, Detroit, MI 48201
- Public
- Year Founded: 1868
- Tuition, 2003-2004: In-state: $17,728; Out-of-state: $35,969
- Enrollment, 2003-2004: 1,049
- Website: http://www.med.wayne.edu/Admissions
- Specialty ranking: drug/alcohol abuse: 19

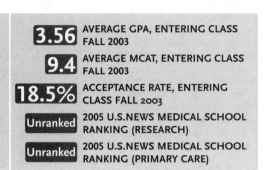

3.56	AVERAGE GPA, ENTERING CLASS FALL 2003
9.4	AVERAGE MCAT, ENTERING CLASS FALL 2003
18.5%	ACCEPTANCE RATE, ENTERING CLASS FALL 2003
Unranked	2005 U.S.NEWS MEDICAL SCHOOL RANKING (RESEARCH)
Unranked	2005 U.S.NEWS MEDICAL SCHOOL RANKING (PRIMARY CARE)

ADMISSIONS
Admissions phone number: **(313) 577-1466**
Admissions email address: **admissions@med.wayne.edu**
Application website: **N/A**
Acceptance rate: **18.5%**
In-state acceptance rate: **37.2%**
Out-of-state acceptance rate: **6.2%**
Minority acceptance rate: **14.8%**
International acceptance rate: **9.6%**

Fall 2003 applications and acceptees
	Applied	Interviewed	Accepted	Enrolled
Total:	2,722	784	504	257
In-state:	1,082	571	402	227
Out-of-state:	1,640	213	102	30

Profile of admitted students
Average undergraduate grade point average: **3.56**
MCAT averages (scale: 1-15; writing test: J-T):
 Composite score: **9.4**
 Verbal reasoning score: **8.8**, Physical sciences score: **9.5**, Biological sciences score: **9.8**, Writing score: **O**
Proportion with undergraduate majors in: Biological sciences: **47%**, Physical sciences: **29%**, Non-sciences: **10%**, Other health professions: **2%**, Mixed disciplines and other: **12%**
Percentage of students not coming directly from college after graduation: **15%**

Dates and details
The American Medical College Application Service (AMCAS) application is accepted.
School asks for a school-specific application as part of the admissions process.
Oldest MCAT considered for Fall 2005 entry: **2001**
Earliest application date for the 2005-2006 first-year class: **June 1, 2004**
Latest application date: **December 15, 2004**
Acceptance dates for regular application for the class entering in fall 2005:
 Earliest: **October 22, 2004**

Latest: **August 5, 2005**
The school considers requests for deferred entrance.
Starting month for the class entering in 2005-2006:
 August
The school has an Early Decision Plan (EDP).
A personal interview is required for admission.

Undergraduate coursework required
Medical school requires undergraduate work in these subjects: biology, English, organic chemistry, inorganic (general) chemistry, physics.

ADMISSIONS POLICY
(TEXT PROVIDED BY SCHOOL):
The Committee on Admissions will select those applicants who, in its judgment, will make the best students and physicians. Consideration is given to the entire record, grade-point average, Medical College Admission Test scores, recommendations, and interview results as these reflect the applicant's personality, maturity, character, and suitability for medicine. Additionally, the committee regards as desirable certain healthcare experiences, such as volunteering or working in hospitals, hospices, nursing homes, or doctor's offices. The committee also values experience in biomedical laboratory research.
 Following an initial screening process, students with competitive applications are selected to complete a secondary application. Special encouragement is given to candidates from medically underserved areas in Michigan.

COSTS AND FINANCIAL AID
Financial aid phone number: **(313) 577-1039**
Tuition, 2003-2004 academic year: **In-state: $17,728; Out-of-state: $35,969**
Room and board: **$18,413**
Percentage of students receiving financial aid in 2003-04: **87%**
Percentage of students receiving: Loans: **86%**, Grants/scholarships: **36%**, Work-study aid: **2%**
Average medical school debt for the Class of 2002: **$104,637**

STUDENT BODY

Fall 2003 full-time enrollment: 1,049
Men: 53%, Women: 47%, In-state: 93%, Minorities: 34%,
    American Indian: 0.2%, Asian-American: 19.3%,
    African-American: 13.0%, Hispanic-American: 1.2%,
    White: 66.3%, International: 0.0%, Unknown: 0.0%

ACADEMIC PROGRAMS

The school's curriculum gives first-year students
    substantial contact with patients.
There are opportunities for first- or second-year students to
    work in community health clinics.
Program offerings: AIDS, drug/alcohol abuse, family
    medicine, geriatrics, internal medicine, pediatrics,
    women's health
Joint degrees awarded: M.D./Ph.D.
Total National Institutes of Health (NIH) grants awarded to
    the medical school and affiliated hospitals: **N/A**

CURRICULUM

(TEXT PROVIDED BY SCHOOL):

The Medical School curriculum is a four-academic-year
course of study, beginning in August of one year and ending in May 45 months later.

Traditionally, the first two years are designated as the
basic science curriculum. The curriculum in Year 1 deals
with normal structure and function of the human body. It
includes courses in human gross anatomy, histology,
embryology, biochemistry, physiology, neuroscience, genetics, nutrition, and clinical medicine. Neuroscience is the
only integrated course in the first year, combining portions
of neuroanatomy, physiology, psychiatry, and biochemistry.
All courses include problem-solving sessions as part of their
curriculum. The clinical medicine program is largely a
problem-based course that is integrated over all four years.

The Year 2 curriculum focuses on the abnormal structure and function of the human body. The first term is composed of courses in immunology/microbiology/infectious
disease, psychiatry, pharmacology, pathobiology, and clinical
medicine. The second term is made up of eight pathophysiology units that integrate pathology, medicine, and pharmacology for gastrointestinal, hematology, connective
tissues/dermatology, neurology, respiratory, cardiovascular,
and endocrine systems. Running concurrently with this program is Clinical Medicine, which involves twice-weekly sessions in area hospitals where students work in small groups
with teams of physicians to learn physical diagnostic skills.

Upon completion of the basic science curriculum, students must pass the United States Medical Licensing
Examination Step 1 before promotion to the third year of
medical school.

The clinical science curriculum includes eight required
clerkships during 11 months in the third year and three
required courses during the eight months of study making
up the fourth year.

The third-year required clerkships are pediatrics (two
months), internal medicine (two months), family medicine
(one month), and continuity of care (six months, concurrent
with other clerkships), general surgery (two months),
obstetrics and gynecology (two months), neurology (one
month), and psychiatry (one month). One month is
reserved for an elective.

The fourth-year required clerkships are Emergency
Medicine (one month); Inpatient Medicine (adult or pediatric, one month); and Outpatient Medicine (adult or pediatric, one month).

During the clinical science curriculum, students must
take a minimum of six electives, typically taken as one elective in the third year and five in the fourth year. It is
required that students plan a balanced program of study.

Midway through the third year, students typically begin
to choose an adviser and focus on postgraduate (residency)
training. The residency application process begins in the
summer of the fourth year, with interviews for most specialties in the fall and early winter. Match lists for the National
Residency Matching Program are due in February of the
senior year, with results announced in mid-March. Senior
students are required to take the USMLE Step 2 before
graduation, and, beginning with Class of 2005, passage of
this examination will be a requirement for graduation.

FACULTY PROFILE (FALL 2003)

Total teaching faculty: **906 (full-time)**, **62 (part-time)**
Of full-time faculty, those teaching in basic sciences: **18%**;
    in clinical programs: **82%**
Of part-time faculty, those teaching in basic sciences: **18%**;
    in clinical programs: **82%**
Full-time faculty/student ratio: **0.9**

SUPPORT SERVICES

The school offers students these services for dealing with
stress: expanded-hour gym access, peer counseling, professional counseling, support groups.

RESIDENCY CHOICES

Most popular residency and specialty programs chosen by
the 2002 and 2003 M.D. graduating classes: emergency
medicine, internal medicine, orthopedic surgery, pediatrics,
surgery–general.

WHERE GRADS GO

43.4%

*Proportion of 2001-2003 graduates who entered primary
care specialties*

60.6%

*Proportion of 2002-2003 graduates who accepted in-state
residencies*

West Virginia University

- 1146 Health Sciences N, Morgantown, WV 26506-9111
- Public
- Year Founded: 1902
- Tuition, 2003-2004: In-state: $13,440; Out-of-state: $31,180
- Enrollment, 2003-2004: 382
- Website: http://www.hsc.wvu.edu/som/students
- Specialty ranking: rural medicine: 13

3.65 AVERAGE GPA, ENTERING CLASS FALL 2003

9.0 AVERAGE MCAT, ENTERING CLASS FALL 2003

19.5% ACCEPTANCE RATE, ENTERING CLASS FALL 2003

Unranked 2005 U.S.NEWS MEDICAL SCHOOL RANKING (RESEARCH)

Unranked 2005 U.S.NEWS MEDICAL SCHOOL RANKING (PRIMARY CARE)

ADMISSIONS

Admissions phone number: **(304) 293-2408**
Admissions email address: **medadmissions@hsc.wvu.edu**
Application website: **http://www.aamc.org**
Acceptance rate: **19.5%**
In-state acceptance rate: **50.0%**
Out-of-state acceptance rate: **8.3%**
Minority acceptance rate: **N/A**
International acceptance rate: **N/A**

Fall 2003 applications and acceptees

	Applied	Interviewed	Accepted	Enrolled
Total:	845	256	165	111
In-state:	228	149	114	82
Out-of-state:	617	107	51	29

Profile of admitted students

Average undergraduate grade point average: **3.65**
MCAT averages (scale: 1-15; writing test: J-T):
  Composite score: **9.0**
  Verbal reasoning score: **9.1**, Physical sciences score: **8.7**,
  Biological sciences score: **9.4**, Writing score: **O**
Proportion with undergraduate majors in: Biological sciences: **70%**, Physical sciences: **20%**, Non-sciences: **6%**, Other health professions: **4%**, Mixed disciplines and other: **0%**
Percentage of students not coming directly from college after graduation: **N/A**

Dates and details

The American Medical College Application Service (AMCAS) application is accepted.
School asks for a school-specific application as part of the admissions process.
Oldest MCAT considered for Fall 2005 entry: **2003**
Earliest application date for the 2005-2006 first-year class:
  June 3, 2004
Latest application date: **November 15, 2004**
Acceptance dates for regular application for the class entering in fall 2005:
  Earliest: **October 15, 2004**

Latest: **July 1, 2005**
The school considers requests for deferred entrance.
Starting month for the class entering in 2005-2006:
  August
The school has an Early Decision Plan (EDP).
A personal interview is required for admission.

Undergraduate coursework required

Medical school requires undergraduate work in these subjects: biology/zoology, English, organic chemistry, inorganic (general) chemistry, physics, behavioral science, social sciences, general chemistry.

ADMISSIONS POLICY
(TEXT PROVIDED BY SCHOOL):

The Medical College Admission Test and a minimum of three years of college in an accredited U.S. or Canadian school (minimum of 90 semester hours or equivalent) are required. All required courses must be passed with a grade of C or better by January 1 of the matriculation year. College work must include: eight semester hours each of biology or zoology, inorganic chemistry, organic chemistry, and general physics, all with lab; six hours of English; and six hours of behavioral or social sciences.

We highly recommend that applicants complete courses in biochemistry and cellular/molecular biology. Fundamental competence in communication skills is a great need. Additional coursework should be designed to provide breadth leading toward a bachelor's degree in a major field of the applicant's own choosing, not necessarily in the natural sciences or in a premedical curriculum. Computer literacy is required.

Applicants are strongly encouraged to (and early-decision applicants must) take the MCAT no later than April of the year before they hope to enter medical school. Applicants must apply through the American Medical College Application Service no later than the posted cutoff date. Interviews are held only on-site beginning in September. No applicant is admitted without an interview. Acceptances will be issued throughout the interview period.

West Virginia residents receive priority consideration. Applicants with ties to West Virginia will be strongly considered, as well as those with strong interest in rural medicine.

The choice of students is based upon scholarship, MCAT scores, community service, leadership, medical experience, personal qualifications as judged by interviews, and recommendations from qualified persons.

The 2003 entering class had the following profile: residency, 74 percent West Virginia residents; mean overall GPA, 3.65; mean MCAT scores, verbal reasoning 9.1, physical sciences 8.7, biological sciences 9.4, writing sample O; gender, 44 percent women; undergraduate major, 81 percent in biological sciences, chemistry, or preprofessional curriculum; and undergraduate schools, 66 students attended West Virginia schools.

COSTS AND FINANCIAL AID

Financial aid phone number: **(304) 293-3706**
Tuition, 2003-2004 academic year: **In-state: $13,440; Out-of-state: $31,180**
Room and board: **$10,005**
Percentage of students receiving financial aid in 2003-04: **85%**
Percentage of students receiving: Loans: **78%**, Grants/scholarships: **37%**, Work-study aid: **0%**
Average medical school debt for the Class of 2002: **$77,747**

STUDENT BODY

Fall 2003 full-time enrollment: **382**
Men: **58%**, Women: **42%**, In-state: **87%**, Minorities: **15%**, American Indian: **0.8%**, Asian-American: **13.1%**, African-American: **0.5%**, Hispanic-American: **1.0%**, White: **84.0%**, International: **0.3%**, Unknown: **0.3%**

ACADEMIC PROGRAMS

The school's curriculum gives first-year students substantial contact with patients.
There are opportunities for first- or second-year students to work in community health clinics.
Program offerings: AIDS, drug/alcohol abuse, family medicine, geriatrics, internal medicine, pediatrics, rural medicine, women's health
Joint degrees awarded: M.D./Ph.D., M.D./M.P.H., M.D./J.D.
Total National Institutes of Health (NIH) grants awarded to the medical school and affiliated hospitals: **$12.1 million**

CURRICULUM

(TEXT PROVIDED BY SCHOOL):
The educational program of the School of Medicine is designed to provide students with a strong foundation upon which they can base preparation for any branch of medicine—specifically, primary care, other specialty practice, teaching, research, or a combination of these career objectives.

In the first and second years, the plan of study is directed toward the principles and methodology of the basic medical sciences. However, the basic courses are modularized and designed so that the student begins to synthesize concepts

of patient care. The first-year basic science courses are integrated through lectures, common test methods, and problem-based-learning clinical applications. Clinical experiences are introduced the first semester of the first year. Summer externships are available in most primary-care fields. Additional early exposure to patient-oriented instruction is through the introduction to clinical medicine, community medicine, and other behavioral medicine courses during the second basic science year.

The third-year curriculum gives the student a foundation in history taking, examination, patient relations, laboratory aids, diagnosis, treatment, and use of medical literature in the major clinical disciplines.

The fourth year is composed of required selectives (60 percent) and electives (40 percent). Requirements include critical care medicine; anesthesia; surgical subspecialties; and a medicine, family practice, or pediatrics subinternship. Three months of rural rotations during the third and fourth years are also required.

Students with interest in research will be considered for the medical scientist M.D./Ph.D. program. The Ph.D. is offered in over eight disciplines. An M.D./M.P.H. program is also offered.

A grading system of honors/satisfactory/unsatisfactory plus narrative is used in the School of Medicine. One hundred hours of community service are required for graduation. Students are expected to demonstrate professionalism at all times.

FACULTY PROFILE (FALL 2003)

Total teaching faculty: **510 (full-time), 95 (part-time)**
Of full-time faculty, those teaching in basic sciences: **14%**; in clinical programs: **86%**
Of part-time faculty, those teaching in basic sciences: **2%**; in clinical programs: **98%**
Full-time faculty/student ratio: **1.3**

SUPPORT SERVICES

The school offers students these services for dealing with stress: expanded-hour gym access, professional counseling, support groups.

RESIDENCY CHOICES

Most popular residency and specialty programs chosen by the 2002 and 2003 M.D. graduating classes: anesthesiology, emergency medicine, family practice, internal medicine, obstetrics and gynecology, pediatrics, psychiatry, surgery–general, internal medicine/pediatrics.

WHERE GRADS GO

35.3%
Proportion of 2001-2003 graduates who entered primary care specialties

38.0%
Proportion of 2002-2003 graduates who accepted in-state residencies

Wright State University

■ PO Box 1751, Dayton, OH 45401-1751
■ Public
■ Year Founded: 1974
■ Tuition, 2003-2004: In-state: $17,532; Out-of-state: $24,426
■ Enrollment, 2003-2004: 364
■ Website: http://www.med.wright.edu
■ Specialty ranking: family medicine: 26

3.49 AVERAGE GPA, ENTERING CLASS FALL 2003

8.7 AVERAGE MCAT, ENTERING CLASS FALL 2003

14.7% ACCEPTANCE RATE, ENTERING CLASS FALL 2003

Unranked 2005 U.S.NEWS MEDICAL SCHOOL RANKING (RESEARCH)

50 2005 U.S.NEWS MEDICAL SCHOOL RANKING (PRIMARY CARE)

ADMISSIONS
Admissions phone number: **(937) 775-2934**
Admissions email address: **som_saa@wright.edu**
Application website:
   https://somms2.med.wright.edu/saa/oasys/login.asp
Acceptance rate: **14.7%**
In-state acceptance rate: **21.2%**
Out-of-state acceptance rate: **2.3%**
Minority acceptance rate: **N/A**
International acceptance rate: **N/A**

Fall 2003 applications and acceptees
	Applied	Interviewed	Accepted	Enrolled
Total:	2,774	409	409	91
In-state:	886	343	188	80
Out-of-state:	1,888	66	44	11

Profile of admitted students
Average undergraduate grade point average: **3.49**
MCAT averages (scale: 1-15; writing test: J-T):
   Composite score: **8.7**
   Verbal reasoning score: **8.6**, Physical sciences score: **8.5**,
   Biological sciences score: **9.0**, Writing score: **O**
Proportion with undergraduate majors in: Biological
   sciences: **66%**, Physical sciences: **13%**, Non-sciences:
   15%, Other health professions: **3%**, Mixed disciplines
   and other: **3%**
Percentage of students not coming directly from college
   after graduation: **11%**

Dates and details
The American Medical College Application Service
   (AMCAS) application is accepted.
School asks for a school-specific application as part of the
   admissions process.
Oldest MCAT considered for Fall 2005 entry: **2001**
Earliest application date for the 2005-2006 first-year class:
   June 1, 2004
Latest application date: **November 15, 2004**
Acceptance dates for regular application for the class
   entering in fall 2005:

Earliest: **October 1, 2000**
Latest: **August 15, 2000**
The school considers requests for deferred entrance.
Starting month for the class entering in 2005-2006:
   August
The school has an Early Decision Plan (EDP).
A personal interview is required for admission.

Undergraduate coursework required
Medical school requires undergraduate work in these subjects: biology, English, organic chemistry, inorganic (general) chemistry, physics, mathematics, general chemistry.

ADMISSIONS POLICY
(TEXT PROVIDED BY SCHOOL):
It is the policy of the School of Medicine to seek a student
body of diverse social, ethnic, and educational backgrounds.
Women, minority students, and applicants from rural Ohio
backgrounds are particularly encouraged to apply. However,
applicants are admitted solely on the basis of individual
qualifications without regard to race, religion, gender, sexual orientation, disability, veteran status, national origin,
age, or ancestry.
   Dedication to human concerns, compassion, intellectual
capacity, and personal maturity in the applicant are of
greater importance than specific areas of preprofessional
preparation. The Admissions Committee, which is broadly
based, also seeks positive evidence of motivation, altruism,
selflessness, and human empathy in the prospective student.
   Upon receipt of the application from the American
Medical College Application Service, all applicants are
invited to submit secondary applications and letters of recommendation. After review of all submitted material, applicants are selected for interviews. The committee carefully
reviews the application, the academic record, Medical
College Admission Test performance, letters of recommendation, and the results of personal interviews (by invitation
only) in making its final selections. Ohio residents are given
preference, but nonresidents are encouraged to apply.

COSTS AND FINANCIAL AID

Financial aid phone number: **(937) 775-2934**

Tuition, 2003-2004 academic year: **In-state: $17,532; Out-of-state: $24,426**

Room and board: **$10,560**

Percentage of students receiving financial aid in 2003-04: **N/A**

Percentage of students receiving: Loans: **N/A**, Grants/scholarships: **N/A**, Work-study aid: **N/A**

Average medical school debt for the Class of 2002: **N/A**

STUDENT BODY

Fall 2003 full-time enrollment: **364**

Men: **45%**, Women: **55%**, In-state: **97%**, Minorities: **21%**,

ACADEMIC PROGRAMS

The school's curriculum gives first-year students substantial contact with patients.

There are opportunities for first- or second-year students to work in community health clinics.

Program offerings: AIDS, drug/alcohol abuse, family medicine, geriatrics, internal medicine, pediatrics, rural medicine, women's health

Joint degrees awarded: M.D./Ph.D., M.D./M.B.A.

Total National Institutes of Health (NIH) grants awarded to the medical school and affiliated hospitals: **N/A**

CURRICULUM

(TEXT PROVIDED BY SCHOOL):

The primary goal of the educational program is to educate students to provide comprehensive care to patients and their families.

During the first two years, students are taught in an interdisciplinary fashion using large- group lectures, small-group discussions, computer-based instruction, case-based learning, and team learning. The curriculum introduces students to normal structure and functioning in an integrated fashion. Instruction progresses through various organizational levels from molecular to organ.

Throughout the first two years, the curriculum integrates the behavioral sciences, humanities, wellness, and disease prevention. Regular didactic instruction by clinical faculty is provided. Students are taught medical history taking, physical examination skills, and evaluation of patients' concerns, and they are provided an understanding of catastrophic illnesses. Students meet regularly with preceptors to develop clinical skills. To provide additional opportunities for clinical exposure and enrichment, clinically based electives are offered in the first two years.

In the third year, students are exposed to the basic disciplines of medicine through six clerkship rotations. Primary-care clerkships are offered as part of block rotations to coordinate instruction among multiple disciplines.

The fourth year includes rotations, time for board study, and junior internships. Students may choose from over 140 monthly electives.

FACULTY PROFILE (FALL 2003)

Total teaching faculty: **311 (full-time), 1,308 (part-time)**

Of full-time faculty, those teaching in basic sciences: **14%**; in clinical programs: **86%**

Of part-time faculty, those teaching in basic sciences: **2%**; in clinical programs: **98%**

Full-time faculty/student ratio: **0.9**

SUPPORT SERVICES

The school offers students these services for dealing with stress: professional counseling, support groups.

RESIDENCY CHOICES

Most popular residency and specialty programs chosen by the 2002 and 2003 M.D. graduating classes: emergency medicine, family practice, internal medicine, obstetrics and gynecology, pediatrics, psychiatry, surgery–general, internal medicine/pediatrics.

WHERE GRADS GO

56.0%

Proportion of 2001-2003 graduates who entered primary care specialties

54.0%

Proportion of 2002-2003 graduates who accepted in-state residencies

Yale University

- 333 Cedar Street, PO Box 208055, New Haven, CT 06520-8055
- Private
- **Year Founded:** 1810
- **Tuition, 2003-2004:** $34,175
- **Enrollment, 2003-2004:** 507
- **Website:** http://info.med.yale.edu/education
- **Specialty ranking:** drug/alcohol abuse: 3, geriatrics: 9, internal medicine: 11, pediatrics: 11, women's health: 12

3.71	AVERAGE GPA, ENTERING CLASS FALL 2003
11.4	AVERAGE MCAT, ENTERING CLASS FALL 2003
5.7%	ACCEPTANCE RATE, ENTERING CLASS FALL 2003
10	2005 U.S.NEWS MEDICAL SCHOOL RANKING (RESEARCH)
Unranked	2005 U.S.NEWS MEDICAL SCHOOL RANKING (PRIMARY CARE)

ADMISSIONS

Admissions phone number: **(203) 785-2643**
Admissions email address: **medical.admissions@yale.edu**
Application website:
   http://info.med.yale.edu/education/admissions
Acceptance rate: **5.7%**
In-state acceptance rate: **15.2%**
Out-of-state acceptance rate: **5.1%**
Minority acceptance rate: **5.8%**
International acceptance rate: **8.6%**

Fall 2003 applications and acceptees

	Applied	Interviewed	Accepted	Enrolled
Total:	3,325	809	189	100
In-state:	197	75	30	22
Out-of-state:	3,128	734	159	78

Profile of admitted students

Average undergraduate grade point average: **3.71**
MCAT averages (scale: 1-15; writing test: J-T):
   Composite score: **11.4**
   Verbal reasoning score: **10.8**, Physical sciences score:
   11.8, Biological sciences score: **11.7**, Writing score: **R**
Proportion with undergraduate majors in: Biological
   sciences: **41%**, Physical sciences: **28%**, Non-sciences:
   27%, Other health professions: **0%**, Mixed disciplines
   and other: **4%**
Percentage of students not coming directly from college
   after graduation: **58%**

Dates and details

The American Medical College Application Service
   (AMCAS) application is accepted.
School asks for a school-specific application as part of the
   admissions process.
Oldest MCAT considered for Fall 2005 entry: **2002**
Earliest application date for the 2005-2006 first-year class:
   June 1, 2004
Latest application date: **October 15, 2004**
Acceptance dates for regular application for the class
   entering in fall 2005:

Earliest: **March 31, 2005**
Latest: **August 31, 2005**
The school considers requests for deferred entrance.
Starting month for the class entering in 2005-2006:
   August
The school has an Early Decision Plan (EDP).
A personal interview is required for admission.

Undergraduate coursework required

Medical school requires undergraduate work in these subjects: biology, organic chemistry, inorganic (general) chemistry, physics.

ADMISSIONS POLICY

(TEXT PROVIDED BY SCHOOL):
Applicants to the Yale School of Medicine must submit the
American Medical College Application Service application
(online) no later than October 15. The Yale admissions office
will invite students to submit a supplemental application
(online) by November 15. Students accepted into the M.D.
program must have satisfied the following before matriculation: attendance for four academic years at an accredited
college of arts and sciences or institute of technology, at
least one year of which must be completed in the United
States; and completion of full-year courses, including lab
work, in general biology or zoology, general chemistry,
organic chemistry, and general physics.

   Review of applications begins in September. Personal
interviews with the Committee on Admissions are required
for admission. There are no rigidly enforced cutoffs for
grade-point average or Medical College Admission Test
scores, and no specific college majors required of applicants. Yale seeks to enroll a broadly diverse class of accomplished, mature, motivated students. The committee
considers academic record, MCAT scores, essays, recommendations, extracurricular and community contributions,
interpersonal skills, and motivation for medicine. The applicant's state of residence is not a factor.

   Final decisions are sent at same time, on or before March
31. If offered admission, applicants must respond by the
first week of April. The Second Look Weekend is held at

Yale in April to help accepted students become better acquainted with the school. If placed on the waiting list, applicants must indicate by the first week of April whether they wish to stay on the list or withdraw; admissions offers may be made through the spring and summer. Deferred matriculation is allowed in some cases. Students who are not U.S. citizens or permanent residents are welcome to apply. Joint degree programs are offered in collaboration with Yale's schools of public health, law, management, and divinity.

COSTS AND FINANCIAL AID

Financial aid phone number: (203) 785-2645
Tuition, 2003-2004 academic year: $34,175
Room and board: $9,650
Percentage of students receiving financial aid in 2003-04: 80%
Percentage of students receiving: Loans: 64%, Grants/scholarships: 53%, Work-study aid: 0%
Average medical school debt for the Class of 2002: $94,955

STUDENT BODY

Fall 2003 full-time enrollment: 507
Men: 49%, Women: 51%, In-state: 12%, Minorities: 41%, American Indian: 0.6%, Asian-American: 23.3%, African-American: 10.3%, Hispanic-American: 6.5%, White: 49.1%, International: 6.1%, Unknown: 4.1%

ACADEMIC PROGRAMS

The school's curriculum gives first-year students substantial contact with patients.
There are opportunities for first- or second-year students to work in community health clinics.
Program offerings: AIDS, drug/alcohol abuse, family medicine, geriatrics, internal medicine, pediatrics, rural medicine, women's health
Joint degrees awarded: M.D./Ph.D., M.D./M.B.A., M.D./M.P.H., M.D./J.D.
Total National Institutes of Health (NIH) grants awarded to the medical school and affiliated hospitals: $267.1 million

CURRICULUM

(TEXT PROVIDED BY SCHOOL):

Yale School of Medicine's educational mission is to train physicians to become leaders in their chosen field, whether in the basic medical sciences, academic clinical sciences, or medical practice in the community. Guiding the mission since 1931 is the Yale System, which provides the educational and intellectual environment for students to become leaders. At the core of the Yale System is the supposition that medical students are already strongly motivated to learn, requiring guidance and stimulation rather than pressure or competition; examinations are given anonymously, and class ranks are not calculated. Students are thus inspired and encouraged, rather than compelled, to take responsibility for their learning. Freed from the anxieties

provoked by competition, students experiment and stretch their interests by participating in electives. The Yale System also encourages students to challenge conventional wisdom by completing an original research project (thesis). Yale trained physicians emerge as independent, creative, and bold thinkers.

The M.D. curriculum is composed of two-year preclinical and clinical segments. In years 1 and 2, the scientific basis of health and disease is presented in the core curriculum, including courses in Human Anatomy and Development, Molecules to Systems (biochemistry, cell biology, and histology and physiology), Neurobiology, Pharmacology, Child and Adolescent Development, Epidemiology and Public Health, and the organ- and system-based Modules. Complementing the core curriculum are opportunities to explore the edge of science and master scientific reasoning. The art of medicine is taught in small-group, skill-building sessions and meetings with a clinical tutor. Students also study ethical and informed medical decision making.

In years 3 and 4, students rotate through clerkships in internal medicine, ambulatory medicine, surgery, anesthesiology, pediatrics, clinical neuroscience, obstetrics and gynecology, psychiatry, primary care, and integrative clinical medicine. A preceptorship program matches students with senior clinical faculty. Students have ample time to participate in electives and continue their thesis research.

FACULTY PROFILE (FALL 2003)

Total teaching faculty: 1,488 (full-time), 1,577 (part-time)
Of full-time faculty, those teaching in basic sciences: 24%; in clinical programs: 76%
Of part-time faculty, those teaching in basic sciences: 5%; in clinical programs: 95%
Full-time faculty/student ratio: 2.9

SUPPORT SERVICES

The school offers students these services for dealing with stress: expanded-hour gym access, peer counseling, professional counseling, religious support, support groups.

RESIDENCY CHOICES

Most popular residency and specialty programs chosen by the 2002 and 2003 M.D. graduating classes: dermatology, emergency medicine, internal medicine, neurological surgery, ophthalmology, orthopedic surgery, pediatrics, psychiatry, radiology–diagnostic, surgery–general.

WHERE GRADS GO

40.0%
Proportion of 2001-2003 graduates who entered primary care specialties

18.6%
Proportion of 2002-2003 graduates who accepted in-state residencies

Yeshiva University

ALBERT EINSTEIN

- 1300 Morris Park Avenue, Bronx, NY 10461
- Private
- Year Founded: 1955
- Tuition, 2003-2004: $36,425
- Enrollment, 2003-2004: 730
- Website: http://www.aecom.yu.edu
- Specialty ranking: N/A

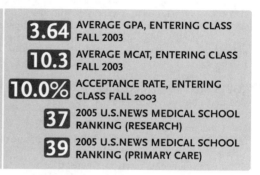

3.64 AVERAGE GPA, ENTERING CLASS FALL 2003

10.3 AVERAGE MCAT, ENTERING CLASS FALL 2003

10.0% ACCEPTANCE RATE, ENTERING CLASS FALL 2003

37 2005 U.S.NEWS MEDICAL SCHOOL RANKING (RESEARCH)

39 2005 U.S.NEWS MEDICAL SCHOOL RANKING (PRIMARY CARE)

ADMISSIONS

Admissions phone number: **(718) 430-2106**
Admissions email address: **admissions@aecom.yu.edu**
Application website:
   http://www.aecom.yu.edu/home/admissions
Acceptance rate: **10.0%**
In-state acceptance rate: **14.0%**
Out-of-state acceptance rate: **8.7%**
Minority acceptance rate: **N/A**
International acceptance rate: **5.4%**

Fall 2003 applications and acceptees

	Applied	Interviewed	Accepted	Enrolled
Total:	5,757	1,526	576	180
In-state:	1,445	477	202	84
Out-of-state:	4,312	1,049	374	96

Profile of admitted students

Average undergraduate grade point average: **3.64**
MCAT averages (scale: 1-15; writing test: J-T):
   Composite score: **10.3**
   Verbal reasoning score: **9.6**, Physical sciences score:
   10.5, Biological sciences score: **10.7**, Writing score: **Q**
Proportion with undergraduate majors in: Biological
   sciences: **47%**, Physical sciences: **17%**, Non-sciences:
   27%, Other health professions: **7%**, Mixed disciplines
   and other: **2%**
Percentage of students not coming directly from college
   after graduation: **22%**

Dates and details

The American Medical College Application Service
   (AMCAS) application is accepted.
School asks for a school-specific application as part of the
   admissions process.
Oldest MCAT considered for Fall 2005 entry: **2000**
Earliest application date for the 2005-2006 first-year class:
   June 1, 2004
Latest application date: **November 1, 2004**
Acceptance dates for regular application for the class
   entering in fall 2005:

Earliest: **January 15, 2004**
Latest: **August 15, 2004**
The school considers requests for deferred entrance.
Starting month for the class entering in 2005-2006:
   August
The school has an Early Decision Plan (EDP).
A personal interview is required for admission.

Undergraduate coursework required

Medical school requires undergraduate work in these subjects: biology, English, organic chemistry, inorganic (general) chemistry, physics, mathematics, general chemistry.

ADMISSIONS POLICY

(TEXT PROVIDED BY SCHOOL):

The M.D. Committee on Admissions considers several
thousand applicants to the Albert Einstein College of
Medicine each year and recommends to the dean the
acceptance of 180 first-year students. Approximately 15 of
those students are selected for the Medical Scientist
Training Program, which leads to the M.D. and Ph.D.
degrees.

   The goal of the committee is to select for admission a
diverse and well-prepared group of students who show great
promise of becoming respected and distinguished members
of the medical community in all areas, including teaching,
research, clinical practice, and administration. Serious consideration is given to participation in extracurricular activities, service orientation, research and other scholarly work,
practical experience in clinical settings, and sincere and
realistic motivation for pursuing a career in medicine.

   The undergraduate experience should not be considered
primarily as preparation for entrance to medical school.
Students are encouraged to take advantage of the diverse
educational opportunities provided at their college or university and are urged to pursue a course of study in which
they are particularly interested.

   It is essential that students begin their medical studies
with a firm foundation in the biological and physical sciences. In addition to completing the minimal requirements
in these subjects, it is recommended that students take at

least another year of instruction in disciplines such as molecular biology, genetics, or neurobiology. Acquisition of a knowledge base in these subjects is not only beneficial to the effective learning of biomedical science during medical school; it also provides a basis for appreciating and understanding numerous remarkable advances in clinical medicine.

In order for medical students to learn many important concepts of biological science, especially in physiology and pathophysiology, an adequate preparation in mathematics is necessary. Additionally, a working knowledge of statistics and an understanding of the concepts of probabilistic science are recommended.

The continuing rapid growth in the volume and complexity of medical information is beyond the range of human cognitive abilities. It is becoming increasingly necessary, therefore, for students of medicine and practicing physicians to be acquainted with computer-based information systems and use computers to manage and access information.

The education of students seeking careers in medicine should also include courses in the social and behavioral sciences because physicians need to focus no less attention on preventing illness and promoting health than on diagnosis and treatment. Successful practice of clinical prevention and health promotion requires knowledge of the sociocultural and behavioral factors that increase the risk of illness and influence the course of disease.

A strong knowledge base in the sciences and mathematics is very important but not sufficient for a successful outcome of the physician-patient encounter; equally important are the physician's communication and interpersonal skills. The quality of such skills determines to a large extent whether the physician is able to conduct a proper history, change a patient's maladaptive behavior, or obtain a patient's compliance with therapeutic advice. Students interested in medicine should seek extracurricular and workplace activities that enable them to interact with people in various ways.

COSTS AND FINANCIAL AID
Financial aid phone number: (718) 430-2336
Tuition, 2003-2004 academic year: $36,425
Room and board: $13,100
Percentage of students receiving financial aid in 2003-04: 80%
Percentage of students receiving: Loans: 80%, Grants/scholarships: 45%, Work-study aid: 0%
Average medical school debt for the Class of 2002: $90,000

STUDENT BODY
Fall 2003 full-time enrollment: 730
Men: 50%, Women: 50%, In-state: 48%, Minorities: 31%, American Indian: 0.1%, Asian-American: 25.3%, African-American: 5.5%, Hispanic-American: 5.6%, White: 58.5%, International: 2.3%, Unknown: 2.6%

ACADEMIC PROGRAMS
The school's curriculum gives first-year students substantial contact with patients.
There are opportunities for first- or second-year students to work in community health clinics.
Program offerings: AIDS, drug/alcohol abuse, family medicine, geriatrics, internal medicine, pediatrics, rural medicine
Joint degrees awarded: M.D./Ph.D., M.D./M.S.
Total National Institutes of Health (NIH) grants awarded to the medical school and affiliated hospitals: $184.1 million

CURRICULUM
(TEXT PROVIDED BY SCHOOL):
The preclerkship curriculum, comprising approximately the first 19 months of study, is devoted primarily to courses in biomedical sciences that take place in lecture halls, conference rooms, and laboratories. During this phase of the curriculum, there are also significant opportunities for students to interact with patients in clinical settings, learn the basics of patient-doctor communication, acquire physical examination skills, and learn how psychosocial and cultural factors affect patient behavior.

During the last two years of the curriculum, students learn the rational application of basic knowledge and communication skills to problems of disease and the treatment of patients in outpatient and inpatient clinical environments.

FACULTY PROFILE (FALL 2003)
Total teaching faculty: 2,452 (full-time), 317 (part-time)
Of full-time faculty, those teaching in basic sciences: 13%; in clinical programs: 87%
Of part-time faculty, those teaching in basic sciences: 6%; in clinical programs: 94%
Full-time faculty/student ratio: 3.4

SUPPORT SERVICES
The school offers students these services for dealing with stress: peer counseling, professional counseling, support groups.

RESIDENCY CHOICES
Most popular residency and specialty programs chosen by the 2002 and 2003 M.D. graduating classes: anesthesiology, emergency medicine, family practice, internal medicine, neurology, obstetrics and gynecology, pediatrics, psychiatry, radiology–diagnostic, surgery–general.

WHERE GRADS GO

55.0%
Proportion of 2001-2003 graduates who entered primary care specialties

60.0%
Proportion of 2002-2003 graduates who accepted in-state residencies

College of Osteopathic Med. of the Pacific

■ 309 E. Second Street, Pomona, CA 91766-1854
■ Private
■ Year Founded: 1977
■ Tuition, 2003-2004: $31,155
■ Enrollment, 2003-2004: 700
■ Website: http://www.westernu.edu
■ Specialty ranking: N/A

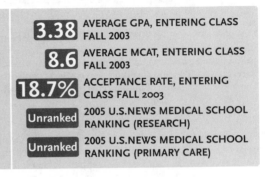

3.38 AVERAGE GPA, ENTERING CLASS FALL 2003

8.6 AVERAGE MCAT, ENTERING CLASS FALL 2003

18.7% ACCEPTANCE RATE, ENTERING CLASS FALL 2003

Unranked 2005 U.S.NEWS MEDICAL SCHOOL RANKING (RESEARCH)

Unranked 2005 U.S.NEWS MEDICAL SCHOOL RANKING (PRIMARY CARE)

ADMISSIONS
Admissions phone number: **(909) 469-5335**
Admissions email address: **admissions@westernu.edu**
Application website: **http://www.aacom.org**
Acceptance rate: **18.7%**
In-state acceptance rate: **30.6%**
Out-of-state acceptance rate: **13.2%**
Minority acceptance rate: **18.9%**
International acceptance rate: **N/A**

Fall 2003 applications and acceptees
	Applied	Interviewed	Accepted	Enrolled
Total:	1,994	478	372	174
In-state:	624	242	191	126
Out-of-state:	1,370	236	181	48

Profile of admitted students
Average undergraduate grade point average: **3.38**
MCAT averages (scale: 1-15; writing test: J-T):
  Composite score: **8.6**
  Verbal reasoning score: **7.4**, Physical sciences score: **8.3**,
  Biological sciences score: **9.0**, Writing score: **P**
Proportion with undergraduate majors in: Biological
  sciences: **48%**, Physical sciences: **17%**, Non-sciences:
  10%, Other health professions: **8%**, Mixed disciplines
  and other: **17%**
Percentage of students not coming directly from college
  after graduation: **16%**

Dates and details
Oldest MCAT considered for Fall 2005 entry: **2000**
Earliest application date for the 2005-2006 first-year class:
  June 2, 2004
Latest application date: **February 1, 2004**
Acceptance dates for regular application for the class
  entering in fall 2005:
  Earliest: **September 15, 2004**
  Latest: **August 7, 2005**
The school considers requests for deferred entrance.
Starting month for the class entering in 2005-2006:
  August

The school has an Early Decision Plan (EDP).
A personal interview is required for admission.

Undergraduate coursework required
Medical school requires undergraduate work in these subjects: biology/zoology, English, organic chemistry, inorganic
(general) chemistry, physics, behavioral science.

ADMISSIONS POLICY
(TEXT PROVIDED BY SCHOOL):
COMP accepts applications from all qualified candidates.
More applications are received from qualified candidates
than can be admitted. While grades and Medical College
Admission Test scores are important in selecting candidates
for admission and may suggest future academic success,
the Admissions Committee recognizes that these statistics,
by themselves, do not guarantee later success as a physician. Therefore, nonacademic criteria are also important in
making the selection.

COMP seeks a diverse and balanced student population
and considers factors such as well-rounded background,
work experiences, letters of recommendation, interest in
and knowledge of osteopathic medicine, and professional
promise. To ascertain these factors, an on-campus interview
is required prior to action on an application. The college
may exercise its discretion to rely upon additional consider-
ations. COMP is committed to admitting competitive, qualified individuals with disabilities.

COSTS AND FINANCIAL AID
Financial aid phone number: **(909) 469-5350**
Tuition, 2003-2004 academic year: **$31,155**
Room and board: **$10,220**
Percentage of students receiving financial aid in 2003-04:
  91%
Percentage of students receiving: Loans: **90%**,
  Grants/scholarships: **14%**, Work-study aid: **0%**
Average medical school debt for the Class of 2002:
  $145,608

STUDENT BODY

Fall 2003 full-time enrollment: **700**
Men: **55%**, Women: **45%**, In-state: **75%**, Minorities: **47%**,
  American Indian: **0.3%**, Asian-American: **38.6%**,
  African-American: **2.1%**, Hispanic-American: **5.1%**,
  White: **44.4%**, International: **1.1%**, Unknown: **8.3%**

ACADEMIC PROGRAMS

The school's curriculum doesn't give first-year students
  substantial contact with patients.
There are opportunities for first- or second-year students to
  work in community health clinics.
Program offerings: AIDS, drug/alcohol abuse, family
  medicine, geriatrics, internal medicine, pediatrics, rural
  medicine
Total National Institutes of Health (NIH) grants awarded to
  the medical school and affiliated hospitals: **$.3 million**

CURRICULUM

(TEXT PROVIDED BY SCHOOL):

The D.O. curriculum is divided into three phases: introduction to the basic sciences; correlated system teaching, incorporating basic and clinical sciences in the study of 10 organ
systems of the body; and clinical experiences.

The four-year curriculum has been developed to appro-
priately prepare the graduate for the postdoctoral training
years of their choice, with an emphasis on primary care.

In addition to the regular curriculum, COMP offers elective courses. These focus on the art of medicine and seek to
sensitize the future physician to the important aspects of
life and to instill a greater sense of ethics and human values. Various extracurricular activities also contribute to the
personal and professional growth of students, among them
a student drama troupe called SANUS.

Phase 1: The first semester of the first year is designed to
introduce the students to the basic concepts of anatomy
(gross, embryology, and histology), biochemistry, microbiology, pathology, pharmacology, and physiology. Interwoven
throughout the curriculum are osteopathic principles and
practice.

Phase 2: This phase begins in the second semester of the
first year and continues throughout the second year. The
basic and clinical sciences concerned with one particular
organ system of the body are integrated in classroom
instruction. This approach emphasizes the relevance of
basic sciences to clinical practice. The osteopathic approach
is continually emphasized by lecture and laboratory demonstration including manipulative techniques. Other courses
not directly related to a system are also included in Phase 2
as family medicine core courses.

Phase 3 (clinical training): Clinical training via rotation
through each of the major medical disciplines (family practice, internal medicine, surgery, pediatrics, obstetrics/gyne-
cology, pathology, psychiatry, emergency medicine, and
radiology) is accomplished in the third and forth years of
training. Twenty-two rotations of four weeks each provide

an opportunity for clinical skills development in primary-
care medicine. Several elective options are also offered during this two-year period.

The goal of COMP's clinical curriculum is to prepare
each and every student with the knowledge, attitudes, and
skills to excel in his or her chosen postdoctoral training program. Specifically, the student will be able, among other
skills, to: identify the wide range of normal human functioning; recognize, diagnose, and treat the most commonly
encountered health conditions in a primary-care practice;
recognize, diagnose, and treat the acute, life-threatening
conditions encountered by the primary-care physician; dif-
ferentiate health and common health problems from less
common diseases; recognize conditions or situations that
are best handled by consultation and/or referral; provide
continuity of healthcare beginning with initial patient contact; assess and treat chronic health conditions; develop
appropriate, professionally intimate relationships with
patients; understand a patient's individual concerns and
incorporate them into routine care; integrate osteopathic
philosophy and practices into routine patient care; and
understand and work with the family unit to improve the
health and welfare of the individual patient and his or her
family.

FACULTY PROFILE (FALL 2003)

Total teaching faculty: **29 (full-time)**, **9 (part-time)**
Of full-time faculty, those teaching in basic sciences: **69%**;
  in clinical programs: **31%**
Of part-time faculty, those teaching in basic sciences: **11%**;
  in clinical programs: **89%**
Full-time faculty/student ratio: **0.04**

SUPPORT SERVICES

The school offers students these services for dealing with
stress: expanded-hour gym access, peer counseling, professional counseling, religious support, support groups.

RESIDENCY CHOICES

Most popular residency and specialty programs chosen by
the 2002 and 2003 graduating classes: anesthesiology, dermatology, emergency medicine, family practice, family practice–sports medicine, internal medicine, internal
medicine–sports medicine, obstetrics and gynecology,
orthopedic surgery, pediatrics.

WHERE GRADS GO

72.0%

*Proportion of 2001-2003 graduates who entered primary
care specialties*

55.0%

*Proportion of 2002-2003 graduates who accepted in-state
residencies*

Des Moines University

OSTEOPATHIC MEDICAL CENTER

- 3200 Grand Avenue, Des Moines, IA 50312
- Private
- Year Founded: 1898
- Tuition, 2003-2004: $27,400
- Enrollment, 2003-2004: 795
- Website: http://www.dmu.edu
- Specialty ranking: N/A

3.50 AVERAGE GPA, ENTERING CLASS FALL 2003

8.4 AVERAGE MCAT, ENTERING CLASS FALL 2003

25.0% ACCEPTANCE RATE, ENTERING CLASS FALL 2003

Unranked 2005 U.S.NEWS MEDICAL SCHOOL RANKING (RESEARCH)

Unranked 2005 U.S.NEWS MEDICAL SCHOOL RANKING (PRIMARY CARE)

ADMISSIONS

Admissions phone number: **(515) 271-1499**
Admissions email address: **doadmit@dmu.edu**
Application website: **N/A**
Acceptance rate: **25.0%**
In-state acceptance rate: **47.8%**
Out-of-state acceptance rate: **23.8%**
Minority acceptance rate: **9.7%**
International acceptance rate: **17.2%**

Fall 2003 applications and acceptees

	Applied	Interviewed	Accepted	Enrolled
Total:	2,161	617	541	201
In-state:	113	66	54	40
Out-of-state:	2,048	551	487	161

Profile of admitted students

Average undergraduate grade point average: **3.50**
MCAT averages (scale: 1-15; writing test: J-T):
Composite score: **8.4**
Verbal reasoning score: **8.2**, Physical sciences score: **8.2**,
Biological sciences score: **8.7**, Writing score: **O**
Proportion with undergraduate majors in: Biological
sciences: **57%**, Physical sciences: **28%**, Non-sciences:
11%, Other health professions: **3%**, Mixed disciplines
and other: **1%**
Percentage of students not coming directly from college
after graduation: **48%**

Dates and details

Oldest MCAT considered for Fall 2005 entry: **N/A**
Earliest application date for the 2005-2006 first-year class:
May 10, 2004
Latest application date: **February 1, 2004**
Acceptance dates for regular application for the class
entering in fall 2005:
Earliest: **October 1, 2004**
Latest: **July 1, 2005**
The school considers requests for deferred entrance.
Starting month for the class entering in 2005-2006: **N/A**
The school has an Early Decision Plan (EDP).

A personal interview is required for admission.

Undergraduate coursework required

Medical school requires undergraduate work in these subjects: biology/zoology, English, organic chemistry, inorganic (general) chemistry, physics, general chemistry.

ADMISSIONS POLICY

(TEXT PROVIDED BY SCHOOL):

The admissions policies of the College of Osteopathic Medicine ensure selection of students with appropriate preparation. The policies define acceptable premedical education and designate admission procedures. All admission requirements must be completed prior to matriculation. Prospective students should carefully note specified deadlines.

The practice of osteopathic medicine requires good communication skills, an understanding of individuals within their social environment, logical and quantitative thinking, and a solid background in the sciences. To meet these requirements, students are encouraged to complete a diversified undergraduate program.

The application process culminates with a personal interview at the college. Because of limited openings, the Admissions Committee invites only those candidates considered to have the greatest professional promise. The committee bases decisions on academic achievement, activities, personality, character, motivation, and promise shown by candidates.

The college's curriculum integrates basic and clinical sciences. COM does not advise prospective students to enroll in courses during their undergraduate years that must be taken during their osteopathic medical curriculum. Advanced standing based on prior coursework is not given.

COSTS AND FINANCIAL AID

Financial aid phone number: **(515) 271-1470**
Tuition, 2003-2004 academic year: **$27,400**
Room and board: **$12,454**
Percentage of students receiving financial aid in 2003-04:
96%

Percentage of students receiving: Loans: 90%,
   Grants/scholarships: 21%, Work-study aid: N/A
Average medical school debt for the Class of 2002: $141,114

STUDENT BODY

Fall 2003 full-time enrollment: 795
Men: 56%, Women: 44%, In-state: 25%, Minorities: 9%,
   American Indian: 0.4%, Asian-American: 4.4%, African-
   American: 1.6%, Hispanic-American: 28%, White:
   87.9%, International: 0.5%, Unknown: 2.4%

ACADEMIC PROGRAMS

The school's curriculum doesn't give first-year students
   substantial contact with patients.
There are opportunities for first- or second-year students to
   work in community health clinics.
Program offerings: AIDS, drug/alcohol abuse, family
   medicine, geriatrics, internal medicine, pediatrics
Total National Institutes of Health (NIH) grants awarded to
   the medical school and affiliated hospitals: N/A

CURRICULUM

(TEXT PROVIDED BY SCHOOL):
The College of Osteopathic Medicine has developed a highly
integrated systems approach that reflects the interrelationship and interdependence of body systems. The curriculum
combines case-based discussion, lecture, and laboratory
studies with clinical experience in teaching hospitals, college
and private clinics, and community service agencies.

The four years of osteopathic medical school preceding
graduate medical education are divided into a preclinical and
a clinical phase ("2+2" curriculum). The preclinical phase
occupies the first two years, and the clinical phase occupies
the third and fourth years. Basic science departments are
largely responsible for the preclinical curriculum in the first
year. During the second year, basic and clinical sciences are
integrated into a case-based, organ-systems approach. The
principal method of instruction in the first two years is lecture, along with small-group discussion, self-instruction, case-
based learning, and laboratory experiences. Concentration of
basic and clinical sciences in this integrated systems
approach ensures a strong base of knowledge that enables
students to function at the highest level in the clinical years.

As an extension of the college's primary-care emphasis,
the curriculum includes a focus on preventive medicine as
a component of Year 2. A series of preventive-medicine
sources are presented as a corollary to the integrated systems sequence. Prior to clinical rotations, a short course
designed to prepare students for the practical requirements
of clerkships is also presented.

The clinical phase of the curriculum begins in
September of the third year and continues until graduation.
The periods of instruction are called clerkships.

Preclinical phase—Year 1 includes these courses:
Behavioral Science/Psychiatry, Introduction to Osteopathic
Medicine, Introduction to Community Clinical Medicine,
Introduction to Medline and the Internet, Biochemistry,

Problem-Based-Learning Biochemistry (elective),
Osteopathic Manipulative Medicine I, Anatomy, Histology,
Neuroanatomy, Microbiology/Immunology, Physiology,
Physical Diagnosis I, Basic Life Support, Pharmacology,
Pathology, Radiology, and Introduction to Medical Ethics
and the Doctor-Patient Relationship.

Year 2 courses include: Pharmacology II; Introduction to
Case-Based Medicine I: Evidence-Based Medicine, Nutrition;
Integrated Systems I: Cardiology, Renal; Preventive Medicine
II: Infectious Disease, Alternative and Complementary
Medicine; Integrated Systems II: Respiratory, Hematology,
Oncology; Preventive Medicine III: Public Health, Geriatrics;
Integrated Systems III: GI, Endocrine, Neurology,
Psychiatry; Preventive Medicine IV: Pediatrics, Occupational
Medicine; Integrated Systems IV: Reproduction,
Neonatology, Rheumatology, Orthopedics, Ophthalmology,
ENT, Dermatology, Allergy; Osteopathic Manipulative
Medicine II; Medical Ethics II; Advanced Cardiac Life
Support; Neonatology Laboratory; Ophthalmology
Laboratory; ENT Laboratory; Physical Diagnosis II; Basic
Surgical Skills; and Introduction to Clinical Clerkships.

Clinical phase (Total: 76 weeks minimum)—Year 3 clerk-
ships include: Family Practice, General Medicine,
Psychiatry, General Pediatrics, Obstetrics/Gynecology,
General Surgery, Emergency Medicine, and electives.

Year 4 studies include: Family Practice, surgery specialty
selective, internal medicine selective, and electives.

FACULTY PROFILE (FALL 2003)

Total teaching faculty: 39 (full-time), 28 (part-time)
Of full-time faculty, those teaching in basic sciences: 72%;
   in clinical programs: 28%
Of part-time faculty, those teaching in basic sciences: 4%;
   in clinical programs: 96%
Full-time faculty/student ratio: 0.05

SUPPORT SERVICES

The school offers students these services for dealing with
stress: professional counseling.

RESIDENCY CHOICES

Most popular residency and specialty programs chosen by
the 2002 and 2003 graduating classes: anesthesiology,
emergency medicine, family practice, internal medicine,
obstetrics and gynecology, pediatrics, physical medicine and
rehabilitation, psychiatry, radiology–diagnostic,
surgery–general.

WHERE GRADS GO

49.8%
*Proportion of 2001-2003 graduates who entered primary
care specialties*

10.5%
*Proportion of 2002-2003 graduates who accepted in-state
residencies*

Edward Via Virginia
COLLEGE OF OSTEOPATHIC MEDICINE

- 1919 Kraft Drive, Blacksburg, VA 24060
- Public
- Year Founded: 2003
- Tuition, 2003-2004: In-state: $29,500; Out-of-state: $29,500
- Enrollment, 2003-2004: 154
- Website: http://www.vcom.vt.edu
- Specialty ranking: N/A

3.39 AVERAGE GPA, ENTERING CLASS FALL 2003

7.6 AVERAGE MCAT, ENTERING CLASS FALL 2003

N/A ACCEPTANCE RATE, ENTERING CLASS FALL 2003

Unranked 2005 U.S.NEWS MEDICAL SCHOOL RANKING (RESEARCH)

Unranked 2005 U.S.NEWS MEDICAL SCHOOL RANKING (PRIMARY CARE)

ADMISSIONS
Admissions phone number: **(540) 231-6138**
Admissions email address: **mprice@vcom.vt.edu**
Application website: **http://www.aacom.org**
Acceptance rate: **N/A**
In-state acceptance rate: **N/A**
Out-of-state acceptance rate: **N/A**
Minority acceptance rate: **N/A**
International acceptance rate: **N/A**

Fall 2003 applications and acceptees

	Applied	Interviewed	Accepted	Enrolled
Total:	657	N/A	N/A	154
In-state:	99	N/A	N/A	45
Out-of-state:	558	N/A	N/A	109

Profile of admitted students
Average undergraduate grade point average: **3.39**
MCAT averages (scale: 1-15; writing test: J-T):
  Composite score: **7.6**
  Verbal reasoning score: **7.9**, Physical sciences score: **7.2**,
  Biological sciences score: **7.7**, Writing score: **N/A**
Proportion with undergraduate majors in: Biological sciences: **50%**, Physical sciences: **11%**, Non-sciences: **7%**, Other health professions: **14%**, Mixed disciplines and other: **18%**
Percentage of students not coming directly from college after graduation: **N/A**

Dates and details
Oldest MCAT considered for Fall 2005 entry: **2001**
Earliest application date for the 2005-2006 first-year class: **N/A**
Latest application date: **N/A**
Acceptance dates for regular application for the class entering in fall 2005:
  Earliest: **October 1, 2004**
  Latest: **June 1, 2005**
The school considers requests for deferred entrance.
Starting month for the class entering in 2005-2006: **August**

The school doesn't have an Early Decision Plan (EDP). A personal interview is required for admission.

Undergraduate coursework required
Medical school requires undergraduate work in these subjects: biology, English, organic chemistry, inorganic (general) chemistry, physics.

ADMISSIONS POLICY
(TEXT PROVIDED BY SCHOOL):
Applicants for admission must meet the following requirements prior to matriculation in fall 2004:

1. Applicants must have completed 90 hours or three fourths of the required credits for a degree in a college or university accredited by a regional educational association. The candidates must earn a baccalaureate degree prior to matriculation. No exceptions currently exist.

2. To be considered a competitive applicant of VCOM, candidates should have achieved at least a 3.0 science and cumulative grade-point average, on a 4.0 scale. Although the minimum GPA is 2.75, the admissions process is competitive, and a much higher grade-point average results in improved chances for acceptance. VCOM places emphasis on the last 120 credit hours, including the science and required courses. The average GPA for VCOM's first-year class is 3.4.

3. The required undergraduate courses for entry are: biological sciences, one year with laboratory (eight semester hours/12 quarter hours); physics, one year with laboratory (six to eight semester hours/nine to 12 quarter hours); inorganic chemistry, one year with laboratory (eight semester hours/12 quarter hours); organic chemistry, one year with laboratory (eight semester hours/12 quarter hours); and English, one year (six semester hours/eight quarter hours). Courses with equivalent content will be reviewed.

4. Applicants must submit scores from the Medical College Admission Test. For the current-year admissions cycle, the college will accept the April MCAT administration from three years prior or later. A competitive MCAT score usually begins at 24. However, the MCAT does not weigh in

importance as highly as the interview and the science and overall GPA.

5. VCOM offers special consideration for practicing nurse practitioners, physician assistants, pharmacists, and graduates of foreign medical colleges who hold a master's, doctoral, or professional degree. For candidates with this professional and academic background, we are willing to review graduate transcripts to ensure our undergraduate course requirements are met. We will require that these applicants take the MCAT. We will be unable to offer advanced standing.

To be considered for an interview, an applicant must meet the admissions requirements and have a complete file, including the American Association of Colleges of Osteopathic Medicine Application Service application, a secondary application, a letter of recommendation from an osteopathic physician, and a letter of recommendation from a premedical or prehealth committee. After the Office of Admissions receives these materials, the applicant's file is reviewed to determine eligibility for an interview, based on the established criteria of the Admissions Committee. Each applicant who interviews with VCOM will be reviewed by the Admissions Committee. An admissions decision, based on academic performance, professional experience, and interview, will usually be provided to the applicant within two weeks of the interview date.

COSTS AND FINANCIAL AID

Financial aid phone number: **(540) 231-6021**
Tuition, 2003-2004 academic year: **In-state: $29,500; Out-of-state: $29,500**
Room and board: **$20,000**
Percentage of students receiving financial aid in 2003-04: **N/A**
Percentage of students receiving: Loans: **N/A**, Grants/scholarships: **N/A**, Work-study aid: **0%**
Average medical school debt for the Class of 2002: **N/A**

STUDENT BODY

Fall 2003 full-time enrollment: **154**
Men: **52%**, Women: **48%**, In-state: **29%**, Minorities: **21%**, American Indian: **0.0%**, Asian-American: **11.0%**, African-American: **7.1%**, Hispanic-American: **3.2%**, White: **74.0%**, International: **0.6%**, Unknown: **3.9%**

ACADEMIC PROGRAMS

The school's curriculum gives first-year students substantial contact with patients.
There are opportunities for first- or second-year students to work in community health clinics.
Program offerings: **N/A**
Total National Institutes of Health (NIH) grants awarded to the medical school and affiliated hospitals: **N/A**

CURRICULUM
(TEXT PROVIDED BY SCHOOL):
The early clinical experiences in years 1 and 2 occur in many sites, from the core hospital sites to ambulatory sites, where individual preceptors work with students to aid in learning clinical skills.

Medical student years 3 and 4 occur primarily at the core hospital sites for inpatient experiences and at the ambulatory family practice and rural family practice sites for outpatient experiences. Geriatric centers provide an educational experience for second- and fourth-year students and are considered imperative for training physicians for the care of patients in the upcoming decade. All scheduling in the hospital sites as well as the educational program in each institution is provided through the college, and therefore the college is the main point of contact for each site regarding the educational programs for prospective students.

SUPPORT SERVICES

The school offers students these services for dealing with stress: expanded-hour gym access, professional counseling, religious support.

Kirksville College of Osteopathic Med.

- 800 W. Jefferson Street, Kirksville, MO 63501
- Private
- Year Founded: 1892
- Tuition, 2003-2004: $30,395
- Enrollment, 2003-2004: 626
- Website: http://www.atsu.edu
- Specialty ranking: family medicine: 22, rural medicine: 10

3.53 AVERAGE GPA, ENTERING CLASS FALL 2003

8.5 AVERAGE MCAT, ENTERING CLASS FALL 2003

17.9% ACCEPTANCE RATE, ENTERING CLASS FALL 2003

N/A 2005 U.S.NEWS MEDICAL SCHOOL RANKING (RESEARCH)

N/A 2005 U.S.NEWS MEDICAL SCHOOL RANKING (PRIMARY CARE)

ADMISSIONS

Admissions phone number: **(660) 626-2237**
Admissions email address: **admissions@atsu.edu**
Application website: **http://www.aacom.org**
Acceptance rate: **17.9%**
In-state acceptance rate: **34.8%**
Out-of-state acceptance rate: **16.9%**
Minority acceptance rate: **17.0%**
International acceptance rate: **23.1%**

Fall 2003 applications and acceptees

	Applied	Interviewed	Accepted	Enrolled
Total:	2,423	534	434	168
In-state:	135	52	47	30
Out-of-state:	2,288	482	387	138

Profile of admitted students

Average undergraduate grade point average: 3.53
MCAT averages (scale: 1-15; writing test: J-T):
 Composite score: **8.5**
 Verbal reasoning score: **8.5**, Physical sciences score: **8.2**,
 Biological sciences score: **8.8**, Writing score: **O**
Proportion with undergraduate majors in: Biological
 sciences: **59%**, Physical sciences: **21%**, Non-sciences:
 8%, Other health professions: **12%**, Mixed disciplines
 and other: **0%**
Percentage of students not coming directly from college
 after graduation: **20%**

Dates and details

Oldest MCAT considered for Fall 2005 entry: **2000**
Earliest application date for the 2005-2006 first-year class:
 June 2, 2004
Latest application date: **February 2, 2004**
Acceptance dates for regular application for the class
 entering in fall 2005:
 Earliest: **October 8, 2003**
 Latest: **March 30, 2004**
The school considers requests for deferred entrance.
Starting month for the class entering in 2005-2006:
 August

The school has an Early Decision Plan (EDP).
A personal interview is required for admission.

Undergraduate coursework required

Medical school requires undergraduate work in these subjects: biology, English, organic chemistry, inorganic (general) chemistry, physics.

ADMISSIONS POLICY
(TEXT PROVIDED BY SCHOOL):

The Admissions Committee seeks those individuals capable of meeting the college's academic rigor.

Applicants are screened for academic achievement, clinical involvement, interpersonal relations, leadership and service, maturity, motivation, and osteopathic awareness. Applicants who reach the final phase of the selection process will be invited to visit the college for an interview. All applicants selected for admission are interviewed prior to acceptance. As a private institution and the national college of osteopathic medicine, the Kirksville College of Osteopathic Medicine seeks students from all parts of the United States who are interested in a career in osteopathic medicine; no preference is given to in-state applicants. The college seeks students who are underrepresented in today's current physician population.

The Admissions Committee reserves the right to accept, reject, or defer an application. Applicants are notified as soon as the Admissions Committee decides on their status. Successful applicants are granted a specified time period to notify the Office of Admissions of their intention to enroll. This letter of intent must be accompanied by payment of a nonrefundable acceptance fee. Complete official transcripts from each school attended must be on file with the Office of the Registrar prior to matriculation. Admission, after acceptance, is subject to the satisfactory completion of all academic requirements.

COSTS AND FINANCIAL AID

Financial aid phone number: **(660) 626-2529**
Tuition, 2003-2004 academic year: **$30,395**
Room and board: **$11,398**

Percentage of students receiving financial aid in 2003-04: **94%**

Percentage of students receiving: Loans: **94%**, Grants/scholarships: **19%**, Work-study aid: **18%**

Average medical school debt for the Class of 2002: **$146,350**

STUDENT BODY

Fall 2003 full-time enrollment: **626**

Men: **64%**, Women: **36%**, In-state: **15%**, Minorities: **13%**, American Indian: **0.8%**, Asian-American: **11.2%**, African-American: **0.0%**, Hispanic-American: **1.1%**, White: **81.5%**, International: **1.3%**, Unknown: **4.2%**

ACADEMIC PROGRAMS

The school's curriculum doesn't give first-year students substantial contact with patients.

There are opportunities for first- or second-year students to work in community health clinics.

Program offerings: AIDS, drug/alcohol abuse, family medicine, geriatrics, internal medicine, pediatrics, rural medicine, women's health

Total National Institutes of Health (NIH) grants awarded to the medical school and affiliated hospitals: **$.4 million**

CURRICULUM

(TEXT PROVIDED BY SCHOOL):

Kirksville College of Osteopathic Medicine offers a four-year program leading to the degree Doctor of Osteopathic Medicine (D.O.). The curriculum is discipline-based and begins with a year of medical basic science courses, including cadaver-based human gross anatomy (with an introduction to radiology), histology and embryology, biochemistry, medical physiology, medical microbiology, and immunology. Each unit in anatomy is accompanied by instruction in physical exam skills (in The Complete DOctor course) and osteopathic techniques for diagnosis and treatment (in Osteopathic Theory and Methods) of the same body region. During the summer of the first year, students participate in a two-week preceptorship with a primary-care physician in Missouri that requires performance of a complete history and physical on a patient.

The second year includes more clinically related basic science courses on infectious diseases, medical pharmacology, and neuroscience. Neuroscience is an integrated course that includes the foundations of neuroanatomy and neurophysiology, along with clinical neurology and neuropharmacology. Psychiatry is also closely aligned with neuroscience. The remainder of the second year is devoted to introductions to the medical specialties. Pathology, internal medicine, and surgery are multiquarter sequences, while other specialties are taught in smaller blocks. These classes

provide a framework for each specialty prior to clinical rotations. A unique feature of the second year is a manikin-based surgical skills lab in which students learn suturing techniques, airway management, operating room protocols, maintaining sterile fields, and other basic surgical skills.

The Complete DOctor is a longitudinal 'doctoring' course. It engages students in topics such as medical interviewing, physical exam skills, discussing difficult topics with patients, medical ethics, death and dying, caring for geriatric patients, issues surrounding human sexuality, and topics in epidemiology and community medicine.

Students are assigned to clinical regions for the third and fourth years. Each region has a regional dean and other clinical faculty. Currently, KCOM students are training in Missouri, Michigan, Ohio, Arizona, Colorado, Utah, Florida, New Jersey, Pennsylvania, and New York. Required third-year rotations include family medicine (with a month in a rural or medically underserved area), internal medicine, obstetrics/gynecology, pediatrics, surgery, psychiatry, radiology, and anesthesiology. The fourth year requires additional time in family medicine, internal medicine (critical care), emergency medicine, and pediatrics. The balance of the fourth year is reserved for electives.

FACULTY PROFILE (FALL 2003)

Total teaching faculty: **76 (full-time)**, **12 (part-time)**

Of full-time faculty, those teaching in basic sciences: **34%**; in clinical programs: **66%**

Of part-time faculty, those teaching in basic sciences: **0%**; in clinical programs: **100%**

Full-time faculty/student ratio: **0.1**

SUPPORT SERVICES

The school offers students these services for dealing with stress: expanded-hour gym access, peer counseling, professional counseling, religious support, support groups.

RESIDENCY CHOICES

Most popular residency and specialty programs chosen by the 2002 and 2003 graduating classes: anesthesiology, emergency medicine, family practice, internal medicine, transitional year.

WHERE GRADS GO

43.0%

Proportion of 2001-2003 graduates who entered primary care specialties

8.0%

Proportion of 2002-2003 graduates who accepted in-state residencies

Michigan State University

COLLEGE OF OSTEOPATHIC MEDICINE

- A308 E. Fee Hall, East Lansing, MI 48824
- Public
- Year Founded: 1969
- Tuition, 2003-2004: In-state: $20,951; Out-of-state: $44,751
- Enrollment, 2003-2004: 533
- Website: http://www.com.msu.edu
- Specialty ranking: family medicine: 19

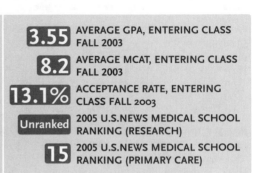

3.55 AVERAGE GPA, ENTERING CLASS FALL 2003

8.2 AVERAGE MCAT, ENTERING CLASS FALL 2003

13.1% ACCEPTANCE RATE, ENTERING CLASS FALL 2003

Unranked 2005 U.S.NEWS MEDICAL SCHOOL RANKING (RESEARCH)

15 2005 U.S.NEWS MEDICAL SCHOOL RANKING (PRIMARY CARE)

ADMISSIONS

Admissions phone number: **(517) 353-7740**
Admissions email address: **comadm@com.msu.edu**
Application website: **http://www.aacom.org**
Acceptance rate: **13.1%**
In-state acceptance rate: **35.6%**
Out-of-state acceptance rate: **3.5%**
Minority acceptance rate: **8.0%**
International acceptance rate: **N/A**

Fall 2003 applications and acceptees

	Applied	Interviewed	Accepted	Enrolled
Total:	1,609	332	210	143
In-state:	481	254	171	132
Out-of-state:	1,128	78	39	11

Profile of admitted students

Average undergraduate grade point average: **3.55**
MCAT averages (scale: 1-15; writing test: J-T):
  Composite score: **8.2**
  Verbal reasoning score: **8.0**, Physical sciences score: **7.9**, Biological sciences score: **8.7**, Writing score: **O**
Proportion with undergraduate majors in: Biological sciences: **64%**, Physical sciences: **8%**, Non-sciences: **14%**, Other health professions: **7%**, Mixed disciplines and other: **7%**
Percentage of students not coming directly from college after graduation: **18%**

Dates and details

Oldest MCAT considered for Fall 2005 entry: **2000**
Earliest application date for the 2005-2006 first-year class: **June 2, 2004**
Latest application date: **December 2, 2004**
Acceptance dates for regular application for the class entering in fall 2005:
  Earliest: **October 1, 2004**
  Latest: **April 1, 2005**
The school considers requests for deferred entrance.
Starting month for the class entering in 2005-2006: **August**

The school has an Early Decision Plan (EDP). A personal interview is required for admission.

Undergraduate coursework required

Medical school requires undergraduate work in these subjects: biology, English, organic chemistry, inorganic (general) chemistry, physics, behavioral science, general chemistry.

ADMISSIONS POLICY
(TEXT PROVIDED BY SCHOOL):

MSUCOM primary application review: Academic minimum standards for receiving a secondary application are 2.70 science and overall grade-point average, and total Medical College Admission Test score of 18, with subject-area minimums of 4 in verbal reasoning, 5 in physical sciences, and 6 in biological sciences. Applicants eligible to receive a secondary application are given a list of any prerequisite credits they have not yet completed. Applicants are given one month to submit all application materials.

Admissions Committee review: Applicant lists are generated each week. The weighted ranking, which is used to determine the order in which applications are reviewed, is 60 percent academic and 40 percent nonacademic. Applications are divided among admissions advisers for in-depth review. Reviewers identify and attempt to answer any concerns the committee might have. Each application is then presented to the interview subcommittee of the Admissions Committee by these admissions advisers. The subcommittee will invite to interview, reject, or hold for later review pending further information, such as new MCAT scores and/or fall semester grades.

Interviews: Selected candidates will be scheduled for a single one-hour interview; the visit will also include meeting with admissions advisers, a financial aid representative, and MSUCOM students. Candidates with afternoon interviews may have the opportunity to observe osteopathic manipulative medicine groups. Interviews are Monday through Thursday between 9:30 a.m. and 3:30 p.m.

Final evaluation: The full Admissions Committee reviews applicant credentials when the interview evaluation is completed. Review criteria include: academic ability as evidenced by the grade-point average, level and types of coursework, academic honors, and MCAT scores; commitment to service; and demonstrated skills in communication, leadership, collaboration, problem solving, and critical thinking. Consideration is also given to abilities and experiences such as fluency in multiple languages, military service, participation in varsity sports, research, and appreciation for diversity and cultural competence in healthcare. The committee will recommend admission, denial of admission, or placement on the alternate list. The dean may review some applications before the decision is conveyed to the candidates.

The committee uses a rolling admission process. The goal is to fill the class as early as possible. Alternates will be told in which quartile of the alternate list they have been placed. This is intended to encourage those alternates who most likely will need to reapply to seek counseling from the Admissions Office.

COSTS AND FINANCIAL AID
Financial aid phone number: **(517) 353-5188**
Tuition, 2003-2004 academic year: **In-state: $20,951; Out-of-state: $44,751**
Room and board: **$11,184**
Percentage of students receiving financial aid in 2003-04: **96%**
Percentage of students receiving: Loans: **95%**, Grants/scholarships: **89%**, Work-study aid: **0%**
Average medical school debt for the Class of 2002: **$117,221**

STUDENT BODY
Fall 2003 full-time enrollment: **533**
Men: **52%**, Women: **48%**, In-state: **93%**, Minorities: **17%**, American Indian: **0.2%**, Asian-American: **12.0%**, African-American: **1.7%**, Hispanic-American: **3.4%**, White: **82.7%**, International: **0.0%**, Unknown: **0.0%**

ACADEMIC PROGRAMS
The school's curriculum gives first-year students substantial contact with patients.
There are opportunities for first- or second-year students to work in community health clinics.
Program offerings: AIDS, drug/alcohol abuse, family medicine, geriatrics, internal medicine, pediatrics, rural medicine, women's health
Total National Institutes of Health (NIH) grants awarded to the medical school and affiliated hospitals: **$7.2 million**

CURRICULUM
(TEXT PROVIDED BY SCHOOL):
The college is dedicated to assist in meeting the ever growing public demand for physicians who can provide comprehensive and continuing healthcare to all members of the family.

While the educational program of MSUCOM is geared to the training of primary-care physicians, the curriculum is also designed to meet the continuing need for medical specialists and teacher-investigators.

Traditionally, osteopathic education seeks to prepare physicians who are especially concerned with maintaining continuing personal relationships with patients, their families, and their optimum interaction with the community environmental patterns. This emphasis is reflected in the nature of the curriculum and particularly reinforced during clinical clerkship rotations through a variety of clinical disciplines in both hospital and nonhospital settings.

Early clinical involvement in patient care enables students to study the biological and behavioral sciences that are relevant to what they are seeing and doing in the clinical area. With the help of the faculties in the biological and behavioral sciences, students learn to apply current concepts and principles to clinical problems related to patient care. The entire teaching program emphasizes an important cooperative relationship between basic sciences and clinical practice.

During their medical undergraduate and graduate education, students must develop the foundation and motivation for a lifetime of learning, and the ability to apply new knowledge and skills as they evolve.

FACULTY PROFILE (FALL 2003)
Total teaching faculty: **140 (full-time)**, **22 (part-time)**
Of full-time faculty, those teaching in basic sciences: **34%**; in clinical programs: **66%**
Of part-time faculty, those teaching in basic sciences: **14%**; in clinical programs: **86%**
Full-time faculty/student ratio: **0.3**

SUPPORT SERVICES
The school offers students these services for dealing with stress: expanded-hour gym access, peer counseling, professional counseling, religious support, support groups.

RESIDENCY CHOICES
Most popular residency and specialty programs chosen by the 2002 and 2003 graduating classes: emergency medicine, family practice, internal medicine, obstetrics and gynecology, pediatrics, psychiatry, radiology–diagnostic, surgery–general.

WHERE GRADS GO

79.0%
Proportion of 2001-2003 graduates who entered primary care specialties

87.2%
Proportion of 2002-2003 graduates who accepted in-state residencies

New York

COLLEGE OF OSTEOPATHIC MEDICINE

- Old Westbury, Northern Boulevard, Long Island, NY 11568
- Private
- Year Founded: 1977
- Tuition, 2003-2004: $30,678
- Enrollment, 2003-2004: 1,161
- Website: http://www.nyit.edu
- Specialty ranking: N/A

3.42 AVERAGE GPA, ENTERING CLASS FALL 2003

8.0 AVERAGE MCAT, ENTERING CLASS FALL 2003

18.0% ACCEPTANCE RATE, ENTERING CLASS FALL 2003

Unranked 2005 U.S.NEWS MEDICAL SCHOOL RANKING (RESEARCH)

Unranked 2005 U.S.NEWS MEDICAL SCHOOL RANKING (PRIMARY CARE)

ADMISSIONS

Admissions phone number: **(516) 686-3747**
Admissions email address: **admissions@nyit.edu**
Application website: **http://www.aacom.org**
Acceptance rate: **18.0%**
In-state acceptance rate: **41.2%**
Out-of-state acceptance rate: **11.2%**
Minority acceptance rate: **27.7%**
International acceptance rate: **7.4%**

Fall 2003 applications and acceptees

	Applied	Interviewed	Accepted	Enrolled
Total:	2,808	670	505	296
In-state:	634	349	261	180
Out-of-state:	2,174	321	244	116

Profile of admitted students

Average undergraduate grade point average: **3.42**
MCAT averages (scale: 1-15; writing test: J-T):
  Composite score: **8.0**
  Verbal reasoning score: **7.4**, Physical sciences score: **8.4**,
  Biological sciences score: **8.4**, Writing score: **N**
Proportion with undergraduate majors in: Biological
  sciences: **51%**, Physical sciences: **10%**, Non-sciences:
  10%, Other health professions: **4%**, Mixed disciplines
  and other: **25%**
Percentage of students not coming directly from college
  after graduation: **N/A**

Dates and details

Oldest MCAT considered for Fall 2005 entry: **N/A**
Earliest application date for the 2005-2006 first-year class:
  April 3, 2004
Latest application date: **February 4, 2004**
Acceptance dates for regular application for the class
  entering in fall 2005:
  Earliest: **N/A**
  Latest: **N/A**
The school considers requests for deferred entrance.
Starting month for the class entering in 2005-2006:
  August

The school doesn't have an Early Decision Plan (EDP).
A personal interview is required for admission.

Undergraduate coursework required

Medical school requires undergraduate work in these subjects: biology, biology/zoology, English, organic chemistry,
inorganic (general) chemistry, physics.

ADMISSIONS POLICY

(TEXT PROVIDED BY SCHOOL):

Applicants for first-year-class admission to the college must
meet the following requirements prior to matriculation: 1)
hold a baccalaureate degree from an accredited college; 2)
have an overall grade-point average and a preprofessional
science GPA of at least 2.75 on a 4.0 scale; 3) submit
Medical College Admission Test scores; 4) complete an academic science sequence; and 5) complete a personal interview process.

COSTS AND FINANCIAL AID

Financial aid phone number: **(516) 686-7960**
Tuition, 2003-2004 academic year: **$30,678**
Room and board: **N/A**
Percentage of students receiving financial aid in 2003-04:
  91%
Percentage of students receiving: Loans: **91%**,
  Grants/scholarships: **5%**, Work-study aid: **0%**
Average medical school debt for the Class of 2002:
  $154,000

STUDENT BODY

Fall 2003 full-time enrollment: **1,161**
Men: **46%**, Women: **54%**, In-state: **67%**, Minorities: **43%**,
  American Indian: **0.1%**, Asian-American: **28.1%**,
  African-American: **8.9%**, Hispanic-American: **5.8%**,
  White: **56.2%**, International: **0.3%**, Unknown: **1.0%**

ACADEMIC PROGRAMS

Program offerings: family medicine, geriatrics, internal
  medicine, pediatrics, rural medicine

Total National Institutes of Health (NIH) grants awarded to the medical school and affiliated hospitals: **N/A**

CURRICULUM
(TEXT PROVIDED BY SCHOOL):
New York College of Osteopathic Medicine is committed to training osteopathic physicians for a lifetime of medical practice and learning based on established science and critical thinking, integrating osteopathic philosophy, principles, and practice.

FACULTY PROFILE (FALL 2003)
Total teaching faculty: **40 (full-time)**, **1,620 (part-time)**
Of full-time faculty, those teaching in basic sciences: **60%**; in clinical programs: **40%**
Of part-time faculty, those teaching in basic sciences: **0%**; in clinical programs: **100%**
Full-time faculty/student ratio: **0.03**

SUPPORT SERVICES
The school offers students these services for dealing with stress: expanded-hour gym access, peer counseling, professional counseling.

RESIDENCY CHOICES
Most popular residency and specialty programs chosen by the 2002 and 2003 graduating classes: anesthesiology, emergency medicine, family practice, internal medicine, pediatrics, surgery–general.

WHERE GRADS GO

63.0%
Proportion of 2001-2003 graduates who entered primary care specialties

75.0%
Proportion of 2002-2003 graduates who accepted in-state residencies

Nova Southeastern University

COLLEGE OF OSTEOPATHIC MEDICINE

- 3200 S. University Drive, Fort Lauderdale, FL 33328
- Private
- **Year Founded:** 1981
- **Tuition, 2003-2004:** $22,490
- **Enrollment, 2003-2004:** 760
- **Website:** http://medicine.nova.edu
- **Specialty ranking:** N/A

3.42 AVERAGE GPA, ENTERING CLASS FALL 2003

8.0 AVERAGE MCAT, ENTERING CLASS FALL 2003

15.7% ACCEPTANCE RATE, ENTERING CLASS FALL 2003

Unranked 2005 U.S.NEWS MEDICAL SCHOOL RANKING (RESEARCH)

Unranked 2005 U.S.NEWS MEDICAL SCHOOL RANKING (PRIMARY CARE)

ADMISSIONS

Admissions phone number: **(954) 262-1101**
Admissions email address: **marlaf@nova.edu**
Application website: **http://hpd.nova.edu**
Acceptance rate: **15.7%**
In-state acceptance rate: **34.8%**
Out-of-state acceptance rate: **11.1%**
Minority acceptance rate: **14.4%**
International acceptance rate: **54.5%**

Fall 2003 applications and acceptees

	Applied	Interviewed	Accepted	Enrolled
Total:	2,059	383	324	202
In-state:	399	163	139	111
Out-of-state:	1,660	220	185	91

Profile of admitted students

Average undergraduate grade point average: **3.42**
MCAT averages (scale: 1-15; writing test: J-T):
  Composite score: **8.0**
  Verbal reasoning score: **7.9**, Physical sciences score: **7.8**,
  Biological sciences score: **8.3**, Writing score: **Q**
Proportion with undergraduate majors in: Biological
  sciences: **37%**, Physical sciences: **8%**, Non-sciences: **8%**,
  Other health professions: **15%**, Mixed disciplines and
  other: **32%**
Percentage of students not coming directly from college
  after graduation: **27%**

Dates and details

Oldest MCAT considered for Fall 2005 entry: **2001**
Earliest application date for the 2005-2006 first-year class:
  June 1, 2004
Latest application date: **January 15, 2004**
Acceptance dates for regular application for the class
  entering in fall 2005:
  Earliest: **November 1, 2005**
  Latest: **December 31, 2005**
The school considers requests for deferred entrance.
Starting month for the class entering in 2005-2006:
  August

The school doesn't have an Early Decision Plan (EDP).
A personal interview is required for admission.

Undergraduate coursework required

Medical school requires undergraduate work in these subjects: biology, English, organic chemistry, inorganic (general) chemistry, physics.

ADMISSIONS POLICY
(TEXT PROVIDED BY SCHOOL):

For entrance to the first-year class, a bachelor's degree from a regionally accredited college or university is preferred, but at least 90 semester hours are required. Prerequisites include the completion of eight semester hours each in general biology, general chemistry, organic chemistry, and physics as well as three semester hours in both English composition and literature. Medical College Admission Test scores must be submitted that are no more than three years old.

A personal interview is required; however, not all applicants will be granted an interview nor does an interview guarantee acceptance. A letter of evaluation is required from the preprofessional committee. If one does not exist, letters from two science professors and one from a liberal arts professor must be submitted instead. A letter of evaluation must also be submitted from an osteopathic physician. Admission is highly competitive. Florida residents are eligible to receive reduced in-state tuition.

COSTS AND FINANCIAL AID

Financial aid phone number: **(954) 262-3380**
Tuition, 2003-2004 academic year: **$22,490**
Room and board: **$11,590**
Percentage of students receiving financial aid in 2003-04:
  84%
Percentage of students receiving: Loans: **89%**,
  Grants/scholarships: **14%**, Work-study aid: **3%**
Average medical school debt for the Class of 2002:
  $154,498

STUDENT BODY

Fall 2003 full-time enrollment: 760

Men: 55%, Women: 45%, In-state: 74%, Minorities: 32%, American Indian: 0.8%, Asian-American: 16.4%, African-American: 3.8%, Hispanic-American: 11.2%, White: 62.1%, International: 0.9%, Unknown: 4.7%

ACADEMIC PROGRAMS

The school's curriculum gives first-year students substantial contact with patients.

There are opportunities for first- or second-year students to work in community health clinics.

Program offerings: AIDS, drug/alcohol abuse, family medicine, geriatrics, internal medicine, pediatrics, rural medicine, women's health

Total National Institutes of Health (NIH) grants awarded to the medical school and affiliated hospitals: N/A

CURRICULUM

(TEXT PROVIDED BY SCHOOL):

The NSU-COM curriculum is designed to fulfill its mission of training primary-care physicians. It emphasizes interdisciplinary collaboration, guiding students to develop a holistic and osteopathic approach to medicine.

Basic scientific information is correlated with fundamental clinical application. Students are exposed to clinical settings in their first semester, giving them an opportunity to prepare for the 'real world' of medicine. The clinical exposure continues into the second year, when students have an increased opportunity to interact with standardized patients and with real patients under the supervision of physicians in office and hospital settings. A notable aspect of the clinical program is a required three-month rotation in a rural practice setting, providing care to patients who are medically underserved. Students learn to treat various patients whose lifestyles, practices, and attitudes toward health differ from those seen in more traditional training sites.

NSU promotes interdisciplinary cooperation whenever possible. Students share faculty members and facilities with NSU's pharmacy, dental, optometry, physician assistant, physical therapy, occupational therapy, public health, nursing, and medical science students.

FACULTY PROFILE (FALL 2003)

Total teaching faculty: 89 (full-time), 727 (part-time)

Of full-time faculty, those teaching in basic sciences: 34%; in clinical programs: 66%

Of part-time faculty, those teaching in basic sciences: 0%; in clinical programs: 100%

Full-time faculty/student ratio: 0.1

SUPPORT SERVICES

The school offers students these services for dealing with stress: professional counseling.

RESIDENCY CHOICES

Most popular residency and specialty programs chosen by the 2002 and 2003 graduating classes: dermatology, emergency medicine, family practice, internal medicine, obstetrics and gynecology, orthopedic surgery, pediatrics, psychiatry, radiology–diagnostic, surgery–general.

WHERE GRADS GO

83.9%

Proportion of 2001-2003 graduates who entered primary care specialties

47.9%

Proportion of 2002-2003 graduates who accepted in-state residencies

Oklahoma State University

COLLEGE OF OSTEOPATHIC MEDICINE

■ 1111 W. 17th Street, Tulsa, OK 74107
■ Public
■ Year Founded: N/A
■ Tuition, 2003-2004: In-state: $14,550; Out-of-state: $30,920
■ Enrollment, 2003-2004: 350
■ Website: http://healthsciences.okstate.edu
■ Specialty ranking: family medicine: 17, rural medicine: 13

3.62 AVERAGE GPA, ENTERING CLASS FALL 2003

8.7 AVERAGE MCAT, ENTERING CLASS FALL 2003

36.8% ACCEPTANCE RATE, ENTERING CLASS FALL 2003

Unranked 2005 U.S.NEWS MEDICAL SCHOOL RANKING (RESEARCH)

Unranked 2005 U.S.NEWS MEDICAL SCHOOL RANKING (PRIMARY CARE)

ADMISSIONS

Admissions phone number: **(918) 561-8421**
Admissions email address: **labgood@chs.okstate.edu**
Application website: **http://www.aacom.org**
Acceptance rate: **36.8%**
In-state acceptance rate: **58.9%**
Out-of-state acceptance rate: **15.4%**
Minority acceptance rate: **25.0%**
International acceptance rate: **N/A**

Fall 2003 applications and acceptees

	Applied	Interviewed	Accepted	Enrolled
Total:	410	188	151	88
In-state:	202	152	119	80
Out-of-state:	208	36	32	8

Profile of admitted students

Average undergraduate grade point average: **3.62**
MCAT averages (scale: 1-15; writing test: J-T):
  Composite score: **8.7**
  Verbal reasoning score: **9.0**, Physical sciences score: **8.0**,
  Biological sciences score: **9.0**, Writing score: **O**
Proportion with undergraduate majors in: Biological
  sciences: **34%**, Physical sciences: **13%**, Non-sciences:
  12%, Other health professions: **7%**, Mixed disciplines
  and other: **34%**
Percentage of students not coming directly from college
  after graduation: **39%**

Dates and details

Oldest MCAT considered for Fall 2005 entry: **2001**
Earliest application date for the 2005-2006 first-year class:
  May 1, 2004
Latest application date: **February 15, 2004**
Acceptance dates for regular application for the class
  entering in fall 2005:
  Earliest: **October 15, 2004**
  Latest: **August 15, 2005**
The school considers requests for deferred entrance.
Starting month for the class entering in 2005-2006:
  August

The school doesn't have an Early Decision Plan (EDP).
A personal interview is required for admission.

Undergraduate coursework required

Medical school requires undergraduate work in these subjects: biology, biology/zoology, English, organic chemistry,
inorganic (general) chemistry, physics, molecular and cell
biology, biochemistry, general chemistry.

ADMISSIONS POLICY

(TEXT PROVIDED BY SCHOOL):

Preference is given to applicants from Oklahoma. Non-U.S.
citizens who do not have a permanent resident visa (green
card) at the time of application cannot be considered for
admission. The Admissions Committee recommends applicants for admission. Final selection of candidates to be
offered admission is made by the dean.

The college considers all qualified candidates without
regard to age, gender, religion, race, or national origin. The
college actively recruits qualified minority students.

At the time of application, the applicant must have an
overall grade-point average of 3.0 (on 4.0 scale), a minimum of 7.0 on the Medical College Admission Test, and a
preprofessional science GPA of at least 2.75 (on 4.0 scale).
Under special circumstances, the College of Osteopathic
Medicine may use discretion to admit students who do not
meet these minimum requirements. The average MCAT
and GPA of recently admitted students are 9.0 and 3.5,
respectively.

At the time of entry, the applicant must have completed
at least three years (90 semester hours) and not less than 75
percent of the courses required for the baccalaureate degree
at a regionally accredited college or university. The applicant
must have completed the following courses, including laboratory, with no grade below C: English (six to eight semester
hours); biology (eight to 10 hours); physics (eight to 10
hours); general chemistry (eight to 10 hours); organic chemistry (eight to 10 hours), and at least one of the following
undergraduate courses (three to five are strongly recommended): biochemistry, microbiology or molecular biology,

histology, embryology, and comparative anatomy or cellular biology.

MCAT scores must be on file before an interview will be granted. An on-campus interview (by invitation only) is required. Interviews are conducted by clinical and basic science faculty members.

FINANCIAL AID

Financial aid phone number: **(918) 561-8278**
Tuition, 2003-2004 academic year: **In-state: $14,550; Out-of-state: $30,920**
Room and board: **$6,459**
Percentage of students receiving financial aid in 2003-04: **97%**
Percentage of students receiving: Loans: **94%**, Grants/scholarships: **69%**, Work-study aid: **25%**
Average medical school debt for the Class of 2002: **$120,000**

STUDENT BODY

Fall 2003 full-time enrollment: **350**
Men: **57%**, Women: **43%**, In-state: **89%**, Minorities: **20%**, American Indian: **11.1%**, Asian-American: **4.9%**, African-American: **2.6%**, Hispanic-American: **1.4%**, White: **78.0%**, International: **0.0%**, Unknown: **2.0%**

ACADEMIC PROGRAMS

The school's curriculum gives first-year students substantial contact with patients.
There are opportunities for first- or second-year students to work in community health clinics.
Program offerings: AIDS, drug/alcohol abuse, family medicine, geriatrics, internal medicine, pediatrics, rural medicine, women's health
Total National Institutes of Health (NIH) grants awarded to the medical school and affiliated hospitals: **$.5 million**

CURRICULUM

(TEXT PROVIDED BY SCHOOL):
The curriculum includes hands-on clinical experiences, student-centered and problem-based methods of instruction, and frequent consultation with faculty members and community-based physicians. Development of problem-solving and information-retrieval skills are emphasized to produce osteopathic physicians with the capacity to be lifelong learners. In a spiral curriculum, study matter is continuously reintroduced to the student in greater depth and complexity, reinforcing prior learning and promoting meaningful retention. The curriculum emphasizes integration of basic sciences with clinical and behavioral sciences to permit full comprehension of the clinician's work and promote a holistic approach to the care of patients and their families.

The curriculum is designed to implement a 22-month clerkship program within the four-year program of professional education.

The first year is designed to bring all students to desired levels of competence in the biomedical sciences and prelim-

inary clinical knowledge and skills. Here, students learn the terminology of medicine and acquire the knowledge for problem solving. During the first year, students are introduced to core concepts in anatomy, physiology, biochemistry, and microbiology. Students begin to develop competence in osteopathic clinical skills including physical examination, diagnosis and patient interviewing, and recognition of normal and abnormal patterns of physical conditions and diseases.

The second year emphasizes case-based learning, clinical problem-solving strategies, and recognition and understanding of common diseases and conditions. Small-group learning and independent study are keys to students' development of the critical thinking required for the clinical context. Students' clinical skills are honed through interactive lab sessions and simulated clinical experiences.

The final 22 months are clinically oriented and community based, consisting of clerkship experiences in hospitals and clinics, where students observe patients on a daily basis under physician-faculty supervision. The student rotates through primary-care services including surgery, obstetrics/gynecology, pediatrics, psychiatry, internal medicine, family medicine, and emergency medicine. The balance of the clerkship program consists of supervised patient contact in small towns and rural areas throughout Oklahoma.

FACULTY PROFILE (FALL 2003)

Total teaching faculty: **72 (full-time), 292 (part-time)**
Of full-time faculty, those teaching in basic sciences: **29%**; in clinical programs: **71%**
Of part-time faculty, those teaching in basic sciences: **11%**; in clinical programs: **89%**
Full-time faculty/student ratio: **0.2**

SUPPORT SERVICES

The school offers students these services for dealing with stress: peer counseling, professional counseling, religious support, support groups.

RESIDENCY CHOICES

Most popular residency and specialty programs chosen by the 2002 and 2003 graduating classes: anesthesiology, emergency medicine, family practice, internal medicine, internal medicine–pediatrics, obstetrics and gynecology, otolaryngology, pediatrics, psychiatry, surgery–general.

WHERE GRADS GO

63.0%
Proportion of 2001-2003 graduates who entered primary care specialties

60.0%
Proportion of 2002-2003 graduates who accepted in-state residencies

Philadelphia College of Osteopathic Med.

- 4170 City Avenue, Philadelphia, PA 19131
- Private
- Year Founded: 1899
- Tuition, 2003-2004: $31,101
- Enrollment, 2003-2004: 1,008
- Website: http://www.pcom.edu
- Specialty ranking: N/A

3.39 AVERAGE GPA, ENTERING CLASS FALL 2003

8.0 AVERAGE MCAT, ENTERING CLASS FALL 2003

12.0% ACCEPTANCE RATE, ENTERING CLASS FALL 2003

Unranked 2005 U.S.NEWS MEDICAL SCHOOL RANKING (RESEARCH)

Unranked 2005 U.S.NEWS MEDICAL SCHOOL RANKING (PRIMARY CARE)

ADMISSIONS
Admissions phone number: **(800) 999-6998**
Admissions email address: **admissions@pcom.edu**
Application website: **http://www.aacom.org**
Acceptance rate: **12.0%**
In-state acceptance rate: **49.4%**
Out-of-state acceptance rate: **7.1%**
Minority acceptance rate: **6.8%**
International acceptance rate: **45.5%**

Fall 2003 applications and acceptees

	Applied	Interviewed	Accepted	Enrolled
Total:	3,396	684	409	263
In-state:	399	268	197	147
Out-of-state:	2,997	416	212	116

Profile of admitted students
Average undergraduate grade point average: **3.39**
MCAT averages (scale: 1-15; writing test: J-T):
 Composite score: **8.0**
 Verbal reasoning score: **8.0**, Physical sciences score: **8.0**,
 Biological sciences score: **8.5**, Writing score: **O**
Proportion with undergraduate majors in: Biological
 sciences: **70%**, Physical sciences: **11%**, Non-sciences:
 13%, Other health professions: **5%**, Mixed disciplines
 and other: **1%**
Percentage of students not coming directly from college
 after graduation: **62%**

Dates and details
Oldest MCAT considered for Fall 2005 entry: **2001**
Earliest application date for the 2005-2006 first-year class:
 May 3, 2004
Latest application date: **February 3, 2004**
Acceptance dates for regular application for the class
 entering in fall 2005:
 Earliest: **September 15, 2004**
 Latest: **August 18, 2005**
The school doesn't consider requests for deferred entrance.
Starting month for the class entering in 2005-2006:
 August

The school doesn't have an Early Decision Plan (EDP).
A personal interview is required for admission.

Undergraduate coursework required
Medical school requires undergraduate work in these subjects: biology, English, organic chemistry, inorganic (general) chemistry, physics, general chemistry.

ADMISSIONS POLICY
(TEXT PROVIDED BY SCHOOL):
Admission to PCOM is competitive and selective. We seek
well-rounded, achievement-oriented persons whose character, maturity, and sense of dedication point to a successful
and productive life as an osteopathic physician. We are an
institution that has historically sought diversity in our student population. We actively recruit underrepresented
minority students and nontraditional students, who often
offer exceptional potential for becoming outstanding physicians.

 Grades and Medical College Admission Test scores are
important to us, as they are some of the best predictors of
success in medical school; however, we also look very carefully at extracurricular activities, community involvement,
motivation to study medicine, and letters of evaluation.

COSTS AND FINANCIAL AID
Financial aid phone number: **(215) 871-6170**
Tuition, 2003-2004 academic year: **$31,101**
Room and board: **$13,190**
Percentage of students receiving financial aid in 2003-04:
 92%
Percentage of students receiving: Loans: **91%**,
 Grants/scholarships: **51%**, Work-study aid: **16%**
Average medical school debt for the Class of 2002:
 $149,813

STUDENT BODY
Fall 2003 full-time enrollment: **1,008**
Men: **51%**, Women: **49%**, In-state: **59%**, Minorities: **20%**,
 American Indian: **0.2%**, Asian-American: **10.2%**,

African-American: **5.5%**, Hispanic-American: **2.9%**,
White: **79.6%**, International: **0.7%**, Unknown: **1.0%**

ACADEMIC PROGRAMS

The school's curriculum gives first-year students
substantial contact with patients.

There are opportunities for first- or second-year students to
work in community health clinics.

Program offerings: AIDS, drug/alcohol abuse, family
medicine, geriatrics, internal medicine, pediatrics, rural
medicine

Total National Institutes of Health (NIH) grants awarded to
the medical school and affiliated hospitals: **$.5 million**

CURRICULUM

(TEXT PROVIDED BY SCHOOL):

A fundamental educational goal of Philadelphia College of
Osteopathic Medicine (PCOM) is to prepare students for
excellence in the practice of osteopathic medicine. The
course of medical study is a practitioner's program, with a
strong emphasis on primary care, prevention, and osteopathic concepts.

Each PCOM student progresses through a uniform and
comprehensive curriculum. Elective clinical clerkships
expose students to specialty or subspecialty fields, and later
they may specialize. At PCOM, students are trained first as
family practitioners and thus build solid foundations for
their careers. Throughout the curriculum, osteopathic concepts and methods are stressed.

Efficiency is also an educational goal. Innovations such
as computerized tutorials, classroom videos, and simulated
patient encounters will sharpen skills as a physician. Our
curriculum revision bridges departmental divisions and
joins related disciplines so that students relate different perspectives to a variety of conditions taught in a common
time frame.

The first two years lay the foundation with intense concentration on the basic sciences, anatomy, biochemistry,
molecular biology, neuroscience, physiology, microbiology,
pathology, and pharmacology. Coursework in ethics, patient
communication, human sexuality, medical law, public
health, and medical economics rounds out the curriculum.

The basic sciences are complemented by instruction in
clinical subjects. All students attend small-group sessions
during the first and second years to develop communication
and diagnostic skills. In addition, an active standardized
patient program introduces first- and second-year students

to patient care through examinations of patient-actors in a
simulated practice setting.

The last two years emphasize clinical training experiences. The program is designed to afford progressive student responsibility for all phases of patient care under the
direction of experienced physicians. Students rotate through
services in medicine, family practice, manipulative medicine, surgery, cardiology, obstetrics/gynecology, pediatrics,
psychiatry, otorhinolaryngology, and office-based preceptorships. All students receive additional training in osteopathic
manipulative medicine in the third year.

Each senior student serves 12 weeks in a healthcare center clerkship. Eight weeks are in our urban clinics, and four
weeks are in one of several rural centers. An alternative
rural selective is offered to a limited number of students in
an area of alternative healthcare delivery or a rural area of
intense medical need, such as India, Israel, Africa,
Appalachia, and Indian Health Service sites.

FACULTY PROFILE (FALL 2003)

Total teaching faculty: **70 (full-time)**, **48 (part-time)**
Of full-time faculty, those teaching in basic sciences: **37%**;
in clinical programs: **63%**
Of part-time faculty, those teaching in basic sciences: **6%**;
in clinical programs: **94%**
Full-time faculty/student ratio: **0.1**

SUPPORT SERVICES

The school offers students these services for dealing with
stress: expanded-hour gym access, peer counseling, professional counseling, support groups.

RESIDENCY CHOICES

Most popular residency and specialty programs chosen by
the 2002 and 2003 graduating classes: emergency medicine, family practice, internal medicine, obstetrics and gynecology, pediatrics, surgery–general, transitional year.

WHERE GRADS GO

42.0%

*Proportion of 2001-2003 graduates who entered primary
care specialties*

50.4%

*Proportion of 2002-2003 graduates who accepted in-state
residencies*

Pikeville Coll. School of Osteopathic Med.

- 147 Sycamore Street, Pikeville, KY 41501
- Private
- Year Founded: 1997
- Tuition, 2003-2004: $26,000
- Enrollment, 2003-2004: 253
- Website: http://www.pc.edu
- Specialty ranking: rural medicine: 23

3.31	AVERAGE GPA, ENTERING CLASS FALL 2003
7.5	AVERAGE MCAT, ENTERING CLASS FALL 2003
15.9%	ACCEPTANCE RATE, ENTERING CLASS FALL 2003
Unranked	2005 U.S.NEWS MEDICAL SCHOOL RANKING (RESEARCH)
Unranked	2005 U.S.NEWS MEDICAL SCHOOL RANKING (PRIMARY CARE)

ADMISSIONS

Admissions phone number: **(606) 218-5400**
Admissions email address: **ahamilto@pc.edu**
Application website: **http://www.aacom.org**
Acceptance rate: **15.9%**
In-state acceptance rate: **46.0%**
Out-of-state acceptance rate: **11.2%**
Minority acceptance rate: **12.7%**
International acceptance rate: **N/A**

Fall 2003 applications and acceptees

	Applied	Interviewed	Accepted	Enrolled
Total:	641	187	102	75
In-state:	87	74	40	33
Out-of-state:	554	113	62	42

Profile of admitted students

Average undergraduate grade point average: **3.31**
MCAT averages (scale: 1-15; writing test: J-T):
　Composite score: **7.5**
　Verbal reasoning score: **7.8**, Physical sciences score: **7.0**,
　Biological sciences score: **7.6**, Writing score: **N/A**
Proportion with undergraduate majors in: Biological
　sciences: **51%**, Physical sciences: **9%**, Non-sciences: **13%**,
　Other health professions: **6%**, Mixed disciplines and
　other: **19%**
Percentage of students not coming directly from college
　after graduation: **36%**

Dates and details

Oldest MCAT considered for Fall 2005 entry: **N/A**
Earliest application date for the 2005-2006 first-year class:
　June 1, 2004
Latest application date: **February 1, 2004**
Acceptance dates for regular application for the class
　entering in fall 2005:
　Earliest: **October 15, 2003**
　Latest: **June 15, 2004**
The school considers requests for deferred entrance.
Starting month for the class entering in 2005-2006:
　August

The school doesn't have an Early Decision Plan (EDP).
A personal interview is required for admission.

Undergraduate coursework required

Medical school requires undergraduate work in these subjects: biology, English, organic chemistry, inorganic (general) chemistry, physics, general chemistry.

ADMISSIONS POLICY

(TEXT PROVIDED BY SCHOOL):

The school considers all applicants for admission and financial aid without respect to age, gender, sexual orientation,
race, color, creed, religion, handicap, or national origin.
Applicants are considered on their intellectual ability,
scholastic achievement, commitment, and suitability to succeed in the study of osteopathic medicine.

　The PCSOM Admissions Committee will consider applications from all qualified individuals, but preference is
given to students who will provide medical healthcare for
Kentucky, other Appalachian regions, and rural, medically
underserved areas.

　The minimum academic requirements for admission to
the first-year class are:

　1. A baccalaureate degree, or completion of at least three
fourths (90 semester hours or 135 term credit hours) of the
required credits for a baccalaureate degree, from a regionally accredited college or university. The baccalaureate
degree is preferred.

　2. Medical College Admission Test scores.

　3. Satisfactory completion of the following college
courses, including laboratory work: English composition
and literature (six semester hours), general chemistry (eight
hours), organic chemistry (eight hours, four of which can
be biochemistry), physics (eight hours), and biological sciences (12 hours).

　Applications to PCSOM are made by submitting a primary application through the American Association of
Colleges of Osteopathic Medicine Application Service. A
secondary application will be sent directly to students who
designate PCSOM on their AACOMAS application.

Applicants must obtain letters of recommendation from a physician (preferably a D.O.), a science faculty member who is familiar with the applicant's academic work, and a premedical source (a premedical adviser or committee).

COSTS AND FINANCIAL AID
Financial aid phone number: **(606) 218-5407**
Tuition, 2003-2004 academic year: **$26,000**
Room and board: **N/A**
Percentage of students receiving financial aid in 2003-04: **87%**
Percentage of students receiving: Loans: **96%**, Grants/scholarships: **67%**, Work-study aid: **N/A**
Average medical school debt for the Class of 2002: **$121,000**

STUDENT BODY
Fall 2003 full-time enrollment: **253**
Men: **59%**, Women: **41%**, In-state: **63%**, Minorities: **8%**, American Indian: **0.4%**, Asian-American: **4.0%**, African-American: **1.2%**, Hispanic-American: **24%**, White: **91.7%**, International: **0.0%**, Unknown: **0.4%**

ACADEMIC PROGRAMS
The school's curriculum gives first-year students substantial contact with patients.
There are opportunities for first- or second-year students to work in community health clinics.
Program offerings: AIDS, drug/alcohol abuse, family medicine, geriatrics, internal medicine, pediatrics, rural medicine, women's health
Total National Institutes of Health (NIH) grants awarded to the medical school and affiliated hospitals: **N/A**

CURRICULUM
(TEXT PROVIDED BY SCHOOL):
The curriculum is structured around nine competencies to maximize the student's opportunity to train for a career in osteopathic primary care.
  1. Osteopathic advocate: The PCSOM graduate is knowledgeable about, and an advocate for, the unique nature of the osteopathic medical profession. This includes integrating the four key principles of osteopathic philosophy into clinical practice. Those principles are: (A) the body is a unit—the person is a unit of body, mind, and spirit; (B) the body is capable of self-regulation, self-healing, and health maintenance; (C) structure and function are reciprocally interrelated; and (D) rational treatment is based upon an understanding of the basic principles of body unit, self-regulation, and the interrelationship of structure and function.
  2. Effective communication: The PCSOM graduate will listen attentively and communicate clearly with patients, families, and other healthcare team members.

  3. Basic clinical skills: The PCSOM graduate will obtain an appropriate history and perform skillful, comprehensive examinations. The graduate will correctly select, proficiently perform, and accurately interpret clinical procedures and laboratory findings.
  4. Use of basic science to guide therapy: The PCSOM graduate will recognize, explain, and treat health problems based upon current scientific knowledge or understanding.
  5. Diagnosis, management, and prevention: The PCSOM graduate will diagnose, manage, and educate in the prevention of common health problems of individuals, families, and communities in collaboration with them.
  6. Lifelong learning: The PCSOM graduate actively sets clear learning goals, pursues them, and applies the knowledge gained to his or her practice of osteopathic medicine.
  7. Self-awareness and self-care: The PCSOM graduate approaches the practice of osteopathic medicine with awareness of his or her limits, strengths, weaknesses, and personal vulnerabilities.
  8. Social and community contexts of care: The PCSOM graduate provides guidance to patients by responding to the many factors that influence health besides those of a biological nature.
  9. Moral reasoning and ethical judgment: The PCSOM graduate combines a willingness to recognize the nature of the value systems of patients and others with commitment to his or her own system and the ethical choices necessary to maintain his or her own ethical integrity.

FACULTY PROFILE (FALL 2003)
Total teaching faculty: **22 (full-time)**, **678 (part-time)**
Of full-time faculty, those teaching in basic sciences: **50%**; in clinical programs: **50%**
Of part-time faculty, those teaching in basic sciences: **0%**; in clinical programs: **100%**
Full-time faculty/student ratio: **0.1**

SUPPORT SERVICES
The school offers students these services for dealing with stress: peer counseling, professional counseling, religious support, support groups.

RESIDENCY CHOICES
Most popular residency and specialty programs chosen by the 2002 and 2003 graduating classes: anesthesiology, dermatology, emergency medicine, family practice, internal medicine, ophthalmology, pediatrics, surgery–general, internal medicine/family medicine, internal medicine/pediatrics.

WHERE GRADS GO

82.0%
Proportion of 2001-2003 graduates who entered primary care specialties

27.0%
Proportion of 2002-2003 graduates who accepted in-state residencies

Touro University
COLLEGE OF OSTEOPATHIC MEDICINE

- 1310 Johnson Lane, Vallejo, CA 94592
- Private
- Year Founded: 1997
- Tuition, 2003-2004: $31,500
- Enrollment, 2003-2004: 500
- Website: http://www.tumi.edu
- Specialty ranking: N/A

3.50	AVERAGE GPA, ENTERING CLASS FALL 2003
8.7	AVERAGE MCAT, ENTERING CLASS FALL 2003
15.9%	ACCEPTANCE RATE, ENTERING CLASS FALL 2003
Unranked	2005 U.S.NEWS MEDICAL SCHOOL RANKING (RESEARCH)
Unranked	2005 U.S.NEWS MEDICAL SCHOOL RANKING (PRIMARY CARE)

ADMISSIONS

Admissions phone number: **(707) 638-5270**
Admissions email address: **haight@touro.edu**
Application website: **http://www.tumi.edu**
Acceptance rate: **15.9%**
In-state acceptance rate: **18.3%**
Out-of-state acceptance rate: **7.0%**
Minority acceptance rate: **9.9%**
International acceptance rate: **N/A**

Fall 2003 applications and acceptees

	Applied	Interviewed	Accepted	Enrolled
Total:	1,942	470	308	131
In-state:	525	230	96	56
Out-of-state:	1,417	240	99	75

Profile of admitted students

Average undergraduate grade point average: **3.50**
MCAT averages (scale: 1-15; writing test: J-T):
  Composite score: **8.7**
  Verbal reasoning score: **8.4**, Physical sciences score: **8.6**,
  Biological sciences score: **9.0**, Writing score: **O**
Proportion with undergraduate majors in: Biological
  sciences: **60%**, Physical sciences: **26%**, Non-sciences:
  6%, Other health professions: **3%**, Mixed disciplines and
  other: **5%**
Percentage of students not coming directly from college
  after graduation: **N/A**

Dates and details

Oldest MCAT considered for Fall 2005 entry: **2001**
Earliest application date for the 2005-2006 first-year class:
  June 1, 2004
Latest application date: **February 14, 2004**
Acceptance dates for regular application for the class
  entering in fall 2005:
  Earliest: **September 1, 2004**
  Latest: **May 31, 2005**
The school considers requests for deferred entrance.
Starting month for the class entering in 2005-2006:
  August

The school has an Early Decision Plan (EDP).
A personal interview is required for admission.

Undergraduate coursework required

Medical school requires undergraduate work in these subjects: biology, English, organic chemistry, inorganic (general) chemistry, physics, humanities.

ADMISSIONS POLICY
(TEXT PROVIDED BY SCHOOL):

1. TUCOM has no mandate to enroll any percentage of
in-state residents.

2. Complete the primary online application with the
American Association of Colleges of Osteopathic Medicine
Application Service. TUCOM's code number is 618.

3. Qualified applicants will be instructed to complete
TUCOM's supplemental application.

4. If eligible for a supplemental application, submit an
evaluation from a preprofessional advisory committee or letters of recommendation from two science faculty members
familiar with your work.

5. Submit a letter of recommendation from a physician
(D.O. or M.D.).

6. If invited to do so, schedule a formal interview with
the Admissions and Standards Committee.

COSTS AND FINANCIAL AID

Financial aid phone number: **(707) 638-5280**
Tuition, 2003-2004 academic year: **$31,500**
Room and board: **$12,750**
Percentage of students receiving financial aid in 2003-04:
  94%
Percentage of students receiving: Loans: **93%**,
  Grants/scholarships: **11%**, Work-study aid: **10%**
Average medical school debt for the Class of 2002:
  $149,500

STUDENT BODY

Fall 2003 full-time enrollment: **500**
Men: **52%**, Women: **48%**, In-state: **46%**, Minorities: **29%**,
  American Indian: **0.0%**, Asian-American: **26.0%**,

African-American: **0.8%**, Hispanic-American: **2.6%**, White: **55.8%**, International: **0.0%**, Unknown: **14.8%**

ACADEMIC PROGRAMS

Program offerings: AIDS, drug/alcohol abuse, family medicine, geriatrics, internal medicine, pediatrics, rural medicine
Total National Institutes of Health (NIH) grants awarded to the medical school and affiliated hospitals: **N/A**

CURRICULUM

(TEXT PROVIDED BY SCHOOL):
TUCOM students take courses in all of the subject areas one would expect any physician to master, including anatomy, pathology, microbiology, histology, osteopathic principles and practices, pharmacology, immunology, clinical skills, and doctor-patient communication, as well as systems courses that focus on each major system of the body, such as cardiovascular, respiratory, gastrointestinal, and so on.

Our goal is to prepare students for the realities of medicine as it presently exists, as well as how it is likely to be in the future. Practice in problem solving is part of the daily classroom clinic experience as we strive to deliver a curriculum consistent with emerging directions of healthcare.

FACULTY PROFILE (FALL 2003)

Total teaching faculty: **40 (full-time)**, **0 (part-time)**
Of full-time faculty, those teaching in basic sciences: **65%**; in clinical programs: **35%**
Of part-time faculty, those teaching in basic sciences: **N/A**; in clinical programs: **N/A**
Full-time faculty/student ratio: **0.1**

SUPPORT SERVICES

The school offers students these services for dealing with stress: expanded-hour gym access, peer counseling, professional counseling, religious support, support groups.

WHERE GRADS GO

62.0%

Proportion of 2001-2003 graduates who entered primary care specialties

40.0%

Proportion of 2002-2003 graduates who accepted in-state residencies

UMDNJ

SCHOOL OF OSTEOPATHIC MEDICINE

- 1 Medical Center Drive, Stratford, NJ 08084
- Public
- **Year Founded:** 1977
- **Tuition, 2003-2004:** In-state: $21,962; Out-of-state: $33,133
- **Enrollment, 2003-2004:** 352
- **Website:** http://som.umdnj.edu
- **Specialty ranking:** geriatrics: 17

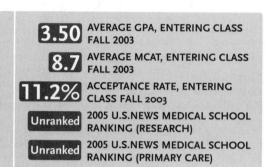

3.50 AVERAGE GPA, ENTERING CLASS FALL 2003

8.7 AVERAGE MCAT, ENTERING CLASS FALL 2003

11.2% ACCEPTANCE RATE, ENTERING CLASS FALL 2003

Unranked 2005 U.S.NEWS MEDICAL SCHOOL RANKING (RESEARCH)

Unranked 2005 U.S.NEWS MEDICAL SCHOOL RANKING (PRIMARY CARE)

ADMISSIONS

Admissions phone number: **(856) 566-7050**
Admissions email address: **somadm@umdnj.edu**
Application website: **N/A**
Acceptance rate: 11.2%
In-state acceptance rate: 29.2%
Out-of-state acceptance rate: 7.3%
Minority acceptance rate: 12.1%
International acceptance rate: **N/A**

Fall 2003 applications and acceptees

	Applied	Interviewed	Accepted	Enrolled
Total:	1,737	290	195	96
In-state:	312	131	91	55
Out-of-state:	1,425	159	104	41

Profile of admitted students

Average undergraduate grade point average: 3.50
MCAT averages (scale: 1-15; writing test: J-T):
  Composite score: 8.7
  Verbal reasoning score: 8.0, Physical sciences score: 9.0, Biological sciences score: 9.0, Writing score: Q
Proportion with undergraduate majors in: Biological sciences: 58%, Physical sciences: 13%, Non-sciences: 14%, Other health professions: 10%, Mixed disciplines and other: 5%
Percentage of students not coming directly from college after graduation: 16%

Dates and details

Oldest MCAT considered for Fall 2005 entry: **2001**
Earliest application date for the 2005-2006 first-year class: **May 3, 2004**
Latest application date: **February 1, 2004**
Acceptance dates for regular application for the class entering in fall 2005:
  Earliest: **September 22, 2004**
  Latest: **August 1, 2005**
The school considers requests for deferred entrance.
Starting month for the class entering in 2005-2006: **August**

The school doesn't have an Early Decision Plan (EDP). A personal interview is required for admission.

Undergraduate coursework required

Medical school requires undergraduate work in these subjects: biology, English, organic chemistry, inorganic (general) chemistry, physics, mathematics, behavioral science.

COSTS AND FINANCIAL AID

Financial aid phone number: (856) 566-6008
Tuition, 2003-2004 academic year: **In-state: $21,962; Out-of-state: $33,133**
Room and board: **$10,000**
Percentage of students receiving financial aid in 2003-04: 89%
Percentage of students receiving: Loans: 83%, Grants/scholarships: 61%, Work-study aid: 4%
Average medical school debt for the Class of 2002: **$88,835**

STUDENT BODY

Fall 2003 full-time enrollment: 352
Men: 46%, Women: 54%, In-state: 98%, Minorities: 49%, American Indian: 0.3%, Asian-American: 23.9%, African-American: 18.2%, Hispanic-American: 6.8%, White: 50.9%, International: 0.0%, Unknown: 0.0%

ACADEMIC PROGRAMS

The school's curriculum gives first-year students substantial contact with patients.
There are opportunities for first- or second-year students to work in community health clinics.
Program offerings: AIDS, drug/alcohol abuse, family medicine, geriatrics, internal medicine, pediatrics, rural medicine, women's health
Total National Institutes of Health (NIH) grants awarded to the medical school and affiliated hospitals: **$3.7 million**

FACULTY PROFILE (FALL 2003)

Total teaching faculty: **163 (full-time), 37 (part-time)**
Of full-time faculty, those teaching in basic sciences: **13%**; in clinical programs: **87%**

Of part-time faculty, those teaching in basic sciences: **14%**; in clinical programs: **86%**

Full-time faculty/student ratio: **0.5**

SUPPORT SERVICES

The school offers students these services for dealing with stress: expanded-hour gym access, professional counseling, religious support.

RESIDENCY CHOICES

Most popular residency and specialty programs chosen by the 2002 and 2003 graduating classes: emergency medicine, family practice, internal medicine, obstetrics and gynecology, orthopedic surgery, pediatrics, psychiatry, surgery–general, internal medicine/emergency medicine.

WHERE GRADS GO

46.3%

Proportion of 2001-2003 graduates who entered primary care specialties

53.5%

Proportion of 2002-2003 graduates who accepted in-state residencies

University of New England
COLLEGE OF OSTEOPATHIC MEDICINE

- 11 Hills Beach Road, Biddeford, ME 04005
- Private
- Year Founded: 1978
- Tuition, 2003-2004: $31,355
- Enrollment, 2003-2004: 488
- Website: http://www.une.edu
- Specialty ranking: rural medicine: 25

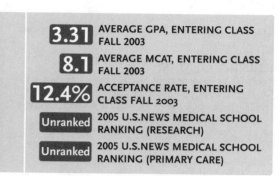

3.31 AVERAGE GPA, ENTERING CLASS FALL 2003

8.1 AVERAGE MCAT, ENTERING CLASS FALL 2003

12.4% ACCEPTANCE RATE, ENTERING CLASS FALL 2003

Unranked 2005 U.S.NEWS MEDICAL SCHOOL RANKING (RESEARCH)

Unranked 2005 U.S.NEWS MEDICAL SCHOOL RANKING (PRIMARY CARE)

ADMISSIONS
Admissions phone number: **(800) 477-4863**
Admissions email address: **admissions@une.edu**
Application website: **https://www.applyweb.com/aw?une**
Acceptance rate: **12.4%**
In-state acceptance rate: **N/A**
Out-of-state acceptance rate: **N/A**
Minority acceptance rate: **2.7%**
International acceptance rate: **N/A**

Fall 2003 applications and acceptees

	Applied	Interviewed	Accepted	Enrolled
Total:	1,867	299	232	121
In-state:	39	33	N/A	16
Out-of-state:	1,828	266	N/A	105

Profile of admitted students
Average undergraduate grade point average: **3.31**
MCAT averages (scale: 1-15; writing test: J-T):
  Composite score: **8.1**
  Verbal reasoning score: **8.1**, Physical sciences score: **7.6**,
  Biological sciences score: **8.3**, Writing score: **Q**
Proportion with undergraduate majors in: Biological
  sciences: **51%**, Physical sciences: **18%**, Non-sciences:
  16%, Other health professions: **5%**, Mixed disciplines
  and other: **10%**
Percentage of students not coming directly from college
  after graduation: **79%**

Dates and details
Oldest MCAT considered for Fall 2005 entry: **2000**
Earliest application date for the 2005-2006 first-year class:
  January 5, 2004
Latest application date: **N/A**
Acceptance dates for regular application for the class
  entering in fall 2005:
  Earliest: **September 15, 2004**
  Latest: **July 30, 2005**
The school considers requests for deferred entrance.
Starting month for the class entering in 2005-2006: **July**
The school doesn't have an Early Decision Plan (EDP).

A personal interview is required for admission.

Undergraduate coursework required
Medical school requires undergraduate work in these subjects: biology, English, organic chemistry, inorganic (general) chemistry, physics, molecular and cell biology, biochemistry.

ADMISSIONS POLICY
(TEXT PROVIDED BY SCHOOL):
All Maine residents meeting the college's stated minimum entrance requirements are guaranteed an interview. Preference is given to residents of the New England region. Factors taken into consideration when determining appropriateness for interview include academic ability, level of healthcare experience, extracurricular activities, applicants' level of knowledge, and commitment to the profession and to primary-care medicine.

COSTS AND FINANCIAL AID
Financial aid phone number: **(207) 283-0171**
Tuition, 2003-2004 academic year: **$31,355**
Room and board: **$10,700**
Percentage of students receiving financial aid in 2003-04:
  90%
Percentage of students receiving: Loans: **89%**,
  Grants/scholarships: **35%**, Work-study aid: **0%**
Average medical school debt for the Class of 2002:
  $143,000

STUDENT BODY
Fall 2003 full-time enrollment: **488**
Men: **48%**, Women: **52%**, In-state: **25%**, Minorities: **9%**,
  American Indian: **0.0%**, Asian-American: **7.6%**,
  African-American: **0.6%**, Hispanic-American: **06%**,
  White: **89.8%**, International: **1.4%**, Unknown: **0.0%**

ACADEMIC PROGRAMS
The school's curriculum gives first-year students
  substantial contact with patients.

There are opportunities for first- or second-year students to work in community health clinics.

Program offerings: AIDS, drug/alcohol abuse, family medicine, geriatrics, internal medicine, pediatrics, rural medicine, women's health

Total National Institutes of Health (NIH) grants awarded to the medical school and affiliated hospitals: **N/A**

CURRICULUM

(TEXT PROVIDED BY SCHOOL):

The four-year curriculum leading to the degree Doctor of Osteopathic Medicine is as follows:

Year 1: Basic sciences—gross anatomy, histology, embryology, biochemistry, immunology, nutrition, virology, bacteriology, parasitology, physiology, pharmacology, and pathology; Osteopathic Principles and Practices I; Medical Jurisprudence; Population Health; and Basic Life Support. Foundations of Doctoring is a yearlong course focusing on traditional physical diagnosis and medical humanities. Students in this course also gain early clinical exposure through the preceptor program. The Dermatology System course occurs at the end of the first year.

Year 2: A neuroanatomy course is followed by systems courses—nervous, psychiatry, musculoskeletal, respiratory, hematology, cardiovascular, renal, gastrointestinal, endocrine, and reproductive. Yearlong courses include Pharmacology and Therapeutics (I and II), Osteopathic Principles and Practices II, and Experiences in Doctoring, a skills-based course. Emergency Medicine, Advanced Cardiac Life Support, and Clinical Decision Making (a capstone course) complete the year.

Year 3: Core rotation requirements include 12 weeks of internal medicine and six weeks each of surgery, obstetrics/gynecology, pediatrics, family practice, and psychiatry.

Year 4: Additional clinical requirements include four weeks each of internal medicine, surgery, osteopathic manipulative medicine, and rural and emergency medicine. The balance of the student's schedule is elective.

FACULTY PROFILE (FALL 2003)

Total teaching faculty: **108 (full-time)**, **363 (part-time)**

Of full-time faculty, those teaching in basic sciences: **17%**; in clinical programs: **83%**

Of part-time faculty, those teaching in basic sciences: **2%**; in clinical programs: **98%**

Full-time faculty/student ratio: **0.2**

RESIDENCY CHOICES

Most popular residency and specialty programs chosen by the 2002 and 2003 graduating classes: anesthesiology, emergency medicine, family practice, internal medicine, obstetrics and gynecology, pediatrics, physical medicine and rehabilitation, psychiatry, surgery–general, internal medicine/pediatrics.

WHERE GRADS GO

74.6%

Proportion of 2001-2003 graduates who entered primary care specialties

13.9%

Proportion of 2002-2003 graduates who accepted in-state residencies

U. of North Texas Health Sci. Center

TEXAS COLLEGE OF OSTEOPATHIC MEDICINE

- 3500 Camp Bowie Boulevard, Fort Worth, TX 76107-2699
- Public
- Year Founded: N/A
- Tuition, 2003-2004: In-state: $9,030; Out-of-state: $22,130
- Enrollment, 2003-2004: 492
- Website: http://www.hsc.unt.edu
- Specialty ranking: N/A

3.59 AVERAGE GPA, ENTERING CLASS FALL 2003

8.8 AVERAGE MCAT, ENTERING CLASS FALL 2003

11.5% ACCEPTANCE RATE, ENTERING CLASS FALL 2003

Unranked 2005 U.S.NEWS MEDICAL SCHOOL RANKING (RESEARCH)

26 2005 U.S.NEWS MEDICAL SCHOOL RANKING (PRIMARY CARE)

ADMISSIONS

Admissions phone number: (800) 535-8266
Admissions email address:
TCOMAdmissions@hsc.unt.edu
Application website:
http://www.hsc.unt.edu/education/tcom/Admissions.cfm
Acceptance rate: 11.5%
In-state acceptance rate: **N/A**
Out-of-state acceptance rate: **N/A**
Minority acceptance rate: **9.3%**
International acceptance rate: **N/A**

Fall 2003 applications and acceptees

	Applied	Interviewed	Accepted	Enrolled
Total:	1,350	447	155	127
In-state:	1,186	416	N/A	120
Out-of-state:	164	31	N/A	7

Profile of admitted students

Average undergraduate grade point average: 3.59
MCAT averages (scale: 1-15; writing test: J-T):
  Composite score: **8.8**
  Verbal reasoning score: **8.5**, Physical sciences score: **8.7**,
  Biological sciences score: **9.2**, Writing score: **N/A**
Proportion with undergraduate majors in: Biological
  sciences: **69%**, Physical sciences: **4%**, Non-sciences: **9%**,
  Other health professions: **17%**, Mixed disciplines and
  other: **2%**
Percentage of students not coming directly from college
  after graduation: **6%**

Dates and details

Oldest MCAT considered for Fall 2005 entry: **2000**
Earliest application date for the 2005-2006 first-year class:
  May 1, 2004
Latest application date: **October 15, 2004**
Acceptance dates for regular application for the class
  entering in fall 2005:
  Earliest: **September 1, 2004**
  Latest: **July 1, 2005**
The school considers requests for deferred entrance.

Starting month for the class entering in 2005-2006:
  August
The school has an Early Decision Plan (EDP).
A personal interview is required for admission.

Undergraduate coursework required

Medical school requires undergraduate work in these subjects: biology, biology/zoology, English, organic chemistry, inorganic (general) chemistry, physics, mathematics, demonstration of writing skills, calculus, general chemistry.

ADMISSIONS POLICY

(TEXT PROVIDED BY SCHOOL):

A minimum of 90 semester credit hours (or equivalent) toward a bachelor's degree from a regionally accredited college or university in the United States is required at the time of application (some courses may be in progress). The following prerequisite courses in the sciences and humanities must be satisfactorily completed: general or inorganic chemistry (eight credit hours), organic chemistry (eight hours), general biology (14 hours), general physics (eight hours), English or creative writing (six hours), and calculus or statistics (three hours).

Strong preference will be given to those who have completed all requirements for the bachelor's degree before entering medical school. Applicants are also encouraged to complete their prerequisite coursework with letter grades rather than a pass/fail option. Science courses must include labs. Prospective students should strive to become proficient in scientific problem solving, critical thinking, and writing.

Although an applicant's academic record is important to us, we look for students who demonstrate the greatest promise of becoming skilled osteopathic physicians. Applicants will be evaluated on their personal integrity, maturity, creativity, and motivation for a career in medicine, ability to work cooperatively, and dedication to service of others. These attributes will be evaluated by several means, including letters of evaluation, the scope and nature of extracurricular and volunteer activities, the breadth of the applicant's undergraduate education, and personal interviews.

As a state-supported medical school, TCOM is required to admit 90 percent Texas residents for each entering class. Up to 10 percent of each entering class may be filled with nonresidents with outstanding credentials.

COSTS AND FINANCIAL AID

Financial aid phone number: **(800) 346-8266**
Tuition, 2003-2004 academic year: **In-state: $9,030; Out-of-state: $22,130**
Room and board: **$10,098**
Percentage of students receiving financial aid in 2003-04: **91%**
Percentage of students receiving: Loans: **91%**, Grants/scholarships: **46%**, Work-study aid: **0%**
Average medical school debt for the Class of 2002: **$80,172**

STUDENT BODY

Fall 2003 full-time enrollment: **492**
Men: **48%**, Women: **52%**, In-state: **94%**, Minorities: **34%**, American Indian: **0.6%**, Asian-American: **25.6%**, African-American: **1.6%**, Hispanic-American: **6.5%**, White: **65.7%**, International: **0.0%**, Unknown: **0.0%**

ACADEMIC PROGRAMS

The school's curriculum doesn't give first-year students substantial contact with patients.
There are opportunities for first- or second-year students to work in community health clinics.
Program offerings: AIDS, drug/alcohol abuse, family medicine, geriatrics, internal medicine, pediatrics, rural medicine, women's health
Total National Institutes of Health (NIH) grants awarded to the medical school and affiliated hospitals: **$7.9 million**

CURRICULUM

(TEXT PROVIDED BY SCHOOL):
The D.O. medical school curriculum is a four-year program leading to the degree of doctor of osteopathic medicine. In the first two years, students are taught basic and clinical sciences in an integrated systems approach. The second two years consist of specific clinical rotations in hospital and outpatient settings combined with classroom lectures and computerized exercises to develop and refine practical skills necessary for medical practice.

Years 1 and 2 of the curriculum integrate the basic and clinical sciences. During this time students develop the skills necessary to diagnose illness and learn the context within which medicine is practiced. This integrated systems approach is built on the same strong foundation of scientific and clinical knowledge that has long characterized TCOM's outstanding academic program.

The instructional program includes classroom presentations, early clinic/hospital experiences, laboratory exercises,

computer-assisted instruction, small group "pbl" education and the use of state of the art computerized mannequins along with simulated patients. Central to all educational activities in the curriculum is teaching critical thinking and helping each student develop the skills required to make decisions in the clinical setting.

For those students interested in rural medicine and family practice, special tract programs begin in these years that provide increased clinical and didactic exposure to these challenging fields.

The clinical years of the curriculum provide students a comprehensive education in the practices of modern medicine. Students complete over 3,800 hours of medical training in hospitals and clinics. During these clinical training years, students participate in daily ward rounds, primary and specialty clinics, and elective rotations. Didactics include lectures, computer-based exercises, grand rounds, and special seminars and conferences. Using a multi-discipline clinical education methodology, the clinical years build upon the strong foundation achieved in years 1 and 2. Students in the "rural tract" program spend time on rotations specifically designed to meet the educational needs of future rural physicians.

FACULTY PROFILE (FALL 2003)

Total teaching faculty: **185 (full-time)**, **15 (part-time)**
Of full-time faculty, those teaching in basic sciences: **31%**; in clinical programs: **69%**
Of part-time faculty, those teaching in basic sciences: **13%**; in clinical programs: **87%**
Full-time faculty/student ratio: **0.4**

SUPPORT SERVICES

The school offers students these services for dealing with stress: expanded-hour gym access, peer counseling, professional counseling, religious support, support groups.

RESIDENCY CHOICES

Most popular residency and specialty programs chosen by the 2002 and 2003 graduating classes: anesthesiology, family practice, internal medicine, obstetrics and gynecology, pediatrics, physical medicine and rehabilitation, psychiatry, radiology–diagnostic, surgery–general, transitional year.

WHERE GRADS GO

79.8%
Proportion of 2001-2003 graduates who entered primary care specialties

59.3%
Proportion of 2002-2003 graduates who accepted in-state residencies

West Virginia

SCHOOL OF OSTEOPATHIC MEDICINE

- 400 N. Lee Street, Lewisburg, WV 24901
- Public
- **Year Founded:** 1972
- **Tuition, 2003-2004:** In-state: $15,272; Out-of-state: $37,794
- **Enrollment, 2003-2004:** 336
- **Website:** http://www.wvsom.edu
- **Specialty ranking:** family medicine: 17, rural medicine: 8

3.37 AVERAGE GPA, ENTERING CLASS FALL 2003

7.4 AVERAGE MCAT, ENTERING CLASS FALL 2003

18.6% ACCEPTANCE RATE, ENTERING CLASS FALL 2003

Unranked 2005 U.S.NEWS MEDICAL SCHOOL RANKING (RESEARCH)

57 2005 U.S.NEWS MEDICAL SCHOOL RANKING (PRIMARY CARE)

ADMISSIONS

Admissions phone number: **(800) 356-7836**
Admissions email address: **admissions@wvsom.edu**
Application website: **http://www.aacom.org**
Acceptance rate: **18.6%**
In-state acceptance rate: **50.6%**
Out-of-state acceptance rate: **14.7%**
Minority acceptance rate: **108%**
International acceptance rate: **N/A**

Fall 2003 applications and acceptees

	Applied	Interviewed	Accepted	Enrolled
Total:	1,432	376	267	102
In-state:	156	110	79	49
Out-of-state:	1,276	266	188	53

Profile of admitted students

Average undergraduate grade point average: **3.37**
MCAT averages (scale: 1-15; writing test: J-T):
   Composite score: **7.4**
   Verbal reasoning score: **7.8**, Physical sciences score: **7.0**,
   Biological sciences score: **7.5**, Writing score: **N**
Proportion with undergraduate majors in: Biological
   sciences: **54%**, Physical sciences: **9%**, Non-sciences: **9%**,
   Other health professions: **11%**, Mixed disciplines and
   other: **18%**
Percentage of students not coming directly from college
   after graduation: **43%**

Dates and details

Oldest MCAT considered for Fall 2005 entry: **2001**
Earliest application date for the 2005-2006 first-year class:
   June 1, 2004
Latest application date: **January 2, 2004**
Acceptance dates for regular application for the class
   entering in fall 2005:
   Earliest: **September 1, 2004**
   Latest: **August 1, 2005**
The school doesn't consider requests for deferred entrance.
Starting month for the class entering in 2005-2006:
   August

The school doesn't have an Early Decision Plan (EDP).
A personal interview is required for admission.

Undergraduate coursework required

Medical school requires undergraduate work in these subjects: biology/zoology, English, organic chemistry, inorganic (general) chemistry, physics.

ADMISSIONS POLICY
(TEXT PROVIDED BY SCHOOL):

Students are the key to the West Virginia School of Osteopathic Medicine's commitment to improving healthcare. The Admissions Committee strives to fill the class each year with men and women who are motivated toward small-community or rural primary care.

Students come to Lewisburg with diverse academic and professional backgrounds, ranging from those possessing the minimum admission requirements to those holding advanced degrees in various fields. First preference is given to West Virginia residents.

The admission process is initiated by completing the American Association of Colleges of Osteopathic Medicine Application Service online application. Supplemental applications are provided only to those applicants who are granted an interview. The interview process begins in the latter part of August of the year preceding entry and continues through mid-April.

The basic requirements for admission to the first-year class include:

1. Ninety semester hours or three fourths of the credits required for a baccalaureate degree from an accredited college or university.

2. Medical College Admission Test scores.

3. Six semester hours (or its equivalent) of English; eight semester hours each in general biology or zoology, physics (algebra and trigonometry based), inorganic or general chemistry, and organic chemistry (including aliphatic and aromatic compounds), all with laboratories; and 52 semester hours of electives.

4. Cardiopulmonary resuscitation (CPR) certification prior to matriculation.

5. Letters of evaluation from the student's premedical adviser, premedical advising committee, or approved science faculty member and an osteopathic physician.

It is strongly recommended that a prospective applicant consider the following courses: biochemistry, cell biology, cell physiology, microbiology, modern genetics, comparative anatomy, embryology, histology, human anatomy, and mammalian physiology.

The Admissions Committee has the responsibility of accepting applicants on the basis of aptitude, maturity, ability to relate to people, motivation for osteopathic medicine, personal conduct, and scholarship. A personal interview is required.

COSTS AND FINANCIAL AID

Financial aid phone number: **(800) 356-7836**
Tuition, 2003-2004 academic year: **In-state: $15,272; Out-of-state: $37,794**
Room and board: **N/A**
Percentage of students receiving financial aid in 2003-04: **97%**
Percentage of students receiving: Loans: **92%**, Grants/scholarships: **10%**, Work-study aid: **16%**
Average medical school debt for the Class of 2002: **$146,813**

STUDENT BODY

Fall 2003 full-time enrollment: **336**
Men: **51%**, Women: **49%**, In-state: **63%**, Minorities: **8%**, American Indian: **0.3%**, Asian-American: **6.8%**, African-American: **0.0%**, Hispanic-American: **09%**, White: **92.0%**, International: **0.0%**, Unknown: **0.0%**

ACADEMIC PROGRAMS

The school's curriculum gives first-year students substantial contact with patients.
There are opportunities for first- or second-year students to work in community health clinics.
Program offerings: AIDS, drug/alcohol abuse, family medicine, geriatrics, internal medicine, pediatrics, rural medicine, women's health
Total National Institutes of Health (NIH) grants awarded to the medical school and affiliated hospitals: **N/A**

CURRICULUM

(TEXT PROVIDED BY SCHOOL):
The West Virginia School of Osteopathic Medicine provides two curricular tracts for students, Systems and Problem-Based Learning. In the Systems track, students spend the first year taking basic science courses, including both lab and lecture formats with a full-body dissection lab in anatomy. Second-year students take an integrated systems approach to medicine, plus courses such as pharmacology, physical diagnosis, and physician skills. An Osteopathic Principles and Practice course is given in both years. First- and second-year students participate in a unique, community clinic experience, where local community patients are diagnosed and treated osteopathically free of charge by the students, under faculty supervision.

In the Problem-Based Learning track, students are taught through the small-group learning process. Each group of seven or eight students is presented patient cases, which are revealed through progressive disclosure. Each group has two faculty facilitators, one basic scientist and one clinician. Students research issues, discuss their findings, and the case continues until all issues have been covered. Students also work on specific problem sets that help direct their learning. They have a full anatomy dissection course and participate with Systems students in the Osteopathic Principles and Practices course. These students begin physical diagnosis in the first year, and this expands into a physician skills course the second year. PBL students also participate in the free community clinic.

Promotion to the clinical curriculum requires passage of Part I of the National Osteopathic Board Examination. The clinical years are identical for both programs. Students are scheduled with clinician preceptors for their clerkships. Students are required to do three months of rural rotations and five months of family medicine throughout their third and fourth years. Other required rotations include obstetrics/gynecology, surgery, emergency medicine, pediatrics, internal medicine, psychiatry, and geriatrics. Graduation requires successful passage of Part II of the National Osteopathic Board Examination

FACULTY PROFILE (FALL 2003)

Total teaching faculty: **35 (full-time)**, **99 (part-time)**
Of full-time faculty, those teaching in basic sciences: **51%**; in clinical programs: **49%**
Of part-time faculty, those teaching in basic sciences: **1%**; in clinical programs: **99%**
Full-time faculty/student ratio: **0.1**

SUPPORT SERVICES

The school offers students these services for dealing with stress: expanded-hour gym access, peer counseling, professional counseling, religious support, support groups.

RESIDENCY CHOICES

Most popular residency and specialty programs chosen by the 2002 and 2003 graduating classes: anesthesiology, emergency medicine, family practice, internal medicine, obstetrics and gynecology, pediatrics, physical medicine and rehabilitation, surgery–general, transitional year, internal medicine/pediatrics.

WHERE GRADS GO

40.7%			

Proportion of 2001-2003 graduates who entered primary care specialties

N/A			

Proportion of 2002-2003 graduates who accepted in-state residencies

Additional Schools

Basic contact information for those schools that did not respond to the U.S. News survey is provided below.

FLORIDA STATE UNIVERSITY
- Tallahassee, FL 32306
- Public
- Website: http://www.med.fsu.edu

HOWARD UNIVERSITY
- 520 W Street NW, Washington, DC 20059
- Private
- Year Founded: 1868
- Website: http://www.med.howard.edu

LOMA LINDA UNIVERSITY
- School of Medicine, Loma Linda, CA 92350
- Private
- Website: http://www.llu.edu/index.htm

LSU SCHOOL OF MEDICINE–NEW ORLEANS
- Admissions Office, 1901 Perdido Street, New Orleans, LA
- 70112-1393
- Public
- Year Founded: 1941
- Tuition, 2003-2004: In-state: $10,703; Out-of-state: $24,851
- Website: http://www.medschool.lsumc.edu

MARSHALL UNIVERSITY
- 1600 Medical Center Drive, Huntington, WV 25701-3655
- Public
- Year Founded: 1977
- Tuition, 2003-2004: In-state: $12,704; Out-of-state: $32,534
- Website: http://musom.marshall.edu
- Specialty ranking: rural medicine: 25

MERCER UNIVERSITY
- 1550 College Street, Macon, GA 31207
- Private
- Year Founded: 1982
- Tuition, 2003-2004: $26,372
- Website: http://medicine.mercer.edu
- Specialty ranking: family medicine: 16, rural medicine: 25

PENN STATE UNIVERSITY COLLEGE OF MEDICINE
- 500 University Drive, Hershey, PA 17033
- Public
- Year Founded: 1967
- Tuition, 2003-2004: In-state: $26,422; Out-of-state: $36,592
- Website: http://www.hmc.psu.edu

ROSALIND FRANKLIN UNIVERSITY OF MEDICINE AND SCIENCE
- 3333 Greenbay Road, North Chicago, IL 60064
- Private
- Tuition, 2003-2004: $11,891
- Website: http://www.finchcms.edu

RUSH UNIVERSITY
- 600 S. Paulina Street, Chicago, IL 60612
- Private
- Year Founded: 1837
- Tuition, 2003-2004: $32,268
- Enrollment, 2003-2004: 487
- Website: http://www.rushu.rush.edu/medcol

SUNY–BROOKLYN
- 450 Clarkson Avenue, Box 60, Brooklyn, NY 11203
- Public
- Year Founded: 1860
- Tuition, 2003-2004: In-state: $17,145; Out-of-state: $30,245
- Website: http://www.hscbklyn.edu

UNIVERSITY OF ARIZONA
- 1501 N. Campbell Avenue, Tucson, AZ 85724
- Public
- Year Founded: 1967
- Tuition, 2003-2004: In-state: $11,578; Out-of-state: $20,348
- Website: http://www.medicine.arizona.edu

UNIVERSITY OF HAWAII–MANOA BURNS
- 1960 East-West Road, Honolulu, HI 96822
- Public
- Year Founded: 1967
- Tuition, 2003-2004: In-state: $15,574; Out-of-state: $29,278
- Website: http://hawaiimed.hawaii.edu

UNIVERSITY OF MISSOURI–KANSAS CITY
- 2411 Holmes, Kansas City, MO 64108
- Public
- Year Founded: 1971
- Tuition, 2003-2004: In-state: $19,905; Out-of-state: $38,938
- Website: http://www.med.umkc.edu

UNIVERSITY OF NEVADA–RENO
- Manville Building, Mailstop 357, Reno, NV 89557
- Public
- Year Founded: 1967
- Tuition, 2003-2004: In-state: $11,607; Out-of-state: $29,185
- Website: http://www.unr.edu/med

UNIVERSITY OF SOUTH ALABAMA
- 307 University Boulevard, 170 CSAB, Mobile, AL 36688
- Public
- Website: http://southalabama.edu/com

UNIVERSITY OF TENNESSEE–MEMPHIS
- 800 Madison Avenue, Memphis, TN 38163
- Public
- Tuition, 2003-2004: In-state: $16,271; Out-of-state: $32,185
- Website: http://www.utmem.edu/com_admissions

UNIVERSITY OF TEXAS
HEALTH SCIENCE CENTER–SAN ANTONIO
■ 7703 Floyd Curl Drive, San Antonio, TX 78229-3900
■ Public
■ Website: http://www.uthscsa.edu

ARIZONA COLLEGE OF OSTEOPATHIC MEDICINE
■ 19555 N. 59th Avenue, Glendale, AZ 85308
■ Private
■ Year Founded: 1995
■ Tuition, 2003-2004: $32,451
■ Website: http://www.midwestern.edu

CHICAGO COLLEGE OF OSTEOPATHIC MEDICINE
■ 555 31st Street, Downers Grove, IL 60515
■ Private
■ Year Founded: 1900
■ Tuition, 2003-2004: $28,142
■ Website: http://www.midwestern.edu

LAKE ERIE COLLEGE OF OSTEOPATHIC MEDICINE
■ 1858 W. Grandview Boulevard, Erie, PA 16509
■ Private
■ Year Founded: 1992
■ Tuition, 2003-2004: $25,195
■ Website: http://www.lecom.edu

OHIO UNIVERSITY
COLLEGE OF OSTEOPATHIC MEDICINE
■ Grosvenor and Irvine Halls, Athens, OH 45701
■ Public
■ Tuition, 2003-2004: In-state: $18,015; Out-of-state: $26,253
■ Enrollment, 2003-2004: N/A
■ Website: http://www.oucom.ohiou.edu

UNIVERSITY OF HEALTH SCIENCES
COLLEGE OF OSTEOPATHIC MEDICINE
■ 1750 Independence Avenue, Kansas City, MO 64106-1453
■ Private
■ Year Founded: 1916
■ Tuition, 2003-2004: $32,265
■ Website: http://www.uhs.edu

Resources for Late Starters

Postbaccalaureate programs for nonscientists

What if you come late to your decision to apply to med school and have little or no science background? Here are several highly regarded postbaccalaureate programs designed to help career-changers make their dreams come true. They offer all the science courses you'll need as well as advice and support when it comes time to apply to medical school; students who successfully complete the coursework are "sponsored" by the program, meaning the program vouches for their readiness to go on. (For a complete list of postbac premed programs, go to www.aamc.org.) Once you complete a program, it usually takes another year to apply to medical school, unless the program has "linkage" with one or more medical schools—an arrangement that allows qualified students to go directly to those med schools when they complete the postbac program.

BRYN MAWR COLLEGE

Canwyll House
101 North Merion Avenue
Bryn Mawr, PA 19010-2899
(610) 526-7350
Website: www.brynmawr.edu/postbac
Year started: 1972
Description: One-year program. Full-time, days only. Three courses per semester. Each usually has a laboratory. Classes are predominantly postbac classes although some are open to undergrads.
Enrollment: 75
Admissions requirements: Minimum undergradu-

ate GPA of 3.0; standardized testing required. Interview required for competitive applicants.
Acceptance rate: 60%
Average MCAT score of those who apply to medical school: 31.5
Acceptance rate into medical school in 2003: 100% (over past 5 years: 99%)
Tuition: $17,280; $1,550 per summer session
Financial aid: (610) 526-5267
Linkage with: Brown University School of Medicine, Dartmouth Medical College, Drexel University College of Medicine, George Washington University School of Medicine, Jefferson Medical College, SUNY at Downstate College of Medicine, SUNY Stony Brook School of Medicine, Health Sciences Center, Temple University School of Medicine, University of Rochester School of Medicine

COLUMBIA UNIVERSITY

Lewisohn Hall, Room 408
Mail Code 4101
2970 Broadway
New York, NY 10027
(212) 854-2772
Website: www.columbia.edu/cu/gs/postbacc
Year started: 1955
Description: Two-year program. Full-time or part-time, days or evenings. General chemistry prerequisite for both bio and organic chemistry. Minimum 120 hours of clinical volunteer work; 18–20 hours research volunteer work required. Postbac students are mixed with undergrad premed students.
Enrollment: 427

Admissions requirements: Minimum undergraduate GPA of 3.0; standardized testing, if taken, must be submitted. Interview not required.

Acceptance rate into program: 50–60%

Average MCAT score of those sponsored: 31

Acceptance rate into medical school of those sponsored in 2001 (last year available): 92%

Tuition: $10,000 per year ($976 per credit; need 20 credits to get certificate). Full program is 38 credits: $37,088.

Financial aid: (212) 854-5410

Linkage with: Ben Gurion University of the Negev; Brown University School of Medicine; Jefferson Medical College of Thomas Jefferson University; Drexel University College of Medicine; National University of Ireland, University College, Cork; New York Medical College; SUNY Brooklyn School of Medicine; SUNY Stony Brook School of Medicine; Temple University School of Medicine; Trinity College–Dublin; UMDNJ–New Jersey Medical School; UMDNJ–Robert Wood Johnson Medical School

GOUCHER COLLEGE

Postbaccalaureate Premedical Program

1021 Dulaney Valley Road

Baltimore, MD 21204-2794

(800) 414-3437

Website: www.goucher.edu/postbac

Year started: 1980

Description: One-year program. Full-time, days only. Classes separate from undergrads. Three courses per semester; intensive general chemistry over the summer. Volunteer work required.

Enrollment: 25–30

Admissions requirements: Standardized testing required. Interview required.

Acceptance rate into program: 20–30%

Average MCAT score of those sponsored: 32

Acceptance rate into medical school for those sponsored in 2003: 100%

Tuition: $2,590 per course. The typical curriculum consists of eight courses, bringing total tuition to $20,720.

Financial aid: (410) 337-6430

Linkage with: Brown Medical School, George Washington University School of Medicine, Drexel University College of Medicine, SUNY Stony Brook School of Medicine, Temple University School of Medicine, Tulane University School of Medicine, University of Pittsburgh School of Medicine

HARVARD UNIVERSITY

Health Careers Program

Harvard University Extension School

51 Brattle Street

Cambridge, MA 02138

(617) 495-2926

Website: www.extension.harvard.edu

Year started: 1980

Description: Two-year program, part-time evenings only. Postbac students are separated from undergrad premed students. Standard load is two courses per term. Students expected to find patient-contact work, either paid or volunteer.

Enrollment: 200 plus

Admissions requirements: Minimum undergraduate GPA of 2.7, no standardized test required. No interview required.

Acceptance rate into program: 90%

Average MCAT score of those sponsored: 32

Acceptance rate into medical school for those sponsored in 2003: 89%

Tuition: $800 per course

Financial aid: (617) 495-4293

JOHNS HOPKINS UNIVERSITY

3400 North Charles Street
Wyman Park Building, Suite G1
Baltimore, MD 21218
(410) 516-7748
Website: www.jhu.edu/postbac
Description: One-year program. Full-time, days only. Four or five courses with no more than two lab science courses each semester. Students participate in a "journal club" and "mini-medical school" to learn about and discuss contemporary medical/health care issues. Students engage in a wide choice of clinical activities, including medical tutorials with medical school faculty, structured hospital internships and volunteer programs, and volunteer work in the community. Postbac students are mixed in with undergrad premed students.
Enrollment: 25–30
Admissions requirements: Minimum undergraduate GPA of 3.0 plus; standardized testing (SAT, ACT, or GRE) required. Interview required.
Acceptance rate into program: 19%
Average MCAT Score of medical school applicants: approximately 31
Acceptance rate into medical school of applicants in 2003: 100%
Tuition: $22,600
Financial aid: (410) 516-4688
Linkage with: George Washington University School of Medicine, UMDNJ–Robert Wood Johnson Medical School, and University of Rochester

MILLS COLLEGE

5000 MacArthur Boulevard
Oakland, CA 94613
(510) 430-2317
Website: www.mills.edu

Year started: 1979
Description: One- or two-year program. Full-time or part-time, days only. Students take two or three courses per semester. Volunteer work not required, but encouraged. Postbac students are separated from undergrad premed students.
Enrollment: 60
Admissions requirements: Minimum undergraduate GPA of 3.0; standardized testing required. No interview required.
Acceptance rate into program: Varies considerably from year to year; approximately 75%
Average MCAT score of those sponsored: 31
Acceptance rate into medical school for those sponsored in 2003: 87.5%
Tuition: $15,000–$25,000 per year, depending on number of courses
Financial aid: Need to respond on application; Mills College will not discuss aid over the phone.
Linkage with: Tulane University Medical School

SCRIPPS COLLEGE W.M. KECK SCIENCE CENTER

925 N. Mills Avenue
Claremont, CA 91711
(909) 621-8764
Website: www.jsd.claremont.edu/postbac
Year started: 1994
Description: One- or two-year program. Full-time or part-time, days only. Postbac students are mixed with undergrad premed students. Students in the one-year program take three or four courses per semester and two summer courses each summer. Students in the two-year program take two courses per semester and are required to work at least 20 hours a week. Internships and volunteer work required.
Enrollment: 12–15

Admissions requirements: Minimum undergraduate GPA of 3.0; standardized testing required. Interview required.

Acceptance rate into program: 27%

Average MCAT score of those sponsored: 31.2

Acceptance rate into medical school for those sponsored in 2003: 100%

Tuition: $20,000–$26,000 per year, depending on number of courses

Financial aid: (909) 621-8275

Linkage with: University of Pittsburgh School of Medicine, Drexel University College of Medicine, George Washington School of Medicine, Temple University School of Medicine, Western University School of Medicine, College of Osteopathic Medicine of the Pacific

TUFTS UNIVERSITY

419 Boston Ave.

Dowling Hall

Medford, MA 02155

(617) 627-2321

Website: http://studentservices.tufts.edu/postbac

Year started: 1988

Description: 11 to 20 months depending on student. Full-time, days only. Two laboratory science courses per semester and other electives available. Volunteer or paid part-time work recommended. Postbac students are mixed in with undergrad premed students.

Enrollment: 40

Admissions requirements: Minimum undergraduate GPA of 3.0; standardized testing required. No interview required.

Acceptance rate into program: 30–40%

Average MCAT score of those sponsored: 30–31

Acceptance rate into medical school of those

sponsored in 2003: 90%

Tuition: $10,001–15,000 per year, depending on number of courses

Financial aid: Once admitted, students can discuss it with counselors.

Linkage with: Tufts University School of Medicine and University of New England College of Osteopathic Medicine

UNIVERSITY OF PENNSYLVANIA

3440 Market Street, Suite 100

College of General Studies

Philadelphia, PA 19104-3335

(215) 898-3110

Website: www.sas.upenn.edu/CGS/postbac/premed

Year started: 1977

Description: One- or two-year program. Full-time or part-time, days, or evenings. Postbac students are separated from undergrad premed students.

Enrollment: 50–70

Admissions requirements: Minimum undergraduate GPA of 3.0; standardized testing required. Interview required.

Acceptance rate into program: N/A

Average MCAT score of those sponsored: N/A

Acceptance rate into medical school of those sponsored in 2003: 100%

Tuition: $12,000 per academic year

Financial aid: www.sfs.upenn.edu/home

Linkage with: George Washington University School of Medicine, Jefferson Medical College, Drexel University College of Medicine, Temple University School of Medicine, UMDNJ–Robert Wood Johnson School of Medicine, University of Pittsburgh School of Medicine

Overseas Options
Foreign medical schools that welcome Americans

If you don't get into an American medical school, one possible alternate route is a foreign or "offshore" school that accepts a significant number of U.S. applicants (see Chapter 6, page 55). Before you make a choice, be sure you know what you're getting into: Visit the school, find out what kind of program it offers and how many Americans attend, how students do on the United States Medical Licensing Examination (USMLE), and how many end up with residencies in the States. Below is a sampling of programs that accept Americans.

AMERICAN UNIVERSITY OF THE CARIBBEAN SCHOOL OF MEDICINE

Jordan Road
Cupecoy
St. Maarten, N.A.

Admissions: Medical Education Information Office
901 Ponce de Leon Boulevard, Suite 201
Coral Gables, Florida 33134
(866) 372-2282
Website: www.aucmed.edu
Year founded: 1978. AUC offers basic medical sciences in St. Maarten and clinical rotations at affiliated hospitals in the U.S., U.K., and Ireland. Graduates include more than 3,500 licensed physicians practicing in the U.S. Semesters begin in January, May, and September.
Enrollment: 380 in basic sciences; 235 in clinical sciences (May 2004)
Percentage of U.S. citizens (or permanent residents): 88.4%
Admissions information: Entering class 2003: average GPA: 3.1; average MCAT: 22
Acceptance rate: 51%
Language: Courses taught in English
Pass rate on USMLE Step 1: N/A
Percentage of first-year residency placements in U.S.: 81.5% (110 of 135 graduates)
Tuition: $9,500 per semester (semesters 1–5); $10,000 per semester thereafter
Financial aid: (305) 446-0600, ext. 22 or 23

BEN-GURION UNIVERSITY OF THE NEGEV

Beer Sheva, Israel
M.D. Program in International Health and Medicine in collaboration with Columbia University Medical Center
Admissions: 630 W. 168th Street, PH15E-1512
New York, New York 10032
(212) 305-9587
Website: http://cpmcnet.columbia.edu/dept/bgcu-md
Year founded: 1996
Enrollment: Average entering class size is 30; currently 123 students in the four-year program.
Percentage of U.S. citizens: 66%
Admissions information: Average undergraduate GPA of 3.4 ; average MCAT score: 27. Interview is required.
Acceptance rate: 46%
Language: Courses taught in English
Pass rate on USMLE Step 1: more than 95% for U.S. students

Percentage of first-year residency placements in U.S.: 100% in 2004

Tuition: $25,850 (2003–2004)

Financial aid: American students may use Stafford and alternative loans; and after the first semester, all students may apply for limited scholarships based on financial need.

Average attrition rate: From 1998–2004, about 4%. The rate this year for the 2003 entering class is 3.4%.

ROSS UNIVERSITY SCHOOL OF MEDICINE

Dominica, West Indies

Admissions: 499 Thornall St., 10th Floor

Edison, NJ 08837

(732) 978-5300

Website: www.rossmed.edu

Year founded: 1978

Enrollment: 2,500 plus

Percentage of U.S. citizens: 93%

Admissions information: Mean undergraduate GPA of 3.25; MCAT score: N/A (though now required). Interview is required.

Acceptance rate: Approximately 55%

Language: Courses taught in English

Pass rate on USMLE Step 1: 88% for 2002 first-time test takers; 94% for first- and second-time test takers.

Percentage of first-year residency placements in U.S.: 64.2% through the match; 16.3% prematch; 19.5% outside the match. Typically, 96% of eligible graduates achieve a residency position in the States.

Tuition: $20,200

Financial aid: (732) 978-5300

Average attrition: 17%

ST. GEORGE'S UNIVERSITY MEDICAL SCHOOL

Grenada, West Indies

Admissions: The North American Correspondent c/o University Services, Ltd.

1 East Main Street Bay Shore, NY 11706

(800) 899-6337, ext. 280 or (631) 665-8500

Website: www.sgu.edu

Year founded: 1976

Enrollment: 2,349

Percentage of U.S. citizens: 75%

Admissions information: average undergraduate GPA for the 2003 entering class of 3.3; MCAT Score: 24. Interview required

Language: Courses taught in English

Pass rate on USMLE Step 1: 90%

Percentage of first-year residency placements in U.S.: 99% of those eligible U.S. graduates who applied obtained residency positions in 650 hospitals throughout 50 states.

Tuition: $30,000

Financial aid: 1-631-665-8500, ext. 232

TECHNION-ISRAEL INSTITUTE OF TECHNOLOGY

The Technion American Medical Students (TEAMS) Program

12th Efron St., P.O. Box 9649

Haifa, 31096, Israel

011-972-829-5248

Website: http://teams.technion.ac.il

Year founded: 1983

Enrollment: 60 Americans

Percentage of U.S. citizens: 100% in the TEAMS program (U.S. citizens make up 10–15% of Technion student body).

Admissions information: Average GPA of above 3.4 and average MCAT score of 24 are required Interview is required.

Acceptance rate into program: 70%

Language: Courses taught in English

Pass rate on USMLE Step 1: 98%

Percentage of first-year residency placements in U.S.: 100%

Tuition: $19,120

Financial aid: Federal and private

Attrition rate: Less than 1 percent

TEL AVIV UNIVERSITY SACKLER SCHOOL OF MEDICINE

New York State/American Program

Ramat Aviv Israel

Admissions: 17 E. 62nd Street

New York, NY 10021

(212) 688-8811

Website: www.tau.ac.il/medicine

Year founded: 1976

Enrollment: 300

Percentage of U.S. citizens: 100%

Admissions information: Minimum undergraduate GPA of 3.0. MCAT score: minimum of 8 on each section. Interview required.

Acceptance rate: 50%

Language: Courses are taught in English.

Pass rate on USMLE Step 1: 98%

Percentage of first-year residency placements in U.S.: 100%

Tuition: $22,000

Financial aid: Federal Stafford loan and several private loans

UNIVERSIDAD AUTÓNOMA DE GUADALAJARA

Av. Patria # 1201, Lomas del Valle, 3a. Sección

Guadalajara, Jalisco, México C.P. 44100

Admissions: 4715 Fredericksburg Road, Suite 300

San Antonio, TX 78229

(800) 531-5494

20 Corporate Woods Boulevard, Suite 205

Albany, NY 12211-2370

(866) 434-7392

Website: www.uag.mx

Year founded: 1935

Enrollment: 4,000 plus

Percentage of U.S. citizens: 20%

Admissions information: Average GPA of 2.9; MCAT: 24. Interview required.

Acceptance rate: 33%

Language: Lectures and some labs taught in English for only the first two years, then Spanish.

Pass rate on USMLE Step 1: 82%

Percentage of first-year residency placements in U.S.: 92%

Tuition: $17,580

Financial aid: Yes

Alphabetical Index of Schools

Index of Schools by State

Missouri

Kirksville College of Osteopathic
Medicine, 326
St. Louis University, 188
University of Health Sciences,
College of Osteopathic
Medicine, 351
University of Missouri-Columbia,
260
University of Missouri–Kansas
City, 350
Washington University in St.
Louis, 308

Nebraska

Creighton University, 126
University of Nebraska, College of
Medicine, 262

Nevada

University of Nevada–Reno, 350

New Hampshire

Dartmouth Medical School, 128

New Jersey

University of Medicine &
Dentistry of New Jersey, New
Jersey Medical School, 204
University of Medicine &
Dentistry of New Jersey, Robert
Wood Johnson Medical School,
206
University of Medicine &
Dentistry of New Jersey,
College of Osteopathic
Medicine, 342

New Mexico

University of New Mexico, 264

New York

Albany Medical College, 113
Columbia University, College of
Physicians and Surgeons, 122
Cornell University, Weill, 124
Mount Sinai School of Medicine,
170
New York, College of Osteopathic
Medicine, 330

New York Medical College, 172
New York University, 174
Stony Brook University, 190
SUNY–Brooklyn, 350
SUNY–Syracuse, 192
University at Buffalo–SUNY, 210
University of Rochester, 276
Yeshiva University, Albert
Einstein, 318

North Carolina

Duke University, 132
East Carolina University, Brody,
134
University of North
Carolina–Chapel Hill, 266
Wake Forest University, 306

North Dakota

University of North Dakota, 268

Ohio

Case Western Reserve University,
120
Medical College of Ohio, 160
Northeastern Ohio Universities,
College of Medicine, 176
Ohio State University, 180
Ohio University, College of
Osteopathic Medicine, 351
University of Cincinnati, 228
Wright State University, 314

Oklahoma

Oklahoma State University,
College of Osteopathic
Medicine, 334
University of Oklahoma, 270

Oregon

Oregon Health & Sciences
University, 182

Pennsylvania

Drexel University, 130
Jefferson Medical College, 150
Lake Erie College of Osteopathic
Medicine, 351
Penn State University, 350
Philadelphia College of
Osteopathic Medicine, 336

Temple University, 194
Temple University, 194
University of Pennsylvanis, 272
University of Pittsburg, 274

Rhode Island

Brown University, 118

South Carolina

Medical Universary of South
Carolina, 164
University of South Carolina, 278

South Dakota

University of South Dakota, 280

Tennessee

East Tennessee State University,
J.H. Quillen, 138
University of Tennessee–
Memphis, 350
Vanderbilt University, 302

Texas

Bayer College of Medicine, 114
Texas A&M University System,
Health Science Center, 196
Texas Tech University, Health
Science Center, 198
University of North Texas Heal
and Service Care, 346
University of Texas, Health
Science Center–Houston, 266
University of Texas, Southwestern
Medical Center–Dallas, 290
University of Texas Health Science
Center
University of Texas Medical
Branch–Galveston, 288

Utah

University of Utah, 292

Vermont

University of Vermont, 294

Virginia

Eastern Virginia Medical School,
Edward Via Virginia, College of
Osteopathic Medicine, 324

University of Virginia, 296
Virginia Commonwealth
  University, Medical College of
  Virginia, 304

Washington, D.C.
George Washington University,
  144

Georgetown University, 142
Howard University, 350

Washington
University of Washington

West Virginia
Marshall University, 350

West Virginia, School of
  Osteopathic Medicine, 348
West Virginia University, 312

Wisconsin
Medical College of Wisconsin, 162
University of Michigan–Madison,
  300

About the Authors & Editors

Founded in 1933, Washington, D.C.–based *U.S.News & World Report* delivers a unique brand of weekly magazine journalism to its 12.2 million readers. In 1983, *U.S. News* began its exclusive annual rankings of American colleges and universities. The *U.S. News* education franchise is second to none, with its annual college and graduate school rankings among the most eagerly anticipated magazine issues in the country.

Josh Fischman, the book's lead writer and one of its editors, covers health and science for *U.S.News & World Report*. His weekly health column, "Pulse," appears on www.usnews.com. Previously, he was editor-in-chief at *Earth*, deputy news editor at *Science*, and a senior editor at *Discover*. He has also cowritten the children's book *101 Things Every Kid Should Know about Dinosaurs*. He has won the Blakeslee Award for excellence in medical reporting from the American Heart Association.

Anne McGrath, editor, is a senior writer at *U.S.News & World Report*, where she covers higher education as well as primary and secondary education. Previously, she was managing editor of "America's Best Colleges" and "America's Best Graduate Schools," the two *U.S. News* annual publications featuring rankings of the country's colleges and universities.

Robert Morse is the director of data research at *U.S.News & World Report*. He is in charge of the research, data collection, methodologies, and survey design for the annual "America's Best Colleges" rankings and the "America's Best Graduate Schools" rankings.

Ulrich Boser is an associate editor at *U.S. News & World Report*, where he writes about higher education as well as primary and secondary education. He is also a writer for the magazine's Science & Society section.

Sara Sklaroff is the education editor of *U.S.News & World Report*, where she manages the magazine's education journalism, both in the weekly magazine and in "America's Best Colleges" and other guides. She is also an editor of the magazine's weekly Science & Society section. Sklaroff has written for *Education Week* and the *Chronicle of Higher Education*, among other publications.

Brian Kelly is the executive editor of *U.S.News & World Report*. As the magazine's No. 2 editor, he oversees the weekly magazine, the website, and a series of newsstand books. He is a former editor at the *Washington Post* and the author of three books.

Other writers who contributed chapters or passages to the book are **Carolyn Kleiner Butler, Kristin Davis, Justin Ewers, Helen Fields, Dan Gilgoff, Vicky Hallett, Bernadine Healy, Caroline Hsu, Katy Kelly, Samantha Levine, Jill Rachlin Marbaix, Stacy Schultz, Nancy Shute, Rachel K. Sobel, Amanda Spake**, and **Marianne Szegedy-Maszak**. The work involved in producing the directory and *U.S. News* Insider's Index was handled by senior research analyst **Sam Flanigan**, with associate research analyst **Meadow Yerkie**. Thanks to **David Griffin**, creative director at *U.S. News*, for his work in designing the book. Thanks as well to **James Bock** for his copyediting assistance and to members of the *U.S. News* **factchecking team** for making sure we got it right.

A NEW CANCER VACCINE • KEEPING DNA'S SECRETS

U.S.News & WORLD REPORT

IRAQ AFTER SADDAM
INSIDE AMERICA'S POSTWAR PLAN

Save 90%*

Find out where the story is going...not simply where it's been

Subscribe to *U.S. News* for only 40¢ an issue

News and events can affect you in a very personal way, whether something happens on the other side of the world or in your own community. And that's where *U.S.News & World Report* can help you. You get valuable information you can use to make better choices for yourself and your family.

And now you can get *U.S. News* at the special rate of just 40¢ an issue. That's over a year (60 issues) for only $24—you **SAVE 90%** off the cover price. Plus, by subscribing you also receive our Special Guides on *Best Colleges, Best Hospitals, Careers, Retirement*, and more.

So call today and get ahead of the news for only 40¢ a copy.

To subscribe, call:
 **1-800-436-6520** *(MENTION CODE: 04SPE4)*

 **U.S.News** & WORLD REPORT

*Savings off the cover price. *U.S. News* publishes weekly except for six special double issues per year.